D1627661

A Social History of British Broadcasting

For
Sonia, David and Leo
and
Theo and Rosie

A Social History of British Broadcasting

Volume One 1922–1939
Serving the Nation

Paddy Scannell
and David Cardiff

LOCATED
BY B M B

Basil Blackwell

Copyright © Paddy Scannell 1991

First published 1991

Basil Blackwell Ltd
108 Cowley Road, Oxford, OX4 1JF, UK

Basil Blackwell, Inc.
3 Cambridge Center
Cambridge, Massachusetts 02142, USA

All rights reserved. Except for the quotation of short passages for the purposes of criticism and review, no part of this publication may be reproduced, stored in a retrieval system, or transmitted, in any form or by any means, electronic, mechanical, photocopying, recording or otherwise, without the prior permission of the publisher.

Except in the United States of America, this book is sold subject to the condition that it shall not, by way of trade or otherwise, be lent, re-sold, hired out, or otherwise circulated without the publisher's prior consent in any form of binding or cover other than that in which it is published and without a similar condition including this condition being imposed on the subsequent purchaser.

British Library Cataloguing in Publication Data

A CIP catalogue record for this book is available from the British Library.

Library of Congress Cataloging in Publication Data

Scannell, Paddy.
    A social history of British broadcasting/Paddy Scannell and David Cardiff.
        p.   cm.
    Includes bibliographical references.
    Contents: v. 1. 1922–1939, serving the nation.
    ISBN 0-631-17543-1 (v. 1)
    1. Radio broadcasting—Great Britain—History.   2. British
Broadcasting Corporation.   3. Radio in politics—Great Britain.   4. Radio
broadcasting—Social aspects—Great Britain. I. Cardiff.
David.   II. Title.
PN1991.3.G7S28   1991
302.23'44'0941—dc20

Typeset in 10 on 12 pt Ehrhardt
by Graphicraft Typesetters Ltd., Hong Kong.
Printed in Great Britain by TJ Press Ltd, Padstow, Cornwall

Contents

———◦◦◦———

Contents

Illustrations and Plates

—————◦◦◦—————

Illustrations

ILLUSTRATIONS AND FIGURES

Map

Tables

Plates (between pages 204–205)

Preface

———◦❈◦———

ALTHOUGH THIS book is all about the BBC it is not a history of the British Broadcasting Corporation.[1] It is the first volume in a series that attempts to account, historically, for the impact and effect of broadcasting on modern life in Britain. There are two parts to this project: the first is to describe the actual ways in which broadcasting developed and interacted with the society it was intended to serve; and the second is to reflect on those accounts and their wider political, social and cultural implications. This first volume begins to trace the development of broadcasting in Britain in its classic form – as a state-regulated national service in the public interest. It reconstructs the foundation of a service familiar to us today in the output of the BBC and IBA.

If that output on radio and televison has by now come to seem like second nature to us, from a commonsense point of view it does seem to amount to much. 'Anything on telly tonight?' 'No, nothing.' This familiar conversational exchange is, of course, neither a criticism nor a disincentive to viewing. It merely expresses what everyone knows, namely that tonight's television is, as it always is on this particular night of the week, nothing in the least bit out of the ordinary. It consists of the usual programmes, on the usual channel, at the usual times. Maybe there's a good film, an interesting documentary or favourite drama or comedy series as punctual pleasures. But more than that is neither expected nor desired. This seeming ordinariness conceals a long and continuing effort by broadcasters to discover formats, styles and modes of address which ceaselessly reiterate effects of familiarity which give to daily output the same unquestioning routine character that daily life possesses.

Broadcasting mediates a seemingly unmediated reality, but the world that is organized in programme output is not a reflection, a mirror of a reality that exists elsewhere. It is a unique totality, a social whole constituted in the range of output, a universe that exists nowhere else. That totality mediates the commonsense knowledge, the practical experience and the everyday pleasures of whole societies. How it is done, and with what social, political and cultural implications, is the central concern of this historical study of broadcasting.

Any broadcast channel is based upon a set of assumptions about the audience for whom its bill of fare is intended, an audience that is figured in the individual programmes and the overall repertoire that makes up the content of the channel. Particular kinds of social identities are projected, particular stocks of knowledge and tastes presumed, particular communicative styles assumed in relation to absent listeners or viewers. The sum of the material transmitted in a national radio or television channel amounts to a socio-cultural universe, a complete world, whose content seems exhaustive. What lies outside its programme repertoire – what is *not* broadcast – is not part of the normal range of the social experience and interests of the audiences as expressed in the totality of output. The output of the four nationally networked television channels today, or of the pre-war National Programme with which this volume is concerned, may be taken as normative expressions of the day-to-day interests, tastes and concerns of a whole society. If it is reasonable to claim that the routine character of a country's politics, entertainment and culture is embodied in the daily output of its broadcasting services, then the historical study of broadcasting offers an unprecedented insight into the character of twentieth-century life, public and private, for whole populations.

But broadcasting is not simply a content – what this or that programme is about, or might mean. It embodies, always, a communicative intention which is the mark of a social relationship. Each and every programme is shaped by considerations of the audience, is designed to be heard or seen by absent listeners or viewers. Programmes are the highly determinate end-products of broadcasting, the point of exchange between the producing institutions and society. In their form and content they bear the marks of institutional assumptions about the scope and purposes of broadcasting and about the audiences for whom they are made. Judgements about the adequacy or otherwise of broadcasting are always based on assessments of the character and quality of output.

It is for such reasons that we have chosen to locate our historical study of the impact of broadcasting at the level of production, by which we mean programme planning as well as programme-making and the policy considerations that shaped them both. The social relations of production and consumption – as between institutions, programmes and audiences – embody the emerging character and impact of broadcasting on modern societies. To maintain this perspective we have inevitably neglected many other important aspects of broadcasting. We have not dealt with the technical or engineering side of broadcasting and their continuing, vital contributions to programme production and distribution.[2] Overseas broadcasting falls outside our remit.[3] Specialist areas of programme-making aimed at particular audiences – religion, education, sport, children's programmes – have been excluded from this volume.[4] So too has television since it was a purely experimental service reaching no more than 20,000 television sets in the Greater London area.[5] Although much incidental evidence of the internal organization of the BBC will be found in this book – and it is clear there was a major management crisis in the mid-thirties – staff relations have been of concern only in so far as they directly affected programme-making.[6]

We have chosen to concentrate on those areas of production that made up the great bulk of general programme output aimed at general listeners especially in peak listening times. We offer accounts of the formation of news, talks, features and documentaries, variety, music and outside broadcasts. We have nothing much to say about drama, for although we researched it we found little in its development that was not covered by our accounts of features, talks and variety.[7] Thus the accounts that follow do not claim to be, in any sense, full and exhaustive. Many aspects of Talks, for instance, have been omitted – on science or literature for instance. We have studied broadcasting's presentation of what we take to be the two major social and political issues of the thirties – unemployment and foreign affairs. But there are many other important issues – housing, health, industrial relations, the environment – which could be studied in similar detail.[8] Again, there is much more to be written on regional broadcasting than our single chapter on the work of the Manchester station. What we hope emerges, however, from the areas we have studied is a clear sense of the main critical factors – internal and external – that shaped the development of the service in its parts and as a whole for local, regional and national audiences.

In every case that we have studied we have tried as best we can to situate developments within the BBC in relation to the larger social, political or cultural environment. In some instances this has not been too difficult: there is much now written on the general character of the politics of the period and the issue of particular interest to us – news management and the orchestration of public opinion – has received scholarly investigation. But when we came to music or variety we had virtually to reconstruct for ourselves, from contemporary magazines, biographies and the like, the character of the wider musical culture or of entertainment for the period. Large aspects of twentieth-century social history still remain under-explored; and although music and variety are not exactly wholly uncharted terrains, their detailed contours have yet to be filled in.

Preface

There is of course an inescapable paradox at the heart of this project of which we have been acutely aware all along – our object of study no longer exists. The early pioneers of radio as an art-form lamented the 'ghastly impermanence' of their medium. Radio and, later, television developed first as live systems of transmission and recording technologies came later. Thus, although there are recordings of some of the more significant programmes broadcast from the mid-thirties onwards, the vast bulk of output perished in the moment of transmission. The fleeting, unrecorded character of early radio seems obstinately to resist the possibility of historical reclamation. Hence reconstructing the character of output has been more akin to archaeology in which shattered fragments allow a conjectural piecing together of what the whole must have been like. That we have been able to do so with some success in the areas of production studied is due almost wholly to the magnificent records of the BBC Written Archives, which must surely be one of the most important historical depositories in Britain on all aspects of twentieth-century British life.

At present the Written Archives, in the grounds of the BBC Monitoring Service at Caversham Park, Reading, contain at least 200,000 files on all aspects of broasdcasting from the early twenties through to the early sixties. New material is constantly being acquired and sorted. For our purposes it has been possible to reconstruct in detail many aspects of programme policy, planning and production from the 50,000 or more files on the inter-war period. Much of this material is fully indexed and catalogued, and it is a great deal easier now to locate the kind of information one is looking for than when we began working in the Archives at the end of the seventies. From the minutes of BBC management boards and departmental meetings, from the policy files on all aspects of programmes, from production files and transcriptions of programmes-as-broadcast, from contributors' files, from Listener Research reports, from the splendid press cuttings collection, as well as from *Radio Times* and *The Listener* – from all these sources, accounts of the routine work of broadcasting can patiently be pieced together like a vast jigsaw puzzle.

Yet for all the wealth of material evidence in the Archives the detailed character of pre-war broadcasting is forgotten today. We are ruefully aware that the films, magazines and literature of our period of study have remained in circulation both as points of reference for understanding the period and as cultural objects in their own right. *The Road to Wigan Pier, Picture Post* or *Night Mail* are today familiar 'texts' from the thirties, not only to students of the period but to a wider and more general public. But who knows, for who has heard, *Crisis in Spain, Steel* or *The Classic Soil*, three notable radio feature programmes from the same period? Even the classic entertainment programmes of the thirties, *In Town Tonight, Monday Night At Seven* and *Band Waggon*, remain only as a trace memory with older members of the population. There are real difficulties in the lack of any continuing process of discussion and evaluation of the character of broadcast output compared with other areas of cultural production. We very much hope that one effect of this book – indeed of the project as a whole – will be to stimulate an interest in the historical recuperation of the character of broadcast output, and a study in depth of all aspects of production.

David Cardiff and I began work on this project over ten years ago. We divided up between us the task of researching the different areas of output and we both were granted a year's study leave by the Polytechnic of Central London. We have published articles separately and together on particular aspects of out work, mainly in *Media Culture & Society*, and much of that material has been incorporated into the present volume. In its general scope and intention *Serving the Nation* expresses a shared perception, but in the end I have assumed responsibility for writing this book and for seeing it through to publication.

Paddy Scannell

Acknowledgements

———◦❀◦———

This book is based on the holdings in the BBC Written Archives and we have a huge debt of gratitude to Mrs Jacqueline Kavanagh and all her staff for their unfailing help and courtesy which made our work there so enjoyable. Margaret Kirby and the staff of the BBC Picture Library were equally helpful when it came to finding illustrative material for the book. Our thanks are due to the BBC for permission to use the map on page 306 from E. Pawley, *BBC Engineering, 1922–1972*, and more generally for permission to make full use of their historical resources. Our thanks to the proprietors of *Punch* for permission to reproduce cartoons from the period. At the very beginning, when we were tentatively thinking of looking into the history of broadcasting, James Curran encouraged us both to believe that it was worth doing and that it might be publishable. Much later, John Cain was a friend and help in one or two tricky moments. Olive Shapley and the late Felix Greene provided fascinating memories of their work in the pre-war BBC. Asa Briggs, John Corner, Anthony Smith and Nancy Wood read the manuscript and provided helpful, critical comments. We are grateful to the Polytechnic of Central London for granting us both a year's study leave in the early eighties; this volume is the fruit of that precious research time.

Our students at PCL, in their final year research projects, provided us with some extremely useful dissertations on topics that touched on our field: to Monica Delaney and particularly Martin Head and Shaun Moores for their invaluable studies of, respectively, Radio Luxembourg before the war and of memories of early radio and everyday life, we offer our thanks. *Media Culture & Society* has provided, over the years, a base in which to publish our work in progress and we are grateful for permission to incorporate material first published in its pages into the body of our book. Leo Scannell provided the idea for the cover. Vicky Williams offered advice and guidance at the proof reading stage. Gwyniver Jones produced the index, a labour of love for which we are deeply grateful. Suzanne Williams provided the inspiration to finish the thing and bring it – at last – to completion.

Broadcasting brings relaxation and interest to many homes where such things are at a premium. It does far more: it carries direct information on a hundred subjects to innumerable people who thereby will be enabled not only to take more interest in events which formerly were outside their ken, but who will after a short time be in a position to make up their own minds on many matters of vital moment, matters which formerly they had either to receive according to the dictated and partial versions and opinions of others, or to ignore altogether. A new and mighty weight of public opinion is being formed, and an intelligent concern on many subjects will be manifested in quarters now overlooked. I have heard it argued that, insofar as broadcasting is awakening interest in these hitherto more or less sheltered or inaccessible regions, it is fraught with danger to the community and the country generally. In other words, I gather that it is urged that a state of ignorance is to be preferred to one of enlightenment ... To disregard the spread of knowledge, with the consequent enlargement of opinion, and to be unable to supplement it with reasoned arguments, or to supply satisfactory answers to legitimate and intelligent questions, is not only dangerous but stupid.

J. C. W. Reith, Broadcast Over Britain (1924)

INTRODUCTION

CHAPTER ONE

Public Service Broadcasting

━━━▶❀◀━━━

 Today it seems that an epoch in the history of broadcasting is coming to a close. For most of this century nationally networked radio and television services, subject to some degree of state regulation, have supplied a wide and varied range of programmes on a small number of channels to whole populations. Now it seems we are on the threshold of a new era in which channel scarcity is a thing of the past, in which state regulation is no longer necessary or desirable, and in which individuals have access not merely to an indefinite number of television channels but to a wide range of interactive video services. A second electronic revolution is promised which will, it is claimed, transform the wired home of the twentieth–century into a self-servicing base from which people in the twenty-first century will manage much of their business and consumer affairs, as well as their leisure needs.

 The extended social and political implications of the new information technologies are, at present, largely a matter of conjecture, for they have yet to achieve a wide social distribution and acceptance.[1] Nevertheless it is clear that the kind of broadcasting service that most of us have known all our lives will no longer continue to define the social uses of broadcast technologies. As the classic era in broadcasting begins to pass away it becomes possible to see more clearly what its features were and are. What once was deeply taken for granted now emerges as one historical form of media usage, one that was part of, that constituted, an epoch; that was deeply implicated in the familiar texture of life for whole populations – the box in the corner, treated with that familiar disrespect reserved for the deities of the hearth.

 Ever since radio and television unobtrusively intruded into the day-to-day life of whole societies there has been controversy about their effects. Much heat and dust has been generated, from the beginning through to the present, about the impact on audience members and society in general of violence or bad language on radio and television. Broadcast politics has, from the beginnings, given rise to unending acrimonious complaint – from governments, political parties, lobby and pressure groups, academic researchers and members of the public – about the treatment of controversial issues on radio and television. Accusations of bias and distortion are as much a commonplace of television in the eighties as they were of radio in the thirties. In all such discussion there has been a tendency to 'personalize' the relationship between the content of radio and television programmes and their effect on listeners and viewers. The live immediacy of broadcasting makes it seem real and present in day-to-day life, a shared topical resource enmeshed in the experience of all. As such it is argued and gossiped about, abused and shouted at, regarded as a friend and companion – in short treated as an interactive, interpersonal resource in a wide range of contexts by most of us most of the time.

To get beneath the massively obvious and taken-for-granted character of programme output we have returned to the beginning, when nothing could be presumed, when the enterprise of broadcasting was, in John Reith's words, a voyage in uncharted seas.[2] We wished to recover the arguments and ideals that informed the way in which broadcasting was established in this country and, more particularly, to study the ways in which a form and content for broadcasting was discovered in the day-to-day business of programme-making. To that end we have tried to reconstruct the histories of most of the major areas of general programming in order to understand the factors that shaped policy and practice in each area and in output as a whole. We have tried to catch the unity in diversity of broadcasting, the parts and the whole, and to understand it as the expression of a new set of social relations between broadcasters, programmes and audiences.

But before turning to detailed accounts of programme output, the framework within which it developed must first be sketched in. It is well known that broadcasting in Britain is based on the principle of public service, though what exactly that means can prove elusive. The most recent Parliamentary Committee to report on broadcasting, the Peacock Committee, noted in 1986 that it had experienced some difficulty in obtaining a definition of the principle from the broadcasters themselves.[3] A quarter of a century earlier, the members of the Pilkington Committee on Broadcasting were told by the Chairman of the BBC's Board of Governors that it was no use trying to define good broadcasting – one recognized it.[4] With the passing of time the concept has become more and more obscure. Most commentators rightly attribute a central role in its definition to John Reith but few have attempted to go much further. Moreover, retrospective judgements of Reith's personality have become entangled with judgements of his ideas, and since the former has been viewed unsympathetically so have the latter. What has been emphasized has been Reith's religious zeal, highmindedness and authoritarianism, and these have been found to be characteristic of the service he created.[5] What is frequently pointed to as a critical absence both in Reith and the service he founded was any concern with the political role of broadcasting or sense of its importance.[6] Briggs summarizes Reith's concept of public service as follows: it should be a non-profit-making monopoly with a programme service animated by high standards and available throughout the nation.[7] There is no mention of its political significance.

Public service was a concept grafted onto an initial pragmatic set of arrangements between the Post Office and the British radio industry to establish a broadcasting service that would create a market for radio-receiving apparatuses. Control of wireless technologies rested with the state through the Wireless Telegraphy Act of 1904. The Act declared that all wireless transmitters and receivers must be licensed by the Post Office, which had the power to define the terms and conditions upon which licences were granted. Thus, in the aftermath of the Great War, when the radio manufacturers began to perceive a domestic market for their products, they were obliged to apply to the Post Office for permission to broadcast. The Post Office, anxious to avoid the chaos that had arisen from unrestrained broadcasting in the United States and unwilling to have to arbitrate between rival interests in the British radio industry, persuaded the manufacturers to form themselves into a cartel which represented the interests of the industry with which the Post Office would negotiate. In the end they did, and formed the Broadcasting Company, licensed to broadcast in 1922, with a working capital of £60,000 and revenues derived from a ten shilling licence fee on receivers payable to the Post Office (which retained half and passed the rest to the Company) and from a percentage of the royalties on the receiving sets sold by the manufacturers.[8]

At this point two of the key features of the British broadcasting system had been established, but without any ideological rationale: the licence fee and the monopoly. There was little perception at the time of the possibility of profit from broadcasting as such: that lay in the creation and exploitation of a market for radio-receiving equipment. The manufacturers capitalized the initial costs of setting up and equipping the broadcasting service. Its day-to-day running costs (staff salaries and programme costs) would be met by extending the principle of the licence fee which the Post Office already collected annually from the radio hobbyists whose wireless transmitter-receivers cluttered up many a suburban spare room or garden shed. The Post Office, as the state's major revenue-producing department, foresaw the possibility of considerably increasing its revenues through the licence fee. Indeed, one of the most scandalous features of early broadcasting was the percentage of the licence fee retained by the Post Office to increase the annual amount it earned for the Treasury.[9]

It was at first denied that the British Broadcasting Company was a monopoly, because entry into the company was allowed to any genuine British manufacturer in the radio industry. The thinking at first was all on the trade side of broadcasting and the creation of a market, and not on the broadcasting side and the nature and content of a programme service. The outcry against a programme monopoly, when the BBC began transmitting programmes, came from those who feared radio would seriously affect their health. The loudest cries came from the popular press which believed that a radio news service would harm its circulation.

The wider social implications of broadcasting were first given detailed attention in the deliberations and report of the very first Broadcasting Committee, under the chairmanship of Major-General Sir Frederick Sykes. The Sykes Committee was set up by the Post Office in 1923 to deal with the difficulties and confusions that had arisen in the first months of broadcasting over the collection and distribution of the licence fee and royalties. But the committee had a much wider remit. It was asked to consider broadcasting in all its aspects and the future uses to which it might be put. In the minuted proceedings of this committee and its report we find the earliest attempts to formulate what the general purposes of broadcasting should be. A crucial move was the definition of broadcasting as 'a public utility' whose future should be discussed as such. 'The wavebands available in any country must be regarded as a valuable form of public property; and the right to use them for any purpose should be given after full and careful consideration. Those which are assigned to any particular interest should be subject to the safeguards necessary to protect the public interest in the future.'[10] Bearing in mind the cheapness and convenience of radio, and its social and political possibilities ('as great as any technical attainment of our generation'), the committee judged that 'the control of such a potential power over public opinion and the life of the nation ought to remain with the state'.[11] The operation of so important a national service ought not to be allowed to become an unrestricted commercial monopoly. The report rejected direct government control of broadcasting. Instead, indirect control should be operated through the licence which by law must be obtained from the Post Office for the establishment of any broadcasting station. The terms of the licence, laid down by the Post Office, would specify the general responsibilities of the broadcasters and hold them answerable for the conduct of the service to that state department.[12]

Thus the definition of broadcasting as a public utility to be developed as a national service in the public interest came from the state. The interpretation of that definition, the effort to realize its meaning in the development of a programme service guided by considerations of national service and the public interest, came from the broadcasters and above all from John Reith the Managing Director General of the British Broadcasting Company from 1923 to 1926, and the first Director General of the British Broadcasting Corporation from 1927 to 1938. The Sykes Committee had made only short-term recommendations about the development of a broadcasting service and the BBC had been granted a licence to broadcast for only two more years. The Crawford Committee, set up in 1925, was intended to establish guidelines for the future of broadcasting on a more long-term basis. Reith was invited by the committee to present a statement of his views about the scope and conduct of broadcasting and he did so in a memorandum which he wrote as an impartial statement, presented in the interests of broadcasting not the British Broadcasting Company, and intended to show the desirability of the conduct of broadcasting as a public service.

In Reith's brief and trenchant manifesto for a public service broadcasting system there was an overriding concern for the maintenance of high standards and a unified policy towards the whole of the programme service supplied. The service must not be used for entertainment purposes alone. Broadcasting had a responsibility to bring into the greatest possible number of homes in the fullest degree all that was best in every department of human knowledge, endeavour and achievement. The preservation of a high moral tone, the avoidance of the vulgar and the hurtful, was of paramount importance. Broadcasting should give a lead to public taste rather than pander to it: 'He who prides himself on giving what he thinks the public wants is often creating a fictitious demand for lower standards which he himself will then satisfy.'[13] Broadcasting had an educative role and the broadcasters had developed contacts with the great educational movements and institutions of the day in order to develop the use of the medium of radio to foster the spread of knowledge.

Here we find a cogent advocacy of public service as a cultural, moral and educative force for the improvement of knowledge, taste and manners, and this has become one of the main ways in which the concept is understood. But radio, as Reith was well aware, had a social and political function too. As a national service broadcasting might bring together all classes of the population. It could prove to be a powerful means of promoting social unity particularly through the live relay of those national ceremonies and functions – Reith cited the speech by George V when opening the British Empire Exhibition: the first time the King had been heard on radio – which had the effect, as he put it, of 'making the nation as one man'.[14] But more than this, broadcasting had an immense potential for helping in the creation of an informed and enlightened democracy. It enabled men and women to take an interest in many things from which they had previously been excluded. On any great public issue of the day radio could provide both the facts of the matter and the arguments for and against. Reith had a vision of the emergence of 'a new and mighty weight of public opinion' with people now enabled by radio to make up their own minds where previously they had had to accept 'the dictated and partial versions of others'.[15] The restrictive attitude of the Post Office which, at the time, had forbidden the BBC to deal with any matters of public controversy, was severely restricting the development of this side of broadcasting, and Reith sharply criticized the shackles imposed on radio's treatment of news and politics. Only when freed from such chains would broadcasting be free to realize one of its chief functions. The concept of public service, in Reith's mind, had, as a core element, an ideal of broadcasting's role in the formation of an informed and reasoned public opinion as an essential part of the political process in a mass democratic society.

Finally, Reith argued strongly for continued 'unity of control' in broadcasting, i.e. for the maintenance of the BBC's monopoly of broadcasting in the United Kingdom.[16] The monopoly granted to the BBC in 1922 was merely for the administrative convenience of the Post Office and there had been a considerable outcry (particularly from the popular press) against this 'trade monopoly' as a restrictive practice which inhibited the development of a range of competing programme services for listeners to choose from. But Reith defended what he later called the 'brute force of monopoly'[17] as the essential means of guaranteeing the BBC's ability to develop as a public service in the national interest. The monopoly was, Reith argued, the best means of sorting out a technically efficient and economical system of broadcasting for the whole population – and universal availability was the cornerstone of the creation of a truly national service in the public interest. Second, unity of control was essential ethically in order that 'one general policy may be maintained throughout the country and definite standards promulgated'.[18]

Reith favoured changing the status of the BBC from a company in the private sector, set up originally in the interests of the British radio industry, to a corporation in the public sector under the authority of the state because he believed it would give broadcasting a greater degree of freedom and independence in the pursuit of the ideals of public service. On the one hand, it was necessary to be freed from commercial pressures. If radio continued to be part of a profit-oriented industry then the programme service would be influenced by commercial considerations and the need to appeal to popular demand. Entertainment, a legitimate aim of broadcasting, would become a paramount consideration to the detriment of other kinds of programming with a more educative or culturally improving aim. On the other hand, broadcasting needed to be free of interference and pressure from the state in order to develop its political role as a public service. Reith's advocacy of a public service role for broadcasting in 1925 had the support of Post Office officials.[19] Public opinion too had come round in favour of continuing broadcasting as a monopoly in the custody of the BBC and there was no opposition to its transformation into a Corporation at the end of the following year. Thereafter, for nearly thirty years, secure in its monopoly, the BBC was uniquely empowered to develop a service along the lines envisaged by its first Director General.

The ideal of *service* has been identified by Raymond Williams as one of the great achievements of the Victorian middle class, and one that was deeply influential on later generations.[20] It was certainly a crucial component of the ideal of public service broadcasting in its formative period from the twenties to the fifties. The Victorian reforming ideal of service was animated by a sense of moral purpose and of social duty on behalf of the community, aimed particularly at those most in need of reforming – the lower classes. It was institutionalized in the bureaucratic practices of the newly emerging professional class, especially in the reformed civil service of the late nineteenth century, whose members thought of themselves as public servants. At its best this passion for improving the lot of those below had a genuinely humane concern to alleviate the harsh consequences of a newly industrialized society. But it did nothing to change the balance of power in society, and maintained the dominance of the middle classes over the lower ranks.

One strand in this general concern for the conditions of the poor focused on their educational and cultural needs. A key figure in this development was Matthew Arnold whose definition of culture as 'the best that has been thought and written in the world' was echoed by Reith in his advocacy of public service broadcasting.[21] The radical element in Arnold's thinking was his claim that the state should use its authority to act as the guardian of culture in the national interest. Culture, for Arnold, was a means of alleviating the strain and hostility between classes in a deeply divided society, and the task of 'civilizing' the masses had a prudent political basis. It was a means of incorporating the working classes within the existing social and political order, and thus preventing the threat of revolt from below. Arnold's best-known essay, *Culture and Anarchy*, expressed that fear in its very title.

The idea that the state should intervene on the terrain of culture and education, so daring in Arnold's time, had won a much wider acceptance some fifty years later when government laid down the conditions under which broadcasting would operate and prescribed its general purpose. Victorian ideals of service laced with Arnoldian notions of culture suffused all aspects of the BBC's programme service in the thirty years of its monopoly. Such attitudes, in broadcasting, as elsewhere, did not outlast the fifties – or at least not with the degree of unself-critical aplomb that they had hitherto possessed. 'The ideals of middle-class culture', as the Annan Report noted in 1977, 'so felicitously expressed by Matthew Arnold a century ago ... found it ever more difficult to accommodate the new expressions of life in the sixties.'[22] Even so it noted that at some levels the old Arnoldian belief in spreading 'sweetness and light' still inspired the BBC some fifty years after its establishment.[23]

Underlying Arnoldian ideals of 'sweetness and light' was a concern for social unity mingled with national pride. In the epoch of the BBC's monopoly both concerns were central to its role as a public service in *the national interest*. The linking of culture with nationalism – the idea of a national culture – was given new expression in broadcasting through those kinds of programme that had the effect of, in Reith's words, 'making the nation as one man'. From the twenties to the present day the BBC has continued this work of promoting national unity through such programmes. Sir Michael Swann, chairman of the BBC's Board of Governors, told the Annan Committee that 'an enormous amount of the BBC's work was in fact social cement of one sort or another. Royal occasions, religious services, sports coverage and police series, all reinforced the sense of belonging to our country, being involved in its celebrations, and accepting what it stands for.[24] The Report described the BBC as 'arguably the most important single cultural institution in the nation', and recommended preserving it as 'the natural interpreter of [great national occasions] to the nation as a whole'.[25]

Such occasions, exemplified by, say, a royal wedding, may indeed be moments of national unity in which all sections of society participate. But what of moments of crisis? The question then arises as to whose interests, in the last resort, broadcasting is there to serve – those of the state or the people? Governments claim the right to define the national interest and expect the broadcasters, particularly in a crisis, to uphold their definition of it. To defend the public interest may mean challenging the government of the day – a risky enterprise for institutions that derive their authority to broadcast from the state.

The concept of the public interest has a very different history from that of public service. It relates to the news function of modern media and was elaborated in the struggles for press freedom from the late eighteenth through to the mid-nineteenth century. Against the power of the state radical opinion publics – bourgeois and proletarian – emerged to claim universal political and civic rights; the right to vote, to free speech and free assembly.[26] New kinds of 'public sphere'[27] were formed independent of church and state, claiming the right to criticize both and committed to the establishment of public life, grounded in free and open discussion, in which all members might participate. The struggle to establish an independent press, both as a source of information about the activities of the state and as a forum for the formation and expression of public opinion, was part of this process, and an important aspect of the long battle for a fully representative system of democratic government.

The establishment of broadcasting coincided with the moment that the vote was finally conceded to all adult men and women, and the development of mass democracy is closely connected with broadcasting's role in that process. The concession of universal suffrage after the Great War was a recognition of long and bitter struggles for basic political equality for all, irrespective of class or sex. At the start of the twenties Britain was faced with a truly mass electorate and with a central government whose actions and decisions impinged increasingly on the lives and circumstances of the population. These changed circumstances catalysed a sense of unease about the efficacy of contemporary democracy. In the decade after the war it had again become fashionable for superior persons to sneer at democracy.[28] Political theorists were wont to look back with regret to earlier models of democracy expressed in the Athenian *polis* or the writings and debates on liberty and freedom of the seventeenth century – the celebrated discussions between the Army and Cromwell, or those of the Puritan settlers in New England – on how to constitute their religious and political rights and freedoms. All these debates about government by consent took place in what seemed like a knowable community in which consensus might be achieved through open public debate and consultation. By contrast the size and scale of modern society had dissolved that sense of community, while the corresponding complexity of modern government – 'the vast elaboration of the subject matter of politics', as Walter Lippmann put it – made it well-nigh impossible for ordinary citizens to have any adequate knowledge of the activities of the state as they impinged upon their lives.[29]

The dilemma for liberal theory concerned the effective means of achieving democratic citizenship in modern conditions. The need to know on the part of individuals about the actions of central government, if they were to use their newly-won political rights effectively, pointed not only to an 'information gap' between state and citizenry, but also to the crux as to how that gap should be bridged and from which direction. The establishment of mass democracy implied a new imperative for parties and governments to secure, through the control and management of public opinion, the acceptance by the electorate of their programmes and policies. For the electorate it meant a new imperative to impress upon their political representatives their wishes and opinions in relation to the management of the nation's affairs. From the start, public opinion was the site and stake of struggle in mass democratic politics, and of crucial importance in the whole history of broadcasting's role in the politics of twentieth-century society.

Traditionally it had been argued that it was the responsibility of the press to act, ideally, as an indispensable link between government and people. By the late nineteenth century it could comfortably be assumed, by legitimate opinion, that an independent press in its role of Fourth Estate was the watchdog of government, the guardian of the public interest and the guide and informer of public opinion.[30] But by the early twenties such reassuring assumptions had been eroded. For Walter Lippmann in America the present crisis of Western democracy was a crisis in journalism, while in Britain the prestige and incorruptibility of newspapers was tarnished by Lloyd George's antics in press manipulation and his purchase, in 1918, of the *Daily Chronicle* to advance his own political causes. The sensationalism and triviality of post-war popular journalism was denounced for its irresponsible evasion of the serious political and public issues of the day. The most outspoken British critic of the tabloid press was Norman Angell, who had worked for eight years on Northcliffe's *Daily Mail* and who saw a reformed popular press as a means of creating a reasoned, reasonable public opinion:

> If any progress ... was to be made against the prevailing disorders of the public mind, that mind had to be reached largely through the Press. How could this be done? How could sense and rationalism be made as attractive as the Hearsts and the Harmondsworths seemed to make nonsense and irrationalism? ... In seeking some solution of that problem it did not help very much merely to abuse the Press lords – which the highbrows and intelligentsia did so plentifully. If the 'big' public, as distinct from the small minority, simply would not read the better type of newspaper, it became an impossibility to reach that public through that paper. This was the dilemma.[31]

Angell believed, though with diminishing enthusiasm, that better education was the best defence against the sensationalism of the press. There were widespread hopes, even before the end of the war, that a reformed educational system would redeem its unprecedented miseries by helping to bring about greater social justice and harmony. Threaded through the educational reports of the time were two underlying concerns; for the cultural enrichment of individuals and for greater social unity. The former might deliver the latter. Rich and poor might be united if both had equal access to the treasures of their common cultural heritage. As the Newbolt Report on the teaching of English put it in 1921:

> An education of this kind is the greatest benefit which could be conferred upon any citizen of a great state, and that common right to it, the common discipline and enjoyment of it, the common possession of the tastes and associations connected with it, would form a new element of national unity, linking together the mental life of all classes by experiences which have hitherto been the privileges of a limited section.[32]

There was a renewed emphasis on the 'apostolic' and 'missionary' task of humanizing the masses whose contempt for culture and enlightenment pointed to a morbid condition of the body politic: 'the nation of which a considerable portion reject this [i.e. literature's] means of grace, and despises this great spiritual influence must be assuredly heading to disaster.'[33] There was a prudent politics behind the call for a more humanely-tuned education. In the words of one contemporary, 'Deny to working-class children any common share in the immaterial and presently they will grow into the men who demand with menaces a Communism of the material.'[34] Common access to spiritual wealth might forestall any need or demand to redistribute more equitably material wealth.

Such current political, cultural and educative concerns, though only lightly sketched in, provide a framework within which to understand contemporary responses to the arrival of broadcasting and the rapidly emerging public philosophy with which it was invested. Radio appeared at the beginning of the twenties as one expression of a new age into which Britain was emerging after the war – the neotechnic age, as Lewis Mumford called it, the age of electricity and petrochemicals.[35] Wireless technology was one potent symbol of the marvels of science applied, in its broadcast form, to general social needs. Progressives like John Grierson saw the new media of radio and cinema as potential solutions to the dilemmas of democracy.

Many of us after the war (and particularly in the United States) were impressed by the pessimism that had settled on Liberal Theory. We noted the conclusions of such men as Walter Lippmann that because the citizen under modern conditions could not know everything about everything all the time, democratic citizenship was therefore impossible. We set to thinking how a dramatic apprehension of the modern scene might solve the problem, and we turned to the new wide-reaching instruments of radio and cinema as necessary instruments both in the practice of government and the enjoyment of citizenship.[36]

Radio, in an organized social form, seemed to be one significant and unprecedented means of helping to shape a more unified and egalitarian society. Through radio a sense of the nation as a knowable community might be restored by putting people in touch with the ceremonies and symbols of a corporate national life. A common culture might be established by providing listeners with access to music and other performing arts and cultural resources from which most had previously been excluded. A sense of civic responsibility and a wider knowledge of public affairs might be encouraged through common access to the discourses of public life, through the balanced presentation of the facts and the issues at stake in current political debates and policies. These interlocking processes were to be the desired effects of a conception of broadcasting as an instrument of democratic enlightenment, as a means of promoting social unity through the creation of a broader range of shared interests, tastes and social knowledge than had previously been the portion of the vast majority of the population.

Reith's achievement was to transform ideals into reality. There were two crucial decisions about how to organize and deliver a programme service. The mandate of national service was interpreted most basically as meaning that anyone living anywhere in the United Kingdom was entitled to good quality reception of the BBC's programmes. They should be universally available. To achieve this a small number of high-powered twin transmitters were set up in strategically chosen locations to deliver two programmes to listeners: a Regional Programme produced from a handful of provincial stations, and a National Programme produced from London. Wherever they lived listeners had the choice of the National or their own Regional programme. Second, the policy of mixed programming offered listeners a wide and varied range of programmes on each channel over the course of each day and week. Typically it included news, drama, sport, religion, music from popular to classical, talks, variety and light entertainment. Not only did this mix cater for different needs (education, information entertainment), but for different tastes and interests within the listening public.

These decisions had far-reaching consequences. They brought into being a radically new kind of public – one commensurate with the whole of society. On behalf of this public the broadcasters asserted a right of access to a wide range of political, cultural, sporting, religious, ceremonial and entertainment resources which, perforce, had hitherto been accessible only to small, self-selecting and more of less privileged publics. Particular publics were replaced by the *general* public constituted in and by the general nature of the mixed programme service and its general, unrestricted availability. The fundamentally democratic thrust of broadcasting – of which Reith was well aware – lay in the new access to virtually the whole spectrum of public life that radio opened up for everyone. Broadcasting equalized public life through the principle of common access for all. As we shall see, in nearly every case, the broadcasters had a hard fight to assert that right on behalf of their audiences. In some cases, most notably access to the House of Commons, the principle has only just been extended to the television cameras more than sixty years after the idea of live coverage of Parliament was first canvassed by the BBC.

One key consideration to which broadcasters were sensitive from the beginning was the circumstances within which listening-in took place. Wireless reception from the earliest days had been naturalized as a domestic activity. The radio in the living room had become, by the end of the thirties, part of the furniture of everyday domestic existence. It was in this context that the broadcasters recognized their audience, not as an aggregated totality (a mass audience) but as a constellation of individuals positioned in families. Radio, it was felt, enlarged and enriched the sphere of private life linking it to the public world and its discourses, broadening horizons, extending informally the education of family members and providing them with new interests and topics of conversation. The 'listener-in' was recognized as carrying a range of social and cultural needs and interests, as having domestic and social responsibilities both in the home and the local community; and beyond that as having a role to play – a more public role as citizen – in the larger community of public affairs and national life.

The BBC came to see its audience both as a unity and a diversity. It presumed a national community whose general interests it had a duty to serve. It must always be the case that 'the general needs of the community come before the sectional.'[37] As for those sectional needs (whether political – as between different legitimated parties; or regional – as between different areas of the country; or cultural – as between different taste publics from high to low), the BBC thought of itself as an impartial arbiter of their various claims, assessing their relative importance and catering for them accordingly. Policy was based on the basic principle that broadcasting 'should be operated on a national scale, for national service and by a single national authority'.[38]

Broadcasting had started up on a local basis. Between 1922 and 1924 nine 'main' stations and ten 'relay' stations had been set up in strategically populous centres of England, Wales, Scotland and Northern Ireland. Between them they provided a service which reached nearly 80 per cent of the population. A network system was introduced whereby each station could take, via Post Office trunk lines, 'simultaneous broadcasts' of news and important programmes from the London station which was also Head Office. Alternatively any one station in the network might 'feed' the rest with one of its own local products. These initial arrangements rationalized developments already in train. Three of the largest manufacturers already had licensed experimental broadcasting stations before the British Broadcasting Company was formed: Marconi transmitted from Marconi House in the Strand with the call sign 2LO, Metropolitan Vickers from Manchester with 2ZY and Western Electric from Birmingham with 5IT. When the BBC officially began broadcasting, these became the first three main stations to provide a regular service for listeners, using the same call signs, in the three largest urban centres of England.[39]

There were solid reasons for not continuing to extend broadcasting piecemeal by adding more and more local stations to the network. On technical and economic grounds it made much more sense to concentrate on a smaller number of stations with high-powered transmitters to extend reception to the whole of Great Britain. To allay the obvious criticism of the monopoly – that it restricted programme choice – it was necessary to provide listeners with at least an alternative choice of programmes. But thirdly, and most crucially, greater unity and centrality of control permitted a more effective organization of programme output to fit the concept of public service.

For Reith unity of control through the monopoly, and centrality of control

15

from London, were inextricably linked. The absence of competition allowed for the rapid, efficient and planned expansion of broadcasting guided by policies embodying the concept of public service formulated by Reith and a small nucleus of senior personnel in Head Office. Reith had stressed, in his memorandum to the Crawford Committee, the importance of one general policy and one set of standards for the whole country. That meant bringing all the local stations into line. Ultimately it meant their elimination. The regime of control was to replace informality by a studied formality; to replace local variety and differences by a standardized conception of culture and manners; to replace audience participation by a more distanced, authoritative and prescriptive approach to broadcasting; to replace ordinary people and amateur performers in the studios by authorities, experts and professionals. The diversity of the early radio stations, and the sometimes heterodox activities of their directors, were carefully brought to heel. By 1930 local radio had vanished. In its place was the National Programme from London and the Regional Programme produced from five centres serving the Midlands, North, South-East, West and Scotland. Northern Ireland and Wales were added in later.

In the formative period of British broadcasting three different models – local, regional and national – were tried, with quite different social and cultural values implicated in each. Early local broadcasting emphasized a friendly interpersonal relationship with its listeners. This was quickly superseded by the National and Regional service. London, in line with Arnoldian notions of sweetness and light, would provide the best that was available in music, talks, drama and entertainment. The standards and values of metropolitan culture were taken for granted. It seemed self-evident that London could provide better quality in musical performance, bigger stars for entertainers, more important speakers than the rest of the country. The national culture that the National Programme claimed to embody was of the educated, south-east English variety. If the Regional service, rooted in provincial centres, could not match the quality that London could draw upon, its task was to give expression to the everyday life and variety of the areas served by the regional stations – culture 'as a way of life' in Raymond Williams' phrase.[40]

Aesthetic theory, from the early nineteenth century, had stressed the autonomy of culture. A work of art was the expression of the free play of the creative genius of the artist. This creative principle was the mark of the integrity of artistic producers and their products. Art as an end in itself was a defence against and resistance to the growing penetration of economic rationality and the industrial process into all spheres of life, including culture itself. In the early twentieth century the new media of cinema, broadcasting and the mass circulation press were seen as completing this process. The 'culture industry', for Adorno and Horkheimer exiled in the United States, marked the liquidation of autonomous individuality and art by impressing the stamp of

sameness on everything and everybody.[41] In Britain Leavis produced exactly
the same critique, from a different political stance, of the standardization of
culture by the mass media.[42] Cultural critics feared both the levelling-down
effects of the modern media and their power to beguile the innocent, the
uneducated and unwary. If broadcasting in Britain emerged relatively
unscathed from such withering criticism it was because the BBC, like the cultural critics, rejected the profit motive as the basis of its institutional existence.
Nevertheless under Reith's management the spirit of bureaucracy began to
pervade its activities as the size and scale of its enterprise grew in the thirties,
with consequences for programme-makers and their products.

Once established in 1927 as the Corporation with a mandate of national
service, the BBC embarked on the expansion and consolidation of its
institutional position within the established political and social order. When
Reith resigned as Director General in 1938 one newspaper congratulated him
for making the BBC into a national institution as thoroughly typical and representative as the Bank of England – safe, responsible, reliable, the guarantor
of the nation's cultural capital. The implementation of a coherent programme
policy began in the days of the Company but was greatly accelerated thereafter. 'Uplift' was the code word that covered a complex set of developments
which included the establishment of more authoritative styles and modes of
address in the presentation and announcing of programmes; the pursuit of
social and cultural prestige, most notably in the fields of music and talks; the
arbitration of the claims of different taste publics in the National and Regional
programmes; the trimming of the wayward tendencies of departments or
individuals; the moulding of each area of production into the bearer of an
articulate set of intentions, consonant with the ongoing activities of other
areas, collectively working together to produce, in a complex unity, the corporate ethos of public service broadcasting in the national interest.

In the first decade of its existence the BBC was in constant flux. It was not
until the early thirties that the arrangement of the service settled into the
National and Regional programmes, that programme techniques began to be
developed systematically and considerations of the audience began to be taken
seriously. To put production on a regular footing Reith undertook a thorough
reorganization of the BBC. Control over programme policy passed from the
production departments and their staff into the hands of a small nucleus of
senior administrators and planners who now, in consultation with Reith or on
their own initiative, determined the overall objectives of programme-building
(i.e. scheduling) and programme-making from the mid-thirties onwards.
Reith, who had been so vitally involved in the shaping of broadcast policy for
the first ten years of his regime, was less and less involved in the routine running of the BBC in his last few years as Director General.

To bring production in line, new personnel were brought in from outside to establish orthodoxy. Departments were dismantled and regrouped. 'Progressives' were eased out of programme making by 'promotion' or banishment to the provinces. In the mid-thirties the BBC was a troubled, unhappy place in which to work. It was riven by internal feuds and rivalries; by dissatisfactions with conditions and terms of employment, pay and promotion; by the lack of adequate mechanisms for bargaining and negotiating on these matters; by corporate meddling in the private affairs of staff members; by the growing gap between rulers and ruled within the institution. By the end of the decade programme-makers had become, in the view of one contemporary, 'the creative helots of broadcasting'.[43] They had begun to learn the rules, to recognize what goes and what does not, to accept the limits of the possible, to develop strategies and routines that would protect their flanks and smooth their way to a less troubled life within the institution. 'Referral up' – seeking guidance and official clearance from senior personnel on potentially sensitive subjects – became a standard practice.

Bleak though it was, this rationalization of production was a necessary, if difficult, period of adjustment to the complexities of the production process itself and to the pressures on production from broadcasting's two constituencies, the state on the one hand, the audience on the other. The problem of production was twofold: how to supply a continuing, uninterrupted output to fill the ether, and how to arrange that output in temporal sequences through the days and weeks in ways that suited listeners. Programme planning became increasingly important, both in scheduling programmes and in trying to balance the competing claims of different areas of output for the scarce resources of time and money. Political pressures were felt earlier than those from audiences and impinged on different areas of production. News, features and talks, each with a different history and rate of growth, drew most of the flak from politicians, parties, governments and state departments. By the mid-thirties continuing, often covert pressures from such sources, combined with well-orchestrated campaigns in the right-wing national press, contributed to a retreat from controversy which reached crisis point, for the BBC, in 1938.

The pressure to accommodate programmes to audience demand was felt at first more indirectly and only came to bear upon the Corporation in a concerted way from about 1934 onwards. There was a growing recognition of the need to modify uplift in order to cater more for the circumstances and tastes of the listening public. The force of this pressure came to bear most urgently upon the Variety Department and the Music Department, and their competing claims for time and money. To arbitrate between such claims in a reasonable manner required more detailed knowledge of listeners' habits and tastes than the broadcasters had hitherto possessed. The establishment of the Listener Research Unit in 1936 to provide such information on a systematic basis was crucial in settling programme planning on a rational basis and in providing criteria for arbitrating between the competing claims of different production departments.

The subtext, in all the accounts that follow, is of a learning process in which the broadcasters discovered what their business as broadcasters was. In the first instance this meant discovering how to make programmes that worked. It also meant grasping, in the day-to-day business of programme policy, planning and production, the thresholds of tolerance that marked the boundaries of their activities. Such thresholds are not fixed, and the extent of openness or closure in broadcasting – the scope of the permissible and possible – varies according to the social, economic and political climate. In this formative period, from a beginning without guidelines or precedents through to the outbreak of war when a secure niche in national life had been achieved, the development of the programme service showed marked unevennesses. As one area of production flowered, another wilted. The scope of what could be done in London could differ markedly from what might, at the same time, be achieved in the regions. But within the determinate pressures of external and internal constraints the fundamental characteristics of broadcasting as a public service in the national interest had been secured by the outbreak of war. A wide and varied range of programmes had been established for audiences throughout the country, and the lineaments of a common culture of broadcasting had begun to emerge.

Part I

BROADCASTING AND POLITICS

CHAPTER TWO

The Containment of Controversy

—————————

'IF ONCE you let broadcasting into politics, you will never be able to keep politics out of broadcasting.' So said the Postmaster General in November 1926, explaining to the House of Commons why the terms of the new charter and licence which would transform the British Broadcasting Company into the British Broadcasting Corporation included a clause forbidding it to deal with controversial matters in its programme service.[1] From the moment he became General Manager in 1923, Reith fought hard to win the right to deal with political controversy and to establish some degree of independence for the BBC. He was anxious to develop the political role of broadcasting which he saw as one of the most important aspects of the service, but in almost everything he tried to do he was thwarted by the evasiveness and procrastination of his political masters in the Post Office.[2]

It would be too simple however to blame the Post Office as the source of the confusion, compromise and expediency that characterized the developing relationship between the British state and the BBC. Governments, parties, state departments and politicians showed little principled concern with the definition or conduct of a system of public service broadcasting. In general they were guided by immediate advantage and self-interest. A perusal of *Hansard* shows that there was no discussion in Parliament of major matters of broadcast policy until late 1926. There was a handful of individual MPs with an interest in broadcasting who periodically put questions to the Postmaster General, but little more than that. Far more time and energy were given to debating the protracted and ultimately fruitless negotiations with the Marconi Company over the setting-up of an Empire Wireless Communications Network. 'Why does Parliament take so little interest in Broadcasting?' was the plaintive question asked in *Radio Times* (31 December 1926) by Captain Ian Fraser, one of the few MPs who actually did show an interest in the matter. Against the indifference of the Commons and the negative temporizing of the Post Office the thrust to formulate an articulate concept of public service broadcasting as a force for democracy in the political and cultural life of the nation came from the early committees of inquiry into broadcasting and from within the BBC, above all from Reith.

The licence granted to the Company by the Post Office in 1922 required it to broadcast programmes 'to the reasonable satisfaction of the Postmaster General'.[3] What did this mean? It soon became clear that it did not include dabbling in the clash of ideas and opinions. In March 1923 an objection was raised in the House of Commons to a BBC talk about a strike in the London building trade while the strike was in progress.[4] In reply, the Postmaster General declared that it was undesirable for broadcasting to be used to allow speculation on controversial matters, adding that he had made his view known to the BBC.

A month or so later the Sykes Committee attempted on several occasions to unravel the implications of this response.[5] It was put to Post Office officials questioned by the committee that this statement amounted to 'a censorship far more severe than was exercised during the War by the Censor's Department'.[6] If not censorship, it amounted to an influence, possibly intimidation. Their response was legalistic and circumspect. J. F. Brown, the Secretary to the Post Office, was more specific when asked if the BBC could be as partisan as it pleased about political, economic or any other questions. 'During the limited period of its licence', he replied, 'I suppose it could, but if it went contrary to what the Postmaster General conceived to be the public interest I am quite sure the licence would never be renewed. Whether this is intimidation or not, I do not know, but this is the kind of line we should take.'[7] The representatives of the Company, Sir William Noble and A. M. McKinley, when questioned, showed that they had drawn the obvious conclusion from the attitude of the Post Office. The BBC was on trial and must not do anything without the consent of the Postmaster General. It was better to steer clear of controversy altogether in order to safeguard the interests and the survival of broadcasting as presently constituted.[8]

Reith wanted greater freedom for the Company in the areas of news, talks, outside broadcasts and the coverage of the proceedings of Parliament in order to give listeners access to the political processes and public events and debates of the day. The development of the BBC's news service exemplifies the ways in which the Post Office, with the established vested interests of the press owners and press agencies, combined to frustrate the development of a key area of programme output. The major issue had been decided in 1922 before the Company-to-be had been formally constituted. In May, the Secretary of the Post Office, Sir Evelyn Murray, prepared a policy memorandum for the Postmaster General who was about to begin talks with the wireless manufacturers about establishing some kind of licensed broadcasting service. Murray argued that among the conditions which the Post Office should lay down was one that forbade the broadcasting of any news that had not previously been published in the press. And this was because 'the wireless companies should not, without very careful consideration, be allowed to enter into active competition with the news agencies, as considerable capital is invested in those undertakings and a large amount of Post Office revenue is derived from them.'[9] In November, Murray chaired the first meeting between representatives of the Newspaper Proprietors' Association and the BBC. A draft agreement was drawn up whereby Reuters, on behalf of the press agencies, would supply the Company, for a flat annual fee, with a daily half-hour summary of world news, to be transmitted between six and eleven o'clock each evening. The BBC would use this material only in its broadcast programmes and would preface every bulletin with a statement that the material was the copyright of the agencies that supplied it. A week later, in deference to the wishes of the Newspaper Proprietors' Association, the BBC agreed informally not to broadcast news before seven o'clock in the evening so as not to compete with the provincial evening newspapers.[10]

Under such restrictions a nightly news bulletin was part of the programme service provided by the Company from the beginning. Reith, who had taken no part in these arrangements, pressed strenuously to break out from their constraints. Within a year of his appointment he was seeking approval for the BBC to cover daytime public ceremonies; 'descriptions' of the Boat Race, the Derby and the Cup Final 'by a reporter into the microphone on the scene', and speeches at important dinners and other functions before and after seven o'clock in the evening.[11] These issues were raised in the hearings of the Sykes Committee and Reith vigorously questioned Lord Liddell, representing the Newspaper Proprietors' Association. But Liddell refused to budge, declaring that the BBC's desire to transmit racing and football results and similar matter would seriously interfere with the sale of newspapers. Any live transmissions would take the edge off press news, making it stale and thereby reducing circulation.

Some minimal concessions were gained however: the right to cover, without introduction or commentary, certain sporting or public events, including speeches, before the evening news bulletin. The transmission of the Derby from Epsom was allowed on condition that only the sounds of the race itself should be heard. There could be no mention of the results. Under these constraints the BBC's first coverage of the race, in 1926, was a fiasco. It rained solidly all day, 'and during the race, not only were there no sounds from the hoofs in the soft going, but even the bookies, tipsters and onlookers were more occupied in taking shelter under their umbrellas than in speeding home the winner.'[12] The opposition of interests between the BBC and the newspaper owners was so great that Reith referred the matter to the Post Office for arbitration. Negotiations remained deadlocked throughout 1925 and 1926. It was not until January 1927, when the BBC became the Corporation, that it was granted the freedom to arrange early news bulletins during the day, running commentaries and eye-witness accounts of sporting fixture and public events.

Although the BBC had no control over the bulletins it received from Reuters, complaints about their form and content invariably tended to land on the broadcasters' doorstep. From 1923 onwards there was a steady flow of letters from the London Office to Carey Clements, Managing Editor of Reuters, on the treatment of politics in broadcast news. The earliest letter to Reuters on this forever to be vexed topic claimed that the news bulletins were supposed to be entirely impartial, but the Company had received complaints from listeners of 'an anti-Labour bias'. It had also received protests (from Surrey) about broadcasting socialist and communist propaganda under the guise of 'news'.[13] Clements was asked to ensure that on every occasion when political issues were touched on, the three parties should be given as nearly as possible equal attention. And when no news was forthcoming from any one party the bulletin should made it clear that it had had no special meeting on that day. The question of balance was raised again over the use by the agencies of news items taken from foreign newspapers. Reuters was asked, when using such material, to identify in the bulletins the political complexion of the particular newspaper and to balance it with the views of opposing newspapers. Clements demurred that this might be difficult since the papers might object to the way they were described.

One particular accusation of bias was made at the time of the notorious Zinovieff letter, in relation to a statement in the news bulletin that 'the only point now is the authenticity of the letter and, as the Foreign Office was originally satisfied on this account, it is difficult to see what further material can be produced.'[14] This was broadcast on Sunday, 2 November 1924, a week after the story was first splashed in the *Daily Mail* and four days after the election in which the first Labour Government was defeated. Burrows, for the BBC, referred the matter to Clements with the comment that the paragraph was unnecessary and exposed the Company to the charge of bias. Clements replied that the item was taken from an agency press-slip and that it appeared to the Broadcasting Editor, at that time, to be perfectly true and no more than a resumé of what had been generally stated on both sides.[15]

Nor did the bulletins escape the attention of the Post Office, which also directed its complaints to the BBC rather than the press agencies. The bulletin of 28 May 1924 was, for reasons unspecified, 'obviously controversial' and, in the view of the Post Office, might well have been omitted.[16] A few months later the Post Office again wrote to the BBC to say that it had received a complaint from Oswald Mosley that announcements in the news bulletins of forthcoming political meetings amounted to a form of free advertising with the object of securing large audiences. The Postmaster General instructed the Company to stop such announcements forthwith and to convey this injunction to the agencies.[17] Reith objected that this order was a very serious handicap to broadcasting and highly prejudicial to the service. As a compromise he suggested that announcements be confined to important occasions when men of acknowledged standing were speaking on matters of national interest. He took the opportunity again to remind the Postmaster General of the recommendation of the Sykes Report that the Company should be allowed greater latitude in its handling of news and controversy, and repeated that the BBC was suffering considerably from restrictions in these areas.[18] J. F. Brown, on behalf of the Postmaster General, replied that during election times the ruling must stand, but that in normal times it might be relaxed along the lines suggested by Reith.[19]

'It is well to be politic and like Agag to tread delicately,' Reith wrote in *Radio Times*.[20] In order to press the claims of broadcasting to handle controversy at all, such issues would have to be treated in a carefully balanced way. 'Great discretion has to be exercised in such matters', Reith noted in his column, 'but if on any controversial matter the opposing views were stated with equal emphasis and lucidity, then at least there can be no charge of bias.'[21] In the very early days one or two broadcasts on controversial political issues had somehow slipped through. In February 1923 there was a debate on Communism with a real live Communist taking part. 'It produced not revolution, but an interesting discussion.'[22] But subsequent efforts to develop more routine formal arrangements for political discussion were to fail completely. In August 1924 Reith asked permission to arrange a debate on some subject of current political interst between leading representatives of the three political parties under the chairmanship of some person of national repute, such as the Speaker of the House of Commons. The Post Office did not think this was a good idea. It might antagonize the public and, since the potentiality of broadcasting for propaganda was so great, the Postmaster General would have to put such a proposal to the Cabinet.[23]

Some weeks later Reith wrote once more to the Post Office to 'represent again our desire for permission to handle outstanding controversial subjects, providing we can guarantee absolute impartiality in the act'. He continued:

I feel very strongly that the utility of broadcasting as a medium of enlightenment is prejudiced owing to the ban on such matters. People have to take the views which are given them either in the Press or from the Party with

27

which they are connected, and practically never have an opportunity of hearing all sides of a question from the lips of the exponents of them, and they will not trouble to read what is written. I submit that broadcasting in this way might be a national service of great value, and that it would be a great advantage if the present restrictions were, under suitable safeguards, relaxed.'[24]

He was fobbed off with a brief note that now was not an opportune moment to revive this question since an election was imminent. Reith nimbly responded with an immediate request to broadcast speeches by the leaders of the three parties, strongly urging that such broadcasts would be in the national interest. Vernon Hartshorn, Postmaster General in the first Labour Government, gave his permission and three uncensored political speeches were broadcast by Baldwin, MacDonald and Asquith within the next ten days.

But that was about the only significant concession gained at the time. In January 1925 Reith wanted to relay a speech on housing by Neville Chamberlain from a banquet in Plymouth. He wanted to relay, from the Oxford Union, the debate on the King's Speech, and a little later to arrange a balanced discussion on unemployment which would be 'of the greatest interest' and a proof of the public service character of broadcasting. All were refused.[25] By now Reith was becoming wise in his dealings with the Post Office. He wanted to relay a speech by Churchill, then Chancellor of the Exchequer, to the Engineers' Club, but before writing to the Post Office he obtained a written confirmation from the secretary of the club that the speech would not contain anything controversial. Armed with this, his request for permission from the Postmaster General was granted. Churchill, as always, was highly polemical and complaints poured in to the BBC. In justification Reith replied, 'there is always a great public demand to hear public men, and Churchill is perhaps a better draw than any other Minister or ex-Minister. The occasion on which he spoke was a non-party one, and I think that our staff were well advised in not switching off Churchill in the middle of his speech.'[26]

By the autumn of 1925 Reith was reaching a pitch of exasperation. In October, after unsatisfactory replies to all his letters of the previous twelve months, he wrote indignantly in reply to the latest evasive missive from the Post Office:

Your letter does not reply to what was the main point, namely our desire, and as we see it, the necessity for some progress being made immediately, particularly in connexion with the handling of controversial matters ... We urgently require to develop new lines and to keep opening new fields, and this seems about the only direction in which we can improve our programmes ... The matter is of great urgency to us ... I know of nothing we can do unless we get permission and authority to move in the direction for which we have so frequently sought permission. The service is being badly prejudiced.[27]

While much time and effort was taken up by the quest for controversy, Reith was equally, if not more, anxious to secure permission for the BBC to present live relays of important public events and ceremonies, especially those in which the monarchy figured. The importance he attached to such broadcasts points up the way in which he thought of broadcasting as a *national* service in the public interest, a concept which became increasingly central to his advocacy of the role of the BBC. In 1923 he was busy trying to get permission to broadcast the King's speech at the Opening of Parliament, and to relay the service at the Cenotaph on Armistice Day. When he failed to secure the former, he commented in his *Radio Times* column, 'What's on the Air?', that there were many functions of national importance which might be broadcast, carrying interest of the highest order into countless homes, but that unfortunately not everyone seemed to grasp this.[28] When the Home Office turned down his request to cover the Cenotaph service (they relented a few years later, providing neither microphones nor equipment were visible at the ceremony) he complained: 'If broadcasting is a national service, our function is revealed on such occasions as these ... I am not criticizing the Department concerned. I am indicating that the position which broadcasting as a national service is able, destined, and will probably be bound to fulfil is not yet in all quarters appreciated.'[29] As a hint in the direction of those quarters he mused, in his column: 'Is it realized that if say a Prime Minister conceived the necessity of delivering a personal message of vital urgency to the people of this country at any reasonable hour after 6 pm he could have an audience of two million people simply by giving us five minutes notice.'[30] He said the same thing to Baldwin a year or so later at one of their first meetings to prove he had powers as great, if not greater, than the Prime Minister.[31] The point was not lost on Baldwin, who was soon to grasp its wider implications during the General Strike of 1926.

At the same time Reith was pressing for permission to provide listeners with daily coverage of the proceedings of Parliament.[32] Peter Eckersley, the BBC's Chief Engineer, had devised a plan for a system of double transmission whereby each main station could carry its normal output on one channel and the proceedings of the House of Commons on the other. Though there were some technical problems, he was confident they were not insuperable. Concealed fixed microphones could quite easily catch both front benches, but catching the voices of back-benchers would be more tricky since the optimum range of the microphones then in use was only five feet. Eckersley however had an ingenious solution in the shape of a moveable microphone: 'It would be quite easy to have a gracefully designed carriage on rubber tyres by which the microphone could move quite unobtrusively to whatever corner of the House was required.' He noted that this might cause some merriment at first.[33]

Eckersley subsequently modified his proposals to eliminate that last absurdity. Otherwise he continued to advocate the scheme, assuring *Radio Times* readers that BBC coverage of Parliament would be an integral part of broadcasting in the future. In these days of enlightenment, he declared, we were all politicians. 'Let broadcasting teach us to be better ones.'[34] The issue had been raised in Parliament some weeks earlier and was subsequently widely canvassed in the national press. At Question Time Ian Fraser had asked the Prime Minister if he would give the House the opportunity to decide the desirability of allowing the BBC to broadcast the Budget Speech, and if they could consider the whole question of broadcasting the proceedings of the House. Baldwin replied with a flat no to the first point and said he would refer the wider question to a select committee made up of members of the Lords and Commons.[35]

The BBC released a press statement, to coincide with Fraser's question, which outlined again the Eckersley scheme. The *Morning Post* reviewed the difficulties this involved, including the temptation to keen party men to withdraw a political enemy's plug unobserved while he stood wrapt in the spell of his own oratory. More pertinently it wondered whether there was any real demand for politics to be broadcast, noting that the BBC had admitted in its release that until the experiment was in being it was impossible to gauge public interest.[36] The *Daily Mail*, in a long article, discussed the feasibility of the scheme and the extent of public demand, pointing out that those moments that might have most appeal to listeners, such as Question Time, took place when most listeners would be unable to hear them. At the times when the majority of listeners could use their sets the House of Commons was usually at its dullest. It wondered whether the presence of the microphone might stir those private members who did not often speak to rouse themselves to catch the Speaker's eye more frequently.[37]

While the issue was under consideration by Baldwin's committee it continued to be discussed, and the expectation remained that the BBC might soon be broadcasting Parliament. In reply to questions from Captain Ian Fraser during the sittings of the Crawford Committee, Reith declared that the BBC had the technical and engineering know-how to relay broadcasts from the House of Commons and would like to do so. When Budget time came round Maynard Keynes argued forcefully, in *Radio Times*, for it to be broadcast and the politicians gave their views.[38] But two weeks later Baldwin killed the issue stone dead in the House of Commons. After consultation with the leaders of the other parties he had come to the conclusion, he said, that opinion was strongly against broadcasting the proceedings of the House.[39]

By 1925 Reith had come to the view that the constitution of the BBC needed to be changed. Its present position was, he felt, increasingly at odds with its professed intentions. In the first place the Company's monopoly, which was essential for Reith's vision of public service, was compromised by its association with the private interests of the radio manufacturing industry. From the beginning the popular press had attacked the BBC on this score. *Broadcast Over Britain* had stoutly defended the monopoly, or 'unified control' as Reith preferred to call it, as essential to the rapid, efficient and rational extension of broadcasting. By 1925 there was widespread acceptance in the press, and among influential opinion, of the BBC's monopoly. The Company was no longer seen as an ordinary business enterprise. Even so, in order fully to justify the BBC as a public service, Reith wanted it to be freed from its connections with trade and the taint of the profit motive. More crucially, in the light of experience, he wanted a position of greater independence from government, particularly in the areas of finance and political broadcasting. What ideally he wanted was an institutional space for broadcasting that was tied neither to commerce nor to the state.

Reith first formally addressed himself and his Board of Directors to this issue on 19 March 1925 at a special meeting held to consider the line to be taken with regard to a change of constitution for the BBC. He felt acutely embarrassed by his own position as he tried to explain to the representatives of the wireless industry how anomalous and absurd the present constitution was. The meeting was not a success: 'Very stupid, lots of them talking at once,' Reith noted in his diary.[40] Still, it was agreed that he should write to the Postmaster General to let him know that the BBC was willing, if required, to discuss its present position.

This was a calculated move in anticipation of the next official inquiry into broadcasting, for the Sykes Report had recommended the extension of the BBC's original licence for only two more years and it was due to expire at the end of 1926. The Postmaster General announced, in the Commons, the setting-up of a new committee, under the chairmanship of the 27th Earl of Crawford, on 20 July 1925, and it began hearing evidence in November. Its day-to-day proceedings and recommendations are less interesting than those of its predecessor. By now there was a general consensus that broadcasting should continue as a monopoly run by a single authority and subject not to trade but to some kind of public control. Most significantly, Post Office officials upheld the case for 'unity of control' while rejecting any suggestion that broadcasting should be run by itself or any other state department. It wanted to re-establish the BBC as a corporation with a widely representative governing body. This view, strongly supported by those who gave evidence to the committee, formed its major recommendation.

In his Memorandum of Information Reith was sharply critical of the present constraints on the treatment of politics and controversy. The recommendations of the committee on this issue were, for Reith, disappointingly vague and tentative. Its members felt themselves unable to lay down a precise policy or to assess the degree to which political argument could be safely transmit-tedd. They felt that, in the absence of authoritative evidence, advice and recommendations on the matter would be premature. But in general they believed that if the material was of high quality, not too lengthy or insistent and distributed with scrupulous fairness, listeners would probably desire 'a modicum of controversy'. With such provisos it recommended that a moderate amount of controversy should be broadcast.[41] The Report was published on 15 March 1926, and in July the Postmaster General announced that he accepted its main recommendations. But in the meantime there had been a major crisis, both for 'the nation' and the BBC.

Much has been written about the General Strike, and there are several accounts of the part played in it by the BBC,[42] so there is no need to rehearse again the details of those days of May. What Reith had been wanting more and more was an opportunity for radio to play its full part in national life. Now, and in a most unexpected manner, the opportunity arose. The strike focused the attention of everyone – government, parties, trade unions, churches and the general public – on the importance of radio. For the Government it showed the importance of radio as *the* means of controlling public opinion during a crisis. For Labour and the trade union movement it established a deep-rooted suspicion of the bias of the BBC in favour of the powers that be. For the public it became an indispensable source of infor-mation, in the absence of the national press, to which everyone turned to find out what was happening. For Reith it provided the chance to prove the 'responsibility' of the BBC in a moment of crisis and a 'golden opportunity' to win a greater degree of freedom for broadcasting. But although the strike per-manently underlined the political importance of this new social form of communication it did little, at the time, to strengthen the position of the BBC itself.

The BBC was not directly commandeered by the state though the Government had the power to do so. Opinion in the Cabinet was divided between those who, like Churchill, wanted to use the BBC as a government tool to crush the strike, and those who held it would be more prudent to allow the BBC the formal appearance of independence so that its seeming impar-tiality would be acceptable to the public. Baldwin favoured the latter view, and it prevailed. Reith then found himself in the unenviable position of having to take independent decisions during the strike but knowing that if his judgement was wrong, Churchill's demand to take over the BBC would be forcefully raised again. It was for this reason that, against his own better judgement, he refused the requests from the Archbishop of Canterbury and from Ramsay MacDonald, leader of the Labour Party, to be allowed to broad-cast during the strike.

But Reith supported the Government because he believed it was acting in the national interest against disruptive sectional interests. After the strike he circulated a memorandum in the BBC defending the position the Company had taken during the crisis in which he proposed his notorious syllogism; 'Since the BBC was a national institution, and since the Government in this crisis were acting for the people ... the BBC was for the Government in this crisis too.'[43] That was to set a major precedent for the BBC's position in future crises. What it did not mean was that the BBC would henceforth automatically accept the Government's definition of the national interest, as the Munich crisis in 1938 would show.

The position from which the BBC presented the strike in its news bulletins was one detached from both sides of the conflict. It sought a tone that was calm and cheering. 'It helped to dispel rumours of riots and violence and to undermine belligerent elements in the government's side. It avoided talk of Bolshevism or Revolution; it took a very down-to-earth attitude to the strike, and attempted to generate a cheerful stoicism among the rest of the population.'[44] Its aim was conciliatory, to reconcile opposing factions to each other, to maintain the morale of the population and to restore national unity. This position was, of course, far less innocent and disinterested than it professed to be, for what it systematically filtered out was any account or explanation of the causes that had put a large section of the population in conflict with central government. And they were bitter and angry about the BBC's presentation of the strike. The next couple of issues of *Radio Times* after the strike was ended were infused with a heady spirit of self-congratulation and letters from prominent men of goodwill praising the BBC's performance during those troubled days. But one letter, from Ellen Wilkinson the Labour MP for Middlesborough, punctured the general air of euphoria:

> The attitude of the BBC during the strike caused pain and indignation to many subscribers. I travelled by car over two thousand miles during the strike and addressed very many meetings. Everywhere the complaints were bitter that a national service subscribed to by every class should have given only one side of the dispute. Personally I feel like asking the Postmaster General for my licence fee back.[45]

In one sense the BBC could not have done more to present the cause of the strikers than it did, for its hands were tied by the Government. The more damaging charge is that there were few, if any, in the BBC who even understood the causes of the strike, 'the realities of working-class life, the sense of solidarity, struggle and occasional triumph which the strikers felt'. But then, as Asa Briggs notes, 'the straight facts of working-class life were not well known to most members of the early BBC.'[46]

The golden opportunity which the strike had presented was the chance to develop its own news service. With Fleet Street silenced, the BBC's news bulletins were the only available source of information for the population. They were assembled by a small scratch-team of BBC staff from the London office, working from the offices of the Admiralty. The bulletins were put together from official statements and press agency tapes, and included, from the first day onwards, an 'appreciation' of the situation written by BBC staff. This editorial comment was a new gain for the BBC and Reith was keen to maintain it. These comments continued for some days after the general strike was called off, but complaints from the newspapers and in the Commons, coupled with delays in getting them vetted, led to their rapid demise.[47]

Still, in the aftermath of all this, Reith was optimistic that he could now win a little more freedom for the BBC in the matter of controversy and politics. On 26 May he had a long conversation with J. C. C. Davidson, the Deputy Chief Civil Commissioner, who had been the link between the BBC and the Cabinet during the strike. Though the conversation was very vague he understood Davidson to say that he could arrange things so that the BBC would not revert to 'pre-strike conditions'. Later the same day he received a letter from Sir Evelyn Murray, for the Post Office, telling him that Davidson was no longer liaising between the BBC and the Government, and that Davidson agreed that the BBC should return to 'non-controversy etc.'. Reith cross-checked this with Davidson, who confirmed that Murray was right.[48]

Next day Reith wrote a long letter to the Post Office proposing that the Company should run a major series of talks and discussions on British industry in which prominent leaders of capital and labour would take part:

> The recent Emergency proved conclusively, if proof were required, how important a factor Broadcasting can be in the life of the community, and we have, as you know, long felt that it is much to be regretted that the influence of the Service should be so restricted ... We are anxious to take a lead in ordinary times, as we were through force of circumstances bound to take it in the Emergency ... While there is no doubt that the talks given on all manner of subjects have a high importance they have little or no bearing on history in the making.

Murray replied that the existing policy of avoiding the broadcasting of controversial matter should be maintained during the remaining period of the Company's licence.[49]

Briggs calls this attempt 'to introduce regular controversial broadcasting by a backstairs route, a curious epilogue to the strike'.[50] In fact it was but one further incident in a consistent campaign which Reith had kept up for over two years. In this particular case he was sure that his request to deal with history in the making was strengthened by the responsible conduct of the

Company during the strike. But by now he had further worries. On 6 July he wrote to the Post Office protesting that

> on practically all subjects of first-rate importance the Service is silent. The Advisory Broadcasting Committee recommended more latitude, so specifically did the recent Committee of Inquiry. It was understood that the restrictions were due to the non-representative character of our constitution, and that this was one of the determining factors for a change. The change is coming, and I earnestly represent that nothing should be incorporated in the Charter which might prevent an extension of activities in a direction of such paramount value.[51]

He had received the Post Office's draft proposals a few days earlier and his diary records the depth of his feelings on reading them – 'absolutely rotten and ridiculous'. Next day he met the Postmaster General at the Post Office and argued very emphatically against the iniquity and absurdity of the financial proposals, and against the continued ban on controversy. 'Their attitude is dreadful.'[52] Back in 1922 the Post Office had contemplated reserving for itself 75 per cent of the licence fee. But it decided, when the Company began operating, to take only half of the ten shillings annual fee.[53] From the beginning of 1925 this was cut back to 25 per cent: seven shilling and sixpence to the BBC, two shillings and sixpence for the Post Office. The methods of payment were not standardized, changing four times between 1922 and 1926 and always operating to the financial advantage of the Post Office.[54] But now a quite different scheme was proposed. There would be a fixed charge of $12\frac{1}{2}$ per cent on the gross annual sum raised, for the administrative costs of collecting the licence fees. When this had been deducted a sliding scale of charges per million licences would come into effect, the revenues of which would go direct to the Treasury: 10 per cent on the first million, 20 per cent on the second, 30 per cent on the third and 40 per cent on the fourth and each subsequent million licence fees collected.[55] Between 1927 and 1935 the gross income from licence fees was just under eighteen million pounds, of which two million went to the Post Office, six million to the Exchequer and ten million to the BBC.[56]

The effect of this progressively punitive scheme, which so outraged Reith, was substantially to decrease the proportionate income that accrued to the BBC as the size of its audience grew. There were other hidden ways in which this levy and the methods of payment worked against the BBC.[57] Reith was not alone in being scandalized by the way in which the financing of broadcasting was being treated. The *Financial Times*, in a leading article headlined 'Grab', described the Post Office's attitude to broadcasting as no more than a means of obtaining revenue for itself while doing nothing in return. And when the financial arrangements became known publicly, the representatives of the wireless trade protested that the enormous possibilities of broadcasting would never be fully realized while the Post Office had the power to make such arbitrary raids on licence revenue.[58]

Reith did his best to forestall the imposition of these arrangements. In July he took 'the highly unorthodox step' of sending a memorandum on 'The Broadcasting Service' to all Members of Parliament arguing against the curtailment of its financial resources.[59] This secured a considerable amount of scattered Parliamentary support, but the Post Office was not well pleased by this attempt to exert pressure on it.

Throughout the preparation of the Charter and Licence the Post Office kept its cards close to its chest. Though Reith learned on 12 June 1926 that the elderly Lord Clarendon was to be the chairman of the new Board of Governors for the Corporation, it was not until 25 October that he, and the House of Commons, learnt who the other four Governors were to be. Three days later Reith went to the Post Office with Lord Gainford, Chairman of the Company, where they met two of the Governors-designate. They were all there to meet Sir William Mitchell Thompson, Postmaster General, and senior Post Office officials, for the first detailed discussion of the terms of the Charter. 'We were handed out copies of the Royal Charter and went through many points, particularly regarding finance. The position is most unsatisfactory and the new body is not getting any more autonomy than the old, which is a deliberate ignoring of the Crawford recommendations, apart from anything else. The treatment of finance is abominable.' Reith noted in his diary.[60]

Next afternoon he returned to the Post Office where he struggled for two and a half hours with Mitchell Thompson and Sir Evelyn Murray, particularly over finance. They were very annoyed by his attitude. For his part Reith said that the Governors would put in writing their anxieties about the financial arrangements, to which Mitchell Thompson replied that in that case he had better get five other Governors. The very next day Mitchell Thompson summoned Clarendon and threatened to dismiss him and the rest of his board if they did not agree to the terms of the Charter. 'What a sickening business it is. Clarendon is so weak and stupid that he immediately accepted the terms,' Reith exploded in his diary.[61] He at least persuaded Clarendon to write, on behalf of the Governors, expressing 'their considerable anxiety as to whether the funds at the disposal of the Corporation under the agreement will prove to be sufficient for the proper development of the Service on progressive lines.'[62]

On 12 November the Post Office published the Charter and three days later the Commons, meeting in Committee of Supply, had the chance to discuss it. The Postmaster General spoke at some length about the financial proposals and the continuing ban on controversy.[63] It was a performance of masterly blandness. Mitchell Thompson defended his financial scheme on three grounds. First, he claimed that the cost of broadcasting did not increase as the number of listeners grew. Second, the state, having granted a privileged monopoly, 'had the right to a consideration in return as a favour for granting that monopoly.' Lastly, since other forms of entertainment had to make their contribution to the general revenue of the country, why should radio be immune. He admitted that the BBC was a little unhappy with his arrangements and quoted in full the letter of 4 November he had received from Lord Clarendon. With the air of one who was being reasonable and generous, he announced that, in response to this, the Post Office had decided to include a clause in the provisions which would allow discussion of the BBC's financial arrangements after two years had passed.

On controversy Mitchell Thompson said that he knew continuation of the ban would provoke discussion and criticism. That was precisely the objective of the Government, because 'this subject as yet has received quite imperfect consideration at the hands of the public in general, and I do not think it has even received a great deal of consideration in this House.' The Government wanted the fullest public discussion of the matter before it ventured to let politics into broadcasting to a greater extent than was desirable. 'Because', he added sagely, 'if you once let politics into broadcasting you will never be able to keep broadcasting out of politics.'[64]

In the desultory discussion that followed – it was late in the evening – the financial arrangements were quite sharply criticized and the BBC's right to handle controversy was defended. Opinion generally favoured it, it was said. Captain Fraser called it the breath of life and essential for the WEA movement and for adult education. Broadcasting was being treated in the same way as the printing press had been in the sixteenth century. The restriction amounted to a censorship over the free expression of opinion and knowledge.[65] Members might criticize but that was all for, when the House was constituted as a Committee of Supply, they were there simply to approve the annual estimates of government expenditure for the various departments of state. They had no control over expenditure. What such occasions afforded was no more than a general discussion of the work of a department. The Commons was not assembled to ratify the Charter, nor could they propose amendments to it. One or two Labour members protested that the new constitution for the BBC ought to have been brought in by Act of Parliament which would have allowed both for significant discussion of the Charter and significant alteration of its terms if so demanded. But Mitchell Thompson had already rejected such a proposal, because to do so might give the public the idea that the new Corporation was in some way 'a creature of Parliament and connected with political activity'. Thus the Government allowed the House the luxury of expressing what opinions it had without in any way being obliged to take heed of them.

Reith's anger on the following day knew no bounds:

The PMG put the Broadcasting business up in the Commons last night, but there was very little comment about it. I cannot express my opinion on the way the Post Office has treated us; they have been unfair, arbitrary and positively dishonest. They have printed outside the document that the terms were mutually agreed. I wonder whether I should not make some public protest about it. The constitution was to be changed to admit of more scope and more autonomy, but none of these has materialized.[66]

On the two crucial matters of financial and political independence, the Charter was the denial of all that he had worked for since becoming General Manager of the British Broadcasting Company.

CHAPTER THREE

The Management of News and Political Debate

———◦❀◦———

THE CHARTER and Licence mark the turning point in the BBC's history, the moment from which it developed in its present form as a major political and cultural influence on national life. But this growth was not accompanied by a strengthening of its financial or political independence. It was transformed from a company in the private sector serving the interests of the British radio industry to a corporation in the public sector under the auspices of the state. As it crossed the political threshold the BBC became, to borrow Keith Middlemas's phrase, a 'governing institution' with aims and functions delegated to it by Parliament, committed to cooperation with government and sharing its assumptions about what constituted the 'national interest'.[1] The limits to this collaboration were set by the broadcasters' sense of responsibility to their audience and a realization, hardwon in the light of experience by 1939, that in the last resort their task was to serve the interests of the people not the government of the day.

In the inter-war period the new conditions of mass democracy foregrounded the critical importance of public opinion and the role of the modern mass media as information and opinion brokers between state and people. Public opinion was something that governments and parties increasingly sought to influence now that they were, in an unprecedented way, subject to the will of the whole adult population at election times. Radio offered a direct and immediate access to the electorate which the parties wished to exploit during election campaigns in order to get their message across. At the same time central government began to discover the art of orchestrating opinion. New techniques of crisis management, censorship and the routine control of information were systematically developed and applied by the Prime Minister's office and all the major Departments of State.[2] These discreet skills were backed up by a series of Acts curtailing civil liberties which culminated in the Incitement to Disaffection Act of 1934 and the Public Order Act of 1936.[3] The management of opinion meant patrolling the boundaries of legitimate politics and the tactical use of force – direct and indirect, overt and covert – to quell activity and expression that was beyond the pale.

Central to this process was the normalization of relations with the media, the establishment of continuous, routine contact with the press and broadcasting and the creation of agreed procedures for the use of official information. In the late twenties Whitehall departments began to lay down guidelines for the continuing production, circulation and control of information about their activities. Publicity Departments were set up in each Ministry, with press officers and public relations officers who now openly sought access to the press and radio. Routine press releases, ministerial briefings, the advanced circulation of official reports and white papers, the arrangement of press tours and visits, the supply of information to individual journalists on request – these were the new means whereby continuous contact with the media was established and maintained. And, as the *Report on the Press* noted in 1938, only the last of them favoured the journalist. The rest placed the initiative firmly with the Government. The report summarized its views on these developments as follows: 'The Government tends to regard publicity as its own prerogative, and when a newspaper seeks to throw light on any department's activity the characteristic reaction is too often that the newspaper is up to no good.'[4] It is not a paradox to argue that official secrecy and control of information became more stringent as the state became more liberal with the flow of information to the media. The latter, we might say, protected the former more effectively.

At the same time Whitehall began to propound the doctrine that all this work, being in the national interest, 'was politically and ideologically neutral'[5] – a doctrine to which the broadcasters also subscribed as they took the first tentative steps in the direction of political broadcasting. The General Strike had incorporated broadcasting into the arts of crisis management. It set a precedent of discreet high-level liaison with central government and of working together 'in the national interest'. If the strike was, for the BBC, its political apprenticeship, the Charter was its passport into the state domain. As a company in the private sector the BBC had been small fry, snubbed by the Post Office and ignored by government and parties. That now began to change as parties, government and state departments started to use broadcast news and talks for their own ends.

The terms of the Charter had included an injunction against editorial comment and the broadcasting by the Corporation of its own opinions on matters of public policy. But it withdrew restrictions on the broadcasting of news, declaring one of the objects of the Corporation to be 'to collect news and information relating to current events in any part of the world and in any matter that may be thought fit and to establish and subscribe to news agencies.'[6] Protracted diplomacy with the Newspaper Proprietors' Association and the press agencies ensued. In January 1927 the Corporation was allowed to bring forward its first General News Bulletin to 6.30 in the evening and also to broadcast at any time a certain number of eye-witness accounts and running commentaries. This was fixed, in 1928, at a quota of no more than 400 a year. In February 1927 the first news bulletin crept forward to its new time, followed by a second at 9 pm. In October that year a new agreement with Reuters allowed the BBC to install an Exchange Telegraph machine in its offices at Savoy Hill, so that the Corporation could check the bulletins supplied by Reuters against the orginal tapes from the Creed machine. It also allowed the BBC to supplement the bulletins, if it wished, with extra material from the tapes. In September 1928 a further agreement with the agencies and the newspaper owners advanced the first bulletin to 6 pm and increased the annual allowance of eye-witness accounts and running commentaries. News was still to be obtained from the four agencies through Reuters, and this agreement was to be binding for two years only, subject thereafter to three months' notice from either side. A week later the first bulletin edged back to 6.15 and the second to 9.15 in the evening.[7]

A year later a further, crucial agreement with the news agencies gave the BBC decisive control over the selection and arrangement of the bulletins. Reuters and the Press Association agreed to supply their full services direct to the BBC. This entailed provision of all the necessary Creed tape machines, as well as the complete hand delivery service of supplementary material supplied to the newspapers. Direct telephone lines linking the BBC to Reuters' Parliamentary Correspondents in Westminster were installed shortly afterwards. For this service the BBC agreed to pay an annual fee of £14,000. The immediate consequence of these arrangements was the formation of a small News Section within the Talks Department, under Hilda Matheson, Head of Talks.

Reith, though bitterly angry about the ban on controversy in the Charter, prudently allowed a year to pass before renewing his efforts to get it lifted. Early in 1928 he wrote again to the Post Office, setting out all the arguments for lifting the restriction.[8] Under the present terms the BBC was falling behind enlightened practice in other countries. In Italy and Russia radio the national broadcasting systems were used for political and cultural propaganda, in Holland radio was used for religious propaganda, in the United States there was complete freedom, and in Germany – which Reith regarded as the most relevant example – controversial subjects were positively encouraged. In contrast with all this the BBC, and the country, had to endure the devitalizing effects of the absence of controversy.

Reith gave assurances that, if permitted, the Corporation would introduce controversial programming with care. There could be no expression of views contrary to the interests of the state, or on subjects likely to offend religious or moral susceptibilities. Topics would be presented with adequate safeguards for impartiality and equality of opportunity. And responsibility for this might safely be left to the broadcasters for 'it appears from universal experience that the broadcaster himself is the most important censor of the form and extent of controversial matter, and that even where government control is so remote and loose as to be negligible, the self-interest or sense of responsibility of the broadcaster requires that controversy should be prudently and tactfully introduced.' In sum Reith submitted that the right to deal with controversy was a natural and logical development of the service, that the power would not be misused, that no partisanship would be shown, and that any controversial matter would be introduced gradually and experimentally.

This letter succeeded where all previous ones had failed. On 5 March 1928, in reply to a question in the House from Sir Ian Fraser, the Prime Minister announced that, while the ban on editorial opinions from the BBC on matters of public policy remained, the veto on matters of political, industrial or religious controversy would be withdrawn immediately.[9] On the same day Reith received a letter from the Secretary for the Post Office informing him of this decision.[10] It acknowledged the loyal and punctilious manner in which the BBC had conformed to the terms of the Charter, which had persuaded the Government that the time had come for an experiment in greater latitude. The responsibility for the exercise of this new freedom would devolve solely on the Board of Governors, and it was not the intention of the Postmaster General to fetter them in this matter. The Government reserved the right to modify their decision in the light of further experience. The provisions for direct control of broadcasting in case of National Emergency were to remain in full vigour.

Thus by the end of the twenties the BBC had won from its political masters what it had desired from the start: the right to provide the new listening public with news and debate on the major issues of the day. What had now to be determined, in consultation with parties, ministries and governments, were the terms on which official information and political debate were available for broadcasting. At first, in their eagerness to establish links with Westminster and Whitehall, the broadcasters assumed that there was a common commitment, on the part of all concerned, to the national interest and the public good. They innocently thought of themselves as equal partners with the state in a joint enterprise of educating the listening public to participate in the democratic process. All participants were new to the game of information management, but the power to determine the rules rested with the politicians. What the broadcasters had to learn was how to embody the rules in news and talks.

The first efforts to establish links with government bodies arose from dissatisfaction with the service provided by Reuters in the aftermath of the General Strike. In November 1926, G. S. Strutt, who had worked on the bulletins during the strike, was in touch with a Parliamentary contact, Sir Ronald Waterhouse, about the possibility of government departments sending their official news direct to the BBC.[11] Waterhouse advised Strutt to contact the Postmaster General directly with an official request. A few months later Strutt wrote to Hilda Matheson setting out the reasons for attempting to establish such contacts. The possession of official press releases would enable the BBC to check agency accounts against them. It was often desirable that the news of government activities should be 'shorn of journalistic embellishments'. If the Corporation had the originals, it could safely revert to using them. Moreover, he argued, news of government activities would carry more weight with listeners if it came in the form, 'We are asked by the Colonial Office to announce ...', than if it came in the middle of the general news. This might seem to make the BBC the mouthpiece of government, but Strutt concluded that 'given common sense in editing, we need not fall into the bog of partiality.'[12]

His proposals got strong backing from Matheson, and two months later she was telling Roger Eckersley how much things had improved. The Foreign Office was being particularly helpful, allowing BBC representatives to secure any news that might be going, a privilege not given to any of the agencies. Downing Street, London County Council and the Guildhall were all offering a quite new and close liaison with the BBC. The staff were being inundated with invitations to dinners and exhibitions. But of course, she added, 'we do not put out all the stuff we receive from such sources, though it gives us a wide field of choice, much of it of definite public service and interest.'[13]

Most of the material now supplied by departments was in response to a clause in the Charter affirming that the Corporation would 'if so requested by any department of His Majesty's Government at the Corporation's own expense, in all respects transmit from all or any of its stations any communiqués, weather reports or notices issued thereby as part of any programme, or programmes of broadcast matter.'[14] This provision, which reiterated that in the original licence of 1923, was designed originally to cover routine announcements such as police messages, gale warnings, outbreaks of foot and mouth disease, and annual reminders from the Post Office when to put clocks back and forward and to Post Early For Christmas.[15] But the bulletins soon began to fill up with litter warnings, Road Safety notices, traffic

warnings from Scotland Yard, Buy British appeals from the Empire Marketing Board, along with S O S messages to missing persons and appeals for
witnesses to crimes and accidents.[16] The news bulletins were becoming an
unofficial notice board for the authorities to which they could pin anything
they wished to bring to the attention of the British public. By 1931 the
bulletins were getting so cluttered with this kind of thing that a ten-minute
period was set aside each Thursday evening to announce Armed Forces
reunions which had hitherto been included in the bulletins, as well as other
matters such as air mails, motor licences and traffic arrangements. This
relieved the pressure on the bulletins and became a permanent arrangement.[17]

The use of the bulletins by the authorities for such publicity purposes may
seem unexceptionable. But it was only a short step to using them in other
ways and for more questionable purposes. For instance, on the evening before
Good Friday, 1930, the press had printed a report of an interview with the
Home Secretary which the Home Office wanted immediately to deny. Since
the newspapers would not be published over the Easter break, the Home
Office turned to the BBC to issue its denial in the main bulletin that night. In
August the Duke of York and doctors attending the confinement of the Duch-
ess turned immediately to the BBC to issue a denial of a statement in a
Sunday newspaper concerning the royal birth. And later that year Emanuel
Shinwell, Secretary for Mines, telegraphed direct to the BBC a denial of
statements attributed to him by the press.[18]

It was an easy slide from letting officialdom use the bulletins to correct the
errors of the press to complicity with the authorities in the management of
news on radio. The case of the Ministry of Mines and the Board of Trade is
instructive. News Section's involvement with these departments began with
Shinwell's 'correction' of press statements. It continued with a government
statement (released simultaneously to the press agencies) being specially wired
through to catch the main radio news.[19] The Labour Government was, at this
time, preparing to bring in its new Mining Bill, but was encountering hostile
tactics from the mine owners and the National Federation of Employers
Organization who, in early 1931, were again advocating wage-cuts in the
industry as the best solution to the deepening recession.[20] The Government
was desperately anxious to avoid the spectre of 1926. Faced with the hostility
of the employers, backed up by a right-wing press, it seemed natural to turn to
the radio to defuse the situation. So, in the first three months of 1931, 'when
the situation in the South Wales coalfields was very unsettled', the Ministry of
Mines and the Board of Trade were, on several occasions, in direct contact
with the News Section. On 11 January 1931 William Graham, the President of
the Board of Trade, made a special request to the BBC to carry his statement
on the South Wales negotiations so that it would reach the miners at the
earliest opportunity. And a few days later, dissatisfied with 'the rather frag-

mentary' agency reports on the negotiations, the duty News Editor telephoned Shinwell and Graham at their homes to obtain personal statements from both which clarified 'all the doubtful points' in the agency reports.[21]

Within months the Labour Government was plunged in crisis by a run on the pound which led the Treasury to propose emergency economies, including a 10 per cent pay cut in the public sector and in unemployment relief. This was unacceptable to a majority of the Labour Cabinet who resigned, leaving Ramsay MacDonald to form a hasty National Government with a Cabinet dominated by Conservatives to approve what Labour had been unable to stomach. The cuts produced the first mutiny in the Navy since 1797. Within a couple of months there was a general election and a National Government was returned with a huge majority.

If 1926 had, under duress, educated the BBC in the rudiments of crisis management, 1931 was the first occasion that the lessons then learnt were voluntarily applied. Looking back over the year News Section's second annual Review of News claimed:

> There is no doubt that the Corporation may claim not only to have maintained its high position as a supplier of unbiased information, but also by means of its news service to have contributed materially to the steadying of public opinion during the financial crisis. During this dangerous period the public received, in the News Bulletins, without any comment, the first notification of the formation of the National Government, the official statements of the Government on the course of events, and objective non-sensational accounts of the results of the crisis on the pound and on the country's economic life.[22]

While the popular press had carried wild stories about the Invergordon mutiny, BBC news had exercised 'a steadying influence by its reports of unrest in the Atlantic Fleet'. At the height of the discontent, the Admiralty released a detailed explanation of the cuts in naval pay to the press agencies and at the same time telephoned through a request to the BBC News Section asking it *not* to broadcast this statement. It was not included in the news.[23] Two weeks later the Ministry of Labour asked News Section to broadcast a notice of the reduced rates of unemployment relief, thoughtfully providing a specially condensed version of the new terms for transmission. It was included in the bulletin. After the resignation of the Labour Cabinet, Downing Street telephoned through the names of the new Cabinet members as they were being appointed, for inclusion in the main evening bulletin. This gave the BBC a notable *coup* over the newspapers, much resented in Fleet Street, which were unable to run the details until the following morning.[24]

By the end of 1930 the News Section could boast that, in its first year's work, it had established good relations with the Foreign Office, the Treasury, the Prime Minister's Office, the India Office, the Department of Overseas Trade, the Ministry of Agriculture and Fisheries, the Meteorological Office, the Air Ministry, the Home Office and Scotland Yard. It had looser contacts with the War Office, the Ministry of Health and the Post Office.[25] By the end of 1931 the Board of Trade, the Ministry of Mines, the Ministry of Labour and the Admiralty had been added to the list.[26] To maintain these newly-made contacts in good working order the News Section let it be known that it was and would continue to be 'sympathetic towards suggestions made privately to us by Government Departments about our handling of news material'. An exchange of letters between the Home Office and Reith, which exemplifies this willingness to modify the bulletins on official request, needs contextualizing to bring out its full implications.[27]

On 31 October 1932 the Home Office wrote to Reith querying the inclusion in the previous night's bulletin of a protest from the Metropolitan Police Federation about proposed cuts in police pay. Reith replied next day that the item came from the usual agency sources but that he had given instructions that 'no stuff from the agencies re cuts in pay, protest etc. is to be broadcast ... only HMG's official statements in future.'

Four days before this exchange of letters the national hunger march of the unemployed had arrived in London. It was organized by the National Un-employed Workers Movement (NUWM), led by Wal Hannington and other prominent members of the British Communist Party. From the start the march had been kept under close surveillance by the authorities. All along the route to London the marchers were secretly checked to discover if they had criminal or political records, while reports flowed in to Scotland Yard from workhouse masters and public assistance officers about their physical condition and whether they were armed (with walking sticks, said one report). Meanwhile working-class districts of London, and especially the haunts of the Communist Party and the NUWM, had been infiltrated by informers and plain clothes police and fine-combed for evidence of Moscow gold behind the march.[28] When the marchers arrived in London they were greeted with a great display of solidarity from fellow members of the working class, and of force from the London police.[29]

By now the right-wing press was baying for the arrest of Hannington and his co-plotters of revolution. Subversive leaflets and stickers had appeared in the streets addressed to the police force: 'Policemen!' Defeat your own pay cuts by supporting Tuesday's demonstration against the Economies!' On the day the Home Office queried the news item about police protests against cuts in their pay, Hannington had made an impassioned appeal to them, in Trafalgar Square, not to use their batons against the marchers and the large supporting crowd. 'Let the working class in and out of uniform stand together in defence of their conditions,' he pleaded.[30] But violence broke out and two days later Hannington was arrested and charged with attempting to cause disaffection among members of the Metropolitan Police contrary to the Public Act of 1919. This incident was one of the factors leading to the Incitement to Disaffection Act of 1934 and the formation of the National Council for Civil Liberties in response to this curtailment of civic freedom.[31]

In these circumstances the anxiety of the Home Secretary about news items hinting at dissent in the ranks of the police becomes understandable. Reith in his reply added, by way of reassurance to the Home Office, that the same queried bulletin had also included a message specially telephoned through to News Section from the Commissioner of Police, asking the public not to go out to watch demonstrations. Thus by exhortation and judicious censorship did the news, in conjunction with the authorities, strive to prevent disorder and to maintain the King's Peace. There was, however, a muted account of the police baton-charging the crowd in Hyde Park a few days later, in an eye-witness talk after the news by Howard Marshall.

The early thirties were years of considerable popular unrest and civil commotion, triggered by the social consequences of the recession and the largely negative responses of the National Government. As the BBC was increasingly absorbed, in these years, into the orbit of central government, senior personnel at times found themselves drawn into the hidden workings of the state within the state. In 1934 a somewhat bemused Cecil Graves, then Controller of Programmes, was invited to attend a secret meeting at the Board of Education. The meeting was called by the Secretary of the Board but acting on this occasion, as Graves discovered when he got there, in his other capacity as publicity officer to the Chief Civil Commissioner.

The purpose of the meeting was to ensure that the methods and techniques for the control of information in an emergency, first used during the General Strike, were still in good working order. In a comprehensive review of the whole supply, control and dissemination of information, the role of the BBC was discussed and it was agreed that a BBC official should be attached to the Board of Education (whence any future emergency would be coordinated) with the necessary secretarial assistance and a specially laid on direct line to Broadcasting House. Present at the meeting were representatives from the Stationery Office, the Post Office, the Foreign and Colonial Offices, the Board of Education and Graves for the BBC.[32] The point to notice is the significance of the uninvited guest. There was no press representative there. It was not just that in a crisis the state could control broadcasting more easily than the press, assuming they were still running. The BBC was more useful. It was more authoritative and reliable. It spoke to and for 'the settled community'. If the press in a crisis tended to be divisive and panicky, the BBC remained calm and rallied the nation – a point which had not gone unnoticed in the crisis of 1931 by St John Ervine, writing in *Time and Tide*:

The reason why we came off the Gold Standard was because a number of neurotics in Fleet Street filled their papers with panicky 'streamers' about the revolt in the Navy. That revolt did not disturb anyone in Great Britain, but it frightened the wits out of foreigners who began to pull their piles of gold out of the Bank of England in a great hurry. Do you recollect, ladies and gentlemen, how calm we remained during the General Strike? Has it occurred to you to account for that fact, in part at all events, by the absence of newspapers from the country at that time? Our news was delivered to us in the calm and even tones of the BBC's announcer. Not a nerve was fretted then. We might still be on the Gold Standard if there had not been any newspapers published on the day the Navy 'mutinied' and we had received the news from Mr Hibberd, the announcer.[33]

In normal times, however, the state tended to favour the newspapers at the expense – or so it seemed to the BBC – of broadcast news. As the crisis of 1931 passed, the newspapers returned to attack the privileges won by radio news as they had done in 1926. The first signs of this came after the general election in October in which the BBC was again 'first with the news' of results in some 210 constituencies.[34] But when the second National Government was formed in November details of the new ministerial appointments, which a few months earlier had been telephoned through to News Section as they were being made, were withheld from the BBC and reserved for the morning papers. By the end of the month the News Section was convinced that a conspiracy was afoot to embargo departmental releases to the disadvantage of broadcasting and to the advantage of the press.

Departmental news releases were normally made in the late afternoon, thus allowing the BBC to nip in and pick the plums for its evening bulletins before they got into the newspapers the following morning. Now, it seemed, the press agencies were putting pressure on government departments to add a caption to their afternoon releases stating that the material was 'Not For Broadcasting'. The formation of the last Cabinet was cited as a major instance. There was an aggrieved sense in News Section that the Government was not playing fair by them. They had gone out of their way on innumerable occasions to include in the bulletins, at the request of state departments, material that could hardly be called of major importance. It was unfair, to say the least, that the very same bodies were now tending to withhold from News Section announcements of major issues which ought to be brought to the notice of the public as soon as possible. In sum, Rose-Troup, one of News Section's two editors, complained to Reith, the state did not seem to appreciate the advantages which the broadcast news service offered. On radio their announcements were made without misleading comments or headlines, 'and the effect on the General Public of receiving material in this form before seeing the headlines, was undoubtedly most valuable to the Government.'[35]

Exhaustive enquiries followed to uncover the origin of these embargoes. It appeared that they went back to the September crisis, as a special measure on an extraordinary occasion, which was then taken as a precedent by the Press Association and subsequently routinely applied. On the day that Britain went off the Gold Standard MacDonald had summoned the press to Number 10 to inform them of this decision. He was most anxious that this should not be known before Monday morning – an advance leak might have disastrous consequences for sterling on the New York Stock Exchange – and was particularly eager that the story should not get into the BBC news before that time. The editor-in-chief of the Press Association suggested that Reith be telephoned immediately and, in response to MacDonald's insistence, assured him that agency tapes would make it absolutely clear that this news item must not be broadcast overnight in this or any other country.[36]

The 'Not For Broadcasting' caption was imposed thereafter on a whole range of quite routine stories. The BBC was at endless pains to uncover who was imposing these embargoes, the agencies or the original information source, and in either case, for what reasons? There ensued for the rest of the decade an interminable lobster quadrille in which state departments, agencies and newspapers appeared – to the BBC – to be treading on its tail. It would be tedious to detail all the particular wrangles: the affair of Princess Marina and the Balmoral Ghillies Ball, the Peterson-Gains fight at the White City, a row with the Lobby over jumping the gun on a departmental Command Paper, a long-running feud about the announcement of racing results, occasional brushes with the Royal Press Office with whom it was hard to keep up since it seemed forever to be on the move from one royal residence to another.[37] These and other points of dispute rumbled on through the thirties, slowly building up paper mountains of memoranda, charges and counter-charges.

Midway through, an attempt was made to thrash the whole thing out, first with the agencies then with the Government. On 12 October 1935 there was a long meeting in the offices of Reuters. The agencies began by demanding that the BBC should respect to the letter the 'Not For Broadcasting' caption while they, for their part, guaranteed never to impose it unless told to by the original source of the item. The BBC refused, in principle, to accept this and wanted to reserve the right to check back with the original source. It undertook to do this in a responsible way and not to try to 'get one over the newspapers' when trouble seemed the likely outcome.[38] A month later there was a meeting at 10 Downing Street with George Steward, press officer for the Prime Minister and the Treasury. In this final attempt to get to the root of the matter senior BBC officials were anxious that the importance of its news service should be recognized and not overlooked when important government or departmental announcements were to be made. They wanted some agreed set of captions to be used by state departments which alone would be recognized by the BBC as debarring their immediate usage. Such embargoes should only be used in cases of intrinsic need.

Steward's response was friendly but equivocal. He readily granted the immense value of the BBC as a channel for conveying unbiased and unadulterated information to the nation. At the same time he appreciated the conflict of interests facing the agencies. He felt obliged to tread warily so as to avoid creating any impression of giving preferment to the BBC over the press, for this would lead, inevitably, to accusations that the BBC was the mouthpiece and publicity organ of the government.[39] Later Steward met with Sir Stephen Tallents, whom Reith had recruited as the Corporation's own public relations officer, and between them they drew up three alternative captions for departmental releases. Tallents tried to get all departments to observe the new arrangements, but had little evident success. The bickering continued sporadically through to the outbreak of war, when the whole issue flared up again in the novel and complex circumstances of wartime broadcasting.

From these procedural disputes the rules of the game in the normalization of relations between government, press and broadcasting began to emerge. The BBC was the weakest of the players in the game, a fact which it had scarcely grasped by the mid-thirties. Moments of crisis gave it the illusion of cooperation with government on an equal footing, but when the danger passed it was bemused to find itself passed over in favour of the newspapers. The press was far less easy to control than the BBC. If the state now turned 'naturally' to broadcasting in moments of crisis, in normal times it prudently gave precedence to the senior news medium which it had threatened and cajoled for centuries. The establishment of the ground rules for political controversy took a different path only to come to a similar result that emphasized again the power of the politicians and the powerlessness of the broadcasters. Here the BBC was asked to act as referee between the parties in drawing up the terms under which political issues were to be discussed at the microphone. The parties, however, defined those terms and made it plain to the referee that there would be trouble if he failed to interpret the rules correctly.[40]

Immediately after the ban on controversy was lifted the Labour Party wrote to the BBC asking when a pronouncement would be made in connection with the next General Election and requesting in advance that Ramsay MacDonald be allowed to make a speech through the channels of the BBC. Reith replied that the BBC was under an obligation to preserve impartiality and so must offer equal facilities on such an occasion to the other two parties. He then wrote to the Conservatives and Liberals. J. C. C. Davidson, replying for the Conservatives, asked whether the BBC 'could draw up rules of general application which would enable the various political parties to know the scope of the privileges to which they were entitled and enable them to make their plans accordingly.'

Reith addressed himself to this task with characteristic skill, perseverance and patience. His first proposals, in April 1928, were acceptable to Labour and Conservatives but not the Liberals, and so for the time being a proposed rota for political broadcasts by the parties, in and out of election times, was shelved. In the meantime Churchill, as Chancellor of the Exchequer, had persuaded Reith to let him make a fifteen-minute broadcast about his budget the day after he had unveiled it in the Commons. He promised to stick to a factual account and to avoid controversy. What he delivered, in Reith's view, was a good defence of his budget, but uncontroversial it was not. MacDonald protested on behalf of the Labour Party and the following year, with an election in the offing, the BBC did not renew its invitation to the Chancellor to speak on his Budget.

Over the next few years an agreed set of procedures was arrived at for the presentation and discussion of the Budget on radio. Meanwhile the need to settle the more general arrangements of political broadcasting became a pressing matter as another election loomed. In early 1929 there was enough inter-party agreement to allow the occasional discussion of political issues – Chamberlain's Local Government Bill, for example. The election was held on 30 May 1929. After much prior discussion it was finally agreed, under protest from Liberals and Labour, that they should both have two addresses before Parliament was dissolved, while the Government should have four. After the dissolution there were six more broadcasts, two for each party of which one in each case was by a woman representative to appeal to the newly enfranchised female electorate.

By the end of 1931 some preliminary agreement had been reached about schedules for the various categories of political broadcasting which had emerged. For party political speeches the BBC would allocate two months each year in which a slot would be available one night a week for the parties to fill in the order of their choice. November and May (for the Budget) were proposed. The selection of subjects and speakers would rest with the parties. In election periods there would be special series on a rota basis before, and with equal access after, dissolution. Provisions were made for occasional ministerial broadcasts on 'national occasions', and for factual talks by ministers of state or independent experts on legislation which had recently been passed by Parliament. The choice of speakers, in all these arrangements, rested with governments and parties, the BBC merely providing the facilities and the occasion.

There remained the question of talks and discussions on radio dealing more generally with contemporary political life and affairs. The BBC proposed periodically to arrange one-hour discussion programmes on current party political issues of general public interest. There would be a speaker from each party, with a right of reply reserved for the government spokesman if the matter at issue was a government measure. The BBC would choose the topic, though the parties might make joint recommendations, while the parties would decide which speakers to field, 'subject to microphone suitability'. On more general political issues, but not of current party dispute, the BBC would choose the topic and the speakers who would be picked to cover 'representative group opinions', whether party or otherwise. When talks series involved party political issues the BBC, while selecting the topic, would invite the parties to nominate their official representatives to take part in the symposium while the BBC would choose the other speakers. On issues that did not involve definite party issues the parties would not necessarily be consulted.

Here were the seeds of doubt and confusion. What was and what was not a party issue, and who was to decide? The party representatives, at the meeting in which this schedule was discussed and broadly agreed, noted that the BBC did not feel bound in every case to secure the agreement of the three parties as a preliminary to proceeding with a political broadcast. They made it plain that if the BBC proceeded with such arrangements in spite of failing to secure the agreement of the parties, they for their part might feel obliged to end the present concordat and to reopen the question of the Corporation's proper use of its discretionary powers in political and controversial matters.

Already however, the Talks Department had been exercising its discretion with some effect while Reith and the Governors battled it out with the parties. Their first major incursion into the field of controversy was a symposium called *Points of View* which ran in autumn 1929. The series was trailed in *Radio Times* as a broadcast symposium of individual opinions on the trends of the time by six of the leading thinkers of the day. Its aim was the personal expression, by each speaker, of his general philosophy of life. None of the speakers was a politician, though most made plain their general political inclinations. They were not asked individually to give a balanced talk – balance would reside in the spread of opinion across the series as a whole – but they were asked, in the letter of invitation, to bear in mind that children and old ladies, the educated and uneducated, would all be listening. Subject to that reminder the speakers were allowed complete freedom of expression.

The series was regarded by Talks as a great success, despite the fact that H. G. Wells, who had a very squeaky voice, apparently got so carried away in the course of his forty-minute talk that there was some controversy about what he actually did say towards the end. The format was repeated, with minor variations, for some years afterwards. However, the original series did not escape comment from the political parties. J. C. C. Davidson, for the Conservatives, complained that the opening talk by Lowes Dickinson was partly political in character, and should not have been given without the

A SOP TO CERBERUS ;
OR, THE DOGS' CHANCE.

[Uncensored talks by political leaders will be broadcast by the B.B.C. on nine
consecutive Thursdays, beginning next month.]

chance to reply by the parties. But what more concerned Davidson, ahead of the series as a whole, was that the list of speakers seemed more weighted towards Liberal and Socialist points of view than towards those of his own party. He declared that while the BBC had every right to invite eminent men of science and letters to express their views on general subjects, if politics, even in the broad sense, came within the scope of such talks, then there should be a fair and equal representation of all three party positions and opinions.

In 1931 the Talks Department was planning a symposium on India at a time of mounting crisis in the dominion. Against the background of wide-spread civil disobedience organized by Gandhi and the Nehrus, the BBC series was conceived as 'purely informative', aiming simply to explain to listeners the problems involved without any attempt to present the range of party views on the crisis in the sub-continent. At an early stage the Party Whips were consulted in the hope that this would produce an agreed plan, and the India Office was consulted about the timing of the series. Churchill was outraged at the spectacle of a Labour Government discussing terms with Gandhi and his Congress Party, and extremely anxious to make his views on the matter known through the microphone. He was deeply offended when he was not invited to speak in the series. He wanted to mobilize public opinion against making concessions to India; the Government wanted to keep him quiet.

A year or so later, along with Lloyd George and Sir Austen Chamberlain, Churchill complained of the whole basis on which the BBC negotiated its political talks. It introduced, they claimed, 'an entirely new principle of discrimination in British life, namely the elimination and silencing of any Members of Parliament who were not nominated by the Party Leaders or Party Whips.' If the same principle were applied in the House of Commons, it would reduce debate to the mere regimentation of machine-controlled opinion, and would deny fair expression to independent and non-official views. This argument would be forcefully reiterated by Churchill in the wake of the Munich crisis, by which time the baneful consequences of the gagging of non-party men were becoming apparent to the broadcasters. What triggered his initial protest was another talks symposium, *The Debate Continues*, which began in October 1933. *Radio Times* described it as 'free from censorship or preliminary arrangement' and intended to give controversy free reign. The series had been – and this was the point of Churchill's protest – planned in consultation with officials of all three parties. Such collaboration was becoming routine.

By the time this series got off the stocks an attempt had been made to regularize relations with the parties. *Ad hoc* consultations with Whips and Party officials for every occasional talks series was a clumsy, time-consuming procedure. In late 1932, at the suggestion of the Prime Minister, Ramsay

MacDonald, the BBC set up a small Parliamentary Advisory Committee, an unofficial body consisting of party representatives from both Houses, to advise it on political talks other than those at election times. The committee was not a success. It was used by the Talks Department, but the advice it received was usually non-committal or negative. There were endless difficulties in convening meetings at which all members could be present, and within a couple of years it had dwindled out of existence.

But what made the Parliamentary Advisory Committee a broken-backed beast from the start was the refusal of the Labour Party to take part in it. This was partly due, no doubt, to hatred of MacDonald, but more particularly because Labour felt aggrieved that its claims to be recognized as the Official Opposition, as distinct from the Liberals and Independents, was neither properly acknowledged nor given fair treatment in the right of reply to government and ministerial broadcasts. Moreover the Labour Party wanted to broaden the definition of accredited political speakers on radio to include representatives of the labour movement. In June 1933 the National Joint Council produced a Memorandum on Broadcasting which advocated equality of opportunity for broadcasting between the Government, the Opposition and the Trade Union Movement. It expressed the hope that reasonable provision would be made for responsible working-class organizations to initiate discussions on radio when, in their view, there were important matters that needed airing. Reith regarded this as absurd, and working-class Points of View, official or otherwise, on the political issues of the day were rarely allowed free range of expression.

What emerged from all this consultation and negotiation was, in effect, a hierarchy of political discourses on radio. First came the government, more particularly the Prime Minister, who could, at any time, address the nation on matters of national importance. Ministers of state could claim the right to explain matters of government policy for which they were responsible or to provide the facts about newly enacted legislation. The right of reply was not, before the war, guaranteed to opposition parties except at Budget time. This was the terrain of government, statesmanship and the national interest. Below this came the level of politics, of disagreement between, but not within, the legitimate, constitutional parties. Provision was made for the airing of partisan positions at election times and, in a very limited way, at other times. The choice of issues and speakers rested with Party Leaders and Whips. Last came the general discussion of contemporary affairs where the choice of topic and spokesmen lay with the broadcasters.

Ideally the task of the BBC was to accommodate the demands of the government in power, to balance out the interests of parties and to devote its main energies to the cultivation of open discussion of the issues of the day across the whole spectrum of opinion. But it never worked like that. The interests of government lay largely in manipulating news to its own advantage and suppressing talk on issues that might cause it embarrassment or give rise to criticism. The parties were concerned to annexe political debate as their prerogative which, apart from elections, they preferred to exercise in the House of Commons rather than at the microphone. The BBC's own efforts to open up the field of controversy on a broader basis were hampered by its commitment to consultation with the authorities, by complaints in the Commons and attacks in the national press, by outraged public opinion, by interference from government and – under the combined impact of all these pressures – by self-censorship, increasing caution and a retreat to safer ground.

CHAPTER FOUR

Broadcasting and Unemployment

━━━━◗❀◖━━━━

THERE IS a well-established consensus in historical accounts of broadcasting that the BBC in the thirties avoided involvement in the political issues of the decade. The standard student textbook on the British media deals with pre-war broadcasting in a chapter called 'Reith and the denial of politics'.[1] Tom Burns characterizes the BBC throughout the thirties as 'ridden on a tight rein, amounting to no more than mild incursions into foreign politics and genteel discussions between political figures'.[2] Krishan Kumar makes similar points,[3] and Jonathan Dimbleby has accused the BBC of turning a blind eye to the reality of that decade. 'In an age of economic crisis, of political uncertainty, and of unemployment – where the poor "have no possessions, but pawn tickets and debts" – the BBC was content to purvey the general goodwill of a country vicar at a vestry tea party.'[4] Asa Briggs has rightly pointed out that the BBC was far more anxious than many of its critics genuinely to probe the conditions of England in the divided 1930s, but offers little evidence in support of his claim.[5]

Such accounts seriously distort a much more complex reality which we have tried to recapture by studying broadcasting's involvement in the two political issues that defined the decade: unemployment at home and the rise of Fascism in Europe. By offering detailed accounts of how broadcasting dealt with the most important domestic and foreign issues of the time, we hope to correct a prevalent misconception of Reith and the BBC as steering clear of direct political confrontations. At the same time we offer them as classic instances of the nature and effects of external and internal pressures on broadcast news and controversy which, to this day, remain much as they were when broadcasting began to engage in contemporary political life.

Today we remember the social conditions in the thirties from the mass of contemporary documentation in films, literature and journalism: Priestley's *English Journey* and Orwell's *Road to Wigan Pier*, Mass Observation, *Picture Post*, and the films of Rotha, Cavalcanti, Elton and Jennings. These, not to mention the 'dole' novels and the activities of the poets, have shaped our readings and our memories of the period.[6] One historian has argued that such sources, more than anything else, shaped 'the myth of the hungry thirties', adding that 'it is easy in the age of television, to forget that one of the major barriers to public action on behalf of the unemployed was sheer ignorance.'[7] But the pioneering efforts of the BBC, now wholly forgotten, to dispel such ignorance and to arouse public debate and action on unemployment, poverty and housing came before these better remembered social documents, nearly all of which come from the second half of the decade. Broadcasting's interventions came when the problems were most serious and potentially explosive as political issues. None was more so than unemployment about which programmes were made throughout the period, but especially between 1932 and 1934 when the number of unemployed rose to its peak.

In its first engagements with the topic the Talks Department relied on the standard methods of straight talks by individual speakers or symposiums of experts and politicians. A series early in 1931 included Sir Henry Clay, Maynard Keynes, Alexander Loveday (leader of the Economic Intelligence Unit at the League of Nations), Professor D. McGregor, Seebohm Rowntree, H. B. Butler (Deputy Director of the International Labour Office), Herbert Morrison, Sir Francis Acland and Stanley Baldwin as leader of the Conservative Party to wind it all up. It was followed by six 'lectures' by Sir William Beveridge which diagnosed the 'disease of unemployment', traced its origins back to before the Great War, examined whether labour or credit was the main culprit, dealt with the problem of 'social malingering' and finally considered the cost of the cure. On reflection Beveridge wished he had been able to make his talks a little more human.[8] This need to humanize such subjects, to make them more accessible to the public by cutting through abstract debate and statistics to reveal their real human consequences, was addressed by the Talks Department in two major series on unemployment and the slums – *S.O.S.* and *Other People's Houses* – which ran in tandem for three months from the beginning of 1933. In the following year Talks ran another twelve-part series on unemployment called *Time to Spare*.[9]

All three series introduced new methods of presenting social problems through the medium of radio, and all drew sharp reactions from the press, politicians and the listening public. The intention behind them was the same: they were appeals to the conscience of the nation, a cry for voluntary effort to mitigate the worst consequences of these social evils. Yet they drew sharply contrasting responses. Though not intended as political interventions, the timing of all three series and the techniques they used undercut their professed neutrality. The two series on unemployment, fundamentally similar in conception, created almost diametrically opposite political problems for the broadcasters. *S.O.S.* was regarded by a section of the Left as evidence of a ruling-class conspiracy, while *Time to Spare* was so effectively appropriated by the Labour Party in the House of Commons as a stick with which to beat the National Government that the Prime Minister, Ramsay MacDonald, attempted to stop the series.

Beveridge had originally defined unemployment as a problem particular to the unemployable. In his early study he had dealt with the issue largely in terms of those residual categories in the labour pool who were unfit for work because of physical, mental or moral deficiency.[10] But in the crisis years of the Great Depression the collapse of industry and trade was seen to have thrown on the scrap-heap many fit and able workers, skilled craftsmen, black-coated workers, professional people. Now unemployment was a disaster which could befall anyone – neighbours, friends, perfectly respectable people. 'There is not a special class or kind of people who constitute the unemployed. They come from almost every calling and have as great a variety of interests and capacities as any other member of the community. They are ordinary decent people like ourselves to whom an extraordinary misfortune has happened.'[11] Thus Dr A. D. Lindsay, Master of Balliol, assured the listening public in the summer of 1932. He drew attention to the work of the National Council of Social Services in organizing schemes to help the unemployed put their enforced 'leisure time' to good use.[12] *The Listener* often carried information on the work of the NCSS and other voluntary agencies, and in early December a leading article dwelt on the urgent need for a unified social service to coordinate and extend recreational, social and occupational facilities for the unemployed. At the same time it announced that the BBC had invited Mr S. P. B. Mais to provide a series of talks on what was being done by way of voluntary relief.[13] His talks would provide first-hand accounts of the situation, based on his own travels up and down the country to investigate the problem and how it was being dealt with.

The National Government was beginning to provide encouragement and some piecemeal financial support for all this voluntary activity and on 19 December, broadcasting from his home in Lossiemouth, MacDonald announced the Government's decision to ask the NCSS to strengthen and widen the scope of their organization for the purposes of coordinating all the voluntary bodies engaged in this field. The Government said MacDonald was doing what it could, but was hampered – like the employers – by the recession in world trade. He called for personal service, a community of friendship, 'the human hand supplementing the state machine'.[14] Two weeks later the Prince of Wales, an active supporter of the voluntary movement, came to the microphone to introduce the BBC's series of talks. Some might argue, the Prince declared, that we were not facing the problem the right way, that voluntary service was starting at the wrong end, but there was a need in times of national crisis for all to cooperate. The causes of unemployment were beyond our control, and we might differ in our estimate of them, but it was largely within our power to control the effects of unemployment. The unemployed were just our fellow men, the same as ourselves, only less fortunate. Our aims in relation to them must be practical not theoretical.[15]

Thus heralded, Mais began his series of eleven reports in a dramatic fashion:

> Here is an S.O.S. message, probably the most urgent you will ever hear and it vitally concerns you. You are called upon to create an entirely new social order. The bottom has apparently fallen out of the old world in which everything was subordinated to the day's work. We are now faced with a world in which one of the major problems is how best to occupy the day's enforced leisure. Some millions of our neighbours, without any preparation for it, have now got this leisure enforced upon them and, not unnaturally, are unable to cope with it. They do not understand how it has come about any more than you or I…. We are not dealing here with unemployables, but with first rate workmen, at least as capable as ourselves…. It is not charity but a practical expression of friendliness that is needed…. There is plenty for you to do and you must do it at once if you care about your fellow countrymen. What therefore can you do at once? Make yourself known to the Manager of your local Labour Exchange, or if you live in a village, to the Schoolmaster or Parson. With their help collect a small number of unemployed who show any interest; find a hut for them to work on, and remember once it is started the men must run it entirely by themselves …[16]

The construction of this discourse, its mode of address, its positioning of the audience as middle-class like itself, its exclusion of the unemployed, its transformation of the problem into the politics of the parish pump, should all be noted. But before showing a little more of the style and content of the reports that followed, the series must be more adequately placed in the context of the politics of unemployment at that time.

Six weeks before MacDonald's broadcast, London had witnessed the arrival in the capital of the National Hunger March organized by the National Unemployed Workers Movement. The reception given the marchers by the authorities has been briefly described above.[17] Its leader, Wal Hannington, had been jailed for three months for attempting to incite the police to disaffection. While serving his time Hannington was told by a friendly prison padre that the march had not been altogether unproductive – it had stirred the conscience of the other class to the need for providing some kind of social life for the unemployed. What this meant more specifically, Hannington inferred, was the Government's launching of the national campaign for the provision of social centres for the unemployed, following hard on the departure of the hunger marchers from London. The radio speeches by MacDonald and 'Edward Windsor' he regarded as part of a subtle and astute change of tactics by the ruling class in order to hold the working class more firmly in their grip.[18]

With such arguments in mind the NUWM wrote, immediately after the broadcast by the Prince of Wales, to J. H. Whitley, Chairman of the Board of Governors asking for the right to broadcast in the talks series on unemployment.[19] The request was turned down. The BBC stated that the talks were based on the actual experience of those who had been in the unemployed areas, and that it wished to avoid controversy. 'In other words', wrote the *Daily Worker*, 'they want only one point of view, a point of view acceptable to the capitalist class and directed against the mass organization of the unemployed.'[20] Unabashed, a deputation from the NUWM went to Broadcasting House to press their claims. There they were met by two detectives on the doorstep, and a member of the BBC management who promised to pass on their request.[21] They were invited to return for discussions by the Director of Talks, Charles Siepmann, who added that the presence of the two CID men was in no way connected with any action on the part of the Corporation.[22] When the deputation of four (including Hannington just released from jail) returned, they found a full-scale police guard surrounding the building: two uniformed police inspectors, a sergeant and plain clothes men in the lobby, and in the side street behind Broadcasting House, a number of uniformed constables. After a ninety-minute discussion their request to broadcast was again turned down. In a subsequent press statement the deputation declared that by their decision the BBC had shown itself to be a supporter of die-hard starvation and the National Government. It promised to organize a strong protest from the workers' movement.[23]

Siepmann was however sufficiently struck by the force of their arguments to refer the series, the following week, to the Parliamentary Advisory Committee. He suggested that, since the series might reasonably be seen as controversial, the talks by Mais should be reduced in number and replaced by a number of speakers giving their views on what politically should be done about unemployment. His provisional list of speakers included Lloyd George, Harold Macmillan and Ernest Bevin for the three parties, plus I. M. Sieff, G. D. H. Cole and a government spokesman to round it off. If this list scarcely represented the position of the NUWM, it had a distinctly progressive whiff about it. Siepmann was anxious to know if the committee thought it represented an equitable balance of interests, but neither Reith nor the committee liked the proposal or anything very much like it.[24] So the idea was dropped and Mais continued his talks, all on the theme of voluntary relief.

To gather material for his talks Mais travelled all over the country. He visited the Out of Work Clubs, the settlements and the Labour Exchanges: he talked not only to the organizers of such schemes but extensively to the unemployed themselves. He dealt not only with the obvious aspects of the problem (the industrial workers in the cities) but with its less visible effects in the countryside, among women, among the black-coated workers and the professions.

It would not be hard to present Mais and his endeavours in such a way as to endorse Hannington's view of the project. Indeed a North Region play dealing with unemployment and blackleg labour a few years later, contained a succinct parody of Mais's manner:

> MARSHALL: I just thought you chaps might like to know what I heard at the [Out of Work] club last night.
> JOCK: I'll tell you what you heard: the capitalist class is the poor man's friend. Teach the unemployed lace-making and keep them cheerful. (*He produces a free imitation of S. P. B. Mais on the wireless*) What these fellahs need is occupation. Make 'em feel they're wanted. Stout fellahs when you get to know them. Really grateful for all that's done for them ...[25]

Yet Mais listened attentively to what the unemployed said and thought, and reported it back to his audience, even if he did not understand or agree with what was said to him. His reports are shot through with statements from the objects of all this middle-class concern which uncomfortably subvert their intentions. At Brynmawr Mais tried to get a message from an old miner to pass on to the listening public: '"The people are all longing to know what to do," I said. "What do you want done? What can people do?" He seemed surprised by the question and then repeated several times, "more honesty". But he didn't hold out any chance of getting that without a revolution.' In the Rhondda he was told that the bosses looked at you 'as though you were a piece of sicked up fat'.[26] At Lincoln he attended a meeting to discuss the formation of more clubs for the unemployed, in the course of which

> a black-haired very frail young man got up and asked how anyone could expect an unemployed man to do physical jerks on 15/- a week, or play ping-pong while his wife was sitting at home before a half empty grate with only margarine to eat. I was more interested in him than in anyone else, so when the meeting was over I talked with him. He wouldn't allow that these clubs were doing any good at all. 'They're only meant', he said, 'to keep us quiet by people who are afraid.' He was right of course in suggesting that ping-pong does not provide a final solution. But he was wrong in denying that the service does no good at all.[27]

A true innocent abroad, Mais was struck, while watching a women's keep-fit class at Byker (Tyneside), by the neatness of their clothes. 'It's perhaps as well', he was told, 'that you can't see what they've got on underneath'.[28]

While Mais was meeting the unemployed, Howard Marshall was meeting the slum dwellers. *Other People's Houses* was originally designed to throw light on the housing problem and to arouse public interest by eye-witness accounts of housing conditions up and down the country. Marshall, normally a BBC sports commentator, was briefed to visit those places where the problem was most serious and to report his findings to the listening public. These talks would alternate with discussions and talks by experts on the subject. But,

62

when it became known that the Minister of Health, Sir Hilton Young, was to put before the House, in late 1932, a new Bill to speed up slum clearance, the BBC decided to make the series more explicitly political. It was referred to the Parliamentary Advisory Committee for guidance on the subjects to be discussed,[29] and Siepmann made informal contact with Sir Hilton Young (who gave the last talk in the series) for advice on the selection of speakers.

The series began on the National Programme in January 1933 with an account by Marshall of slum conditions in Tyneside. In three subsequent reports – there were to have been six, but Marshall had flu in February – he described the slums of London, Manchester and Glasgow, taking care to mention what was being done to alleviate the problem, but stressing that the conditions he described were typical and representative, not exaggerated or selected instances. His accounts were passionately praised and denounced by the press, by listeners and by some of the experts with whom his reports alternated. After his description of the East End *The Everyman* fiercely attacked 'the misleading and mischievous effects of the one-sided, reckless and inaccurate statements broadcast to the world regarding London's housing conditions ... One must remember – and this is important – that these talks are picked up abroad. What splendid propaganda for Bolshevism! Moscow will glory in it. London, a city of slums where people live with rats in underground dwellings! All this is the natural and inevitable product of capitalism!'[30] The *Daily Worker* picked up this article, describing *The Everyman* as a paper under the control of strong personal supporters of MacDonald, which was foaming at the mouth because a faint glimmer of truth was accidentally slipping through the BBC censorship.[31]

In *The Listener* and *Radio Times* correspondents attacked Marshall for being too emotional ('speaking with a tear in his voice') and thus confusing the facts of the matter which could be more accurately and dispassionately put by experts on the subject, or defended his reports for their truthfulness and honesty in presenting the real facts of slum conditions. Some greeted his accounts with frank disbelief. 'Either you are the world's biggest liar, or you are trying to play the funny man,' wrote one anonymous correspondent of Marshall's description of the East End.[32] Others felt it was the fault of the slum dwellers themselves. Many of them were of low mentality, in the opinion of an anonymous letter writer to *Radio Times*, who, unlike most of the self-respecting working class, did not limit their families to numbers they could hope to bring up decently.[33] And Sir Cecil Levita MP, one of the expert speakers in the series, took the opportunity at the microphone to criticize Marshall's methods: 'All old towns contain worn-out and bad houses. It is an unhappy fact. Probably they always will, and eye-witnesses will always, as ever, be able to harrow your feelings about such properties,'[34] Marshall defended himself against the critics and the doubting Thomases by offering to arrange, for all disbelievers, a tour of the East End to prove the accuracy of his accounts.[35]

Neither *S.O.S.* nor *Other People's Houses*, for all the debate to which they gave rise, probed a raw nerve of the state. The Mais series evidently supported the actions of the Government and outraged only those most actively engaged on behalf of the unemployed. And they could easily be discounted as Bolshevik extremists. What drew most of the flak in the housing series were the counter-claims of eye-witness versus expert which arguably distracted attention from the implications of the Bill placed before the House by the Minister of Health on 18 December 1932. It was to be the next series on unemployment which triggered the most explosive row between the BBC and the Government, for seeming to expose (quite unintentionally) the inadequacies of the National Government's handling of the problem.

In 1934 the Talks Department launched its second major series on unemployment, which this time relied not on an outside observer, but on the unemployed themselves to come to the microphone and describe the human consequences of unemployment, how they managed living on the dole.[36] The series was produced by Felix Greene who solved the initially difficult task of finding appropriate speakers by contacting societies and individuals all over the country who were constantly in touch with the unemployed, asking them to suggest speakers. But Greene came to feel that he could not hope to organize the series from behind his desk in his London office. He could get the facts of unemployment, but not the *feeling*. So for three months he toured the country. He met the unemployed in their homes and clubs and sat up into the night talking with them. He selected the speakers from the hundreds he met, not because they were the saddest cases, but because they were most typical and representative. Some found it difficult to write down their story, though they could tell it well. When Greene tried to copy down what they said he found they spoke less freely. So he invited them to Broadcasting House, took them into a studio and got them talking. Meanwhile, unknown to them, their words were transcribed by secretaries in another room listening to them over a loudspeaker. There was no censorship, Greene claimed. The BBC altered or deleted nothing that the speakers wished to say.[37]

Time to Spare started on the National Programme on 11 April 1934 with an introduction by Mais who began with a quotation from J. B. Priestley's just published *English Journey*. Although things had improved since last year, Mais declared, there was still no room for complacency. Reiterating the theme of his own series, he called upon the listening public to dedicate themselves anew to the unemployed by searching about in town or village for some unemployed family in need of friendship and not resting until they had been found.[38] In the weeks that followed the unemployed themselves came to speak of the way they lived: John Bentley, a tramp; John Evans, a miner from the Rhondda; John Rankin from the Clyde; Mrs Pallis from Sunderland; John Evans from

Birmingham. There were eleven all told, and each speaker's fifteen-minute talk was followed by a shorter postscript given by a suitably official person to point the moral of their tale.

From the beginning the series attracted considerable attention from the left-wing press. The *Daily Worker* headlined the talk by John Evans of Birmingham, 'Forced to Live on $3\frac{1}{2}$ d a Day',[39] and after Mrs Pallis gave her talk the *Daily Herald* and the *Daily Worker* had the same headline – '16/- a Week to Feed a Family of Five'. But it was the row in the House of Commons about the truth of these talks that made them headline news in the national press as a whole.

The series had started shortly before the third and final reading in the Commons of the Unemployment Bill. In the course of the debate Labour back-benchers took the Government to task over the way the Means Test was administered. George Daggar, the MP for Abertillery, attacked the Minister of Labour's claim that the unemployed were better off at present in view of the fall in the cost of living over the last three years. He produced as supporting evidence extracts from the talks in the *Time to Spare* series, as reprinted in *The Listener*, whose testimony, he claimed, could be accepted as reliable because they were broadcast by the BBC and hence were free from political theory or bias. Daggar quoted verbatim from the talks by John Evans of Birmingham and John Evans from the Rhondda. In both passages the speakers told how their families managed on the dole money, which worked out at eight shillings a week to feed four in the first case, and twelve shillings and sixpence a week for three in the second case. R. S. Hudson, Parliamentary Secretary to the Minister of Labour, replied that he had made enquiries, and could assure the Hon. Member that the whole story was not given. Pressed on this point Hudson insisted that in two cases – John Evans of Birmingham and Mrs Pallis of Sunderland – there was no need whatever for there to have been any tragedy at all; that if those speakers had told the whole story of their circumstances it would have put a very different complexion on the matter. In neither case would it have been possible to say they were very hard cases. They were not living on the amount they claimed.[40]

That exchange was picked up by the press and a war of words ensued between the BBC and the Ministry of Labour. After a hasty internal review, the BBC issued a public statement that not only were the claims in the talks as broadcast correct, but there was nothing omitted that could justify Hudson's assertions. His statements in the Commons were based on a misunderstanding. Hudson however refused the offer of that escape clause and, in a letter to Reith, which was reprinted in *The Times*, repeated his assertions that the speakers were untypical and had not stated the full facts. The Government was by now becoming alarmed. The *Daily Herald* carried a story on 5 June 1934 that the Cabinet was thinking of stopping the series: '*Time to Spare* is shattering too many illusions. Millions are being turned against the Government.' Reith in fact, though this was not public knowledge at the time, was summoned to Number 10 and told by MacDonald that the talks must stop. Reith replied that it was within the power of the Government to order the BBC to discontinue the series but that if it did he would, at that time in the schedule when the talks should be given, instruct the announcer to declare that the next twenty minutes would be silent because the Government had refused to allow the unemployed to express their views.[41] MacDonald backed off, and the series continued.

But to placate the Prime Minister, Reith and the Governors were anxious that the series should be rounded off with a talk which would balance out the objections he had raised against the series and which gave the Government what credit it was due.[42] The Prime Minister's office was asked to submit the kind of material it would like to have incorporated in the closing talk, and MacDonald's private secretary sent Siepmann a complete script which expanded on what the Government had already done for the unemployed and elaborated on the extra benefits of the new Act. Siepmann wanted the talk to make it clear that the series was *not* a reflection on the Government of the day. Reith and the Governors were eager to see the script, and Siepmann worked hard to get the manuscript in final shape well in advance of the day it was broadcast. It was written and presented by the Master of Balliol who was, as we have seen, a supporter of the voluntary relief movement. Lindsay made little use of the Downing Street material in preparing his script, but covered in a general way the points that Siepmann wanted establishing. He summarized the series as 'an eloquent sermon addressed to each one of us, recalling us to our personal responsibilities'. He went on smoothly to explain the gap between what was, and what was intended; between the responses of the unemployed to their situation and especially to their treatment by authority, and the strains on the official machinery (designed mainly to handle seasonal, or short-term unemployment) which resulted in people not always getting the help the administration was ready to give them.[43]

At the same time as this concluding talk was being prepared, Siepmann was conducting his own inquiry into the specific charges made by Hudson against some of the speakers, and in early July presented his report to Reith. Hudson had made three points against the BBC; that it took insufficient care to check the facts and figures mentioned by the speakers; that those selected were exceptional and in no way representative; and that certain essential facts were omitted giving a distorted picture of the particular case, in consequence of the general lot of the unemployed. These general complaints were embodied in specific instances of whom two, Mrs Pallis and John Evans of South Wales, were the most significant.

Mrs Pallis's case was exceptional, Hudson asserted, in that her husband had been out of work for a much longer period than average, and he was moreover a left-handed riveter and as such at a disadvantage when it came to getting jobs. As regards the first point Siepmann had established that Mr Pallis's term of unemployment was, for his trade and for the area, not unusual. And as to the second, 'we have it from Mr Brown, the Chief Engineer of Palmers of Jarrow, that left-handed rivetters [sic] stand an equal chance with right-handed rivetters when seeking employment.' Descending to the details of Mrs Pallis's talk Hudson complained that she made capital out of the absence of facilities for advice on birth control, omitted to mention that her children received free school meals, mentioned that her husband shared an allotment at 22 shillings a year which he could have achieved at a cheaper rate through the Society of Friends, and did not avail herself of the maternity facilities in the district. On the first of these points Hudson had got his facts all wrong, said Siepmann. Mrs Pallis knew all about birth control. What she said was that poor people could not afford it, and only incidentally remarked that some people did not know about facilities for advice. Hudson had flatly asserted that Mrs Pallis could have obtained advice on the subject from her local birth control clinic. Siepmann had carefully checked this and found that there was no local authority clinic in Sunderland; that the nearest voluntary clinic was in Newcastle, and that the local medical officer was against such clinics and advice on birth control being given on anything other than medical grounds. The second and third points he dismissed as being really too trivial and the last was irrelevant because Mrs Pallis made no reference at all to the maternity service in her talk.

John Evans, Hudson claimed, had stated in his talk that his daughter was earning seven shillings a week, but the local Public Assistance Committee said she was earning twelve shillings a week. Both facts were wrong, at least as broadcast. The child was earning thirteen shillings a week. Evans had referred to her wages in relation to the weekly sum she contributed to the running of the household. She paid seven shillings to the home, keeping six shillings for her maintenance, clothing and other expenses. While Evans' statement was, in law, an error of fact, it conveyed the sense he intended and was in any case a trivial point in relation to the talk as a whole.

The other two cases that Hudson raised were nitpicking and obscure but Siepmann sifted the evidence and concluded that he was satisfied, after very careful investigation, that no case could be made against the BBC either for careless or irresponsible action, or for a distortion of the truth.[44] Reith wrote the following day to MacDonald's secretary stating that the BBC believed that the talks had presented a substantially accurate and representative picture of the hardships of the unemployed, but admitted that the series might have created the impression that the talks represented the lot of the average unemployed, which impression the BBC had carefully asked the Master of Balliol to remove. Reith regretted that party capital had been made out of the series, but felt it was unfair to blame the BBC for this. 'We should more than regret that anyone should imagine that either with malice aforethought or through negligence on our part, the Government had suffered a prejudice.' And that, officially, closed the matter.

Perhaps the most disgraceful aspect of this whole affair was the harassment by the Ministry of Labour of those speakers whose statements it had challenged, which underlined the pusillanimous spirit in which it interpreted state relief for the unemployed. In a *Radio Times* article written at the height of the row, Felix Greene had emphasized that it took courage to come to the microphone and describe the facts of one's existence, when that existence was a struggle for the bare necessities: 'There are neighbours who will gossip, and the Press who will worry one, and the Public Assistance Officers who will make enquiries.'[45] The full glare of press publicity fell on Mrs Pallis and John Evans of Birmingham; and the former was subjected to persistent questioning by social workers and ministry officials who went to her children's school to find out if they were receiving free meals.[46] Evans was brought back from Ireland to undergo detailed questioning by a committee which included the area relief officer and the chairman of the Public Assistance Committee. And Greene himself was obliged to write to a contact in South Wales asking him to investigate, in confidence, how much the daughter of the miner, John Evans, actually earned.[47]

The Talks Department at that time, though its outlook was certainly progressive, could scarcely be described as left-wing. Yet the effect on some of those directly involved in making these programmes was to transform their social or political perspectives. Marshall was deeply moved by his encounters with the slums and the people who lived there. When the series finished he wrote a documentary book, called simply *Slum*, in which he declared: 'Once you have seen the slums you will find your values change. You will be haunted. The shadow of the slums will fall over everything you do.' To write the book, to get the proper *feel* of the subject, Marshall chose to cut himself off entirely from his normally comfortable way of life; so he rented a room in a cheap lodging house in Poplar and struggled to set pen to paper. 'Do you really care much? I dare say you do. I dare say it is foolish of me to be writing here at all. I should be sitting in my club in St James Street, surrounded by familiar things, looking down at Poplar with detached benevolence. That would give me the right perspective: I should see the East End as a statistical problem – houses to the acre, families to a room, the infant mortality rate, and the whole complex tale of suffering set out to three places of decimals.'[48] Greene's response to the unemployed was much the same. 'Statistics we can read and put aside unmoved. The story of unemployment in terms of bread and worn out boots, rent that cannot be paid and hands that daily lose a little of their skills, and "unstretched intellects" that know they rust from want of use – such stories cannot be put aside.'[49] His encounter at first hand with the way the poor lived was the source of Greene's awakening left-wing sympathies. He began to feel that there was something very wrong in a society enormously rich at one end and abjectly poor at the other extreme.

Time to Spare was the last big talks series on unemployment for the general listening public. By 1934 the economy was reviving, and it was becoming apparent that long-term unemployment would be confined to the old industrial regions, the so-called 'distressed areas' of South Wales, the North-East, Clydeside and the textiles areas of Lancashire and Yorkshire. Their special needs were recognized by the appointment of two Commissioners for the Distressed Areas, one for England and Wales, the other for Scotland. Their brief from MacDonald was vague, their powers ill-defined, and the burden of alleviating the problem continued to be shouldered by voluntary bodies, notably the Society of Friends, working independently or with the National Council for Social Services. The NCSS continued to direct its efforts largely at the unemployed clubs and occupational centres which, by late 1934, numbered nearly 2500.[50]

That Autumn, in collaboration with the NCSS, the Talks Department launched a series of daytime talks, *For the Unemployed* (later renamed *Off Duty*), which were to continue – though in an increasingly diluted form – to the outbreak of war.[51] At first there were three sessions each week: one on industrial and economic matters, one on club organization and activities, and a third by Professor John Hilton on Friday afternoons called *This and That*. The scheme was introduced on the wireless by George Lansbury, full of windy benevolence, urging the men not to get into a muddle about their circumstances, to think for themselves and not to blame the Government.[52] It was soon discovered that most of the intended audience was queuing for its dole money at the time of Hilton's little chats, which were rescheduled to a time when the unemployed were available to listen. And subsequent inquiries disclosed that less than half the occupational centres had radio sets, so the talks were addressed more to people listening at home than in the centres. By 1938 the BBC's Regional Education Officers were in general agreement that the economic situation had improved and that the best of the men had found work. But in the depressed areas it remained true that many able-bodied men who were too old for re-training remained on the dole. The afternoon talks were transferred to the Regional Service to cater for such men.[53]

In 1935 there was a major reshuffle in the Talks Department and, after a brief interregnum, Sir Richard Maconachie was appointed as the new Director of Talks.[54] This was a deliberate move to trim the progressive character of the department under Hilda Matheson and Charles Siepmann, and there was a marked retreat from dealing with contentious issues in talks programmes in the second half of the thirties. The last major intervention by the department on the subject of unemployment came in 1936 when it was decided to present a discussion of the Means Test before it was debated in the Commons.[55] Elaborate precautions were taken to ensure that it caused no outcry. The idea for the programme was referred upwards for approval by Reith and the Chairman of the Governors who gave it the go ahead with the suggestion that the Ministry of Labour be informed. The Ministry was duly contacted and discussions were held. The Ministry accepted the idea for the programme and its proposed date and offered, at a later point, to go through the briefs for the discussion to check them for facts. Finding speakers was not easy. At first it was thought that one of the three members of the Independent Labour Party in the House of Commons might be a good choice to speak against the Means Test. But Mrs Hamilton, one of the Governors, suggested that this should be checked with Attlee first, who might be offended that the BBC had gone outside the official Labour Party for speakers. At this point it was decided to abandon the use of MPs as speakers. It would tend to make the discussion purely political as well as give rise to all sorts of other problems.

The Unemployment Assistance Board was contacted early on for advice. This Board, a product of the 1934 Unemployment Act, was responsible for administering the Means Test and was deeply disliked by many working-class people. Mr Eady, for the Board, advised the BBC that the speakers in the discussion should be anonymous because the defenders of the Means Test could only say what needed saying provided they were guaranteed against 'unhappy personal consequences'. This recommendation was accepted. Two speakers were eventually found, scripts were drawn up and sent to the Ministry of Labour with a note that careful consideration would be given to any observation which the Minister might care to make. It was returned with a few pencilled corrections on points of fact, and the broadcast went ahead on 15 May 1936 with two anonymous speakers. The following day a Mr Thomas from the CID attached to the Unemployment Assistance Board, called in at the Talks Department offices. He wanted the name of the unemployed man who had spoken against the Means Test. 'Not for any purpose directly relative to the man himself', so he said, 'but in order that enquiries might be made in the area of which he was speaking, to discover what facts would substantiate what the man said.' The files do not disclose whether or not Mr Thomas got the name he was after.

The cautiousness at every stage in the planning of this discussion contrasts strikingly with the approach to *Time To Spare*. In the same year, 1936, Talks had plans for an ambitious social survey of Britain which eventually collapsed, apparently from problems of coordination between London and the regions. But at the outset all those concerned were warned that 'we do not want to get into the difficulties such as a couple of years ago when we were doing a series dealing with the actual conditions of the unemployed.'[56] The pioneering commitment to new forms of social reportage which had animated the department under Matheson and Siepmann had withered and died. It is indicative of the growing crisis at the heart of public life in Britain that at the same time as the BBC's attempted inquiry into the state of the nation failed, two young graduates were launching an independent fact-finding movement called Mass Observation. The immediate impulse behind it was the abdication crisis and the realization, as Tom Jefferey has argued, that 'ordinary people were being misled by a complacent press and indifferent government, both deeply ignorant of the needs of working people and the desires of "people of goodwill". Against this people needed to know the facts about international affairs, government policies and about themselves; only if people were given the facts could democracy work.'[57]

'Facts were wanted about everything and everybody – cross-sections of society, symptomatic opinions and observations, detailed investigations and statistics,' wrote Malcom Muggeridge.[58] The felt need for information grew stronger as the thirties progressed. In 1937 a new monthly magazine called *Fact* was launched. The editorial, in the first issue, compared its aim with that of the French Encyclopaedists – to produce and spread information, in a language that all could understand, as a catalyst for action. In the later thirties facts were gathered in all kinds of ways.[59] Social surveys were undertaken by philanthropic individuals and private trusts, or by independent research groups like Political and Economic Planning. There were workers' film, theatre and photography groups, and new publishing ventures such as Penguin Books, *Picture Post* and the Left Book Club founded in May 1936 with the declared objective of giving 'all who are determined to play their part in the coming struggle [for world peace and a better social order] such knowledge as will immensely increase their efficiency'.[60]

The information generated by such activities nourished the ferment of radical opinion publics, the ebb and flow of public platforms, campaigns and mass marches (against unemployment, against fascism: for peace, for the republican cause in Spain) – all indicating a widespread mobilization of public opinion as the noise of history grew ever louder and more implacable. A sense of being hounded by the pressure of external events dogged the Auden generation. As British culture was radically politicized the gulf between public and private, government and people, rulers and ruled became more starkly apparent. John Stevenson has pointed out that one of the remarkable features of the investigation of unemployment in the thirties was that it was conducted entirely by voluntary groups or on the initiative of individuals or publishers. Central government 'made no serious attempt to investigate the social consequences of unemployment'.[61] We have seen its response to the BBC's well-meaning efforts in this direction, a response which contributed to a retreat into caution by the broadcasters on sensitive political issues. The muffling of open debate, the silencing of dissent by the Government and the complicity of broadcasting and the press, created a vacuum at the heart of public life whose baleful consequences would become apparent, within the BBC, during and after the Munich crisis of 1938.

CHAPTER FIVE

Broadcasting and Foreign Affairs

<del>━━━━◉◈◉━━━━</del>

T HE BBC'S difficulties with the presentation of foreign affairs at the microphone can be traced back to the Vernon Bartlett row in 1933.[1] Bartlett became the BBC's 'foreign correspondent' in 1932, having previously worked for the *Daily Mail*. His brief included establishing personal contacts with European broadcasting stations, recruiting stringers in foreign capitals, and regular fifteen-minute weekly broadcast talks on foreign affairs for the National Programme and schools broadcasting. He was attached to the Talks Department. On 15 October 1933 Germany pulled out of the Disarmament Conference at Geneva convened by the League of Nations. After the six o'clock news that evening, which gave full coverage of the story, Bartlett made a short broadcast commentary, the general tenor of which was that the German action was understandable given the intractability of the Allies and their failure to honour the pledge of Versailles. Britain, argued Bartlett, would have done the same thing if it had been in Germany's shoes.

This sounded very much like editorial comment, which the Charter had forbidden, and the Government was displeased, for beyond these shores the BBC was regarded as a semi-official voice. MacDonald rang Reith at once to declare that the BBC was turning his hair grey. Who was the Government he wanted to know – he and his colleagues, or the BBC? He followed this up with a letter of complaint to the Board of Governors. The Foreign Office was perturbed. Press comment ranged from the *Daily Telegraph*'s condemnation of Bartlett's 'grave indiscretion' to the *Daily Herald*'s praise for 'a courageous and outspoken broadcast'. In the short term the BBC quietly dispensed with Bartlett's services, and he was not asked to talk again on radio for several years. The Foreign Secretary was alarmed by the 'terrible power' of such a broadcast to create public panic and wondered whether such power should be left in the hands of the BBC. The Cabinet concluded that it could not do otherwise without challenging the independence of the Corporation – a fear which the left-wing press raised at the time. *Reynolds News* expressed its worries at the machinations of the establishment and defended radio correspondents from 'kid-glove dictators' at the Foreign Office.

The Foreign Office was sensitive to being branded as censoring or interfering with free speech. In a private conversation with Rex Leeper of the Foreign Office's News Department, Alan Dawnay, the Controller of Programmes, admitted that 'a serious blunder had been made' and that, in the wake of Bartlett's departure, the BBC was eager to clear with the Foreign Office the nature of future talks on sensitive areas. On 2 February 1934 Reith discussed with MacDonald, apropos of the Bartlett affair, the whole question of BBC liaison with government departments which MacDonald felt could be much improved without prejudice to the autonomy of the BBC. Less than two weeks later Reith had a 'very helpful meeting' with Sir Robert Vansittart and Sir Warren Fisher at the Foreign Office which did much to ease the strained relations between the BBC and that department. Vansittart was 'most affable and anxious to arrange all sorts of contacts'. By the end of the month he and Reith had agreed to meet monthly for regular discussions on foreign affairs.[2]

At the request of Reith, Leeper had drawn up some suggestions for the handling of talks on foreign affairs. He put forward three main options: one or two regular speakers, a panel of experts or reports from foreign capitals. Although Leeper preferred the first, the Foreign Secretary and his colleagues were less keen. Their main concern was the tendency of listeners – especially foreign listeners – to accept the broadcast voice as official. John Salt, for the Talks Department, suggested a series of talks by 'intelligent travellers' giving their strictly personal views and thereby neutralizing the effect of a single expert speaker. During 1934 no one voice dominated the foreign scene as Bartlett had done, and a variety of travellers expressed a variety of opinions. This arrangement was, in the end, to prove as unsatisfactory as the use of the single accredited expert. During a visit to Germany, Richard Crossman broadcast his impressions of the country. His trip coincided with the 'night of the long knives'. Crossman's view of Hitler's bloody *coup* as 'a personal triumph' over factional intrigue, with his word now law 'in the sense of burning public approval' caused the Foreign Secretary to despair of 'the vein of exultant approval' running through the talk, and Vansittart to dismiss it as 'go-getter, sensation-mongering Hearstliness, man on the spot and red-hot stuff'. Though Dawnay defended the talk, pointing out the difficulties of reporting in censor-ridden countries like Germany, the Foreign Office reaction put an end to Salt's proposal.

The major crisis in the relations between the BBC, the Government and the Foreign Office came a year later. In 1935 the BBC's Adult Education Advisory Committee had recommended a balanced series of twelve educational talks under the title *The Citizen and His Government*.[3] The first seven talks by Captain Harold Balfour MP and Mrs Agnes Headley-Morlam were to be expository. The last five were to begin with two talks on Fascism and Communism by Sir Oswald Mosley and Harry Pollitt, respectively, followed by three talks critical of the preceding two by MPs representing the constitutional parties – Isaac Foot (Liberal), Herbert Morrison (Labour) and Kenneth Pickthorn (Conservative). The outline of the series was approved by the Board of Governors, and submitted informally, in the summer of 1935, to the Foreign Office, who raised no objection at the time. By the autumn it had become apprehensive. On 13 September Leeper rang Dawnay urging the BBC to drop the Pollitt talks, and a little later Vansittart expressed to Reith his concern that Mosley should be allowed to broadcast. The Foreign Office's main worry, as Reith put it in a letter to Lord Elton, was that when in future they protested to the Soviet Ambassador about the flow of communist propaganda into this country, they would have the Pollitt talk held up to them. So many foreigners, he complained, either could not or would not differentiate between the BBC and the British Government and maintained – when it suited them – that the voice of the BBC was the voice of government. Foreign Office fears over Mosley were prompted by Mussolini's recent attack on Abyssinia.

These points were considered by the Board of Governors but, after careful thought, rejected. The Board took the view that it was their duty to allow expression to all shades of political opinion with any substantial backing, and the issue at stake in the series was not the point of view of individual speakers, but the claims of differing systems of government. Mosley would not be allowed in his talk to refer to Abyssinia. There was no connection, the Governors felt, between Pollitt's talk and any flow of Comintern propaganda into Britain. The overall structure of the series would do more to discredit and weaken Communism in Britain than any measure to check the spread of subversive propaganda. It was agreed unanimously that, subject to such safeguards, the series should proceed.

The Foreign Office now threatened to take the matter further, but an imminent general election gave a pretext for postponing the last five talks in the series which had already started. After the election the Adult Education Advisory Committee again pressed for the inclusion of the talks in the spring schedule for 1936. Negotiations reopened with the Foreign Office and Lord Stanhope, Under-Secretary of State, declaring that the policy of His Majesty's Government remained the same, and adding that it would be extremely embarrassing to the Government if the BBC allowed Mr Pollitt to broadcast his views. By now the Board of Governors was prepared to abandon the series provided the BBC could state it was doing so because the Government was anxious the talks should not be given. Stanhope countered by asking if the Governors had considered the effect of such an announcement on Parliament shortly before the new Charter was due for discussion in the House, in response to the Ullswater Report. It would strengthen, he suggested, the case for those who demanded more Parliamentary control of the BBC.

The Foreign Office continued to insist that government intervention should not be mentioned. Anthony Eden prepared a memorandum which was discussed in Cabinet on 12 February 1936. After setting out the story so far, Eden concluded:

> Though it is still desirable that the BBC should withdraw the objectionable items of their programmes without bringing in His Majesty's Government, it seems impossible to induce them to do so; and if the talks are, in fact, withdrawn through Government intervention, it would seem difficult, and in fact undesirable, to refuse to permit them to say so. It would however be neither true nor desirable to state publicly that the talks 'would be an embarrassment to the Government' at the present time; but it would be true to say that 'they were not in the national interest'.[4]

In the discussion that followed it was agreed that Baldwin, the Prime Minister, should get the new Postmaster General, Major G. C. Tryon, to find a final solution, and that he should make it quite clear that the Government would not permit the broadcasts. A week later Baldwin was able to report back that the BBC had agreed to withdraw the Pollitt and Mosley talks and that 'no public reference would be made to government intervention'.[5] The Cabinet formally recorded its congratulations.

The agreed public formula for cancelling the talks was: 'In view of the effect which the proposed talks might have on an international situation already aggravated by recent developments, the Corporation has decided to cancel the talks.'[6] The Adult Education Advisory Committee was not much impressed by this resolution of the matter. Cecil Graves tried hard to persuade its members of the wisdom of the BBC's decision, 'since occasions must from time to time arise when to do otherwise would quite possibly cost a considerable set-back to the work of the Corporation, and to the objectives which it shared in common with the committee.' But the committee was not to be persuaded. At a meeting on 14 February 1936 Graves was asked if the BBC had capitulated in the end because of the imminent publication of the Ullswater Report, and Graves replied that the BBC was naturally not anxious, at the present juncture, for a great deal of public attention to be focused on such an issue. Graves was then asked to withdraw from the meeting while the committee passed a resolution expressing its deep concern at the decision to cancel the talks, and the hope that this did not represent any narrowing of the field over which balanced controversy might be permitted. In its reply the Board of Governors confirmed unanimously that, subject to adequate safeguards being taken, controversial talks should take a prominent place in the programmes of the BBC. This did not answer the point about narrowing the field of controversy.

The matter did not rest there. It was resumed a few months later by the new General Advisory Committee who considered the resolution of the Adult Education Advisory Committee, at that committee's request, on 29 June 1936. The Chairman of the Governors gave a confidential resumé of the whole story, and reaffirmed BBC policy on controversial broadcasting. In the discussion that followed there was general concern at the implications of the affair for the future, and at the danger to the freedom of broadcast speech from government intervention. Its power to intervene was acknowledged, but the consensus of opinion was that the BBC would not be justified in accepting such intervention unless satisfied, with or without the necessary information, that a course advised by the Government was in the public interest, or unless the Government was openly prepared to accept responsibility for enforcing its will. There was general apprehension in regard to future possibilities of veiled interference by the Government.

A recent Director General has written of the clause in the Charter that empowers Ministers to require the BBC either to broadcast or to refrain from broadcasting particular material, that 'in either case the BBC is free to announce that such a direction has been received'. He continues a little later:

> The power to require the BBC to refrain from broadcasting particular material is the famous 'unused' veto. This arouses immense suspicion in the minds of visitors to Britain, who are not accustomed to the force of convention in British society. The fact that the power exists leads them to suspect that it must be used, or that its use must, at times, be threatened in order to secure desired objectives. This is simply not the case.[7]

But the force of convention in British society is sometimes established by force, and *The Citizen and His Government* was one such instance. Nor can it be dismissed as an accidental hiccup in a normally smooth set of relations. It was in effect the culmination of a series of disparate pressures to which broadcasting had been subjected ever since the ban on controversy had been lifted in 1928. It clearly narrowed the field of controversy within the narrow confines of the differences between the three constitutional parties. Opinion to the right or left of these was not acceptable to the Government. It was the Government, not the broadcasters who claimed the right, and exerted their power, to define the boundaries of the field of political controversy. Secondly, it gave the Foreign Office *de facto* control over the discussion of foreign affairs on radio. The BBC, in the aftermath of the Vernon Bartlett row, had been progressing comfortably enough with routine consultation and advice. Now it knew that if the Foreign Office felt strongly enough it both could and would make its wishes prevail. Thirdly, and most inexcusably, the Government had made the BBC carry the burden of responsibility for the whole business, and had successfully concealed its exercise of power from the public. This was a flagrant violation of the basic principles on which broadcasting in Britain was supposed to rest, and made nonsense of the supposed independence of the BBC.

It cannot be said that the talks were in any sense a danger to some vital aspect of state policy. For the Foreign Office they were an embarrassment, since the BBC was widely regarded overseas as a semi-official mouthpiece of government. They had uneasy visions of the propaganda mileage certain foreign governments might get from the seeming legitimation, via the microphone, of communist and fascist viewpoints. To say the talks were not in the national interest was a convenient smokescreen for a government more concerned with controlling than with informing public opinion, and fully prepared to exercise its power to contain it.

Once again this incident points to the vulnerability of the BBC. It could not have come at a worse time. There had been noises in the press, and from the Conservative back-benches, about left-wing bias in the Talks Department. The Corporation had just been subjected to a Committee of Inquiry – always an anxious moment – whose report was due before Parliament. The Foreign Office had given the plainest of hints that if the BBC went against its wishes there might be demands for tighter parliamentary control of broadcasting. Though a Labour MP raised the matter of the cancelled talks in the course of the debate in the Commons on the Ullswater Report,[8] there is no indication that the Labour Party was prepared to make an issue of defending the independence of the BBC. The press was always more ready to blame than praise the Corporation for which its lack of public relations skills with Fleet Street, and its own internal disorders, were partly to blame. Public opinion in a more general sense is hard to judge, but there was never any widespread enthusiasm for radio talks, still less for adult education programmes on such unengaging subjects as *The Citizen and His Government*. Most citizens preferred light music and variety.

The Ullswater Committee's Report on Broadcasting was published four weeks after the Cabinet recorded its satisfaction at the cancellation of the talks by Mosley and Pollitt. The report declared: 'We have no reason to suppose that, in practice, divergent views of the lines of public interest have been held by the Corporation and by government departments, or that the Corporation has suffered under any sense of restraint or undue interference.'[9] Its praise of the BBC for exercising responsibility for controversy confided to it by the state 'with outstanding independence' had a distinctly hollow ring for those few at the time who knew of the extent to which that independence had been compromised.[10]

In the aftermath of this affair the BBC maintained an extremely low profile on all political issues. Talks was still in a state of shock after its reshuffle. News, still in its infancy, was having teething troubles. When the Spanish Civil War broke out in July 1936 it produced a non-interventionist response from the British Government, a sharp polarization of public opinion and another political minefield for the BBC. There were no symposiums on the subject from the Talks Department, not even of the purely informative and educative variety. There were no further *Crisis in Spain* feature programmes to follow up that remarkable production of 1931 and bring it up to date.[11] There were plenty of people in the BBC who cared passionately about the events in Spain and who wanted to say something about it, but precisely because it was the most explosive and divisive issue of the decade, because it split government and opposition, because it polarized right- and left-wing opinion, because it brought bitterness and class-consciousness into foreign policy and so into domestic politics – for all these reasons it was an untouchable subject for all areas of programming other than news. And news found itself in trouble soon enough.

By 1937 accusations were flying to and fro yet again of bias in the BBC, this time over news coverage of the war in Spain. There were all the usual signs: a ramp in the popular press, letters of complaint from public persons and questions in the House of Commons. The *Daily Mail* set the ball rolling with a campaign against 'The menace of the red bias on radio'. 'Who', it demanded in a leader article, 'is responsible for the conspicuous and persistent pro-red bias given to the BBC's service of news bulletins dealing with the Spanish Civil War?'[12] The left-wing press replied with their own content analysis of the bulletins to show that items of 'rebel' news outweighed government news by two or three to one, and so were helping to damp down any sympathy in this country for the forces of democracy in Spain. The tone of voice of the announcers was adduced by some as evidence of bias, and the exact terminology for describing both sides was a matter of the nicest diplomacy. F. A. Voigt, in *The Listener*, commented on the impossibility of calling anything nowadays without someone objecting, and went on to discuss the complexities of the terminology of Rebels, Patriots, Insurgents and Loyalists.[13] The news room followed the Foreign Office in referring to the Madrid Government as 'the government', 'and every recognized handbook on International Law in calling the Burgos government "the insurgents".'[14]

Jonathan Dimbleby has written that the whole of the news room wanted

" SAY, MR. AMBASSADOR, DON'T BE TOO DEPRESSING WITH YOUR 'EUROPEAN CRISIS,' 'COS I FOLLOW YOU WITH 'WE'RE ALL GOING ON THE RICKETTY RACKETTY RAZZLE.' "

some one of them to be sent out to report on the war from the front line, but that this was not permitted, although every newspaper had a reporter on the scene.[15] As it was, the news room had to rely on agency reports as its main source of information. Here there were all kinds of difficulty which the BBC explained in some detail in response to complaints from Victor Cazelet MP and from the Nottingham Diocesan Branch of the Catholic Women's League.[16]

The quality of agency material was admitted to be very unsatisfactory, and John Coatman, Chief Editor of News, had already complained about the matter. Unfortunately, there was no well-balanced flow of information from either side. Each of the four agencies had their man in Madrid. There was none with Franco in Burgos. News from both sides was highly partisan and strictly censored, but the flow of information from government sources outran that from the insurgents by six to one. Communiqués received from the same side on the same day frequently contradicted each other. Many were undated. The insurgents tended to withhold information from all correspondents except those of the one or two papers friendly to their cause. Their main means of disseminating information was through their own radio station, and these were not regularly quoted by the agencies. To frame a true and fair picture with such material was no easy matter, it was pointed out to the Catholic Women's League.

What the News Department fell back on was maintaining an equal balance. With no reporters of its own in Spain, it relied on occasional accounts from those who had been to the fronts. The main news bulletin for 20 January 1937 contained two eye-witness accounts of life in Spain: one from Professor J. B. S. Haldane about Madrid, and one from G. H. Keeley MP, who had visited Franco territory. This is how Haldane ended his brief talk:

> The citizens of Madrid have put themselves under voluntary discipline. They believe that their efforts and sacrifice will mean the death of fascism, and the birth of a new social order. They are determined that their fight shall be noble, not only in its main plan, but in its tiniest details. And that is why, if I lived for a thousand years, it might still be my proudest boast that on Christmas Day, 1936, I was a citizen of Madrid.

And this is how Keeley concluded his account:

> I have no time to speak of the causes for which the two sides are fighting, and I express no opinion on the probable result of the war. But I return home convinced of one thing. The less England takes sides and the more she uses her influence to limit the intervention of other Powers, the better it will be for England, for Spain, and for the world.[17]

In spite of the rousing sentiments expressed here by one of the leading left-wing intellectuals of the time, the *Daily Worker* denounced the BBC as an 'Ally of Reaction' for its policy of balance. 'The BBC's standard on impartiality in its reporting on Spain would be funny if it were not tragic. Its plan is to have an equal number of items from each side. This would not be so bad if the supply of news worked out that way, but frequently Exchange Telegraph tapes have two items from the rebels and four from Madrid. So two Madrid items are omitted. The result is shamefully misleading.'[18] It was an insoluble dilemma. Newspaper coverage was so partisan and public opinion was so inflamed that belief had become more important than the events themselves. The strain on the department was such that at one point R. T. Clark, Deputy Editor, marched into Reith's office and declared in no uncertain terms that the pressure on 'his boys' must stop, and came out slamming the door behind him. For this, says Jonathan Dimbleby, he was nearly sacked.[19]

By the autumn of 1937 Spain was beginning to fade as a news story. The Government's attention turned increasingly in the direction of Hitler's Germany. In the summer a new British ambassador, with pro-German views, had been sent to Berlin. Later in the year top-level contact was made, for the first time, with the Nazi leaders. In November Lord Halifax went to Germany and met Hitler. Hitler blamed the British press and anti-German elements in the Foreign Office for the increasing tension between the two countries.[20] The two most prominent offenders were swiftly removed by Chamberlain. Sir Robert Vansittart, the Permanent Head of the Department and intransigently anti-German, was promoted out of the way in December 1937. Two months later Chamberlain forced the resignation of Anthony Eden, his Foreign Secretary, who favoured a firm line with dictators. Halifax, more complaisant to Chamberlain, became Foreign Secretary and attention now turned to Hitler's other complaint – the media.

The German press had been fulminating for some time over the coverage of Germany in the British press and BBC News. On 13 February 1937 the *Berliner Börsen-Zeitung* had accused the BBC news service of taking

> every opportunity of tendentiously corrupting German press comment, of underlining any alarmist or questionable report. In England's internal politics, socialism is always preferred. Lectures giving another point of view merely serve as a convenient foil. In Spain there is only one legal government – at Valencia. The BBC bears the chief responsibility for misleading the English public during the Abyssinian War. Recently they have endeavoured to mislead in regard to Spain.

In January 1938 Chamberlain ordered a special watch to be kept on the BBC after statements in its news bulletins that no steps towards the improvement of Anglo-Italian relations were intended in the near future. The BBC news statement was 'corrected' on the orders of the Prime Minister's Press Secretary, and denied in the main news bulletin the following day.[21] There was a flurry in the press two weeks later as Germany denied rumours of unrest in the Army, blaming Polish Jews and the BBC for the story. The German Foreign Office strongly attacked the BBC suggesting that the reports were inspired by the new British Propaganda Committee set up by Chamberlain and chaired by Vansittart.[22] On the same day *The Times* pointed out that the new committee had not yet met, and that BBC bulletins were compiled from agency tapes. On 3 March Sir Philip Henderson, the British Ambassador in Berlin, told Hitler that Halifax had that same day arranged a press conference with responsible newspaper editors, and had also talked with the President of the Newspaper Proprietors' Association and senior BBC officials. To all he had emphasized their responsibility in the maintenance of peace.[23] A week later the Foreign Office, immediately before Hitler's annexation of Austria on 9 March, informed the press that no pressure could or would be exercised over newspaper content, but that personal attacks on German leaders, as distinct from reports and policy criticism, would make Halifax's negotiations more difficult.[24] The policy of appeasement thus began with discreet surveillance of and diplomatic pressure upon the British media.

As Hitler marched into Austria the BBC Talks Department was running a series called *The Way of Peace* which had started in February 1938. Its progress however was less peaceful than its title and a minor furore arose when one of the speakers, Sir Josiah Wedgwood MP, was not allowed to deliver the talk he had originally written. Wedgwood had included in his script a long shopping list of Hitler's territorial demands and ambitions which the BBC insisted he should cut: 'Concrete charges of this sort, which are at the most conjecture, ought not to be given the great publicity of the microphone.'[25] Wedgwood refused to omit the offending passage and another more amenable speaker was fielded in his place. Wedgwood made a fuss in the newspapers and wrote a pamphlet protesting that he had been gagged, and denouncing BBC censorship. The BBC's Home Intelligence Unit, organized by Sir Stephen Tallents, noted that the widespread impression created by this incident was that the BBC, due to recent political events, would not let dictators be criticized. In an important memorandum, written seven months later, John Coatman, now Director of North Region, bitterly attacked this series as playing about on 'the academic, idealistic fringes of the subject of war and peace. It bore as much relation to the necessities of the moment as the chatter of elderly spinsters at a Dorcas Society's tea-party bears to the fight against sin.' What had really been needed at that moment, Coatman maintained, were 'realistic' talks by Liddell Hart, Admiral Richmond, Seton Watson, Harold Nicholson, Voigt, Haldane and others telling simply and clearly the decisions this country would certainly have to take in the near future, and the state of our military, economic and other resources in relation to those decisions.[26] What Coatman meant by realism will become plain later.

At the same time the BBC was under pressure from two directions over political talks on radio; from the Labour Party and its own Talks Advisory Committee. It had still not succeeded in establishing an agreed code of practice between the parties over the right of reply to government broadcasts outside election periods. It had been trying hard to do so since the Ullswater Report urged more progress in this direction, but so far without success. In this it was urged on by the Talks Advisory Committee, formed early in 1937 under the chairmanship of Sir Walter Moberly. This superseded the Adult Education Advisory Committee, and marked a shift in policy away from the specialized listening groups for adult education talks towards the general audience.[27] Its brief was to advise the BBC on major matters of talks policy, to make suggestions for talks, to consider and comment on the Corporation's proposals and to act as consultants in the planning of particular series. One of its most active members was Megan Lloyd George MP who, at the second meeting of the committee on 1 July 1937, had put down the following resolution which the committee accepted:

> That this committee desires to reaffirm its view previously expressed as to the importance of the discussion before the microphone by whatever methods the BBC finds practicable, of live political issues which are actually under consideration.[28]

Even before this resolution, the BBC had been pressing the Postmaster General for some agreed formula for political talks on radio, but the Post Office simply stalled. On 7 February 1938, A. C. Norman, Chairman of the Governors, wrote to Major Tryon asking again for an answer to the letter he had written nearly a year earlier on 1 March 1937. Tryon replied to this on 18 February 1938 with the unhelpful statement that 'there is no prospect of agreement being reached between the Parties in the present circumstances, and consequently there are no further steps which can be taken at the present time.'[29]

A week later, immediately after Eden's resignation, the Secretary of the Labour Party, J. S. Middleton, wrote to request, in the general public interest, the right, as the Official Opposition, to broadcast its views on the present international situation in special relation to the Government's new declaration of policy. Letters went back and forth, with the BBC arguing that the views of both sides were fully and fairly presented in the news bulletins, that if the opposition were allowed to broadcast the Government would wish to do so, and that a balanced discussion, *if* it could be arranged, might be the best thing. The Labour Party wanted to put forward its own views, not to solicit or convey the views of the Government on this or any other matter and, after several letters expressing dissatisfaction with the BBC's attitude, requested a meeting with the Board of Governors. This took place on 30 March 1938. It would seem that this was the first time that an opposition party had asked for the right to make a policy statement outside election time – apart from the agreed procedure for the Budget – and it put the BBC in a quandary. Should it accede to this request, at the same time offering the right of reply to other parties or the opportunity to make some other policy statement? How often should this be allowed? In its official reply to the Labour Party the BBC stated that it had always held the view that there should be greater opportunity for the broadcast discussion of controversy, but that its efforts in this direction had so far, and not for want of trying, proved abortive. It would now look into the whole matter afresh with its Talks Advisory Committee.[30]

That committee was again agitating for talks by MPs on live political issues. But Tallents advised Reith of the necessary constraints upon such demands. The BBC had lately, of its own initiative and not at the suggestion of the Foreign Office, felt obliged to exercise special care in the organization of debates on live international political issues. The problem was, Tallents said, that BBC programmes designed purely for internal consumption were likely to be overheard some 400 miles into Europe where the BBC was regarded as officially controlled and inspired. Though the BBC did its best to remove that supposition it could not, without irresponsibility, be disregarded and hence the need for discretion in the treatment of international affairs in home programmes.[31]

In the wake of the Austrian crisis Reith, at a Control Board Meeting on 5 April 1938, had raised the question of the effect on the public of the generally sensational tenor of the news.[32] This was not the BBC's fault he declared, but he wanted everyone to give serious thought to ways and means of formulating a positive policy to keep the country in better morale. The nation needed heartening. The Outside Broadcasts Unit had few ideas other than Royal broadcasts 'to give an idea of foreign goodwill towards this country and a belief in its future'.[33] For Features Moray McLaren was bubbling with ideas. He put forward a four-part historical programme on *The Defence of Christendom* to show the rape of Europe in the past by ancient Goths, Huns, Vandals and Infidels. He followed this with a medley of programme ideas on the themes of Liberty and Freedom as exemplified by the Armada, Trafalgar, Mount Everest, Nansen, Abraham Lincoln, Florence Nightingale, Henry V, Scott of Antarctica and the *Golden Hind*. For Talks, Maconachie was more sombre and realistic. In reply to Cecil Graves, upon whom had fallen the task of implementing Reith's scheme, he declared:

I have been thinking over this proposal since you mentioned it to me, and feel that propaganda of this kind is full of pitfalls. If, for instance, we were dealing with subjects of real importance, such as the military strength of this country, it would surely be futile, if not dishonest, to leave out the black spots, and emphasise merely the bright ones.

He suggested that Features or Variety might create a series built round a pessimistic character who, through a series of misadventures, was made to look ridiculous – the idea being to kill pessimism by ridicule. He also suggested that John Hilton might give a series of monthly talks. These would probably be crude and emotional with an appeal most likely only to the working class with whom they might be very effective.

For the News Department, R. T. Clark's reply was the darkest of all:

As far as News is concerned, it is very difficult for me to put up any suggestion on the matter of improving the morale of the country. I am afraid that at present the majority of people would admit that the main items of news are, in themselves, depressing ... It seems to me that the only way to strengthen the morale of the people whose morale is worth strengthening is to tell them the truth, and nothing but the truth, even if the truth is horrible.[34]

Reith's own scheme for national 'heartening' was that the BBC should dispense 'a cheerful tonic calculated to remove any inferiority complex latent in the mind of the man in the street' about Britain's industrial efficiency.[35] He wanted the news bulletins to carry a regular Industrial Report which, in a break with precedent, would give a pat on the back to British industry by naming individual firms that were holding their own in world markets – the Reith Award for Industry. This fatuous scheme was practically the last thing Reith did in the BBC. On 30 June 1938 he left the Corporation to go to Imperial Airways and the fruitless task of pursuing his idea fell to others. It was greeted with no enthusiasm in the news room, and collapsed entirely at the end of August after protracted wrangles with the Federation of British Industry whose competitive instincts disliked the idea of free publicity for some but not others.

Meanwhile Basil Nicolls, Controller of Programmes, was grappling with the rather more important and intractable question of political programmes. In two long memoranda he tried to set out policy guidelines on the matter, drawing a sharp distinction between two different categories of political broadcasts and the different treatment they might receive.[36] Category (A) was politics in the narrow sense of the word, that is party politics. In essence this involved the treatment of controversial subjects at a time when they were most forcibly before the attention of the public. This was what the Labour Party was after and one faction of the Talks Advisory Committee (Megan Lloyd George) without much support from anyone else. In Category (B) were political broadcasts in a wider social sense, broadcasts which served to educate the electorate on broad issues not acutely controversial or actively before Parliament or the public. The majority of the Talks Advisory Committee wanted more of this kind of programme.

For Category (A) the accepted and only acceptable treatment was that of uncensored and emotional appeals by front-benchers. The BBC did not, so to speak, guarantee the broadcast matter, which was the responsibility of the parties. For Category (B) the normal BBC standards of impartial, authoritative and balanced presentation must apply. Speakers should be chosen for their expertise and not because they happened to be politicians. This second category – of which *The Way of Peace* was the most recent example – was altogether an easier proposition than the first and a series on *The Mediterranean* was planned for the autumn. All the difficulties lay with the first category. It would always be virtually impossible for foreign politics to be treated in this manner, while certain domestic issues, such as defence or conscription, would almost certainly be turned down by the Government. That left a residue of dull domestic subjects which were often not controversial enough to warrant the parties sending their leaders to the microphone. Nicolls had scanned the programme for the next session of Parliament and it yielded – apart from foreign politics and defence – not a single Bill of any controversial significance. There were highly technical subjects like rent restrictions and dull subjects like bacon. The best of a thoroughly bad lot seemed to be the Milk Bill, but after due consideration at Control Board, it was felt it would be a bad start, if not a downright absurdity, to write to the parties and ask them to come to the microphone to spill milk. Nicolls concluded that it would be best to defer efforts in this direction until the autumn session when the Prisons Bill might offer a better opportunity. In the meantime the situation would be kept under review and if something interesting cropped up, to which the Category (A) treatment might be applied, the chance would be seized upon.

At the same time, in a desultory and leisurely fashion, the awareness was growing that the BBC had rather been caught napping by the Austrian crisis. At a Programme Board on 26 May, it was agreed that the BBC would give the impression of being more wide awake if programmes were broken into in order to include topical items. A month later the Assistant Controller of Programmes, just back from America, reported that over there the BBC's handling of the Austrian crisis was felt to have been disappointing. Felix Greene, the BBC's North American Representative, thought that the Corporation had much to learn from the American networks.[37] Nicolls confirmed that departments must take a more topical attitude to their programmes at the expense, if need be, of the advanced schedule. There was a long discussion of the Austrian crisis at Programme Board on 4 August. It was realized that the American companies had greater freedom of action at such times than the BBC. There was agreement that, News apart, the BBC had failed to give listeners, especially listeners overseas, adequate information on the course of events. There should have been much more information about the historical background to the annexation of Austria, and much more objective interpretation of events as they occurred.[38]

Not everyone in the BBC approved, though, of American news methods. In the moritorium on Munich a few months later the Director of Overseas Services declared that, while he was not blindly opposed to broadcasts from the scene of the action, he felt there were times when such things were liable to be unhelpful, misleading and purely sensational, 'and therefore not in accordance with the principles which guide our action as a British organization'. The American networks had made a great splash in print about their coverage of the Munich crisis, presumably with a view to impressing their sponsors. The question was how far the BBC could preserve its principles if it decided to follow in the wake of American broadcasting.[39]

The Czechoslovakia crisis was now coming to a head. In August and September Nicolls was pursuing attempts with the Party Whips to come to some arrangement over Category (A) broadcasts for the autumn schedule, but these negotiations were overtaken by events and had to be postponed. As the crisis deepened Nicolls wanted permission from Reuters to set up loudspeakers in public places so that the BBC's 'sober and objective' bulletins might be as widely available as possible. This was taking a leaf out of Goebbels' book, who was already using radio in Germany in this way as an instrument of propaganda. But Sir Roderick Jones, who owned Reuters, flatly turned down the idea, and events were moving too swiftly for it to be worth pursuing.[40]

Outwardly at least the BBC's performance during the critical period appeared to be much as might now be expected. A report compiled some years later in the BBC registry on the Corporation's handling of the Munich crisis declared that:

Broadcasting naturally played an important part in the Czechoslovakia crisis of September/October 1938, and was commended afterwards on all sides for its efficient news service and for its steadying effect on anxious listeners, only too ready to seize on wild rumours and to believe the most sensational news-paper stories ... There was no censorship by the Government of the BBC news bulletins or broadcast material, though the Corporation naturally kept in close touch with the appropriate departments and the bulletins fell in line with

Government policy ... The news bulletins became the most important sections of the programmes to a world-wide audience during those anxious days and the calm voice of the BBC announcers evoked special comment from abroad in contrast to the excited accents of American commentators, and the extreme anti-Czechoslovak propaganda from Germany.[41]

Within the BBC, however, a critical debate arose in the immediate aftermath of the crisis led by John Coatman, first head of the News Department, who had moved to Manchester at the beginning of the year to become the Director of BBC North Region. In a lengthy memorandum called *The BBC and National Defence*, Coatman raised the crucial question of the extent of government control of the BBC's news service.[42] The BBC was, Coatman argued, in times of crisis, the most important public institution in the country. Its prestige was unique since the mass of the people believed that the BBC could speak for the Government and yet was independent of it. This entailed a special responsibility on the broadcasters of 'playing fair' with the people of this country, which meant being truly independent of improper coercion or control by Government. What gravely troubled Coatman was that it was common knowledge in the BBC and had been, he declared, for at least a year, that war with Germany was inevitable. Yet this knowledge, and the magnitude of its implications and consequences, had not been communicated to the listening public. The BBC had been making its own arrangements for wartime broadcasting since 1937 and these had been finalized, down to the details of wartime pay-scales, only the week before the crisis broke.[43] It was in this context – of behind-the-scenes planning based on the inevitability of war, and a front-of-house policy that continued to evade that certainty – that Coatman expressed his deep dismay at the ignorance of the people of Britain and the Empire of much of the essential information that they should have had, not just at the moment of Munich, but well beforehand.

I say, with a full sense of responsibility and, since I was for over three years Chief News Editor, with a certain authority, that in the past we have not played the part which our duty to the people of this country called upon us to play. We have, in fact, taken part in a conspiracy of silence. I am not saying for a moment that we did this willingly or even knowingly, and most certainly there is not a word of accusation against any individual in what I am saying. In view of our history and our peculiar relationship to the Government, and also the very short time, comparatively speaking, during which we have been at work, I think even the sternest critic can hardly have expected us to have behaved differently. But now things have changed. The position of this country is infinitely more dangerous than it has ever been in modern times, and the past few weeks have invested the BBC with a new importance, given it a more vital role in the national life, and have, therefore, laid a new responsibility on us who are its servants. This responsibility is to let the people of this country know, as far as the sources available to us allow, just what is happening. Again I will make a necessary explanation. I am not for a moment suggesting that the BBC should have a rival foreign policy to that of the Government. In any case it is impossible, and even if it were not impossible it would be grossly improper and irresponsible. What I mean is that we should make it our duty to get the most authoritative and responsible non-official students of foreign affairs to expose the development of events frankly and fearlessly in our general talks and news talks. We should, of course, keep full liaison with the Government, but we would never allow ourselves to be silenced except when we are taken into that confidence which our position and sense of responsibility entitle us to, and are given specific, valid reasons for not following out some course of action on which we had decided.

Coatman gave examples of the ways in which the Corporation had been drawn into the Government's web of silence. More than a year earlier, at a private gathering, a member of the Government had said that Britain would almost certainly be at war with Germany over Czechoslovakia by September 1938. That view, and the facts on which it was based, was known to many people outside official circles, including several people in Broadcasting House. But the BBC had been unable to let the public know of such opinion in any way. The other instances he cited were the Abyssinian War and the first discussion in Parliament of German militarism, when Churchill revealed the extent of German rearmament. From time to time, said Coatman, the News Department had got as close to the truth as it could in its news talks, but their liberty of action was subject to close limitations.[44] His memorandum was not intended merely as a review of the past. The Munich Agreement had given this country, he wrote, a breathing space not a permanent peace, which the BBC must use to rethink its responsibilities to the country and its relations with Government. He concluded with 'a plea for realism in our talks and news, and a determination to keep our people informed of developments at home and abroad, developments which concern them vitally, using that word in its literal sense'.

If reactions to the Austrian crisis earlier in the year had been sluggish, this time the response was swift. At the height of the crisis the BBC's handling of it was discussed at Programme Board on 29 September. The matters raised were largely technical and administrative, including the allegation that the recording of Chamberlain's speech at Heston, on his return from Godesburg, had been played at too fast a speed, thus altering the pitch of his voice and the impression of what he was saying.[45] At the next meeting, on 6 October, the implications of the crisis were beginning to sink in. After noting that the Foreign Office had expressed high appreciation of the work of the News Department, the next matter raised by Coatman was that of government control. On this Nicolls declared that there was a clear distinction between interference with broadcasting by the Government on its own behalf, of which there had been none, and advice from the Foreign Office on matters concerning the national interest, which would have to be sought by the BBC if it were not offered in the first place. There was some discussion as to whether there had been enough topical talks on the factors leading up to Munich and the personalities involved, and Maconachie stated that there had been a talk on Czechoslovakia and a brief portrait of Dr Benes, the Czech Prime Minister. It was agreed that, in the wake of events, there should be a series of talks on 'After the Crisis' which would begin with the reactions of ordinary people to the crisis and be followed by authoritative speakers to answer the points they made. It was hoped that the series would not be so edited, especially as regards politics, as to make them uninteresting.[46]

Next day at Control Board, under a minute headed 'Broadcasting in time of war', it was agreed that the lessons of the crisis should be recorded and present programme arrangements should be revised where necessary and given wider publicity.[47] The issue came up again at Programme Board on 3 November, when the BBC's handling of the crisis and the implications of Coatman's memorandum were discussed at length. It was agreed that the value of a post-mortem would be greatly enhanced if it led to a definition of policy in advance of the next crisis.[48] This was deferred until 17 November, when the whole question of the BBC's relationship with government was reviewed.[49] It was resolved that the BBC neither could nor should attempt an 'editorial policy' of its own; that it should try to give expression to informed opinion even though critical of the government, balanced with the official view; should anticipate events as far as possible and try to give listeners the necessary background information before matters became so critical that there was opposition to them being treated at all; should broadcast more topical material during the actual crisis and lastly, should treat current events more regularly and in greater detail than at present, possibly by a general extension of talks.[50]

The immediate response of Maconachie and the Talks Department was to run a symposium called *Everyman and the Crisis*[51] along the lines suggested by Programme Board. Valuable though this may have been in restoring the nation's morale, it did little to add to its political education as to the real implications of Munich. The change in the BBC's attitude showed up most plainly in the News Department led by R. T. Clark who had taken over when Coatman went North. In November the BBC received a private letter – 'or at any rate a very semi-official one' – from A. P. Ryan in the Offices of the Cabinet, complaining of the tendentious nature of the news bulletins and the predominance of commentators who in the past were of a pacifist nature but had lately become ultra-bellicose. Ryan observed that the news of late 'while perhaps containing nothing to which specific objection could be taken, has managed to convey a sort of leaning in one direction'.[52]

By early 1939 listeners had become accustomed to hearing in the nightly news 'actual recordings of fiery foreign dictators making their speeches'. And what was more, according to Mr F. Washington Flatt in a letter to *The Times*, 'the BBC makes a point of recording the most vehement part of the speech, which of course is greeted with wild cheering'.[53] Were they trying to foment fear and turmoil in the minds of English listeners? This correspondent was at least a month behind *The Times* for, during the whole of February, there had been a long and hostile correspondence in that newspaper about the tenor of BBC news.

It began on 2 February with a letter from Mrs E. Hester Blagden of Peterborough complaining that:

> Some of us ordinary citizens are troubled and perplexed that while our Prime Minister and Foreign Secretary do all in their power to bring about friendly cooperation between this country and the peoples of Germany and Italy, we are subjected every night in BBC news bulletins to hearing only those words from abroad which must aggravate ill feelings and exasperate tired minds, so that nightly we can go to bed more certain that war must come.

This struck some deeply responsive chord in the readership of *The Times* for there followed an avalanche of mail, of which those published were but a fraction, and in which the critics far outnumbered the supporters of the BBC.[54] One early correspondent put it mildly: 'Everybody must have been filled with admiration for the restraint shown by the BBC at the time of the crisis, but since then it does seem inclined to yield to the temptation to dramatize the news.' Others were less inhibited: alarmist, emotional, sensationalist, rumour-mongering, 'giving folk the jitters', one-sided (every item tending to place the fascist nations in an unfavourable light), left-wing … these were the charges, tirelessly repeated, with evidence thrown in for good measure from previous occasions. It did not escape the memory of some correspondents that it had been exactly the same during the Spanish Civil War. Atrocities on Franco's side had always been given prominence in the bulletins while nothing was said about Republican outrages. On and on it went for a whole month with the babble of voices increasing in numbers and shrillness.

The popular press soon weighed in: 'The fat boys of the BBC who try to make our flesh creep are under fire. They are the news announcers who have been sending the country to bed at night convinced of immediate catastrophe. Now they are being criticized and it is right and proper they should be, for the manner and substance of much of the news broadcast is deplorable.'[55] Thus,

PANDORA'S BOX

" Be a bit less gloomy—or I'll—"

and much more, the *Daily Mail*. Soon after this commotion died down there was another as the press splashed a spate of 'BBC suicides' said to have been caused by hearing 'bad news' on the wireless.[56] There were no reported instances of newspaper suicides.

The BBC was undeterred. Nor was it without some support. The professor of Prehistoric Archaeology at Edinburgh, wrote to congratulate the Corporation on its objective news: 'The present correspondence in *The Times* is the best testimony to your success in separating news from propaganda. Personally I confess I find the decipherment of the ruling oligarchy's tortuous aims, by applying to the skilfully selected half-truths of *The Times* the methods of criticism of ancient authors taught at Oxford, a better guide to the conduct of my own affairs than any attempt to discover what is really happening.'[57] This latest press ramp was discussed at Control Board, with Clark present for the news room, who agreed that it was not the job of the BBC to send people comfortably to bed.[58]

While this was going on attempts to establish an agreed procedure on political talks of the Category (A) variety had been resumed. These had been postponed when the Munich crisis blew in, but by the beginning of 1939 senior BBC officials had returned to the task of rolling this particular stone uphill. From then until the summer, continuous efforts were made to bring the opponents of government foreign policy to the microphone, above all Churchill and Eden, and to mobilize public opinion to prepare for war. Both are evidence of a new-found determination, in the aftermath of Munich, 'to play fair' with the British people by keeping them informed on issues which, as Coatman had put it, concerned them vitally in the literal sense of the word.

Immediately after the crisis in October 1938 Churchill had broadcast from London to America a powerful and sustained attack on government policy, appealing for American support as the lights in Europe went out.[59] The following week Control Board, noting that Lord Halifax had agreed to broadcast to America after Churchill, proposed that it might be desirable to get a talks series along the same lines by Government and Opposition speakers for the National Programme. Frederick Ogilvie, the new Director General, agreed to take the matter up with Sir Horace Wilson, Chamberlain's faithful civil servant. The time was scarcely opportune however, 'owing to the preoccupations of Whitehall', and further attempts to arrange political talks were deferred until the new year. On 10 January 1939 Ogilvie wrote to Captain Margesson, Conservative Chief Whip, saying he was most anxious to straighten out arrangements for political broadcasting, and asking for a meeting at his earliest convenience.[60]

After a meeting with Margesson on 18 January, a new initiative began though with 'foreign policy definitely excluded in the meantime'. What was now accepted in principle by the parties were regular Category (A) broadcasts on domestic issues by front-bench spokesmen. Ogilvie contacted the Labour Party for suggestions and Attlee proposed a debate on 'Problems of Old Age Pensions', which was accepted by the other parties. The news of regular radio discussions on political issues by the parties was publicized in the newspapers. This prompted Churchill to write again to the Chairman of the Governors asking if, alongside these, some provision ought not to be made for public men who had held high office but who were unlikely to be selected as spokesmen of their parties. He gave a list of those who, like himself, were unlikely candidates for the microphone under the present arrangements. They included Eden, Duff Cooper, Lord Cecil, Amery, Lloyd George, Stafford Cripps and Lansbury. He reiterated the point that he had made several years earlier that it was an indefensible public policy to exclude from the microphone those public figures not acceptable to the Party Whips. Ogilvie replied in most conciliatory terms. The BBC had long been anxious to increase its facilities for political broadcasting, and it seemed best at first to ask the parties to choose the subjects and the speakers. 'But', he went on, 'we are closely considering further stages in the development of political broadcasting, including the one you are good enough to outline.'[61]

What Ogilvie now tried to establish was the right to discuss, at the microphone, issues over which the parties were *internally* divided. He began by trying to persuade the Labour Party to air some of its differences on radio. That pretext having been established, the next move would be, presumably, in the direction of the Government. Accordingly, Ogilvie wrote to Attlee suggesting that he, or anyone else, might be willing to take part in a microphone debate with Sir Stafford Cripps. Cripps, who figured on Churchill's little list of party offenders, had been seriously at odds with the Labour leadership for some years now. Since 1937 he had been prominent in the Popular Front organized by the Communist Party, the Socialist League and the Independent Labour Party, all of whom had been anathematized by the Labour Party. In January 1939 he had tried to reactivate the Popular Front campaign, which was rejected again by the National Executive of the Labour Party. Cripps persisted however, and was expelled from the party for his pains. Thus Ogilvie's proposition was not only highly topical and controversial, but probed as well the Party's divided attitude to that most forbidden of subjects – foreign policy.

Attlee however sent the proposal smartly packing:

> It would be setting an entirely new precedent in political broadcasting to initiate discussions on domestic differences between members or ex-members of the same political party. No suggestion has been made, as far as I know, in the cases of MR EDEN or MR DUFF COOPER who have differed with the Conservative Party on the issue of foreign policy. I think you will find that similarly the various occasions on which MR CHURCHILL, during recent years, has differed from the Government have not been made occasions for such a debate.

94

He went on to say that political broadcasting had always been confined to the discussion of matters at issue between recognized parties. 'The difficulty of admitting fortuitous collections of individuals has always been recognized as opening the door to all kinds of cranks.' He and his colleagues would not entertain the idea. Ogilvie wearily replied that 'the way of broadcasting is hard!'. He reminded Attlee how hard the BBC had tried to open up political debate on radio. He hoped Attlee did not think that the new arrangement was the sum total of what could or should be done. He replied that the line between cranks and non-cranks (Attlee's terms, not his) might be difficult to draw, but it was one which it was the business of the BBC to face. He said there was a general feeling in the BBC that the public demand occasionally to hear a Churchill, a Lloyd George, a Lansbury or a Cripps was by no means unreasonable. He hoped to be able to approach Attlee and the other leaders when the times were a little rosier. In the meantime, he concluded, 'May I ask you to extend your sympathy to the BBC for its present inability, through no fault of its own, adequately to discharge what it believes to be its duty to listeners and to the country.'[62]

As that door closed the BBC was trying another way in. At a Controllers Meeting on 10 March the Chairman of the Governors was asked to contact the Postmaster General about the possibility of a debate on Eden and Churchill's request for a wider form of National Government. Before he did so the crux of the matter was raised in the Commons on 27 March by Sir Richard Acland. Acland, a Liberal MP and another prominent supporter of the Popular Front, raised a question which he had twice already tried to put, and which had been twice postponed by the Government. At just after eleven o'clock that night he was at last able to put his question, 'which only the Prime Minister can answer'. 'Why is he entitled to state [on radio] his views on foreign affairs when he chooses, and why is no other leader entitled, on any occasion, to make any reply?' Chamberlain left the answer to his Postmaster General, Major G. C. Tryon. This provided Norman with a pretext for raising the matter, and he wrote to Tryon on 5 April.

Tryon, using the classic ploy of all Postmasters General when awkward questions on broadcasting were raised in the House, had replied that the matter of who should broadcast was for the Governors of the BBC to decide. This, said Norman, was of course the true constitutional doctrine to which he unreservedly adhered. However, he found himself wondering whether the practice which had grown up with regard to political broadcasting really did accord with this doctrine. Norman was very tactful, but he made clear all the critical points. There were difficulties, he granted, in the BBC policy of balanced controversy. The Prime Minister of the day, whatever his political colour, was more than a party leader and was entitled sometimes to speak as the leader of the nation. So the BBC had gladly allowed Mr Chamberlain to make a number of broadcasts in the past few months, and had withheld the right of reply 'though not infrequently the speeches included passages of a party nature'. It was a good thing that, after years of trying, the BBC was able at last to arrange broadcast debates on Old Age Pensions and Municipal Trading. Encouraging though this was as a start, no one could claim that these were the issues on which the mind of the public was concentrated, or that any of the issues which had been before the public for many months now had been adequately discussed on the air. They were issues frequently debated in Parliament and canvassed daily in the press; but the vast audience of thirty million who listened to the wireless were deprived of any opportunity of getting, through the unrivalled instrument which the BBC controlled, such an education in the most controversial questions as was in the sole power of broadcasting to offer.

Acland was, said Norman, uncomfortably near the truth in saying that who should speak at the microphone was in the hands of the Prime Minister. And matters were made worse by the fact that although many prominent politicians outside the Government had spoken over the air to the United States, they remained unheard in this country – a fact that exposed the BBC to much criticism. It could not be right, at a time like this, that the British people had no chance of hearing statesmen of the standing of Churchill, Lloyd George or Eden. It was essential that they, along with leading members of the Government, should come to the microphone. 'I gravely doubt', said Norman, 'whether we are doing our duty and exercising properly the discretion which, as you truly say, lies with us under the Charter.' Norman ended by noting that though he was shortly to lay down his chairmanship he had not wanted to depart without registering his sense of the urgency of the matter, and he hoped that Tryon would discuss the whole issue with the new Chairman. Tryon's reply was as curt as it was short. He thanked Norman for his views, and was glad to have them before he departed. So the door was almost bolted shut against the efforts of the BBC to bring the opponents of government policy to the microphone. There remained one other possibility. It might yet try to mobilize public opinion to prepare for war and, in so doing, bring in Churchill and Eden as speakers. This it tried to do in the spring and summer of 1939.[63]

Back in December 1938 the Ministry of Labour had contacted Sir Stephen Tallents, in charge of Public Relations for the BBC, over its preparations for a general publicity campaign to launch its new National Service scheme. In the early months of 1939 Whitehall and the military moved into action and the News Department found itself up to its neck in Army propaganda schemes and the plans of the War Office which, as Richard Dimbleby confided to Donald Boyd, 'are more or less of a compulsory nature as far as we are concerned'.[64] By Easter the campaign was well and truly bogged down through lack of any coordinated government plans or any established means of liaison between Whitehall, the Army and the BBC.

At the end of April Charles Siepmann, now Director of Programme Planning, wrote to advise Basil Nicolls that there was considerable puzzlement and anxiety in Broadcasting House at the lack of any emerging policy. Gielgud and the others were sick, he said, of half-measures and a policy which seemed to vacillate between appeasement and half-hearted propaganda. He summed up the general mood as follows: 'If we wait upon the Government the immense influence of broadcasting for mobilizing public opinion and a proper appreciation of our present state, recruitment and National Service will all be deferred until the bombs are dropping.'[65]

Siepmann suggested that the BBC should take the initiative and at once devote a portion of the daily programme schedule to a concerted scheme of professional propaganda. He wanted every section of the community to be made aware of its particular danger; to launch a major campaign for Army recruitment, air raid precaution and local emergency services; to exploit the appeal of Eden and Churchill, and the combined resources of Features and Talks as a spearhead for the whole exercise. It would need cooperation from government departments, but the BBC must take the lead.

This idea was immediately accepted and over the next six weeks the BBC went ahead. It was hampered by fairly continuous examples of Whitehall inefficiency and stupidity in banning items for broadcasting when they were 'obviously of urgent public interest'.[66] But in spite of this the project moved ahead. Lindsay Wellington grappled with plans for a big talks series to support the recruitment drive. His jotted notes reveal an almost equal concern to persuade the Government of the gravity of the situation as to persuade the country, with the added worry that to initiate a big campaign was worse than useless if the administrative machinery to handle a sudden big influx of recruits was not in existence. He began from the assumption that a great many people still did not believe that Britain was on the brink of war and that until they understood this they would be unwilling to volunteer for national service. So the indispensable first step must be a statement of the real situation and the necessary objectives, coupled with a direct and unequivocal appeal for concrete action. He then sketched out a sequence of such appeals, starting with Eden and Churchill, and spread over successive days of one week. At the same time Lawrence Gilliam was drafting detailed proposals for a features series that would recreate the events leading to Munich, the crisis itself and its implications through to the present. It would combine news bulletins, public speeches, foreign press and radio bulletins with public reaction to these events drawn from *Everyman and the Crisis*, the Institute of Public Opinion and Mass Observation reports. It might have been brilliant had it ever been done.

By the end of May detailed plans had been drawn up for a two-week campaign which the BBC wanted to place in the schedules between 18 June and 1 July. The short-list of speakers included the leaders of the three parties, then a sample drawn from Baldwin, Churchill, Lord Derby, Morrison, Gracie Fields (for women recruits), Lloyd George, Dorman Smith, Eden, Halifax and Anderson. All was ready. Only the official green light was needed. On 31 May, Nicolls wrote to the Ministry of Labour enclosing the preliminary draft of the scheme. He asked the Ministry to give it a general blessing on behalf of the Government, and two aspects of it in particular. The BBC wanted to be able to tell its speakers that the scheme had general government approval, and that the suggested guidelines they should take in their talks had been drawn up in consultation with the Ministry of Labour. Secondly, if the BBC was to make this big effort, it would be useless unless it could go all out to convince the country – without necessarily being very alarmist – that the need was urgent and the crisis still remained. Nicolls pointed out that time was of the essence: speakers needed to be recruited, and if the plan was to make the *Radio Times* it must be with the printers within a week at the latest.

On 5 June there was a meeting at the Ministry of Labour between the department, the Lord Privy Seal's office, and Maconachie and Nicolls for the BBC. Before the meeting began Nicolls had been tipped off that the Ministry of Labour was very keen on the idea but there were grave doubts about the attitude of the Lord Privy Seal's office which had policy control over the Ministry of Labour. Mr S. H. Wood, speaking for the Lord Privy Seal, said that he was very grateful for the BBC's scheme but felt it was rather like taking a steam hammer to crack a nut. He objected to having in all the big guns – Churchill, Lloyd George, and so forth – since it would make people think that the Government was in a hole and must have mismanaged its recruiting campaign in the past. The truth was that the present campaign was the most phenomenally successful campaign ever launched in this country. Wood went on to say that the Lord Privy Seal objected to this 'crisis' programme as being likely to give people the idea that they might be involved in a war in a few months time – by, say, September.

Reading between the lines Nicolls inferred that these objections were prompted by party political considerations (jealousy of the likes of Lloyd George and Churchill being called upon to pull the irons from the fire), and by appeasement, or some shade of it. It seemed that if Britain were to be ready, it must not be at the expense of saying that Germany was prepared to go to war. At one point a Ministry of Labour official stated that the Department only expected to get 150,000 recruits out of the target of half a million. Wood replied that this was better than alarming people. Nicolls had no option but to withdraw all the major ingredients of the scheme. There was a good deal of further discussion among the government representatives at the other

" My dear, could you sleep a wink without dear. Mr. Chamberlain? "

end of the room, much of which was inaudible to Maconachie. Nicolls reassured him afterwards that he hadn't missed much.[67]

So this last effort, like all previous ones, was squashed. Nicolls sent round a memorandum to all concerned telling them of his very great disappointment that the plans, due to political or other extraneous motives of the Government, would have to be very considerably watered down. Nearly all the features were cancelled, along with the 'elder statesmen' talks and the 'What can I do?' talks planned to advise ordinary citizens about air raid precaution, and so on. Nicolls was angered at the waste of time and effort that staff had been put to. He was now no longer prepared to put the BBC to any great expense or inconvenience on behalf of a government that saw no need for urgency.

The summer that year was glorious. In July and August the BBC did all the things it usually did at that time of year. There was plenty of tennis, cricket and golf. There were the usual August Bank Holiday special feature programmes, and Outside Broadcasts from the seaside. Features did a programme on Oxford – *Undergraduate Summer*, produced by Stephen Potter – from its backwaters to its common rooms. John Betjeman talked about *How to Look at Books*. North Region launched a new series called *Mr Mike Walks In*, in which the microphone turned the audience into broadcasters by calling on them informally in their own homes. John Pudney produced a *Modern Pastoral* about the coming of electricity to a remote Essex village, and J. B. Priestley began reading in instalments his new novel, *Let the People Sing*, before it was released by the publishers. There were new quiz programmes and parlour games – *Noah's Ark*, *All in Bee* and *For Amusement Only*. *Radio Times* carried details of what Autumn had in store for listeners by way of talks, music and entertainment. At last this hypnotic trance – as if warm days should never cease – was broken. On Sunday, 3 September 1939, Neville Chamberlain came to the microphone, which he had so jealously preserved as his own exclusive property, to tell the people that Britain was now officially at war with Germany.

This then was the legacy of the developing relationship between the British state and the BBC. At the critical moment, when the public vitally needed access both to facts and to informed debate about events in Europe, broadcasting was unable to meet those needs. If it was a conspiracy, then John Coatman was right to say that it was one into which the BBC was drawn unwittingly. But there was no grand strategy behind it. It was rather the cumulative effect of precedents established and powers imposed piecemeal by central government in the decade following the lifting of the ban on controversy.

After the General Strike Reith had rationalized the role of radio in the matter by arguing that 'since the BBC was a national institution, and since the

Government in the crisis were acting for the people ... the BBC was for the Government in the crisis too.'[68] Munich was the first test of that syllogism as a precedent for the role of broadcasting in a national crisis. The BBC was confronted with the fundamental dilemma as to whose interests it had a prior duty to serve, and it rightly decided that its final responsibility was to the British people not the government of the day. It came to see that the listening public was, at the very least, entitled to hear on radio, from leading British statesmen, views that opposed official government policy. But the extent of the BBC's powerlessness became apparent when, having grasped the nettle of responsibility to the public, it tried to do something about it. For what compounded its difficulties and prevented it from breaking the deafening silence was its own absorption within the state domain. The continuous routine contact that had built up over the years between senior personnel in Broadcasting House, Whitehall and Westminster meant that they all abided by the same rules and code of conduct. The Corporation had become the shadow of a state bureaucracy; closed, self-protective and secretive. No one in the BBC spoke out publicly at the time of Munich about the extent to which broadcasting was being gagged. But then *The Citizen And His Government* affair had disciplined the broadcasters to accept covert government interference in their programme arrangements and to pretend publicly that it had not happened.

As for society and public opinion, Munich was the last and perhaps the most striking proof of the extent to which it remained confused and uninformed by the Government before war was declared. *Britain by Mass Observation*, a Penguin Special produced in 1939 on 'the state of the nation', contained a survey which showed the uncertain and volatile condition of public opinion before, during and after the Munich crisis. 'The urgency of fact, the voicelessness of everyman and the smallness of the groups which control fact getting and fact distribution' was the motivating thrust behind the book. This pioneering study of public opinion identified two kinds of focus in society: 'One is the ordinary focus of the ordinary man or woman which centres on home and family, work and wages. The other is the political focus, which centres on government policy and diplomacy. What happens in this political sphere obviously affects the sphere of home and work. But between the two there is a gulf – of understanding, of information and of interest.'[69]

The early broadcasters thought of themselves as bridging the gulf between state and citizenry and saw no fundamental clash of interest between themselves, the world of politics and the everyday world of work, home and family inhabited by listeners. Painfully they came to understand not only the power of governments, parties and state departments to impose their definitions of political realities, but their own complicity in that process. For over thirty years, throughout the era of the BBC's monopoly, political broadcasting was structured in deference to the state. The struggle to make politicians answerable and accountable to the electorate through broadcasting was not joined until the establishment of commercial television and the new forms of broadcast journalism inaugurated by Independent Television News in the late fifties.

Part II

THE PRODUCTION OF INFORMATION: NEWS, FEATURES AND TALKS

CHAPTER SIX

News Values and Practices

———◁❋▷———

T HE METHODS and techniques of broadcast journalism with which we are familiar today were barely established before the war. The pre-emptive arrangements, for their mutal self-interest, between the Post Office, the news-paper owners and the press agencies delayed the entry of broadcasting into the field of journalism for a number of years. A proper news department was not created until the end of 1934. Despite a rapid expansion of staff between 1935 and 1939, the department was only beginning to discover the methods and routines of news gathering and presentation when war was declared. The eye-witness, on-the-spot report from where the story was breaking at home or abroad and the use of recorded interview material had just been introduced to the news bulletins by this time. The studio interview with politicians, pundits or experts was still an undiscovered resource. Throughout this period radio remained a live medium. The earliest recording facilities, ponderous and clumsy, were ill-suited to the special requirements of news gathering with its tight schedules and deadlines. But by 1939 recorded excerpts from political speeches were a regular feature of the bulletins. The difficulties of the broad-casters in getting access to official sources, compared with the newspapers, was a source of vexation, as were the shortcomings of the material supplied by the press agencies, the main source of information from which the bulletins were compiled throughout the period. Finally, the continuing political pressures on the broadcasters – the very real sense of being watched – affected the scope of the service and the kind of news that it felt able to provide.

Within such constraints the broadcasters began to develop their own sense of what a broadcast news service might consist of. The basic issues were the nature of broadcast news, its presentation and its difference from the popular press. Radio news was thought of, at first, as a purely informational resource, without entertainment or dramatic programme values. It should avoid sensationalism altogether. Such beliefs were influenced by a commitment to the educative role of broadcast news in a modern democracy and by considerations of the audience. What were the implications of the domestic circumstances within which people listened to the news? How should one create a news service designed for the ear rather than the eye?

We can begin to glean an understanding of how broadcast news values evolved from the earliest extant correspondence between the BBC and Reuters. In the first few years of the Company there was a steady flow of complaints and requests from the London office to Carey Clements, the manager of Reuters, which began to lay down a set of guidelines for broadcast news. This was, and remains, an incremental process whereby practices are established on the basis of pragmatic solutions to particular problems as they arise, and are subsequently made routine as taken-for-granted rules and standards. Like the common law, a piecemeal series of precedents creates broadcasting custom and usage which may justify later courses of action. One of the very first letters from Arthur Burrows, Director of Programmes in London, to the Broadcasting Editor of Reuters, established some general principles, and an embryo definition for broadcast news, which subsequently were consolidated as guidelines for BBC news for many years.[1]

The letter asked all those concerned in the preparation of the bulletins to take special care about what they included in the scripts, and asked them to bear in mind the subtle difference between news printed in a newspaper and news read into the ears of listener, since it was felt to be more shocking to hear of a crime or disaster than to read of it:

> We are discovering that a certain class of persons is very sensitive to this sort of thing, and we think it a good policy as far as possible to eliminate from bulletins all crimes and tragedies that have not national or international importance. The hanging of a criminal, the burning of a child, or the assaulting of a woman are not news items suitable to a broadcast service.

Subsequent correspondence elaborated on this. There was no need to disclose the religion of persons mentioned in the news, particularly if they were Jewish. In cases of illness, nothing should be said which might upset listeners who suffered from the same complaint.[2] Royalty was a sensitive subject. The BBC was not well pleased by the Reuters coverage of the Prince of Wales' visit to the United States in 1924. It was 'distinctly American in flavour', and the account of HRH clambering aboard the royal yacht at four in the morning might well be associated 'with what we vulgarly term "a night out"'.[3] A later item, 'Princess Mary's Babes Come to Town', was strongly deprecated:

> We feel for instance that it was unnecessary to use two particular phrases in last night's bulletin – (1) that the babes were in a reserved carriage with two nurses, and (2) that the younger one, nine weeks old, was carried on a white silk cushion. This sort of information, we believe, only helps to stimulate feelings akin to Bolshevism.[4]

It was however perfectly acceptable to mention that this was the first time that the Queen had seen her grandchildren, that their identity was unrecognized and that the elder boy waved a chubby hand to the by-standers. Such things were of general interest.

There was continuing trickle of requests to eliminate the unpleasant, harrowing or gruesome from the bulletins – vitriol throwing, for instance, or the Nuneaton Bus Disaster ('Seven Lives Lost in a Blazing Bus!').[5] The long-suffering Carey Clements usually replied that the particular point was taken ('We will carefully avoid in future anything that might stimulate feelings akin to Bolshevism'). In February 1924 he reported to Admiral Carpendale, Reith's second-in-command, that he had given orders to all agencies to eliminate from the bulletins all harrowing or distressing details; not to chronicle a murder or suicide unless very sensational and then only with the briefest mention; and to avoid anything that might offend sensitive ears.[6] But on the particular matter of the Nuneaton bus disaster, the worm turned and Clements fired off a long and testy reply quoting Thackeray's Mr Yellowplush along the way – that in the long run it is best to call a hat a hat – and pointing out that it was in fact a blazing bus and that seven people died in it. He pertinently reminded Burrows that probably nine-tenths of listeners travelled by that means of transport, so that a general interest in the matter was surely obvious.[7]

This desire to avoid sensationalism had a cluster of reasons behind it. In the first place it sprang from the BBC's concern with the power of the new medium with which it had been entrusted, and from a recognition of the conditions in which listeners received the service. What was fit to print was not necessarily fit to hear. A sense of tact was in part, at least, grounded in a proper respect for the conditions of domestic listening. But the question of good taste was also part of a process of establishing the respectability of the BBC. The concern with the avoidance of the hurtful and harmful in news was consonant with changes in the style and mode of address of BBC announcers, with the tightening up on vulgarity in entertainment, with cultural assumptions about 'good' music and drama. Most generally, however, these attitudes to broadcast news were the means whereby the BBC distanced itself from major changes that were taking place in the newspaper industry at that time. In setting their face against the new journalism the broadcasters sought to define an informational role for broadcasting that was deliberately opposed to the trends in the popular press.[8] Radio served no particular interest, but the interests of all. It aspired to be, in Reith's phrase, the integrator for democracy.[9] Just how problematic that role might be, the BBC discovered during the General Strike of 1926.

During the strike the news bulletins were compiled from two main sources: Reuters and information supplied by the Deputy Chief Civil Commissioner's Office in the Admiralty. These were supplemented by items taken from the British and foreign press and, occasionally, news stories from BBC staff about the impact of the strike on London life. After the first day most bulletins included the BBC's 'appreciation of the situation' written by Gladstone Murray or Reith and vetted by J. C. C. Davidson, the Deputy Chief Civil Commissioner.[10] These editorial comments were thought of as standing in for the leading article in the newspapers, and are particularly revealing of the BBC's attitude to its own role not just in the strike, but as an institution in relation to the country as a whole.

Within a day or so the structure of each bulletin had a settled format. They began with special messages, if any, from official sources (the Prime Minister or the Home Office). Then came the appreciation of the situation, 400 words or more on the general state of national affairs. This was followed by official notices and exhortations from government departments, and then general news about the strike and its impact on the country. This section usually started with a long report from the Home Office or the Chief Civil Commissioner before turning to news items from Reuters and from unofficial sources of various sorts. The bulletins ended with briefer details of Parliamentary proceedings, general domestic and foreign news and lastly, the weather.

The bulletins began on 4 May and were broadcast at ten in the morning and thereafter each day at one, four, seven and nine-thirty in the evening. It is not surprising that, in the unprecedented circumstances in which the BBC began its own news service, the results were at first 'pretty rotten', as Reith put it.[11] But in a day or so, the news was coming in better and Reith fussed over the bulletins, vetting many of them and even, on occasion, reading them after complaints that the announcers had sounded panicky. The avoidance of panic, the scotching of wild rumour, and the maintenance of law and order were consistent emphases in the bulletins produced by the BBC during and, for a few days, after the strike.

In attempting to assess the way in which the broadcasters themselves framed and interpreted the strike it should be remembered that the bulk of what went into the bulletins was not written by BBC staff. Essentially the bulletins were a scissors-and-paste job compiled very largely from official sources and from Reuters. Official news items were always clearly attributed. The announcer would introduce them by saying, 'We are instructed by the Civil Commissioners to announce', or 'We are informed by the Railway Information Bureau that', or 'I will now read you some announcements from various Government Departments.' Thus listeners could hardly be unaware that the BBC was a mouthpiece for the authorities during the strike. The BBC's own attitude to the strike can be inferred from the items it picked from Reuters, the occasional stories and press cuttings it selected from other sources and, above all, from its own the appreciations of the situation.[12]

Throughout its duration the strike was presented within a 'law and order' framework. Official statements emphasized the degree of calm and order in the country, and went out of their way to deny rumours of large-scale disorder and commotion. Thus on 7 May a communiqué from the War Office noted that rumours continued to circulate that the Army had come to the end of its resources, that the troops on strike duty had refused to obey orders and that the reserves had been called up. The bulletin continued: 'We are requested by the War Office to notify for general information that, with the exception of guards for a few vulnerable points in Great Britain, no troops have yet been called up in aid of the Civil power, but as previously stated, certain units have been moved to districts to be available if their services are required. The spirit of the troops is excellent, the Army Reserve has not been called up.'[13] Listeners were advised to disregard any reports not officially issued, and the bulletins contained official denials of, for instance, 'serious disturbances at Hammersmith, Putney, Chiswick and Poplar' and of the unfounded rumour that two policemen had been killed at Canning Town.[14]

Violence invariably appeared as the product of hooligans, gangs of working-class youths or the isolated outbursts of 'disaffected' individuals. The police were presented by contrast as intervening to stop disorder, or as the recipients but never the dispensers of violence. Reporting on the prison sentences imposed on people arrested during 'strike scenes at Shoreditch and Bethnal Green', a BBC news item announced that 'the offences included assaulting the police, endangering the safety of police constables by discharging dangerous missiles, damaging police tunics and throwing stones to the public danger'.[15] And an item written by BBC staff headlined, THE LONDON BOBBY, quoted a statement from a leading Paris paper 'with which all of us, especially Londoners, will be in full agreement. This French observer writes: "London owes its tranquility largely to its admirable police. To all who know these English Bobbies – always courteous, smiling and strong – it is not astonishing that he is equal to his hard task." '[16]

Items selected by the BBC from *The British Worker*, the official strike bulletin of the General Council of the TUC, often dealt with the efforts of the

TUC to keep the peace. Thus, under the headline, ALARMIST SUG-GESTIONS, the one o'clock bulletin, for 8 May, quoted from the editorial of an issue intended to show that acts of disorder by the strikers were few and far between. 'To drop into the public ear suggestions that violence is increasing and ruffianism loose should be made a crime.' On another occasion, under the headline ADVICE TO WORKERS, the bulletin quoted the *British Worker's* tips to its readers on how to behave in these difficult times. 'Do all you can to keep everybody smiling. The way to do that is to smile yourself. Do your best to discountenance any ideas of violent or disorderly conduct. Do what you can to improve your health. A good walk every day will keep you fit. Do *something*! Hanging about and swapping rumours is bad in every way.'[17]

Through the course of each day, and from one day to the next, the BBC's appreciations of the situation wove together the threads of events and their implications into a text whose motto was that everything was under control thanks to the good offices of those in authority. This editorial, from the last bulletin on 9 May, is typical:

> The position is much the same as it was at 5.30 when we last gave you an account of the state of the country. There are no serious disturbances to report anywhere. The isolated hooliganism of previous days has definitely diminished. Trade Union leaders are increasingly active in their efforts to prevent violence. The government measures proceed quietly and effectively.

And when the strike was over a 'retrospective appreciation' in the seven o'clock bulletin, of 18 May, assessed the implications of the past two weeks:

> While we have been solving our domestic troubles, the world has been following its usual course and presenting day by day its patchwork of light and dark for those who have time or opportunity to look at the picture.
>
> Today, with the resumption of ordinary publications by the great national journals, we begin again to see the wider world and our relations to it in some-thing like the proper proportions. Do we see it with the same eyes as before May 4th? Not altogether, for meantime we have passed through a test and passed through it in a way that astonishes both ourselves and the rest of the world.
>
> As a nation we are apt to be complacent and self-satisfied, and other nations are not in the least unaware of this trait in us. They regard it, in fact, as one of our stock attributes. For once, our self-satisfaction is universally allowed to be justified, but we must remember that we have earned our self-satisfaction and the world's praise quite as much by our national adaptability as by mere solidity. The capacity we have shown for handling even the gravest internal difficulties calmly, is something that we owe to a long course of political evolution that is not yet ended; there are, unhappily, contemporary events in Warsaw that point the moral of *continuity*. There, a political change of regime has been effected at a

cost of killing and wounding 1,000 persons, not to mention those who may suffer in possible counter-offensives. Warsaw is the capital of a new country, or rather an old country very recently revived after a long subjection that was brought about by the decay of the capacity for self-government. And for the fact that *our case* is different from that of Poland, we have to thank much less *ourselves* than the *continuity of our institutions*. But continuity is not the same as fixity; it is the same as growth.

The echoes of the great strike are dying away, but the problem which aroused to it [sic] has not yet been solved. The task before us all is to help solve it constitutionally, and to remember all the time that the constitution is not a machine but an organism, not only something traditional but something that develops new faculties to meet new needs.

What is striking here, apart from the general air of self-congratulation, is the assumption of a national position; the claim to speak as a national institution, to represent national opinion, to speak for and on behalf of the nation as community. The rhetoric of constitutionalism deployed here was consonant with that of the Government and especially of the Prime Minister Stanley Baldwin; a rhetoric which, as Bill Schwarz has shown, 'was able both to displace and neutralize the antagonism between the people and the state'.[18] That this rhetoric was common both to the Government and to the BBC is shown in a revealing incident recorded by Reith in his diary at the time. On 8 May Baldwin came to the BBC's London studio to broadcast to the public. He invited Reith's comments on 'the tripe' he had prepared, and especially the ending which he wanted to finish on a personal note. Reith suggested, 'what about this – I am a man of peace; I am longing and working and praying for peace; but I will not compromise the dignity of the British constitution.' 'Excellent', replied Baldwin, and it went in his speech.[19] For a moment, government and broadcasting institution spoke with a single voice.

During and immediately after the strike there was much discussion, among those directly involved, about public perceptions of the news service and how it should be reorganized in the light of experience. It was accepted that the bulletins had, unquestionably, become suspect in the eyes of many people. The second general news bulletin of 7 May had acknowledged that:

> Certain people are attempting to discredit the authenticity of our news because it does not include a description of incidents that they themselves have witnessed. It must be appreciated that our attempt is to give objective and national news and that incidents which to individuals may appear important have little or no bearing upon the general situation.

Behind the scenes, though, it was admitted that that objectivity had been compromised. C. F. Atkinson noted that the BBC had been dubbed the BFC

(British Falsehood Company) and that he had heard several public protests against the 'doped' news bulletins. It was impossible to estimate the degree to which public confidence in the BBC's impartiality was shaken, but there was no doubt, Atkinson wrote, that it was considerably affected. He conceded that the news was doped – by suppression, not fabrication – but hoped that the public recognized that the BBC was not a free agent and that, with all its imperfections, the news had been a great steadying influence throughout the country.[20]

There was general agreement that there should be no return to the old arrangement with the press agencies and that a new concordat with Reuters should be sought giving much greater autonomy to the broadcasters. Roger Eckersley argued for the creation of a small News Section, within Stobart's Education Department, whose main responsibilities would include the editing of agency material, the writing of a daily editorial, the arrangement of topical talks and, if a break could be made with the newspapers, the collection of news by BBC staff.[21]

The handful of staff who had prepared the bulletins during the strike responded to Eckersley's proposals and elaborated on them. They began by emphasizing that the strike had foregrounded radio as a new kind of 'national platform.' The rejection by the politicians of the idea of broadcasting the proceedings of Parliament had reduced that proposal to the level of the picturesque Outside Broadcast. Instead, the radio studio had become recognized as an alternative national platform, and utterances from that source had been at least as important as those coming from Parliament throughout the crisis. A fully developed news service would be able to stage the problems of the day for democracy far better than the mere broadcasting of Parliament. Everyone wanted to keep the editorial as part of the news service. The bare substance of the news bulletins needed to be fleshed out with an 'appreciation' of the day's events, and supported by debates and talks symposiums. The role of broadcast news was to be 'a popular and nation-wide analogue of "The Times"'. That newspaper provided a leading article which corresponded to the BBC 'appreciation'; special articles corresponding to general and topical talks; news corresponding to the broadcasters' dressing of Reuters material, and correspondence to which broadcast debates and symposiums were equivalent. In the combination and interplay of such functions broadcasting could continue to do for the nation what it had done in the last fortnight.[22]

What was conceived here, in the heady flush of the moment, was a fully developed structure for news and talks (what much later would be called news and current affairs), which depended on a daily news service to provide a pool of information for comment and discussion of contemporary affairs in topical talks, debates and symposiums. The ban on editorializing and on controversy, the continuing reliance on Reuters for the time being, all postponed the realization of this role for broadcast news. Nevertheless the strike was the moment that hardened the resolve of the broadcasters to develop their own news service and confirmed their sense of its central importance to their work. A tiny News Section was created, at first within Stobart's Education Department, but quickly switched to the Talks Department when Hilda Matheson became its head in 1927.

At first its responibilities were taken up with the selection of speakers and subjects for topical talks and in liaising with government departments over the supply of special news items. In late 1927 Matheson was looking for a staff replacement in News Section to assume special editorial responsibility for Parliamentary News. She wanted someone with a good knowledge of politics and public affairs, coupled with a non-partisan outlook. What she emphatically did *not* want, she informed Reith, was anyone with 'ordinary popular journalistic experience, as it is so difficult to get our totally different outlook and methods into their heads.'[23] As Geoffrey Strutt, who headed the Section, put it a few days later: 'The whole aim and object of our news service is to avoid the errors into which journalists, as such, seem inevitably to fall (sensationalism, inaccuracy, partiality and overstatement), and to present news of all that is happening in the world in a clear impartial and succinct language.'[24] Matheson decided to sound out the Royal Institute for International Affairs, or Dawson at *The Times*, to see if they could suggest a suitable candidate.

By now the News Section had begun to exercise a limited degree of editorial control over the agency bulletins. There were occasional complaints, from the BBC high command, that they were dull and priggish and lacking in what Roger Eckersley called 'snappy news'.[25] In response to this, and in anticipation of the day when the BBC would assume full editorial responsibility for the preparation of bulletins from agency tapes, Matheson commissioned a report on the bulletins and how they might be improved. She invited Philip Macer-Wright, formerly assistant editor of the *Westminster Gazette*, to work in News Section during the summer of 1928 and then to present his observations and recommendations based on his experiences.[26]

Macer-Wright's eleven-page report offered an incisive assessment of the problems with the existing Reuters bulletins, and a full description of the ways in which the BBC should begin the establish its own news service.[27] He began by arguing that a News Department in the BBC should be established within the Corporation as an autonomous and self-contained organization with a News Editor directly answerable, not to the Head of Talks, but to the Controller of Programmes. The News Department, as he foresaw it, should contain in miniature the machinery and resources of a newspaper office: telephones for incoming and outgoing calls, typists, tape-machines, a cuttings collection and a reference library. He described in detail the machinery needed for a fully-fledged news room: private lines with Reuters and their Parliamentary

Correspondents at the House of Commons; the delivery by hand of the latest agency material; methods for handling news 'as it comes'; a greater access for senior staff to 'accredited experts' on financial, sporting, legal and scientific matters; the importance of contact with 'responsible and sympathetic government officials'. These recommendations confirmed and endorsed trends already under way, and stiffened managerial resolve to gain control of news in their tortuous negotiations with the press agencies.

The report's comments on news presentation, style and content are of particular interest. Noting that the radio audience was widespread, cutting across all shades of class, religious and political opinion, Macer-Wright declared that the bulletins should contain something for everybody. The most damaging charge that could be brought against the bulletins was that they were dull. Playing for safety led to dullness; so too the refusal to recognize the legitimate needs of the great mass of unsophisticated people. If the BBC wanted to make the news service an irresistible attraction to the millions, it could not afford to ignore the appeal of news that contained human interest simply expressed. Listeners wanted to hear and feel the news, to exercise their intuition as well as their intellects. Radio news must have 'news values'.

He offered two contrasting examples of what was and what was not of news value, based on his own experience during his three months with News Section. He had himself reluctantly included in one of the bulletins an inconclusive message from the League of Nations' headquarters in Geneva about the aspirations of the Hungarian Optants, and was later told that its inclusion was strictly in accordance with precedent. Such an item, in his view, had no news value. There was, however, definite news value in the story of the murder of a Burmese elephant driver in his flat above the Tapir House at London Zoo. After this item, which Macer-Wright had put in the bulletin, was broadcast he received an 'unofficial protest' about the inclusion of such an 'unedifying story'. The fact that the elephant driver was a familiar figure to hundreds of thousands of school children and their parents who had seen the elephant perform his tricks with buns and pennies only compounded the error, so he was told, of putting out a story so calculated to harrow the feelings of unprotected listeners. But these points, Macer-Wright argued, actually intensified the news value of the story. He was not saying that murder *ipso facto* was a good thing; merely that the Zoo story was an item that could not possibly be excluded from any efficient news service. A pencilled note in the margin of his report, possibly by Reith, declared that this was 'contrary to policy'.

If that aspect of Macer-Wright's report was not acceptable his comments on the organization and presentation of news found a more receptive response. The bulletins, he declared, did not arrange the news items according to their intrinsic value. The sequence in which they were arranged was arbitrary and

" Anyone there? "   " No one of any news-value. "

fragmented. A story on the departure of the Prince of Wales from England appeared as an item of Home News, while his arrival at a French port on the same day made up an item under Foreign News. Stories were split up and dispersed across the whole bulletin in this way. On important issues this arbitrary system of classification employed by Reuters reduced them to absurdity. The Kellogg Pact, a major international anti-war treaty, was reported on 27 August 1928 in the following way: preliminary services of thanksgiving in English churches came under Home News; political comment came under a separate Home News item covering a Labour Party meeting; preparations in Paris came under Overseas News; the signing of the pact in Paris came under French News; the response of the Swedish Government was a separate item of Swedish News, while an item of Russian News recorded the fact that a copy of the Pact had been handed to the Soviet Government. Finally, a wireless message from Mr Kellogg, despatched a few days before his arrival in Paris, was ingeniously classified by Reuters as Mid-Atlantic!

Macer-Wright wanted the bulletins to be arranged in fixed major categories – Home News, Overseas News, Sports News – and the news editors to arrange their material within each category in order to obtain as arresting and harmonious a bulletin as possible. As for presentation, the key was to construct a bulletin specially written for listeners' ears. This was already well recognized within the Talks Department, but the Reuters material was still written in involved, cumbersome and flowery journalese. It was often hard to grasp its meaning even when reading the typescript. All Reuters material needed to be rewritten to make it suitable for reading aloud. Strange sounding foreign names should be avoided. Adapted headlines and every possible kind of pointer should be used to let the listener know first what the subject was, and secondly what was going to be said about it. The listener, unlike the reader, could bot refer back.

In the absence of records it is impossible to assess the impact at the time of these recommendations on the form and content of the bulletins. The first news bulletin prepared entirely by News Section was transmitted on 10 February 1930. The position of News Section within the Talks Department was quite lowly. Discussions and decisions about news styles and presentation were taken by others. In November 1930 the idea of an experimental radio newsreel was floated by John Watt, recently brought over to London from Belfast to head the newly-formed Revue Section. The suggestion was not taken up immediately, but three years later an experimental newsreel programme was broadcast on 1 July 1933 and continued on a weekly basis every Saturday from 14 October to the end of the year. The programmes were produced by Lionel Fielden, regarded by his contemporaries as one of the most creative people working in Talks at that time.[28]

Each weekly programme lasted thirty-five minutes, starting at 9 pm with the weather and the news in brief. At 9.05 there was a twenty-minute 'roving commentary', at 9.25 Economic Background, and at 9.30 a five-minute sports bulletin to round the programme off. Introducing this venture, *Radio Times* proclaimed that the news of the day would be more fully and vividly presented in Roving Commentary than in the usual bulletins because the full resources of radio would be used to give events a greater immediacy and vividness. These included short topical studio talks, eye-witness reports and 'sound pictures' either live or recorded, and 'such other methods of presentation, expanding and illustrating the news as opportunity affords'.[29] Among the items included in Roving Commentary were recorded extracts from the World Economic Conference in London, Hitler's declaration of Germany's withdrawal from the League of Nations, and memorial services for the Battle of the Somme. Occasionally recordings of commentaries on sporting events were included in the sports bulletin, and there were regular talks by Vernon Bartlett (until his downfall) and other public figures, politicians and commentators on the contemporary political scene. Charles Siepmann, the Head of Talks, described these developments in a newspaper article as 'an effort to substitute for a news bulletin a minor drama of events, to give to the recital of the disjointed and apparently irrelevant happenings of the day the elements of a story, a flow, a sequence, a dramatic setting.'[30]

By now news had become taken for granted as an essential feature of the service offered by broadcasting. If the great virtue of the bulletins was, as Lawrence Gilliam suggested in *Radio Times*, their unvarnished directness, their faults shadowed their merits. Listeners could not, as with newspapers, select the facts they wanted.[31] The items selected for the bulletins seemed arbitrary and fragmented. The general import of unadorned news without explanation, illustration or commentary was hard to grasp. What was at stake here, Gilliam suggested, was conservatism versus experimentalism. This was not merely an internal matter of attitudes within the Talks Department, but involved taking account of listeners' opinions. His analysis of letters to *Radio Times* about Newsreel showed that six to one correspondents favoured it. The minority view was tersely put by one writer: 'I want the News as short as possible, at the regular time, and then I want to get on with my Bridge.' But the majority encouraged the BBC to go ahead. 'Do all you can to make News colourful, interesting, surprising. We don't mind if we have to wait a little longer. It's well worth it,' wrote one supporter. 'The news reel', wrote *The Times*, 'exploited the element of surprise, and a conception of news as something more than facts. News in this wider sense is facts present, plus facts past, plus human reactions, and the experiment showed something of what may be done in presenting such news for the ear alone.'[32]

The experiment did not last. It was too big and costly, as Briggs notes, at a time when there were not enough staff in the Talks Department and none with journalistic experience. The use of recording was, of necessity, thought of then as an expensive luxury rather than a necessary component of news. The bulletins continued to be compiled from the agency tapes by the two or three members of News Section who did their best, within the limitations of their own inexperience and the material available to them, to improve the selection and presentation of news. Items were briefly and simply worded. Particular attention was paid to the needs of Announcers. Sentences were made as easily readable as possible, and efforts were made to help them further by checking in advance the pronunciation of foreign names.[33]

An austere conception of news values continued to govern the selection of material for broadcasting. When news of the quality required was lacking no efforts were made to pad out the bulletins to a standard length. On Good Friday, 1930, in the view of the news editors, 'there was no news of the normal type or standard for broadcasting, and as a result no news bulletin was given'. The announcer simply declared 'there is no news tonight'.[34] The press of course saw a good story in the BBC's 'no news' news bulletin and comment ranged from amusement to astonishment. The *Sunday Chronicle* pointed out that there was plenty of news on the day: 'The BBC could have announced the death of Lady Glanely, the fire at Lord Haddo's mansion, the mountaineering accident to Professor Julian Huxley and the motor collision involving Lady Diana Cooper, among other items.'[35] The *Sunday Graphic* was amazed that the BBC should waste such an opportunity on a day when there were no newspapers,[36] and for the *Newspaper World* it simply proved that radio news was no threat to the newspapers.[37] It certainly perfectly encapsulated the gulf between the BBC's ideas about news values at that time and those of the popular press.

In 1935 a separate News Department was created.[38] The newspapers saw the separation of news from Talks as the BBC's 'Answer to Tory Suspicions of Radicalism'.[39] Within the BBC it was seen as a result of a sustained campaign by the right-wing press against alleged BBC 'redness'.[40] The appointment of John Coatman as the head of News was both a political decision to 'balance' the erring leftward tendencies in the Talks Department, and a part of the wider reorganization of programme-making along bureaucratic lines.[41] Coatman – a Conservative by intellect, a Radical by temperament – insisted from the start that News be separated from Talks and answerable only to the Controller of Programmes and the Director General.[42] Although he himself had no professional journalistic experience he made clear his intentions to establish broadcast news on professional lines.

The first efforts of the new department drew a mixed response from the press, and point to much initial uncertainty about the appropriate style and format for broadcast news. The use of experienced journalists for talks and eye-witness commentaries was welcomed, and *Newspaper World* commended a vivid account of the launch of the Queen Mary.[43] But the dramatization of events was more dubious. 'Grand Guignol Bulletin', declared the *News Chronicle*, reporting the dramatization of a car crash 'whose realism made listeners' blood freeze'.[44] The techniques of radio features and the Newsreel were borrowed in a determined effort to liven up the bulletins. Some idea of what they were like can be got from one surviving script of a fortnightly news round-up, *News from Yesterday*, produced by news-room staff for a few months in early 1935. Caption voices declaim the day of the week and the headlines for that day:

1st:	WEDNESDAY!
4th:	Heavy fog all over the country.
	MIX TO:
	Noise of traffic and motor horns
	FADE THIS BEHIND
2nd:	(a common, busybody type with slight cockney accent)
	Hullo! How do you like the fog?
3rd (G)	(*refeened, Kensington house mistress*)
	Like it? I loathe it!
2nd:	Then why have it? Do you know …
3rd (G)	Don't you start lecturing me. I know all about it. London's on the river and in certain conditions (*cough*) you are bound to get fog.
2nd:	Not this sort, stinging your eyes so that you can hardly see. Never get a fog in the country like that.
3rd (G)	What's the remedy?
2nd:	Give up your coal fire.
3rd (G)	Give up my coal fire! (*laughs and coughs*)
2nd:	If you want to stop it that is. Do you know that for every pound you chuck on the fire an ounce goes up the chimney? About $2\frac{1}{2}$ million tons of coal go up the chimney every year! And that's household coal; it doesn't count factories, railways and so on. $2\frac{1}{2}$ million tons at 45/- a ton! It's a good bit of money to throw away isn't it? It costs about 15 million a year to the community – your coal scuttle. [*and so on*][45]

The *Manchester Guardian* deplored the use of such methods for presenting important foreign news. The first duty of the BBC, it declared, was to report them plainly. Dramatic techniques were all very well in retrospective feature programmes such as the highly successful *Crisis in Spain*, but were quite out of place for presenting urgent immediate news.[46]

The same newspaper praised the use of caption headlines, such as 'News in Brief' or 'Opinions of Today', but objected to the sudden inclusion of a heavily facetious item between two serious bits of news – a practice that was widely condemned:

4th:	TUESDAY!
2nd:	In Russia.
	Intense cold freezes signals.
4th:	Moscow – Leningrad train crashes into Tiflis express.
3rd (G)	Many people killed and injured.
2nd:	In India.
	An aeroplane dives into a platoon of soldiers and kills 11.
3rd (G)	In Germany.
	Charlie Chaplain's masterpiece, 'The Gold Rush', is banned. It does not fit in with the present world philosophy of Germany.
4th:	Recipe for a free meal from a gentleman in Spezia.
1st:	Enter a restaurant, consume the meal –
2nd:	– approach the Pay Desk, opening upon it the box of snakes you have brought with you –
3rd (G)	– The attendant will run away screaming Vipers! Vipers!
4th:	Replace snakes, rob till, and move on.
2nd:	Repeat thrice daily until arrested.[47]

Hilda Matheson strongly criticized the bittiness of the new news. 'It is clearly with a view to being bright and intriguing', she wrote in *The Observer*, 'that items are thrown next to each other to suggest contrast, or are linked, often small with great, with a forced chattiness or humour. I have yet to find the listener who likes his news as a salad of all the courses. In my experience he likes his courses in some recognizable sequence.'[48] But what most offended Matheson was the seeming collapse of the standards of news selection that she, more than anyone, had tried to establish. Serious news was being replaced by trivia, a view endorsed by the editor of the *Children's Newspaper*. 'We confess our astonishment', he declared, 'that the BBC Announcer should think it well, at a time when grave issues are in the balance, to begin his news items with a long account of a horse race. Not content with giving the result of the race, he even told us who trained the winning horse.'[49] Similarly, Matheson deplored that, on a day of momentous news at home and abroad, the bulletin had led with a detailed analysis of the day's play in the latest Test Match.

The News Department had to find, by trial and error, an appropriate form and content for the bulletins that it now prepared. Professional standards and practices had yet to be discovered. When Coatman joined the BBC he had a staff of five. By the end of 1938 News Department had grown to thirty-one, and by the outbreak of war to thirty-nine members of staff.[50] The senior staff he appointed were able and experienced journalists – Kenneth Adam from the *Manchester Guardian* to the new post of Home News Editor and R. T. Clark from the same stable to be Foreign News Editor. Younger men, mostly from Oxford and Cambridge, some with journalistic experience, were appointed as

Sub-Editors: Michael Balkwill, Ralph Murray, Tony Wigan and last, but in no way least, Richard Dimbleby – the only non-graduate in the department. Coatman ran the department until the end of 1937 when he moved to Manchester to become the Director of North Region. Clark took his place. Between them all they began to establish broadcast news on recognizably journalistic lines.

As staff expanded so did the amount of time given to news in the evening schedules. By the end of 1937 there were ninety-five minutes of news time on the National and Regional programmes between 6 pm and midnight.[51] From 1931 onwards the times of the two main bulletins on the National Programme had been set at six and nine o'clock in the evening, though these times varied at certain points of the year, especially during the six-week Promenade Season in the summer. One of Coatman's first decisions was to make the second national bulletin as far as possible free from any verbatim repetition of the earlier six o'clock transmission. In the summer of 1938 the 9 pm bulletin was pushed back an hour to 10 pm, a move which brought a flood of protests from listeners (and a letter to *The Times* from the irrepressible George Bernard Shaw) that this was too late.

By 1938 the content of the bulletins broke down into three sections – news, news talks and sport – each the responsibility of a small group of journalists within the department. The main news was still, of course, compiled almost exclusively from agency tapes. Sports news became a regular feature, and one greatly welcomed by many listeners, after the appointment in 1936 of a Sports Sub-Editor. By 1939 there were four full-time staff responsible for two daily sports bulletins, a sports talk for the Saturday evening bulletin and for developing suitable contacts with sporting personalities. News talks were drastically improved. So-called topical talks had been included in the bulletins since before the Department was created in 1934, and a separate group in the Talks Department – quite independent of News Section – had supplied talks to go in the news period. These were often merely talks that could not be slotted into other periods and which bore only tenuous links with the news of the day. On one occasion a talk on a 'completely non-news subject' took up eight of the fifteen minutes of the bulletin. When Coatman took over he soon put a stop to this. Responsibility for news talks was transferred to his department and delegated to Ralph Murray. By 1937 the principle of no talks except *news* talks had been accepted, but only after a good deal of resistance from the Talks Department. A ten-minute news talk became a regular feature of the main evening bulletins.

Although the department did not have the resources for special overseas correspondents Murray occasionally acted as a roving reporter abroad, providing eye-witness reports from the League of Nations in Geneva which were either recorded or fed live into the bulletins. On the home front Kenneth Adam covered such varied events as the lying in state of George V, a speech by Lloyd George to the Trades Union movement, the Spring Show at the Old Horticultural Hall and a new play by Shaw at the Malvern Festival. Such accounts introduced a new immediacy and vividness to the measured tones of the bulletins. But the most enthusiastic and indefatigable exponent of a new art of radio news was the young Richard Dimbleby.

Dimbleby had cut his teeth as a reporter working for his father's newspaper, *The Richmond and Twickenham Times*, and then as News Editor of *Advertisers Weekly*. But he was ambitious and restless for better things. In 1936 he wrote to Coatman asking for a job in the News Department. At his first interview with the BBC it was made plain to him that his services were not immediately required. Unperturbed, a few weeks later, he wrote a long letter to Coatman setting out his ideas about how radio news might be improved.

It is my impression, and I find it shared by many others, that it would be possible to enliven the News to some extent without spoiling the authoritative tone for which it is famed. As a journalist, I think I know something of the demand which the public makes for a 'News angle', and how it can be provided. I suggest that a member or members of your staff – they could be called 'BBC reporters or BBC correspondents' – should be held in readiness, just as are the evening paper men, to cover unexpected News for that day. In the event of a big fire, strike, civil commotion, railway accidents, pit accidents, or any other major catastrophes in which the public, I fear, is deeply interested, a reporter could be sent from Broadcasting House to cover the event for the bulletin.

At the scene, it would be his job, in addition to writing his own account of the event, to secure an eye-witness (the man or woman who saw it start, one of the survivors, a girl 'rescued from the building') and to give a short eye-witness account of the part he or she played that day. In this way, I really believe that News could be presented in a gripping manner, and, at the same time, remain authentic.

Everyone, I think, finds the agency reports a trifle flat after a time, as, indeed, they are bound to be. It is for that reason, I take it, that you keep an observer at Geneva, and incorporate a short talk in the bulletin on some topic of the day. But these talks are always academic – they come from some authority on the subject. There can be no vital authority on a sudden news event, unless it be the man in the street who was on the spot ...

The principle of enlivening news by the infusion of the human element is being followed in other spheres, as you know. The newspapers, of course, have demanded interviews for their big stories for many years, and I myself have had to obtain eye-witness accounts and personal interviews for hundreds of stories of all types.

The newsreels are following suit. The March of Time being an example. In this, as you may have seen, the method followed is not only that of showing the news, but telling why, and how, it happened. That is what I suggest the BBC could do with great success, not only with sudden events or catastrophes, but with all types which at present come to the listeners from the pen of a Press Association or Exchange Telegraph man who gives the same story to hundreds of provincial evening papers and London dailies ...

If you put this scheme into operation, or even included part of it in your future scheme, I should be happy if I were able to play a part.[52]

Dimbleby's persistence paid off, and within six months he landed a job in the BBC News Department. Many years were to pass before the kind of broadcast news service outlined in his letter was finally established. The on-the-spot report, the use of recorded actuality sounds from the scene of the action, location interviews with eye-witnesses – these things which are today the very stuff of broadcast news were all pioneered by Richard Dimbleby who, more than any other individual in the BBC, laid the foundations of modern broadcast journalism.

In 1936 he was years ahead of his time and was regarded, as Jonathan Dimbleby's excellent biography reveals, with some amusement and condescension by his more sophisticated graduate colleagues. But he remained undeterred. From the moment he joined the BBC he worked irrepressibly to realize his vision. His first eye-witness report, in October 1936, covered the Annual Conference for the Preservation of Rural England. Next he interviewed a cow. His first big story was the fire at Crystal Palace, when listeners heard his excited voice, from a public telephone booth on the spot, describe the scene with the sounds of the flames, the crowds and the fire engines in the background. It was the first up-to-the-minute, on-the-spot radio report of a major news story and it scooped the newspapers.

In this particular case Dimbleby was lucky to be able to rush to the scene for his live broadcast, but to cover such kinds of news story on a regular basis required the use of mobile recording equipment. In Germany cars fitted with equipment for this purpose had been in use since the mid-thirties, and *Echo Des Tages* – sound recordings of events of the day – was one of the most popular features of German news programmes. It was a matter of comment in the press that the BBC lagged behind the Germans in this respect.[53] In fact, mobile recording equipment for the News Department had been an urgent request since 1934 and in September 1936 the Engineering Division of the BBC delivered two prototype recording vans for use by news.[54] These however were so large and heavy that they were useless for coverage of sudden or rapidly changing events. Moreover bureaucratic regulations governing three different sectors of BBC staff (engineers, drivers, producers) further impeded their effective usage. When Dimbleby did find a story that would stay there long enough for him to get there with the van (the Fen floods in March 1937) he was frustrated again and again in his two-week coverage of the floods by the van driver sticking to his shifts and refusing to take the van out at other times.

In August 1938 Clark was still awaiting the delivery, expecting it at any time, of a car fitted with recording equipment.[55] He acknowledged Dimbleby's special contribution to such developments: 'It is most emphatically Dimbleby's province, and I think I ought to say here how greatly I value his services in this connection, and also to pay tribute to him for the devotion with which he has succeeded in making himself a first-class broadcaster in this type of programme.'[56] Clark envisaged the routine use of the recording car on lines very similar to *Echo Des Tages*. He wanted to experiment with a tri-weekly, ten-minute recorded news magazine which, if successful, might be extended and given a definite regular place in the bulletins. Its prime purpose though would be in the service of general news and anything of particular news value – the arrival of a trans-Atlantic flyer, a fire at Canterbury Cathedral or an interview with an important personality.

But what was a news personality? For years news, following BBC policy, had avoided the 'infusion of the human element' which Dimbleby advocated. By 1938 policy was beginning to shift and Basil Nicolls, Controller of Programmes, was asking for the provision of more personalities in the news. This in itself, Clark replied, was simple enough but it did raise awkward questions of policy and organization:

It is rather difficult to get straightforward cases. You may remember that Sir John raised the question why, when the Anglo-Turkish Agreement was signed, we did not get the chief Turkish delegate, because he was a personality. That is just the point. Actually the chief Turkish delegate was not a personality at all. No one knew him, and it is very doubtful whether he could speak anything but Turkish, while getting him involved a complicated negotiation with both the Foreign Office and the Turkish Legation. Where we are dealing with politics or that type of thing, the subject matter is the chief concern, not the personality ... I think that what we should aim at is the getting to the microphone (a) of people who in themselves are of interest to a large section of the public (and I am afraid this means in the main film stars and people prominent in sport), (b) distinguished visitors to this country (statesmen, soldiers, artistic people and the like) or well-known people here who just at the moment have something very definite to say, as for instance we got Ellen Wilkinson on her Hire Purchase Bill, and (c) people who have suddenly become news, like record breakers or heroic life-savers, or even at a pinch beauty queens![57]

On the organizational side Clark was worried about competition for such personalities with *In Town Tonight* and *The World Goes By* which might give rise to conflict. If it came to that, the final say should be with his department but Clark did not expect such a situation to arise in the ordinary run of things. There was no need, in his view, for a 'personality period' in the bulletins. Their news value would be clear from the way they were contextualized and the amount of time given to them. That should scotch possible criticisms that news was being either more dignified than *The Times* or indulging in *Daily Mirror* publicity stunts. 'I think', Clark told Nicolls, 'that we have just got to take risks here, and within the limits suggested by ordinary intelligence be, like the Apostle, "all things to all men".'

All these matters, now under discussion in the summer of 1938, concerned the treatment of domestic news. There remained the great unspoken problem of coverage of foreign news which the Munich crisis brought to a head in the last weeks of September. When Chamberlain flew to Germany for a third time to meet Hitler, on 29 September, fear and rumour were rife. The first evening bulletin advised people to listen to the next bulletin at eight o'clock, and the special announcements which would precede it, with pencils and paper at the ready to make note of addresses and other points of public safety in the bulletin. At the same time it begged listeners not to flood the BBC in the meantime with questions that would be answered in the later bulletin. The following day, 30 September, there were brief news flashes in the morning and afternoon culminating in the announcement at ten to three of the text of the official communiqué issued twenty minutes earlier by the German News Agency. Chamberlain touched down at Heston Airport a couple of hours later and the first evening bulletin contained an account of his arrival. The second and third bulletins continued with his reception at Buckingham Palace, and later at Downing Street:

> Mr Chamberlain was given a tremendous reception when he stepped out of the plane at Heston. Crowds had travelled out to the airport from London hours before he was due to arrive. The adjoining fields were crowded with cars and cycles, and the thousands who could not get into the airport itself lined the route from the main gateway through which Mr Chamberlain's car was to pass. The houses of the neighbourhood were decorated with bunting and flags, and many people had brought Union Jacks to wave. Inside a special enclosure were members of the Cabinet, the Dominion High Commissioners, the Ambassadors to Britain and the Lord Mayor of London. The cheering began, as soon as the Prime Minister's plane was sighted, and it rose in a terrific crescendo as it landed, taxied to the tarmac and Mr Chamberlain stepped down. He seemed almost dazed by the tremendous warmth of the greeting. The cheering and the shouting almost drowned the noise of the plane and in those first few moments of welcome Mr Chamberlain stood smiling and looking very happy, but still a little nervous. Then the Lord Chamberlain, on behalf of the King, presented a personal letter from the King, and after he had read it, members of the Cabinet

rushed forward to congratulate him. Lord Halifax led the Ministers, the Ambassadors and the great crowd round the aerodrome in cheer after cheer. After it had subsided, Mr Chamberlain spoke to the microphone.

[2'50" extract from recording of Chamberlain's speech]

The news given in the document read by the Prime Minister was the signal for another outburst of great enthusiasm and it was some time before the Prime Minister's car could move from the aerodrome. People jumped on to the running board, many tried to open the car doors to shake the Premier's hand, and there were warmhearted cries of 'Well done, Neville' and 'Peace at last through you sir'.

Then began the journey to Buckingham Palace, where the King and Queen were waiting to receive the Prime Minister. Mrs Chamberlain had already arrived. Again there were thousands of people to greet Mr Chamberlain and even household officials at the Palace ran out through the forecourt to cheer as the car drove in. It must have been one of the greatest receptions any visitor to the Palace has had. The cheering continued while Mr Chamberlain was in the Palace and eventually the King and Queen, with the Prime Minister and Mrs Chamberlain, appeared on the balcony. They remained there for some minutes, and the King persuaded Mr Chamberlain to go forward and stand alone in the very front of the balcony. He stood smiling for some moments and waved his hand in acknowledgement. A few minutes ago the Prime Minister and Mrs Chamberlain left the Palace and arrived at Downing Street where there is to be a Cabinet Meeting.[58]

The bulletins that evening contained other items. On the domestic front messages from The Home Office to Local Authorities advised them to continue distributing gasmasks, to stop digging trenches (but not to fill them in) and to continue to improve First Aid Posts. Shopkeepers all over the country were being asked by the public to take back the extensive emergency purchases of the last few days, but this drew a stony response from the Secretary of the Retail Distributors' Association. The authorities at the Universities of Oxford and Cambridge decided not to postpone the start of term, while at Lloyds the rates of insurance for war risks had fallen to a twentieth of the figures quoted two days earlier. The sports report which ended each bulletin contained details of golf, rugby, snooker and motor racing. In the Special Announcements some extra advice was offered to the population on the proper use of gasmasks:

In spite of the Air Raid Precaution Handbook and other official warnings there are still many reports of people misusing the gasmasks that have been distributed. It is even stated that some people have been testing them in gas ovens or by motor car exhaust pipes. This misuse of the masks carries its own punishment, but as this is quite likely to be unintentional suicide the suggestion is that masks should be kept for gases they *are* designed to deal with.

Foreign responses to the day's momentous events were also given, especially those from Czechoslovakia, the second item in the bulletins after the accounts of Chamberlain's tumultuous reception. The reports were brief and stark describing the utter astonishment of the Czechoslovak Government at the shortness of the time allowed them by Chamberlain to respond to the terms agreed by the Four Powers in Munich. 'The Czecho-Slovak Cabinet met at 10 o'clock this morning and shortly after 1 o'clock it was unofficially stated in Prague that the Czecho-Slovak Government, having considered the decision of the conference in Munich, taken without and against them, found no other means but to accept and had nothing to add.' There were brief accounts of public alarm in Prague, of demonstrations against the agreement and of police patrols dealing with the demonstrators. Later bulletins added that all wireless programmes except news had been cancelled as a sign of national mourning.

Newspaper reactions from Moscow and the United States were given. *Izvetsia* described the Four Power Conference as 'a committee for the coordination of Fascist aggression', and the leading article from the *New York Times* was quoted:

> Let no man say too high a price has been paid for peace in Europe until he has searched his soul and found himself willing to risk in war the lives of those nearest and dearest to him. But no man who is honest will attempt to pretend to himself that a high price has not been paid. It is a price which enables a dictator who would willingly destroy the last vestige of democracy in Europe to claim that he has scored over the democracies of Europe the greatest diplomatic triumph of modern times; that he accomplished by a mere ultimatum what Bismarck failed to accomplish with armies.

American historians of broadcasting agree that network coverage and commentary on the European crisis brought radio news in the United States to maturity. According to David Culbert radio news created mass interest in foreign affairs beginning with the Munich crisis and, as a result, radio emerged as the principal medium for combating isolationism in America.[59] Radio commentators not only became household names, but figures courted internationally by politicians and government officials. The coverage of CBS in particular reveals the huge gulf between the robust political independence of broadcasting in the United States compared with Britain. It was perhaps a stroke of luck that, when the Austrian crisis broke in March 1938, CBS had two brilliant reporters in Europe – William Shirer and Ed Murrow – but there was nothing fortuitous about their presence there. As the signs pointed to a European war, Edward Klauber, Vice President of CBS and formerly night city editor of the *New York Times*, had already begun to build up a team of foreign correspondents and stringers in Europe.[60]

"We've missed the news, Edith."

On 13 March 1938 listeners to CBS news heard Murrow in Vienna describing the air of tension in the city as everyone waited and wondered when Hitler would arrive. In the same broadcast they heard reports from Shirer in London, Edgar Ansel Mowrer in Paris, Pierre Huss in Berlin, Frank Gervasi in Rome and Robert Trout in New York. The 'news round-up', a CBS creation, was born in crisis. Two days later, broadcasting from London, Murrow continued his Vienna story:

> Later Herr Hitler arrived, made a speech, took the salute of the big parade, and Austria ceased to exist. Vienna became a provincial town; faithful party members, most of them Germans, were placed in all the important posts. It was called a bloodless conquest and in some ways it was, but I'd like to be able to forget the haunted look on the faces of those long lines of people outside the banks and travel offices. People trying to get away. I'd like to forget the tired, futile look of the Austrian army officers, and the thud of hobnail boots and the crash of light tanks in the early hours of the morning on the Ringstrasse, and the pitiful uncertainty and bewilderment of those forced to lift the right hand and shout 'Heil Hitler' for the first time. I'd like to forget the sound of smashing glass as the Jewish shop streets were raided; the hoots and jeers aimed at those forced to scrub the sidewalk.
>
> Well, those are a few of the things that happened in Austria. People in England are wondering when similar things may happen here.[61]

Doubtless they were, but not as a result of listening to the BBC. American commentary on the Munich crisis was equally forthright, and news coverage was continuous throughout those September weeks. All the leading figures – Hitler, Mussolini, Chamberlain, Daladier, Benes, Masaryk – were heard on the air. CBS made 151 short-wave pick-ups of transmissions from European stations which Eric Kaltenborn, their New York news analyst and fluent in French and German, immediately translated for listeners, placed in context and assessed their significance. Within a month of the resolution of the Czechoslovakia crisis Kaltenborn published a book, *I Broadcast the Crisis*, containing excerpts from the September newscasts. In Kaltenborn's view the Munich settlement was a defeat for Britain and France which boded ill for the long-term prospects of peace in Europe. He quoted Robert Walpole – 'Today we ring the Bells. Tomorrow they will wring their hands!'[62]

More radio sets were sold in America during the three weeks of the crisis than in any previous three-week period in the industry's history. *The Nation*, commenting on the enormous public interest in radio's handling of the crisis, declared that it had become the dominant system of news communication. For the first time history had been made in the hearing of its pawns. Public opinion polls confirmed the intense interest that the American people had taken in the events and found that, for 70 per cent of those polled, radio had become their preferred news source during the European crisis.[63]

In the BBC attitudes to American network coverage varied. Felix Greene, the BBC's representative in North America, had urged that the BBC should follow the example of American network coverage of the annexation of Austria. But in the moratorium on Munich the Director of Overseas Services sniffed that NBC and no doubt the other American chains had made a great splash in print about their coverage of the crisis, presumably with a view to impressing sponsors. He was not blindly opposed to broadcasts from the scenes of action, but thought there were times when they were liable to be unhelpful, misleading and purely sensational and therefore not in accordance with the principles that guided the BBC's action as a British organization. Some British newspapers had adopted American news styles to achieve notoriety and popularity, 'but "The Times" and other papers have not emulated the example of their more popular contemporaries with a view to their own circulation.' The most important thing at issue was how far BBC principles could be preserved if it was decided to follow in the wake of the trend of American broadcasting.[64]

In the News Department there was a comprehensive review of the impact of the crisis and the problems they faced in adequately responding to it. For Clark Munich brought to a head all the dissatisfactions with the news agencies which had been accumulating over a decade. In a four-page memorandum he reviewed the whole problem.[65] For home news the Press Association was largely excused since it was in the same boat as everyone else – a complete inability to get any information at all from Downing Street. In the absence of official information it had fallen back on Lobby talk and club gossip, but this of course could not be used in broadcast news. The bulk of Clark's report dealt with the inadequacies of Reuters.

He began by pointing out that, as a commercial organization, Reuters had had to adjust its service to please its customers, and as such it had changed enormously from the service it had been before the Great War. Its main clients today were the popular press which published very little foreign news, and then only the most sensational – the birth of a baby with four heads in Bulgaria was of more interest than the fall of the French Cabinet. As a result Reuters concentrated increasingly on non-essential and picturesque stuff. The result of these changes was predictable. Reuters coverage of the crisis was poor and perfunctory. When the Czechoslovakia situation looked like growing into a big news story the agency had sent out one of its senior men, three of whose stories were cancelled in their entirety within eight hours of their dispatch. For the first four or five days he had relied entirely on Sudeten German sources. Godesberg was badly covered and Munich was worse. During the whole of the crisis the service of the three agencies supplying foreign material (the other two were Central News and Exchange Telegraph) was totally inadequate for the purposes of the kind of news service the BBC was trying to give.

There were two ways to overcome this problem. The BBC could either subscribe to the services of the British United Press agency or build up its own team of foreign correspondents. In the teeth of opposition from the British press agencies the American United Press, which supplied foreign news to the United States press, had established the British United Press in London as an extension of its service. Not only was its coverage of the crisis infinitely fuller that Reuters, it was consistently faster in getting the key details of developments as they unfolded. Clark however had a characteristically British mistrust of American journalism and journalists. On the whole, he allowed that United Press correspondents were exceedingly able news-getters. The trouble was they knew nothing about politics and rarely distinguished between the value of news from official and unofficial sources. For them the story was the thing, not the source from which it came, so their material would have to be double-checked. If British United Press copy were given to untrained people it would be like entrusting a child with a stick of dynamite.

Clark thought that the four-figure sum needed to buy the services of British United Press would be better spent in building up a team of foreign correspondents. *The Times* and the *Manchester Guardian* used agency material mainly as a check and cover, relying on their own staff to provide nine-tenths of foreign news. The quality of their coverage of Munich was streets ahead of the agencies. Although it would cost too much to build up a service as comprehensive as that of *The Times*, BBC foreign correspondents would be able to provide a separate and reliable source of news from places and at times when such a service was essential.

Among the other problems for the News Department highlighted by the crisis was the role of Announcers.[66] There was none with special training in or responsibility for news reading. It was just one of the many things announcers were called upon to do in the course of their daily rota. It was absurd, Clark felt, for them to arrive in the studio only minutes before transmission to read a forty-minute news bulletin. Moreover, without going into personalities, it had become obvious that some announcers were temperamentally very much better suited to tackling news at a moment of crisis than others. Instead of the present arrangements in which the bulletins were read by anyone from the pool of thirteen announcers, Clark wanted to select three for secondment to his department to build up experience in the specialized task of reading the news. He wanted them to feel they were part of the news process and that they shared in its work.

But the most pressing matter was to improve the news service in the light of Coatman's memorandum and Clark's belief that the job of the department

was to go on plugging away at the truth no matter how horrible. The admini-
istrative decision-making process in the BBC ground slowly and it was not
until March 1939 that Clark's request for more staff, especially foreign
correspondents, was accepted as an imperative necessity. In the meanwhile
Clark had got what available resources he had to the European trouble spots.
Ralph Murray left for Prague on 1 October 1938 and a week later Dimbleby
and the news car (which had at last arrived) headed off in the same direction.

At the beginning of 1939 Dimbleby was on the Franco-Spanish borders to
witness the last stages of the Spanish Civil War.[67] At the end of January he
was in the village of Le Perthus, high in the Pyrenees, to report on the flight of
those who had fought to defend the republic from Franco's forces as they
advanced northwards into Catalonia. It was cold and wet. At the border there
was no food, no water and little shelter. In one week nearly half a million
refugees, many of them women and children, crossed from Spain into France.
Dimbleby described their plight for British listeners:

> Some of them are in the last stages of exhaustion. They're hungry – starving,
> many of them – and numbed with cold ... There was an old woman at the inter-
> national station last night, the colour of deep sunburn, with dirt and with dried
> blood on her face from a deep gash in the cheek. She told me how she and her
> children, and eight other old people, lay down in the open to sleep. It was she
> said – and for this I can vouch – bitterly cold. In the morning three of the
> group, one of them her daughter, were dead ...[68]

Two days later at the frontier itself, 'with one foot in France and the other in
Spain', he broadcast live into the ten o'clock news. For the first time British
listeners heard the sounds of gunfire and bombing in the background as he
spoke.

> Since early to day – early this morning when we got here – there have been
> crowds, masses, lines of wretched torn and tattered soldiers going by, throwing
> down their guns, their rifles and their pistols at the guards on the frontier ...
> There are machine guns by the dozen stacked up just behind me – I'm sorry
> I'm pushing my way past the *Garde Mobile* in order that I can get well onto the
> frontier line: he didn't like it very much ... Now here comes another procession
> of lorries. I'm going to stop for a moment and let you hear it go by. The first one
> is a Russian lorry piled high with soldiers ... The second carries a heavy gun ...
> and behind it is another lorry with two soldiers in it, four or five sheep and a
> cow piled up in the back of the lorry. This would be almost comic if it weren't
> such an appalling tragedy to watch down here.[69]

Such unscripted reports show that in Dimbleby the BBC had a reporter equal
to the best of the American correspondents. He returned to London, deeply

shaken by the experience, to the congratulations of his colleagues and – unprecedented tribute – a commendation for his work from the Board of Governors. For all that, in the last months before the outbreak of war Dimbleby's skills as a reporter remained under-used, as the kind of broadcast journalism he advocated remained unacknowledged and undeveloped.

CHAPTER SEVEN

Features and
Social Documentaries

———◦❀◦———

'DOCUMENTARIES', says Felix Felton, 'are known in the BBC as "Features"', and certainly that was the preferred term in broadcasting before the war.[1] Their development was chequered and uneven, and they never amounted to more than a fraction of the programme output in London or in the Regions. Their importance lies not in their bulk, but in the ways they took the lead in exploring the form of the medium of radio and its potential to communicate new social topics to a new kind of public. Aesthetics and politics came together in radio, as elsewhere, under the pressure of the times to register the issues of the day for a newly democratized society.

Three lines of development can be discerned in London between the late twenties and the mid-thirties. There was first a concern with the possibilities of the medium itself in which the exploration of form took priority over content or subject matter. Here the influences of contemporary modernism in the arts and cinema shaped developments. This gave way to the discovery of new forms of reportage for dealing with the urgent issues of the day as the Talks Department addressed itself to the social consequences of the recession. From this it was a short step to a concern with – a then novel concept – 'actuality' broadcasting and the use of sound effects and talk recorded on location as the material from which to construct programmes. Initial developments in the radio feature ranged from avant-garde aestheticism to more plain-spoken direct forms of social documentation and reportage.

In the first few years of broadcasting it had been a continuous scramble simply to fill the hours of transmission with suitable music or voices and to maintain an uninterrupted flow of scheduled material. But by the late twenties the BBC's system of distribution and the content of its programme service had begun to settle. Attention now turned towards a more defined social purpose and towards more considered forms of expression. Radio began to be talked of not only as a new form of communication, but also as a potential artform. It was linked in discussion with film, especially the pioneering work of contemporary Russian film-makers. At the same time comparisons were made with the theatre of Shakespeare where, in the absence of any realistic visual staging, the combination of the poetry (which conjured the scene in the mind's eye) and the highly flexible open stage, allowed a form of drama which was able with ease to 'cut' from one location or storyline to another. The purely auditory nature of radio seemed to offer similar possibilities. Broadcasting might combine techniques drawn from cinema with a poetic style to build 'sound pictures' that appealed to the listener's inner eye.

The radio feature – the term being borrowed from cinema's feature film – began to be developed in the BBC from about 1928 onwards. Features were special programmes in that they required, it was claimed in *Radio Times*, research and thought as 'original forms of expression, peculiar to radio and not suited to the public stage or concert platform'.[2] They combined words and music to produce an artistic effect which could not have been produced by either separately. With music, talks or variety programmes it was largely a question of engaging speakers or performers and then rehearsing them in front of the microphone. But the feature programme arranged its material into original forms that exploited the potential of the medium. They were the first kind of programme to be put together and produced by people working in the BBC. In all these ways they were what Lance Sieveking referred to as 'the stuff of radio'.[3]

In 1928 Sieveking was hand-picked by Reith to do research into the form of radio. He was given a brief to prepare special programmes as occasional features and to build suitable programmes for broadcasting's special dates in its calendar – Christmas, New Year's Eve and so on. Later in that year the Productions Department in London was reorganized and Val Gielgud was put in charge. A small research group was established within the department whose task was an extension of that given to Sieveking: 'to give any help or suggestion in the presentation of any kind of programme ... [to] experiment and do specialized research work in regard to the techniques of radio drama.' In sum, its responsibilities were 'research, creation and experiment'.[4] These developments marked the start of a self-conscious intention within the BBC to explore and extend the artistic scope of programme output.

Sieveking was the most grandiose and loquacious exponent of a new art of radio. He was passionately interested in the cinema and the theories of Pudovkin which he tried to transpose to radio production. Techniques of slow motion, close-ups, dissolves, fades, mixes and montage were all combined in the plays and features he wrote for radio in the late twenties and early thirties. The difference between a play and a feature, for Sieveking, was that a feature had a theme but no plot. If it had a plot it was a play. His book on the art of radio should certainly be read as a modernist curio of the period. Innocently self-absorbed, Sieveking saw himself as a pioneer of 'pure radio'. But he declared himself worried by

> the curious habit that exists in England of presuming and asserting that *any* attempts whatsoever at doing anything in a new way proclaims its author as a member of some political party of the Left. Modern painters, sculptors, poets, architects and composers are all supposed by popular opinion to be paid to do what they do by cheque from Moscow.... The difficulty is to convince anyone that one is just tremendously interested for its own sake in the thing on which one is working, and that one doesn't relate it to any politics whatsoever.[5]

The dramatic control panel was the most sophisticated tool for radio production at that time. Sieveking has written a vivid account of his own great moment in radio when, on 4 September 1928, he produced his first big feature programme, *Kaleidoscope*, at the control panel.[6] For the new kind of large-scale feature production one studio was not enough to accommodate all the various components – actors, musicians, choruses and sound effects – that made up the whole. Each element was placed in a separate studio and all were linked to the dramatic control panel at which the producer sat like a musical maestro (or so Sieveking saw himself) orchestrating the whole performance.

There are no recordings of Sieveking's work and no production files or scripts of his programmes in the BBC Written Archives. So an impression of his work must be gleaned from the examples of his plays and features that he chose to put in his book. Without knowing what they sounded like it is hard to be entirely fair. From the printed evidence it must be said that the experimental techniques swamp the substance of the narratives whose content seems banal or pretentious. *Kaleidoscope* was conceived as a 'rhythm representing the life of man from the cradle to the grave' and the struggle of Good and Evil for his soul. Both these agencies were represented by music: Beethoven for Good, Jazz for Evil. Evil is inclined to whisper seductive Romantic verse into the hero's ear, while Good breathes more sober stuff recalling Duty. A farrago of short impressionistic scenes swirl in and out, sketching in fragments in the life of a modern (middle-class English) man.[7]

But when not plundering his own imaginative resources, Sieveking could turn his techniques to produce a fast-moving historical narrative. Perhaps his best and certainly his most ambitious production was *The End of Savoy Hill*, broadcast on 14 May 1932. This panoramic survey of the first ten years of radio lasted over two and a half hours. It was 'too purely radio' (and too long) to be printed, but this extract from an appendix in *The Stuff of Radio* gives a good idea of the Sieveking style:

Flick 2 .... (Trumpet)
Flick 4 .... (Announcement)
1ST VOICE: *The End of Savoy Hill!*
2ND VOICE: Here is a panorama of the years from 1922 to 1932.
1ST VOICE: Ten years of broadcasting in 161½ minutes.
2ND VOICE: We present for your entertainment an historical pageant in sound. The complicated process of ten years, full of experiments and shots in the dark, is about to unwind before you, so that you may observe how the broadcasting service which you enjoy today has come about. Unfortunately not all the voices in our pageant can be living voices ...
Flick 2 .... (Trumpet)
Flick 4 – *1st Voice*: A Panorama of the First Ten Years.
                                    (Pause)
Flick 4 – *Voice*: THE CAT'S WHISKER TREMBLES!
VOICE: Back we dart to 1922, before there was any official broadcasting. With the amateurs of those days, we hear the voice of P. P. Eckersley from the experimental station at Writtle ——
Effects .... (*FADE UP* Eckersley —— *Writtle*.)
Flick 4–1ST VOICE: May the 4th, 1922. The Postmaster-General, the Right Honourable F. W. Kellaway, M. P., is speaking in the House of Commons ... [8]

The vogue for such baroque performances was quite short-lived. By the late thirties they were more a matter of parody than an accepted method of production.[9] The problem they posed was their suitability in a medium that addressed itself not to the avant-garde public but a much wider audience with simpler tastes. A *Radio Times* article pinpointed the dilemma, remarking that radio producers were trying on the one hand to create a distinctive type of broadcast drama, and on the other to bring theatre within the reach of everyone. These were irreconcilable aims.[10] Val Gielgud was strongly opposed to Sieveking's approach. He had a low opinion of the merits of the dramatic control panel and later returned to single studio production for radio drama.[11] There were others in the BBC who felt that Sieveking's work should be considered as backstage 'laboratory' experiments which ought not to be conducted in public. Sieveking spluttered against these prosaic attitudes but his work on the whole, after the initially dazzling effect of all their fireworks, had little significant content and was probably more bewildering to listeners than anything else. 'Recalled one's impression of gas in the dentist's chair' was one response to *Kaleidoscope*. By the mid-thirties the kind of radio production espoused by Sieveking was a spent rocket, and so was its exponent.

In an effort to pinpoint the artistic mood of the late twenties, Orwell recalled the *Punch* joke of around 1928 in which an intolerable youth is pictured informing his aunt that he intends to write. 'And what are you going to write about, dear?' his aunt enquires. 'My dear aunt,' says the youth crushingly, 'one doesn't write *about* anything. One just *writes!*'[12] A response which neatly captures Sieveking's attitude as well as a more general mood. A rueful sense of modern life as lacking in fine ideals treads softly through Sieveking's writings (*Intimate Snapshots* is exemplary)[13] and Tyrone Guthrie's *The Squirrel's Cage*[14] which is usually hailed as one of the first real radio plays. A successful, and much repeated, adaptation of Karel Capek's futuristic fantasy, *R. U. R.*, explored the horrors of a machine civilization.[15] The taste for allegorical fantasy was well represented by Charles Croker's *Speed*, a parable of gods and mortals, in which the gods above looked down on the speed-crazy frenzy of modern mortals on earth below.[16] The gods spoke in blank verse, the mortals in colloquial prose, and *Radio Times* asked listeners to be in their 'listening chairs' by 9.35 prompt and ready to pay as much attention as they would in the theatre.[17]

This 'twilight of the gods' mood was abruptly shattered by the economic crisis of 1929 whose political and social consequences defined the next decade. In the face of the march of events in the thirties it was increasingly difficult to maintain a purely aesthetic stance towards art. Sieveking's protest, in 1934, that he was just tremendously interested, for its own sake, in what he was doing, was a plaintive cry against the prevailing winds. The motives for writing had changed. It was not so much a matter of choice as 'the forcible intrusion of social issues'.[18] There was a conscious sense of a break with the past under the clamour of the times, which disrupted the privacy of the individual and the closed little enclave of art and literature. Poverty, unemployment and the looming threat of another war drove art into politics. Under pressure the intellectuals could not shut their ears to the noise of contemporary history. It would no longer do just to write. One must write about something: with a purpose, to a purpose.

Sieveking described himself as a Christian and a loyal subject of the king. 'All the politics I have can be summed up in a few words: if the excellent civil service could be left to administer the wide liberties of the British constitution, we might be rid of these jigging politicians for ever.'[19] By contrast his close colleague and fellow member of the Research Unit, A. E. Harding, was well known in the BBC for his left-wing views. While sharing Sieveking's modernist tastes, Harding's work was far more political than Sieveking's allegorical whimsies. His productions were wide-ranging and included special features for the major feastdays in the BBC calendar and a varied mix of literary productions including a memorable feature on the sixteenth-century French poet, Francois Villon, written in collaboration with Ezra Pound.[20]

Harding's more historical and political productions included The *Republic*

138

of Austria, Crisis in Spain, and *New Year Over Europe.*[21] *The Republic of Austria* was a history of that country from the eighteenth century to the present. It was billed in *Radio Times* as a 'Poster in Sound', and the programme blurb gave a plan of the narrative, translations of German words and phrases used in the programme, and an acknowledgement that 'for many of the ideas the author is deeply indebted to the works of T. S. Eliot, Valery, D. H. Lawrence and G. K. Chesterton'.[22]

Crisis in Spain was a brilliant programme which broke new ground in many ways. *Radio Times* hailed it as the first British example of the reporting in radio form of contemporary events. The Talks Department had arranged a studio discussion of the recent Spanish crisis – the abdication of the King, the establishment of a republic – but proposed to precede it with a dramatic feature to provide colour and a factual chronological background to the debate. The narrative, it was claimed, had no other aim than to record what actually happened during the momentous weeks of March and April.[23] There was no single narrator to control and guide the narrative. Events spoke themselves via 'caption voices' in French, Spanish, German, English and American as events in Spain were relayed round the world by international press agencies, radio and news reporters. Music, with strong royalist or republican associations, was used to build momentum into the sequence of events. Impressionistic montage was used to generate the sense of an inexorable march of events towards the proclamation of the republic, as a direction in the script makes plain:

GENERAL NOTE: (The following sequence expresses the irresistible advance of the revolutionary movement in terms of announcements from radio stations all over Spain, interrupting rather ironically the even tenor of daily commercial broadcasting of dance music. The tempo should be deliberate down to the end of Basque Announcer's last speech, and then quicken to end, suspended only for a moment by Cabinet Minister's ineffectual attempt to stem the tide. After Marseillaise tempo slows up for next sequence which is more or less a realistic shot, taking the place and precising the preceding impressionism.)[24]

The style of the programme is strongly reminiscent of the 'symphonic' documentary techniques developed by European film-makers such as Ruttman and Cavalcanti. The mode of presentation avoided rendering down the issue in terms of personalities and the decisive actions of a small number of significant individuals. It avoided the peculiar ability of later current affairs journalism instantly to digest history by reducing it to a cud chewed over by politicians, reporters and pundits. It succeeded in realizing a contemporary event as a dynamic, historical process by a complex cross-cutting between events taking place in different parts of Spain and, at the same time, the global distribution of accounts of those events via modern media and communications systems.

Thus the narrative was simultaneously presented as a national and an international event. The crisis of Spain was not simply a crisis in Spain. Its significance was opened up beyond its own frontiers by the formal techniques of the narrative itself.

New Year Over Europe on the last day of 1932 was Harding's final fling in London. The tradition of a special feature on that evening had been established in the late twenties. It was usually a bland medley of events from the year that was passing, but Harding's programme sounded a more ominous and overtly political note whose underlying topic was peace or war in Europe. It began with a sequence of bells ringing and time signals from all over the world that dissolved into an exchange between two caption voices:

VOICE 1:   1932 has still an hour to run.
VOICE 2:   How will it be spent?
VOICE 1:   In reviewing the events of the past year?
VOICE 1:   Unemployment, debts, disarmament, riots, re-armament, Empire Unity at Ottowa and economic war.
VOICE 2:   Or at a cost of anything from 17/6 to £2 a head in supping and dining to the dance tunes of the day ...[25]

A quotation from H. G. Wells on the need to take hold of the 'war problem' more courageously than hitherto led into the main body of the programme – a sixty-minute tour of various European countries and capitals showing how the old year was being ushered out and the new year ushered in.

The original script appears to have been modified for transmission with several more contentious references pencilled out. Thus Italy, though described as a fascist state, had details of the size of its armed forces removed. One statement that did remain in the script was an assertion that Poland still delivered one third of its national income to the Ministry of War. This aroused the ire of the Polish Ambassador in London who protested to the Foreign Office and the BBC and managed to stir up a political storm in a teacup on the matter. There were questions in the House of Commons, letters to *The Times*, and the upshot of it all, if Bridson's account is to be believed, was that Harding was summoned before Reith and banished to Manchester as Programme Director, North Region. 'You're a very dangerous man, Harding. I think you'd be better up North where you can't do so much damage,' so Reith is supposed to have said.[26]

Harding's departure marked the demise of the research group and of formalist experiments in 'pure radio'. By now the Talks Department was more concerned with the social consequences of the recession, and the search for new ways of presenting them to the listening public. *Other People's Houses* and *S.O.S.* were their first attempts to humanize the treatment of social issues.

Hilda Matheson, then Head of Talks, regarded them both as a radical break with the established literary, rhetorical and formal methods of illustrating and explaining such topics: 'In both instances the speakers were not official experts using official language, still less politicians; but broadcasters capable of surveying the field as a whole and of presenting it in this new way to the widest possible audience.'[27] Through such novel forms of presentation the radio talk was becoming *relevant*, as a correspondent in *Radio Times* put it, expressing his delight that the BBC had left behind its milk-sop policy of not touching on controversial issues.[28] And a *Radio Times* leading article hailed the two programmes as 'placing the serious talk in the category of "things to be heard"'. No talks series, it was claimed, had ever aroused such general interest, or had dealt with matters of such urgent human concern. The article concluded with a prophecy that in this live yet dispassionate reporting of facts, no less than in the elaboration of theories, lay the future of the broadcast word.[29]

When Howard Marshall came to the microphone on 9 January 1933 to describe the slums of Tyneside his report struck a quite new note for broadcasting. He had been into the homes of the slum dwellers, had seen the conditions in which they lived and listened to what they had had to say. Now he told the general listening public what he had heard and seen.

> The first house [in Gateshead] at which I knocked was opened by a woman who was wiping her hands – she had been washing something in a bucket of greasy dirty water – and a bunch of undernourished, ragged children stared at me open-mouthed. The old grandfather was huddled by the fire, a very sick man, and the husband pointed to a lump of plaster a foot across, which had just fallen from the ceiling onto the rickety bed. Bare boards, with rat holes here and there, a wooden box or two, uncurtained windows with broken sash-cords, permanently closed, a great patch of moisture where damp had soaked through several layers of wallpaper by the baby's cot: this was the room I saw by the cheerless light of an unshaded gasmantle. And always it was the same story: no water, no conveniences ... One woman told me her story: not bitterly, but with a dispirited resignation which was far more terrible than any bitterness. Things were like that she said. The children ailing, all water and slops to be carried, the washing to be dried over a rope slung across the room, damp everywhere, cockroaches swarming over the bread when she put it on the table; but how could she hope to move out into the new housing estate when her husband had been unemployed for three years?[30]

In its selection of individual detail, in its representation of the experiences of those living in the slums, such reporting anticipated the methods and intentions of later and today more well-known documentaries dealing with the subject – the documentary film *Housing Problems* made in 1935, and Orwell's *Road to Wigan Pier*, published in 1936. It is an early example of that developing mode of documentation which, in the course of the decade, spread across film, radio, print journalism, photography and literary prose writing. Its general characteristics included an emphasis on ordinary life and the condition of the masses; a concern with social conditions detailing the symptoms rather than their causes; a belief that increased general awareness of the problems would give rise to their reform; and lastly, a stress on the factual, indicative of a widespread feeling that social reportage was the most relevant and immediate means of presenting the problems of the age.[31]

This new kind of witnessing was a good deal more than simple factual description. It was witnessing by the representative of an institution and on behalf of an audience. The style of reporting reveals the ways in which the relationships between the BBC, audience and subject matter were organized in the talks themselves. Consider the language and imagery with which Marshall began that very first report on conditions in Tyneside.

When we travel to strange places I suppose most of us try to picture what we are going to see. I know I did when I was rattling up through the night to Newcastle, and I know how utterly my imagination failed me. Perhaps the gaps between fact and imagination were caused largely by contrast; it is odd to break-fast comfortably, as I did, in a Newcastle hotel, and then immediately after-wards to cross the great suspension bridge over the Tyne into the dreary Gateshead streets. We are apt to think of the slums as localized areas – a few alleys here; a bunch of houses in a condemned area there – but it isn't like that in the towns and boroughs which lie strung along the Tyne. If you look through the carriage window of the little train which chugs from Newcastle, through Gateshead and Jarrow, to South Shields, you see a continuous belt of roofs below you; roofs which cover, not alway adequately, hundreds upon hundreds of families suffering from unemployment and poverty and hunger and ill-health.

It was this little train which carried me one night to High Shields Station, where I got out and made my way toward George Street, Holbourne and Rackondyke Lane. An unpleasant night, rather: a piercing wind whistled round the corners, which may have explained why the streets were quiet, peculiarly quiet with so many people only the thickness of a wall away. And perhaps because a day in Gateshead had made me impressionable, I felt, as I turned up my coat collar, that there was a strange quality about the stillness, a kind of dumb expectancy, so that it was almost startling in Cornwallis Square to hear a woman shout, 'looking for anyone mister?'

Cornwallis Square – it sounds well enough doesn't it? Plane trees, Georgian houses, expensive cars, orderliness, dignity – that is the sort of picture the name evokes. But Cornwallis Square hardly lives up to its name. You approach it, stumbling along a pitch dark passage which leads off a dingy alley, and you emerge into a muddy courtyard, perhaps fifteen yards across. This is the square; round it, just discernible in the flare of a flickering gas light, squat a dozen mis-shapen houses, with a kind of verandah on wooden posts giving access to the top rooms, and making the whole place look like a collection of mud huts in an African swamp. I went into every room in those houses, and in practically every one of them lives a family. And I didn't go because I wanted to – to see one was quite enough – but because family after family begged me to come and see their surroundings.[32]

It is the *otherness* of *Other People's Houses* that is most strikingly underlined. It is not merely a feature of the descriptive language – the strangeness of the slums, their likeness to darkest Africa (a commonplace image from the nineteenth century for the unknown continent within). It is more pervasively an effect of the relationship between speaker and listener that is organized by appeals to assumed common social attitudes and stocks of knowledge. Thus the space between the imaginary evocation of Cornwallis Square and its reality discloses not only an implied world in common between speaker and listener but also its distance from the slums of Tyneside and the people who live there. The use of the personal mode of address was part of a deliberate attempt to cut through the established discursive forms for dealing with such issues. The Talks Department knew that people listened in households, in family contexts, in moments of relaxation and leisure. Hence personal, intimate and informal modes of address seemed the best way of establishing an acceptable relationship between institution and audience.[33]

One simple but effective method was to invite the people themselves to come to the microphone to describe their experiences and feelings in their own words, a technique first employed in *Time to Spare*. These fifteen-minute talks, with their five-minute postscript by a doctor, a parson, a politician, were all reprinted in *The Listener*. They express quite different attitudes and experiences and the example chosen should not be regarded as representative of the tone of the series. It illustrates some interesting and problematic aspects of this new kind of radio talk. The speaker is John Evans, an out-of-work miner from the Rhondda, and the extract gives the beginning and end of his talk. It should be noted that, as printed in *The Listener*, the idioms of speech and the traces of working-class accent or dialect of the speakers are all lost and beyond conjecture. It is impossible to determine the extent to which speakers were 'helped' by people in Talks in the production of their scripts, but the occasional literary turn of phrase arouses suspicion.

People often ask us, who are out of work, how we manage. Well, the answer is easy. We manage by doing without. You have probably heard how we have to scrape together a few bones and cabbage leaves and odds and ends, and so on, to make a dinner, but I wonder whether you know the effect a sordid struggle of this kind has on people's minds, apart from the effect on their bodies. It is not a question of 'the unemployed struggling to make both ends meet', but of men and women struggling to live. Please do not think of us as 'the unemployed', but as individuals like yourselves. We have the same ambition to get on in the world: we have just the same feelings as you have.

Why should this sordid struggle for mere existence take place? My wife and I have often gone out on Saturday night without a single penny in our pockets. We walk along the streets and see plenty of everything in the shop-windows, so can you blame us for getting bitter? This goes on, not for a short time, but day after day, month after month, and as far as I can see it is going on for the rest of my life. I sometimes feel like throwing a brick through a window ...

As I've said, I've been out of work for eight years, and I've only managed to get eleven days work in all that time. I am forty-seven years old with no hope of work in the future. Work used to shape the whole of my life and now I've got to face the fact that this won't be so any more. Somehow or other I've got to live my life independent of the industrial machine. It takes a lot of doing because for years we've been told over and over again that work was the only really necessary virtue. I've tried to make use of my 'time to spare' by reading and so on, but don't for a moment look on unemployment as a heaven-sent opportunity for ramming education down the throat of many who may not want it. There are other things which they may need much more desperately. I know how difficult it is to be keen on one's education when one's mind is constantly worried and preoccupied by the facts of food and mere existence. The question that's in my mind is whether people in comfortable circumstances are really concerned with the troubles and trials of those who are out of work. Have *you* done anything toward solving the unemployment problem? What are you going to do about it? Do you think that because some of you have sent us clothes you no longer need, the problem no longer exists? I wonder what is going to happen! There's a quotation I often think of, 'Poverty is that state in which a man is perpetually anxious for the future of himself and his dependants, unable to pursue life on the standard to which he was brought up, tempted both to subservience and sour revolt and tending inexorably toward despair.'

That expresses much better than I can what unemployment makes me feel. One moment I could almost lick a man's boots for a favour: another time I could bash him in the face.[34]

The extent to which John Evans speaks here in his own voice is a difficult question. Obviously the production of talk of this kind is for him – as distinct from, say, Howard Marshall – a very rare, if not unique, act and one with which he is not fully at ease. We might reasonably feel the claim he makes that the quotation he often thinks of (if indeed he does) as expressing his feeling much better than he could, is immediately belied by the unadorned expression of his feelings in his own words in his final sentence. The difference here is one between institutional and individual forms of talk which pose questions about their authenticity, sincerity and truth. It can be seen that Evans speaks at times as a representative (para. 1) and at times as a person (para. 2). As a representative he speaks on behalf of others like him (the unemployed) to a generalized other unlike him (those in comfortable circumstances). As a person he speaks individually, directly to an absent particularized listener. Moving back and forth between these two positons Evans expresses a fierce resentment of his situation and a hostility towards the middle-class listening public. At the same time he must appeal for their understanding and help. These irreconcilable tensions give the talk its discomforting force and energy.

All the programmes considered so far were produced and broadcast live from the BBC's London studios. Yet the impulse of documentary is to show people in their normal ordinary lives, and to talk to them in their own everyday milieu rather than the artificial and inhibiting environment of the broadcasting studio. A *Radio Times* article published in 1932 and headlined, 'Wanted! A Microphone at Large', forcefully made the point:

> Real life is news and the more people feel it is real the better it is as news. That is why the arts have gone realistic; why tragedies are no longer written only about rich people, and the film cameras have come out of the studios and begun haunting the factories, the stokeholes and the docks. Yet there is the microphone, tending more and more to stay at home in its snug unreal studio, or at least going out only to the people it knows. New techniques are needed, that do not rely simply on commentators, not to come between the real stuff and the listeners, but to help reality out.[35]

The difficulty was, of course, the absence at this time of equipment that would permit speech and sound to be recorded on location and subsequently edited, like film, into extended narratives.

In the absence of such facilities, broadcasting relied on the extensive live coverage of events by the tiny Outside Broadcasts Unit. By the early 1930s the BBC was transmitting many hundreds of OBs, as they were called, each year. But nearly all of them were parasitic on already established social, cultural or sporting events over which the broadcasters had no control and which they sought simply to relay to the listening public. Gradually there emerged what was later called, in BBC television, the 'built OB' – a live transmission from one or more locations with some kind of thematic or narrative structure organized and imposed by the broadcasters. Such a programme was *Fleet Street Symphony*, broadcast from London on 16 December 1929. This was a microphone tour of the offices of the *Daily Express* in the late evening as it went through the final preparations for the next day's issue.[36] Microphones were installed in various parts of the building – the Creed room, news room, the Chief Editor's office and the printing rooms. Nothing, it was claimed, was specially staged for the programme. The intention was to show the ordinary routines of the newspaper industry. The transmission was not entirely uneventful however, for at one point an excited fanatic attempted to impose his political opinions on the world. But he mistook a light fitting for a microphone and was hurried away before he could make good his error.[37]

Such programmes were produced only very occasionally in London, and the lead in their development came from the Regions. But they were the first attempts to make programmes out of 'actuality' itself, and pointed the way towards more sophisticated developments. By 1934 'actuality' was a much used word in *Radio Times*. Commenting on a built OB from Battersea Power Station in which Howard Marshall described the new generating station, a leading article called 'Actuality' claimed that one of the main lines along which broadcasting was most likely to develop was outside broadcasts of wider scope than relays of music and organized arts. The same issue praised a documentary drama of the trial of Charles I (*The King's Tryall*, written and produced by Peter Creswell) for a realism 'that pulses with actuality'.[38] A few weeks later two 'dramas of actuality' (*Quarrel Island* and *Egypt's Gold*) were each described as drawing freely on dialogue actually spoken by the original actors in the events they recounted. There was the appeal of 'actuality' in the lines themselves. 'Art', the article declared, 'can never consist in the bare reporting of events, but, as far as the microphone is concerned, the most effective art does consist in the sure selection and vivid presentation of the facts.'[39] Both were billed as contemporary documentary drama.

At the beginning of June there was a special Outside Broadcast number.[40] A leader on OBs and actuality claimed that the former were now a matter of course in broadcasting. The next step would be 'actuality' – i.e. the sort of relay that depended more on the inherent quality of the event itself than the degree of artifice with which it was presented. The skill would lie mainly in the selection of material and its juxtaposition with other material; a technique parallel to what the film world called 'cutting'. The actual material must speak for itself. The movement towards actuality, it was claimed, had many manifestations and a number of articles elaborated on what was presently being done. Lawrence Gilliam allowed that developments in actuality broadcasting had come from the regions and their persistent efforts to mirror the everyday life of the country. Archie Harding confirmed the special need of regional broadcasting to go out after 'the stuff'. He claimed that Manchester's pioneering work in outside broadcasts was leading to a revolution in the presentation of actuality material. The next big development would be, he predicted, the introduction of recording techniques. Actuality recordings would be taken on location and then edited, back in the studio, into 'a pattern of significant sound'.[41]

In the mid-thirties sound recording on disc or the Blattnerphone was possible only in the London studios and was used exclusively for 'bottling' examples of significant broadcast material. There were no facilities for location sound recording – indeed, the first documentary film to use location sound was *Housing Problems* in 1935. But in the summer of 1934 Lawrence Gilliam hired a recording van from a film company to make the first radio feature using actuality sound recordings taken on location.[42]

'Opping 'Oliday was broadcast on 15 September 1934 on London Regional.[43] It offered a 'sound picture' of East Enders harvesting the hops in the Kent fields. The programme was broadcast live from the studio with a narrator, the recorded 'microphone snap-shots', two short talks giving personal side-lights on hop picking, and finally an outside broadcast link-up for a singsong from a Kent pub where the pickers were celebrating the end of their 'oliday. This was the first broadcast programme to realize that populist impulse at the heart of documentary which allows people to speak for themselves. No longer are they merely described by another in a studio talk, or else read a scripted talk from the studio in which they express the viewpoint of 'the ordinary person'. Now they speak from their own everyday environment, and produce impromptu talk, via an interviewer, for the microphone. Broadcasting has gone out into everyday life to capture 'the essence' of that reality as lived by those who speak of it in order to re-present this experience to listeners.

The nature of that representation needs to be considered with some care. What Stuart Hall has called 'the conditions of recognition'[44] are framed in a preliminary way in broadcasting by the timing, placing and titles of programmes. Note first the knowing cockney idiom of the title which situates the programme as an exercise in folk culture. Pat Forrest, who worked on the programme with Gilliam, described its aim as giving listeners 'an 'opping 'oliday without the work'.[45] It is thumbmarked as a lighthearted look at an aspect of the lives of cockney folk.[46]

Such conditions of recognition have to be worked into the manner and tone of the discourse itself. Here's how John Watt, the narrator, sets the opening scene at London Bridge station where the people have assembled overnight to wait for an early morning special train to take them down to Kent:

It was 2.30 in the morning. People were lying huddled in gutters, and near the walls which bear poster pictures of expensive continental resorts. But they're nor going to Monte Carlo. The crowd consists mainly of women and children of all ages, but more men this year. We all know the reason for that. I wish you could have seen the children – poor little things, some of them huddled up in perambulators. There was a bright moon which, together with the dusty station lights, showed how pathetic a thing like this can be.

Here the language of address – particularly the use of I, you and we – establishes a common way of looking at the programme's subject matter, a similar set of social and cultural dispositions. You and I, institution and audience, know how pathetic the sight of poverty can be. We all know – don't we? – why there are more men here this year. We hardly need mention unemployment ... This knowing collusion embraces the speaker and the listener but excludes the subject of the programme. The hop pickers are not included in the audience. The programme is *about* them but not *for* them. They have been taken up as an interesting topic, and made to reappear for another audience, another class, in another context.

For Gilliam the main point of this programme was as an experiment in a new technique. He had recently moved from working in *Radio Times* to Gielgud's new Drama Department, replacing Archie Harding and assuming responsibility for the production of the kind of special feature productions that had led to Harding's departure from London. In 1936 Gielgud divided the Drama Department in two. He retained sovereignty over a Drama Section under Howard Rose and a small Features Section under Gilliam. Features did not become a full-fledged department in its own right until after the war. In the early thirties the radio feature had not yet been recognized as an autonomous kind of production requiring specialist staff with specialist skills. Until the creation of the Features Section in 1936, the Talks Department continued to produce occasional features-type programmes along with the more run of the mill talks and symposia.

As a follow-up to the Outside Broadcast about Battersea Power Station, the Talks Department launched, later that year, an occasional series about various public utility services. The Port of London Authority, the National Grid, the Sea Fish Commission and the Metropolitan Water Authority were among the topics initially suggested.[47] They were intended to combine civic education with entertainment value; to give, within the compass of thirty minutes, a vivid impression of some particular aspect of modern life. Modest though this intention was it raised, for the first time, a number of policy problems about balance in dealing with such topics that have remained crucial dilemmas for programme-makers of documentary and current affairs programmes through to the present.

The subjects, though not directly political, were important public institutions or powerful commercial services of a quasi-national kind. The issue of balance arose over the programme on the national grid. In the thirties there was fierce competition between the three major energy resources of gas, coal and electricity over sales to domestic and industrial consumers and over their respective images and merits. So, when a commitment to a programme about electricity was agreed, the BBC, to forestall complaints from the Gas Board that this would be tantamount to free advertising for their arch-rival, informed them that this would be followed by a programme on gas and invited their cooperation.

To avoid giving offence the programme on the grid had all references to electricity consumption reduced to the barest minimum, and such that remained in the script covered spots where gas made little or no effort to compete – 'slums and out of the way parts of the contryside'. Nevertheless the net effect of the programme was to raise hostile suspicion in the gas industry, and an extreme sensitivity to any broadcast reference to electricity. When it came to the programme on gas, things soon bogged down in the mire of mutual antipathy between those in the BBC working on the programme and the representatives of the industry. The method of presentation wailed the producer, John Salt, was not suited to the subject. It was difficult to be lyrical about a subject associated with bad smells and vulgar jokes, yet the Gas, Light & Coke Company regarded any script in which the word 'gas' occurred less than once a line as showing an anti-gas bias. He complained that the Company withheld historical material about gas for fear that references to the past would give listeners the impression that gas was not modern.[48]

The programme never saw the light of day. Surveying retrospectively the wreck of the project Salt wrote, in a memorandum, that he had explained the BBC's concern with balance and fairness, and that he had carefully avoided establishing the awkward precedent of broadcasting one programme as compensation for another. In his view it was best to avoid making programmes that raised the spectre of commercial rivalry. If further experiments in this kind of programme were required he suggested they should be planned well ahead and spread out at intervals over a year so that the problem of balance could be worked out from the start and repercussions anticipated and prepared for. 'And as for gas', he concluded, 'I feel that nothing short of a "Gas Week" would heal the running sore of the gas industry, but that flow of matter – at least into our trays – might be stemmed by a judicious talk. Professor Allan Fergusson would do it admirably, and it should be not less than twenty minutes. Less than this, I fear, would but rub salt into the wound.'[49]

The Grid was broadcast on 12 December 1934 on London Regional. It was preceded by *Moonstruck Fish*, on research by the Ministry of Agriculture and Fisheries into the autumn shoaling of the herring. It appears from a note in *Radio Times* that there was to be a regular feature of this kind once a month throughout the next year with programmes on 'gas, water, lifeboats, hospitals and things like that'.[50] But the gas programme proved an abortion and, although there were occasional successors such as *The Weather Forecast* about the Metereological Office, no regular series was sustained.[51] At the same time Gilliam produced occasional programmes – *Gale Warning*[52] and *Cable Ship*[53] – along the same lines as *'Opping 'Oliday*, which aimed to give the flavour of some little known aspect of life or work in terms of the actual sounds of the job and the speech of the men who did it.

Details of all these programmes are scanty so it is impossible today to assess their style or quality. But John Grierson, at the time, had no doubts.

He roundly took the BBC to task for the conservative use of its great resources:

> Its producers have used the microphone very much as the early film makers used the camera. They have accepted it as an essentially immoveable object to which all action or comment must be brought; as a reproductive instrument capable of repeating speeches, talks, music, fairy stories, readings of poetry and the like, but without creative power of its own. A few simple deviations there have been in the so-called 'actuality' programmes (in this borrowing from our documentary example), but they have been so tentative and ill-equipped, that for all its years of work and national fields of opportunity the BBC has created no art of microphone sound and, in its own technique, not a single artist.[54]

This begged as many questions as it raised, particularly to do with art and authorship in radio. Perhaps narrative cinema, as an analogue of the novel, could be thought of as an art-form and its creator-directors as 'authors'. Whether radio could be thought of in the same way was another matter. Neither in features nor in drama did the BBC succeed in persuading the leading writers of the day, with reputations established in other mediums, to apply their talents to radio. It is true there was a trickle of feature programmes by the leading literati of the day – Pound and Auden made very occasional contributions – but in general they ignored radio.[55] For one thing the financial returns were meagre in the extreme. It might be an incidental confirmation that one had arrived to be asked to do the odd talk or to take part in some portentous symposium, but literary reputations were still to be made elsewhere through established forms and the usual agencies of legitimation.

From the mid-thirties there was a perceptible tendency for those recruited to features work in the BBC to have a literary pedigree (Geoffrey Bridson, Rayner Heppenstall and John Pudney, for example), but it was the Second World War which enabled the BBC to recruit writers with established reputations. Louis MacNeice, who joined the BBC in 1941 and remained with Features until shortly before his death in 1963, confessed that before the war he had thought of radio as 'a degrading medium, both vulgar and bureaucratic, and not even financially rewarding'. He added that he might well have been a snob at the time.[56] Perhaps, but a further factor was that ghastly impermanence of the medium to which Sieveking had referred. A thing of beauty might well be a joy forever in the shape of an urn or poem, but a radio feature was written on the wind. It is not mechanical reproduction as such that destroys the aura of the aspiring art object in broadcasting, but the ceaseless ebb and flow of a varied output. Broadcasting has no sense of occasion, of a time and place set apart from the routines of day-to-day life, which affirms the difference of the work of art. The demands of continuous production, the constant need to feed the voracious appetite of the microphone, and the pressures on producers from a bureaucratic hierarchy are all inimical to the service of the Muses. In the several books by or about individuals who have worked in radio features there is a palpable sense of the gradual erosion of creative flair under the cumulative burden of such pressures.[57]

By the mid-thirties, the techniques of radio had scarcely been established let alone consolidated. The achievements of Harding were isolated and terminated with his departure. There was no continuity either in the dramatic presentation of political events that *Crisis in Spain* initiated, nor in the social documentation of public matters of general concern. The *routine* treatment of such issues by broadcasting is a phenomenon of the late fifties and after. The new methods of reportage developed by Talks existed in a vacuum. When the political pressures on the department increased, their response was to draw in their horns and refrain from such kinds of programme.

Features production in London was affected by those pressures. Gilliam and his colleagues continued to produce programmes along the lines of *'Opping 'Oliday* and *Summer Over the British Isles*, made in 1937, is representative.[58] Features about notable British institutions continued, and there is a complete recording of *Scotland Yard* made in 1938.[59] Both this and *Summer Over the British Isles* sound alien to contemporary ears. It is not just the clipped middle-class accents and the facetious treatment of working people that makes them repellent. Today they sound lifeless, wooden and poorly written. And that is how they sounded to informed opinion within the BBC at the time. R. S. Lambert lamented the 'dreary Feature Programmes which are such an outstanding and deplorable characteristic of British broadcasting'.[60] In *The Listener* Grace Wyndham Goldie donned the mantle of Zola to denounce the feature programmes made in London. 'Surely something can be done, surely something *must* be done', she declared, 'to prevent the ruck of them being as feeble, as spineless, as weakly and abominably and intolerably dull as many of them are.'[61] Features had got worse in the last twelve months, not better. Nor was this, she went on, merely her opinion. A panel of listeners had been invited to listen and comment on the output of the drama department for three months in 1937. In this period there were eighteen feature programmes, not one single one of which was more than mediocre. The verdict of the drama panel was clearly against the kind of feature they were being given. There were continual complaints of scrappiness and disjointedness and a strong dislike of the 'relay system of narrating by several voices'.

Goldie singled out one lone swallow for praise, as she had often done before, and that was Geoffrey Bridson. Bridson was Features Producer for North Region. In the second half of the thirties most of the interesting and innovative work in features and documentaries was being done in Manchester.[62] The centre of gravity, as far as programme-making was concerned, had shifted from London to the Regions. It was not that there was no talent in London, but that there was no longer any chance or incentive to express it. A pall of mediocrity descended on those area of production that dealt with – or that once deal with – contemporary social and political life. If there were no interesting programmes being made it was because there was nothing to be interesting about. A memorandum from Lawrence Gilliam, in March 1939, to Val Gielgud reveals quite clearly what the problem was. Gilliam wanted to persuade the top brass in the BBC to sanction a regular features series on the lines of the well-known American *March of Time* programmes. He recognized that for policy reasons the major political events of the time were out of court, but still felt this left a vast field of non-controversial issues which could be worked up into a regular feature series: 'If we can prove to the authorities that we can tap a new source of topical features, without running them into a lot of trouble, we can go a long way to filling one of the Corporation's biggest gaps – that is, topicality.'[63] Topicality is the oxygen of those areas of broadcasting – news, talks and features – that deal with contemporary life and affairs. Starved of the possibility of making programmes that dealt with the vital issues of the day, it is scarcely surprising that the features produced in London were boring or banal. The blight of irrelevance infected the activities of features and talks producers in the late thirties.

CHAPTER EIGHT

Forms of Talk

————◦✴◦————

No DEPARTMENT in the pre-war period had a more troubled, turbulent history than the London Talks Department. From its inception in 1927 through to 1935 Talks was probably the most exciting area of broadcasting to work in. Thereafter it became the dullest. Under Hilda Matheson (1927–32) and her successor Charles Siepmann (1932–5) the Department was inspired by a common commitment to the importance of radio as a new form of social communication, and a common interest in developing effective methods of communicating via the spoken word. Matheson was a woman of courage, originality and culture, and she brought these qualities to broadcast talks.[1] She was, thought R. S. Lambert, a typical post-war liberal with an enthusiasm for feminism, socialism and modernism in the arts and literature.[2] She was liked and admired by her staff who noted her vision of the possibilities of broadcasting as an influence on people's minds and hearts and her capacity to kindle enthusiasm in others. She made the Talks Department into a live, energetic and humane place to work. In its brief golden age, talks 'kept abreast of topical developments in literature and politics, experimented with education, provided listeners with a service of informed criticism of books, films, plays, music and farming, opened up the field of debates and discussions, improved and expanded the news, and sought even to train the politicians to make better use of broadcasting.'[3]

Hilda Matheson was recommended to Reith because she had contacts in that social world which, as yet, the BBC had failed to penetrate. She had been Lady Astor's personal secretary, and through this office had formed a large circle of friends and acquaintances in the worlds of fashion, letters and politics. The staff she picked to work with her at the BBC had access to this world, and thus it came about, as one contemporary commentator put it, that it was now possible for the younger dons to mention broadcasting at the high tables of Oxford Colleges without fear of ridicule. The intelligentsia began to be interested in the microphone. Society was mildly intrigued, and the great ones of the world no longer shrank from crossing the threshold of a BBC studio.[4] Talks schedules now included the names of Wells and Shaw, Vernon Bartlett and Harold Nicolson, Churchill and Lady Astor, Beveridge and Keynes, Huxley, Sydney and Beatrice Webb – a roll call of the great and good who flocked to the studio to speak of many things to do with contemporary life and affairs. Such speakers were mostly progressive in outlook, but not *too* progressive. They were often politically non-aligned, but committed to efficiency in social administration and the benefits of a planned economy. Their outlook was generally consonant with the ethos of the department which Hilda Matheson encouraged and nurtured.

Both Matheson and her successor, Charles Siepmann, were anxious to develop the role of radio talk in the creation of an informed public opinion, and we have described their efforts to bring a greater immediacy and realism to radio talk. *Crisis in Spain* was designed to illuminate a studio discussion on the abdication of the Spanish monarchy and its aftermath. Similarly, though in a more distanced historical way, a talks series on the history of trades unionism introduced by J. L. Hammonds in April 1934 was supplemented by carefully documented dramatizations of the Tolpuddle Martyrs and the Sheffield riots of 1867, written by R. S. Lambert.[5] The kind of reportage inaugurated by Howard Marshall's series on housing was followed by a major series of talks by Professor John Hilton on *Industrial Britain*. To prepare this 1934 series Hilton visited factories in many parts of Britain and, in his talks, made it plain that he was treating the subject from the point of view of the workforce as much as the management.[6]

For Matheson such programmes demonstrated and confirmed the social role of broadcasting as a mediating agency between the state and people; they were a means of bridging the gulf between expert and citizen, and of reducing the awkward time lag between official perceptions of the remedies for social ills and making them understood by the population.[7] But what series like *Time To Spare* tended to do, through exposing the very urgency of the problems, was to highlight the inadequacies of the official remedies proposed. The National Government was far removed from Matheson's idealistic conception of 'the modern state' which, like a true progressive of the time, she based on the Stalinist model of efficient, centralized state planning.[8] What was not anticipated was the extent to which such interventions by broadcasting might affront the ignorance and prejudices of conservative opinion or tread on official toes.

A series of memoranda on complaints of bias in talks, prepared for the Ullswater Committee, claimed that a careful examination of the balance of talks would show that there was, in fact, no bias in any direction, but that misapprehensions arose from the nature of broadcasting. Talks series on topical and controversial issues were carefully arranged so that all main points of view got their proper share of time, but it could not be guaranteed that the same audience would hear them all. Listeners of Conservative tendencies might hear only a Liberal or Labour contribution, and vice versa. To hold the scales evenly, to give minorities their innings, to let in the breath of criticism on matters where otherwise complacency might reign – these were not simple tasks, and mistakes were sometimes made. Moreover it was often the case in the world of ideas that talent tended to be, if not subversive at any rate highly critical. It was quite natural that people with specific gifts of observation or expression should think they could improve the world a little, and broadcasting drew such people like a magnet. It was a pity that those 'who lose sight of the wood of British oak because their gaze is riveted on an occasional piece of what they take for Russian timber cannot see, for a brief salutory moment, what might be in the programmes if it was true that those who drew them up favoured subversion and degeneration and the dissolving of standards and the remodelling of the life of Britain according to the paper plans of intellectuals with no roots in the country.'[9]

While complaints about controversy increased Reith was reorganizing the running of the BBC. The Talks Department, more than any other, was subject to boundary changes and the lines of its responsibilities were frequently redrawn. When Matheson took charge she was responsible for general and 'topical' talks. Responsibility for news was soon added and remained with the department until a separate News Department was established in 1935. In 1928 Adult Education was hived off from Stobart's Educational Department and became a powerful sub-kingdom run by Charles Siepmann who transferred from Stobart's department to be Matheson's deputy. The growing complexities of BBC administration imposed a severe strain upon her, as upon other departmental heads, and in 1931, ostensibly to ease the pressure on her, it was proposed that a larger share of administrative responsibility should be delegated to Siepmann. Matheson agreed but subsequently found that in effect Siepmann now appeared to be a co-director of the department rather than her deputy. The stink of intrigue went up and factions formed in the first big internal row in the BBC. In the end Matheson resigned – was forced into resignation according to Lionel Fielden – to be succeeded by Siepmann.[10]

Siepmann had risen in Reith's favour, while Matheson's relations with him became increasingly fraught, so his succession was inevitable. But if Reith thought that Siepmann was a 'safe' choice he was mistaken. Siepmann increased the size of the department, bringing in many new recruits of advanced views including Mary Adams, a scientist and adult educator, who set a high standard of broadcast science talks. Siepmann also energetically pursued the development of controversy, and it was during the three years of his stewardship that the major rows over broadcast talks blew up. Lambert has suggested that Talks blossomed forth in an era of liberal optimism when a Labour Government ruled at Westminster, and that the ill winds began to blow after the fall of the second Labour Government and its replacement by a National Government of conservative character:

> From that time onwards, a steadily growing wave of attacks upon the BBC for the 'redness' or the 'pinkness' of broadcast talks rose up in the Press, and extended even to Parliament. The *Daily Mail* and the *Morning Post* lost few opportunities of picking holes in the BBC's choice of speakers and topics. Again and again the most trivial errors were magnified into examples of 'left-wing bias'. Such press 'stunts' took a form which we in Broadcasting House came in time to predict as easily as one can predict a thunderstorm on a sultry day. First, some 'special correspondent' would write suggesting that malign, dark, conspiratorial forces were at work to spread the gospel of the Third International through broadcast talks. Then would follow a spate of letters from 'readers', all of the same colour, adducing examples of BBC Bolshevism – sometimes slips in the news, sometimes extracts from talks torn from their context or isolated from the symposium of which they formed part. Lastly, the moral would be rubbed in by leading articles of a Pecksniffian character. Then the cycle would be complete, and after a lull could commence again on a slightly different orbit.[11]

Things came to a head in 1935, a year in which the BBC, with its Charter and Licence due for renewal, was under the scrutiny of a Parliamentary Committee of Inquiry, headed by Lord Ullswater. At such a moment Reith did not want trouble in the ranks for there were quite enough complaints and criticisms – particularly on regional and musical policies – floating about in the various submissions, written and verbal, to the committee from outside interests. The battening down of the hatches was made clear to all departmental heads by Gladstone Murray, Assistant Controller of Programmes, at the first Programme Board meeting of 1935. Murray began by laying down the general principles to be observed in framing programmes for the year. He stressed the need for a greater sense of collective responsibility and the avoidance of narrow departmentalism. He spoke of the importance of intelligent censorship and the need for prudence, and called for special efforts to interpret the doctrine behind all controversial broadcasting. He ended by reminding all present of the confidentiality of Programme Board meetings. He re-emphasized these points a few weeks later to an enlarged Programme Board meeting which included the Head of the Empire Service and all the Regional Directors. Murray again underlined the special importance attached to the

B.B.C. CALLING

work of 1935 and 1936 and the need for collective responsibility. 'The circum-stances did not call for an irrational application of negative censorship, but rather the exercise of vigilance and discerning judgment.'[12]

The effect of this internal tightening up on all sensitive matters was felt immediately by the Talks Department. At the beginning of the year there were plans for a series called, provisionally, 'What Price Freedom', a title which would take on a certain irony in the course of its chequered develop-ment.[13] The original idea was for a series on the topic in relation to politics, religion, literature, industry, education and finally the individualist point of view. As representative of various shades of political opinion on the subject the names of Stanley Baldwin (Conservative), H. G. Wells (Liberal), Herbert Morrison (Labour), Sir Oswald Mosley (Fascist) and John Strachey (Commu-nist) were proposed at an early stage. Felix Greene however felt that Strachey was too academic and that the political leader of the British Communist Party, Harry Pollitt, would be much preferred by working-class listeners. There was, Greene claimed, referring to his own work with unemployed and working-class listeners, a widespread feeling there that the communist point of view was not given a square deal by the BBC. The *Time To Spare* series and the new special talks for the unemployed had done a great deal to make the work-ing-class audience sympathetic to the BBC, but the William Ferrie incident was still fresh in many people's minds. 'There is no getting away from the fact', Greene concluded, 'that countless numbers of unemployed and working-class listeners are still suspicious and unfriendly towards us, and I can think of nothing that we could do that would alter this more effectively than a decision to allow Pollitt for once to have his say.'[14]

This suggestion was accepted, but the Department was no longer master of its own domain. All through its planning stage the series was referred upwards, through Gladstone Murray, to Reith and the Board of Governors who were the final arbiters of who should and should not speak on the topic of Freedom. Siepmann had wanted to include Ernst Toller – a leading German left-wing dramatist and intellectual who had left Germany when Hitler came to power – as one of the speakers with Mosley and Pollitt in the initial list passed up for consideration. In due course the Department was informed, via Gladstone Murray, that the series idea was accepted by the Board of Governors, that Communism and Fascism were not to be included, that Ernst Toller was not acceptable and that there were doubts about Mr Bernard Shaw (for the individualist point of view) who had, it was felt, about reached the end of his (broadcasting) tether.[15]

The Department's response was one of unease and disappointment. Lionel Fielden, in a memorandum to Siepmann, expressed the strongly felt general opinion that the banning of names without reason in a series that had been carefully thought out was becoming more and more common, and was leading to considerable difficulty and discouragement in the work of the department.[16]

But no explanations from above were forthcoming and Siepmann had to bow to the continuing interference with, and dilution of, the original proposal. He gathered that Toller was rejected because he was regarded as a Communist not because he was a foreigner. He therefore proposed to replace Toller with Professor Schroedinger who, he informed Gladstone Murray, had a delightful sense of humour, spoke very good English, had left Germany voluntarily because he did not agree with Nazi politics and was not Jewish. Reith accepted Schroedinger. 'So long as he is not going to talk against Nazism, but only to discourse on English freedom, there is no objection.'[17]

Siepmann continued to try to retrieve something of the original intentions of the series and put it to Reith that many people would see the range of speakers proposed by the Board of Governors as unrepresentative of anything but very bourgeois opinions. He felt it would be just and safe to include a working man as one of the speakers and, he went on, 'I am making myself personally responsible for the series and ['I think' deleted] I can guarantee to you no repetition of the Ferrie incident.' Reith was deeply suspicious of this suggestion.[18] He did not think that the working man's view of British freedom was necessarily different from the bourgeois one, and thought it better not to secure an opinion from a quarter where, almost inevitably, a party political point of view would be imposed. However, he accepted the idea, and told Siepmann to contact Walter Citrine, General Secretary of the TUC General Council, for advice on a suitable exponent of the working-class view of freedom. Citrine suggested a Mr Moore who eventually spoke in the series, receiving an unusually high fee of £20 for his contribution.

By now Siepmann's days as Head of Talks were numbered and in June 1935 he was moved to the newly-created post of Director of Regional Relations. This was discussed in some detail by the Governors and H. A. L. Fisher queried whether it in fact was a promotion. He was informed by Sir Charles Carpendale (Controller, Administration) that it was not, and that Siepmann would not regard it as such. It had become necessary, according to Carpendale, because of friction between Siepmann and those above and below him, and particularly Alan Dawnay, Controller of Programmes, who was on the verge of quitting. Dawnay had been carefully picked for this key job by Reith in 1933, but within a year his health was severely affected by the strain of it. According to Carpendale, Dawnay had felt he could not trust Siepmann's judgement and this entailed an awful lot of work reading manuscripts, etc., which was probably the primary cause of his breakdown. Fisher thought Siepmann was exceedingly able and declared that in Oxford, where there was an intelligent audience which mattered, talks were regarded as by far the best part of the BBC's programmes. It was essential to have someone like Siepmann in Talks to keep it in the van of new movements of thought, and so on. Carpendale accepted this last point and the need for virile, intense enthusiasm, but felt these were qualities better found in junior staff in the charge of someone more level-headed to keep the balance. With Siepmann, he suggested, it was like having Noel Coward as Director of Programmes. Coward would of course be excellent so far as ideas, etc. went, but after a while everyone would feel that they could not sleep at night with him in charge and that they could not put up with the temperament, friction and so on. Mrs Hamilton agreed that Siepmann was everything that Fisher said he was, but added that the trouble was he had no sense.[19]

So Siepmann was told to pack his bags to tour the provinces and write a report on their activities. Nor was he the only member of the Talks Department to depart from Portland Place that summer. Felix Greene went to New York to be the BBC's North American representative. Lionel Fielden went to India to set up a broadcasting service in the subcontinent. Tony Rendall went to Palestine. The cream of the Department were all offered posts that took them a very long way from Head Office. Hilda Matheson, still a keen observer of events in the BBC, described it as 'a dispersal and disintegration unparalleled in any other department'. Writing a few months after the diaspora she recorded her impression of widespread arrested development in the work of Talks.[20] Looking back to this period, Lionel Fielden noted that the programme was no longer the thing. 'It was wiser in the BBC of 1935 to be a good administrator than to have any original ideas; better to spend your time cutting down artists' fees than rehearsing the artist; more paying to use a blue pencil than your mind.'[21]

There is no doubt that the new postings, with the exception of Siepmann's, were attractive and advanced the careers of those who took them up. Equally there is no doubt that the newly vacant posts in Talks were not filled by people with the same imaginative qualities or progressive outlook.[22] Now, according to Lambert, the 'orthodox public schoolboy type' was preferred, who knew the difference between a nod and a wink; and an apparatus of close personal contact with other official bodies – government departments, public utilities, big corporations, trade associations – was built up for their benefit. The young talks assistant of the later thirties was trained to regard himself as a civil servant 'with a difference'.[23] He was answerable to Sir Richard Maconachie, whom the Governors appointed as Head of Talks in 1936.

There had been a brief interregnum in Talks before his appointment, which Briggs describes as a period of anarchy when contending forces struggled against each other.[24] Maconachie's arrival put a stop to that. He had served as British Minister at Kabul from 1930 to 1936, and his appointment was seen as part of a swing to the right in the BBC, an indication of a further retreat into caution.[25] Paul Bloomfield, who joined the Talks Department a year after Maconachie's appointment, described it as

> notoriously the unhappiest department in the BBC ... The little band of assistants were as dispirited a company as I ever expected to make one of.... Our relationship with one another was in some degree affected by the well-known Hidden Hand atmosphere of Broadcasting House, which high managerial personnel did so little to dispel (by using plain good manners for instance) that one was apt to suspect them of being purposefully responsible for it. The decent people in Talks Department were terribly correct ... on the whole their instinct of self-preservation kept them anxiously diplomatic.[26]

In the last few years of the peace 'dullness lifted its head once again, and rejoiced to think of its escape from extinction. Talks ran again in series, more solid than ever; topicality was eschewed; assistants continued to spend their days laboriously twiddling their pens in little white-washed rooms, thinking out ways of combining the edifying with the innocuous.'[27] Controversy was avoided rather than sought. Instead, Briggs suggests, there was a renewed interest in the techniques of the spoken word as the approach of Hilda Matheson and Siepmann seemed to be out of date, particularly in its emphasis on the formal script and the single speaker. However, attempts to enliven broadcast talk by experimenting in alternatives to the straight lecture were as much a feature of the Matheson-Siepmann era, as the later thirties when Maconachie ruled.

When Hilda Matheson took up her post wireless talks were regarded as an inferior kind of entertainment, a poor relation to the more lively parts of programme output such as variety, plays and music. A certain touchiness on the subject can be detected behind the suggestion in the *BBC Hand Book* for 1928 that listeners should try to meet the BBC halfway and be more open-minded about its talks and lectures. Contrary to popular surmise, the article declared, it was not the policy of the BBC 'wantonly and arbitrarily to cut the audience off in the middle of a delightful concert, and announce a talk by Professor Haxan on Prehistoric Crustaceans without any rhyme or reason'.[28] In the new Talks Department there was a growing realization that talk on radio needed to take into account the kinds of people who might be listening and the circumstances in which they did so.

Matheson conducted a series of experiments with broadcast talk which led her to the view that it 'was useless to address the microphone as if it were a public meeting, or even to read it essays or leading articles. The person sitting at the other end expected the speaker to address him personally, simply, almost familiarly, as man to man.'[29] Broadcasting could not treat its audience as a crowd. It had to learn to speak to them as individuals. Its task was the domestication of public utterance. Available models of public talk – the sermon, lecture or political speech – were all unsatisfactory. The 'holy voice' used by the clergy to read the lessons in church had a double purpose: it was used to project to the back of large, echoing buildings, and appeared as a special voice set apart for religious purposes, more devout than the ordinary voices of everyday life. But the 'parsonical drone' was peculiarly unsuited to radio, and had a tendency to make listeners switch off immediately. The BBC's Central Religious Advisory Committee was well aware of this problem, and efforts were made to establish a standard for the reading on radio of lessons and biblical extracts. A passage was read to a select group of listeners first in a completely ordinary voice as if it were an extract from a newspaper, next in a 'holy' voice, and finally in something between the two, as a piece of good literature. The third voice was the one preferred and a number of bible readings in this voice were subsequently recorded on disc as a guide and model for readers of the scriptures on radio.[30]

Matheson noted the problems of another special voice – the declamatory, 'poetic' voice used for acting or for public readings of poetry and literature. This voice, with its polished elocution and exquisite pronunciation, seemed mannered and affected to the listening ear. Again, the political voice and the rhetoric of the platform put the speaker at a disadvantage when used for broadcasting. 'The microphone', Matheson noted, 'has a curious knack of showing what is real and unreal, what is clear and what is woolly, what is fact and purpose and what is stock phrase, what is sincere and what is an appeal to the gallery, what is constructive and what is destructive.'[31]

The art of radio talk as it came to be understood by the Talks Department is easily summarized. Since it was received by family groups it should be conversational in tone rather than declamatory, intimate rather than intimidating. The personality of speakers should shine through their words. But because all broadcasting was live, talks needed to be scripted. Otherwise what they gained in colloquialism and personal idiom they would lose in clarity and succinctness. As Briggs put it, 'what was natural had first to become artificial before it would sound natural again.'[32] This 'natural' style of talk was perfected by John Hilton, Professor of Industry at the University of Cambridge, and one of the best-known speakers on radio before the war. In 1937 Hilton gave a radio talk about talk on radio in which he simultaneously employed the technique of writing for the ear and revealed how it was done. Referring to newspaper critics who had praised him for simply talking rather than reading from a script, he continued, 'Oh yes, I like that. For, of course, I read every word. If only I could pull it off every time – but you have to be at the top of your form. Yes, of course, every word's on paper even now – this – what I'm saying to you now – it's all here.'[33]

If the technique of writing for the ear was an art it found its expression in such skilled practitioners as Hilton. But there were those who felt that the Talks Department was creating a mystique about the spoken word. Some critics felt that, far from being a new art-form, the style was simply an artificial compromise which interfered with the direct transmission of information; that there was a tendency for the aims of informing and attracting listeners to come into conflict. It was also alleged that powerful or prestigious speakers were allowed to deliver their scripts as they wished, while lesser fry were subjected to detailed revision. The insistence on all talk being scripted and checked before transmission could easily be seen as a means of censorship. A style intended to ease listening became a means of controlling contributors. While evidence can be cited to support such criticisms, none of them reached to the heart of the matter. The careful attention to scripts signalled an anxiety to be understood by listeners while differentiating between different kinds of speaker and different categories of talk.

The tension between the need to inform and the need to attract listeners to listen presented producers with a problem. The style of talk perfected by Hilton was simply unsuitable for putting over the complex information and ideas which made up the staple content of many a talks 'syllabus'. Paul Bloomfield, a talks assistant in the late thirties, amused himself by imagining how Einstein might deliver a talk on the stars in the approved idiom. 'Well, I suppose all of us at some time or another have – er um – looked up on a clear night and seen the stars overhead. Of course when I say "stars" I mean planets too. It would never do to leave out the planets!'[34] It was a style which, Bloomfield admitted, important speakers were able to resist having thrust upon them. There was a growing tendency to distinguish between serious and popular categories of talk and talker. The speaker who had perfected the intimate, informal style might find himself relegated from the league of radio authorities respected for their expertise, to the league of radio personalities liked for their homely touch. John Hilton's radio career exemplified this slide. He began, in 1934, with a major talks series on his own academic field, industrial relations. By the end of the decade he was responsible for a kind of agony column of the air, championing the cause of 'the little man' against the predations of fraudsters and confidence tricksters.

The way in which serious and popular speakers were distinguished from each other can be seen in a problem the Talks Department had with one of the BBC *National Lectures*. These were instituted in 1928 and were intended 'to hold the blue ribbon of broadcasting and to provide, on two or three occasions in the year, for the discussion of issues of major importance and the interpretation of new knowledge by men of distinction in the world of scholarship and affairs'.[35] An advisory panel of academic, scientific and literary luminaries was set up to propose suitable speakers. The first was the poet laureate, Robert Bridges, who spoke for three-quarters of an hour on *Poetry*, in the form of an imaginary dialogue with a typical poet. The second National Lecture was by Dr Arthur S. Eddington, the Plumian Professor of Astronomy at the University of Cambridge, on the subject of *Matter in Interstellar Space*. The lecture dealt chiefly with the cosmic cloud – 'a cloud of extremely rarefied gas which occupies the space between the stars' – its temperature, density and probable composition.[36] In 1935 it was noticed that one of these lectures, by Lord Macmillan on *Law and the Citizen*, was to be followed a few weeks later by a talk on *The Rule of Law* to be given by a young barrister, Maurice Healy.

Healy was very much a popular speaker who had contributed to a series of imaginary court cases, *Consider Your Verdict*, and had read short stories on the air. There was a minor panic when it was realized that listeners might, even after a five-week interval, suppose that his contribution was as authoritative as the *National Lecture*. Healy's talks producer wrote to him that 'Lord Macmillan's talk will be very much a lecture and I think it would be a good thing if you were to keep in mind the fact that your short address is very much a talk, full of that touching on "I" and "you" which comes so easily from yourself ...' He wanted Healy to make it quite clear that he was talking on a subject that was near to his heart but on which he was not an expert.[37] To this Healy objected that, as a barrister, he was an expert, and he took umbrage at the idea of being labelled in *Radio Times* as 'a layman'. In the end he was credited as a lawyer 'speaking on this occasion as a layman'. But from the BBC's point of view an appropriate distinction between the two talks and talkers had been achieved. Lord Macmillan discussed 'the reign of law' as follows. 'The conception of what it embodies is the conception of certainty as opposed to arbitrariness. To know what we can lawfully do and what we cannot lawfully do; to be subjected to laws constitutionally enacted and enforced ...' etc.[38] Healy began, 'Well, freedom is a vague word and you may well ask what I mean by freedom. For nobody is free to do exactly as he would like. The baby stretches out his hand for every toy he fancies and cries if he does not get it.'[39]

The personal style, with its 'I's and 'you's, was by now reserved for radio personalities offering diversion or mild entertainment, rather than information. But in the case of serious or controversial talks, the approach was very different. In the same year as Healy's talk on law, Harold Laski gave a series on *What is the State?* Laski had first been invited to come to the microphone in 1928 and at the time it was noted that, as a prominent left-winger, he would need 'careful vetting'. In the 1933 series it was felt that he had not sufficiently stressed interpretations of the role of the state that were opposed to his own. He was asked to insert 'some sort of statement from the "authoritarian" point of view', and to make stylistic changes which involved 'cutting out the "I thinks" and "my views" and rephrasing in such a way that your point of view

" WHEN IN THE COURSE OF HUMAN EVENTS IT BECOMES
NECESSARY FOR ONE PEOPLE TO DISSOLVE THE POLITICAL
BANDS WHICH HAVE CONNECTED THEM WITH ANOTHER,
AND TO ASSUME, AMONG THE POWERS OF THE EARTH, THE
SEPARATE AND EQUAL STATION TO WHICH THE LAWS OF
NATURE . . ."
"SAY, IT'S A TALK ABOUT SOMETHING! "

is put over impersonally'.[40] The impersonal style became the rule for expert speakers precisely because the BBC wished to avoid the accusation that it allowed them to use radio to promote their personal views. Little effort was made to alter their scripts unless, as happened occasionally, they took part in talks of a lighter kind. For instance, Sir William Beveridge, who broadcast frequently on social and economic issues, agreed in 1937 to contribute to a light historical series of eye-witness accounts called *I Saw the Start*. He was to talk on the origin of labour exchanges. The producer complained that his script was stilted and 'unsuitable for an audience that wants to be talked to rather than at'. But Beveridge was 'not very easy to deal with because apparently he's used to being treated casually and having things left to him.' The producer was advised by his superior to 'do nothing more'.[41]

Matheson had wanted to develop accessible, informal styles of talk for dealing with serious issues, but this lapsed after a few years. It was not simply that the original commitment to the role of radio talk in contemporary life and affairs had caved in. Most of the experts invited to speak by the BBC were busy men with established reputations who were not prepared to spend a great deal of time adapting their scripts and rehearsing their performance. More to the point, the use of a personal, populist style seemed a breach of the conventions of learned discourse and argument. Only a dispassionate, academic mode of presentation would legitimate and authenticate what was being said. Thirdly, and perhaps most importantly, the use of the personal style semed to undermine the ethic of impartiality; impersonal speech *sounded* more neutral. The sometimes byzantine diplomacy over the style of talks scripts was as often as not concerned with establishing the credentials of speakers (their *right* to speak) and with situating them in a particular relationship with their audience, rather than a covert form of censorship.

Even when the objections of members of the Talks Department to scripts amounted, in effect, to censorship, they were liable to be directed to matters of style and manner of expression rather than content. This is unsurprising, since style was the one thing that the producer could claim to know more about than the speaker. To question the content of what the expert said might be to overstep the mark. Talks producers were in fact called 'talks assistants' – a title which implied a minimal degree of interference in helping speakers to produce and deliver their contributions. This image of the producer's role was important in preserving good relations with outside speakers. But as considerations of the audience became more important, people in Talks began to value those speakers who could be 'produced' and take advice, above those whose august status placed them beyond editorial guidance. In 1938 the number of *National Lectures* was reduced, because the BBC no longer felt such need for the aura conferred by distinguished men of knowledge. By now attention in the Talks Department, as elsewhere in the BBC, was increasingly directed at ways of presenting talk on radio that appealed to ordinary listeners.

There was always more to radio talk than the straight talk, and a number of alternatives were explored as more stimulating than lectures delivered at listeners by preachers, politicians and pundits. These included the discussion, the debate, the interview and the magazine format. They were regarded both as means of relieving the monotone of monologue, and of introducing greater balance within programmes where controversy might arise. They also offered the possibility of escape from scripted speech into impromptu talk.

Before the ban on controversy was lifted in 1928 there had been experiments with both scripted and unscripted studio discussions, and with relays of debates before live audiences from public halls in London. Studio discussions were intended to capture the quality of good 'table talk', rather than the clash of opinion. That was more the province of the public debate which, in the absence of serious matters for disagreement, invited opposing speakers into the lists to tilt at such topics as 'Are critics taken too seriously?', 'Is chivalry dead?' and 'The menace of the leisured woman'. Speakers such as G. B. Shaw, G. K. Chesterton and Bertrand Russell were well known as opinionated, witty public performers. Their speeches were scripted and, if the results were often awkward, this was partly because the distinguished speakers were unwilling to rehearse or consider the requirements of broadcasting. But the real fact was, as Hilda Matheson admitted, that the Department had rapidly exhausted the supply of people of any standing willing to talk to topics that smacked of the undergraduate world of the Oxford and Cambridge Unions. Duff Cooper had refused an invitation to take part in a debate, she told Roger Eckersley in February 1928, because he 'sees no use in doing it until we can talk about things in which people are interested'.[42]

When the ban on controversy was lifted a month later, however, the studio discussion was the preferred alternative to the straight talk for dealing with controversial topics. These 'hammer and tongs' discussions, as Hilda Matheson called them, were defined as 'challenging and opposing points of view on a controversial subject expounded in prepared statements in sequence'.[43] The clash of opinion could be engineered either by a laborious exchange of manuscripts between speakers or by allowing one contributor to devise both sides of the argument. In 1932 Sir William Beveridge prepared both sides of the case on the topic of The Family which he was to discuss with Professor Ginsberg. He assured Mary Adams, his Talks producer, that 'it leads up to quite a good difference of opinion between me and Ginsberg as to whether one can or should equalize opportunity for every individual ... Of course we've go to make Ginsberg take it, and drill him and rehearse till we're tired. But I'm sure we can.'[44]

The scripted discussion was used throughout the decade, but in 1935, greatly daring, Talks ran a series of unscripted, impromptu debates before live audiences on controversial topics. The only precautions taken were to make the non-participating audiences by invitation only, and to ensure that the debates were chaired by experienced broadcasters who were carefully briefed 'to make good any misunderstandings that may have arisen during the course of the debate, i.e. to protect the BBC's interests if they seem to be at stake'.[45] In part this venture seems to have been intended to counter criticisms of BBC censorship. Gladstone Murray, Head of Public Relations, informed Controller of Programmes that 'Bertrand Russell expressed astonishment that there was really no rehearsal or censorship. He said he had fully expected to be closely examined about what he proposed to say. The fact that he had such a free hand considerably altered his opinion of the BBC.'[46] The Programme Committee also noted the goodwill that had been gained by the absence of censorship and welcomed a new method for dealing with controversial questions.

But the goodwill gained did not, presumably, extend to Harold Laski who had agreed to take part in a debate on Proportional Representation only to be informed that the idea had been dropped because Charles Siepmann, Director of Talks, was not sure whether the topic was suitable for the new experimental free debates.[47] In fact, as Laski realized, there had been other objections to his inclusion. The Controller of Programmes had suggested he was not qualified to talk on the subject but could be invited to debate on 'Academic Freedom'. But as Laski had often spoken on political subjects in the past, Siepmann was forced to adopt an argument in relation to the style of presentation. After a minor row, Reith eventually allowed him to debate the issue of the Second Chamber with Bob Boothby MP, and when this too was cancelled because of an imminent general election, Laski could only congratulate the BBC on a technique so delicate and ingenious that he thought it deserved its victory. Mary Adams, who produced the series, noted that although the absence of censorship was stressed to participants, it was clear that they considered their obligations seriously and were most restrained in language and ideas. This, she observed, was a general attitude to broadcasting and it was not without its problems. 'Speakers do in fact censor themselves before they begin to write for broadcasting and it is this moral censorship which in fact endangers the freedom of the microphone.'[48]

The shackles of scripted speech were lifted from the studio discussion in a 1937 Talks series, *Men Talking*, modelled on an American series *The Chicago Round Table*. Its producer, Roger Wilson, hoped that these unrehearsed and unscripted discussions would reveal the way people *felt* about subjects rather than a potted scientific analysis of the problem, and that listeners would recognize that here at least the BBC was departing from its general policy of passionless exposition of logical positions.[49] It was decided to opt for a regular team consisting of John Gloag and Sinclair Wood, both advertising agents, and James Whittaker, an unemployed working man and author, but in the end only Gloag was kept as a regular. He soon adopted the role of chairman and much was made of his 'nice sense of public relations'. Wilson noted how difficult it was for people talking naturally, even on 'safe' subjects like Football or Manners, to avoid references to dictatorships, Hitler, Stalin, capitalists, trade union demagogues, puritanical spoilsports, etc., but Gloag had the knack of always being able to carry off such references with a soothing one from the opposite point of view.[50] The Director of Talks, Sir Richard Maconachie, welcomed this series for 'speakers of the "man-in-the-street" type of intelligence'. He had recently attended conferences in Birmingham and Leeds at which the public had offered their comments on broadcasting and felt sure that that the 'naturalness and vigour' of treatment together with the choice of subjects 'of everyday interest' made them of very lively interest to the working-class listener.[51]

Speakers for this series were chosen more for their personality and communicative style than any specialized knowledge they might possess. One speaker was referred to as a '50-year-old journeyman bookbinder, who writes admirable short stories of Lancashire life. A robust Lancashire voice, pungent, fundamentally liberal but hard hitting about bogus or academic views of things.' Another was hailed as 'a young lawyer, self-consciously epigrammatic, who will be cynical about anything. A good broadcaster.'[52] But as a consequence, serious topics were ruled out of court. Maconachie turned down proposals from Wilson to discuss topics such as Russia or Isolationism because subjects of such importance required a different method of treatment. He was prepared to allow a discussion of the Means Test only because it had already received the 'full dress treatment' in a formal talk.[53] As a result expert speakers tended to be wary of taking part. Cyril Burt, the psychologist, explained to Wilson that, while he would try like the other speakers to give replies that were intelligible to the general audience, he had to bear in mind the possible reaction of colleagues only too willing to seize on and criticize loose, popular statements.

The usefulness of a chairman in such discussions had been a matter of internal, and sometimes arcane, debate within the BBC. It was acknowledged that the introduction of 'a third party' to mediate between speakers and listeners might prove helpful in guiding and controlling the discussion. In 1928 Hilda Matheson had wanted to include 'a "plain man" asking severely practical questions' in a discussion on science and philosophy.[54] A little later Roger Eckersley, then Director of Programmes, criticizing a discussion which had drifted and contained mutual interruptions, suggested that a third party might have been helpful 'not necessarily named as taking part in discussions but merely a voice, who would have controlled the discussion to the point of keeping speakers to their subjects – telling them, perhaps, not to speak at the same time – steering them off dangerous ground – acting in point of fact as an umpire but not taking part in the discussion itself.'[55] The interest of the Talks Department in the role of the third person had been aroused by an article in the *Berliner Tageblatt* on 'The Broadcast Tertius' which cited classical authority for such an addition to the dialogue. 'The old Romans, the well-known masters of intellectual battles of flowers, had a dictum, *Tres faciunt collegium*. Such a dictum must have an appeal to the unknown and distant listener.'[56]

From such considerations the broadcast interview gradually emerged. The role of the interviewer was at first thought of as the 'plain man' and mediator between expert and public. In 1933 R. A. Rendall of the Talks Department, advising the Director of the newly created Empire Service on the current range of broadcasting techniques, recommended the use of the plain man as 'a purely educational device'. 'The idea is to keep the expert on a low level so that he is intelligible to the inexpert listeners and also to add lightness and entertainment to a serious subject by adopting the dialogue form. The ordinary man must be chosen above all for his *ability as a broadcaster*.'[57]

The usefulness of such a mediator in controversial broadcasts was not established until later in the decade. Controversy had been dealt with largely through the symposium – a series of straight talks with a different speaker each week. This method was defended by Alan Dawnay, Controller of Programmes, in verbal evidence to the Ullswater Committee in 1935. 'It resulted of course that each talk in a controversial series, taking it in isolation, was in fact strongly biased and very often highly tendentious. This was because the BBC were seeking to provide the balance through the preceding or succeeding talk which put the opposite points with equal emphasis and equal freedom.'[58] Dawnay felt that the BBC would always attract criticism until the public became educated to the point of taking a controversial series as a whole and not in isolation, speech by speech.

The Ullswater Report commended the BBC's handling of controversy, but discussion about how best to present it continued within the Corporation. In 1938 Maconachie wrote a memorandum to Basil Nicolls, Controller of Programmes, on the Interlocutor Technique – a method which required an interviewer to interject critical questions throughout the talk in order to provide an immediate element of balance. Its use was justified in quite explicit terms:

> When I came here I was informed on the highest authority that 'balanced controversy' was regarded as the most important element in serious talks, and one which should be introduced to a greater extent in future. The problem then was to discover the best form in which such 'balanced controversy' could be presented to the public so as –

(a)   to allow the speaker the greatest possible freedom of speech
(b)   to forestall the tiresome charges of political bias, etc., to which our discussions of controversial subjects had too often given rise in the past.

Both these objects, in my opinion, have been achieved by the free use of the 'interlocutor technique', and cannot be achieved by any other method.[59]

On the same day that he received this memorandum, Nicolls wrote to the North Region Director to complain that an interlocutor in one of his programmes had not intervened enough. He was advised to ensure that 'the interlocutor acts as we expect an interlocutor to act, not merely asking questions but bringing out other points of view on controversial subjects'.[60]

The techniques of debate, discussion and interviewing were largely developed to enliven the talk of public persons and to introduce balance to controversy. The Talks Department was always more at home with public figures and men of letters. It was less successful than other departments in bringing ordinary men and women to the microphone, though not for want of trying. In 1929 Talks put on a scripted series called *My Day's Work*, in which working people described their routine. Their talks showed all the signs of literary embellishment at the hands of the producer. For instance, 'Bill', a docker, ended his talk as follows:

Arriving at Higham Bight in the early grey of the morning I have looked at the Hulks and across the Essex shore – where stretches that strange, level country which seemed so much to fascinate Charles Dickens – and fancied in the rising mists the faces of hunted convicts and Joe Gargery and Pip and remembered that it was somewhere in this reach of the river that David Copperfield said adieu to his Mrs Peggotty and Mrs Gummidge, where little Em'ly waved her last farewell ... etc.[61]

At some point the absurdity of these talks must have come home to its producer(s), for the series ended with a spoof piece from 'a burglar' who retired to bed with Spinoza after his night on the tiles.

The difficulties of the Talks Department with working-class speakers was highlighted by the William Ferrie incident in 1934 and again by the 1937 series, *Men Talking*. The series, designed at first for the unemployed, gave rise to objections from its audience. A listening group in Morecambe, for instance, complained that, in a discussion on education, all the speakers appeared to belong to the same minority group and evidently did not have children in state schools. The producer admitted that 'this question of working classes is very difficult indeed. We know very few broadcasters who would fulfil the role without sounding like *In Town Tonight* or the *Punch* idea of the workingman.'[62] He informed Maconachie that Gloag, the regular chairman, 'was

171

astonished when I told him about the storm of protest about the middle-class atmosphere of the discussion. At first he was suspicious that this was due to what he called "the inverted snobbery of left-wing intellectuals", but I ... persuaded him that there was much more to it than this and that we must in the next few talks at any rate, have an unlettered voice.'[63] The BBC's Leeds Education Officer reported that the next broadcast did appear to have 'the common touch' which the previous one had so lamentably lacked, but some of the regular contributors now began to complain that the quality of the conversation was suffering as a result.[64] Luker found himself wondering whether for once, as an experiment, 'to let all this about the common touch go hang and just have three good talkers in the studio'.[65] But it was acknowledged as patently absurd to have 'men with "thousand-a-year voices" discussing the details of a family budget', though the problem remained that there were few working-class speakers who could live up to the standard of conversation set by the middle-class regulars. One exception was an unemployed miner and county councillor who was, according to Gloag, the chairman, a 'splendid character' who provided listeners with a 'valuable illustration of the way people can live their lives in economic adversity'.[66]

In the late thirties there was a new emphasis on public participation in broadcasting, though it was manifest more in the activities of the Variety Department and the Regions than in London Talks. One aspect of this trend was the series *Everyman and the Crisis* which Talks put on in the immediate aftermath of Munich to show the impact of the crisis upon individuals, especially those for whom it posed some kind of moral dilemma. 'A young man who didn't know whether he ought to honour the Peace Pledge; an unemployed man for whom war would mean work; even a lady with ample pets who didn't know whether to destroy them or not' – this was the sort of thing the producer, Christopher Salmon, had in mind.[67] From such unpromising material a remarkable set of documents was produced. The talks were delivered anonymously in groups of three, with a five-second interval between each one and a minimal introduction. According to Salmon this austere method of presentation helped make the talks seem unusually sincere and spontaneous. They were published in *The Listener* and reveal an interesting and varied range of responses, including one particularly dignified and moving contribution from a German woman married to an Englishman.

If this series did little to inform the general public of the causes of the crisis, it pointed to the revaluation of the point of view of Everyman and its inclusion in the programmes. This process had clearly reached canonical status when *Radio Times*, on 24 March 1939, carried a supplement on The Man in the Street. One article pointed out that the common man was a veteran broadcaster but that his 'communal voice has been essentially a background voice'. He had been heard as an incidental sound effect in countless outside broadcasts. At church services, for instance, he was to be heard coughing and shuffling his feet as he settled in his pew, and his loyal cheers had been heard at times of public festivity. But, the article went on, there had gradually developed 'the notion that the Man-in-the-Street makes an excellent foreground broadcaster'. *In Town Tonight* was mentioned, and the North Region features of D. G. Bridson and Olive Shapley. The most recent development hailed by the article was the occasional use of vox pops (impromptu street interviews) on topical issues – during the Munich Crisis for instance – on *In Town Tonight*. Hitherto the Man-in-the-Street 'was always selected beforehand and rehearsed. Probably he spoke from a script. Impromptu broadcasts are only the very latest development in his entertainment value.'

Entertainment value had never been a high priority in the Talks Department, but it was by now recognized that the audience for talks was stratified, and accepted that some listeners had a low tolerance for demanding, difficult fare. A departmental memorandum on Talks Standards, written by Norman Luker in 1938, divided listeners into three groups. Group A were 'intelligent and well-informed', and therefore needed to be catered for only occasionally. Group B were 'the intelligent and not so well-informed' whom Luker identified as the most important target for Talks. Briefly discussing the characteristics of this group Luker pointed to the increase in secondary, adult and university education, the huge sales of Pelican and Left Book Club publications devoted to serious issues, and the success of the newly established *Picture Post*. All this indicated that there was now a 'considerable serious-minded public anxious for mental pabulum which we are well placed to give them'. Group C, the largest part of the potential audience, included the 'not-so-intelligent and mostly uninformed' who, because of their extreme simplicity would only listen to 'adventure' or 'personality' talks. They were well served by *In Town Tonight*, though Talks should continue to educate unobtrusively through the personality of men like John Hilton. Finally, Luker noted, it should not be supposed that this stratification split along straight class lines: group C might contain customers from Harrods and group B, artisans and farm labourers.[68]

The techniques for enlivening talk by public speakers and for balancing controversy could also be applied to lighter purposes and by other departments. In 1931 Hilda Matheson had launched a series called *Conversations in the Train*. The plan was that the conversation, with suitable sound effects, should seem to arise out of casual encounters in a train and its content could be topical, general or of purely entertainment value. Instead of approaching authoritative speakers, Matheson went for literary figures such as Roger Fry, Aldous Huxley, E. M. Forster and Dorothy L. Sayers in the hope that they could both write and perform witty, occasional dialogue. But it soon became clear that writers of amusing dialogue did not necessarily make good performers, so actors were employed in their place and the programmes were produced in cooperation with the Drama and Features Department. The conversations ran, off and on, from 1932 to 1938 and within a couple of years it was claimed, in the Talks Department, that they vied with *Music Hall* on the alternative programme and made the Variety Department nervous at their competing entertainment value. By the late thirties the hybrid form of the series was creating administrative problems and it passed into the hands of Felix Felton of the Drama Department who promised that in their hands the series would deal with private and human problems rather than such cosmic topics as Fixed Easter or the Metric System. He planned to start with a conversation on Dogs.[69]

By 1936 Talks had become interested in broadcasting 'Slices of Life'. Paul Bloomfield, fresh from 'St Beadles' – the BBC's new staff training school run jointly by Gerald Beadle and Archie Harding – was informed by an official that the BBC was looking for someone with journalistic experience to handle these talks: 'We want a man – someone upstanding and dignified, a gentleman by all means – but the sort of person who can go into the public bar without the conversation drying up as soon as he goes in.' Bloomfield obliged by finding a saddler called Luddock, with something of a reputation in poetry. He seemed to fit the bill, but Bloomfield felt that he was too much of a local celebrity and that a true 'Slice of Life' should involve 'someone who enjoyed no fame or notoriety or even any particular local reputation. Then what should we have? Simply character, I suppose. Plenitude of life.' He approached a friend, a 'Wodehouse character' and a good conversationalist who simply offered random observations on life under the heading of *A Good Grouse*. This got good notices in the press, but aroused anxieties in Talks about the level at which it was pitched. When Bloomfield proposed more talks on the same lines to his departmental head, Sir Richard Maconachie, the following exchange took place:

> 'The idea is, sir, to express the common life, without ... as it were ... any ulterior motive ..., the common life, even perhaps low life ...'
> 'Not *too* low life,' said the Director of Talks; and that was all he did say.

Bloomfield himself was suspicious of the motives behind such talks. He felt that 'realistic broadcasts of the "Slices of Life" nature tend to involve one in making people make an exhibition of themselves more than the results justify'.[70] One of the few regular working-class speakers used by Talks to provide a slice of life was the London taxi driver, Herbert Hodge. He too was dubious about the ways in which the common life was expressed in London talks and pointedly suggested, in a letter to his producer, that the BBC might consider a series treating working-class life as *natural* – instead of just quaint. Battersea Bridge Road is being repaired and as I write, everybody's dashing out with baths and boxes and perambulators to get wood blocks for their winter fires. There's nothing extraordinary about it. It's the thing to do. But the middle-class commentator either denounces it as a crime; or weeps over the wrongs of the noble proletariat compelled to get their firing in this way; or treats it as a quaint custom of the Battersea aborigines ...[71]

The influence of entertainment values on talk is most clearly seen in the rise of the magazine programme whose embryonic form goes back to *In Town Tonight*, one of the handful of radio shows from before the war that people over fifty might still remember. It started in 1933 and ran until the mid-fifties. The show was devised by Eric Maschwitz, Head of Variety, as a shop window for any topical items that might bob up too late to be included in *Radio Times* each week.[72] It was, from the start, intended to appeal to human interest, presenting a mix of items that reflected 'the simple, fascinating things that humble folk do, and the high points achieved by men and women of distinction'.[73] This kind of contrast – the marquess and the chimney-sweep; the hawker, the sewer-man and the fruitseller counterposed to the film star and famous author – was deliberately aimed at. The magazine as a literal format for a radio programme was first adopted by a North Region series called *Owt Abaht Owt* that started in 1934. Each series of the programme was a 'volume' and each programme a 'number', complete with 'cover illustration' by the Northern Studio Orchestra and a table of contents to introduce it. *At the Black Dog*, which began in 1937 with a pub setting and genial host, could perhaps be called the first British chat show. Meanwhile the Talks Department had started its own magazine, *The World Goes By*, presented by Freddy Grisewood, one of a new breed of professional all-rounders, whose personality soon became intrinsic to the programme.

All these programmes emphasized that human interest approach which BBC News was at such pains to avoid. *In Town Tonight* discovered Mrs Wheelabread, the Chocolate Lady of Kensington Gardens; Mrs Nelson, the female chimney-sweep and the cat's meat man with his strange street cry. It was open to the advances of publicity-seekers like Jack Morgan, the Boy with Big Ears, whose earlier exploits included wangling an invitation to 10 Downing Street from the Prime Minister's daughter on the grounds that he was 'puzzled about political happenings in the last few years'.[74] North Region's more folksy *Owt Abaht Owt* might offer a table of contents containing 'an aerial flood-shooter, a harmonizing boy's club, a well-known Northern itinerant bagger of gags, an inveterate drummer, a master of mistletoe and a pantomime star'.[75] Even *The World Goes By*, which was staid compared with *In Town Tonight*, used 'Gipsy Petulengro' as a regular contributor.[76]

The BBC was a middle-class institution, and it sounded like one – especially in London. Its institutional voice, expressed through its announcers, was often aloof and supercilious. The announcers were on the one hand the voice of the BBC, and on the other an essential link with the public. As symbols of the institution they were anonymous voices whose speech and pronunciation were trained and vetted to be formal, correct and unvarying. But as links with the public their voices needed qualities that were attractive to listening ears. Their role was defined by the Announcements Editor in a quite mystical fashion:

> The BBC is one corporation and can only be thought of by the listener as individual. It has many voices but one mouth. It can speak in many styles, but the variety is due to the difference in subject matter and must not betray any inconsistency of treatment. It is common place that 'announcers sound alike'. That is a tribute to their training.[77]

The selection and training of announcers was partly the responsibility of Professor Arthur Lloyd-James, secretary to the BBC Advisory Committee of Spoken English. It was thought that the influence of broadcasting together with compulsory education for all would lead to standardized speech. It was therefore the task of the BBC to define that standard and Lloyd-James, a phonetician, was asked to advise. The norm set by Lloyd-James was never referred to as middle-class English but as 'educated English'. It was expected to conform to literate standards of syntax and vocabulary. The BBC spoken voice should avoid what Lloyd-James called 'extreme variants', whether they were the broad open vowels of the regions, the closed, over-refined voices of the South or, above all, the affected drawl of public school or Oxford English.[78] The golden mean was an educated, but classless voice that all might find acceptable and none offensive.

The search for the acceptable mean was the thread running through the efforts of the Talks Department to find ways of distinguishing serious and popular styles of talk via impersonal and personal forms of address; techniques for managing controversy and for escaping the limitations of the straight lecture-talk; and methods of presenting ordinary people, their experience and points of view. The common purpose of these developments was to find ways of communicating with a new, unknown audience which took account of the person and status of the speakers, the form and substance of their talk and the circumstances in which it was heard. In addressing such issues the broadcasters were breaking quite new ground as they tried to overcome the limitations of existing practices of public speech and rhetoric. The long-term trend, on radio and television, has been to shift the relationship between communicators and audiences away from distanced, authoritarian patterns

POPULAR MISCONCEPTIONS—A LONDON ANNOUNCER

towards more relaxed, informal and interactive styles of communication. This trend, spread over sixty years, has been the expressive register of the erosion of social deference and of more equal styles of social interaction between people in public and private.

This change in the communicative ethos has been broadcasting's fundamental contribution to the quality of social relations in modern society. In the pre-war period class boundaries were still strongly marked out by subtle and precise indicators of status and position. Voice, dress, tastes and lifestyle were much clearer markers of social class then than now. The BBC, of course, in manifold ways expressed itself as a middle-class institution, but it had to inform, educate and entertain an audience drawn from all classes. To that extent it had to find ways of presenting programmes in accessible ways that might, in principle, appeal to all. This realization was not simply or easily achieved, and provoked considerable internal opposition from those who felt that to court popular tastes and large audiences was to compromise the cultural mission of the BBC and devalue its standards. The search for accessible styles and the struggle over cultural values intensified in the later thirties as a number of factors combined to show the BBC policy-makers that their audience could not just simply be presumed and taken for granted. The unknown audience needed to be known and understood in order to provide it with programmes that satisfied its interests, tastes and wants.

In the period between 1927 and 1935 the most significant developments in programme and policy-making took place in London, and in those areas of programming that dealt with contemporary life and affairs. But thereafter, shorn of the possibility of dealing in any effective way with anything remotely controversial, talks and features production languished. The major focus of interest was now in squaring the circle of differences between the claims of the Music Department and the Variety Department in relation to a clearly perceived need to entertain the listening public while maintaining a commitment to its cultural improvement. It was here that the endeavour to establish a common culture of broadcasting was tried and tested.

Part III

THE PRODUCTION OF ENTERTAINMENT AND CULTURE: MUSIC AND VARIETY

CHAPTER NINE

Music Policy

———⇒❋⇐———

IN MOST other areas of programming, broadcasting, when it started up, found itself up against powerful and well-established business or political interests, but with music it was the other way round. The BBC very soon found itself to be the most powerful single operator in the field and all those who, one way or another, made a living from music were compelled to negotiate with what they saw as 'the broadcasting juggernaut'. When the BBC began regular transmissions, music – with certain exceptions such as music hall – showed little sign of consolidation into unified markets for commercial exploitation. It was not easy to draw a clear distinction between amateurs and professionals in music. It is true that those who made a living from music had, since the late nineteenth century, been forced gradually to combine to protect their interests, but the unionization of professional musicians and the formation of protective cartels and associations increased sharply after the arrival of broadcasting.[1]

By the mid-thirties the BBC was easily the largest single employer of professional musicians and the most powerful patron of music in the country. The Performing Rights Society collected 39 per cent of its total annual revenue from the BBC in 1935; by the end of the decade this was up to 54 per cent. The power of the BBC's purse in the music market was enormous and before the war it, and not the music publishers, unions or other agencies representing the interests of conductors, composers and performers, was usually in a position to fix the price and terms of the job. For it was radio, not the gramophone business, which first consolidated the field of music, and in so doing profoundly disturbed the existing social and economic networks of music-making. Before broadcasting, music did not exist as a unifed cultural field. It was scarcely meaningful to speak of music in general. What existed were particular musics – the choral societies, brass and military bands with their competitions and festivals; the concert publics, elite and popular, in London and the major provincial cities and resorts; the background music performed in cafés, restaurants and cinemas; music hall and the emerging musical shows and revues; the vogue for opera and operetta, the beginnings of the dance music craze. These musics were profusely, though unevenly, distributed throughout the country. The metropolis did not dominate the provinces. Indeed, it could be claimed, as Elgar did, that the living centre of music in Great Britain was not London, 'but somewhere further North'.[2]

Radio uprooted all these musics from their particular social and economic settings and brought them together in a strange new abstract unity. Because the nature of the medium did not favour one kind of music at the expense of another,[3] and because its social direction was towards the whole community, the BBC rapidly found itself undertaking the presentation of *all* forms of music that had any appreciable audience (and some that had none) side by side in a single channel. Thus broadcasting universalized music as a socio-cultural category in a quite unprecedented manner. For the broadcasters this became a highly complex administrative task as they found themselves respon-sible, in effect, for the standardization, classification and evaluation of the whole field of music.

But what was broadcast music? In administrative terms it did not include the music of the dance bands, cinema organ, operetta and musical reviews, all of which was relayed live from outside venues. Responsibility for all this was in the hands of Gerald Cock, in charge of Outside Broadcasts, until 1933. In that year the Variety Department was created and it took charge of such music. The Music Department, under Percy Pitt until 1930 and Adrian Boult from then on, was responsible for symphonies, chamber music, opera and con-temporary 'modern' music. It also administered, but with little enthusiasm, the ambiguous intermediate category of 'light music'.

From the start there was an internal departmental division between 'serious' and 'popular' music. But in either case the essential bureaucratic principle remained the same: define a standard of quality and then establish the means of enforcing it. This entailed the rationalization of criteria by which decisions were taken as to what kinds of music to broadcast, in what quantity, on what channels, at what times and for whom. Though policy for popular and serious music developed separately, the kinds of issue at stake – the poli-tics of culture – were of the same general kind.

In the earliest issues of *Radio Times* the BBC proudly featured its first top-rate dance band to perform regularly on radio – the Savoy Orpheans, led by Debroy Somers. Syncopated music was here to stay and the Savoy

Orpheans, twelve in all, most of them American, would perfectly express the modern style of dancing as well as being much easier to dance to.[4] Soon the BBC's mail-bags were full of letters asking for more, and early in 1924 *Radio Times* announced plans for broadcasts of dance music three times a week.[5] Within a year there was the promise of dance music every night except Sunday. The post-war craze for dancing coincided almost exactly with the arrival of broadcasting. 1923, the first full year of regular BBC programmes, was also the year of the Jog Trot, the Missouri Walk, the Elfreda and, most popular of all, the Shimmy. These were quickly followed by the Charleston and the Black Bottom, with *Radio Times* helpfully providing photographic illustrations as to how to perform the latter.

For the rest of the inter-war period popular music was to be defined by the BBC very largely in terms of dance music. By the mid-thirties, though, the meaning of the term had begun to shift, posing new problems of policy and requiring a closer attention to the divisions within popular music and the ways in which it was enjoyed by audiences. At first it simply meant music supplied by bands for dancing to, and listeners were invited to roll up the carpet at home and take their partners. Loosely speaking it was regarded as the same as jazz, and it polarized contemporary opinion. Opponents saw 'negroid' or 'nigger' music as a sign of moral degeneracy and cultural barbarism. Its devotees regarded it as new and invigorating. The pros and cons were vigorously debated in the early twenties. A *Radio Times* article, 'In Defence of Jazz', claimed that it was not a transient fad but an authentic expression of the spirit of the age. It predicted that in two centuries, time learned professors of music would quote *Alexander's Ragtime Band* alongside the folk tunes of the Middle Ages as examples of important contributions towards music's development.[6] But learned professors of the present day thought otherwise, and there was a famous radio debate in 1926 when Jack Hylton and Sir Landon Ronald clashed on the respective merits of jazz and classical music.[7]

If the beginnings of the dance band era in Britain can be pinpointed by the visit, in 1919, of the Original Dixieland Jazz Band to the Hammersmith Palais (itself the first custom-built dance hall in the country), it is not easy thereafter to trace developments. There were significant variations in taste in different parts of the country, as Henry Hall discovered in his travels up and down the land to the various LMS hotels and their resident bands for whose music, as Musical Director of the whole chain, he was responsible. Manchester and Glasgow were well up to date, whereas Edinburgh and Liverpool tended to be rather more conservative and selective. Turnberry was about two months behind, but Gleneagles, with a large number of American visitors for the pleasures of its famous golf courses, was 'absolutely up to the minute for the very latest numbers'.[8]

Hall's continual chase to be as up-to-date as possible points to the accelerating pace of the popular music business in the twenties. New companies sprang up in Charing Cross Road alongside the older well-established firms to cash in on an expanding market.[9] A BBC checklist of one week's output in 1937 listed twenty-seven different British sheet publishers whose current numbers had been played that week.[10] If previously the creation of a hit tune or song had taken months rather than days, radio, with its insatiable appetite for new material, drastically reduced the turn-over time for hit numbers, so stimulating demand for an unending supply of more and more new tunes. 'Today', lamented William Boosey on behalf of music publishers, 'things are broadcast on Monday, popular on Tuesday. Wednesday they do not know how many to print. By Friday the thing is finished and on Monday they have to find something else to print.'[11] By making dance music continuously available to the general listening public the BBC had unintentionally created a mass market ripe for exploitation, and BBC officials found themselves increasingly drawn into a continuous kind of guerilla warfare with the sheet music publishers and the dance band leaders over the control of the means whereby the supply of popular music on radio was maintained.

The very first issue of *Radio Times* contained a full-page spread for the latest lyric of the sheet music publishers, Aschberg, Hopwood and Crew Ltd:

> The Bridge of Dreams I built for you
> Is made of memories dear.
> The Bridge of Dreams is love come true,
> It brings you always near,
> And so when I am far away
> And silver moonlight gleams,
> I come to you in memory
> Across the Bridge of Dreams.

The *Bridge of Dreams*, the advertisement claimed, would be played on every BBC station that week.[12] Two weeks later another big advertisement from the same firm listed its current catalogue of vocal fox-trots, ballads, waltz songs and fox-trots for piano, urging all readers to ask their local station to broadcast these 'winners'.[13]

Plugging goes back well before broadcasting. Since the last century the publishers had included in the price of their song-sheets a costing for publicity via hired singers, concert promotions, newspaper advertisements and strings of travelling salesmen throughout the country. By the 1920s some firms were spending up to £1000 a week in the summer months plugging their current lists through the dance and concert halls in all the major seaside resorts. They were quick to latch on to the new media. One publisher spent £4000 promoting a tune that netted just over £1000. This included sending lantern slides and words of the song to every cinema in the country, with a free issue of band parts.[14] The exploitation of the first ever issue of *Radio Times* shows just how quick the merchants of Charing Cross Road were to grasp the new opportunities that radio offered. After the first few issues though, there were no more advertisements of this kind (perhaps Reith or some other official intervened), and the attention of the publishers switched from the audience towards the band leaders whom radio was turning into household names.

It was after all far more effective directly to target the source of the music, and soon the practice grew of backhanders to the bandleaders to include a particular number in their nightly broadcasts. Vocal numbers were assiduously pushed since the title was invariably a repeated refrain and hence was a great deal easier for listeners to remember than the names of instrumental numbers. The practice came to the notice of the officials in the late twenties and stern efforts were made to stop it. In 1929 the BBC not only banned vocal numbers in the bands' broadcast programmes, but tried to remove the announcing microphone from the band leaders. 'That', said Gerald Cock, 'will prevent them from telling the public what numbers they have played or are about to play.' And if anyone tried to shout out the names of the numbers, he added, they could be faded out.[15] This pleased no one, least of all the listeners, and within a few months the bandleaders were back at the microphone and vocals were back in the programmes.

It was not until the mid-thirties that sustained attention was given to the administrative problems created by dance music. In a long memorandum on the 'Dance Music Situation', Eric Maschwitz declared that the whole issue had been shirked for the last ten years. Gerald Cock, in charge of Outside Broadcasts, had done a grand job in tackling the plugging situation, but the main problem was that, until recently, there had been no one with a firm and clear responsibility for dance music, Now that all dance music had been brought under the control of his recently established Variety Department the moment had come to be revolutionary, It was time to clean out the stable for the old racket of plugging had given way to a new one – orchestrations.[16]

Whether this *was* a racket very much depended on your point of view. By the mid-thirties the bands heard regularly on radio had become used to having special arrangements of the popular tunes of the day made to suit their particular style, sound and mix of instruments. This required expert musicianship and an intimate knowledge of the band for whom the arrangement was to be made.[17] It was thus a highly specialized field, with a small number of arrangers, most of whom had been bandsmen before switching to this for a living, working in close association with particular bands. It was probably true to say that the arranger had as much to do with the success of a new number as the composer of the original tune. It was also an expensive business. The standard fee for an arrangement was eight guineas, and a band usually got through

"FOR WE'RE TOUGH, MIGHTY TOUGH, IN THE WEST."

eighteen numbers in a sixty-minute broadcast.[18] When Henry Hall left the BBC in 1937 it was agreed that he could take the entire library of arrangements made for the BBC Dance Orchestra under his leadership on the understanding that the BBC could borrow from it, free of charge, at any time. Hall thus acquired around 5000 orchestrations worth over £40,000.[19]

The quality of these special arrangements was not at issue. The question was who should pay for them. The publishers were disgruntled because they, for the most part, bore the burden of the costs. In the United States, the music publishers had got together and agreed to provide no more special arrangements, and the leading bands had either to play from standard arrangements or else pay for their own orchestrations.[20] The British publishers also wanted to transfer the cost of arrangements to the bandleaders, but their position was not strong. A bandleader might boycott a firm that failed to deliver the goods, and play only the numbers of those that continued to supply the arrangements.

So the publishers formed an association, the Society of Popular Music Publishers, as their American brethren had done, to deal with the bands and negotiate with the BBC. The task of dealing with the publishers was passed round inside the Corporation and landed in the lap of the BBC's Business Manager, Jardine Brown. When the bands heard what was afoot, they formed the Bandleaders' Federation to defend their interests. They took the view that the BBC should pay for the arrangements – a view which the BBC was reluctant to accept since it would increase considerably the cost per hour of dance music on radio. Negotiations started cagily, with Jardine Brown having separate meetings with the bandleaders and publishers. He was not helped, he complained, by the confusing and contradictory statements made from time to time by Maschwitz who appeared to be withdrawing from his original position of wanting to eliminate most of the free arrangements paid for by the publishers and to charge the cost of the rest to the Variety Department.[21]

Things began in a muddle and, though meeting after meeting took place in the next three years, the muddle remained. A tentative agreement between the BBC and the publishers early in 1937 to ban orchestrations was neatly sidestepped by the bandleaders who reverted to playing only those old numbers for which they already had arrangements. To stop that the BBC insisted that 80 per cent of their programmes should consist of current numbers.[22] But the publishers found it hard to hold ranks. The market was fiercely competitive and the agreement to ban arrangements favoured the older, established firms but not the newer and smaller fry. Chappells, one of the oldest firms in the business, had opposed the agreement from the beginning, which was never signed, and little by little and one by one the others crept from grace, so that by the end of 1938 things were as bad as they had ever been.

By now the publishers were pressing the BBC to impose some form of proportional representation, according to the size of their current catalogue, on the music played in the dance band programmes. This prompted the BBC to consider that perhaps the only solution was to take charge of planning the programmes itself instead of leaving it, as was the custom to date, in the hands of the bandleaders. But would those appointed to this task prove to be beyond corruption, for they would most certainly be offered bribes by the trade? It was felt, on reflection, that there was little to fear on that score. Other staff members – the booking officials, for instance – were open to the same temptations and had, so far, remained above suspicion. The real problems were not moral but financial. To police the dance band programmes properly would need an extra three staff members at a cost of about £1500 a year. And even if they could clean up the programmes it was likely that the pluggers would simply turn their attentions elsewhere – to variety turns and light orchestral combinations, or to the regions. And to plug those leaks would call for yet more staff. There was, moreover, the certainty that the star band leaders, like Ambrose, would not take kindly to the idea.[23]

Ultimately it had to be asked, was this necessary? Was it worth it? It was decided that it was not. The bandleaders were now asked to submit in advance details of all the numbers they intended to play during their radio sessions, and these would be carefully vetted with a very firm insistence on a balanced bill of fare. In the end, as far as the BBC was concerned, the only important question was the quality of the programmes themselves. By the end of 1939 John Watt, the new Head of Variety, was convinced that everything was all right on that score. He had come to the conclusion that the BBC, having manfully tried and failed over the years to control plugging and associated evils by one means or another, might as well now be realistic. The whole business was slightly immoral but the Corporation might as well wink at it, since the programmes themselves – the only object of concern – were quite satisfactory.[24]

An immense amount of time and paper had been consumed by these issues, but there were other problems to tax the administrative mind. Styles of performance were changing in the thirties, and crooning was a case in point. This had been popularized in the United States by Rudee Vallee and the phenomenal success of Bing Crosby. It was a new style of singing that took advantage of the characteristics of the microphone. The older style of 'legitimate' singing had been developed for the public concert platform. The voice was trained to project to the back of the hall – good delivery, a strong voice and a stout pair of lungs were essential requirements. Legitimate singers always stood a yard or so from the microphone to avoid blasting either that instrument or the listener's eardrums. Crooning was the reverse of this. It was an intimate style, close to the microphone, with the singer whispering rather than bellowing. Those like Maurice Elwin, 'the wizard of the microphone' according to *Radio Pictorial*, who changed to the new style soon discovered that a wealth of vocal expression was at their command while singing at half volume.[25] Al Bowlly, the guitarist in Lew Stone's band and the only British singer of the time to rival the popularity of the Americans, defined the art in terms of the new range of emotions – a smile, a sigh, a frown, a laugh – which crooning allowed the invisible singer to express.[26]

Though the vogue for this kind of singing had reached Britain in the early thirties it did not come to the notice of policy-makers in Broadcasting House until late 1935. Early next year Cecil Graves was insisting to Roger Eckersley and Eric Maschwitz that this 'particularly odious form of singing' must be obliterated right away. But alas, like plugging and orchestrations, it could not be done. The Variety Department played for time and tried tactfully to persuade Graves to change his mind. Lindsay Wellington sought the views of the Music Department, but they batted that one straight back, asking whether anyone had attempted to define crooning. Definition was to prove elusive. At a Programme Board in December 1936 it was agreed that it was hard to find a suitable definition either for crooning itself or for the particular kind of crooning that was thought to be objectionable. It depended so much on the words themselves, how they were sung and the artistry of the performer. Graves wanted to insist that a BBC official should always be present at the final rehearsal of light music combinations with a singer – particularly those with a tendency to improvise their programme at the last minute. But no one wanted to undertake such a hapless task.[27]

Policy, as we have so far considered it, was largely negative. It was mostly to do with stopping graft, as the BBC saw it, in the business. But the question of crooning raised issues of taste and standards, and the attention of the BBC administrators began to turn to attempting to sort out a policy for popular music as a whole and towards greater care in its presentation. Lindsay Wellington, Director of Programme Planning, was arguing in 1937 that it seemed increasingly necessary for the BBC to take strict control of all dance music programmmes.[28] Such control should be guided by aesthetic not administrative criteria, by the BBC's conception of what did or did not make a good programme. But before that, everything that so far had been lumped together as dance music needed more careful classification. This task was now feasible, since the recent inclusion of swing music in the National Programme permitted at last the organization and classification of the whole field of popular music.

Swing music had come to the attention of the policy-makers in London by a curiously indirect route.[29] In 1936 Scottish Regional was running a programme called *Facets of Syncopation*. Its producer, Moultrie Kelsall, was rather proud of it and made the mistake of offering it to London for simultaneous transmission in the National Programme. Graves, the Controller of

DELICIOUS INTERLUDE

Sister Ann (as their favourite crooner comes on the air). " QUICK, CAROLINE— ' SHOE SHINE BOY ' ! "

Programmes, rather baulked at the idea of Aberdeen as the home of syncopation but considered taking it if 'by some curious freak Aberdeen could offer programmes of this kind better than we can contrive here.' Enquiries were made and it turned out that the Regions were already, in a sporadic way, presenting a good deal of swing music while London had not yet formulated a policy on the matter.

Policy was duly formulated. It was decided that swing music 'recitals' were very specialized things, and that it was probably best to confine them to transmissions from London to the Regions, who should be discouraged from producing such programmes. Swing music was declared to be a minority taste, with a specialized appeal mainly to the connoisseur of dance music. As such it should be given a rather different status to ordinary dance music, with the aim of inculcating a standard of taste and an appreciation of quality in jazz music. Someone suggested it should be broadcast only between half past ten and midnight, since to give caviar to the general would only antagonize the majority audience. But it was resolved to introduce swing music to an ever-widening circle of listeners, and the BBC's 'first big excursion into live Swing Music' was scheduled for 8.20 in the evening in March 1937.

The rhythm must have got through to the Announcer who introduced one of these programmes as 'a jam session'. 'A jam session!', exploded Graves, 'What on earth that means I don't know. Is it a new Americanism, or is it some bright(?) idea on somebody's part? In any event this kind of title is quite meaningless. We must introduce some sort of central supervision to prevent this sort of thing.'[30] The Variety Department, which had produced the programme, had its knuckles rapped, and Harman Grisewood, the resident expert on the subject, was asked to write carefully prepared opening announcements, which would put the bands and their music in 'the right perspective'. They were to be given the same kind of presentation as chamber music. They were to interest, not to entertain.

As for poor Moultrie Kelsall in Aberdeen, who had unwittingly roused the slumbering administrative beast, when his programme was eventually heard on the Blattnerphone in London it was judged to be so weak and amateurish that he was ordered to take it off. Roger Eckersley, now Director of Regional Relations, came to its defence, praising the programme and forcefully arguing that local syncopated features were as indigenous as local cinema organs, café music and other such items. The programme was very popular round Aberdeen and it would be a shame to deprive Scottish listeners of something they enjoyed. Graves reluctantly agreed to let it die a natural death rather than kill it off immediately, but he still felt that Aberdeen would be better advised to encourage a local choral society rather than to put its money into a jazz combination.

This saga exhibits the fate of culture when it submits to the spirit of bureaucracy. In particular it shows how a popular form of pleasure is transformed and renominated as a superior pleasure for the cognoscenti. Swing becomes the most legitimate form of dance music, permitting the classification of all music of this kind in relation to the new standard of taste it sets for the genre. After six months of broadcast swing music in the National Programme, Harman Grisewood concluded that 'the importance of Swing to us has been to mark the beginning of serious attention to dance music and an intention to continue improving it within the frame of a declared dance policy ... The purposes we had in mind when we embarked on this Swing venture can best be fulfilled by exercising an enlightened discrimination over the whole field of dance music.'[31] To this end he recommended that the weekly output of dance music should be considered as a whole, and analysed in a way that distinguished between different styles of programme, their audiences and their times of transmission.

This was the task undertaken by Lindsay Wellington, after detailed discussion with Maschwitz and Watt as well as Grisewood.[32] At that time there was about fifteen hours a week of dance music on the National Programme. Wellington proposed dividing it up under three headings: music for dancing, music for entertainment and music for the connoisseur. Music for dancing should continue to be relayed from the London hotels six times a week in the late evening, but there should be little of such music in the daytime or in the main evening schedules. The main evening periods should be filled with four entertainment programmes a week. There should be one connoisseur programme during that time and one during the day each week. The OB relays from the hotels were for dancing only and the bands must play in strict dance tempo without vocal refrains of any sort. For the much larger public that liked dance music just as entertainment the main evening programmes would introduce special methods of presentation and would include popular songs of all kinds. There would be no restrictions – except in terms of quality – on the number of 'vocal refrains', or on any other way of getting the programmes across successfully. As for the connoisseur programmes, these would consist largely of records or relays from America of the musically interesting forms of jazz. Arrangements were being made with the record companies in New York and their English agents for the latest and best recordings of such music to be shipped over to Broadcasting House.

The aim of these proposals was to please the public, to placate the publishers and to put the bandleaders in their place. By introducing a clear distinction between music for dancing and music for entertainment, by defining presentational rules for both to sustain the difference, Wellington undercut the freedom of the bandleaders to organize their own programmes. The repositioning of vocal numbers, their transfer from dance to entertainment slots, was a neat administrative solution to the problems of plugging.

It further acknowledged the rising popularity of songs in their own right, not as incidental material to pep up the programmes of the dance bands.[33] The new arrangements proposed by Wellington included a daytime novelty feature programme consisting entirely of popular songs 'sung as songs and not as dance music', It was recognized that the products of Charing Cross Road were the modern equivalent of the ballads of Victorian and Edwardian days. 'The errand boy', said Wellington, 'has exchanged *Roses of Picardy* for *Little Man You've Had a Busy Day.*' It was hoped that the new daytime 'showcase' programmes for the popular songs of the day would destroy the taste for indifferent singing and casual presentation of this kind of song. They would be presented and sung in the best possible way, with quintet or piano accompaniment but definitely not with dance band backing.

In these accounts of the emergence of a policy for dance music it is noticeable that the planners and policy-makers were unchallenged and untroubled about their ability to make decisions on what was good or bad. Popular music had no priestly advocates to defend its value and integrity, and in such circumstances the educated layman's opinion was, perhaps, as good as anyone else's. But in the case of serious music there emerged, in the course of a decade, a widening gulf between the views of the administrators and of the Music Department about the aims and purposes of broadcast music.

Under Adrian Boult, Music was the largest programme department in the BBC with a staff of fifty-four by 1937.[34] Boult himself combined two jobs after 1931 as head of department and, at Reith's personal invitation, permanent conductor of the Symphony Orchestra. This almost impossible task would have been quite impossible without the loyal support of a nucleus of staff upon whom Boult devolved responsibility for arranging the musical activities and output of the department. Boult's first love was the magnificent orchestra whose reputation he both established and nurtured. Rehearsing and performing with it took up most of his time and though, as Kenyon notes, he was always available for consultation when necessary, he confined himself to directing the Orchestra, to policy decisions and to representing the department within the BBC. Much of the routine administrative work of the department was undertaken by Kenneth Wright, while Edward Clark and Julian Herbage were responsible for planning the overall content of the department's orchestral performances, including the Proms.

Clark was the 'principal programme-builder' in the department until his resignation in 1936. He had studied under Schönberg and had an international reputation for his knowledge, understanding and advocacy of contemporary music. He took the central role in organizing programmes of new music and in arranging for leading contemporary composers to take part in or conduct performances of their work, often for the first time, in this country. To Clark's encyclopaedic knowledge and wide range of contacts, Herbage added meticulous organizational skills and an understanding of broadcasting's needs for detailed forward planning. 'Tommy' Thompson was Concerts Manager, assisted by Dorothy Woods, and together they did all the work of liaison with the concert halls, arranging programme and poster printings, ticket sales and the management of the concerts themselves. Owen Mase (Musical Executive) dealt with artists and rehearsal arrangements. Victor Hely-Hutchinson started *The Foundations of Music*, which Herbage helped him to plan, until he left the BBC in 1934 to become Professor of Music at Birmingham University.

In 1936 Dr Reginald Thatcher was appointed Assistant Director of Music. As Boult's deputy his chief task was to represent the interests of the Music Department to the upper levels of the Corporation.[35] By now the increasing importance of programme planning meant that the department was losing its autonomy with regard to programme selection and planning. For years Clark and Herbage had enjoyed complete freedom to follow their inspirations within broadly allocated blocks of time to be filled each week. But by the mid-thirties the BBC, under a range of external pressures, began for the first time to engage in efforts to assess and monitor the overall balance of output in the National and Regional Programmes. The demands of broadcasting began to override the purely musical concerns of the Music Department and this gave rise to increasing tension between programme planners and leading members of the Music Department.

Throughout the period there were two distinctive aspects of musical policy: the pursuit of standards of excellence in the authentic performance of great music, and a commitment to increasing the new listening public's taste for, and appreciation of, such music. The Music Department showed more enthusiasm for the first ideal, while Reith and senior policy-makers showed more enthusiasm for the latter. At first there was no apparent contradiction between these two positions, but in the end they would prove irreconcilable.

The musical appreciation movement had a well-established history long before the coming of wireless.[36] Since the mid-nineteenth century there had been a growing middle-class concern to educate the people and to promote social harmony by weaning the 'horny handed sons of toil' away from their vicious indulgences towards more rational, moral and peaceable forms of recreation and leisure. Musical education and appreciation was one strand in this pervasive social movement. In Sunday schools and the emerging system of national elementary education the new tonic sol-fa method encouraged group singing with an effect that reached far beyond the classroom. The great Victorian revival of choral singing had, by the end of the century, consolidated into an extensive network of regional and national festivals and competitions. The growth of the works brass bands, with their competitions and festivals, was part of this movement. In the later part of the century a 'music for the people' campaign, designed 'to bring beauty back home' to them, was one thread in the missionary work of those philanthropic middle-class settlements in the working-class ghettoes of the great cities. Cheap musical concerts were arranged in the working-class districts of Manchester and the East End of London to bring high-class music at a low price within the reach of the lower orders.

Broadcasting, the BBC argued, was the final step in the 'true democratization of Music'. Through radio 'the shepherd on the downs, or the lonely crofter in the farthest Hebrides and, what is equally important the labourer in his squalid tenement in our but too familiar slums, or the lonely invalid on her monotonous couch, may all, in spirit, sit side by side with the patron of the stalls and hear some of the best performances in the world.'[7] This concern with putting fine performances of great music within reach of all was the main aim of musical policy under Percy Pitt, appointed Musical Adviser in 1923 and the first head of the Music Department until 1930. Its effect is hard to gauge, but the initial impact of radio, so hard for us now to imagine, should not be under-estimated. Thus a 'listener-in' from Whitstable in 1923 wrote to *Radio Times* to say that 'in these little provincial towns, whose chief items of amusement consist of two or three picture houses, a local struggle on the part of the amateur societies and strong sea air, a feast of good music *is* appreciated.'[38]

It was recognized that the ordinary listener, who had probably never before heard a Beethoven symphony, might need help to appreciate this feast so, in the early years, music teachers and critics were engaged to explain the meaning of music. The BBC was fortunate in its choice of Percy Scholes and Sir Walford Davies. Both had the knack of explaining musical form simply and clearly and without condescension. Sir Walford Davies, who inaugurated Schools Broadcasting in April 1924 with a talk on music, soon established a reputation as a great popular evangelizer of music and as an accomplished broadcaster. His series, *Music and the Ordinary Listener*, which started in January 1926, was very popular with listeners.[39] Scholes was a prolific broadcaster with an encyclopaedic knowledge of musical history. In his book, *Everybody's Guide to Broadcast Music*, which he wrote in 1925, he described in clear and easy language the elements of musical form and advised how to listen to opera, orchestral and chamber music.[40]

In its very first month as a Corporation the BBC began to lay down *The Foundations of Music*, a fifteen-minute programme broadcast five times a week in the early evening, which was to run continuously for the next ten years. The idea for the programme came from Filson Young, appointed as 'critical adviser' to the BBC by Reith in August 1926, a curious post which he kept till his death in 1937. The series started life as an attempt painlessly to provide the ordinary listener with a systematic introduction to the shorter works written for solo instruments and small ensembles by those masters who had laid

M.C. of Village Concert (to famous Pianist). " PERHAPS I OUGHT TO TELL YOU, SIR, THE WIRELESS 'AS MADE US ALL PRETTY CRITICAL 'ERE IN LITTLE WORTLEBURY."

the foundations of music.[41] For Filson Young the original idea was to provide 'a quarter of an hour's pleasant sound, like the bubbling of a fountain, which might be listened to attentively or drowsed over at the end of a tiring day'.[42]

By 1934 the Music Department had become restive with the programme and wanted to give it a complete overhaul. The standard repertoire of 'the present fashion in classics' had been exhausted. Bach-Mozart-Haydn, Bee-thoven-Schubert-Mendelssohn and Schumann-Brahms had all been 'done' but very inconsequentially, with one week pitchforked in after another without any idea more than rough contrast.[43] It was now proposed to present the *real* foundations comprehensively and systematically in due chronological order, paying attention to the historical founders of any school or style of compo-sition, including many minor ones hitherto neglected. This scheme needed a five-year plan, and it was proposed to start with the foundations of English music in the sixteenth century played on the original instruments of the period with the assistance of the Dolmetsch family and the advice of two leading authorities on the music of the period, Sir Richard Terry and Professor E. J. Dent. This departure from the orginal aim roused the wrath of Filson Young who complained that this flood of sixteenth-century music appealed only to the narrowest minority of cultivated musicians and not at all to the general public. Its effect would be to nullify a series that had, until now, been import-ant for 'the humble listener'. But the Music Department replied that the idea was 'an amazing example of historical development such as had never before been available to students in any country, arranged and sponsored at the microphone by the greatest experts in the world.'

In the autumn of 1935 two weeks were devoted to the Italian madrigals of Peter Philips. This, said the Music Department, was a key moment in the his-tory of the programme, since it rediscovered one of the major figures of the madrigal period whose work had completely escaped the attention of modern researchers. They attached much importance to the prestige this would earn for the department. By the end of the year Boult was claiming that the series had never been of such value to the world of music. It was assisted by eminent musicologists, it had enhanced the BBC's reputation at home and abroad (winning plaudits from musicians and critics in Paris and Prague), and had become the object of close attention from 'truly musical listeners'.[44] The changing tune of this series is one clear indicator of a shift of emphasis in the Music Department, a move away from trying to win the ordinary listener to the appreciation of good music towards winning the approval of those who were musically knowledgeable. For the Music Department, under Adrian Boult, prestige and the legitimation of its activities was increasingly sought from musicologists and the educated musical public rather than the general listener.

But the popularization of good music remained a central commitment, and one that was much enhanced by the BBC's acquisition of the Promenade Concerts in 1927. The Proms, which began in 1895, had already become a unique musical institution under the inspired direction of their founder, Sir Henry Wood. Their special success lay in their appeal to a much wider audience than the usual concert-going public. There were several reasons for this. They were considerably cheaper than the usual subscription concert; their social atmosphere was informal and relaxed; and thirdly, it was Wood's particular genius to design a programme for these eight-week festivals which had something for everyone. The Proms drew in, year after year, people who would never have dreamt of attending an ordinary concert. For many of them the Proms meant a broadening of musical experience. Wood succeeded in combining the familiar with the unfamiliar, demanding and undemanding orchestral music, in such a way as to keep good faith with his audiences while maintaining an excellent record at the box office.[45]

In spite of this the Proms were in severe financial difficulties by the mid-twenties, for orchestral music (like opera) is an expensive commodity that needs patronage. They were sponsored by Chappell's the music publishers, but in 1926, having lost £60,000 in three years, they decided to pull out. It was an inspired decision by Reith that the BBC should assume responsibility for sponsoring and financially guaranteeing the Promenade Concerts, a move which Wood greeted with relief and gratitude: 'With the whole-hearted support of the wonderful medium of broadcasting, I feel that I am at last on the threshold of truly democratizing the message of music and making its beneficial effect universal.'[46] Throughout the thirties decisions about the concerts rested largely with Wood, with the BBC exercising only a light control over their content. They knew they had backed a winner. The Proms have remained the most successful single attempt at the democratization of music in this country.

The Music Department had less success in its own efforts at organizing public concerts for simultaneous transmission to the listening public. When the BBC Symphony Orchestra was formed in 1930 Boult knew that it could not be confined to studio perfomances alone.[47] To bring out the best in performance and to maintain the morale of the players a live audience was essential. At the end of their first season of public concerts in 1931 Boult felt obliged to suggest that the title of the concerts and the name of the orchestra should both be changed: instead of BBC concerts by the BBC Symphony Orchestra, they might be called National Concerts by the National Symphony Orchestra. 'I am repeatedly told outside', Boult noted with evident irritation, 'that it is the expression "BBC" that helps to keep people away. Why I cannot imagine.'[48] When the Department locked horns with the administration in 1934 to devise the Five Year Plan for Music it was noted and agreed that the Proms were immensely more successful than any other concerts undertaken by the BBC. This could not be explained away by the personal charisma of Sir Henry Wood. Their atmosphere was less stodgy, the programmes less formal and the prices a lot lower than the BBC's own concerts. Roger Eckersley, Head of Entertainment (a broad fiefdom which made him overlord of the Music Department), emphasized the need for more standard and popular works in the BBC's concerts, and there was unanimous agreement that they should be made more like the Proms, including prices.[49]

In his written memorandum to the Ullswater Committee in 1935, Boult defined the primary duty of his department as providing a programme service of the highest possible standard for the listening public. Sir Walford Davies, in his oral evidence, saw the first aim of the BBC as 'a perfect broadcast', the best rendering of outstanding, exemplary music which could only be got from the best players by a systematic daily perfecting and repetition of studio and public performances.[50]

In the early years most of the efforts of the Music Department had been absorbed by the struggle to get permission for live relays of performances by the major orchestras in London and elsewhere, and the effort to recruit suitable ensembles for studio performances. As these early difficulties were overcome, and as the programme schedule took on a more settled form, attention in the Music Department turned, in the late twenties, to a more careful consideration of the techniques of broadcast music and in particular to higher standards of performance from singers and instrumentalists.[51] 'There are some who may pass muster in public places where the evidence of the ear is outweighed by the seduction of the eye', the *BBC Hand Book* portentously intoned, 'but the sensitive electric instrument's photographic reproduction of the performance shows lamentably how much is lacking in finesse, in delicacy.'[52] The microphone favoured none and allowed no faking. It demanded clean, legitimate execution and beautiful tone. In short the medium of radio called for new standards of professional competence, of technical efficiency combined with quality of tone.

It was because the general level of professional playing in Britain was so low that the BBC formed its own Symphony Orchestra in 1930 to supply its needs. It was set up with the deliberate aim of becoming one of the finest orchestras in the world, and it revolutionized standards of performance in Britain. It was the very first orchestra to offer full-time employment, on permanent contracts, to professional musicians. Previously even the best-known orchestras had been permanent in name only. The Hallé Orchestra, for example, though it had a core of permanent players, was largely assembled from scratch each year for the brief duration of the season. The 'evil tradition' of deputizing allowed players to duck out of any performance for a better contract elsewhere and to field in their place a last-minute substitute. Thus it was impossible to obtain any regular standard of performance, since rehearsals were a waste of time for an orchestra that changed not from year to year, but weekly and even daily during the season.[53]

The BBC contracts contained clauses which, for the first time, banned deputization and forbade the acceptance of any outside work. When the new orchestra was formed Boult was able, not surprisingly, to handpick the best principal players in the country, while the rank and file were selected after exhaustive auditions up and down the country. With Boult as its permanent conductor, and with far more time for rehearsal than any other orchestra (for the rest had to pay extra fees for rehearsal time) the new BBC Symphony Orchestra was well placed to achieve its aims. It was now possible for players to work together over time to build up a repertoire and to raise their standard of performance.

The formation of the BBC orchestra was bitterly opposed by the existing orchestras, which regarded it as unfair competition. When it began to give public concerts Sir Thomas Beecham took the lead in a campaign to confine it to the studio. This was resisted and in a year or so the opposition faded away. In fact the formation of the BBC Symphony Orchestra quickly obliged the other major orchestras to go full-time, offering permanent salaried posts to all members. There is no doubt that this single move improved the general standard of professional playing throughout the country, and deputization gradually became a thing of the past.

By 1935 the Symphony Orchestra had toured abroad and continental critics had, said Boult, unanimously acclaimed it as one of the best orchestras in Europe, on a par with the Berlin and Vienna Philharmonic Orchestras. But the final confirmation of the prestige of the orchestra came when Toscanini – 'probably the greatest conductor who has ever lived', in Boult's opinion – accepted an invitation to conduct in June 1935. His standards were so high that he was normally willing to conduct only the world's best orchestras, and his consent to conduct a particular orchestra was, in itself, a great compliment. After conducting his first concert the great conductor was so impressed that he changed the final programme in the series he had accepted to include more difficult works. When the last concert was over he told Boult that he hoped he would be invited again.[54]

The Symphony Orchestra was the standard bearer of the BBC's quest for musical perfection. Its permanent establishment necessarily entailed a heavy and continuing financial commitment to the standard works in the symphonic tradition. Such a commitment had been given to the Crawford Committee in 1925 when the BBC promised that it was building, on a systematic basis, 'a judicious mixture of classical, modern and popular works on an annual rota, in which would figure prominently the overtures and symphonies of Haydn, Mozart, Beethoven, Schubert, Mendelssohn and Brahms.'[55] It remained, over the years, an administrative article of faith that the BBC would provide the listening public, through the course of every broadcast year, with the standard works that made up the great tradition of symphonic music. Such music was the very cornerstone of the BBC's policy, as 'the guardian of cultural values', to continue expanding 'by worthy means, the number of those capable of enjoying great music'.

It became apparent, however, in the course of time that the members of the Music Department were less enthusiastic advocates than the administration of the standard repertoire. In 1934, the same year that *The Foundations of Music* was given an overhaul, the Five Year Plan stated its forward policy for symphonic concerts: '[1] They will contain the necessary amount of classics, [2] but added to these will be a fairly large proportion of more modern and less hackneyed works, [3] and at the other end we shall not hesitate to include works which are generally considered too "popular" for Symphony Concerts' [figures in parenthesis added].[56] Decoding this composite resolution put together by Eckersley and Boult it can reasonably be assumed that [1] and [2] are the expression of the Music Department's view, while [3] reflects that of the administration. The sentence as a whole is a political compromise designed to square the circle of the differences between both sides. The administration, that is, remains committed to making BBC symphony concerts more appealing to a wider unmusical public. The Music Department, while grudgingly accepting its responsibility for the *necessary* amount of classics is more interested in modern and less hackneyed works that appeal to a much smaller musically educated public.

The Five Year Plan marks the point at which the administration took control of planning for musical programmes and policy. The call for a Plan came from the Controller of Programmes and was delegated not to Boult but to Roger Eckersley, then Director of Entertainment with overall responsibility for Music, Outside Broadcasts, Drama and Variety. Eckersley produced his plan in close consultation with Boult and the Music Department, but it was written by him and he had the last word in one or two matters where he disagreed with the Director of Music. The report laid down 'the syllabus' for symphony concerts, opera, chamber music and contemporary concerts and proposed that a bi-annual or quarterly publication should be produced to give the musical public a really planned idea of what was coming its way. It was intended also to forestall criticisms from the Musical Advisory Committee and elsewhere by revealing in a definite form the future plans for music.

The Music Advisory Committee was another thorn in the flesh of the Music Department. Its members were leading representatives of the British musical profession, and it was set up with the intention of providing the BBC with wise counsel in developing its musical policy. The committee, however, spent most of its time deriding the Music Department as 'amateurs' and attacking its policies. In April 1934 a new Music Programme Advisory Panel was set up in the hope that it might provide more helpful, regular and detailed advice than the parent committee, with its endless rows, had done. There were three members of this panel of whom Arthur Bliss was easily the most important. He quickly developed a close working relationship with Boult, and the two men saw eye to eye on all musical matters. Bliss was soon aware of the troubles of the Music Department. The problem lay, he felt, not inside but outside the department for whose keenness, loyalty and amazingly efficient and disinterested work he had the greatest respect. 'BUT', he wrote to Boult, 'they are being continually checked and thwarted in the main policies which determine the future of music by higher authorities – they have no power.' He forcefully put it to Boult that the difficulties would be reduced only if *he* were Director of the whole Music Department responsible *only* to the Director General. 'It is absolutely essential that Music be an independent entity under yourself,' he wrote.[57]

Boult passed the letter to Reith and Roger Eckersley who commented, 'a highly mischievous letter written apparently without any kind of knowledge of the problems of broadcasting as a whole. It assumes that music *qua* music must as a *sine qua non* have entirely preferential treatment as opposed to all the other activities which go to build the whole programme.' Alan Dawnay, Controller of Programmes, who replied to Bliss, was more conciliatory but made the same point. 'If matters are not always decided in accordance with the recommendations of those directly responsible within the Music Department, you may be certain that an adverse decision has been taken only with the general programme in mind, and in the interests of listeners as a whole.'[58]

By now the small nucleus of senior personnel responsible for policy and programme planning were increasingly directing their attention to the overall balance of the general programme and a perceived need to leaven it with more entertainment. They began to look at the ways in which music was cluttering the schedules, thus preventing the introduction of lighter fare. The Proms were a prime example. During its season the BBC relayed at least the first half of the programme every night for forty-nine successive evenings bar Sundays. The evening schedules, during the summer months, were taken up with symphonic music for at least ninety minutes each night. By 1936 Cecil Graves had decided that this eight-week block of music was not in the interests of listeners as a whole.[59] That year, and thereafter, the Proms were broadcast selectively. In the same year Graves axed *The Foundations of Music*. It had had, he felt, a long innings and was now blocking efforts to make the general programme more lively and popular.[60]

As part of this policy, attention focused on the presentation of music programmes. If converts were to be won to the higher forms of music a more human method of presentation was needed, something that was neither the recitation of Italian tempo directions, nor a bare statement of the number of movements. How improvements were to be achieved was not immediately apparent to those responsible for presentation. At the same time listeners needed active encouragement to try a dose of good music. In 1938 Northern Ireland, not a notable source of new programme ideas, put on a series of weekly discussions in which George Nash, a well-known Ulster humorist, sportsman and musical 'lowbrow', challenged James Denny of the Belfast Music Department to prove to him that there was something in *This Symphony Business*. It was intended as propaganda for serious music, as 'a missionary endeavour among the musically heathen'. In London the Programme Planning Department became interested in the series and early in 1939 transferred it to the National Programme. At the same time it asked the Listener Research Unit to monitor the impact of the programme. Their report showed a steady rise in the listening figures for the series – from 11 to 20 per cent of the total potential audience in England – and that the audience found it informative and enjoyable.[61]

By now the Music Department was being bypassed by the planners. In the same year, 1938, the department became aware of a marked change in the type of music played by the Regional Orchestras in the daytime schedule. Upon investigation it turned out that the Programme Planning Department had sent a memorandum to all regions instructing them to put much lighter music into their daytime programmes and to avoid the Classics. The Music Department had not been informed. Boult regarded this as a deliberate snub, 'an unmistakable sign of disregard of us and our opinions'. The same thing happened when war was declared. Normal programmes were immediately suspended and replaced by an Emergency Policy of continuous light music on records, punctuated by news bulletins and official announcements. The Gramophone Department had been given most precise instructions. Everything must be gay and cheerful. German music must be avoided. Beethoven was banned, though a dash of Mozart was permissible. In the first two weeks of war there was only a quarter of an hour's music, in Boult's opinion, that could be said to cater for the needs of the genuine music lover.

For Boult this was the last straw. Not only had the department not been consulted or forewarned, but administrative policy was in flat contradiction to what he would have recommended had he been asked in the first place. Given the choice he would have conducted Beethoven's C Minor the day war was declared. He had evidence of the irritation of 'thinking listeners' at being plunged into light music the moment they had heard the grave news bulletins during those serious days. His long pent-up grievances were poured out in a seven-page memorandum, 'Decentralization', in which he raised the fundamental question of BBC organization. He protested against a system of administration which had caused considerable irritation and bad work in the years before 1939 and which, if unchecked, would in the end deprive the Corporation of its ablest minds and produce dryness and sterility in programme activity. The bulk of the memorandum reviewed the checks and slights the Department had had to endure, culminating in the recent emergency policy. Boult directed his fire particularly at the Programme Planning Department. He strongly urged that it should restrict its activities to manipulating the spaces available in the schedules *and nothing more.*[62]

PLATE I   Sir John Reith, Director General, July 1928

PLATE 2   Capt P. P. Eckersley,
Chief Engineer, November 1926

PLATE 3   R. H. Eckersley,
Director of Programmes,
September 1932

PLATE 4   B. E. Nicolls,
Controller (Administration),
May 1936

PLATE 5   Sir Richard
Maconachie, Head of Talks,
October 1937

PLATE 6   C. A. Siepmann, Director of Programme Planning, August 1939

PLATE 7   John Coatman, first Head of News, in the news room, 12 February 1936

PLATE 8   Stuart Hibberd reading the news as Michael Balkwill slips him a new
script, 18 January 1939

PLATE 9   Richard Dimbleby and C. J. Gardner checking out new copy,
23 January 1939

PLATE 10   Lance Sieveking (left) and Val Gielgud, July 1930

PLATE 11   A. E. (Archie) Harding, September 1936

PLATE 12 Pipers from South West Ham Social Centre, Talks to Unemployed Clubs, 13 February 1935

PLATE 13 Rehearsing *Conversations in the Train*, May 1935

PLATE 14   Unrehearsed debate: 'That parents are unfitted by nature to bring up their own children'. Bertrand Russell (left) Cyril Burt (centre) chairman, G. K. Chesterton (right)

PLATE 15   The panel of *Men Talking*. John Gloag centre, December 1937

PLATE 16   *In Town Tonight*, Dame Laura Knight with a 92-year-old circus dog
trainer

PLATE 17   Henry Hall and Gracie Fields, farewell concert of the BBC Dance
Orchestra, 25 September 1937

PLATE 18   Checking the results of a Spelling Bee between Harvard, Radcliffe and Oxford Universities. Seated umpires: Derek McCulloch (left) and Thomas Woodruffe. Standing, Felix Felton (left), Miss Botwood and Fred Bate for NBC

PLATE 19   Arthur Askey and Richard Murdoch, *Band Waggon*, 22 February 1938

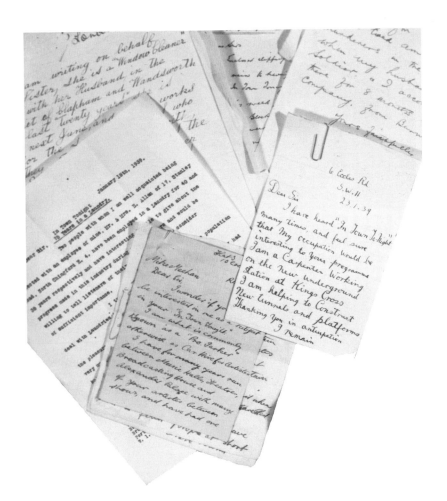

PLATE 20   Letters applying to take part in *In Town Tonight*, 25 February 1939

PLATE 21   Outside Broadcast van, relaying the service at the Cenotaph,
November 1928

PLATE 22   Cricket: The third Test Match at Old Trafford, July 1934

PLATE 23   Robert Wood (standing with headphones), relaying the wedding of the Duke and Duchess of Kent from the crypt, Westminster Abbey. The commentator (seated with plan of the Abbey) was not allowed in the church and had to do it 'blind'

PLATE 24   A family in 'a remote farm kitchen in Essex' listening to the funeral service of George V, January 1936

PLATE 25   Oldham Musical Society, Broadcasting from Studio 2, Manchester,
12 August 1937

PLATE 26   Olive Shapley (standing) at the seamen's mission, South Shields,
researching *Homeless People*, 1938

PLATE 27   Olive Shapley, in Mrs Emmerson's kitchen, preparing *Miners' Wives*,
February 1939

PLATE 28   Joan Littlewood (next to pit pony) and D. G. Bridson (next to her) down
the Brancepath Colliery, preparing *Coal*, 24 October 1938

CHAPTER TEN

Musical Tastes

————◦❉◦————

BEFORE THE coming of the modern media music was a live performing art. But the gramophone and the radio separated the production of music from its reception, thus shattering the immediate, intimate relationship between performers and audience. Many at the time felt that radio in particular would destroy active music-making and that an older *musica practica* would be replaced by passive listening.[1] The leading publishers and members of the profession feared that the habit of concert going would be destroyed, a view expressed by Sir Thomas Beecham with the forthrightness for which he was well known:

> Ever since the beginning of the present century there has been committed against the unfortunate art of music every imaginable sin. But all previous crimes and stupidities pale before this latest attack on its fair name, the broadcasting of it by means of wireless ... The performance of music through this or any other ludicrous contrivance cannot be other than a ludicrous caricature ... If the wireless authorities are permitted to carry on their devilish work, in ten years' time the concert halls will be deserted.[2]

The fears of the musical profession about the impact of radio on their livelihood were put to the Crawford Committee in 1925. The music publishers claimed that radio was damaging the sale of sheet music. William Boosey had from the beginning refused to allow the BBC to relay concerts from Queen's Hall, though by the end of 1927 he had begun to allow a limited number to be broadcast each year. He further refused at first to allow artists under his control to accept broadcasting engagements. He, like Beecham, was convinced that radio spelt the ruination of publicly performed music, a view he put to the Crawford Committee, adding that those who listened in to the wireless gave up practising or playing the piano. Other contemporaries took a different view. The Editor of *Musical Times*, attending a series of BBC concerts in Queen's Hall in 1928, thought it might well turn out that broadcasting, far from killing the public concerts, was giving it a new lease of life. The concerts were tapping a quite new public: 'At each ... I have found myself surrounded by refreshingly unsophisticated folk. Evidently they had heard orchestras at home, and had decided to go and see one – for they took in almost as much pleasure through the eye as through the ear. At first one thought these hearers were Promenaders who had stolen back to their old haunt, but clearly they were quite new hands.'[3]

Musical opinion of the impact of radio on the ordinary listener was similarly divided. Constant Lambert wryly regretted the appalling popularity of music. In an age of overproduction music, of a sort, was everywhere. 'At one time a cautious glance round the room assured one, through the absence of a piano, that there would at least be no music after dinner. But today the chances are that one's host is a gramophone bore, intent on exhibiting his fifty-seven varieties of soundbox, or a wireless fiend intent on obtaining the obscurest stations irrespective of programme.'[4] Dame Clara Butt welcomed the radio as putting an end to dreary musical parties in the drawing room. She wrote in *Radio Times* in 1925 that 'as long as the wireless set brings first-class music into the home, musical people will not permit themselves to be troubled with indifferent amateur performances – except as a social necessity.'[5] But Lambert observed that the more people used the wireless the less they listened to it. He, like many others, deplored the widespread habit of playing bridge with the radio on in the background. 'Were the Last Trump to be suddenly broadcast from Daventry by special permission of Sir John Reith – and I can think of no event more gratifying to the stern-minded Governors of the BBC – it is doubtful whether it would interfere with the cry of "No Trumps" from the card table.'[6]

The BBC was equally disapproving of background listening. It expected people to use the resources it offered selectively and with an open mind. As far as its musical offerings were concerned *Radio Times* declared that it wanted listeners who 'were not only tolerant but eclectic in their taste ... who can listen to and enjoy either Bach or Henry Hall.' This was written, Susan Briggs notes, with no sense of bathos, in a 1935 editorial which jointly celebrated the beginning of the fourth year on the air of Henry Hall and the BBC Dance Orchestra and the 250th anniversary of the birth of Bach. But did this ideal listener, with a catholic musical taste, exist anywhere other than in the hopes of the broadcasting administration? The evidence suggests that the Henry Hall fan loathed Bach, while the lover of Bach loathed Henry Hall.

The universal audience for music of all kinds towards which the BBC directed its efforts was something brought into being by radio itself. Previously there had existed only different kinds of music embedded in particular economic and social networks and produced for particular taste publics. By attempting to cater for all existing musical tastes, through a policy of mixed programming on a single channel – national or regional – the BBC quite unintentionally brought all these musics and their publics into collision with each other. For all must perforce compete with each other for that intrinsically scare commodity, time. Another unintended outcome of the universalization of music and its audience was that different tastes appeared much more than previously to be organized in a hierarchy of values, which ranged from good to bad. The terms highbrow, middlebrow and lowbrow, widely current in discussions of music and radio in the twenties and thirties, only became meaningful systems of classification when different kinds of music were brought into close proximity with each other. A plurality of choices was more likely to produce a negative response to one kind of music in order to affirm a preference for another, rather than an acceptance of them all.

Everyone understood well enough their position within the different taste publics addressed by radio. Thus a listener from Newcastle defined himself with perfect accuracy as 'a lower middlebrow' when sending *Radio Times* his list of 'Six Great Melodies: 1. *Ave Maria*, Schubert; 2. *Liebestraum*, Liszt; 3. *Blue Danube*, Strauss; 4. *Salut d'Amour*, Elgar; 5. *Elegie*, Massenet; 6. *Black Eyes*, Ferraris'.[8] Lowbrows and highbrows defined themselves as much in terms of what they hated as what they liked. For Arthur Bliss, who took over as Director of Music in 1941 when Boult decided he had had enough, popular music was evil. It was the delight of Caliban. The cinema organ was 'dope as insidious as opium', while jazz was fit only for 'artificial excitement and aphrodisiacal purposes'.[9] And here is the voice of Caliban raised against the highbrow:

> You will have to go a long way to hear navvies or dockers whistling the *Rondo Capriccioso*, or your other favourite the Grieg Concerto. But you and the other big pots of the BBC can take it from me that the public don't want it. They want something more tuneful and pleasant. They can always go to a funeral and hear your sort of nice music. The only piece that was tuneful last night was the *Spring Song*.[10]

But it was not simply a matter of antagonisms between different fields of music, the serious and the popular, highbrow and lowbrow. Within each field there was a hierarchy of tastes that fragmented the unity of these categories.

" Listen, dear. Isn't that from 'Lohengrin' ? "
"No, silly! It's from Droitwich."

The different strata of tastes for dance music can best be traced through the magazines devoted to popular music that started up in the twenties and thirties. *Melody Maker* began in 1928 as a trade magazine for professional dance band musicians, but it also assumed through its editorial columns, a responsibility for maintaining quality and standards in dance music. Its contrasting attitudes to the music of Fred Elizalde on the one hand and of Henry Hall on the other exemplifies not only the wider implications of different musical styles in the dance bands, but the contradictions in the magazine's editorial policy. For *Melody Maker*'s defence of standards was not always reconcilable with the bread and butter interests of its clients, the bandsmen in search of a regular living.

Elizalde and his Savoy Band began playing opposite the Savoy Orpheans in late 1927 and broadcast for the first time on New Year's Eve. *Melody Maker* gave it an ecstatic write-up, but patrons of the Savoy Hotel were far less enthusiastic. Many of the dancers complained to the management that they were unable to recognize the tune and that they were left hanging about on the dance floor while the band played long-off tempo introductions. The BBC was bombarded with letters about the lack of melody in Elizalde's performances, though there was some praise from a minority of correspondents. In 1928 complaints from the audience continued and eventually the BBC stopped transmitting its performances.[11]

In a poll conducted among its readers in 1928 to establish an order of merit for the radio bands Elizalde came out clear favourite, with Bert Ambrose and his Mayfair Band second, the Savoy Orpheans third and Jack Payne's BBC Dance Orchestra fourth. Some doubt was subsequently cast on the validity of this poll since it was argued that most of the voters were musicians, and 'lay listeners' had played a very small part in the ballot. To this the magazine replied that its readers represented 'the *intelligentsia* of dance music, and the general public has an instinctive knack of conforming to the tastes of this *intelligentsia* as its voice becomes more and more heard among the masses.'[12]

This was all very well but the magazine was often reminded by its readers that they depended for their livelihood on giving the public what it wanted, and all the public wanted was ' "four-beats-in-a-bar" and that only to support first, last and solely *Melody*'. Rhythm, as far as the public was concerned, came a long way second and could be met simply by supplying a steady tempo. The editor of *Melody Maker* was most reluctant to accept the implications of this. In a style that is infinitely remote from the magazine today he solemnly declared that 'We could not reconcile ourselves to the belief that the public was anything like crude enough in its appreciation and understanding of popular music to be satisfied with the often mediocre melodies of the majority of the numbers issued so prolifically for its edification, seemingly with a delightfully nonchalant disregard of their intrinsic merit.'[13] The essence of good dance music was *style*. It was skill in the individual interpretation of a particular orchestration, the subtlety of difference in phrasing and tempo, which characterized the good dance musician as much as the 'legitimate' symphony player.[14] *Melody Maker* had prized Fred Elizalde above all for his adventurous style. When, to its astonishment, the BBC dropped 'London's Best Dance Band', the magazine could only wonder whether it was something to do with plugging, or because the band had proved 'too hot for provincial listeners-in'.[15]

Throughout the thirties *Melody Maker* continued to epitomize a highly sophisticated metropolitan, not to say cosmopolitan, taste. Its two idols were Duke Ellington and Louis Armstrong, and when these two toured Britain, as they occasionally did, they were given royal coverage. Each, during his first tour, gave one studio performance for the BBC. These scarcely met the demands of the *cognoscenti*, but they were more than enough for an uncomprehending general public who reacted to their music with dislike.[16] For all the best efforts of *Melody Maker* the gap between the intelligentsia of popular music and the masses failed to close. The majority were seemingly well satisfied with Henry Hall.

Informed opinion was rather condescending about Henry Hall, but he was well chosen for the job of setting up and conducting the BBC's first full Dance Orchestra. Hall was the only band leader from the provinces to broadcast regularly from London, and his job with LMS Hotels had given him an unrivalled knowledge of provincial taste the length and breadth of the country. He was an unflagging hard worker, and a good organizer and administrator – all in all, an ideal candidate for the job. *Melody Maker*, while regretting the passing of Jack Payne and his BBC Dance Band ('always a musicianly outfit'), was prepared to welcome Henry Hall as a 'well-liked, competent and reliable musician and administrator with the right social address for the job', and to await his first performance.[17]

The BBC gave its new orchestra a big build-up, and new standards for dance music were promised. To give it the maximum publicity its first broadcast on 15 March 1932 launched the start of programmes from the brand new, purpose-built Broadcasting House. It was headlined in *Melody Maker* as 'The Negation of Dance Music'. The band was tuneful, well balanced, played in nice tempo and avoided vulgarity. It could play current popular songs in a simple, melodic way. But that was all it was – no more than an efficient band playing an ordinary sort of tune in ordinary sort of way. It was not interesting enough to be called bad. It had no personality. It was inoffensively negative.[18]

The intelligentsia might dismiss the new BBC Dance Orchestra but the general public took to it right away, and Henry Hall was one of the biggest stars in the popular radio magazines of the day. The first issue of *Radio Pic-*

torial, on 2 January 1934, contained a give-away portrait of Henry Hall, while a month later the first number of *Radio Magazine* had a feature article on 'this national figure' whose name was synonymous with dance music. 'Tall, slim, dark in appearance, he has quiet thoughtful eyes which flame, on occasion with an eloquent smile.' The magazine praised him for never having been infected with 'the virus of West-Endism' and for his wisdom in catering to the suburban needs and tastes of the majority of listeners. Hall made it plain that he believed in melody rather than 'the cacophonous discords of hot music'. He believed that most people, like himself, disliked the extremes of hot jazz and the music of Schönberg which appealed mainly to Jews. Jazz had been killed by the errand boys of the world – the greatest advertisers of tunes – who could not whistle inverted harmonies, hacked rhythms and insane discords. Hall claimed to play for the errand boys of the world and for the fireside folk who made up his listening public.[19]

Most ordinary listeners wanted not much more than a good tune. 'Hot music means very little in Blackpool,' declared Bertini, the musical director of the Blackpool Tower Ballroom whose stage name belied his cockney origin. Bertini and his men were heard regularly on BBC North Region during the holiday season as they played to a throng of nearly 5000 people a night in this Lancashire palace of the people, and he knew what his genial public liked. It liked melodious dance music full of life, vim and gaiety. Advanced rhythmic music was all very fine but the vast majority of listeners, like the people of the North, preferred jolly music played in a straightforward way to which they could either dance or listen with pleasure as they wished.[20]

All this suggests that the late-night metropolitan dance music which was broadcast throughout the thirties had a strictly limited appeal. The bands had a largely cult following among a knowledgeable minority who could, and did, argue interminably among themselves over the respective merits of Ambrose, Roy Noble, Lew Stone, Harry Roy, Jack Hylton and the rest.[21] The music for the majority was that most neglected of categories, light orchestral. This, as a furrow to be ploughed by the policy-makers, lay fallow until the war when the imperatives of morale demanded close attention to music to keep the nation buoyant. Until then light music, though its volume exceeded both dance and symphony music, had received no serious scrutiny within the BBC.

Light music was a buffer zone, a no-man's land between dance music and serious music. It appealed to that mass of listeners who disliked extremes and required no more than 'soothing melodies and gently undulating rhythms poured out in measured doses of soft lights and sweet music'. That at any rate was how Sam Heppner defined Light Music in a series of articles for *Radio Times* in 1936.[22] It was a catch-all which included the sentimental songs, ballads and instrumental compositions of late Victorian and Edwardian days. Such music was exemplified by the work of Haydn Wood (*Roses of Picardy*,

Love's Garden of Roses), Albert Ketèlbey (*In a Persian Garden, In a Monastery Garden, In a Fairy Realm, With the Rumanian Gypsies*), and Teresa del Riego from Australia whose biggest successes included *O Dry Those Tears, Homing, Slave Song* and *Thank God for a Garden*. Some of these had been enormous successes – *Roses of Picardy* had sheet sales of over a million and netted its author a five-figure royalty – but their appeal in the thirties was largely nostalgic for an older generation of listeners.

By contrast the music of the 'jazz symphonists' was right up to date. The most famous of these was, of course, George Gershwin whose *Symphony in Blue* (1924) influenced a whole generation of younger English composers including Constant Lambert, Eric Coates and George Posford – a versatile musician who wrote film scores for *The Good Companions* and *Goodbye Vienna* as well as an orchestral suite called *Broadcasting House* inspired by the monument in Portland Place. It was, in Heppner's view, a quite enchanting work 'with Stravinsky-like mock jazz movements, orchestral effects and street noises'. The BBC gave it an airing in 1935 and it was subsequently performed in Germany by the Berlin Philharmonic.

Such compositions were straying over the borders into the domain of serious music. They called for performance by decent-sized orchestras, by the BBC's Regional Orchestras at the very least. But the light orchestral combinations most often heard on radio were very much smaller. The Gershom Parkington Quintet was the first to broadcast regularly, while two of the most popular quintets of the thirties were those led by Lesley Bridgewater and Fred Hartley. Hartley was later called upon, during the war, to bring some definition and order to light music. His Novelty Quintet, which started regular studio broadcasts in 1931, was probably the best of its kind on radio at the time.

In an article for *Radio Magazine* Hartley described how he put together programmes to please his absent listeners. He always tried to bear in mind the tastes of the ordinary listener whose music must be neither too weighty nor too long. He aimed to include in each programme samples of the hits of the moment, the older ballads still remembered with affection, the standard solo works for the instruments in his group and the speciality numbers which showed off the abilities of the combination as a whole. Examples of the first included *Sing, Gypsy Sing, Waggon Wheels* and *Little Man You've had a Busy Day*; of the second, *The Rosary, I'll Sing Thee Songs of Araby* and *Love's Old Sweet Song*. The third group included 'the ripened fruits of Chopin's works, the brilliant gems of Liszt and the superb arrangements of Fritz Kreisler', while the last might include fantasias on hornpipes, country dances and similar medleys. The programmes lasted an hour and Hartley attributed the secret of their popularity to their continued variety, the lightness of the arrangements, and the non-stop presentation which not only allowed listeners to switch on at any moment but to continue listening without fear of boredom to the whole programme of more than seventeen items. Summing up the philosophy of his music and his audiences Hartley concluded:

> Quick change is the pass-word today. Contrast is the spice of this twentieth century. We want short fast journeys, short sermons, kaleidoscopic newspapers, short working hours and short shrift with bores. I think I may claim that my programmes fulfill most of the needs of the present day average man. I am neither highbrow, nor lowbrow but broad brow, as one must be in catering for the great wireless audience.[23]

Light music also appealed to the 'lower middlebrows', that self-improving section of the new universal audience brought into being by radio. In the early years Percy Scholes, that most kindly and well-intentioned of musical experts, received a very large mail bag from such listeners who wanted to appreciate good music but did not know how.

> (1) I always envy people who really enjoy classical music, but to me personally it is boring. I know there are many people in the same category as myself, so that if you could put us on the right track I am sure it would be greatly appreciated.

> (2) I have made the acquaintance of music for player-piano in the last two years, and have from the first obtained from the library the music I ought to like, and have stuck to it until I did.

> (3) [*After listening to Elgar's 2nd Symphony in E flat on the radio*] I wondered what it was all about. What was the Composer getting at? Is there an idea running through it all? Is the music conveying something that is beyond me to understand? I like the music for its own sake, but if I could understand what the composer was getting at I think I should enjoy it even more.[24]

These were aptly defined by Basil Maine as 'the conscience-stricken listeners' who felt they *ought* to like good music but were worried that they could not understand it. What at the very least they wanted to know was 'what is good music?' and 'who is the greatest composer?' Having been given the answers they could then buckle down to cultivating a taste for the medicine secure in the assurance that it was good for them. Scholes and Maine would try to point out that these were the wrong sorts of question, that there was good and bad in all types of music. But for those who desired musically to better themselves it was important to know the answers to such questions. Otherwise what was the point of taking the medicine? At least they had, as Maine put it, 'the desire to esteem' and so something could be done to assist them.[25]

Maine saw the relationship between himself and this kind of listener as that between doctor and patient. He and Scholes or Walford Davies might, in their broadcast talks, help a simple liking for melodious orchestral music to develop into a slightly more sophisticated appreciation of musical form, and a greater ability to respond to more demanding music in the classical repertoire. There was something touching in the gratitude of ordinary listeners who felt they were improving under such radio tutelage.

(1) The BBC is teaching us all music. My household are beginning to appreciate good class music in a way that, speaking for myself, I never did.

(2) I enjoyed the overture to the *Nutcracker Suite*, so I suppose I'm improving, for Tchaikovsky used generally to beat me and often to annoy me.

(3) The BBC have been responsible for the expansion of my musical taste. I have learnt to listen patiently to things that once seemed to me only 'musical gymnastics'.[26]

But in spite of all such assistance there still remained formidable obstacles in the way of those who sought to cultivate a true musical appreciation.

Out of all the listeners I do not suppose that there are more than one-third who really understand anything about 'good music', and there must be many, like myself, middlebrows or lowbrows, who would like to. My complaint is that daily we read in the *Radio Times*, in the programmes, the musical terms used, and it would be a boon if we knew what they meant. Articles have lately appeared on melody, rhythm, counterpoint etc. – most interesting and instructive – but cannot someone help us by giving the meaning of all musical terms?[27]

It was Percy Scholes who, in 1935, responded to this plea with 'a little book of First Aid for the Puzzled Listener'. *The Radio Times Music Handbook* was prompted by his sympathy with that huge section of the audience who found themselves constantly baffled by hearing this kind of thing on radio:

As I switch on my set I hear a pleasant voiced announcer persuasively proclaiming: 'the four movements of the composition you are about to hear are as follows: *Allegro; Scherzo-Assai Vivace; Adagio Sostenuto; Largo-Allegro, Prestissimo, Allegro Risoluto, Fugue,*' And having thus flung a chunk of a foreign language at an island population notoriously monoglot, he stands aside with the comfortable feeling of having done what he could to be helpful.[28]

This said Scholes, which the musically educated would recognize as a Bach concerto, was one of the very simplest examples compared with the indigest-

THE NEW CRITICS.

"The *pizzicato* for the double basses in the coda seems to me to
want body, Alf."

ible chunks which the announcers, *Radio Times* and the compilers of concert programme notes frequently rattled off or thrust before the public. His guide book provided clear explanations and translations of no less than 1288 terms or phrases which the fireside listener might expect to encounter. All were carefully sorted into ten classified groupings, which ranged from keys, scales, intervals and chords to 'French, German and Italian particles and other stray words, terminations, etc.'

Fortified with such a helpful compendium, and guided by radio talks, the anxious listener just might, with patience and perseverance, progress so far as a taste for Bach ('I have a conscience however about my inability to care for Bach. I feel the fault is mine. How can I remedy it?').[29] But having got thus far there still remained one last, insurmountable blank rock face which barred access to the commanding heights of truly musical culture.

(1) Following your instructions I carefully listened to the Bela Bartok concert. I love every note and every progression in *Till Eulenspiegel* and all Strauss including the *Alpine Symphony* which I consider magnificent; but last night's Bela Bartok concert was, to me, terrible. Nothing from a melodic, harmonic or structural point of view. In addition, an atmosphere of trivial puerility. What a waste of a Symphony Orchestra's time!

(2) Cut out of your programmes the Bartok-Stravinsky type of organised musical noise as much as you can. In its place pick out say twenty symphonies of the best of Brahms, Schubert, Beethoven, Schumann, Haydn, Mozart, Tchaikovsky etc.; give them over and over again until listeners know them, and then add others until you end up with the rubbish which is called 'modern'.[30]

Such responses are entirely representative of those listeners who felt they could, with time and effort, come to cope with the old masters but were baffled by the moderns. No matter how hard they tried, the music of Bela Bartok (a name that frequently cropped up) remained an impenetrable mystery. This was the real test which winnowed the wheat from the chaff on the riddle of culture, for true musical competence could not be demonstrated by achieving a taste for nineteenth-century symphonic music. Such taste had already become middlebrow.

The administration had defined the missionary work of broadcasting as winning converts to what a later Director General, Sir William Haley, defined as 'the Beethoven – Brahms – Tchaikovsky standards'. But the Music Department was already tired of the standard symphonic repertoire by the mid-thirties. It devoted most of its missionary endeavours to the advancement of chamber music and of certain modern composers. By the end of the thirties the Music Department's loyal advocacy of these two causes had, from the point of view of programme planning, begun to appear as yet another obstacle in the way of lightening and brightening the National Programme.

'Chamber music is not the entertainment of the crowds,' wrote Scholes. 'It is not heard to effect in very big halls, nor does it usually draw big audiences. It is the delight of the performing amateur and of the listening connoisseur, who finds in its very restraint, due to its limitations of tonal variety and volume, something which appeals to them differently (and perhaps beyond) any other musical experience.'[31] The Music Department drew no sharp distinction between classical and modern chamber music and from 1927 onwards it worked hard to win converts to a kind of music that it recognized was 'totally unfamiliar to the average man'.

Contemporary Chamber Music Concerts began in 1927 and consisted of eight a season, broadcast from the studio in homeopathic doses once a month between October and May. 'Contemporary' in this context meant the work of composers whose work was acclaimed as advancing the scope and art of musical composition.[32] Schönberg and Stravinsky were seen by the Department as the most important living composers, 'the two axes around which turned the most significant developments in contemporary music'. They were little known in England and the 1927 season of concerts included performances of some of their key works in the hope of creating a keener appreciation of their music. Hindemith, Berg, Webern and Bartok, and the new wave of younger English composers such as Peter Warlock, were all regularly presented.[33]

From the start, the department knew that there would be protests against such 'controversial' music. But advancing its cause was not just a matter of trying to win public acceptance for modern music. It was also a means whereby the Music Department won prestige for itself and the BBC, as much abroad as at home, as patrons of the contemporary arts. Many of the concert programmes included first performances in this country, with the occasional world premiere when the composer was usually invited to attend, perform in or conduct his own work. Stravinsky, Webern, Bartok and especially Schönberg were so honoured. The department participated in international Contemporary Music Festivals and claimed that in so doing it won excellent publicity for itself in the foreign press and thus enhanced the international reputation of the BBC.[34] The Five Year Plan recommended continuing the programme of eight contemporary concerts a year. A somewhat non-plussed Eckersley commented, 'these concerts it is known appeal only to a minority public, but they serve a valuable purpose. Extreme modernity may be an object of ridicule and execration, but it is generally a live spot. We must continue with this work which, I feel sure, brings us good marks from the really musical public.'[35]

But who was that public? Its voice was extremely elusive and, like a rare species of bird, sightings are very hard to obtain. The *Musical Times* welcomed the inaugural series of concerts in 1927, and provided a regular column to review them each season. But the reviewers were not infrequently baffled. When Webern conducted his own *Five Pieces For Orchestra* on 2

December 1928 it produced this response in *Musical Times*: 'A wisp of sound from this quarter, a ping from that, a pong from somewhere else and (for the listener) a pang as the result.'[36] Or again, when Bartok performed in his Piano Concerto under Sir Henry Wood's baton, the reviewer's response, like that of the audience, was tentative and puzzled. The work

> had a mixed audience, the minority of whom had come especially to see and hear Bartok – if one judged rightly from the number of people who took no part in the applause ... Bartok, like other modern composers, plays the game of musical composition according to principles of his own making, and to appreciate his work one must first understand the local rules and the finer points to which they give rise. We are assured by an expert that this work is, on its own ground, a masterpiece, especially the 2nd movement, a quiet essay in percussive philosophy.'[37]

Before the establishment of the Listener Research Unit the Music Department attached considerable importance to all its public concerts for paying audiences since the box office was their best means of gauging public interest in their programmes. Some of the early Contemporary Chamber Music Concerts had been transmitted from a public concert hall. Scholes notes that the audiences they attracted were the smallest that he, in all his years as a London music critic, had ever observed. As he recalled he had sometimes amounted to one fourth or one fifth of the whole audience and never less than one thirtieth.[38] In 1932 a new series of public Chamber Music Concerts was launched from the new Concert Hall in Broadcasting House. These were intended 'to put the spotlight on the BBC's notable propaganda for chamber music', and were experimental in the way they were arranged. At times they combined with poetry readings – a Mozart quintet, *The Eve of St Agnes*, a Debussy quartet – or else unfamiliar modern works were sandwiched between recognized popular classics. At first this series did rather better than the earlier one and after two years it was claimed that there had been a 15 per cent increase in attendance which showed, or so Aylmer Buesst felt, that the series was definitely putting public chamber concerts on a firm basis. This was perhaps an over-hasty claim, for the 1934 series was not well supported, and a year later the Concerts Committee was reflecting on its difficulties in establishing a public for chamber music concerts.[39]

'Will the BBC never learn from public opinion?' demanded 'Fed Up' in a letter to *Musical Times*. 'Because we won't swallow whatever the Extremist Department of the BBC chooses to perform (or to let its foreign friends try on us, as on the dog) we are treated as naughty children.'[40] But the editor of that journal was prepared to give generous credit for the valuable 'salvage work' performed by the BBC in continuing to offer performances of works which in the ordinary way would never be heard in public. 'It is hardly possible to over-estimate the good work the BBC is doing in widening the listener's knowledge and repertory. The point deserves to be emphasized because this kind of service is not showy or sensational and so is apt to be overlooked by critics.'[41] This was well put, and the Music Department deserved praise for its disinterested service to the cause of such music without bending to the expediencies of popularity, administrative concerns for the 'average listener' or the lash of public opinion. But by 1935 it was under severe pressure from the planners and policy-makers to reduce the number of chamber music concerts.

Such concerts had to be arranged and publicized many months ahead and, since it was standard practice to relay them live to the listening public, they became fixed points in the programme schedule. By the mid-thirties these two factors – fixed points and small audiences – had made them an administrative embarrassment. The Five Year Plan conceded unenthusiastically that 'it was the duty of the BBC to support chamber music' and that the best way to do this was through public concerts. Boult wanted twelve a year but Eckersley, backed up by the Director of Programmes, was unwilling to recommend more than six. Boult strongly advocated one public chamber music concert a month in order to allow enough room for interesting programme building and to build up a regular audience. As a compromise he suggested that only half might be broadcast while the rest be given to the paying public. Eckersley turned that idea down on the less than convincing argument that to give concerts for profit (there was surely none in these!) opened up a big policy issue and laid the BBC open to complaints from other concert-giving bodies. In the end six fixed concerts a year were accepted by the administration as part of the overall plan for the rest of the decade.[42]

In spite of that defeat the department continued to chip away at the administration. The Concerts Committee recommended that there ought to be weekly broadcasts of public chamber music in order to give them a chance both with the concert-going and the listening public. But that, as far as Eckersley and Wellington were concerned, was the negation of programme building for the wider audience of broadcasting. The Department continued to press its case and in 1937 Kenneth Adam, Programme Organizer, accepted a monthly afternoon concert of chamber music from the department, but he and Charles Siepmann (now Director of Programme Planning) categorically refused them a fixed date or time since, from the programme point of view, such a concession would be a definite embarrassment.[43] When at last, from the beginning of the war onwards, Listener Research began to provide routine audience figures for all kinds of music, chamber music concerts regularly recorded the lowest scores of all broadcast programmes. In one two week period in August 1940 they produced audiences of 0.4 per cent, 0.8 per cent and 0.9 per cent.[44]

The divisions between BBC policy-makers, the Music Department and listeners came to focus on the differences between symphonic and chamber music. The symphony has been called 'the large scale novel of musical literature', containing something for everyone.[45] In the course of the nineteenth century it was increasingly dominated by 'programme' values – that is non-musical, representational effects that aimed to arouse a particular emotion, image or scene, or to tell a story.[46] Beethoven's *Pastoral Symphony*, Berlioz's *Symphonie Fantastique* or Tchaikovsky's *1812 Overture* are obvious examples. They can readily be appreciated by the musically uneducated in non-musical terms, as stirring, heroic or tragic, as appealing to the emotions, as offering a point of identification. By contrast, 'absolute' music is pure form and most fully embodied in chamber music. Its values are internal to the logics of its themes and structures. It is void of any literary, pictorial or other non-musical points of reference, and as such it is the exact opposite of programme music. It is 'musicianly' music and, as Scholes points out, 'most musicians make a very clear distinction between absolute music and programme music even though the distinction is more difficult to maintain than is often supposed.'[47]

The distinction transcends the modernist 'break' initiated by Schönberg and Stravinsky at the beginning of this century, for what links that musical revolution with the music of Bach and Mozart, and the small-scale 'musicianly' music of Beethoven (whose late quartets are taken as expressions of his profoundest *musical* ideas) is the effort to resume the exploration of form (and hence of music) in and for itself. The break from the dominant tonal tradition marked its exhaustion and devaluation by the continuing growth of the symphony in the nineteenth century. The symphony, unlike chamber music, was designed for public performance and thus came to depend either on public subscriptions or the box office to sustain it. As the scale of symphonic composition expanded, it called for ever larger orchestras to perform before ever larger audiences. The increasing inclusion of programme values in symphonic compositions can be understood as a response to the need to secure a paying public. Thus the symphony came to contain within itself the values of the market, as it presupposed an expanding public to support it in performance as its scale of composition grew larger.

The break with such music can be seen as a rejection of the intrusion of market values which muddied the dominant musical form of the epoch. As *Britannica* puts it, concerning the music of Stravinsky and Schönberg, 'because both dwelt so much on the importance of musical techniques, they have been dismissed as "formalists" concerned only with pure form devoid of musical expression. Indeed the neoclassicists [Stravinsky and his followers] were particularly condemned for their insistence on "objectivity", but this objectivity was really a way of achieving artistic dignity and distinction by maintaining an aesthetic distance from the emotions portrayed.'[48] In other words, the renewed emphasis on technique and objectivity, which privileged form, was in part a rejection of emotional identification with non-musical reference points as an invitation to the pleasures of music. For that destroyed its dignity and distinction.

This argument is tentatively advanced, for the analysis of the social significance of musical forms is an underdeveloped field, yet it is offered as a way of accounting for the differences between the BBC policy-makers, the Music Department and the listening public. The policy-makers thought of what Sir William Haley called the 'Beethoven-Brahms-Tchaikovsky standard' as defining the norm for 'good' music, as setting the level of taste and appreciation to which the ordinary listener might, with time and effort, aspire. We have seen evidence that the self-improving listener, under the kindly tutelage of Sir Walford Davies or Percy Scholes, might indeed cultivate a liking for such music. The trouble was that this norm was not that of the Music Department, for whom the standard symphonic repertoire was somewhat old hat and vulgar. Chamber music, classical and modern, as the embodiment of absolute music was the norm of the Music Department. This negation of market values in music inevitably entailed an indifference to general considerations of the needs and circumstances of the general listening public.

Thus there was no universal audience for the universe of music on radio. The ideal-typical listener who enjoyed everything from Henry Hall to Bach existed only in the corporate mind, and even then only in the minds of senior personnel, not in the minds of the Music Department. The impact of radio was such as to heighten rather than assuage the social antagonisms of musical tastes. Music, the 'purest' of all the arts, far from fulfilling its Orphean mission of charming all ears and soothing all hearts, divided and fragmented the listening public. The effort to establish a common musical culture through broadcasting – a project dearer to the hearts of the administrators than the musicians within the BBC – foundered on the implacable antipathies of musical tastes. One should not underestimate the depth of the hostility to each other felt by highbrow and lowbrow alike. 'Tastes', says Bourdieu, 'are the practical affirmation of an inevitable difference. It is no accident that, when they have to be justified, they are asserted purely negatively, by the refusal of other tastes... Aesthetic intolerance can be terribly violent. The most intolerable thing for those who regard themselves as the possessors of legitimate culture is the sacrilegious reuniting of tastes which taste dictates shall be separate.'[49]

A similar antagonism divided the publics for dance music. The conflict between rhythm and melody – between complex improvizations and a good simple tune – defined the difference between the connoisseurs of swing music

B.B.C. TONICS FOR ALL

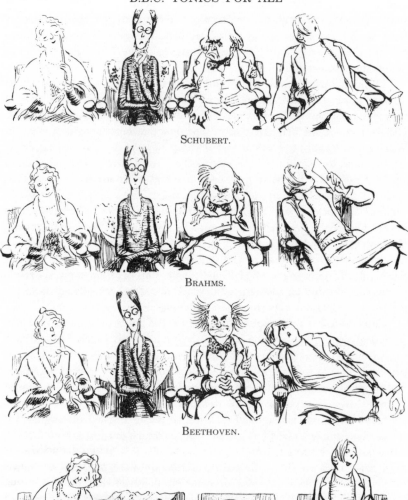

SCHUBERT.

BRAHMS.

BEETHOVEN.

SOMETHING MODERN (VERY).

and the majority who liked a catchy tune. Popular music, like classical music, had no simple unity. It too had gradations of taste with uneven degrees of legitimacy and status. It was only in the late thirties, when swing music was given canonical status, that popular music could be sorted out into a hierarchy of tastes and policy duly formulated. By then the efforts of programme policy-makers and planners were increasingly directed at efforts to lighten and brighten the National and Regional Programmes, and to redress the overall balance of the pattern of output in favour of entertainment. This was reflected in the increasingly tense relationship between the planners and the Music Department on the one hand, and the rise of the importance of the Variety Department and all its works on the other.

CHAPTER ELEVEN

Time and Money, Entertainment and Culture

—————⟶❈⟵—————

LISTENERS ALWAYS wanted more and better entertainment. In late 1923 a letter to *Radio Times* asked for more music hall turns and humorous broadcasts: 'I believe that if you would cater more freely in this direction, many who would hear this winter with apathy, if at all, programmes compiled as at present, will really enjoy listening.' This was followed by a challenge which was often to be repeated. 'If, over "radio", you could invite a consensus of opinion on the point I believe the result would astonish you.' The reply of the editor was that listeners would have to wait until more entertainers adapted their material to 'the special requirements of broadcast telephony'.[1] But apart from fairly regular 'sketches by humorists' there was little to tickle the tonsils of the audience in the early years of radio.

The twenties and early thirties were lean years for broadcast entertainment. 'Let there be no idea that this category is one given grudgingly and under pressure from the public or the press. To provide relaxation is no less positive an element of policy than any other', Reith grimly declared in the *BBC Hand Book* for 1928.[2] But to many it seemed that the transition from Company to Corporation had altered the relaxed and friendly relations between broadcasters and listeners, which had characterized the pioneering years. Thus a listener from Devon described the change:

It is my firm opinion that the root of nearly all the dissatisfaction regarding the BBC policy and programmes lies in the air of lofty condescension which pours from the loudspeakers. How we dislike the person who must always inform us, who is bursting with advice, whose genteelness and etiquette almost induce hys-

teria! At one time you and I were good pals, thanks to your spontaneous naturalness (what larks we had!) but now all has changed and your voice has assumed a
tutorial (and dictatorial) inflection, whilst I have become a small boy again in the
Lower Fourth.[3]

Harry Tate, the comedian, who based one of his sketches on the complexities
of the wireless apparatus, wrote, in *Popular Wireless*, that 'when Sir John
Reith was plain "Mister" and everybody was working much harder than now,
the old British Broadcasting *Company* never thought of "putting over" educational items. It is only since the BBC attained the status of a Corporation
that it has become swollen-headed and put uplift before laughter.'[4]

There was, by the late twenties, a good deal of press criticism of the standard of broadcast entertainment, which accounts for Reith's defensive tone.
Polls of audience preferences in the newspapers consistently showed that
vaudeville and variety were among the most popular kinds of programme on
radio, though they were in very short supply. The variety impresario C.B.
Cochran, writing for *The Graphic* in 1929, declared that he would 'make a
clean sweep of all those nightly mediocrities, those suburban pianists and
mothers' meeting ballad singers, those smoking concert entertainers and
pier-head parrots. I would give stars – quality ...'[5] Cochran might have a professional axe to grind, but not the critic Ivor Brown who complained in
The Saturday Review that 'the programmes today are like elongated penny
readings with orchestral variations and, when I look at the long list, my mind's
eye sees the vicar in the chair and the local concert party in menacing preparation.'[6]

The problem however was only partly to do with corporate attitudes to
entertainment. The field of entertainment itself was in transition when broadcasting came on the scene. Entrepreneurs in the business were deeply suspicious of the new medium, while the entertainers themselves feared radio. It
was not easy for them to adapt their performance to the peculiar context of the
studio microphone. Considerations of the home and family-based context of
listening led to severe restrictions on more robust and earthy forms of
humour. Gradually there emerged, by the late thirties, forms of 'radiogenic'
entertainment that were appropriate to the medium itself and the conditions in
which it was listened to. This development rested upon the emergence of a
clear policy for entertainment within the BBC as well as more settled relations
with management and performers in the entertainment business. At the same
time it pointed to a revaluation not only of the importance of entertainment
within corporate policy as a whole, but to a new attitude towards audience
tastes and wants. The acceptance, within the BBC, of the central importance
of entertainment within the whole range of output led to a change in attitude
towards programme planning that had significant consequences for the

arrangement and presentation of daily output. By the late thirties the success of the Variety Department was beginning to change the relationship between the BBC and its audience (or at least to recapture that earlier friendly quality lost in 'the stuffed shirt era'), and to modify some of the more austere aspects of the corporation's interpretation of its duty as a public service. This complex of developments must first be traced as an essential context within which to consider the development of styles of variety which offered entertainment to all by creating a common broadcast culture.

Relations with the entertainment business were difficult from the start. In April 1923 the executive committee of the Variety Artistes' Federation resolved to urge its members to refuse to cooperate in providing facilities for broadcasting. A month later the Entertainment Protection Association, representing all interested show business parties, was formed to guard their interests against the BBC. Although the BBC set up, in 1925, a joint committee with representatives of the entertainment business, the Variety Artistes' Federation refused to take part and there were few live broadcasts from variety theatres before 1928.

Individual performers and 'turns' faced real difficulties in adapting their acts to the microphone. Comedians in particular faced formidable problems. They lost their live audience and got no direct response from the absent listeners. They could not rely on visual humour, and they worried that they would very quickly use up all their material which was now subject to censorship on grounds of taste and vulgarity. In the earliest years there were complaints about the 'cruelly silent mike', or what George Graves described as 'that soulless and appallingly unsympathetic gadget'.[7] Harry Lauder found it helped to imagine the listeners back home. 'I saw the auld folks; I heard them "niccher" to themselves at "Hairry an' his daffin"; I saw the bairns; the young men and their lasses. I saw the wan faces lying in bed, and I saw the ancient shepherd, wi' his collie at his feet, in the wee biggin on the hillside.'[8] Will Hay referred to 'my friend Mike' whom he treated with some deference. 'You must be on your best behaviour in front of Mike. You must not say naughty words or anything the least bit lurid.'[9]

The BBC forbade jokes containing references to politics and politicians, advertisements, drink and prohibition in the United States, clergymen, medical matters and human infirmities, Scotsmen and Welshmen but not, apparently, Irishmen. In 1931 it was reported that producers were trying to exclude 'such worn-out topics for humour as sea-sickness, flat feet, cheese, kippers, bunions, etc'.[10] The BBC seemed at times more concerned with the susceptibilities of Mrs Grundy than the majority audience. Midland Region was ticked off in 1937 for broadcasting George Formby's, *The Window Cleaner*, and, when they protested that the song had been performed in a film with a U certificate as well as in a local pantomime, they were told that 'the people who complain of vulgarity in broadcasting may be those who think it immoral to go to a pantomime or even to a film'.[11] On one occasion at least the BBC even apologized in the news bulletin for its own lapse of taste. Listeners to the early evening news on 21 January 1935 heard the following announcement:

> The BBC apologizes to listeners for the inclusion in the *Music Hall* programme, broadcast on Saturday night, of certain highly objectionable remarks, violating standards which have been firmly established by the practice of the BBC.

And what were those remarks? An exchange between the popular comedy duo, Clapham and Dwyer: 'What is the difference between a champagne cork and a baby?' Answer: 'A champagne cork has the maker's name on its bottom.'[12] Programme Board disciplined the two comedians by banning them for five months.[13] By now the BBC's prudishness was itself a source of music hall jokes, and in 1937, Cecil Graves, Controller of Programmes, complained to the Variety Department about 'the habit comedians sometimes have of apologizing, so to speak, for not being vulgar because the BBC won't allow it. You probably know well enough what I mean. It is done in obvious ways and I really think it is rather stupid.'[14] Thus comedians who broadcast regularly had not only to seek fresh material but to seek it within a shrinking realm of subjects. John Watt, Head of Variety, confessed in 1939 that there were not many things left to be funny about on radio. 'It is said that there are only six jokes in the world, and I assure you that we cannot broadcast three of them.'[15]

The theatre managers' resistance to radio had a simpler basis. Just as newspaper owners feared the loss of newspaper sales, as the churches feared the loss of congregations each Sunday and the Football Association a collapse of attendance at the match each Saturday, so the show business impresarios feared a collapse of receipts at the box office. At first they combined to prevent the relay of live entertainment from their theatres, but their unity began to crumble in the late twenties when George Black agreed to monthly relays from the Palladium and Sir Oswald Stoll offered broadcasts from the Coliseum and the Alhambra. This infuriated Walter Payne, chairman of Moss Empires and president of the Society of West End Theatre Managers, who had voiced the strongest opposition to the BBC's involvement in entertainment in oral evidence to the Crawford Committee three years earlier.[16] Stoll had also annoyed the Variety Artistes' Federation by proposing to make no extra payment to performers for their appearance in broadcast shows. He argued that radio was providing them with free publicity and that his offer to release contracted artists from the ban on studio work was adequate compensation. The BBC however was anxious not to alienate performers and it insisted on payments to performers in the relayed shows. In the event the concordat with Stoll was short-lived. Early in 1930 the BBC faded out an act which was over-running from one of Stoll's theatres, thereby arousing the wrath of the impresario who withdrew his cooperation. But by now Stoll's business was in decline and the BBC did not suffer from the rift.[17]

More serious was the row with George Black a year or so later. Regular fortnightly relays from the Palladium continued until 1931 when the BBC dropped them 'as an economy measure'. Black suspected other motives since, by his estimation, the cost of the relays, to the BBC, was a mere £40 or £80 a month. His response was to ban from broadcasting all artists under contract to the General Theatres Corporation. This gave rise to some alarm in the BBC for Black was becoming a powerful figure in British show business. In 1932 the film company, Gaumont British, became the parent company for both General Theatres Corporation and Moss Empires, with Black in control of the variety side of the business. Though the BBC tried to bypass Black by seeking the support of the record companies and by going direct to Isidore Ostrer, the head of Gaumont British, these stratagems backfired when Black got to hear of them and took a harder line. By now Black controlled almost 50 per cent of the most popular performers in the British entertainment business, and was trying to use his power to get control of broadcast entertainment.

At the end of 1932 he was reported to be demanding an annual payment of £30,000 from the BBC for the right to engage his artists. He followed this up with a suggestion that he should become involved in the organization of BBC variety programmes in return for half the fees paid by the BBC to his contracted artists. Gerald Cock, who organized Outside Broadcasts, saw a chance here to drive a wedge between management and performers. He drafted a letter to be sent to leading performers, declaring that the BBC would rather deal directly with them, and reminding them again of the loss of potential income from the ban on studio work on their contracts. The letter ended with a call to action: 'By a unanimous refusal to sign such contracts, each of the artists with whom we are communicating would retain complete freedom to broadcast or otherwise, at his or her discretion, with no possibility of individual victimization. Unanimity is therefore of great importance.' This incitement to rebellion was too much for Roger Eckersley, then Director of Programmes, who was unwilling for the BBC to appear 'as a principal in the organization of artists' and the letter was not sent.[18]

It is worth considering why the BBC was so opposed to Black. After all, the £30,000 he asked for was not much more than the annual subsidies paid for opera, and he was in a position to supply the best names in the business. Gracie Fields, Flanagan and Allen, Max Miller, Tessie O'Shea, Billy Bennet, George Formby, Wee Georgie Wood and Hutch were all in his stable, and all were barred from appearing in BBC programmes. By the mid-thirties they were beginning to be heard on Luxembourg. Moreover, Black could undoubtedly organize the booking of artists efficiently. What Cock objected to was that to accede to Black would put the BBC in the position of being a paying customer, while Black effectively had the say as to what variety on radio should be. In effect, as Cock put it, 'BBC variety would be GTC variety'. To allow that would concede control of an area of broadcasting to an outside agent, and that would undermine the autonomy of the BBC.[19]

The real significance of these difficulties with performers and management was, however, to highlight the fact that there was, by the early thirties, as yet no coherent policy for broadcast entertainment. At the same time they showed that entertainment on radio could not rely either on simply getting artists into the studio to do their turns, or in relaying live shows from the halls. On the whole, they did not work and they were not funny. Even when relays of stage shows were allowed they often made awkward broadcasting: loud applause might overpower the microphone and gales of laughter might engulf the point of the gag. The routines of jugglers, conjurers and acrobats were largely incomprehensible to the unseeing listening audience, and the clumsy expedient of providing a commentary to describe and explain such acts hardly helped. Radio needed to discover its own forms of entertainment. But that required a more coherent idea of the role of variety in general programme output, and a properly established production department to deliver it.

Until 1932 responsibility for variety programmes had slipped between the fingers of Gerald Cock, who organized all Outside Broadcasts, and Val Gielgud, in charge of the increasingly unwieldy Production Department responsible for everything apart form talks and music. In 1930 a separate Revue Section was set up within Gielgud's empire, with two newly appointed producers. The following year two more staff were recruited to produce vaudeville and variety, and the BBC Theatre Orchestra was formed. In 1933 the Production Department was split up. A separate Variety Department for entertainment programmes was created, headed by Eric Maschwitz, while Gielgud remained in charge of what was now called the Drama Department. At the same time the BBC purchased St George's Hall in which to stage its own variety performances. By 1936 the Variety Department employed twenty-nine producers and writers.

The restructuring of the production departments, coupled with the separation of administration from programme-making resulted in renewed corporate efforts to achieve overall policy and planning for the whole range of output. Attention focused increasingly on the vexed question of what the audience wanted, what its tastes were and how these might be identified. It began to be perceived that there should be some correlation between the overall balance of output and the preferences of the listening public. As such considerations came to the fore, so too did the Variety Department and support for its activities. What yet needed to be established though, here as elsewhere, was a more sophisticated and precise appreciation of audience preferences within the range of material produced by the department. What was the audience for music hall? For dance music? For revue and cabaret? As answers to such questions were sought and found, the Variety Department readjusted its own output, while successfully claiming more time in the schedules at the expense of other departments.

One powerful external stimulus to lighten and brighten the output was the impact of Radios Normandie and Luxembourg.[20] The possibility of European commercial radio aimed at Britain had begun to emerge in the late twenties. Reith commented then: 'My reaction is why worry when 10 per cent of our listeners are affected? Are we so afraid of competition?' In the early thirties a senior BBC executive could ask: 'Are the threats that Luxembourg holds over us so serious? It is suggested that they are not.' The view was, at first, that it would simply fade away or, if not, that it would be largely taken up by 'the kind of little people who will give remarkably bad programmes'.[21] This soon gave way to efforts to impede the reception of commercial radio in this country. The BBC now found itself in alliance with an old enemy, the Newspaper Proprietors' Association, who feared a loss of advertising revenue if commercial radio became established. The newspapers responded by refusing to carry details of the commercial stations. The BBC tried to dissuade the wireless exchanges from distributing foreign programmes to their customers. In October 1931 a provisional agreement was reached to this effect with Standard Radio Relay Services, the leading company in the business. However, in June the following year, the Postmaster General refused to give his necessary consent to the agreement, taking the view that there was no reason why subscribers to relay exchanges should not be allowed to listen to commercial programmes from abroad when ordinary wireless listeners could receive them. The agreement lapsed, and with it the BBC's efforts to limit the reception of foreign commercial radio.

By 1935 Reith was fuming about 'the monstrous stuff from Luxembourg' and wondering aloud what could be done to put a spoke in their wheel.[22] One thing that was done was to put pressure on BBC performers. When BBC artists started to wonder if they might be sacked for appearing in Luxembourg programmes, Admiral Carpendale had declared himself against such an idea: 'It is not the artist's fault. We don't give them a living, they've got to go to all and sundry where they can earn their money. We must wait and see what Luxembourg does.' But six months later, in September 1934, Carpendale told the Post Office that 'we are now warning artists unofficially that it is not in their interests to broadcast from Luxembourg, and several have declined to do so on this account, in spite of good offers.'[23] Christopher Stone, the world's first 'disc jockey' lost his regular record programme with the BBC when he began to broadcast from Luxembourg, and the *Daily Express* cancelled his weekly review article. The BBC expected a flood of protest when Stone was taken off the air, and were surprised to receive only ten letters in the week his programme was cancelled. One reason for the apparent indifference might have been that he was preferred in his new show. A letter to *Radio Pictorial* declared: 'One misses him from Daventry, but already one hears in his voice from Luxembourg a nuance of greater freedom. Those hampering and petty restrictions at the BBC must have been very difficult to cope with.'[24]

On the whole, performers were better off working for Luxembourg than the BBC. In the early thirties the normal BBC fee for a variety turn was reputed to be as low as two guineas. In 1935, writing for *The Star*, J. B. Priestley complained that the BBC gave too much airtime to second-rate acts and concluded that it was not prepared to pay for talent. 'In spite of its vast revenues, its colossal public, the acres of print at its service, the BBC is never regarded by its talkers, actors, singers as anything more than a half-way house'.[25] For an act in a radio variety show, usually lasting about ten minutes, a real top-liner such as George Robey or Gracie Fields might be paid as much as £150. But the normal fee for the star of the show was £50 and a contract that stipulated numerous rehearsals (though these were often avoided). Performers who owed their reputation to radio were paid less – anything from 15 to 30 guineas per performance. But the BBC found it hard to keep its own 'discoveries' if they happened to make a success on the boards. One well-known double act which made its name on radio was paid a mere 15 guineas per act by the BBC in 1933 but by 1937, when it was reportedly earning up to £400 a week on the stage, the BBC was forced to increase its fee to 52 guineas. An executive in BBC Variety Bookings complained: 'This is all very well in the case of artists who do not owe their success partially to broadcasting but in the case of artists who achieve fame via the microphone I feel we are entitled to be a little less generous in our fees.'[26]

BBC programmes always went out live, but programmes for Luxembourg were produced and recorded by advertising agencies in London and sent to the Grand Duchy on discs. Although the agencies paid a relatively unknown performer little more than the BBC offered – about £20 per show – they recorded four shows in a morning. Thus an artist earned four times as much for working roughly the same hours (including rehearsals) that it took to earn £20 from the BBC. Furthermore, since all commercial shows were arranged in series, the work was regular. Until the BBC began to produce more series, to supply artists with scripts and to offer long-term contracts, it would always seem more attractive to work for commercial radio.[27]

The challenge of Luxembourg could not be met by negative action. Senior policy-makers were aware of this and efforts were made to lighten the programme service. There was one severe obstacle, however, in the way of any attempt to compete directly with Luxembourg, and that was the BBC's Sunday policy. Radio Luxembourg had begun transmissions in English on 16

January 1934 on a powerful longwave frequency, which gave good reception in most parts of mainland Britain. Through the week Luxembourg broadcast in English each evening, but in French, Italian and German during the day. On Sundays however, from eight in the morning until late at night, it provided a non-stop service of entertainment for a British audience. This was a brilliant thrust at the BBC, whose Sunday programme policy had long been notorious. Guided by Reith's strict sabbatarianism, the BBC's Sunday output was severely constrained both in quantity and quality. The BBC Sunday began with a religious service in the morning from 9.30 to 10.45. There was silence then until 12.30, and thereafter a diet of serious music and talks until evening service at eight in the evening. This was followed by more serious music until the Epilogue ended it all at eleven o'clock. When Luxembourg came on air listeners began to desert the BBC in large numbers. Seebohm Rowntree noted that in working-class households in York it was customary to switch on to Luxembourg first thing on a Sunday morning and leave it on all day, with perhaps a break in the evening for the religious service. The Relay Company, which provided a service to 3000 subscribers in York, gave Rowntree a breakdown of the most popular programmes selected by subscribers. Leading the field was the *Littlewoods Pool Programme* from Luxembourg each Sunday at 1.30 pm. It had a 100 per cent load against the BBC on the other channel.[28]

Efforts within the BBC to change the Sunday policy had to take on not only Reith, but the Central Religious Advisory Committee and the Rev. Frederick A. Iremonger, the BBC's Religious Director, neither of whom wished to make any changes to the broadcast Sabbath.[29] But from 1934 onwards the pressure from senior policy-makers increased for more secular programme material on Sunday evenings. Religion was being squeezed in favour of entertainment – to Reith's dismay, as Kenneth Wolfe notes, who lamented that there was not to be one day 'clear of such stuff'.[30] But Iremonger and the Central Religious Advisory Committee blocked all attempts to perform any radical surgery on the body of Sunday programmes. Change, if change was to come, should be gradual. Iremonger, invoking the Lord's Day Observance Society and 'a solid block of English and Scottish conviction' maintained that Sunday broadcasting should continue to be largely different from weekdays. He opposed any proposal that Sunday output should be like that of any other day without the unsavoury material such as jazz. More positively, he favoured a broader definition of plays on Sunday beyond the works of Shakespeare. Though he strongly opposed the music of the Wurlitzer organ as vulgar in the extreme, he was prepared to countenance light opera as a concession to more entertainment on God's day.[31] Against this, the planners and policy-makers made little headway in enlivening the BBC's Sunday before the war.

Such restraints did not however apply to the rest of the week's output, and there attention to the overall balance of output was first addressed in 1934 by a newly constituted Programme Revision Committee whose task was to consider the timing of programmes, the ratio between different kinds of programme and 'the efficiency of the programmes as a whole' – a concept which appeared to mean something like 'cost-effectiveness'. The committee noted that throughout its deliberations it had been conscious of the lack of any reliable data concerning the habits and tastes of the majority of those who listened to BBC programmes. It regarded this lack as 'a serious defect in the equipment of a great national corporation', making planning difficult and preventing the BBC from dealing adequately with its critics in the press and elsewhere who claimed, without fear of contradiction, a comprehensive knowledge of public taste.[32]

In spite of this admission the committee had no apparent qualms in proceeding to analyse the unknown audience in terms of four different categories of demand: the wireless trade, the 'tap-listener', the occasional listener and the serious listener. Each, it appeared, was getting what he or she deserved. There was daytime broadcasting for the trade who could demonstrate the quality of their goods to customers. The tap-listener was the sort that the BBC had always discouraged and therefore 'warranted no further special provision in programmes'. The occasional listener was catered for in the general balance of output as was the serious listener, whose needs were entitled to 'the greatest measure of consideration'. All in all, the committee concluded, without a shred of evidence in support, the existing ratios of programming were 'about right'.

When it turned to consider the activities of particular areas of production the report conveyed a sense of drift, and of enthusiasm and ideals undermined by the effort to maintain a continuous supply of output. Talks had run out of fresh subjects and needed 'new and more imaginative forms of presentation'. Elsewhere greater 'efficiency' could be achieved by simpler production methods. In the early and more experimental days of broadcasting there had been a tendency towards deliberate complexity in the technique of presentation. This was now regarded as highly undesirable. No more could Lance Sieveking rapturously preside over the knobs and switches of the dramatic control panel. The multiple studio production was becoming a thing of the past.

In only one area of production could the committee detect a coherent sense of purpose which it wholeheartedly endorsed, and that was light entertainment. 'The committee believes that on the criterion of numbers light entertainment in its various forms is probably the most popular element in the programmes, and it is in large measure responsible for the Corporation's growing revenue. It therefore deserves a large place in the programmes and an ample financial allocation.' It recommended the employment of more staff writers to increase the output of revue material, and noted that the inclusion of highly paid star artists in all variety programmes was of great value both on grounds of quality and of prestige. A correlation was beginning to emerge between the time and effort involved in programme making, their costs and the size of their audiences. This trend was underlined the following year when Programme Board addressed itself to the question of whether the BBC was trying to produce too many programmes with a consequent loss in standards. This was a sensitive issue, for the Ullswater Committee was about to begin its enquiries, and Reith took it up. He offered for consideration four administrative solutions: an increase in production staff, a reduction in output, simpler and more economic production methods and more repeats of programmes and at closer intervals. Recommending simple production methods, Reith noted that 'there should be efficiency of output in the sense that the return from any particular programme was definitely comparable with the outlay in energy, time and money'.[33]

Reith went on to declare that success should be the criterion for both the effort put into production and for repetition. But what, he asked, was the system for assessing the success of programmes? When the next Programme Revision Committee met in 1936, under the chairmanship of Cecil Graves, it had no satisfactory answer to that question. The tone of this report was, as Briggs notes, far less complacent than its predecessor, as by now something of the magnitude of the task of improving the balance of programmes was beginning to sink in. Graves made three key points. There was a need for a more clearly defined programme policy, and for this to be understood by the London production departments and the regions. Second, more thought and care should be given to programme presentation. Some 'showmanship' was necessary if programmes were to catch and keep the attention of listeners. It was no longer enough simply to expect or exhort listeners to listen. The style of presentation was important. Third, it was now clear beyond a doubt that for programme planning to be a meaningful exercise, those responsible needed much closer knowledge of the social composition of the audience and its listening habits, tastes and preferences: 'In considering programme revision as a whole those concerned were faced at every turn with an absence of reliable evidence on which to base their judgments and recommendations.'[34] Listener research was essential. A few months later R. J. E. Silvey, of the London Press Exchange, was recruited to the BBC to establish audience research on a systematic basis.

Although the full flowering of the Listener Research Department did not take place until the Second World War, the information it began to supply soon became an essential aid to programme planning.[35] For the first time an accurate picture began to emerge of audience tastes and preferences. Though, unsurprisingly, variety was the most popular kind of programme there were some surprises when listener preferences for different types of entertainment became known. Eric Maschwitz had always claimed that straight dance band music was the most popular of all the programmes for which he was responsible.[36] But the first survey of listening to light entertainment, in 1937 and 1938, showed that while 70 per cent of the volunteers who took part in the survey wanted more variety and only 1 per cent wanted less, only 17 per cent wanted more dance music and 28 per cent voted for less. The expensive revues and musical comedies favoured by Maschwitz were found to be very much a minority taste. While the new comedy series and continuity shows were not quite as popular as variety, their audiences were found to increase with familiarity, and by 1939 *Band Waggon* had overtaken the traditional Saturday night *Music Hall* in popularity.[37] In 1938 the Director of Programme Planning was suggesting that the number of continuity shows should be increased, and that dance music should be cut back. In that year the production of sophisticated revue almost ceased and musical comedies were reduced to no more than one or two a month.[38]

At the start of the thirties Variety was under-resourced and under-financed. By contrast, the then powerful Music Department was well staffed and amply funded. The sponsorship of the Henry Wood Promenade Concerts from 1928 onwards and the creation of the BBC Symphony Orchestra had established it at the forefront of musical life in Britain. At the same time the BBC's patronage of music established expensive fixed commitments both in terms of time and money which, by the end of the decade, had become something of an embarrassment for programme planners. By 1939 the Symphony Orchestra employed 119 musicians at a cost of £80,000 a year. Besides this there was now the Theatre Orchestra, Variety Orchestra, Empire Orchestra, Military Band and five regional orchestras, together employing 266 musicians and costing around £120,000 a year.[39] Since they were there, all the orchestras had to be used, and so there was an inevitable commitment to the regular supply of symphonic and orchestral music in the programme schedules throughout the year. In time this began to appear as an oversupply to policy-makers and planners anxious to allocate more time and more resources to variety.

Apart from its investment in its own orchestras, the BBC was subsidizing other outside musical bodies, particularly opera companies. The sponsorship of opera went back to the earliest days of broadcasting and, by the start of the thirties, the BBC was prepared to subsidize Covent Garden to the tune of £25,000 a year. In an extraordinary arrangement with the Treasury, under the Chancellorship of Philip Snowden, the Labour Government underwrote the agreement and offered a subsidy of £7500. All this took place just before the financial crisis which brought the Government down later in the year, and the *Daily Express*, for one, was not amused: 'There are better ways of spending

£17,500 than in subsidizing a form of art which is not characteristic of the British people,' it declared.[40] The size of the BBC's subsidy was reduced, but by the mid-thirties the BBC was paying £10,000 a year to Covent Garden, £6000 to Sadlers Wells and £2000 to the touring Carla Rosa Opera Company. This was in return for just under fifty hours of broadcast opera a year at a cost of around £400 an hour.[41] In 1936 an *ad hoc* Opera Advisory Committee under Sir Landon Ronald was set up to recommend how the BBC should distribute its largesse to the opera companies. It recommended decreasing the subsidy to Covent Garden and increasing the allowance to Sadlers Wells because it was seen as the chief permanent home of opera performed in English by British performers. By the late thirties Sadlers Wells received £8000 a year from the BBC.[42]

The heavy investment in serious music thus tended to clog up the programme schedules to the increasing perplexity of the planners as they tried to make output more lively and entertaining. The Programme Revision Committee in 1934, while endorsing the policy of subsidizing opera, wished 'to stress the damage to programmes which may result if the amount of financial subsidies granted is allowed unduly to influence the number of relays.' At the same time it recommended that the weekly public performances of chamber music in the concert hall of Broadcasting House should be discontinued because of 'the additional element of fixity which they involve'.[43] The following year, it will be recalled, Graves scrapped *The Foundations of Music* in order to ease the early evening schedule and in 1936 he abandoned the practice of broadcasting the first half of every single concert given during the six-week Promenade season. This, as he explained in a public announcement, was in order to make the Promenades fit more into the general scheme of programme planning. The practical reasons for such decisions were amply supported by Listener Research when it began to produce figures for the size of audiences for serious music. The General Listening Barometer for January 1939 showed that during peak hours symphony concerts attracted between 9 and 16 per cent of listeners, opera between 11 and 23 per cent chamber music about 3 per cent. Variety, by comparison, drew between 40 and 68 per cent.[44]

By the mid-thirties resource allocation between different areas of production was becoming a central issue for programme policy and planning. It might be thought that, as annual revenue from licences had risen steadily from the late twenties to the late thirties, the BBC had ample resources to finance all types of programmes and therefore competition between departments for funding need not have arisen. But although the BBC's income correspondingly increased during these years, expenditure on programmes in general and in particular on 'creative labour' increased less rapidly than other types of expenditure.

The BBC has always been notoriously secretive about its finances and

TABLE 1. Proportions of total BBC annual expenditure devoted to different items, 1927–38

Type of expenditure	Percentages of total annual expenditure											
	1927	1928	1929	1930	1931	1932	1933	1934	1935	1936	1937	1938
Programmes	63·07	61·30	57·37	55·89	55·02	47·83	49·77	49·77	51·69	51·91	53·95	53·53
Engineering	16·94	18·25	18·71	18·56	17·70	18·18	18·55	18·22	17·99	19·01	18·68	19·06
Premises maintenance and overhead charges	8·18	8·87	6·17	8·73	8·41	11·15	7·56	8·88	8·49	7·39	5·54	5·47
Administration	6·58	6·39	5·82	5·72	5·35	5·56	5·63	5·05	5·53	5·16	4·55	4·67
Contribution to staff pension scheme, etc.	1·02	0·96	0·98	1·01	1·16	1·61	2·46	1·7	1·75	1·75	2·06	2·12
Governors' fees	0·79	0·69	0·64	0·59	0·50	0·41	0·39	0·33	0·24	0·24	0·27	0·25
Provision for depreciation and renewals	3·41	3·54	4·02	4·68	5·67	7·18	7·91	9·9	8·7	8·92	9·51	8·99
Provision for income tax	—	—	6·27	4·81	6·19	7·93	7·66	6·15	5·59	5·62	5·43	5·89
Total %	99·99	100·00	99·98	99·99	100·00	99·85	99·93	100·00	99·98	100·00	99·99	99·98
Actual total (in 1000s to nearest £1000)	773	879	956	1038	1196	1387	1580	1838	2148	2580	3206	3535

detailed evidence of programme expenditure is hard to come by and difficult to interpret. Nevertheless some broad details of pre-war programme spending can be sketched in. Table 1 gives a breakdown of annual total expenditure (excluding transfers to capital account) for the years 1927 to 1938.[45] It can be seen that the share allocated to programmes fell from 63 per cent in 1927 to 48 per cent in 1932 and by 1938 had only climbed back to 53 per cent. This dip in relative expenditure on programmes was due mainly to the move to Broadcasting House in 1932 and the rising costs of engineering, maintenance and provision for depreciation as the service expanded. Although actual expenditure on programmes nearly quadrupled over the period, the proportion of this spent on creative labour did not rise to the same extent. Creative labour costs refer to expenditure on salaries for the permanent orchestras and choruses, on fees to outside performers, writers and other contributors, and on copyright fees for music, gramophone recordings and news agency royalties. Table 2 provides a breakdown of programme expenditure for the same ten-year period.[46] It can be seen that the proportion spent on creative labour (understood as comprising the first two items listed) declined from 60 per cent in 1927 to 49.5 per cent in 1938. Again, expenditure in this area trebled over the period, but these figures include the Empire Service which began in 1933 and the Television Service which started in 1936. By 1938 over 20 per cent of expenditure on creative labour was absorbed by these two new services.

Once this is taken into account it can be shown that, for home radio, expenditure on creative labour increased by a factor of only 2.7 over the period. The most rapidly increasing area of expenditure was on copyright charges, the bulk of which went to the Performing Rights Society which collected on behalf of copyright music. Payments to the PRS were calculated on the basis of the annual number of licences and so continued to rise across the period. At first this was subject to an upper limit of 5 per cent of the BBC's licence income, but in 1937 this was dropped and the income from radio of the PRS increased dramatically.[47] In 1930 the Society received £60,300 (35 per cent of its total income) from the BBC. In 1935 this had risen to £134,700 (39 per cent) and by 1940 to £337,000 (54 per cent).[48] Expenditure on copyright rose by a factor of 4.7 between 1927 and 1938 but this did not, of course, reflect any substantial increase in the amount of music broadcast. All this suggests that room for manoeuvre between the main programme departments in London over the allocation of budgets for expenditure on creative labour was more restricted than might have been supposed. By the late thirties, as income began to level out, hard decisions had to be faced.

Table 3 shows the distribution of expenditure on creative labour and of hours produced among different areas of output in London for 1934 and 1937, the only two years in the thirties for which such information has survived.[49] The figures are for expenditure on the National Programme and the London

TABLE 2. Proportions of BBC annual programme expenditure devoted to different items, 1927–38

Type of programme	*Percentages of total annual expenditure on programmes*											
	1927	*1928*	*1929*	*1930*	*1931*	*1932*	*1933*	*1934*	*1935*	*1936*	*1937*	*1938*
Artists, speakers, etc.	60·3	62·8	60·2	60·6	62·6	58·6	54·9	36·1	36·1	37·7	37·2	38·0
Permanent orchestras								18·4	18·1	16·7	13·1	11·5
Performing rights, copyright fees and news royalties	12·5	10·0	11·2	12·6	12·4	13·4	15·7	16·3	16·9	15·3	21·0	20·6
Simultaneous broadcast telephone system	2·2	2·2	3·2	3·1	3·6	4·6	6·1	5·2	4·9	4·5	4·0	3·8
Programme staff salaries	21·3	21·9	22·2	20·5	18·3	19·5	19·3	20·4	20·5	21·9	21·2	22·6
Various expenses	3·6	3·1	3·1	3·1	3·1	3·9	3·9	3·6	3·5	3·9	3·5	3·5
Total %	99·9	100·0	99·9	99·9	100·0	100·0	99·9	100·0	100·0	100·0	100·0	100·0
Actual total (in 1000s to nearest £1000)	488	539	549	580	658	663	786	915	1111	1339	1730	1892

TABLE 3. Distribution of creative labour costs and of hours produced for BBC in London, 1934 and 1937

Type of output	Percentage of total hours		Percentage of total expenditure		Average cost per hour (£)		Producing department
	1934	1937	1934	1937	1934	1937	
Serious music	16·19	16·38	38·86	28·59	134·6	107·3	Music
Light music	28·01	26·13	18·83	19·73	37·7	46·4	
Variety and vaudeville	2·46	3·96	7·49	12·3	170·7	190·5	
Revue and musical comedy	2·40	2·09	9·36	7·24	218·7	212·6	Variety
Dance bands	11·97	7·97	7·74	9·87	36·2	76·1	
Gramophone records	9·59	12·64	0·2	0·15	1·2	0·7	—
Serious drama	1·38	1·01	2·46	2·52	100	153·2	
Light drama	1·15	1·23	2·29	3·22	111	161	Drama
Feature programmes	0·79	1·25	1·64	3·49	116·6	172·3	
Children's Hour	3·60	2·62	2·02	1·74	31·5	40·7	
Talks	8·15	8·21	6·26	5·74	43	43	Talks
Outside broadcasts	1·25	2·13	0·67	2·09	30·2	60·4	OB
School education	3·2	3·46	1·29	1·87	22·6	33·2	Schools
News	6·01	7·39	—	0·03	—	0·2	News
Religion	3·65	3·52	0·85	1·4	13·1	24·4	Religion
Total %	99·79	99·99	99·96	99·98			
Actual totals	6149	7542	£344,690	£463,383			
Average overall cost per hour					56	61·4	

Regional Programme, both produced from Broadcasting House by the departmental staff of the National Programme. London Regional notionally supplied a service to the South East. More exactly it served as a 'feed' for all the other regional stations during daytime hours of transmission. The main defect of these figures is that they do not include copyright payments. It was impossible to find an accurate means of distributing the gross royalty paid for copyright music among the different categories of music output. But it can be assumed that if such costs were included, expenditure on light music and dance music would have been at least doubled, and serious music and variety would also come out as more expensive. If news royalties and mechanical copyright charges had been included, the cost of news would have risen to approximately £55 per hour and the cost of gramophone record programmes, on a very rough estimate, to about £40 an hour.

This having been said, the table does give a reasonable indication of the relative costs of different types of programme. It provides an index of the relative value which the BBC placed on different types of output which is in marked contrast to the index of time allocation which has always been used by the BBC itself and by most commentators on broadcasting. Most notably, while few hours of variety, vaudeville, revue and musical comedy were produced, these were by far the most expensive types of programme. By 1937 they accounted for 19 per cent of expenditure on creative labour though they made up only 6 per cent of the hours produced. Light music and dance music, which were the bread and butter of broadcasting, particularly during daytime hours and the late evening, were predictably cheap. Serious music absorbed a high proportion of time and money.

Another interesting aspect of the figures for the two years is that they give some indication of a shift in priorities between 1934 and 1937, though a comparison over a longer period would almost certainly have illustrated this trend more decisively. While expenditure on serious music actually decreased by about £1000 over the four years, expenditure on variety, vaudeville, revue and musical comedy increased by about £31,000. While the amount of time allotted to dance music declined and the proportion of time devoted to light music fell (though there was an actual increase here of 200 hours), there was a considerable rise in the expenditure on both these categories. More time and more money were being devoted to light drama in comparison with serious drama. All these comparisons suggest a shift of resources in the direction of more popular programmes, a shift which can hardly be detected if we simply compare the proportions of time allocated to different types of output.

By the late thirties the slow growth in creative labour expenditure, the high cost of variety programmes and the increase in expenditure on entertainment was creating real difficulties within an overall programme budget which, though adequate to existing commitments, had nothing in reserve for expensive new production proposals. Just how problematic resource allocation had by then become can be seen in the clash between Charles Siepmann, now Director of Programme Planning, and the Music Department over the establishment of a new Music Production Unit in 1938.[50]

The aim of this new unit was to produce opera from the studio, with a view to ending the everlasting problems of late starts and finishes, and of last-minute changes to the programmes by the opera companies whose performances the BBC paid so much for the privilege of occasionally relaying. When Stanford Robinson, the head of the unit, put forward his plans, Siepmann was horrified. The proposal envisaged, on a continuing monthly basis, a full-length opera at a cost of £600, a short opera or excerpt at £350 and an operetta at £250. In addition to this there would be an average of ten concerts a month, from straight Theatre Orchestra broadcasts to arranged productions (like *Victorian Melodies*), at varying costs of up to £150. The annual cost of all this was projected at around £16,000, but Siepmann pointed out that there were further hidden costs. The plan would completely tie up the Theatre Orchestra (which it was planned to augment at a cost of £8000 a year in salaries for the extra players), which had hitherto been mainly used by the Variety Department in its musical shows, comedies and operettas. There would thus be a consequent increase in expenditure on their side of the line. Moreover Stanford Robinson could not do all this by himself and he had already put in a bid for extra staff. Meanwhile the subsidies to the opera companies continued.

Logic and consistency, Siepmann remarked, seemed to have been the last consideration in this scheme, but that perhaps did not matter very much in an institution not wedded to such principles. What did matter were questions of audiences and costs. For whom were these broadcasts intended, and how far should the BBC meet their demands in terms of programme hours? Before any decision was taken, Siepmann asked that Silvey's Listener Research Section should investigate the audience for broadcast opera and whether they would prefer studio or relayed performances. The evidence supplied by Silvey on other matters had been, said Siepmann, so illuminating and so important that he was sure that Listener Research would provide the information necessary to judge whether the activities of the Music Production Unit could claim a legitimate place in the programme. Already Silvey's investigations into the daytime audience had shown that the publics for serious music were significantly smaller than for other major areas of output. Though this was not conclusive, it suggested, Siepmann felt that to provide opera on the lines proposed would be 'to make further concessions to the claims of a minority which was already treated more liberally perhaps than was quite fair to the ordinary listener's needs'. This was the crux of the matter, and Siepmann forcefully stated his growing concern with the cost-effectiveness of programmes in relation both to the size of audience they delivered and to the importance of lighter, entertaining programmes adapted to the needs of ordinary listeners.

> It has been our practice in the last year to relate programme planning more closely than in the past to programme costs. The suggested expenditure on studio opera is very high, higher in fact than for any other department of our work considered on the basis of equivalent hours of output ... While our present programme budget is, I think, adequate to our commitments, it leaves us without any margin or reserve. One of the more serious implications of MPD's proposal is that the higher cost involved can only be met at the expense of lighter programmes. Even if opera is substituted for orchestral music, no economy is

realised in view of our capital liabilities for the maintenance of our main orchestra. Either Variety or Drama will have to foot the bill for MPD's productions,
and if Silvey's [head of Listener Research] figures are even approximately correct, the former commands almost three times and the latter almost twice the
audience which we can assume to be available for opera.[51]

Siepmann claimed there was no proven need for studio opera. Recent
relays from the continent had been technically successful and were ridicu-
lously cheap. If opera from Europe could be got at a cost of about £30 an
hour, why go to all this trouble and expense? There remained the question of
what to do with Stanford Robinson and his new unit, and there Siepmann had
no solution. What seems to have happened is that he was confined to one
opera a month, and devoted the rest of his energies to light music features.
When the war came the BBC reverted to taking regular broadcasts from the
leading British opera companies.

Planning documents for the last two years of the decade reveal the extent
to which the policy-makers had reached stalemate. Notes on the autumn
schedule for 1938 stated plainly that Listener Research statistics 'may be
interpreted as demanding a lightening of the programmes, chiefly at the
expense of serious music', though any such policy should proceed with some
caution in view of 'our traditional policy of giving the public something better
than it thinks it wants'. The document called for more of the accepted classics
and less experimental music from the Music Department, who should also try
harder to 'sell' difficult music with better presentation and publicity. But there
was little room for manoeuvre because of fixed commitments and the need for
BBC musicians to earn their keep by working their full contractual hours. A
small reduction in the output of serious music could be made, however, if the
musicians spent more time in rehearsal and less in performance.[52]

In 1939 it was stated that the two main principles on which programme
planning was based were '(i) to allocate time and money as between the various categories of programmes in relation to listeners' demands and BBC policy and (ii) to provide listeners with well contrasted programmes on
two alternative wavelengths.' In practice this meant more lightening of
programmes and more routinization of schedules, with the latter as the means
of securing the former. Programme Board noted that 'in view of the large
extent to which the available programme time has been "locked" owing to
unavoidable commitments, a solution has been found by way of "locking" the
programme throughout, i.e. by allocating regular times each week for the various programme activities.'[53] Contrasted programming – popular material on
one wavelength against serious fare on the other – tended further to reduce the
size of the audiences for serious music, as the programme planners discovered

that given such a choice the majority would tend always to prefer the light-weight rather than the heavyweight.

By now the competing inter-departmental claims for time and money had reached an uneasy compromise. As far as time goes, Variety was in the ascendant. There was a commitment to increasing its programme share at the expense of serious music. Variety producers liked fixed scheduling since they were by now committed to the series format, whereas music producers preferred to pick and choose outside broadcasts as the occasion arose and to vary the length of their own musical selections. There was a way out, which had in the past occasionally been discussed, and that was the provision of a third programme. This proposal, put on the agenda again by the Director of Programme Planning in 1938, was envisaged as an alternative to the National and Regional programmes. It would be 'of a "universal" (i.e. popular) nature', and would satisfy the undemanding needs of ordinary listeners while allowing serious matter to be scheduled more flexibly in the other two programmes.[54] Such a solution was perhaps, in an underlying sense, becoming inevitable but it was not to be reached until after the war with the creation of the three-tiered radio service which lasted from the late forties through to the late sixties.

As far as money was concerned, although there is no clear evidence of budgetary readjustments between the Variety and Music Departments, it seems likely that any increase in the overall programme budget would have been absorbed by the Variety Department since it was acknowledged to be overstretched.[55] Though variety was seen as a money-earner, attracting new listeners and even beginning to sell the stage rights to some of its shows, it was set to become the money-spender as well, soaking up the extra revenue it generated. But by the late thirties there was little extra revenue to be had. Income from licence fees which had, over the whole period, increased at a steady rate, had now flattened out as the size of the radio audience reached a stable plateau in the late thirties. Nor was there much chance either of persuading the Post Office or the Treasury to part with the quite disproportionate amount of the licence fee that they extracted before handing over the annual residue to the BBC. There was little hope that the Government would agree to an increase in the licence fee.

The growing concern of policy-makers and planners for the needs of 'the ordinary listener' was not merely a matter of expediency and cost-effectiveness, goaded by the impact of commercial radio. The timing of programmes, the establishment of fixed schedules and a routinized output, and the new emphasis on presentation all acknowledged both a pragmatic attention to the realities of listening and a greater consideration for listeners. These concerns came together in the developing output of the Variety Department on whose behalf the policy-makers and planners came into conflict with the Music Department. For, if the thrust of that department's work was to fragment the audience, the thrust of the work of Variety was to unite it. It is not enough merely to note that Variety was popular. Why it was so is intimately connected with the form and content of the entertainment supplied. The development of styles of entertainment which were particular to broadcasting and which, in their form and content, appealed to all sections of an audience differentiated by age, gender and social class, was one crucial means whereby broadcasting created the basis of a genuinely common culture. Broadcast entertainment became socially inclusive because it was culturally inclusive. The gradual discovery of how to produce such 'radiogenic' entertainment before the war culminated in the creation of *Band Waggon*, a landmark programme in broadcast entertainment.

CHAPTER TWELVE

Styles of Variety

———◦❋◦———

Producers of radio variety faced two problems, which were not shared by their contemporaries working in the entertainment business. They had to produce material that would entertain people in their homes, as distinct from the theatre or music hall. Besides this they had to maintain a continuous supply of material on a scale that would soon have exhausted the most energetic impresario. Thus the task for broadcast entertainment was to discover forms that were appropriate to the conditions in which they were heard and that were in principle endlessly reproducible. Existing forms of public entertainment defined themselves in their difference from day-to-day living. The design of the place of entertainment whose name so often expressed a promise of exotic pleasure – The Palace of Variety, The Coliseum, The Alhambra, The Ritz – marked out the visit to the cinema, the theatre or the music hall as something set apart from ordinary life, and the pleasures on offer therein as extraordinary pleasures. The trick for broadcasting to discover, by contrast, was how to offer ordinary pleasures to listeners that interacted with the ordinary circumstances of domestic life and supported its routines. In the process the broadcasters moved away from the stage conventions of existing forms of entertainment as they discovered the techniques and methods that were appropriate to the medium of radio and its situational proprieties. In doing this they found themselves gradually moving from formats of limited appeal to particular groups of listeners, towards entertainment formats of general appeal to all sections of the listening public.

In the early years studio 'variety' programmes were usually billed in *Radio Times* as 'vaudeville'. The distinction is obscure. Barry Took's suggestion

"THERE'S VARIETY AT EIGHT O'CLOCK TO-NIGHT, FRED."

that artists appeared once in vaudeville and twice in variety is not confirmed by *Radio Times* billings.[1] The London *Star* claimed unkindly that the BBC used the term vaudeville because ' "Variety" no longer describes the kind of thing broadcast on Saturday night.'[2] There was some truth in this. Stage variety depended on contrast between acts. Radio vaudeville was restricted to singers and comedians, although speciality acts – a 'siffleur', a virtuoso on saw or wineglasses, Bransby Williams impersonating Dickensian characters – might sometimes be heard. The reproduction of atmosphere and the selection of artists were the two problems that gave variety producers the greatest trouble.

Atmosphere was largely a matter of the relationship between performer and audience. It was discussed within the BBC in an interminable debate, which lasted well into the 1950s, around the pros and cons of broadcasting applause. Most performers felt they needed it if they were to get into the spirit of their act, though some, like Gillie Potter, refused it. All listeners complained when applause or laughter drowned the punchlines. The complete absence of applause left one listener's heart 'aching with a sense of gratitude unexpressed'. Another found it both irritating and unpleasant 'that a claque of invited guests in the broadcasting studio should provide artificial laughter and mechanical applause for everything and anything irrespective of broadcasting merit'.[3] Producers preferred the spontaneous reactions of a theatre audience but the problem with relays from the halls, once they became available, was that some of the acts had a largely visual appeal.

An ingenious compromise was attempted. Outside broadcasts from the theatre were dovetailed into studio vaudeville programmes. As an unsuitable theatre act came on, the stage orchestra was faded down and mixed into the BBC Dance Orchestra in the studio, producing what the *BBC Hand Book* hopefully called 'a not unpleasing welter of sound which at least one listener has mistaken for the prelude to a concert of modern Chamber Music!' While Programme Board took the view that the stage acts tended to 'kill' the studio acts the *Year Book* put a brave face on it, claiming that at the moment of transition, 'the listener feels himself transported, as if by a magic carpet, from studio to packed auditorium, with a stimulating effect on more lively imaginations.'[4] Running commentaries on visual acts were rarely used. One producer left a record of the elaborate preparations he had made for a commentary on the pantomime, *Mother Goose*. First, each separate item in the show had to be timed. Next, notes were prepared of such description as was necessary. Then rehearsals at speaking the commentary at the correct tempo were followed by two trial runs of the whole performance, with sound engineers present.[5]

A remarkably simple way out of these difficulties was discovered when John Watt first produced *Music Hall* in 1932. He used a large music studio in a converted warehouse in which an audience of about 400 could be seated well back from the stage with the Variety Orchestra directly in front and below. The microphone was slung in mid-air in such a way that a balance was maintained between the sounds of performers and audience. In effect, techniques that had been known and used in Outside Broadcasts for some years were applied for the first time to home-produced variety.[6] *Music Hall* was immediately hailed as a triumph and continued to be the BBC's most popular programme for many years. It was soon admitted that the broad type of humour which had seemed out of place in more intimate studio productions, worked very well in its natural context. But because the shows used stars from stage variety, who were expensive and in short supply, *Music Hall* remained the only programme of its kind.

We discussed earlier the difficulties faced by entertainers in adapting their routines to 'the mike'. Those who did broadcast regularly faced not merely the problem of maintaining a supply of fresh material, but of doing so within a limited range of subject matter. Under such constraints broadcasting began to create a special kind of comedian with a special line of humour. In 1925, George Grossmith, the creator of the immortal Mr Pooter and now employed by the BBC as a radio critic and adviser, suggested two ways in which comedians might overcome the limitations of wireless. One was by creating a 'humorous personality'. 'The psychology of this appears to be that when an artist has transmitted the impression of a humorous personality the listeners probably visualize him as a person whom they actually know. They expect something funny and unconsciously invest what the artist says with a life it would not otherwise possess.' The other was to adopt the manner of 'American raconteurs'. 'There is hardly time to think about what they say. Story follows story in machine-gun succession.'[7]

The first of these methods was already being applied by Helena Millais with 'Our Lizzie' and by the Yorkshireman John Henry who introduced listeners to other characters such as his wife Blossom and his friend Joe Murgatroyd. These were soon joined by Jean de Casalis as the scatterbrained Mrs Feather, and by Mabel Constanduros who portrayed not only Mrs Buggins, a put-upon Cockney housewife, but also her quarrelsome relatives, using as many as seven different voices in one performance. When she began on radio Constanduros's previous experience was limited to amateur dramatics in the suburbs. In time she became not only BBC Variety's hardiest perennial but the author of numerous radio plays, including the BBC's first domestic comedy series, *The Robinson Family*. She became the first entertainer to get a foothold on the stage on the basis of a wireless reputation when, in 1929, she took top billing at the Coliseum. She did not, however, prove a success on the halls and thereafter stuck largely to radio work.[8]

With hindsight it is tempting to trace the roots of situation comedy back to these character comedians. As Grossmith foresaw, the creation of stock characters enabled listeners to participate in the comedy by anticipating the character's reaction to a new situation. Because it was a form that relied on familiarity as much as gags, it permitted that economy of comic invention eked out by repetition which was to become the basic way of satisfying broadcasting's insatiable appetite for material. But its potential could not be fully exploited by individual performers appearing irregularly in a mixed bill of fare. The early radio character entertainers were a transitional type of entertainment in between the stock comic character of the halls and the stock comic situation of broadcasting.

Grossmith's second suggestion did not bear immediate fruit. The American gag-merchant with his fast-talking routine was very different from the British red-nosed comic. Since he used up gags wholesale in the course of a performance he depended on a backup team of gag-writers to supply the goods. This type of performance began to find followers in Britain in the 1930s with Ted Ray and Tommy Trinder as notable exponents. It was while struggling to entertain cinema audiences in the intervals between films that Ted Ray realized that he could abandon his comic make-up and ludicrous props and walk on wearing a lounge suit, as himself. He described the result: 'From the moment I made my entrance I felt a warmth between myself and the audience – a warmth I had never known before. I was one of them. I told my jokes casually and intimately as though they were in on the joke.'[9] Classless in manner, democratic in their identification with the audience, such performers were to come into their own during and after the Second World War. Before the war American influences were felt most strongly in styles of music, song and dance. Older home-grown styles of sentimental ballad and comic song could still be heard, and George Formby and Gracie Fields continued the tradition of the halls in their style of delivery if not in the songs they sang. But most vocalists on variety bills sang the refrains made popular by dance bands, and were more at home in hotel ballrooms and recording studios than on the boards. The chorus line with its precision drills, typified in Britain by the Tiller Girls, had its transatlantic origins in the routines created by Florenz Ziegfeld.

Instead of the gag-merchant there emerged a group of radio comedians who relied on verbal dexterity as the basis of their humour – puns, rhymes and rigmaroles, burlesques and bizarre narratives. Tommy Handley was one of the first to exploit this method. Giving away some of his trade secrets, in 1928 he wrote, 'I endeavour to employ every trick of vocal gymnastics, of inflection and of mispronunciation of which I am capable.'[10] By 1931 the variety producer, Bertram Fryer, was extolling the radio comedian's verbal wit, which was sustained not only by the quality of the performance but by the 'invention and writing of material of real wit, absurdity or pathos calculated to amuse the *ears* (and so the brains) of their audience.' In practice such verbal humour could soon become mechanical and dull. Stainless Stephen's radio act was based on speaking out loud the punctuation marks in his script. Fryer cited as successful acts Leonard Henry 'guying the highbrows', Leslie Henson's 'ridiculous commentary on a cricket match' and Ronald Frankau's 'perverted versions of Shakespeare'.[11] Such acts could be indefinitely reproduced without too much inventive strain. More original was the work of two perfectionists, the comedian Gillie Potter and A. J. Alan, the pseudonymous civil servant, the mystery of whose identity tantalized listeners. In the mythical village of Hogsnorton, Gillie Potter evoked not the timeworn stereotypes of eccentric squires and idiot bumpkins but a Lilliputian world of inverted logic and arcane social mores. A. J. Alan elevated the telling of shaggy dog stories to a fine art.

In his study of modern comedians, *Make 'em Laugh*, Eric Midwinter refers to the rise of 'a fascinating group of middle-brow comic performers' in the 1930s. Among them he includes Ronald Frankau, Gillie Potter, Tommy Handley, Claude Dampier and Will Hay – all of them regular broadcasters.[12] While the characters they created and the worlds they evoked varied considerably, what they had in common was a literary allusiveness, revealed in their penchant for self-reflexive verbal humour in a style that was closer to the pages of *Punch* than the broad humour of the halls. Parody and burlesque were essential features of their art and were to become central ingredients of radio entertainment.

These related forms of amusement converged on radio from different sources. One was the concert party whose roots stretched back to the nigger minstrel shows imported from the United States in the late 1840s and still alive, more than a hundred years later, in BBC television's *Black and White Minstrel Show*, an old chestnut which lasted through the sixties until, in a climate now much more sensitive to racism embedded in language and culture, it could no longer be endured. The minstrel shows became, by the late nineteenth century, seaside entertainment for the family, performed on beaches and pierheads, free from the whiff of vulgarity or raciness that clung like stale cigar smoke to the music hall. By the beginning of this century, minstrels were giving way to Pierrot troupes and concert parties which took a variety of forms but always preserved a wholesome quality. Performers were often from middle-class backgrounds. The first Pierrot troupe to perform in the West End, Pelissier's Follies, began as an amateur concert party, raising money for charity in the London suburbs. Another well-known troupe, The Co-Optimists, who numbered Stanley Holloway among their troupers, emerged from Cambridge University. Concert party was the main kind of entertainment on offer for the troops during the First World War and some war-time concert parties, such as The Roosters, retained a military flavour in their postwar peacetime acts.

By the 1920s concert party had become the standard form of amateur performance. Thus we find, in the fiction of the time, Bertie Wooster singing *Sonny Boy* at 'a clean, bright entertainment' staged by the Reverend Beefy Bingham for his Lads' Club in the East End,[13] and Richmal Crompton's William sabotaging a similar jollification in the village hall. In the early thirties, and in a real world that borders on the fiction of an Andy Hardy movie, we find the eleven-year-old Hughie Green and his gang of talented chums getting up a concert in a hired hall in Golders Green – the first step along the road to *Opportunity Knocks!*[14] At the other extreme, concert party could be a fairly large-scale business. Greatrex Newman managed three separate troupes of Fol-de-Rols with large casts and an emphasis on spectacle.[15]

One aspect of concert party fare, to be found particularly in the more sophisticated material of The Follies or The Co-Optimists, was a tendency to parody other forms of entertainment from the legitimate stage and music hall. Pelissier staged Potted Plays and Potted Pageants (as much later, on television, did Morecambe and Wise), spoof music hall acts, with impressions of well-known contemporary artists, and a send-up of a benefit matinée. Max Beerbohm, reviewing The Follies and similar troupes in the Edwardian era, welcomed the parody but wished it could be extended to satirize other aspects of the social scene. But in restricting themselves to theatrical or historical lampoons, The Follies stayed in line with the older tradition of burlesque.[16]

Burlesque has a long history, but in its modern form it was popularized on the London stage in the 1860s by John Hollingshead, manager of the Gaiety Theatre. The Gaiety was designed to attract a middle-class clientele, and in drawing together elements from music hall, operetta and the legitimate stage, Hollingshead initiated a hybrid form of entertainment for the middle classes later to be exploited by Sir Edward Stoll, the creator of the London Coliseum, and George Black of the London Palladium. The Gaiety burlesques could be seen as model forms of middle-class entertainment. Taking as their themes Shakespearean or other classical drama, opera, literature or historical incidents, with titles like *Columbus, Gulliver, Faust up to Date* or *Carmen up to Date*, and peppered with far-fetched puns and topical allusions, they appealed to an audience with a sufficient veneer of education and culture to enjoy their allusive but undemanding pleasures.[17] If it went as far as satire, its object, like the Savoy Operas of Gilbert and Sullivan, was always the extremities of contemporary social, cultural and intellectual fashion – extravagance in manners, intense sensibility, rarefied ideas. It was a form of comedy that at worst descended to crude debunking, and at best rose to a delicate and innocent wit which did not demean its target. Such humour fed through into the type of radio variety labelled 'sophisticated', and it was through parody and burlesque that radio comedy drew on broadcasting itself as an exploitable topical source of amusement for listeners.

In the very early days the scientific complexities of radio and the difficulties of listening were a source of fun. Stainless Stephen began his microphone career by portraying characters with names like Atmos P. Herics and Oscar the Oscillator. The Valve Set Concert Party gave each item in their programme a subtitle such as 'the Mirth Condenser will function' or 'High-Tension again in evidence'.[18] 'What's all that wire for?' somebody asked the comedian Harry Tate in an early 1920s sketch. 'Wireless, you fool!' he replied.[19] A more lasting tradition was sending up the serious elements in the BBC's output. In 1924, *Radio Times* printed a monologue about broadcasting from Our Lizzie:

> Mind you, I don't always 'old with the programmes. They're too 'ighbrow. I like the comics and the Saverloy Band, and some of the Hentertainers ain't bad; but them simfunny concerts and them virtuoso stunts! Of course I'm glad the singers is virtuous, but I'd like 'em to be a bit brighter about it.[20]

In 1928 Tommy Handley wrote:

> The announcer is a constant figure of fun outside the studio; within that grim chamber the announcer must be taken seriously! I have found also that the public enjoy good-humoured skits on the more serious educational features of the programmes, and I even had the impertinence to discourse on such subjects as voice culture, music and dietetics.[21]

An impression of this kind of humour can be gained from some of the earliest surviving variety scripts. A sketch in a 1931 programme called 'Vaudeville' began, 'This is the National Programme whether you like it or not. Miss Helen Halibut will now give a cosy cookery talk on "Chicken Dishes Made From Rabbit".'[22] Another ended as follows:

> Next week we 'ope to present a further startling series of attractions – including Sir Walford Davies and Mr Thomas Handley in that rollicking knockabout act 'Laying the Foundations of Music' – the six genuine Greenwich Pips in Stravinsky's opera 'Time Gentlemen Please' and twelve talks on 'Glue'. These talks will be a bit sticky – they will be found gummed into next week's edition of *The Listener*.[23]

The allusions in these sketches now need glosses, but any regular listener at that time would know of the Savoy Band, Sir Walford Davies' music talks and the long-running series called *The Foundations of Music*. It is notable that

Stravinsky is presumed to be a familiar topical reference – familiar, that is, only through the widely accessible cultural resource that radio itself constituted.

Talks and serious music were favourite targets, but a 1932 programme, *From the Files*, burlesqued a wide variety of radio forms including experimental drama and features. In 'a lowbrow listener's *Nightmare*' the activities of Lance Sieveking, Archie Harding and Tyrone Guthrie were accurately parodied. The feature began with a mix of Chinese music and Stravinsky. The spirit of Sieveking's *Kaleidoscope* was caught in a disembodied chorus wailing 'Nightmare!', by the incongruous use of sound effects (the BBC seagulls were already notorious) and by a montage of loose associations: a chorus of 'January-February-March-March-March' was faded into sounds of marching feet and the skirl of bagpipes. Guthrie's *The Squirrel's Cage* was sent up in the announcement of 'Life in a Boarding House' followed by a chanted dirge: 'Saturday, Sunday, Monday, Tuesday – Bubble and squeak, bubble and squeak – bubble – bubble – bubble – (fade in gargling noises).'[24]

This programme was a medley compiled from a series devoted purely to lampoons of other radio programmes. It was called *Airy Nothings*, and the *BBC Year Book* commented; 'This satire on broadcasting activities strangely enough proved popular with listeners who could hardly have been expected to enjoy such family jokes.'[25] But reading the scripts of such shows one is reminded less of family jokes than of those performances which occur on special occasions in Goffman's 'total institutions', when the inmates are allowed openly to mimic the authorities.[26] The purpose of such muted, institutionalized saturnalia was to provide occasional relief from constant subordination. On radio they seemed to suggest that someone somewhere in the BBC understood the plight of listeners and was prepared to ease for a moment the schoolmasterly tones of all those heavier and demanding programmes. Midwinter has pointed to a whole subgenre of middlebrow comedy set in rundown British boarding schools, from Will Hay's 'Narkover College' in 1930s concert party, to Jimmy Edwards' 'Chiselbury' on the television screens of the fifties.[27] 'Up the cads! Up the college!', drawled the Western Brothers in the BBC's 1938 series, *Cads' College*, 'the only thing we lack is knowledge.'[28]

Self-parody could be a discreet means of laughing off some of the BBC's most acute embarrassments. Shortly after the William Ferrie incident, one of the *Charlot's Hour* revues portrayed an interview, inside Broadcasting House, 'between a "working man" and two extremely polite and blasé officials who were giving his political speech a preliminary hearing.'[29] It was only when the BBC succeeded in producing truly popular entertainment of its own that the almost apologetic tone of self-parody was dropped. Comedians continued to make joking references to BBC programmes and personalities, but they were now more likely to refer to other entertainers and variety shows than to high-brow programmes. By the late thirties Broadcasting House no longer appeared so much as a house divided as a house of fun.

The turning-point in this direction was the establishment of the Variety Department in 1933. The immediate concern of Eric Maschwitz was to reduce his dependence on the entertainment business for the supply of radio variety, and he adopted two strategies towards this end. First, he moved up market from music hall and concert party to the world of revue and musical comedy for a supply of star performers. Justifying the expense of his musical productions in his first year as Head of Variety, he wrote, 'I am not claiming that stage and film stars never appeared for us before, but the constellation has been dazzling this autumn, with consequent artistic results and valuable extra publicity – all of which has gone to convince the listener that "broadcasting is looking up".'[30] At the same time he tried to move away from reliance on outside broadcast relays and studio-based productions of straight variety.

These, Maschwitz predicted, would soon vanish from the air, to be replaced by an ever new supply of 'script features' delivered by BBC staff teams of writers, composers and producers, and by BBC performers.[31] Hitherto the bulk of radio entertainment had been supplied either by relays or by artists hired on a one-off basis who, as part of the deal, supplied their own material. Black's ban on his General Theatre Corporation artists appearing on radio had led the Productions Executive in the BBC to suggest that artists might find broadcasting more attractive if they were offered longer-term contracts. But it was soon appreciated that if they were to broadcast regularly they could not be expected to supply their own material. Maschwitz was keen to employ script-writers but, as he pointed out, 'You can get nothing good without paying – not in a world where film and stage people are hunting madly to snap up every grain of talent and material that's going.'

In response to suggestions that he was overspending, Maschwitz retorted that 'there is no programme estimate that cannot be "pruned" by such simple devices as that of booking second-rate artists, reducing number of choruses etc., all of which results in a reduction in quality.'[32] He countered by asking for a 35 per cent increase in the Variety budget. In fact, from the moment of his appointment large permanent resource and production allocations were committed to the development of this area of broadcasting. There were two Variety producers in 1930. By 1936 there were twenty-nine. Supported by its own Variety Orchestra and its own theatre, St. George's Hall, the new influx of production staff quickly increased the supply of radio entertainment.

Before 1933 only four hours of Variety were broadcast from London each week, consisting of two one-hour vaudeville shows and one hour-long concert party or revue, which was repeated. By the beginning of 1935 the Variety Department was producing 44 hours a month, and by January 1936 this had increased to 59 hours a month. Variety producers felt overworked but had considerable freedom of action, for the BBC hierarchs had no positive recommendations to make about what they should do or how they should do it. Maschwitz recalled that 'the programme planners of those days were merely human timetables: they informed us weekly how many hours, at what times, we were required to fill with entertainment; what went into those hours was our responsibility.' Staff worked as much as possible from St. George's Hall where they escaped the formality and red tape of Broadcasting House. Maschwitz recognized that they could not be confined to 'office hours'. Nor could he keep too strict an eye on their extra-curricular activities:

> I encouraged my band of incorrigible bohemians to call me by my first name and to break into my office at any hour of the day or night with their problems and ideas. I wrote for them and rehearsed with them, even to the humble extent of occasionally assisting with the 'sound effects'. I also drank with them not always to the benefit of my constitution. We were friends.[33]

Maschwitz was described by his old friend Lance Sieveking as 'carrying round with him an aura of nostalgia as real as armour plate.... He saw that owing to the cataclysm of 1914 he had just missed growing up in an England that appealed to everything in him – that chimed with every chord in his temperament – and he *refused* to miss it. In Eric's company it was, by magic, always 1909.'[34] Yet it was as much to the Europe of the *Belle Epoque* as to Edwardian England that Maschwitz was drawn. Like Val Gielgud, he was of Polish extraction, and the two of them were known in the BBC as 'the Polish Corridor'.[35]

The Maschwitz touch was evident in the many revivals of Edwardian musical successes, among them *A Waltz Dream, Floradora, Our Miss Gibbs* and *The Geisha*, as well as his own *Goodnight Vienna*. A characteristically Ruritanian BBC produced musical of that time was *By Royal Appointment*. Written by C. D. Freeman and the (ex-Eton) composer/producer Mark Lubbock, its plot owed more to Anthony Hope's *Sophie of Kravonia*, a tale of a kitchen maid who became a queen, than to his *Prisoner of Zenda*. Naturally the musical's opening scene was set on the Orient Express, steaming off to Molkavia on this occasion. Joanna, a lady's maid from Brixton, is thither bound to inform the Prince of Molkavia that her mistress, an English duchess, has decided to decline his offer of marriage. When Joanna meets the Crown Prince he tells her that, for reasons of state and in order to defeat the evil schemes of Baron Thal, the Molkavian Chancellor, he must go through with the wedding. He begs her to take the place of the duchess. She protests:

> Why have you fixed on
> A girl from Brixton

> To decide affairs of state?
> How can I tell you
> Just how the hell you
> Start to find a mate?

Of course, though, she relents and falls in with the scheme. The Crown Prince Philip declares, 'The coach awaits us!' The BBC's cheering crowd record is faded up and Joanna exclaims, 'When I tell them in Brixton – well...!'[36]

The expatriate yearnings of the Polish Corridor were assuaged by occasional microphone trips to the banks of the Danube and in the new light music features with continental settings, such as *Café Colette* and *Red Sarafan*. In 1934 Maschwitz drew on his experience from musical comedy to evoke in sound the atmosphere of a Parisian café as a suitable setting for the continental dance music of Walford Hayden and his orchestra. Against the background of popping champagne corks and boulevardiers' chatter, the Chef d'Orchestre presented the show in broken English. Early scripts are not available, but something of what it was like can be imagined from a 1940 edition of the show which has the Chef d'Orchestre welcoming listeners as follows:

> But now you all come back to the Café Colette and everything is 'soufflé'. Oh, 'ow you say in English? Ah ... swell. That was a nice piece, no? That is funny, when we would say 'yes' we say 'no', but if you want to say 'yes' you say 'pas demi', er ... 'not 'arf'. C'est extraordinaire.[37]

It was claimed that many listeners believed that the show was an outside broadcast live from Paris. Maschwitz followed it with *Red Sarafan*, another Parisian café, this time the haunt of Russian emigrés. Here the local colour was deepened to include a cast of characters and a rudimentary plot. In the fourth episode we find the very English Mr Gordon, accompanied by his Russian wife Natasha, delivered to the café by a taxi driver who, inevitably, turns out to be a tsarist duke in disguise. They are greeted by the proprietor, Captain Vivien, who introduces Natasha to Countess Loubanoff.

NATASHA: Don't you remember me? I am Natasha Baratova.
COUNTESS: Natasha Baratova! Little Natasha with the long plaits! But my dear, how time flies! How are you, how are your dear brothers, your dear father?
NATASHA: My father and Alesha were killed ... I haven't heard anything from Boris for six years – maybe he is – dead, too.
COUNTESS: Oh, my dear I am so sorry and what gay times you children used to have.

With a typically Russian switch of emotional tempo, they fall to reminiscing about Christmas in old St Petersburg until Natasha's cry of 'Oh look! Here come the Cossacks!' prompts her husband to exclaim, 'By Jove, yes! I wonder what they are going to sing.' Captain Vivien is ready with an answer:

> It is the song of the boatmen of the Volga. Imagine a quiet summer evening, with the sun just setting in a ball of fire. The reeds on the banks of the Volga rustle. Then softly from the distance we hear the boatmen's song.

When the song is over Mr Gordon admits, 'I must say I liked that very much.'[38] But the *Daily Worker* did not: 'This gang of White Russian emigrés has proved one of the most unpopular turns Broadcasting House has ever put on. After every performance protests against their blatant anti-Soviet propaganda have poured in.'[39]

It would be wrong to see Maschwitz's tastes as merely self-indulgent. He was a successful and versatile writer and an astute show business operator, in tune with the more sophisticated tastes of the times. *A Waltz Dream* was revived on the London stage in 1934 after its airing on radio. His own *Goodnight Vienna* was subsequently staged in the West End and made into a film with Anna Neagle and Jack Buchanan in the lead roles. The mood of nostalgia and romanticism which pervaded so much of the entertainment of the thirties – in the later revues by Noel Coward, in the musicals of Ivor Novello, in the films of Greta Garbo – were perfectly caught in two lyrics by Maschwitz for which he is still remembered today: *These Foolish Things* and *A Nightingale Sang in Berkeley Square*.

By now Music Hall and stage Variety were fading blossoms. Concert Party seemed irredeemably amateurish and second-rate. Newer forms of entertainment, taking elements from the older traditions of variety, operetta and burlesque, transformed and revitalized them by bringing them up to date. Fast-paced American musical shows, in which dance was as important as song and with an emphasis on spectacle, pace and a tight-knit plot were beginning to overtake the English musical of the Edwardian era. *Show Boat* and *No No Nanette*, both performed on radio, had long runs in the West End in the thirties. Their energy and vitality had a contemporary, modern quality, which was miles away from the older home-grown high society musicals and Ruritanian romps.

But it was revue and cabaret that introduced an atmosphere and a type of humour that caught the bitter-sweet blend of romanticism and cynicism which characterized the jazz age. Noel Coward was the perfect embodiment of this mood. In lyrics like *Poor Little Rich Girl, World Weary* and *Twentieth-Century Blues* he evoked the restless hedonism and disillusionment of the Bright Young Things so memorably that the impression of decadence could overwhelm the underlying note of cautious disapproval:

Cocktails and laughter,
But what comes after?
Nobody knows ...

Coward could shock with his open allusion to sex. His sketches had a sharper
cutting edge than Edwardian satire on modern manners. But in his taste for
parody of the stage to be found in pieces like *Theatre Guide* and *Red Peppers*,
in the snooks he cocked at the upper classes in *The Stately Homes of England*,
in his antipathy to the avant-garde expressed in *The Swiss Family Whittlebot*
(a squib on the Sitwells), above all in the nostalgia of *Bitter Sweet* and the
patriotic sentiment of *Cavalcade*, Coward revealed himself as the heir of
middlebrow entertainment, though he was its most brilliant exponent.[40]

True decadence was more to be found in the *demi-monde* of cabarets and
night clubs, where socialites mingled with show people and prostitutes. It was
against these that the *Daily Mail* ranted and the Home Secretary wielded the
Defence of the Realm Act, sure signs of conventional outrage. It was cabaret,
rather than the variety stage, which was becoming associated with blue
humour, albeit with a veneer of sophistication. Like the cinema of the
twenties, cabaret explored the boundaries of propriety. By the mid-thirties the
Windmill Theatre had come into being. There, in between displays of what
the manager, Vivien Van Damm, called 'the artistry of nudity', might be seen
the curious suburban figure of Eric Barker, with his unabashed contempt for
the low comedy of 'the fish and chip brigade', performing restrained send-ups
of BBC radio interviews. He was the first in a long line of radio comedians to
serve an apprenticeship in the lonely art of comedy at the Windmill, playing to
an audience of furtive, unresponsive businessmen, concealed behind half-
raised newspapers.[41]

Occasionally, in the further fringes of late night entertainment on radio,
the elements of cabaret were blended with other material in shows known as
'miscellanies'. These might contain material from the old Etonian lyricist
Harry Graham, author of *Ruthless Rhymes* and much fashionable *vers
d'occasion*, or from Elsa Lanchester whose Cave of Harmony night club had
provided offbeat entertainment in the twenties and whose most famous song
was 'I've danced with a man who's danced with a girl who's danced with the
Prince of Wales'. One such programme, which caused an outcry from
listeners, included a performance of Maeterlink's playlet, *The Death of
Tantagiles*; another, sketches by Herbert Farjeon and Robert Benchley, a
poem by Edith Sitwell and an adaptation of an L. P. Hartley short story,
together with songs and orchestral interludes.[42] After 1933 such hybrid
entertainment was rarely broadcast. It was rather too recherché compared
with the more acceptable, comfortable pleasures of revue.

It was in revue that Variety began to evolve a 'radiogenic' style of entertainment. Early revue on radio had consisted of a swift succession of songs and sketches, all vaguely topical, but with no particular theme or compére to hold it together. An article in *The Writer* in 1929 claimed that the BBC wanted revue which dispensed with a compére but relied on a loose theme or setting to hold it together.[43] Much of the work of the tiny Revue Section, created in 1931, was of this type. The thematic revue was developed by Ernest Longstaff, the first producer to build a programme around a central, topical idea such as the rush hour or shop-lifting. Later came 'story reviews' with a slender plot line linking together comedy scenes, 'pretty' numbers and syncopation. In the earliest of such shows, such as *Djinn and Bitters* and *Peep-bo-hemia*, both written by Clifford Seyler, the dramatic control panel was for the first time enlisted in the cause of light entertainment.[44] Typical of this genre was *A Seat in the Park* by C. D. Freeman and Mark Lubbock. Set in Hyde Park, it featured a romance between a young man and a dowager's daughter. Their dalliance was interrupted by comic characters such as the 'Chairman' selling tickets for deckchairs and grumbling about the Rotten Row Brigade ('Every morning you see 'em 'ere – some of 'em with pullovers, most of 'em with 'angovers.') and a woman police sergeant who identifies herself as Florrie the Belle of the Female Force. The Rotten Row Brigade canter by, no doubt to the accompaniment of coconut shells, singing:

> Belted earls and galloping girls,
> With clinging knees between the trees
> Off they go, round Rotten Row.

In the end the young man gets his girl and the story draws to a close at dusk with a chorus of nursemaids singing, 'It's love that makes us linger after dark', echoed by the park-keeper's 'It's love that makes the keepers close the park.'[45]

Other settings included a pub (*Listener's Inn*), rural England (*Bumpkin Pie*) and the industrial North (*The Clatter of Clogs*). John Watt used the dramatic control panel to present a fast-moving montage of different settings. *Toytown* took the form of a pot-pourri of 'toy songs' interwoven with a romantic dialogue between a tin soldier and a doll. More ambitious was *The Stage Revolves* which presented rapid transitions from scene to scene – Vienna, the seaside, Derby Day. The *BBC Year Book* remarked, 'There was only the sound of the stage revolving and the strain of the theme song to assist the listener in the transition from item to item, each one self-contained and each one self-explanatory. It is a tribute to the listener's imagination that he found no difficulty in making these mental jumps.'[46] Such programmes bordered on the methods and effects of Sieveking and the experimental radio feature.

Burlesque and satire were frequent ingredients of radio revue. We have mentioned *From the Files* in the *Airy Nothings* series. Its producer, Gordon McConnel, specialized in such send-ups, and theatre was lampooned in *Pantomimicry* and Hollywood in *Talkie Town*. John Watt introduced satire into *Stop Press* and *World For Sale*, in which an auctioneer tried to dispose of various contemporary ideas, fashions and institutions. Lot 19, a natural complexion ('Surely I can tempt you, madam? Eyebrows warranted unplucked!'), found no buyer. When 'patriotism' came under the hammer the programme, at least in its scripted form, broke the BBC rule against political allusions by including a veiled reference to Mussolini.

AUCTIONEER: Patriotism knocked down for £5 to the gentleman in the black shirt representing the ...
VOICE: Signore, si prego ...
AUCTIONEER: Ah, the gentleman would prefer to remain anonymous.[47]

Satire of a more sophisticated though less risky type was to be found in the occasional *Little Reviews* and *Monthly Reviews* introduced by Maschwitz after 1934. These were often scripted by Maschwitz himself, using his *nom de plume* of Holt Marvell, with music by Jack Strachey. The performers included Nelson Keys, the acknowledged star of review in the inter-war years, Hermione Gingold, then married to Maschwitz, and Arthur Marshall who had fallen like a ripe plum into the lap of the BBC. A sketch from *The World We Listen In* of 1936 used the time-honoured formula of contrasting past with present manners to poke fun at modern educational methods in the age of psychoanalysis. A scene of the bad old days, with a naughty schoolgirl being whacked by her headmistress for stealing, was followed by a version of the same incident in 1935. Today's headmistress is having a cosy chat with the girl, whom she addresses as Babs, and they both come to the conclusion that she is suffering from 'a fixation'. Babs then sings:

> I'm an ultra modern midget.
> If I shriek or sulk or fidget
> Or a pin into the cook I drive,
> I am never smacked or shaken
> But to Harley Street I'm taken,
> I'm a child of 1935
> ...
> Old-fashioned toys are barred me.
> I sit and think instead.
> Angels don't need to guard me
> Now that Freud and Jung watch over my bed.
> Yes my dream life has been sifted
> By those analysts so gifted

261

And to this conclusion they arrive –
I'm unconsciously uncleaner
Than Mae West or Messalina
Just a child of 1935.[48]

When the musical comedies and reviews of the Maschwitz era are sifted we find the latent themes and structures that would shortly provide the foundations of a radio entertainment with universal appeal. There is first the move to writing specially for radio, rather than relying on outside sources for entertainment. The *Manchester Guardian* enthused over *Goodnight Vienna* and the *Daily Herald* declared, 'At last the BBC has put over a winner.'[49] Of two musicals by John Watt and Harry Pepper, *It Seems Only Yesterday* and *It Was in the Papers*, the *BBC Annual* commented: 'They were purely "radiogenic" in technique, the greater part of the story being told by an informal narrator with occasional lapses into dialogue-scenes. This treatment was most effective in that it lent an interest and a realism which are not usually associated with musical comedy.'[50] But the same article acknowledged that the appeal of such shows was mostly to older listeners with memories of bygone theatre productions of musical comedy. By contrast, revue was modern and up to date in ways that much of the rest of BBC output was not. Topicality did not dominate the output of either the Talks Department or Features producers in London. If contemporary life was scarcely yet an established resource for informational and news-oriented programmes, it was beginning to become so for entertainment as it progressed towards the discovery of comedy forms with universal appeal.

The final step in this direction was the appreciation of the significance of serial production and fixed time-slots on the same day each week for entertainment programmes. This development depended on a move away from the earlier corporate attitudes to the audience, which expected them to measure up to the BBC's expectations of them in terms of attentive and selective listening. As it gradually became accepted that a central concern of broadcasting must be to to provide entertainment, attention to the needs and tastes of listeners came to the foreground. The *BBC Year Book* for 1934 acknowledged the importance of radio variety: 'Its appeal is to the majority. It must be "popular", since the audience for which it is intended is that which we know as the People.'[51] The 1935 *BBC Annual* elaborated: 'It is this field that holds the largest popular audience and whatever may be the wider aims of broadcasting, here it must set out specially to *please*.' Its public was:

in the main a tired public, in search of diversion after the day's work, and clever but elaborate programmes that demand concentration may prove more exhausting than diverting to such listeners. This fact must not of course be pressed too far. To assume the state of the 'tired businessman' as permanent and not pass-ing, leads to entertainment becoming slick, glittering – and empty. He is not always 'tired' and in his less exhausted moods he will be prepared to concentrate upon a broadcast talk, an opera, or a symphony concert. There are departments to cater for these moods, and his periods of exhaustion are left to 'Variety' and must be its special care.[52]

Leaving aside how far the 'tired businessman' was representative of 'the People', the attitude here – for all its condescending and uncertain tone – expressed an acceptance of the need for undemanding entertainment as relax-ation after a hard day's work.

Industrial psychologists – and cultural critics – were beginning to argue that monotonous and repetitive work routines led to monotonous and repeti-tive patterns of leisure. But, we would argue, the routinization of radio entertainment, far from leading in such directions, brought about a creative transformation of Variety output and the pleasures it offered to listeners. The *BBC Annual* of 1936 told readers that the shortage of personality artists could only be met by the creation of programme features which, if repeated suffi-ciently often, might become as popular in their own way as any single celebrity. In America, it went on, popularity on radio was the result of regularity:

In that country the 'So-and-So Hour' of which the label at first conveyed nothing but the advertiser's name, came to mean a specific kind of entertainment associated with that name to which people returned regularly. It had the merits of specific radio character, and of depending on itself and its own following rather than on the sporadic appearance of well-known personalities.

Not only regularity, but also continuity:

Of old, the mere fact of being able to listen to broadcasting was enough to ensure attention, but today, after twelve years' experience of almost continuous entertainment at negligible cost, the listener, no less than broadcasting, has changed, and the attack upon his interest must be met and sustained if he is to be engaged and held. A striking opening will keep him in the mood to override the minor distractions which every home provides. If the programme slackens in tempo and interest, if it is broken by ill-timed silences or fumbling pauses, the connexion is lost. True continuity, therefore... is of the greatest importance.[53]

Although the remarks here refer to continuity within programmes, it was a short step to extend the principle to continuity between programmes. What BBC Variety producers perceived in contemporary American radio and cin-ema were qualities of pace and polish – of professionalism in short – which they admired and tried to emulate. Regularity meant that a show could build a loyal audience by becoming known as something that recurred at a predictable time in the week and thus be pleasurably anticipated. Greater attention to maintaining tempo, quality and pace within the show would consolidate audience loyalty. Beyond this, as a show built up a regular audience it could develop and deepen the pleasures it offered. The *BBC Annual* noted that American shows like *The Burns and Allen Show* and *Amos 'n' Andy*, though expensive to produce, allowed the comedians to build and establish a comic personality in true detail instead of putting across a quickly sketched stereotype in an occasional eight-minute turn. The regular comedy show allowed a cumulative elaboration of material.

In retrospect three shows stand out as landmarks in the regularization of radio entertainment: *In Town Tonight*, *Monday Night at Seven* and *Band Waggon*. We have already briefly discussed the content of *In Town Tonight*. The mix of show-biz glamour and human interest stories had a ready appeal, but what ensured the success of the programme was its scheduling and presentation. It was given a fixed slot at 6.30 on Saturday evenings, at the beginning of peak listening time on the most popular night of the week for listening in. It was the first variety programme to be broadcast regularly, week after week at the same time. On top of that its signature tune and introduction had a punch and energy that was rare on radio in the early thirties. Maschwitz thought up the brief opening *mise-en-scène* of the roar of London traffic and the flower girl murmuring 'sweet violets' abruptly halted by the stentorian voice of Freddy Grisewood bellowing 'Stop!', and followed by the studio announcer with 'Once again we stop the mighty roar of London's traffic to bring you *In Town Tonight!*' The music chosen from the record library for the signature tune was the *Knightsbridge March* from a new suite of music by Eric Coates. Within six weeks of the start of the programme the BBC was inundated with thousands of postcards asking for the title of the piece. Its infectious rhythm swept the country. Recorded versions of it were made by every musical combination from a symphony orchestra to an accordion, and Coates, who had hitherto been an obscure though highly successful composer, became a public celebrity. The success of *In Town Tonight* – it ran for nearly a quarter of a century – proved the importance of regular scheduling in a good peak listening slot, combined with a strong identity created by a well-selected signature tune and attention-grabbing introduction.[54]

Monday Night at Seven was the first 'continuity show'. It dispensed with an imaginary location, and tried to overcome the limitations of traditional studio variety by offering a more diverse range of ingredients, while using a studio host as a unifying thread who provided continuity between items and who held the show together. The novel ingredient was the mode of address employed by the show. It spoke directly to listeners, acknowledged the situation in which they listened, and tried to create a communicative bond

"WHAT I SAYS IS, MRS. JONES, THERE'S TOO MUCH OF THIS HERE VARIETY AND MOST OF IT'S ALL THE SAME."

between show and audience by inviting their participation rather than treating them as distant witnesses to a performance they were, unfortunately, unable to attend in person. The show was hosted by a mellow voiced 'commère' who sang the links between items and – with the soft chimes of a clock in the background – the introductory signature tune:

> It's Monday night at seven o'clock,
> Oh can't you hear the chimes?
> They're telling you to take an easy chair,
> To settle by the fireside,
> Look at your *Radio Times*,
> For *Monday Night at Seven*'s on the air.

This was very different from the rousing tune of the *Knightsbridge March*. If that invoked a combination of show-biz razzmatazz with the noise and bustle of public life, the introductory note struck by the quieter, crooning style of the commère's theme song was more intimate and personal – a reaching out to enter into and communicate with the imagined, cosy fireside world of listeners.

Each programme was a compendium of individual variety acts and regular weekly items. There were attempts to introduce short comedy features such as *Thompson and Johnson*, a below-stairs farce involving a cook and a butler, and drama in the shape of *Paul and Virginia*, a serial romance. For a while there was a weekly magazine section, featuring interviews with well-known personalities. In a similar vein, *Youth Takes a Bow* introduced young talent from the worlds of sport and entertainment. But the most durable weekly items were *Inspector Hornleigh Investigates* and *Puzzle Corner*. The former was a short, dramatized detective story to which the audience was invited to 'Listen carefully and see if you can spot the mistake the criminal makes'. The latter was a quizz with answers provided at the end of the show.[55]

Nothing so well illustrates the newfound populism of BBC entertainment in the late thirties as the return of 'listener participation'. This had been a notable feature of the very first few years of radio, when individual stations vied with each other to produce novelty programmes that included competitions, quizzes, stunts, request programmes and even phone-ins. But all that vanished without trace as the easy informality of early radio gave way to the distant formality of the British Broadcasting Corporation. When finally, in 1930, the Board of Governors decided that they were 'in principle not in favour of competitions in our programmes',[56] they lingered on only as a childish memory in *Children's Hour*. *Puzzle Corner*, in 1937, seemed like a new departure and its producers were astonished when an on-air invitation to

" Take your paper and pencil—here is puzzle-corner."

listeners to telephone in their answers to the BBC resulted in telephone exchanges becoming jammed.

Soon radio parlour games, quizzes and competitions abounded. 1938, among much else, was the year of the Spelling Bee craze on radio, followed by tongue-twisting bees, general knowledge bees, agricultural bees and 'humming' bees. The *BBC Year Book* for 1940 noted that there had been radio versions for 1940 of such favourite old parlour games as Clumps, Ghosts, Proverbs, Coffee Pots and 'My Aunt Went to Town'. It added that when the presenter of the 1939 programme, *Lucky Dip*, asked listeners to send in original songs, verses and anecdotes for the *Listeners' Corner* feature, he received them at the rate of 2500 a week. Record requests could be sent to *You Asked For It*. The compère of *Sing-Song* jollied along the home audience to join in the fun with cries of 'Now Granny, put your knitting down!' and, 'There's a woman in Hull not singing!'[57] Programme Board, in 1935, had rejected the idea of a half-hour programme made up of excerpts from listeners' letters as 'quite unsuitable'.[58] But by 1939, in the Midland series, *Listeners Answer Back*, members of the public were allowed to criticize the BBC on air and, in the case of one participant, to cause embarrassment by asking why Sir Oswald Mosley had not been allowed to broadcast.[59]

Monday Night at Seven was the first show which, in its very name, built on the anticipation of pleasures reiterated each week, on the same day at the same time. It had no stars – the singing commère was anonymous – and comedy was not the central focus of the show, but it was soon one of the most popular shows on radio. The first radio comedy series were really extensions of the radio 'character' humorists broadened out into a dramatic context. *The Strange Adventures of Mr Penny* was first broadcast in 1936. Mr Penny, played by Richard Goolden (who immortalized the part of Mole in the stage version of *Wind in The Willows*), was an office worker who lived in Acacia Villas, Tooting Bec, and had been happily married for twenty years. Vague and bungling, his misadventures sprang from commonplace everyday incidents, like forgetting to buy his wife a present on their wedding anniversary. Such was the popularity of the show that *The Times* was moved to offer a sociological explanation of its success. It was 'the noisy emergence of "supermen" with all their uncomfortable possibilities that disposes us to feel kindly towards "little men", those humble heroes of mock heroic fables whose adventures are suggested in the daily comic strips and whose respectable gestures in the face of Nature are, we feel, not much smaller or clownish than our own.'[60] The heroes of the next BBC comedy series, *The Plums*, were even humbler, though hardly respectable – a northern working-class family led by the unemployed and Micawberish Mr Plum whose improvidence was rewarded by a win on the pools – another phenomenon of the age. 'The Plums', said *Radio Times,* 'are anyone and everyone. They're a product which is completely contemporary.

Their world is a world of football pools and film fanaticism, of the can and the co-op, of the cat on the rag mat, of small family loyalty and all its implications.' 'It doesn't matter what the weather, Plums will always hang together,' went the theme song of the show.[61]

The Plums started up in 1937, and in the same year came *Mr Muddlecombe J.P.*, which had Robb Wilton as a bumbling magistrate presiding over absurd cases in the Court of Not-So-Common-Pleases. This affronted the Magistrates Association, which complained that the series was bringing the profession into disrepute.[62] It was a sign of the growing confidence of the BBC that it was winning the loyalty of its audiences that it felt able to laugh off such an objection in the programme itself, adding that it had received an identical complaint from the Burglars' Union (Smash and Grab Section)![63] 1938 saw the start of *Cads' College*, the first radio entertainment based on that peculiarly British institution – the third-rate, ramshackle boarding school. With its seedy headmaster, played by Davy Burnaby, and the lordly Western brothers as its head prefects and chief cads, the humour had, nevertheless, a distinctly modern ring about it. In the second episode the Head has spotted one of the Western brothers in a roadhouse the previous night:

HEADMASTER: And what were you doing at this road house, may I ask?
WESTERN: I went there with a bird.
HEADMASTER: (*staggered*) You went there with a *what*?
WESTERN: A bird! You know, a girl.
HEADMASTER: You went there with a... (confidentially) what's her address?
WESTERN: 15 Cranbrook Gardens.
HEADMASTER: Oh, that one! I could have told you were wasting your time.[64]

Band Waggon first rolled on 5 January 1938. The pre-publicity for the show emphasized its orginality, as this radio causerie in the *Daily Mail* made plain:

NOVEL IDEA

Comedian's Serial
Programme

ARTHUR ASKEY THE
LUCKY MAN

An idea novel in every respect to broadcasting in this country was approved by the BBC Programme Board today.

A Comedian has been selected, material will be written round him, and in the New Year he will broadcast every Wednesday night for twelve weeks. Such a contract has never before been given to a radio comedian in this country. The programme will be in serial form to the extent that the same characters and artists will be retained, but each episode will be complete in itself. Each instalment will present a problem which listeners will be asked to assist in solving.

Great Opportunity

Arthur Askey is the comedian who receives the new contract and there is little doubt that at the end of the twelve weeks his name should be a household word.

It is an opportunity radio artists dream about, a much desired continuity which has – with certain rare exceptions – never been attainable.

It is a step nearer the regularity of programmes which makes for easier and more discriminate listening.[65]

The original idea came from an American radio show called *The Band Waggon*, featuring a dance band of that name. But it was now known in the Variety Department that dance bands, by themselves, were a minority taste. It was decided to enliven the music provided by Phil Cardew and The Band Waggoners and the harmony trio, The Jackdaws, with a comedian as its regular presenter. In other respects the show relied on the compendium format of *Monday Night At Seven*. There was a regular item called *New Voices* which introduced new singing hopefuls, and a variant on *Puzzle Corner* called *Mr Walker Wants To Know*. This featured Syd Walker as a cockney barrow-boy who, with much street wisdom, related a mysterious adventure somewhat in the manner of the Waterman in the W. W. Jacobs short stories. Each tale ended with the same question – 'Well, what would you do chums?' – to which listeners were invited to send in their replies. Besides this there was the regular *Chestnut Corner* in which Murdoch and Askey competed to outdo each other in resurrecting ancient gags.

In Askey's account the first three shows were so uninspired that John Watt threatened to withdraw it after six episodes.[66] At this point, with nothing to lose and free to do what they liked with the scripts, Askey and Murdoch let their imaginations loose, and the comedy took off in a spiral of surrealist fantasy the likes of which had never before been heard on radio. The comedy was a group effort produced by Askey and Murdoch sitting round a table each week with the production staff, throwing out ideas and trying out gags which were then written down and worked into a script. The germ of the inspired development of *Band Waggon* came out of the way that Askey was introduced in the very first show. It was, by now, a standard routine for radio comics to interrupt the Announcer, who explained Askey's barracking as follows: 'Ladies and gentlemen, I must apologize for the interruption – it was Arthur Askey, our resident comedian. Nobody knows why he is called the resident comedian, because he doesn't live here either.' The point was picked up in the second show, when Arthur declared, 'I'm the resident comedian, aren't I?

Ever so nice it is, too. Every night an announcer comes round and tucks me up and brings me a glass of milk.'[67] But the idea took off in the fourth episode with the invention of the famous flat, at the top of Broadcasting House, in which Dicky and Arthur – now truly the BBC's resident comedian – lived. Thereafter, the show never looked back. Watt lifted his threat and, when the first twelve shows were done, immediately invited 'Big' and 'Stinker' (nicknames, by now established in the show, for Askey and Murdoch) to sign up for another series in the autumn.

Arthur and Dicky were soon joined in the flat by a bizarre range of animals and other characters. There were the pigeons, Basil and Lucy, and Lewis the goat, installed because it was too far to go down a flight of forty-nine stairs, followed by seven more floors, to get the morning milk. But why a goat? For the sake of an old chestnut: 'A goat in the flat? What about the smell?' 'Oh, she'll get used to it!' Then there was the charlady, Mrs Bagwash and her daughter, Nausea, whose names came from a laundry van with 'Diploma Bagwash' on the side. Askey spotted it on the way to the weekly programme ideas meeting, and immediately decided that Bagwash was just the name for the character they'd been thinking of, while Diploma would do perfectly for her daughter. At this, the producer, Harry Pepper, demurred – it sounded like advertising. To which Askey retorted, 'Oh you fill me with nausea', and then, a moment later, realized that Nausea Bagwash was even better than Diploma.[68] Neither mother nor daughter ever spoke throughout the series: Mrs Bagwash gave an occasional grunt when spoken to, while Nausea always fainted at the microphone, so that all that was ever heard of her was a thud as she hit the floor.

Up in the flat anything could happen. When Arthur and Dicky vacuumed the floor the BBC Variety Orchestra, practising in the studio below, was sucked up to the ceiling. Sound effects became increasingly unruly. When Big and Stinker found a lump in the upholstery, a ripping of cloth followed by tinklings indicated that a grand piano had slipped down the back of the settee. The loud crash which came to punctuate the show had originally been used, in realistic fashion, to indicate that Arthur had dropped his hiking equipment. But once the convention was established it was used in quite anomalous contexts. At the start of one show Arthur had not yet arrived so Dickie seized the chance to show that 'I am quite capable of carrying the programme on my own shoulders.' As he said this there was a loud crash, and Arthur entered with 'Hello playmates! You've just heard Richard Murdoch dropping the programme.' Some of the humour relied wholly on sound effects, as when the pigeons got into Reginald Foort's cinema organ, producing a medley of coos and chords, or when Dickie read a melodramatic story punctuated by ill-judged thunder-claps and explosions supplied by Arthur.[69]

Band Waggon did make Arthur Askey a household name, though it took eighteen shows, according to Askey, rather than the twelve predicted by the *Daily Mail*, for this to happen. Askey was one of the first authentic radio stars (Henry Hall was perhaps the very first) able immediately to cash his success in other media: a lucrative contract for six films with Gaumont British, a touring version of the radio show organized by Jack Hylton who bought the stage rights from the BBC, the offer of top billing on Sir Oswald Stoll's Variety Hall circuit and, from the Oxford University Press, the unlikely accolade of *The Arthur Askey Annual* produced for the Christmas of 1939. His life story was serialized in *Tit-Bits* and he had a regular humorous column ghosted in the *Sunday Chronicle*. Askey was delighted to have made it into the big time but he hesitated before accepting the invitation to do the Music Hall circuit. He had worked his way up in the summer world of Concert Party and of Panto in the winter, starting with The Filberts in 1923 at £6.10s. a week. By the time *Band Waggon* arrived he was established as 'the king of the Concert world'. He had never felt he was 'broad enough' for the halls and had deliberately avoided Music Hall for that reason. He had seen Mable Constanduros die, before his very eyes, at the Alhambra with Joe Beckett, then reigning heavyweight champion, topping the bill with a boxing exhibition. 'The audience consisted of men with broken noses and cauliflower ears and you can imagine how interested they were in Mabel's chat about Gran' ma!' Askey knew instinctively that his kind of humour was better suited to radio than the halls.[70]

The humour of *Band Waggon* – its aural slapstick, its inverted logic and surreal fantasy – drew on diverse elements in contemporary popular culture, but always nourished by reference back to broadcasting. Earlier radio entertainment had expressed its uneasy relationship with an institution seemingly dedicated to higher things, through burlesque and parody of its serious programmes. But *Band Waggon* drew less on such elements in radio output, and more on its popular shows and characters. If it treated the BBC announcer as a figure of fun, it also drew him into the show as a performer. There were family references to the production team of the show, and listeners came to know its producer, Harry Pepper, by his *Band Waggon* nickname of 'the Bishop'. Arthur and Dickie's tenancy of the flat at the top of Broadcasting House symbolized the occupation of that 'damned awful erection', that monument to Reithian sobriety, by the forces of innocent mayhem and fun. Because the elements of this fantasy world and its in-jokes grew with a crazy logic from week to week its pleasures, for listeners, were cumulative as they learnt its conventions and shared in its laughter. *Band Waggon* was not the first show to use catch-phrases, but Arthur's 'Aythangyow' (picked up from London bus conductors) was the first radio catch-phrase to pass into the language. It became a cult.

Listener Research confirmed that the regularity of shows like *Monday Night at Seven* and *Band Waggon* enabled them to accumulate more and more listeners each week until they reached a stable plateau as the most widely listened to programmes on radio.[71] At the height of its success, the popularity of *Band Waggon* on Wednesday evenings led to church services having to be altered, to a decline in attendance at cinemas and theatres and to a sharp fall-off, noted by the Post Office, in the number of telephone calls made between eight and nine o'clock that evening. The BBC had succeeded in entertainment, where it failed in talks and music, in creating a genuinely common culture on the air. Now it was the regular date with Arthur and Dickie, or *The Plums* or *Puzzle Corner* that united the national audience. Radio had learnt to relax. What came together in the style of radio variety produced in the late thirties were forms of entertainment that blended in with domestic life and the daily round instead of offering, as did other entertainments, a break from that routine. Faced with a vast and socially diverse public, radio variety staff discovered that a common framework of associations could only be achieved by actually inventing it through the mechanisms of catchy signature tunes, well-established characters and situations and familiar voices uttering familiar catch-phrases. This was the real value of the series format, of the stock situation as well as the stock character. Each week a new variation was found for the reiterated theme. The new and the predictable, sameness and difference, were skilfully interwoven. Like the private jokes of a family, radio comedy built up its far-fetched associations, while remaining rooted in the charm of the familiar. One resource that could always be relied on as a shared point of reference available to all listeners was the culture of radio itself.

Part IV

BROADCASTING AND ITS AUDIENCES

CHAPTER THIRTEEN

The National Culture

⟶━⊛━⟶

IF THE culture of radio depended on a shared public life brought into being by broadcasting itself, a central aspect of this process was the creation of a sense of participation in a corporate national life. The BBC fulfilled its mandate of service in the national interest by synthesizing a national culture from components that had begun to converge since the late nineteenth century. There was a national education system to inculcate, as part of the curriculum, the achievements of British history and the glories of English literature.[1] The monarchy had been thoroughly revamped and refurbished with a whole new deck of ritual functions and ceremonies.[2] The land itself was reclaimed as the national heritage by the National Trust.[3] Nationalism found musical expression in the Savoy Operas and more profoundly in the music of Elgar and Vaughan Williams.[4] Many sports, of quite recent origin, began to organize national competitions on an annual basis. But the full convergence of these developments as elements of a unified national life available to all, awaited the establishment of broadcasting and the new kind of public, commensurate with the whole of society, which it brought into being.

A nation, as David Chaney points out, is an abstract collectivity. It is too big to be grasped by individuals. A sense of belonging, the 'we-feeling' of the community, has to be continually engendered by opportunities for identification as the nation is being manufactured.[5] Radio and, later, television were potent means of manufacturing that 'we-feeling'. They made the nation real and tangible through a whole range of images and symbols, events and ceremonies, relayed to audiences direct and live. In the course of the twenties and thirties BBC engineers arranged thousands upon thousands of outside broadcasts from a wide variety of sources for the growing listening public.[6] They included religious services and sacred music from churches; opera and plays from the theatres and entertainment from variety halls; dance music from cafés and concert music from the concert halls; public speeches by public persons from all sorts of public places; and ceremonies and events which ranged from royal occasions to the song of the nightingale. Added to all these was the coverage of sporting events – football, rugby, cricket, horse racing, tennis and boxing.

In presenting this material the broadcasters did not intervene to re-structure it. Most programmes observed real time, the length of the broadcast corresponding to the duration of the event. Radio sought to minimize its own presence as witness, claiming simply to extend the distribution of the event beyond its particular context to the whole listening community. Their appeal, which was very great to an audience unlike today's which takes such things for granted, was that they admitted listeners to public events, to their live pre-sence, in a way no previous technology had been able to do. A letter to *Radio Times* in 1928 poignantly expressed their effect:

> Many of your readers must be office workers. They must know what sort of a life is that of a clerk in a provincial city – a tram-ride to the office, lunch in a tea-shop or saloon bar, a tram-ride home. You daren't spend much on amusements – the pictures and that – because you've got your holidays to think of. We have no Trade Unions and we don't grumble, but it's not an easy life. Please don't think I'm complaining. I'm only writing to say how much wireless means to me and thousands of the same sort. It is a real magic carpet. Before it was a fortnight at Rhyl, and that was all the travelling I did that wasn't on a tram. Now I hear the Boat Race and the Derby, and the opening of the Menai Bridge. There are football matches some Saturdays, and talks by famous men and women who have travelled and can tell us about places.[7]

Such broadcasts unobtrusively stitched together the private and the public spheres in a whole new range of contexts. At the same time the events them-selves, previously discrete, now entered into new relations with each other, woven together as idioms of a common national life. Nothing so well illustrates the noiseless manner in which the BBC became perhaps *the* central agent of the national culture as its calendrical role; the cyclical reproduction, year in year out, of an orderly and regular progression of festivities, rituals and celebrations – major and minor, civil and sacred – that marked the unfolding of the broadcast year. The calendar is based on natural temporal cycles – the lunar month or solar year – and is a means of regulating in the long term the manifold purposes of religious and civil life. It not only coordinates social life, but gives it a renewable content, anticipatory pleasures, a horizon of expectations. It is one means whereby 'the temporality of social life is expressed in the meshing of present with past that tradition promotes, in which the cyclical character of social life is predominant.'[8]

The cornerstone of the broadcast calendar was the religious year: the weekly observances of the Sabbath through church services and a programme schedule markedly more austere than on other days; the great landmarks of Easter, Pentecost and Christmas; the feastdays of the patron saints of England, Scotland and Wales which occasioned special programmes from the appropriate 'region', though what to do with St Patrick's Day was an annually recurring headache for the programme-makers in Belfast. Bank holidays were celebrated in festive mood while the solemn days of national remembrance were marked by religious services and special feature programmes. Sport of course developed its own calendar very quickly. The winter season had its weekly observances of football, rugby and steeple-chasing, climaxing in the Boat Race, the Grand National and the Cup Final. Summer brought in cricket and flat racing, the test matches, Derby Day, Royal Ascot and Wimbledon.

Threaded through the year was a tapestry of civic, cultural, royal and state occasions: Trooping the Colour, the Ceremony of the Keys, the Lord Mayor's Banquet, the Chairing of the Bard, the Dunmow Flitch, the Shakespeare memorial celebrations at Stratford and much, much more. From the late twenties onwards programme-makers kept a watchful eye on impending anniversaries as occasions for a potential talk or feature. The 2000th anniversary of Virgil's death produced a talk on Virgil in English Poetry, while some of the more radical elements conspired to remember republican causes – May Day, the Fall of the Bastille or the hundredth anniversary of the first great Chartist march.

The broadcast year fell naturally into two divisions: the indoor months of autumn and winter and the outdoor months of spring and summer. One of the first things the radio manufacturers discovered was the seasonal nature of the sale of radio sets which increased sharply as winter came on. Hence the annual trade exhibition, Radiolympia, was held in the autumn as heralding the start of the 'wireless season'. By the late twenties output was being planned on a quarterly basis, and the autumn quarter was always carefully arranged to woo the fireside listeners with a varied menu of new plays, concerts and variety programmes. The fireside months were generally better stocked with 'serious' listening matter, but from Whitsun onwards the lighter elements in the programmes were expected to have an increasingly wide appeal. At the same time the broadcasters claimed to have redressed the balance between the seasons of the year, making it possible now to hear good music and plays throughout the summer months when the theatres and concert halls were closed.[9] Thus the programme planners tried to find broadly appropriate material to suit the climate of the year and the mood and leisure activities of the audience. The highpoint of these activities were the annual arrangements for Christmas Day.

From the very beginning Christmas was always the most important date in the broadcast year. It was the supreme family festival, an invocation of the spirit of Dickens, a celebration of 'home, hearth and happiness'.[10] It was no coincidence that Reith had worked hard for years to persuade the King to speak, from his home and as head of his family, to the nation and empire of families listening in their homes on this particular day. The royal broadcast (the first was in 1932) quickly became part of the ritual of the British Christmas, and is a classic illustration of that process whereby tradition is invented. It set a crowning seal on the role of broadcasting in binding the nation together, giving it a particular form and content: the family audience, the royal family, the nation as family.

Though not all these ceremonies and events recurred annually their combined effect was to create an underlying stable temporal framework for broadcasting, working through the weeks and months of the year. Programme output took on a patterned regularity that grew stronger in the National Programme during the 1930s. This was, and continues to be, an incremental process of production and reproduction in which a seemingly diverse range of material – Wimbledon, a Bank Holiday seaside special feature, a commemorative church service, a royal ceremony – becomes sedimented in annual output as the normative expression of an accessible public life. The nation as a knowable community became available to all members with access to broadcasting.

The apparently noiseless and effortless way in which this material slid into place in the schedules of broadcasting conceals the difficulties in many cases of securing access initially, the technical problems to be overcome in successfully relaying live events to listeners and the cracks that the broadcasters discovered in the facade of a common national life in a divided society. The monarchy was one quarter not immediately to be won over to the opportunities which the microphone presented for cementing the bonds of loyalty between the sovereign and his subjects, though Reith had foreseen it from the beginning. In October 1923 he wrote to the King's Private Secretary, Lord Stamfordham, at Buckingham Palace:

No doubt you are aware of the great progress made by Broadcasting in this country in the past nine months. It has developed into a national service, the potentialities of which it is difficult accurately to foreshadow ... It is our earnest desire that His Majesty the King, should honour us by broadcasting a special message on Christmas or New Year's Day, this being heard throughout the British Isles by an audience of between one and two million persons. Such a personal message from His Majesty to all sorts and conditions of people in town and country districts alike would make, in these difficult and anxious times, a national moral impression, the effect of which could hardly be estimated.[11]

It took Reith nearly ten years of patient diplomacy to persuade George V to initiate, in 1932, what became the tradition of the monarch's Christmas Day broadcast to the peoples of Britain and the Empire. Still, he scored a notable *coup* in 1924 when he obtained permission for the BBC to relay the opening of the Empire Exhibition at Wembley, including the speeches by King George and the Prince of Wales. This was the first time that the voice of the monarch had been heard on radio and it was easily the BBC's most successful single broadcast to date. Some ten million people heard the King. This was an audience far greater than the number of households with licensed wireless sets and many millions heard the broadcast relayed in public places by loudspeakers. The newspapers, for once, put aside their own interests and took the lead in promoting the event. The *Daily Mail* made arrangements for massed crowds to hear the speech in major cities such as Leeds, Manchester and Glasgow,[12] while in Oxford a crowd of several thousands gathered in St Giles and the High Street to hear the broadcast courtesy of the *Oxford Times* and the Oxford Wireless Telephony Company. The next day the *Oxford Times* declared:

Many people have realized the wonders of wireless in their own home if they have taken the full opportunity made possible by broadcasting, but it was not until some national function took place like the State opening of the British Empire Exhibition at Wembley ... that the full force of the miracle of science was realised. For the uninitiated to imagine that broadcasting gives them the opportunity to hear spirited music and the spoken word is a very different thing to realising for the first time that it enables them to take part in a ceremony sixty, a hundred miles, or even greater distances away. It gave the sense of unity with a mighty people, the sense of participation in an unseen event.[13]

Reith noted in his diary that everything went most successfully, including the broadcast which went all over the country and was 'the biggest thing we have yet done'.[14]

At the time, though, it remained a lonely portent of things to come, and when Reith came to draft his Memorandum of Information for the Crawford Committee he pointedly expressed his disappointment that broadcasting's potential influence on national life was still being so severely curtailed. The possibility of broadcasting great national occasions remained almost wholly dependent on the individual whim of a Minister or Government Department.

Such events united all classes and linked together town and country. In the future he expected that the relay of any public event or ceremony of general interest should be practically automatic.[15]

The transformation from Company to Corporation opened up access to many public events from which the BBC had formerly been barred. Sport in particular very quickly yielded up its plums. For Robert Wood, the BBC's young engineer in charge of Outside Broadcasts, 1927 was a year in which landmarks came so thick and fast that his life was one long rush to keep up with all the new developments. It was a year of 'firsts': the first live coverage of a rugby match from Twickenham on 15 January, of the Grand National on 25 March and a week later of the Boat Race (one of the most technically difficult broadcasts to date), of the FA Cup Final from Wembley, of the Lincoln and the Derby, of the TT motor cycle races from the Isle of Man and of cricket from Lords and the Oval. As summer approached, Wood began negotiations with the secretary of the All England Club for permission to broadcast from Wimbledon. After much discussion he finally agreed and a permanent soundproof hut was built at the side of the court, wired to a control point underneath the terraces.[16]

The live coverage of outdoor events required meticulous preparation and planning, the skilful selection of microphone placements to catch the natural sounds which conveyed the essence of the event, and the maintenance of a careful balance between these and the voice-over commentary which set the scene and described the event for the blind, invisible listener. When the BBC covered the launching of the *Queen Mary* in 1934, Wood set up thirteen separate microphone placements: two for the King, one each for the Queen, the chairman of Cunard and the christening bottle, three for the commentator, two for the slipway effects, two for the band and one more (in a rubber balloon) for water effects. The engineering task of ensuring that all the equipment worked during the programme, and the production task of mixing together sound effects and commentary to produce a smooth, unbroken account of the event made these the most demanding of all broadcasts and none more so than royal occasions.[17]

The first two royal Christmas broadcasts in 1932 and 1933 were rather stiff and formal, but in 1934 the King, speaking into a special microphone encased in empire walnut, offered his Christmas greeting to all his people on this day which 'with its hallowed memories is the Festival of the Family'. He addressed his listeners as 'all the members of our world-wide family', and hoped that he might be regarded as 'in some true sense the head of this great and widespread family'.[18] King George's last broadcast – he died within a month of giving it – struck a quite new note in the relationship between monarchy and people:

I wish you all, my dear friends, a happy Christmas. I have been deeply touched by the greetings which in the last few months have reached me from all parts of the Empire. Let me in response send to each of you a greeting from myself. My words will be very simple but spoken from the heart on this family festival of Christmas.

The year that is passing – the twenty-fifth since my Accession – has been to me most memorable. It called forth a spontaneous offering of loyalty – and may I say of love – which the Queen and I can never forget. How could I fail to note in all the rejoicing not merely respect for the Throne, but a warm and generous remembrance of the man himself who, may God help him, has been placed upon it.

It is this personal link between me and my people which I value more than I can say. It binds us together in all our common joys and sorrows, as when this year you showed your happiness in the marriage of my son, and your sympathy in the death of my beloved sister. I feel this link now as I speak to you. For I am thinking not so much of the Empire itself as of the individual men, women and children who live within it, whether they are dwelling here at home or in some distant outpost of the Empire.[19]

Deliberately setting aside the symbolic abstractions of Throne and Empire the old King spoke in a simple, direct and personal way to the listeners as individuals and friends. He spoke of his own family as familiar to those whom he addressed, and he spoke of personal feelings, of spontaneous bonds of affection which linked himself and his family to his people. Not all royal broadcasters have successfully brought off this direct and personal mode of address, but this short royal speech, the first fully to deploy an interpersonal style, has a genuine sincerity which makes it still moving to listen to today.

Other modern media, the cinema newsreels particularly, covered the public face of monarchy as well as broadcasting. What the newsreels in the thirties lost in live immediacy they gained in their visual record of state rituals as symbolic spectacles. But only broadcasting could deliver the double face of monarchy, its private as well as its public aspect. Thus uniquely radio first and, later, television presented royalty as near and far, impersonal and personal, extraordinary and ordinary. The mediating metaphor of the personal, private face of monarchy was the family. The Christmas Day broadcasts unobtrusively underwrote a particular version of society; of Britain as a nation of families, fundamentally all alike, and bound together from top to bottom by a newly familiar monarchy as its focus and epitome.

After the Christmas Day broadcast in 1932 permission was given for the microphone to be present at many state rituals and royal ceremonies. Two months of elaborate planning went into the coverage of the wedding of the Duke of Kent and Princess Marina in Westminster Abbey on 29 November

1934. It was the most difficult of all the 13,000 outside broadcasts Wood had arranged. No commentator was allowed inside the Abbey and Wood had to arrange concealed microphone placements throughout the church to convey a coherent presentation of the wedding service without added commentary. Nor could Wood see what was happening for he and all his equipment were tucked away in a small room in the crypt, a few feet away from the Tomb of the Unknown Warrior. For weeks before the ceremony he paced the floor of the Abbey, timing the service and the procession, testing placings and trying to balance the mix of sounds coming through. On the day itself he sat for four hours at his controls praying that his timing and preparations had been exact, and that all parties concerned were in fact standing where he had estimated them to be standing when he switched from microphone to microphone. In the event the transmission was an enormous success and listeners in many countries clearly heard the couple exchange their marriage vows, for the service was relayed to Italy, Yugoslavia, Denmark, Holland, Germany, Austria and the United States. Apart from the King's Christmas Day broadcasts, this very first royal wedding to be covered by broadcasting drew the largest world-wide audience of any transmission to date.[20]

It was followed by others – the Silver Jubilee celebrations of George V and Queen Mary in 1935, and early in 1936 the funeral service of the old King. On this occasion it was felt that commentary would be superfluous and so the whole event was portrayed by sound alone – one of the finest sound portraits ever achieved by radio in Wood's opinion. A few weeks later came the proclamation of Edward VIII as King-Emperor and at the end of the year his extraordinary abdication broadcast, probably the most riveting 'news' actuality broadcast yet heard on radio. The Coronation of George VI received the most elaborate coverage of any broadcast to date, and was the first royal ceremony to be presented on television. Fifty-eight microphones, 472 miles of wire, twelve tons of equipment and sixty BBC engineers were involved, those inside the Abbey doing their job in full morning dress. By now overseas broadcast services were sending their own teams to provide coverage and the service was described in Czech, Danish, Dutch, Finnish, Flemish, French, German, Hungarian, Japanese, Norwegian, Spanish (for South America), Swedish and Serbo-Croat.[21]

There is no doubt that the royal Christmas Day broadcasts along with the coverage of great sporting or ceremonial events were the most popular single broadcasts of all, and they won new listeners and extra revenue for the BBC as it built up its national audience. Mass Observation's survey of the Coronation in 1937 has a fascinating section on how the population listened to the event throughout the day, and the kinds of dilemma it posed. Was it permissible to eat or write or read during a 'sacred' broadcast? Should one stand while listening to the national anthem? Less reverent souls found that they could not

"ALBERT, I'M SURE THE DEAR KING AND QUEEN WOULDN'T WISH US TO STAND TO ATTENTION ALL THE TIME."

quite hear the words of the ceremony 'and some of the phrases sounded like "Gawd blimey" and "swelp me bob". We all joined in mock interpretations and there was much laughter.' One Mass Observer from Nottingham reported her hairdresser's account of the day. 'They'd had the wireless on from half-past ten to half-past four – "And you should have seen my mother – she sat in front of it all day – and all through the service while he was being crowned and that, the tears were pouring down her face and she kept moaning 'Oh, it ought to be Edward – it – it – it ought to Edward – My mother's a scream!" '[22]

Transmissions such as these were the only programmes to attract an audience drawn, as the *BBC Year Book* put it, 'almost equally from all grades of the listening public'.[23] But when the broadcasters themselves began to put together special feature programmes for anniversaries and special days in the BBC calendar they found themselves in difficulties. The art of live commentary took time to develop. The more elaborate attempts to combine narrative with music and actuality material could give rise to uneasy transitions between the symbolic and the real. But the problems went deeper than style. How should such abstract entities as empire or nation be represented? If the broadcasters drew on older cultural traditions, on history or folk music and poetry, the material might bypass large sections of their audience. If they dealt with the contemporary and actual it might give rise to controversy. There were fissures within the imaginary unity of empire and nation: there was India, there was Ireland. To reference such divisions would defeat the purpose of the programmes. Perhaps the idealized and the actual could be combined if the perfect typification could be found; a location that embodied the essence of Britishness, a New Zealand farmer who might serve as a model for colonial virtue and honest loyalty. Producers explored a range of possibilities, but none provided an obvious way out of their difficulties.

The problems were most evident in the special feature programmes made for Christmas, New Year, Empire Day and the national saints' days. A notable feature of their development was a change in style from the symbolic, rhetorical and impersonal to the actual, vernacular and personal. The pervasive unitary metonym that stood in for the social whole was again the image of the family. In the Empire Day programme for 1935 a mother was heard explaining to her daughter, '"The British Empire, Mary, is made up of one big family." "You mean a family like ours, Mummy?" asks Mary. "Yes, darling", Mummy replies, "but very much larger." '[24]

The royal broadcasts on Christmas Day were preceded by an elaborate feature programme which aimed to link nation and empire in a common celebration of the family festival. For the first one, described as a 'poetic juggling in time and space in terms of broadcasting', the British announcer was transmuted into an 'aerial postman' who surveyed the globe from a great height and intoned his greetings to each dominion and colony to the sound of a striking clock.[25] This pitch of poetic elevation was not sustained when the postman set foot on land with his 'Hullo Brisbane' or 'Are you awake Vancouver?' and handed over to a local announcer who might mingle expressions of loyalty to the crown with accounts of butter and cheese production or descriptions of a new hydro-electric plant.[26] While critics welcomed the programme as a technical triumph it was evident that a more intimate style would be needed if a sense of the national and imperial community as family was to be evoked.

In successive Christmas features such as *Absent Friends* in 1933 and *The Great Family* in 1935, poetic narration and the chain of empire greetings played a diminishing part.[27] Instead, listeners were offered slices of life, outside broadcasts from a lighthouse and a coal mine, church services, children's parties and family gatherings, talks from individuals representing different parts of the United Kingdom. But here the issue of what was acceptable as representative posed severe problems. Within the BBC the most successful contributor of this type was reckoned to be 'the grand old shepherd of Ilmington' who introduced the King's talk in 1934. But a critic of the 1933 programme pointedly preferred characterful episodes from a Welsh family, Rhondda miners and Highland Scots to the less distinctive Glasgow and Lancashire Christmas parties which he found 'noisy and tedious'.[28] And it was, characteristically, in Northern Ireland that the gravest exception was taken to the way in which that part of the United Kingdom was presented to the rest of Great Britain.

Belfast's contribution to *Absent Friends* lasted less than four minutes. It was intended to show how 'a distinctively Ulster household might be spending part of Christmas'. In the fortnight that followed the broadcast a long and often highly critical debate about it took place in the letter columns of the Belfast Unionist press. Over seventy letters were published, and the following extracts give something of their tone:

1.   The feelings of thousands of Ulster people must have been outraged when listening to this 'ballyhoo' performance, coming as it did in the midst of an otherwise impressive Christmas message. One listened first to the carefully chosen words of the London announcer and to Mr Howard Marshall, delivered in their delightfully cultured voices, then to the nice, simple messages from hospital children, lighthousemen, miners, crofters, etc., in their natural dialects, musical and unexaggerated in every case. But what a shock, when Ulster was called, to hear what was obviously considered an amusing example of Ulster dialect, but what in reality was mere parody. What must the world think of Ulster when that is the only form of Christmas message we could send on the ether?

2.   It was not Ulster dialect at all, it was an imitation of the dialect of the Free State.

3. We are cut off from the rest of Ireland by the Border. We have not anything to do with it, and we never will have. Erin is Ireland. Ireland is on the other side of the Border: yet we hear the voice of Ulster proclaiming in song 'Come back to Erin'. Ye Gods! Think of it. Who arranged this programme which was of world-wide significance to our province? Who selected 'Father O'Flynn' as a typical Ulster song? Many people have thought for a long time that there is too much of the Irish pipe, the Irish jig, and the Irish atmosphere in the BBC programmes from Belfast.[29]

In an implacably divided community it was an impossible task to find accept-able symbols and images to invoke a shared sense of a common way of life. In London, as Rex Cathcart points out, there had been a tendency to regard the BBC in Northern Ireland as the BBC in Ireland. But in the 1930s the Belfast station became, under its Regional Director, George Marshall, increasingly Unionist in outlook. When North Region proposed to relay a feature in 1937 called *The Irish*, Marshall objected to the title itself as 'highly undesirable, linking under one name two strongly antipathetic states with completely different political outlooks. There is no such thing today as an Irishman. One is either a citizen of the Irish Free State or a citizen of the United Kingdom of Great Britain and Northern Ireland. Irishmen as such ceased to exist after the partition.'[30]

In such circumstances the special programmes for St Patrick's Day became an annual ordeal by fire for programme-makers in the BBC's North-ern Ireland office. *Turf Smoke*, Belfast's effort for 1933, was relayed to the rest of Britain and parts of the empire. It was meant to recall for Irish exiles far from home 'those things in Ireland which have a universal appeal'. There was a Prologue spoken by a number of voices and an Epilogue which referred par-ticularly to Belfast. In between there was music, poetry and songs. All the voices were anonymous. The letter columns of the Belfast newspapers regis-tered Ulster opinion. Exception was taken to 'Father O'Flynn' and to unedu-cated English accents trying to assume a genuine Irish brogue. But there was praise for the clever dialogue – 'one could almost see the hills and the valleys and the little thatched cottages through the mist, and hear the sea-gulls screaming on the shores.' The tone of many of the critical letters was more in sorrow than anger, and registered a feeling that the BBC staff in Northern Ireland, being mostly English or Scottish, could not be expected to under-stand Ireland or the Irish.[31] By 1937 the search for exemplars of Irishness for St Patrick's Day drove the desperate producer of the programme up the Sperrin mountains in a blizzard to bring back to the studio a shepherd, a gamekeeper, an embroidress and a country fiddler.[32]

The production files for all the anniversary programmes reveal the problems producers experienced in trying to square myth with reality. Empire

288

Day was a constant source of embarrassment to producers who were aware that its traditional celebration involved aggressive and ultra-patriotic sentiments which might offend supporters of internationalism and the League of Nations. Yet attempts to devote the programme to current imperial themes such as constitutional change in India were abandoned for fear of controversy.[33] When the New Year's Eve feature in 1932 struck a controversial note, for once, it gave rise to a diplomatic tiff with the Polish Embassy and the banishment, it was rumoured, of its producer to Northern parts. Even the Christmas features were not entirely free of politics. In 1935 it was found that there were too many difficulties in including a representative of the unemployed in *The Great Family*. This programme was criticized within the BBC as too formal and pompous. Significantly the objections came from producers in North Region where more direct and down-to-earth styles of documentary and more populist styles of presentation were being developed.[34] By the late thirties the Christmas Day features were sometimes dropped and the highlight of the day – at least as far as the popular press was concerned – was the radio stars' Christmas Party. The folksiness of the earlier Christmas features was lampooned in a stage review, *Nine Sharp* by Herbert Farjeon, which had Captain Snaggers of the North Sea Bloater Fishing Fleet quoting poetry and a BBC commentator bidding him farewell with 'Goodbye and good bloating'.[35]

In routine, day-to-day output the issues of national identity and culture posed problems which, on the one hand, arose from divisions within the supposed unity of British life and culture and, on the other, from the impact of foreign cultures and their perceived threat to traditional national values. Talks might try to preserve a harmonious vision of the British and Britishness only to have the tranquility of their account exploded by one of the participants. The Americanization of British culture was widely debated outside the BBC, with particular reference to variety programmes and dance music. And the Music Department found itself caught in the double bind of defending a vision of musical culture without national boundaries while trying, at the same time, to promote British musical interests at home and abroad.

Martin J. Wiener in an influential recent analysis of English culture, has a telling account of the prevalent, mythic version of the 'English way of life'.[36] In an industrialized society, most of whose members live urban and suburban lives, the predominant image of Englishness for most of this century has been of a timeless, rural way of life located in the southern parts of the country. This image, cultivated in art and literature in the last century, has been reiterated this century by film, radio and television. Wiener points to the role of the pre-war BBC in this respect: to portentous talks series on the subject, to gardening programmes introduced by 'Our Bill' (Freddy Grisewood) and to a pervasive concern with the preservation of our greatest heritage, the countryside.[37] The conservatism of this nostalgic image of Britain was, he argues, part of the political rhetoric of both Right and Left in the twenties and thirties, most comfortably given voice by Stanley Baldwin and J. B. Priestley.[38]

Both were accomplished broadcasters and in 1933 we find Baldwin introducing an interminable Talks series on *The National Character* by locating the essence of that character in the Normans (who were not really French but 'gallicized Scandinavians'), in the village community, in the writings of Dickens and, 'if I might mention a living writer, I think the truest Englishmen are found in Mr Priestley's novels'.[39] Subsequently, Arthur Bryant elaborated a ripely sentimental account of the trueborn Englishman as embodied in Squire, Parson, Yeoman, Craftsman, Merchant, Adventurer and, last and least, Housewife (who ought to learn to cook better). There was a little muted protest in the letter columns of *The Listener* about halfway through – 'Is not the complacency of Mr A. Bryant beginning to wear thin?' – but it was not until near the end of the second twelve-week run on the subject that the aura of self-satisfaction was torpedoed.

After a break for Christmas the series resumed by broadening its scope. Up to this point the National Character had been located almost wholly in the past, in the countryside and in the home counties of England. Now it was acknowledged that there were significant differences between North and South, that there were Welsh, Scottish and Irish identities as part of the picture and that changes in the last century – the impact of modern industry – had had their effect on the national character. This last point was developed by Sir Herbert Austin, an industrialist, who stressed recent improvements in working conditions and living standards and foresaw an improvement in the mental life of the nation. 'Mechanization is relieving the brain of old tediums and giving it new stimulus. The slaves of metal labour, while the mind of man directs.'[40] After the point of view of Industry it was the turn of Labour and William Ferrie, a representative of the National Union of Vehicle Builders, was invited to put the working-class view. Ferrie strongly disagreed with the previous speaker, and his draft script drew attention to the economic exploitation of the working class. It went on to reject calls for equality of sacrifice in the national interest, referred to the rise of Fascism in Europe and Britain and claimed that the workers were looking to Russia for a solution: 'The dissatisfaction of the workers with their lot is growing. The limitations imposed on us educationally and culturally are making us increasingly determined not to tolerate a social system which denies us the opportunity to develop our material and cultural existence.'[41]

Much of this got the blue pencil from the producer of the series on the grounds that it was off the point, and Ferrie apparently acquiesced in the cuts made to his manuscript. But on the night, when he came to the microphone, he abandoned his script, protested at the way in which his talk had been censored and left studio. In place of his twenty-minute talk there was an embarrassed silence and a realization of the Talks Department's worst night-mare. Critics seized upon the incident as evidence of the censorship they had long suspected, and the *Daily Herald* and *Daily Worker* printed in full the original text indicating the censored passages. In a statement to the *Daily Worker* (which suggests that the walk-out may have been carefully calculated), Ferrie declared:

> I was determined from the commencement of the negotiations that I would not permit the BBC authorities to manoeuvre me into giving expression to Capital-istic propaganda. In order to do this I had to create the impression that I would broadcast this speech, at the same time fighting against the character of this speech.[42]

The BBC argued that Ferrie had been invited to give a broad, representa-tive point of view, and that the deleted passages were not relevant to the actual topic. The following week 'a working woman' was hastily drafted in to offer a pointedly balanced judgement on the national character from the working woman's point of view:

> I believe we're a good deal happier than our mothers were in their day. That doesn't mean to say that things couldn't be better, or that the lot of the British working woman is a bed of roses.... After all, we're all human, and I don't believe there's very much difference between us, rich or poor. The thing that matters is not money or education, but character. The great thing is to be inde-pendent and capable of looking after yourself. Facing up to things – that's character.[43]

Talks did face up to some of the issues raised in the second part of this series – but not, of course, working-class support for Communism – in a short series on Nationalism in the spring of 1936. One consequence of the depression was the rise of the Scottish Nationalist Movement in the early thirties, which provoked much discussion at the time. In late 1935 Reith had promised A. D. Gibbs, the Regius Professor of Law at Glasgow University and an ardent nationalist, that the BBC would bring the subject to the microphone for dis-cussion. He passed this command to Talks via Cecil Graves, Controller of Programmes, and Rose-Troup passed it on to Scottish Region for them to put into shape.[44] Moray McLaren, in consultation with Welsh Region, came up with a scheme for two Scottish and Welsh speakers, one to represent the 'extremist' political claim to home rule and the other to put the moderate cul-tural claim to preserve the heritage of Wales and Scotland and their separate historic identities. It was suggested that an Englishman should introduce and conclude the series, but in Scotland there was a general consensus that while an Englishmen might open the series a foreigner – André Maurois, perhaps – should sum up as the Englishman would be biased 'and tend either to "pooh pooh" the whole affair or to "be superior".' There was some talk of asking Winston Churchill, as an English extremist, to contribute to the debate but prudence prevailed and Arthur Bryant was invited – and agreed – to provide a suitably emollient conclusion.

It was a continuing grievance in other parts of the country that those in London responsible for the content of the National Programme invariably not only defined 'national' issues in purely English terms, thereby rendering invisible Scotland, Wales and Northern Ireland, but then defined 'Englishness' in ways that ignored that North or the West of England, for instance. These differences were again collapsed when confronted with the inroads of foreign cultures, and above all that of the United States. In the early years the major criticism of American broadcasting was directed not at its content but at the 'chaos of the ether' which arose from unregulated transmission. This was always one argument advanced to defend the BBC's monopoly in Britain. For most of the. twenties broadcasting on either side of the Atlantic was quite similar, consisting largely of what became known in the United States as 'potted-palm-court music'. There was, of course, advertising on American radio and sponsorship of programmes to promote a product or a corporate image – a feature which the British always thought of as the quintessence of American vulgarity. But apart from this obvious difference the range of output on both sides remained broadly similar – news, music, variety, drama, etc. What began to diverge sharply, in the late twenties, were the manner and style of broadcasting – modes of address, production values and styles. At the same time the American domination of the emerging entertainment industry – notably cinema and popular music – created widespread alarm in Britain.

In 1929 Gerald Cock, in charge of Outside Broadcasts, wrote a report on 'American Control of the Entertainment Industry'. He warned that the BBC's monopoly would not necessarily protect it from the 'ramifications of the Transatlantic octopus', since American interests were investing in Britain and would attempt to establish monopolies of performers, writers, composers, plays and copyrighted music. 'It is even possible', he declared, 'that the national outlook and with it, character, is gradually becoming Americanized.'[45] To prevent that dire possibility *Radio Times* mounted a sustained campaign against American manners and mannerisms. In 1931 Basil Maine was asking, in its columns, 'Is American Killing Our Sense of Humour?': 'The American invasion of the entertainment world is responsible ... for changes of taste, for the blunting of dialect ... for new manners of thinking, for higher pressure of living, for discontent among normally contented people, for big ideas and for "Oh yeah!" '.[46] In the same year an editorial launched an attack on both British and American newsreel commentators.

Their accent is often painful to the educated ear; they do not seem to have even an elementary notion of how to get their words 'over'; instead of giving point to the silent drama by making it articulate, they are usually little more than a hindering background of jumbled words. The chief offenders in this matter are the Americans. Why must they talk to us as though we were all children? It is not only there feeble jokes and puns that we resent: it is also their condescending intonation. Even in their worst lapses our wireless announcers are never guilty of offences like this. They may occasionally strike us as too impersonal; but better the cold efficiency of the impersonal voice than the halting efforts of some of our English commentators or the condescending puerility America usually offers.[47]

When a straw poll of the readers of the *Literary Digest* showed that educated Americans disliked listening to jazz, crooners, sob-songs and advertisements, *Radio Times* gave the results with approval, 'Again, we have frequently heard admiration expressed for the more personal style of the average American announcer, but the trashy, coy, cute, patronizing and wise-cracking varieties are all pilloried in this poll.'[48]

Modes of address, styles of talk, are always crucial indicators in broadcasting of the relationship between programme-makers and their audience. In the era of uplift the BBC sought to preserve a distance from its audience which contrasted sharply with the more friendly, informal and democratic style of American radio. We have noted occasions when senior BBC personnel tried to root out Americanisms from BBC programmes – Cecil Graves, Controller of Programmes, for instance, ticking off the Variety Department for allowing an announcer to describe a swing music programme as a jam session. Here is Graves again, this time criticizing the commentary from an Outside Broadcast, on the first night of a West End show:

> What depressed me was the fact that it was another example of trying to introduce American methods and American phraseology into our broadcasting. Those of us who have been to the United States realize that there is a certain amount which we can learn from American broadcasting and there are ways in which they can put things over more professionally than we do, but there is absolutely no reason why we should introduce American jargon into our commentaries and announcements.... Such expressions as 'We bring to you', 'We offer you', etc, are examples, but it goes deeper than that and is noticeable in the form used as well as in the actual words.[49]

This incident provoked a wider discussion of the issue at Programme Board. Some felt that 'while any all-round americanization of programmes would be deplorable, certain types of programme called for treatment in the American manner and that these should either be treated in the manner best adapted to them or excluded altogether.' Others disagreed. The Head of News argued that the BBC had a world-wide responsibility for combating American tendencies which had largely captured the press and film industry. The Director of Schools Broadcasting said she would welcome the elimination of American types of entertainment, while the Director of West Region observed that 'P. G. Wodehouse's kind of humour was suggestive of a more characteristically English approach to the problem.'[50]

That there was a problem there can be no doubt. We have traced, in the preceding chapter, the development of radiogenic styles of entertainment which culminated in *Band Waggon* at the end of the thirties. *Band Waggon* was a successful adaptation of American techniques to produce a show with a wholly British flavour. The ancestral beginnings of British soap opera can be traced back to this period and to *The English Family Robinson*, a drama serial of suburban family life, devised by Mabel Constanduros after hearing from a visiting American about a successful series in the USA called *One Man's Family*.[51] *The English Family Robinson* lived in a suburb and consisted of Mr and Mrs Robinson, their three children, a maid called Shirley and a car called Ella. The aim of the serial was to make them a very ordinary family and they were, according to *Radio Times*, 'as near to being real people as you can expect on the radio'.[52] It was, though deplored by Gielgud, a successful home-grown version of an American format. But other efforts to lighten and brighten the programmes with imported American idea seem awkward today.

For instance, when the BBC, as part of its new endeavour to get the audience to join in, imported the American craze for Spelling Bees into the National Programme it managed to make them sound more like a schoolroom test than fireside fun (the results were printed in *The Times* in the style of chess reports). The Director of the Overseas Service, who had been listening to the American originals on short wave, had to advise the Talks Department on ways of livening up their presentation. He pointed out that 'the Americans adopted a slightly new technique by making suitable use of what I might call biographical dialogue with the competitors.... Each competitor was asked where she came from, what precisely her job was, etc., etc. and the words to be spelt were rather woven into this conversation.'[53] Nor was the Director of Overseas Services alone in listening to American radio. It was becoming common practice for British comedians to spend their nights tuning in to the United States on their short-wave sets in search of fresh material.[54]

The BBC sometimes broadcast relays of variety programmes from the United States, though it usually took the opportunity to damn them with faint praise. Recalling a relay of the *Amos 'n' Andy* show on New Year's Eve for 1930, the *BBC Year Book* remarked, 'It cannot be said that at first hearing their humour appealed to the British public, but it must be remembered that even in the United States it took some time for the public to develop a taste for it'.⁵⁵ Of a 1932 relay of a programme called *Stars of American Radio, Radio Times* commented, 'The programme – its precision of presentation, confidential familiarity of its announcement, the hymn tune repeated half a dozen times by way of a trade mark, the almost undiluted sentimenality of its content – presented a flawless picture of the lighter side of American broadcasting.'⁵⁶

The following year BBC put out a series of burlesques of American radio, *America Calling*, featuring Eddie Pola. This was one of the very few BBC variety shows to be relayed to the United States and it was broadcast by the NBC red network under the quizzical title *Is America Calling?*. Send-ups of American films and advertising were a frequent ingredient of BBC revues, and sniping at American radio continued even as the BBC increasingly borrowed its ideas. A 1937 edition of *Monday Night at Seven* featured a dialogue between Uncle Sam and a strangely refined and priggish John Bull who expressed astonishment that American radio could broadcast a symphony concert sponsored by a corset manufacturer and could mutilate a traditional ballad like *Annie Laurie* by playing it in swing tempo.⁵⁷ Sympathetic treatment of American popular culture was hard to find on British radio in the thirties, though Alistair Cooke presented a number of investigations into the roots of American folk music and *Baghdad on the Subway*, a feature by John Watt described as 'A phantasmagoria of New York', celebrated the hectic night life of that American city.⁵⁸

Few British listeners had direct access to American radio before the war. But they did become familiar with American style entertainment through listening to European commercial radio. Something of the quality and character of the output of Radios Normandie and Luxembourg can be got from the pages of *Radio Pictorial*, the only British magazine to publish details of their programmes, and itself a radio advertiser, sponsoring the *Radio Pictorial Celebrity Concert* on Normandie. The magazine was almost exclusively devoted to entertainment and gave as much space to BBC light progammes and personalities as to continental output. But there was a constant vein of criticism of the BBC as an institution. The first issue carried an article headed 'If I Were Governor of the BBC' by Oliver Baldwin, the BBC's renegade ex-film critic, who complained that 'the BBC of today tends to give out the attitude that it doesn't very much care whether its programmes are liked or not',⁵⁹ a recurring refrain in later issues. Godfrey Winn condemned BBC talkers for their lack of personality. 'Oh this "refained" BBC English!', sighed another critic. George Robey pleaded for more 'honest vulgarity by radio', and one of the many articles on American radio claimed that over there there was 'No red tape – or blue pencil'. One essential difference was summed up by Margot Jones in an article titled 'Luxembourg as I saw it', describing a visit to the station in 1938. 'There is a pleasant air of informality about the whole proceedings which perhaps explains some of the difference between Luxembourg and BBC programmes. No atmosphere of strained silence, no warning lights, no deep piled carpets to strike awe into the heart of the broadcaster.'[60]

Luxembourg's programmes were shorter than the BBC's, running for either fifteen or thirty minutes. They were more crisply presented and were arranged in regular series. But in substance most were like the kinds of light music programme put out the by the BBC for background listening. Titles like *The Bile Beans Concert, Mackay's Pools Concert* or the *Palm Olive Concert,* featuring Olive Palm and Paul Oliver, promised little more than the usual selection of dance band and light orchestral music, with a supply of vocalists. Variety could be heard on the *Kraft Cheese Music Hall of Fame* and *Vernon's All Star Variety Concert.* Many regular BBC performers turned up under new guises. Davy Burnaby, who often broadcast for the BBC with his Co-Optimists, could be heard in the *Rinso Concert* with his Rinsoptimists. Jeanne de Casalis, the BBC's 'Mrs Feather', teamed up with Lady Charles Cavendish to present the *Pompeian All Star Concert,* sponsored by Pompeian beauty products. Harry Helmsley, the child-impersonator, whose 'family' often appeared in BBC variety bills, became the presiding genius of the Ovaltiney's concert parties.[61] And perhaps most surprisingly, S. P. B. Mais, who had presented *S.O.S.,* the BBC's first eye-witness series on unemployment, turned up a few years later on Luxembourg on behalf of Scott's Emulsion. Introduced as the famous author and traveller, this 'modern Columbus' came to the microphone to give a series of 'radio snapshots' of modern heroes – ten-minute talks on characters such as Lawrence of Arabia. J. Walter Thompson, the agency that designed and produced the series, described it as 'another example of a keep-fit product allied to a keep-fit programme'.[62]

The American style of commercial radio at first revealed itself in the streamlined regularity of the scheduling, in the cheerful informality of presentation and in the ubiquitous hard-sell advertising of the product in between dance numbers. *The Andrews' Liver Salts Concert,* for instance, opened with a chorus of 'Merry Andrews' singing, to the tune of *See Me Dance the Polka*:

> We're the Merry Merry Andrews
> As fit as fit can be.
> And there's no reason why you
> Should not be as fit as we.
> So drink your Andrews in the morn
> And then you'll sing with glee,
> I'm a Merry Merry Andrew,
> As fit as fit can be.

Captain Merry Andrew then appeared to a small boy and his mother and took them for a ride on his magic carpet. They dropped in to Persia so that mother could do her shopping – a cue for the orchestra to play *In a Persian Market*. After that it was time to give the product another mention.

CAPTAIN MERRY ANDREW:	Well, have you done all your shopping mother?
MOTHER:	Yes I have got my tin of Andrews.
VOICE:	What, in Persia?
WOMAN'S VOICE:	Yes, you can buy it all over the world. Even in a Persian market.

And so time passed until Captain Merry Andrew brought things to an end with an offer of free samples for listeners and 'a fascinating puzzle booklet for the kiddies, which incidentally is very intriguing to the grown-ups as well'.[63]

There was nothing in this modest show that would have brought a blush to the cheeks of a BBC variety producer. And the same could be said for the *Ovaltiney Concert Party* which was aimed at children. Its genteel flavour is best exemplified by the rules of the League of Ovaltineys, the radio club which young listeners were encouraged to join. Members had to promise 'to do the things my parents tell me – because they know what's best for me and I want them to be proud of me' and 'to study hard at school – because I want to have a good keen mind'. Only after five such pious promises did Ovaltineys come to the nub of the matter and promise 'to drink Ovaltine every day – so that I can be healthy, happy and full of vim like all true Ovaltineys' and to 'listen to the Ovaltineys' programme ... every Sunday from Radio Luxembourg'. In 1938 the league had over 1.2 million virtuous little members.[64]

By then regular listeners to Luxembourg could hear American soap operas and programmes like the *Kraft Show*, with Billy Cotton and his band, wise-cracking Ted Ray and the barbed repartee and showbiz ballyhoo which was the hallmark of American radio variety. The bare format of this show was not unlike *Band Waggon*, but its atmosphere and style of humour differed markedly, as Martin Head has shown in a pointed comparison of the introductory announcements to the two shows:

Band Waggon:
ANNOUNCER: Ladies and Gentlemen. Arthur and Dicky have asked to be excused, as they are very busy spring-cleaning their flat, which as you know, is at the top of Broadcasting House. However, we thought you would like to know how they are getting on with it, so we have installed a microphone in the sitting-room, and we are now taking you over for a few minutes so that you can join in the fun. Over we go!

Kraft Show:
TED RAY: Welcome! Welcome to the Kraft Show featuring the one and only – thank goodness! – Billy Cotton, and the beautiful, adorable Phyllis Robins, not forgetting that delightful personality, Lizzie Tish. What fun we do have!

COTTON: Come on.... You're supposed to be the comedian here – make me laugh.
RAY: Mr Cotton, you pain me. You hurt me to the quick.
COTTON: What Ted Ray is trying to say my friends, is that he hasn't got a joke ready. So in order not to embarrass him any longer we'll play a tune.[65]

Band Waggon was a much more sophisticated programme both technically and in its whimsical, innocent humour. The *Kraft Show* was more down-market, more rackety and knowing. Ray and Cotton kept up a nudge-nudge, wink-wink patter between the music and titbits that make up the show. Here they are in the middle of a routine about football:

RAY: But you know, Billy, in the second half I was penalized for holding.
COTTON: But holding players is against the rules, isn't it Ted?
RAY: Well, *I* was penalized for holding the Manager's daughter.... She was cute ... a lovely blonde....
COTTON: Oh – and what did *Mrs* Ray say?
RAY: I wasn't there when she was told about it... but I bet I can guess three out every four words she said....
COTTON: Does your wife swear much Ted?
RAY: No, not much Bill ... but she makes every word count.[66]

This was precisely the kind of thing that the BBC was at such pains to avoid. The show was scripted by Eddie Pola who had graduated from writing burlesques of American radio for the BBC to writing something like the real thing for Luxembourg.

It was Claude Cockburn who pointed out that the attraction of Americanized culture in the thirties lay in its democratic appeal and that it was just that quality which led 'British statesmen, thinkers and leaders of the upper sort in general to observe it with alarm and utter their warnings against it.'[67] American culture, as inflected in film, radio and mass advertising, bespoke a more equal, open society than Britain. It had a democracy of manner and outlook which was as much a matter of communicative style as of content. While American culture implied that one person's views and values were as good as another's the BBC seemed intent on reforming the still *lumpen* majority. While American entertainment offered predictable pleasures, the BBC continued to make easy listening difficult. While American speech was beginning to assume a universal, classless manner, the accents of the BBC continued to exude what Compton Mackenzie called 'finicking, suburban, synthetic, plus-fours gentility'.[68] Anti-Americanism in Britain was, in reality, always more indicative of threatened class attitudes and postures than a threatened national culture. Working people in Britain massively enjoyed and consumed American entertainment because it did not treat them as second-class citizens.

One consequence of the huge success of American cinema and dance music in the twenties was that it created new job opportunities for British musicians. Music, Cyril Ehrlich notes, was one of the very few occupations in Britain dominated by foreigners.[69] Britain had long suffered an inferiority complex as a second- or even third-rate musical nation compared with France, Germany or Italy. Among British performers a resentment of foreigners was as old as the profession. In the nineteenth century British musicians had assumed foreign names to further their careers, but that stopped when the First World War broke out (Gustav Holst, British born and bred, was advised to drop the 'von' from his name by Percy Scholes).[70] The war led to an exodus of foreign musicians accompanied by fits of xenophobia among British musicians, and when it ended they were determined to keep foreigners out as new markets for their talents opened up. Leaders of the profession continued to fulminate against jazz and crooning, and to denounce America as 'the least musical nation in the world'.[71] But most musicians did not mind what music they played so long as *they* were playing it, and their professional bodies – the Musicians' Union and the Incorporated Society of Musicians – worked hard to keep out aliens and to promote the interests of British music and musicians.

The BBC had to deal with persistent lobbying on two fronts: from the bands and popular music publishers, and from the representatives of composers and performers of serious music. In 1930 500 players met to form a Dance Band Section of the Musicians' Union, intent on securing standard minimum wages and on keeping out American players. Foreign bands and rank-and-file players were already virtually excluded, and in the thirties only occasional tours by acknowledged stars such as Louis Armstrong, Sidney Bechet and Duke Ellington were allowed.[72] The BBC was under pressure to maintain a large proportion of British numbers in their dance band broadcasts, and by 1937 it was bombarded with letters on this point from the British Authors and Composers Association.[73] The issue focused particularly on vocal numbers and the recent edict fron Cecil Graves that there should be no more than one in three of these in dance band programmes. This was part of Graves' campaign to eliminate crooning, but it did not go down well with the bands or the publishers.

At a meeting between the BBC and the British Authors and Composers Association in June 1937 an attempt was made to define a British song in the light of the Association's complaint that not nearly enough were being broadcast. Graves ruled that the BBC defined a British song as one of which both author and composer were British subjects, wherever it had been published. The only exception might be when a well-known British composer collaborated with a foreigner who wrote the lyrics.[74] The Association suggested that more records of British numbers should be played and offered to provide the BBC with periodic lists of good current British numbers. The issue, like plugging, was not capable of simple resolution and continued to consume much time and paper until it took on a new complexion during the war.

The Music Department too was constantly harassed by the British music profession. In 1925 a Music Advisory Committee, consisting of leading representatives of the profession, was set up to provide the BBC with wise counsel in developing its music policy. But the committee spent most of its time attacking the Music Department for not doing enough for British music and musicians.[75] In 1933 Boult was under heavy pressure from the committee to include more British music, more British conductors and more British soloists in the music schedules. 'They prefer', he cried in exasperation, 'a second-rate Britisher to a first-rate foreigner and a concert of first-class importance.' Boult's own attitude had changed since he joined the BBC, as he admitted to Reith. 'I realized that for our most important work we, as it were, treat the world as our field, both in respect of compositions and performers, where I have previously looked upon England as my field with occasional excursions abroad.'[76] Boult came to value the Musical Advisory Committee 'most highly' not for any useful advice it had to offer, but because its members were typical of 'the average or perhaps of the rather more stupid kind of professional'. He could take its reactions as a reliable guide to the responses of the music profession in the country generally to the activities of the department.

Boult's anger with the Music Advisory Committee came to a climax in 1935 in a memorandum responding to evidence by three of its members to the Ullswater Committee. He bitterly denounced his Advisory Committee as 'phenomenally ill-informed' of the Corporation's musical activities and as motivated almost wholly by consideration of the immediate interests of the music profession. He protested that the Committee had tried to insist on the BBC broadcasting a far larger quota of British music than was merited by its quality and quantity. It had tried to insist that the BBC employ practically none but British artists. Against this Boult claimed that each year the BBC, on its latest figures, had given an average of 5500 engagements a year to British soloists and 330 to foreign solo artists. He went on to detail the support given by the BBC to numerous musical societies and organizations in London and the provinces. He declared that the BBC Symphony Orchestra had helped to transform the reputation abroad of British music and musicianship which was, until its establishment, extremely low. The BBC's music policy, he claimed, was rapidly building a very high musical reputation for Britain.[77]

There is no doubt that, under Boult, the Music Department was a loyal advocate of the casue of British music at home and abroad. The *BBC Year*

Book for 1930 noted that a great deal was being written these days about our 'national' school of composers who, being English in sentiment and outlook and expressing their inner selves in their art, were creating an essentially 'English' kind of music.[78] A year later, in an article on 'The English School of Music' for *Revue Musicale*, the leading French music magazine, Suzanne Demarquez began: 'No one would have thought of writing down this title a mere score of years ago without exciting in France – and perhaps in England too! – well justified astonishment.' This drew a rather huffy response from the *Monthly Musical Record*, but it did not contradict her.[79]

English music was promoted in a number of ways. Established and up and coming composers could be assisted by judicious patronage. There is the well-known case of the BBC's commissioning of Elgar's never completed Third Symphony.[80] But before the war it was generally decided – after unsuccessful negotiations with Constant Lambert and with William Walton (for a supposedly small-scale piece about Nebuchadnezzar, or The Writing on the Wall) – against commissioning individual compositions. Boult was advised that it was far better to let it be known that the BBC would always perform new works, provided they reached an approved standard. The problem with Lambert and Walton was that they offered 'unsuitable' pieces that they were working on, without regard to any particular suitability for the medium of radio.[81]

An occasional and more successful alternative was to commission incidental music for BBC programmes. In 1935 Geoffrey Bridson commissioned the Sheffield composer, Desmond MacMahon, to write an eponymous symphonic suite, *Steel*, for a feature programme he was preparing about the industry.[82] In 1936 the 23-year-old Benjamin Britten in collaboration with W. H. Auden, was not only hard at work on writing the musical score of *Nightmail*, the best remembered of all pre-war documentary films. He also worked with him on a delightful sounding programme, *Up the Garden Path*, an anthology of bad verse selected by Auden and bad music selected Britten and presented by John Cheadle. The following year Britten wrote the music for *King Arthur*, a dramatic feature written by Bridson and produced by Gielgud. Britten thoroughly enjoyed working on *Up the Garden Path* as well as the programme itself, but he found Bridson's script stilted and dull, and noted in his diary, 'It's a curse having to go on and on with this awful bore of Uncle Arthur.'[83]

A major way of promoting native talent was the decision, from 1929 onwards, to make the Thursday Promenade Concert each season a showcase for British music. The Proms, David Cox notes, made a powerful contribution to the renaissance of creative work in England by providing a popular platform and immense listening audience not only for the music of the older generation (above all the trinity of Elgar, Delius and Holst, all of whom died within months of each other in 1934), but for contemporary composers such as

Ireland, Bax, Vaughan Williams, Tippett, Walton and Rubbra.[84] The BBC received occasional complaints about the Thursday night Proms being too experimental and boring, but Boult would not accept this. In every case, he claimed, there was a balance between the stranger and more experimental music and accepted 'key' works by masters such as Elgar, Delius, Vaughan Williams, Bax, Holst and Ireland.[85]

From the mid-thirties the Music Department was cooperating with the newly created British Council for Relations with Other Countries.[86] This had been set up by the Government, so the BBC understood, with the object of spreading the gospel of British culture abroad. As soon as he heard of it Reith wrote to Sir Robert Vansittart at the Foreign Office suggesting that the BBC be represented on the British Council. Cecil Graves subsequently lunched with Rex Leeper, in charge of the Foreign Office's News Department, who turned down the idea but agreed to close informal cooperation with the BBC in relation to the activities of the British Council. The main form this took was 'propaganda' for British music on the continent.

In September 1935 Bliss and Boult were becoming excited about a proposed 'Foreign Office tour abroad' for the BBC Chorus. Bliss had been approached, at a very early stage, to join a committee for the furtherance of British music abroad which eventually became the British Council Music Committee. Boult thought it wonderful that the Foreign Office was at last interested in such things, though the enthusiasm of the Department waned a little after closer contact with the Music Committee. Its proposal to send the BBC Chorus on a fortnight's tour of Europe, it turned out, included the BBC paying half the costs of the exercise, estimated at £2000. The BBC's Music Executive did not think that it was worth it from the point of view of prestige for the Corporation, but it was the first serious effort by the British Government to put Britain on the musical map of Europe and, as such, deserved all the help it could be given. If there was £1000 to spare it was money well spent.

In the end this scheme did not get off the ground, but thereafter there was continuous liaison with the British Council until the outbreak of war. By 1937 the Music Department was compiling a list of its efforts at propaganda for British music abroad, mainly in terms of persuading foreign conductors and soloists to include British works in their repertoires and concerts here and overseas. Among a dozen leading continental conductors and soloists Casals had been persuaded to include the Elgar Violin Concerto in his standard repertoire, Hindemith had conducted the first performace of the Walton Viola Concerto and Rubinstein had twice played the Ireland Concerto. The great Toscanini had agreed to include Elgar's 'Falstaff' in his programme for the 1937 season and only physical disabilities and great pressures of work had prevented him from doing so.

In order to monitor systematically the cause of British music abroad, a small committee was set up in 1937 with representatives from the Music Department, the Musical Advisory Committee, the British Council Music Committee and the Incorporated Society of Musicians. One question that soon arose was how much British music was being played in other European countries. The Performing Rights Society was asked to report on how much it paid each year for performance rights of copyright composers in European countries and how much it received from Europe for performances of copyright British music. When the figures were produced they made chastening reading. In 1936 The Performing Rights Society paid out £6044 2s 10d, of which £5491 10s 2d were broadcasting fees from the BBC, to corresponding bodies in France, Germany, Austria, Italy, Czechoslovakia, Poland, Denmark and Holland. In the same year it received from those eight countries, for playing copyright British music, the paltry sum of £231 13s 10d. Clearly there was still much work to be done in putting British music on the European map.

In all this, of course, British music was automatically equated with English music. The music of Scotland, Wales and Ireland was marginalized, though each had its own deep-rooted musical traditions. Within England itself regional and local music and tastes were persistently overlooked. The simmering discontents in the rest of the country on such issues came to the boil in 1935 and the Ullswater Committee received many representations about the BBC's policy of cultural centralization, particularly in music, and its harmful effects on local and regional cultures. This was an endemic problem in the policy of centring production on London and the National Programme. Though something like a common national culture and identity was given expression in moments of ritual celebration, it was often at the expense of different cultures and identities within the imposed unity of the United Kingdom and its national broadcasting service.

CHAPTER FOURTEEN

Local and Regional Broadcasting

————◦❀◦————

$\mathbf{R}$EITH HAD, from the start, thought of the BBC as a national service, but this was not achieved until the end of the twenties when the National
and Regional Programmes started to come into operation. The former provided a service produced in London for listeners in all parts of the country
while the latter, produced from a small number of provincial centres, provided
programmes for listeners in the region they serviced. These two programmes
displaced the original single network service, which developed between 1923
and 1925. The character of broadcasting in its very first few years is now long
forgotten. It is not simply a matter of the absence of any records of the
programmes themselves which makes the years of the British Broadcasting
Company seem an inaccessible prelude to a history that properly begins in
1927. It is more that the values and attitudes that began to emerge in the local
stations between 1923 and 1927 were quite deliberately eradicated by the policy of centralization. They remained repressed for many years until the late
sixties and the rediscovery of local radio broadcasting by the BBC in the wake
of the Pilkington Report. Whether the radio stations outside London operated
by the BBC and the commercial stations in the Independent Local Radio network actually amount to a truly local service today is a matter of contention.
There is reason to think that radio was more genuinely local for a few years in
the early twenties than it was some sixty years later in the eighties.

When the British Broadcasting Company began transmitting programmes
in November 1922 it had inherited radio stations in Manchester, Birmingham
and London from Metro Vickers, Western Electric and Marconi. Its immediate and pressing task was to make the radio service more widely available

304

throughout the country. There were three major technical problems to be solved in the task of 'Spreading the Service': first, to ensure that one programme could be heard anywhere in Great Britain without interference; second, to arrange that the sounds heard were a faithful copy of the original; third, eventually, to give the listener a range of choice between different, clearly heard and faithfully reproduced programmes.[1] The last problem was something of a luxury to begin with and was not addressed seriously until 1925. More pressing was the need to deliver a single, interference-free service throughout the country. The solution was to a great extent determined by the limited power both of radio transmitters and receivers. The most obviously practical thing to do was to go on adding to the three initial stations with more low-power transmitting stations. If these were sited in strategically chosen urban centres with a high population density in different parts of Britain, large potential audiences might be attracted to 'listen in'.

Accordingly, stations in Newcastle, Cardiff, Glasgow, Aberdeen, Bournemouth and Belfast were added to those in London, Birmingham and Manchester. These nine 'Main Stations', as they were called, began operating independently, producing about six hours of their own programme material each day. But their effective reception range was no more than a radius of fifteen to twenty miles and many populous areas of the country could not get decent reception from them. So, between 1924 and 1925, a number of 'Relay Stations' were set up to increase coverage: Sheffield first, then Plymouth, Edinburgh, Liverpool, Leeds-Bradford (a unique twin station), Hull, Nottingham, Dundee, Stoke-on-Trent and Swansea. All these stations were linked, not to their nearest main station, but directly to the London station through Post Office telephone lines.

This was not the original intention. It seemed absurd to Reith that Swansea, for instance, should relay programmes from London rather than Cardiff, but he had not reckoned on inter-civic jealousy. When plans were being drawn up for the first relay station, it seemed natural to propose that it should be linked to Manchester, but Sheffield thought otherwise. They wanted first their own programmes and then the pick of the London programmes. What they got was the reverse: a very limited amount of home-produced material and a very large amount of London's output. Subsequently, the other relay stations were one by one wired in to London. It appeared, Reith commented tartly, that no city that was deemed sufficiently important to have a relay station could listen to the programmes of any other station except London without loss of dignity.[2]

The technique of 'Simultaneous Broadcasts' (SBs) was quickly developed by Peter Eckersley whereby a programme from any one station could be taken by all the others at the same time through Post Office landlines. Thus a network was established through which stations could pool resources and supply

305

ABERDEEN

DUNDEE

GLASGOW   EDINBURGH

NEWCASTLE

BELFAST

BRADFORD   LEEDS   HULL
MANCHESTER
LIVERPOOL

SHEFFIELD
STOKE
NOTTINGHAM

BIRMINGHAM
DAVENTRY

GLOUCESTER

SWANSEA
CARDIFF   LONDON

BOURNEMOUTH

SCALE

PLYMOUTH   20 0 20 40 60 80

miles

Simultaneous Broadcasts Line Network (1927)

Station call signs

London: 2LO	Nottingham: 5NG	Liverpool: 6LV
Belfast: 2BE	Aberdeen: 2BD	Sheffield: 6LF
Birmingham: 5IT	Glasgow: 5SC	Stoke: 6ST
Bournemouth: 6BM	Dundee: 2DE	Swansea: 5SX
Cardiff: 5WA	Edinburgh: 2HE	Plymouth: 5PY
Manchester: 2ZY	Hull: 6KH	Daventry: 5XX
Newcastle: 5NO	Leeds/Bradford: 2LS	

Source: Pawley (1972, p. 57)

each other. London held a key position in the network from the start and, while other stations could and did provide SBs for the rest, the principle was established in 1923 that two complete evenings a week should be supplied by London to all the other stations. London, it was claimed, was able to supply not only the news service but also outstanding artists, concerts and public events that could not be matched elsewhere.

This was later to be extended into a larger claim for a broadcasting service controlled by and centred in London as the political, social and cultural heart of the nation. But to begin with Reith envisaged a different development with radio stations eventually grouped according to the regional characteristics of the populations in the areas they covered. Main stations would develop the quality of their services to make them acceptable to relay stations, while London would secure important metropolitan events for simultaneous transmission to the network on London Special Nights. Thus relay stations and main stations would develop their own characteristics in relation to local and regional needs and interests and, at the same time, be able to tap London for cultural and entertainment programmes of more general interest.[3] In this scheme of things London would be first among equals, not in dominance over subaltern provincial stations. And that, to an extent, is how radio did work for the first few years.

Undoubtedly it was, for all station directors, a desperate effort at first to avoid technical disasters and to fill the hours each day. The first radio Christmas in Newcastle was marred by breakdowns in transmission. On 23 December 1923 nothing but howling was heard throughout the area and on Boxing Day there was total silence. Local wireless dealers claimed to have lost several hundred pounds worth of sales. Simultaneous broadcasts (SBs) from London were at first severely distorted by high-speed morse interruptions, repeated clicks from switch movements at the Newcastle Telephone Exchange and induced conversations.[4] In Manchester Robert Wood had to solve the problem of interference from the nearby power station by trial and error. In the early days he gave regular talks asking people to report on the strength of the signal in their area that night.[5] But there were other things that needed explaining to listeners; why, for instance, there were no programmes on Thursday afternoons in Manchester. In reply to a complaint from seven shop assistants in Warrington that there was nothing to listen to on their half-day off, Basil Nicolls (the station director) explained that there was an agreement not to transmit on Thursday afternoons to allow the Manchester College of Technology to continue with experiments in its wireless laboratories without undue interference from the station's transmitter.[6]

As the stations settled to work they were helped out by the SB programmes supplied by London and the touring musicians, singers and entertainers hired by London to go the rounds doing one-night stands for the

307

microphone in a gruelling circuit which took them to stations in Scotland, Northern Ireland, Wales and Northern England within a fortnight.[7] Head Office also sent round the stations in turn a large leather trunk filled with all kinds of sheet music – enough material to provide a musical medley for several weeks.[8] But on the whole the main stations depended, through force of circumstances and limited budgets, on what they could find locally in the way of programme material and talent. Each station supplied talks by local worthies and most had their own amateur drama group. Cardiff specialized in dramatic sketches of local history written and produced by a local man and performed by the Newport Players Society. The Huddersfield Thespians presented *St Simon Stylites* from the Bradford Studio. *Witness for the Defence*, performed in November 1925 was the fiftieth production of the 2ZY Drama Company under the enthusiastic leadership of Victor Smythe. At Christmas, for the first couple of years at least, the stations produced their own pantomimes. *Singbad the Wailer*, from Birmingham in 1924, was offered in *Radio Times*, 'flu permitting'.[9] Cardiff's 1925 panto was such a success locally that it was given a repeat performance, SB, to the whole network.[10]

Music was the staple commodity of the programme service provided by all the stations. Performers, mainly amateur, were recruited locally and augmented by the station orchestra and the special concerts from London which were, occasionally, sponsored by Harrods or the national newspapers. Manchester's first station director was Dan Godfrey Junior whose father had founded the Bournemouth Symphony Orchestra. Under his leadership 2ZY quickly established a thriving musical culture which drew on the wealth and variety of musical life that flourished in the area. 'In Lancashire', Godfrey wrote in *Radio Times*, 'every little district has its bands and choirs, and these choirs are composed of the very keenest of amateur vocalist. And so it has been our principal object to give primarily such musical performances as can be appreciated by so critical an audience.'[11] By the end of 1923 Godfrey had recruited a twelve-piece orchestra, mainly from the Hallé'. Its repertoire included Beethoven, Tchaikovsky, Rimsky Korsakov and Brahms. There was a 2ZY Opera Company, again recruited from the district, which in 1923 had given extracts from *The Barber of Seville, Carmen, Il Trovatore* and *Rigoletto*. Godfrey had plans for much more of this in 1924, including a performance of Beethoven's Ninth with choir. The station had several dance bands – with the Garner Schofield Dance Band reckoned the best – which made a feature of the old-style waltzes and round dances which were much preferred to jazz in the Manchester area.

There was a very rapid turn-over of staff in those early years and Godfrey was soon recruited to London to organize the music programme there, but in his brief term of office in Manchester he laid the foundations of the Manchester station's reputation for high quality music. Even the Company's sales managers in the area commended that side of the programmes. Godfrey planned his music schedules three months ahead and in January 1924 was aiming to 'out-Hallé the Hallé' that summer. His station Opera Company was selected from the Beecham Opera Chorus. Each of the twenty hand-picked members was paid the nominal sum of half a guinea per performance plus six rehearsals. 'The only extra expense, which gave comfort to these willing folk, was the provision of coffee.' Choral music was, of course, very popular in the area, but it did not broadcast too well due, Godfrey believed, 'to concerted air disturbance quite apart from the sound waves', His solution was to suspend the microphone at mid-height in one corner of the studio and then make the singers perform at the other end with their backs to it. This seemed to work well and the technique circulated to all the other stations.[12]

Godfrey was a corpulent man and a keen rugby player who frequently conducted the station's studio orchestra in his rugger shirt – a habit which appears less eccentric when one considers the conditions in the station's cramped warehouse studio. A graphic account of such performances was given to listeners by Basil Nicolls in one of his weekly talks; 'The studio is draped to deaden echo and every door and window is tight shut and covered with baize and drapery – all to exclude noise and, incidentally, air. You will thus realize that if you have a large band in a room which will just about squeeze them in, with everyone practically touching his neighbour and with all windows shut, the atmosphere becomes very heated after the studio has been in use for a quarter or half an hour.'[13] This was by way of explaining, to those who had written to complain of frequent intervals of several minutes between items in studio concerts, why it was absolutely necessary and desirable for all concerned to get out of the studio for a breath of fresh air whenever there was a chance.

An air of improvization and informality characterized the first few years of broadcasting. When Manchester's second birthday came round a large number of staff from Head Office came up by train for the celebrations, and some of them put on an impromptu revue in the Savoy Hotel for the rest of the staff and their guests. This was relayed to listeners, but much of the humour of the event escaped them because they could not see it. The following week Nicolls, in his weekly chat, filled in for the listeners what they had missed: 'The Beauty Chorus consisted of typists from the London Office with Mr Dan Godfrey playing the violin which was six inches long and correspondingly narrow. The funny part about it was that the artists were all dressed up in masks which very effectively disguised them.'[14] The third birthday of broadcasting was marked by a day of Radio Revels with programmes (SB) from London to supplement local festivities. The aim was, according to *Radio Times*, to bring together all over the country like one big family, as many as possible of the vast audience of listeners so that they might in an appropriate spirit celebrate the completion of three years' broadcasting in Great Britain.[15] Newcastle celebrated with a highly successful Children's Revel which was broadcast from a hall filled to capacity. A substantial cheque was handed to the local children's hospital. The Evening Revel for grown-ups was not such a success however, for it clashed with one of the biggest dances of the year in Newcastle. It ran at a loss which meant that a cheque could not be given to the Royal Infirmary.[16]

There was a keen spirit of competition between the stations, which vied with each other to produce novelties, stunts and 'firsts'. Leeds-Bradford was the first to produce a programme from the bottom of a mine – a concert from the coal-bed, 1500 feet below ground, of the Whitewood Colliery in Normanton. London produced the first underwater broadcast by a diver on the bed of the Thames, and Plymouth offered the first 'sound of the sea'. Leeds-Bradford again claimed the first Wireless Charity Concert to raise funds to provide ailing Leeds children with a holiday. It also bagged the first amateur talent show from the Rowntree Cocoa Works in York, and took part in stunts organized by the local radio trade to drum up business, such as the great open-air demonstration in Huddersfield Park.[17]

To these must be added the novelty programmes, quizzes and audience participation programmes which were to vanish without trace within a few years. One enterprising local announcer gave out his car number plate one day, offering a pound to the first listener to phone in to say where they had seen him as he rode around town. Bournemouth had a musical crossword puzzle, Aberdeen a musical acrostic. There were Musical Consequences and Musical Charades. Manchester invited listeners to devise a musical medley around the theme of 'Sea Magic'. The winner, out of more than a hundred entries, was Mr Fairhurst of Bray Nook, Sandy Lane. He received a prize of one guinea and an invitation to the studio to supervise the production of his programme, which was broadcast on 5 January 1925.[18] Edinburgh had a Spot the Deliberate Mistake programme, a short talk containing 'anachronisms, incongruities and factual errors'. There were prizes of three, two and one guinea for the listeners who spotted the most.[19] Birmingham had a novelty half hour of musical guesses with prizes.[20] Manchester organized an Over the Open Mike programme in which a studio audience was invited to select the tunes to be played by the studio concert band[21] and London, in 1926, offered a phone-in programme for listeners to request their favourite items.[22]

There were more elaborate programmes of this sort. London arranged a 'psycho-puzzle' with its drama department, a mystery play competition, in which listeners heard the first three parts of a serial drama and were asked to supply the *denouément*. Called *Which?*, the play was about three men and a girl on a desert island and listeners had to guess which of the three she would marry – the society man, the millionaire or the ordinary seaman. It was a little cameo of popular stereotypes. The aristocrat was a chinless wonder, the millionaire a vulgar parvenu and, yes, she married the able seaman who, in the end, turned out to be a decent middle-class professional in disguise for plot reasons which need not detain us here.[23] There was a prize of £20 for the best solution and it was such a success that it was shortly followed by another psycho-drama called *Wolf! Wolf!*[24] But perhaps the most surprising stunt of those days, given the later character of broadcast news, was the competition again organized by London in which different well-known radio personalities read the main evening news bulletin on five successive nights with a large cash prize for the first listener correctly to identify the readers.[25]

While all this was going on it was the job of the station director to set up good relations with the local civic authorities, churches, universities and schools, societies and clubs for music and other forms of recreation and of course with the public. On the second annual 'At Home' day organized by the Newcastle Station, over 2000 people visited the new premises at 54 New Bride Street. One listener demanded to see the man who was responsible for *Novocastrian Nights*: 'I should just like to tell him something. My wife could not get to sleep after all that stuff about a Black Gate Mystery.'[26] By 1926 Newcastle had a well-established network of local contacts. The Brass Band Committee which organized the annual festival was running smoothly. L. G. Marshall, the station director, had set up a Poor Children's Holiday Camp Committee, with the cooperation of juvenile and welfare organizations. This was taken up as a civic scheme under the presidency of the Lord Mayor. Relations with the civic authorities were cordial and permission had been granted for a live transmission from the Town Hall of a meeting of the City Council. This however was rejected as a programme idea by Head Office, presumably on the grounds that it might be controversial. When Newcastle's fourth birthday came round in December 1926 there were big celebrations in the city. The station put on special birthday programmes. The Mayor made speeches and there was a banquet in the Mansion House to mark the occasion.[27]

The lucky survival of the weekly talks by Basil Nicolls, while acting as Station Director of Manchester 2ZY, gives a unique insight into the working relationship between station and audience for nearly two years from 1924 to 1926. These fifteen-minute talks on Friday evenings were a very early kind of feedback programme and served as a forum for a continuing dialogue between Manchester and its listeners. In the first of these talks, on 18 July 1924, Nicolls invited listeners to have their copy of *Radio Times* and a pencil to hand to note any last-minute alterations to the programmes as listed there. Week by week he dealt with what the station had to offer listeners in the coming days and explained Company policy: 'It is the policy of the Company to give on Sunday what might be called a Sunday programme. That does not mean that the music is to be all sacred and the rest of the programme of a religious nature, but it means that the general aspect of the programme will be quiet and serious without of course being heavy and musical comedy dance music etc. will be excluded.' The apologetic tone was more in tune with the viewpoint of local listeners than that of Head Office.[28]

In his first talk Nicolls emphasized that he welcomed all reasonable criticism and suggestions about programmes and, as the programme became established, Nicolls talked to the audience about a variety of matters to do with the problems and difficulties of broadcasting. Here he is on the vexed subject of oscillation:

> I feel that I am voicing the wishes of nearly all our listeners in asking anyone who is consciously oscillating, if such there be, to live and let live; if a programme annoys you, hang up your receiver and take pen and paper and let off steam on me. I shall be sympathetic as I am more than used to it. Do not punish your neighbours for our shortcomings. To those who may have an uneasy feeling that they have sometimes oscillated unconsciously, and with the best will in the world, I say write in for Captain Eckersley's Anti-Oscillation Pamphlet; or again, if you feel your neighbour needs one, write for it and then let it blow over into his garden, or give it in all innocence to one of his family.[29]

One thing that Nicolls had to point out, at regular intervals, was that the station could not give out notices for every fête and carnival in the district. To the lady who wanted 2ZY to broadcast a personal message to her parents on their wedding anniversary, he replied that these were broadcast only on exceptional occasions, such as a diamond wedding or an eightieth birthday, and they were not done for payment. When things went wrong or when there were lapses in taste Nicolls would apologize, as he did for the studio entertainer who 'was inadvertently permitted to broadcast a piece that many of our listeners must have considered nauseating. Those of you who heard it will know what I refer to. I must ask you to accept my apology for the occurrence and my reassurance that we will always do our best to prevent such pieces being given from the station.'[30] Programme aims and plans were always explained. When the arrangements for summertime were given out in April 1925, the audience was told that the station was trying to make the programmes lighter for the summer, as might be expected:

> I know listeners will disagree with one another as to whether a programme is light or heavy. There is a large number who do not think they are light enough, and many more who think they are too light; it is a matter of arriving at some compromise with the views of all listeners. Anyway, in summer, they will certainly be lighter, and I hope you will notice that as time goes on. This does not mean that the programmes will be 'low-brow' and that there will be no

'high-brow' evenings – there will be a regular number of these, but not as many as in the winter.[31]

The week after Christmas 1924 Nicolls thanked all those who had sent Christmas cards to the station, wished everyone a Happy New Year and expressed his hope that 2ZY's programmes, or at least some of them, would continue to help those who were burdened with problems to forget their little difficulties.

Audience participation was frequently invited and occasionally uninvited. In March 1924 the *Manchester Evening Chronicle* had a story of 2ZY being invaded by students dressed as Red Indians during Rag Week who held the staff captive while they sang 'Yes We Have No Bananas' and broadcast a spoof local news bulletin followed by an SOS for a missing lady with two glass eyes, a transparent skirt and anyone who found her could have her.[32] Listeners were asked to send in toys for Children's Corner to redistribute to local children's hospitals. There were radio charades and musical consequences, and an Open Request Concert for which listeners wrote in to request their musical favourites. One clear favourite was Gilbert and Sullivan, and Nicolls had regularly to explain that they could not perform extracts from the Savoy Operas since their copyright belonged to the D'Oyley Carte Company.

In June 1926 weekly staff meetings were started in Manchester to discuss programme ideas and routine station business. One of the first suggestions to be taken up was a one-hour studio revue programme the theme of which was a charabanc picnic, and this was followed up with 'A Day at the Seaside' based around a Lancashire family, with train noises and conversation, seaside sounds of ice cream vendors, etc.[33] Such 'theme' programmes were common. There was A Trip to Fairy Land which consisted of 'fairy music' and a Little Programme with nothing but small items including a dance of the dwarfs. There was a Hunting Programme with a burlesque play, hunting music and choruses, and music for a Hunt Ball. A Plantation Night had Uncle Remus as the announcer, banjo songs and a plantation play.

The relationship between the Manchester station and its audience was interactive and participatory. The way Nicolls spoke to his listeners presupposed that they were entitled to explanations and apologies if necessary. The audience, in turn, was expected to show understanding and respect for the efforts of Nicolls and his colleagues and to recognize their enthusiasm and commitment to providing as good a service as possible when all the circumstances were taken into account. It was a relationship of equality based on a notion of mutual accountability between broadcasters and audience. The outstanding quality of radio at this time was its cosiness and warmth, reflected both in *Radio Times* and the programmes themselves. Listeners liked its 'personal touch' and Reith, for the moment, took pride in the fact that it

313

was seen as 'a friendly thing'.[34] The radio announcer was the 'Voice with a Smile'.[35] It is possible to look back at this period and dismiss the efforts of the stations as gimcrack stuff compared with the pearls on offer a decade later. Certainly there was a natural tendency to gimmickry and stunts, in line with the activities of the popular press and magazines of the time, in a new medium seeking to draw attention to itself and to build up its audiences. But in spite of the difficulties in filling the ether with a varied and continuous output, in spite of technical hitches and in spite of the growing trend towards duplication, the local stations had each, in their own way, adapted themselves to the areas they served and offered not only entertainment but a public service to their community of a rather different kind to that which was taking shape in London.

When Leeds-Bradford put on a charity concert for ailing children, when Liverpool ran a series of programmes about the city, past and present, during its Civic Week, or when Sheffield let its university students put on a programme in aid of local hospitals during Rag Week, these were unemphatic instances of a kind of public service performed by radio in its infancy which has scarcely yet been recovered. It was inevitable that this kind of radio would be superseded. But something valuable was lost, though it was hardly recognized at the time except by local people, in the growing centralization of control and production in London, and in the plans to reorganize the distribution of the programme service.

In 1923 Reith was telling the Sykes Committee of the very great advantage in having a uniform policy of what could or could not be done in broadcasting.[36] The first smoke signal of this intent was a confidential memorandum he sent to Admiral Carpendale in December that year in which he mused about the need to establish tighter control over the activities of broadcasting at the next Station Directors' Meeting: 'I am not satisfied that there is sufficiently definite central control on the operation of the Stations, and although I am more or less thinking as I dictate, I want arrangements to be put to them in a final shape on Tuesday so that they can go away understanding definitely what to expect.'[37] Crucially, Reith was anxious to have a demarcation line, as he put it, between HQ staff and 2LO staff and the rest of the stations – i.e. between himself and a small number of people in Head Office who would define policy and ensure its implementation, and the rest of the staff in London and elsewhere who were concerned with programme production. The difference between HQ staff and the rest was one of degree only and not of nature Reith insisted, but the military overtones of the distinction were heightened when he stressed the need for HQ staff regularly to visit the stations and check up on their activities. 'The periodic supervision of Stations, the inspection on the spot, the rooting down to all details, and the setting matters right' was of great importance, he declared to Carpendale. This was unmistakably the language of the barrackroom inspection. Reith wanted the station directors to get it into their heads that their actions and initiatives were not being restricted. It was all a question of how it was put to them.

From now on control over the stations began to be applied from London. Programme schedules were to be submitted to HQ in advance and conferences between Reith and the station directors were set up on a regular basis. In 1924 the Control Committee was set up – 'a real management committee' consisting of Reith and four senior HQ staff. Briggs comments, 'However much the BBC changed over the years, two "cardinal" principles were maintained throughout. First that only a handful of people were responsible to the Managing Director. Second that these people were in control.' He continues: 'A newcomer to the BBC in 1924 or 1925 could not fail to notice the existence of a "core" or "stratum" of authority within the organization. There was as yet no clear-cut or even gossipy distinction between "them" and "us", but there was an immediately apparent and definable leadership and direction.'[38] By the end of 1926 however, 'a clear-cut distinction between 'them' and 'us' was beginning to emerge.'[39] Further administrative reorganization earlier that year had strengthened and enlarged the Control Board (its new title), which now met regularly to take all major decisions on broadcast policy.

The beginning of regular SB broadcasts and the possibility of programme exchanges between stations on a network basis led to the establishment in May 1924 of a Programme Board to organize and monitor the activities of the stations.[40] Within a few months it had decided that quiz competitions should not become the staple fare of the new listening public, though their popularity was noted.[41] By 1926 disapproval had hardened into a veto. At the Manchester staff's weekly programme meeting Victor Smythe suggested a half-hour Musical Novelty competition to raise money for the Wireless for the Blind fund. Ted Liveing, the Station Director, agreed this was a nice idea, but added that the need to promote interest in radio through novelties had passed and besides, Head Office had issued definite instructions against running competitions.[42]

At the same meeting Liveing announced that 2ZY's *Children's Hour* was to be given a thorough shake-up in line with Head Office directives and in consultation with the Professor of Psychology of Manchester University. 'The impromptu corner has been abolished and more carefully prepared programmes substituted in its place. The amount of back-chat is now almost negligible and a certain amount of educative material has been introduced in a bright and stimulating way,' Liveing reported. It was hard to tell whether, as a result of these changes, interest in the programme was falling off, but he declared that even if Radio Circle's membership and children's letters to the station declined he would not be too disappointed. It had to be realized that 'a complete re-education of children's tastes had now to be faced'.[43] Stobart, the officer from HQ who made regular on-the-spot inspections of the stations, reported back to Reith in November 1926 that the programme had 'reformed in the direction of greater dignity and less informality'.

It was creeping in everywhere. Reith had already warned station directors of the dangers in letting any Tom, Dick or Harry come to the microphone:

> In some stations I see periodically men down to speak whose status, either professionally or socially, and whose qualifications to speak, seem doubtful. It should be an honour in every sense of the word for a man to speak from any broadcasting station, and only those who have a claim to be heard above their fellows on any particular subject in the locality should be put on the programme.[44]

In November 1924 it was decided that all radio announcers should be anonymous. Hitherto both local and national announcers were quite well known by name to their listening publics. At around the same time staff were forbidden in future to publish books about broadcasting. There were to be no more inside accounts, such as those by Lewis and Burrows, and no one was allowed to publish articles in newspapers or magazines without Reith's express permission. Staff were given detailed instructions about 'personal publicity'.

Earlier in the year, with one dissension, it was decided to insist on a standard form of announcing in all stations as well as London. The American style was explicitly ruled out, and announcers were to build up in the mind of the public a sense of the BBC's 'collective personality'. The anonymity rule was designed to further this end. Station directors were told to think of announcers as 'men of culture, experience and knowledge'. Not only correct speech, but also correct dress. In the autumn of 1925 it was decided announcers should wear dinner jackets at the microphone, for which they were given an initial dress allowance. A new respectability was being imposed on broadcasting.[45]

By 1926 each station had a book of instructions on the do's and don'ts of broadcasting. It prompted D. H. Clarke, the Director of the Belfast Station, to protest that the feeling it engendered, along with the majority of Head Office memos, was that the provincial stations lived by rote and that the slightest departure from the guidelines was sure to involve trouble. The words 'sanction', 'authority' and 'permission' loomed large, and the daily dose of curt, unsympathetic memoranda from Head Office conveying instructions or demanding explanations had a deeply discouraging effect. They compounded the feeling that London simply did not understand the problems or the work of the stations. Clarke ended with a plea for greater understanding and appreciation from Head Office and, as a step in this direction, he suggested some means whereby 'subordinates at stations could meet subordinates at Head Office'.[46]

Reith circulated the gist of Clarke's complaint to all the stations asking for their frank replies. He very much regretted that Head Office had created this impression and asked everyone to appreciate that 'we are all out for the efficiency of the service'.[47] Of the replies filed, Nottingham and Birmingham disagreed entirely, while Dundee felt it was all too true. Manchester discussed it at their regular staff meeting, but agreed unanimously that the case was far too overstated. There is no doubt of the pressures the stations were under from London. At an earlier meeting the Manchester staff had discussed their working hours and the many obstacles in the way of getting home early at night. The two main problems were the shared announcing duties which everyone did on a rota basis, and the work resulting from Head Office telephone calls. The former problem was resolved by the appointment of a specialist announcer who would do three nights a week, but the staff saw no solution to the other problem.[48]

The 'them' – 'us' distinction which Briggs identifies as stealing over the Company had two distinct aspects. The first was internal, an emerging separation between policy-making and programme-making, whereby a small nucleus of senior personnel, answerable only to Reith, controlled all aspects of programme policy and planning. It took time for this to be effectively installed and implemented across the whole range of output, but this hierarchical division of labour within the BBC was installed from very early on and was one of Reith's most lasting contributions to the institutional development of broadcasting. The other form of the divide was between the BBC and its audience. There was a retreat away from direct contact with listeners, from their participation in programmes, from informality, friendliness and easy accessibility into a distanced, anonymous, collective voice. A corporate mode of address was installed to signify the authority and respectability of radio. It was the start of the 'stuffed-shirt era' of broadcasting. The fetishization of correct dress was not an eccentric quirk. It was consonant with a major shift of emphasis on the *manners* of broadcasting. Heard but not seen, the BBC was henceforth always to be on its best behaviour. As Peter Eckersley tartly noted, the BBC was becoming more like a public school than a public serivce.[49]

Eckersley himself was a victim of this trend. In 1929, he was cited as co-respondent in a divorce case and Reith ordered his dismissal. Looking back on his six years with the BBC, he noted 'the gradual tightening of control and the gradual beginning of corporate self-consciousness, resulting in the formation of unsympathetic little rules which turn effort inwards rather than outwards towards the product.'[50] Eckersley, the BBC's Chief Engineer from 1923 until his forced resignation, was a key figure in the early history of broadcasting. There was a suspicion at the time that he had become an overmighty subject in Reith's kingdom whose insubordination contributed to his fall. Certainly an instructive contrast can be seen in the quite different careers in the BBC of

Peter Eckersley and his younger brother Roger, who was recruited to the BBC by Eckersley senior after a spell as secretary of Littlehampton Golf Club and a disastrous venture into chicken farming. Roger rose rapidly in Reith's favour – 'never expressing an opinion, seeing both sides of every question and, with these two safe supports, floating upwards to a resting place near, but never too near, the top,'[51] his brother commented. Each wrote a book about broadcasting: Roger, *The BBC and All that*,[52] and Peter, *The Power Behind the Microphone*. One has only to compare them to see that Roger had not one single idea in his head about radio and its social, cultural and political implications (but it was a lot of fun!), while his brother 'had more ideas about broadcasting than any other man in the country'.[53] The fall of the elder brother and the rise of the younger points the moral of how to succeed in the BBC – and all that!

Peter Eckersley designed what came eventually to be known as the Regional Scheme, although regionalism had precious little to do with it at first. By 1925 it was clear that broadcasting could not continue to develop along its original lines. It was more efficient, and cheaper, to have a smaller number of high-powered stations with a reception radius covering the whole country. The initial system was proving wasteful in the duplication of the same kind of programme material by the nine main stations. Simple and effective economies could be made in the production of music and entertainment by centralizing their production and supply in London, thus releasing extra resources for programme-making from the savings effected. Moreover the problem of interference from continental stations was becoming serious. It was no longer feasible to continue with twenty different stations on twenty different wavelengths. In 1926 the Sheffield station suffered serious interference from Radio Toulouse, which was resolved by Sheffield going up and Toulouse going down one metre on the waveband.[54] Such improvised adjustments could not continue, and international cooperation was needed to establish agreements about the allocation of wavelengths in Europe on a national basis to prevent a 'chaos of the ether', such as had already happened in America. The Geneva Plan of 1926, in which Peter Eckersley played a major role, halved the number of medium wavelengths used by the BBC at that time.[55]

These were the immediate and powerful arguments for reducing the number of stations that produced their own material and for concentrating production in London and a small number of provincial centres. On top of all this a crucial consideration was that any reorganization of the programme service must offer listeners, wherever they were, some degree of choice. The strongest case against the BBC's monopoly was that it eliminated choice, and Eckersley's plan, which he drew up in 1925, was designed to answer such criticism. Eckersley, in committee in Geneva, supported the recommendation that Britain should in effect halve its number of medium wavelength stations. His plan therefore tried to provide all listeners in Britain with a choice of two programmes and at the same time to make the best use of the BBC's existing resources. He proposed to use the ten available wavelengths to establish five twin-wave stations simultaneously transmitting two different programmes. This plan was formally adopted by the Control Board on 17 November 1926, when it was decided to establish twin-wave regional stations in place of the existing main stations at Glasgow, Manchester, Cardiff and London. The fifth station in the scheme, Birmingham, was already operating, on an experimental basis, as a twin-wave station.

It was recognized from the start that the new scheme might seem inimical to local interests as an internal Head Office memorandum noted, while at the same time displaying a characteristic metropolitan bias: 'Those who have not been much in the Provinces cannot assess the extraordinary value placed upon the local station by provincial listeners.'[56] Reassurances were made that local interests would continue to be served by the new scheme, but when Control Board formally accepted it it also recommended the gradual elimination of all stations other than those five designated for the new scheme. Their closure was achieved very quickly, and by 1930 they had all disappeared: the call signs of Bournemouth, Newcastle, Nottingham, Aberdeen, Dundee, Edinburgh, Hull, Liverpool, Leeds-Bradford, Sheffield, Stoke and Swansea were heard no more upon the air.

They all died quietly with one notable exception, and that was Sheffield. This was the more surprising because Sheffield, although the first, was only a relay station and with an undistinguished track record at that. Its programmes were the worst in the country according to the *Sheffield Mail*.[57] Even so when the first whiff of the new regional scheme reached Sheffield its Director of Education, Percival Sharp, wrote to Reith promising that any proposal to close down their local station would be met with 'the full weight of opposition that Sheffield can bring to bear'.[58] Nor was this an idle threat. Reith had already told all directors of Relay Stations that he would be disappointed if they failed to deal effectively with 'embryo local agitation',[59] but the Sheffield agitators went straight to the top. Sharp's letter was shortly followed by letters from the Sheffield Chamber of Commerce and the Sheffield Rollers and Tilters Association both expressing their opposition to any talk of closure. Reith had replied to Sharp at some length, and in conciliatory fashion, though promising nothing. As the protest began to roll in he became vexed and wrote to S. D. Howard, the Sheffield Station Director, asking him to deal with the matter. 'It is so extraordinarily short-sighted and irritating to take a purely local view and to disregard, as they apparently have, almost every statement we have made on the advantages of the new scheme.'[60]

But still the opposition spread, with the local press becoming a vociferous lobby. In 1928 the Town Clerk wrote to the Post Office asking for a reassurance that, in spite of all appearances, the station would not close. The letter was passed back to Reith who replied at length, setting out the problems of interference from the continent and the new European agreements on the allocation of wavelengths. As to the fate of the Sheffield station and its transmitter, Reith remained circumspect: 'If and when the transmitter is shut down, the studio may still remain open, so that any speech or music or other activity in Sheffield may be communicated to the regional transmitting centre. There is no idea of shutting down the transmitter within the next year.' Such equivocations did not satisfy the burghers of Sheffield, and in December of that year a delegation of representatives from the City Council, the Cutlers Company, the Chamber of Commerce, the University and the Education Committee descended on Savoy Hill to exchange further words on the matter with Reith. To no avail. The station was shut down two months later. Now a vigorous rearguard action was mounted to salvage at least the transmitter, and the 'Sheffield Situation', as the BBC administrators came to call it, continued to throw up a sizeable molehill of correspondence throughout the thirties.

This epic in miniature, whereby the civic authorities of Sheffield laid siege to the BBC, was a unique case of official resistance to the scrapping of the original local service and its particular public service character. The Sheffield authorities clearly saw local radio not just as a matter of civic pride (though there was an element of that) but as a means of creating local interest in municipal and industrial life as well as providing entertainment, information and educational material from and for the local community. It was this possibility, as well as the friendly informality of local broadcasting, which was foreclosed in this country for so many years by the implementation of the regional scheme.

Initial discussion of the new scheme, aside from technical arrangements, centred on the alternative programme service. What should be the basis of contrast between the two programmes? The spoken word in contrast with music – a play on one channel, a symphony on the other – was one possibility. Another was majority and minority appeal. Eckersley, in his original discussion paper 'The Distribution of the Service', proposed that the only real principle of contrast was between Universal and Speciality programmes. It was not clear from Eckersley's paper, or the subsequent discussion of it, how in detail this distinction was to work on two different programme channels, but the general idea was clear enough. 'Universal' programme material would be provided by a 'national' programme produced by Head Office in London and supplemented by 'the cream' of provincial programmes. It would consist largely of 'restful' programme offerings, mainly music, of widespread appeal, which did not demand much effort from listeners. 'Speciality' programmes called for some degree of effort and cooperation from the audience. They might come from London or the provinces and were subdivided by Eckersley into two categories, 'service' and 'popular' programmes. The former included news bulletins, education, weather reports, charity appeals and the reporting of Parliament. The latter included drama, variety, poetry, story-telling, children's hour and after-dinner speeches.[61]

There was also discussion of a third alternative, an 'Uplift' programme to transmit 'a really first-class programme appealing to connoisseurs, and taking no notice of other things and events. It would be to broadcasting what *The Spectator* and *The Times* were to British journalism, and would be of the greatest value to the Programme Department in Head Office, allowing them to carry all the matter that we think we *ought* to do, but which is interesting perhaps to only one fifth of our listeners.'[62] The case for a Third Programme, though recognized, was not seriously pressed, so for the time being it remained a programme planner's pipe dream, a wistful gleam in the corporate eye. Attention focused on a two-channel service, one based in London, the other in a small number of provincial production centres. It was generally agreed that local or regional values should be retained in the speciality programmes, but this was not stressed when, in rather uncertain and vague terms, the BBC unveiled the new plan and the idea of contrasted programmes in the *BBC Hand Book* for 1929. 'It is in fact impossible to formulate any one principle which will be an infallible guide in every case of doubt, but it has been found that a useful test to apply is the distinction between items which demand concentrated listening and those which repay more casual listening.'[63]

The need to maximize reception was the most important consideration on the technical side. It meant that the siting of the transmitters and the testing of their potential range and quality of signal was a long and arduous business that went on throughout the thirties. Certain areas remained intractably difficult: North-East England, the Highlands, North Wales and the far West of England. The problems of covering West Region were exemplary. It was supposed to serve Wales and the West of England, and Cardiff was designated as the production centre.[64] It was impossible though to cover this area with one transmitter and, since the bulk of the Welsh population lived in South Wales and a sizeable portion of English listeners in the region lived around Bristol, the transmitter was sited in Somerset and a new production centre for the region was established in Bristol. The service could not be heard in North Wales, though listeners there could receive the programmes from Manchester. In the far South West reception was very poor, and the old relay transmitter at Plymouth was pressed into service again to boost the signal in that part of the country. The extent to which this arrangement, though the most feasible solution to a difficult engineering problem, actually created a plausible and coherent 'region' remained another question. What had Welsh and Cornish men and women in common? Why should people in Devon have to listen to programmes in Welsh, for instance? The design of the regional scheme, and the siting of the transmitters and stations, was determined by administrative, technical and economic considerations before any notion of what regionalism might actually mean in terms of people, places and cultural characteristics.

Peter Eckersley later fantasized that his obituary would give him full credit for the Regional Scheme, adding that he hoped it would say that he designed it technically and the BBC used it stupidly. It was his brother Roger who, along with Reith and a handful of senior programme officials in London, spelled out the programme policy for the new two-channel service and its implications for the provincial production centres.

The master concept which defined HQ policy was 'centralization'. Roger Eckersley, then Director of Programmes, welcomed the new scheme for the economies he could make particularly in entertainment and music, and he wrote a policy paper itemizing the savings he could make. The old practice of hiring variety artistes and musicians to tour the stations was costing £27,000 a year by 1927 of which half went in travelling expenses. By now the studio orchestras in Manchester, Birmingham and Glasgow were costing £38,000 a year while the attempt to subsidize a Welsh National Orchestra attached to the Cardiff station added a further £12,000 to the bill. The plan to establish the BBC Symphony Orchestra, now well advanced in London, depended in part on axing the provincial station orchestras. Allowing for its establishment, Eckersley projected a net saving of £24,000 a year from abolishing the provincial orchestras which, added to the £13,000 saved from scrapping touring performers, amounted to overall economies of around £37,000 a year. Further savings could be made by increasing the number of SBs from London which would mean that not only expensive concerts, but variety shows, extravagant drama productions and the like should no longer be undertaken by the provincial stations.[65]

Roger Eckersley was, as Briggs notes, particularly metropolitan in his outlook.[66] At Control Board, a week after his policy paper had been circulated among senior London officials, he defined the general principle that provincial stations should concentrate on purely local material as far as possible, and eliminate programmes of a character similar to those available from London. A memorandum went out to the newly designated Regional directors setting out the arguments for abandoning touring artists and for drastically reducing their station orchestras. Eckersley summed up the implications of it all as meaning 'take from London what you cannot do better yourself and do yourself what London cannot give you'.[67] This did not imply, he assured them, any curbing of provincial activity or any loss of prestige. But in his earlier memorandum for internal consumption, he had dismissed the earlier policy of giving the old main stations a greater autonomy 'from the point of view of civic pride and *amour propre*'. He did not believe that just because Manchester was given a lesser orchestra listeners in that area would give up their wireless sets, or that it made any difference to the man in Glasgow whether he heard Jock McKay down the line from London or from his own local studio.[68]

The response of the Regional directors was one of cautious agreement, except for the fate of their station orchestras. Ted Liveing, while fully supporting the plan for a national orchestra, still felt that this could be done without axing the provincial orchestras. Apart from the fundamental issue of the BBC's support for the musical life of the rest of the country, Manchester's permanent orchestra of twenty-seven players had made it much easier to deal with programmes and, when augmented for public concerts, was an invaluable public relations ambassador in the area. It had been used to support Civic Weeks in Liverpool and Leeds and the Tuesday Mid-Day Concert in Manchester.[69] Cleghorn Thomson for Scottish Region offered his support for the new scheme, but again with strong reservations about the reduction of the orchestras. He added that a greater degree of reciprocity should be part of future policy – London should be as willing to take programmes from the regions as to supply them. Why should it be London that supplied special programmes on St Andrew's night? There was a strong case for looking to the provinces for added colour, character and variety in the programmes.[70]

Within a year the Regional directors' support for the new scheme was wearing thin as its full implications began to be appreciated. Reith had set up periodic meetings between them and himself and at a Regional Directors' Meeting in January 1929 Liveing, Cleghorn Thomson and Beadle (for Northern Ireland) made a concerted effort to stop the reduction of provincial orchestras, but without success. Cleghorn Thomson was becoming very gloomy and doubted whether Eckersley and the rest in Head Office had any idea of the cramping and depressing effect of the new policy. Programme-making in the provinces was becoming a weary, flat, stale and unprofitable business. It was impossible to maintain variety of local interest on the reduced budgets and he and the others felt that London was always reluctant to look to them for programme ideas or to trust and applaud their judgements when given.[71]

Reith responded to these anxieties by asking them all 'definitely to accept the Centralization policy'. Whatever its disadvantages – of which he, Reith, had been aware all along – the local cultural loss should be offset by the quality of the London programme, and by the activities still open to the regions. This was small comfort, and there was less on the question of the orchestras. They were to be cut down to octets, though a year would be allowed for this to be put into effect. As a sop, Reith offered the possibility of subsidies for collaboration with existing musical facilities in the regions. £2000 spent in helping local musical effort was better than £10,000 spent in the studio. He also held out the prospect of greater cooperation and consultation between the regions and Head Office over policy and programmes, and gave assurances

"They've got the National, Dad. I'd better put on the same."

"No, yer don't—bung on the *Regional*. We've as much right to the river as what they 'ave."

that in view of the rapid growth and changing circumstances of the Corporation's work the present scheme, while the best for the moment, might be reviewed in the future. Meanwhile he wanted all Regional directors to look at their staff requirements, particularly redundancies.[72]

But the signs of greater consultation and cooperation were not immediately evident. Rather the reverse. The attitude of Head Office was to keep a beady eye on the provinces to make sure they did not overstep the mark. In particular, Charles Siepmann for Talks and Val Gielgud for Drama both insisted that they should have authority over regional activities in their particular areas of programme-making, which should in every respect conform to general Corporation principles and policy as well as to quality and standards. Siepmann took a particularly hard line. He wanted Reith to make it plain, 'once and for all', that Regional directors and their staff were subordinate to Eckersley, himself and the other heads of programme branches in London. Otherwise there would be a dyarchy in the Corporation and an increasing divergence of standards and quality between the centre and the provinces. If the regions were allowed to pull away towards independence in programme policy 'we shall live to regret it unless we scotch it now by honestly facing the issue'.[73] Siepmann recommended weeding out inadequate regional staff members, however embarrassing that might be, and replacing them with better programme-makers. Regional staff ought frequently to be in London seeing how production was done there and acquiring 'a single-mindedness with us in methods of negotiation, rehearsal and presentation at the microphone'. It was scarcely tolerable, he felt, that some of the provincial programme people were more or less unknown in London and wholly ignorant of London methods.

Liveing, Beadle and Cleghorn Thomson would have none of this. Control of programmes from the centre would be deadly and the theoretical gain in efficiency would not compensate for the loss of those qualities of character, personality and enthusiasm which existed in the regional stations. Siepmann and Gielgud, said Liveing, knew little about provincial programmes and resources and their suggestions would create endless friction and appeals to Reith for arbitration. He proposed either an impartial commission to examine the whole question of Regionalism versus Centralization or else an extensive reorganization within the BBC entailing the separate direction of regional, national and empire programmes.[74] Beadle proposed that a new post of Regional Assistant Director of Programmes be created under Eckersley as Director of Programmes, to liaise with the Regions and mediate between them and London. The appointee should be someone more programme- than administration-minded.

Reith took up this idea and Lindsay Wellington was appointed to the post in July 1932. A more important step, in the same year, was the creation of the post of Programme Director for each region who would be directly responsible, under his Regional Director, for all aspects of regional programmes and programme-building. The appointees would keep in regular touch with Eckersley and Siepmann and be subordinate to them. They would absorb Head Office outlook and standards on the one hand, and on the other they would safeguard 'justifiable' regional interests. A. E. Harding was appointed Programme Director of North Region early in 1933. Whether his departure for Manchester was intended by Reith get him away from London or to boost programme-making in the North is, in the end, uncertain. It was probably a bit of both. But what is certain is that Harding's appointment was crucial for the flourishing of programme-making in Manchester. He came from London with an established reputation for programme-making, and his impact on Manchester was immediate.

By now something like a satisfactory structure for liaison between London and the regions was beginning to emerge. Yet there were still many uncertainties about programme quality and quantity in the regional schedules, and about financial and staff resources for programme work in the provinces. It has never been intended that the regions should produce all or even most of their own programme material. By the mid-thirties the amount each region produced varied from an upper limit of 40 per cent original material in Midland to a low of about 20 per cent in Northern Ireland. These efforts were concentrated in programmes to fill the peak hours from 6.30 to 9.30 each evening. To fill the daytime and late-night hours all regions drew heavily on the offerings of London Regional, which had never been intended as a true regional programme. It had no separate staff or production centre. Its schedules and content were planned and produced in Head Office, and it was filled with 'overspill' material from the National Programme.

A fair amount of material from the National Programme found its way into the regional schedules. The practice of 'diagonalization' meant that a programme first heard in the National Programme was given a repeat a few days later in London Regional and in one or more of the other regional programmes. The so-called 'phi-system' was an extension of the old SB arrangement whereby a programme from London was simultaneously broadcast on all the other regional wavelengths.[75] But the phi-system was also a means of rating the cultural importance of programmes from London. When Regional directors received the advance schedules for the National Programme around which they must build their own, they would find certain programmes with a starred rating of one to three. A one star programme was good but not obligatory. A two star programme was strongly recommended and should be taken unless there were very good reasons for not doing so. A three star rating meant a programme of outstanding national or cultural singficance which all stations must take.

Briggs offers two significant example of the conflicts this system could create. In 1934 a Sunday Symphony Concert conducted by Casals was given a two-phi rating. Harding had already planned to fill this slot in the North Region schedule with a concert by a Merseyside group of unemployed musicans. A dialogue ensued with Lindsay Wellington who urged the cultural importance of Casals while Harding stressed the social importance of the Liverpool concert for the region. In this case Harding stuck to his guns, and Manchester dropped the Casals concert.[76] The other example came from West Region whose musical resources were, on their own admission, inadequate. Yet when for once they came up trumps with a proposal to transmit a Rubinstein performance from Dartington Hall, it was turned down by London on the grounds that Rubinstein had not yet performed on radio and that, if and when he did, he should make his debut on the National Programme.[77]

With Harding's appointment to Manchester, Liveing began to press for more staff to expand the region's work in news, outside broadcasts, topical features and regional drama.[78] This had become a matter of urgency for, under the new stimulus to programme-making which Harding had inspired, the time and energy of the staff were being severely tested. In 1935 Midland had 14 staff, North Region 13, Scotland and Northern Ireland $12\frac{1}{2}$ and Wales and West $9\frac{1}{2}$ each.[79] These discrepancies, and the variations in the volume of material produced by each region, led Basil Nicolls (then Director of Internal Administration), at Reith's request, to attempt to rationalize output and staffing in the regions.

Nicolls recommended that Midland, Scottish, North and West Regions should be limited to 25 hours of output a week while Northern Ireland and Wales should be limited to 20. While there was some flexibility in this decree it was not a paper limitation to be ignored in practice. Staffing was calculated on the basis of the division of labour within the total number of hours of production allowed. Nicolls put forward a standard establishment of fifteen production staff for each region: one programme director, three music specialists, two announcers, two studio assistants and one specialist producer for OBs, features, drama, variety, talks and Children's Hour, plus one musical accompanist for studio programmes. This would give each region two or three extra staff and put them roughly on a par, in proportion to output, with London. The question of engineering staff to deal with the technical side of OBs – an important part of all regional broadcasting – was dealt with separately.[80]

A memorandum on Regional Staffing prepared for the Ullswater Committee had a significant note on the status of regional staff. Their standing had recently been raised in most cases to a theoretical equivalence with corresponding staff in London. For instance, Regional musical directors enjoyed a status as high as that of any member of the London Music Department except Adrian Boult. But salaries were lower in the provinces than in London for the same kind of work. The reason for this, the memorandum declared, was 'simply that the best of the staff tend to gravitate to London, partly because most staff prefer to serve in London than in the provinces, and partly because London's contributions to the National Programme are intrinsically more important than the local contributions of the regions.'[81] As long as such attitudes prevailed there was bound to be resentment and resistance in the regions to London policies and to metropolitan cultural values.

The problems of the BBC's regional policy was a major issue for the Ullswater Committee, particularly in relation to music. Representatives of the music profession forcefully argued that the BBC's music policy was damaging to active music-making and to provincial musical culture. There was strong pressure from the National Federation of Music Societies and from the Incorporated Society of Musicians, for the decentralization of musical policy and for a new regional autonomy in all matters relating to music. The Incorporated Society of Musicians argued that the BBC was not doing enough to encourage amateurs, young musicians and provincial music societies. It was prepared to spend a fortune on Toscanini in London, but unwilling to support, for example, the Leeds Music Festival at a fraction of the price. What really mattered, the Society suggested, was the music the country as a whole produced.[82]

Sir Thomas Beecham, for the National Federation of Music Societies, made similar points and took North Region to prove his case. The North was, he said, the most musical part of the whole country and between them Lancashire and Yorkshire accounted for more than half the music societies in the country. Speaking as a Lancashire man himself, Beecham claimed there was great dissatisfaction in the region because Manchester paid little heed to what people there wanted to listen to. They wanted to hear a great deal more of their own musical institutions – the Hallé, the Liverpool Philharmonic Society, the choral societies and musical festivals of the region. The regional programmes were more or less dictated by London taste which was very different from the North. Manchester had no proper regional orchestra. It should take more local music from local societies. The North, said Beecham, had been starved of the music it wanted to hear ever since the Charter of 1927.[83]

In response to these criticisms Adrian Boult, on behalf of the BBC, replied that they amounted merely to a scheme of increasing employment in the profession. He declared categorically that no substantial increase in employment could be given by the Corporation in the immediate future without lowering the standards of the programmes. Central control over the whole field of the BBC's musical activities was essential. Regional autonomy would lead to chaos. 'Musically the BBC would not speak with one voice. It would be a house divided against itself with disastrous results in every way.' The BBC had given a great deal of help to the musical societies going back to the first years of broadcasting. The major societies received annual payments from the BBC in return for broadcasting, while the smaller ones were paid per performance. In Manchester, Birmingham and Belfast the BBC helped to maintain the city's orchestra on whole time contract by an annual subsidy of around £14,000 in each case. The Corporation was anxious to do more, but in many cases – particularly in London – its good intentions were treated with suspicion or hostility.[84]

To defend itself on the wider issues raised by the criticism of its music policy the BBC prepared a memorandum for the committee to explain its regional policy 'in view of the serious misunderstandings which may have been created either in ignorance or by intention' by the statements and submissions of the music profession. It reiterated that central control and supervision of programming was essential while accepting the desirability of extending regional activities. Regional directors had been given as much freedom as was possible or desirable. It was claimed that there had been far more central-ization at first than now. It had been essential in the early days when the many problems of premises, plant, technical resources and staffing had all made con-trol from the centre inevitable. But now it was claimed – and this was a quite new argument – that the process of devolution was proceeding as quickly as was compatible with efficiency in the broadest sense.

As to the criteria by which Regional activity was judged, that, said the memorandum, was difficult to define precisely. It was understood as meaning that no region should embark on anything that could be done better in any other region or in London. It should be justifiable on economic and artistic grounds, though a second-rate programme might be permitted locally at the expense of a first-class one from elsewhere. Standards could not be lowered further than that.[85] A more precise definition, as Briggs remarks, would have been helpful. Nor did the report shed much light on the cultural aspects of regional versus national broadcasting, or define what it meant by contrasting programmes on which the regional scheme was said to be based. 'Contrast' by itself was, as Briggs observes, the most inadequate of criteria by 1935 and even this was not adequately achieved.[86]

The memorandum was, in today's bureaucratic jargon, a damage limi-tation exercise. There is no doubt that London was thrown on the defensive by public criticism of its regional policy and the need to justify it to the Ullswater Committee. One immediate outcome was the creation of a new post, Director of Regional Relations, to act as mediator between the margins and the centre. It was a typically cunning move to appoint Charles Siepmann to this post. It plucked him out of the Talks Department, thus opening up the chance to put the brakes on there by replacing him with a departmental head of conservative outlook. It got him away from London for a while, to cool his heels, since the first task of the new appointee was to tour all the regions and write a detailed report on all aspects of regional broadcasting. And lastly, since Siepmann had notoriously advocated a strong centralist line with the regions, it meant that he might have to revise his views in the light of experience or else have them confirmed.

In the event, Siepmann recanted. After spending one to three weeks in every station, interviewing all programme staff, inspecting the premises and listening to the evening output of every region, he now declared that centralization was a short-sighted policy. The regions were the seed-bed of talent and the ultimate source of supply of London's programmes. In particular Siepmann pinpointed as a crucial difficulty the cultural criteria that London took as the measure of the quality of its own work and that of the regions. The value of regional programmes could not be gauged by such standards. Regional programmes had a different rationale from that of the National Programme. Siepmann argued that until now the regions had been slow in adapting to their local resources, that the pattern of their programmes was too uniform and not sufficiently attuned to the particular interests, needs and loyalties of the areas they served. The regional service, in 1936, was only on the threshold of effective action.[87]

The report was read and discussed in detail by senior staff in London and by the Board of Governors, who accepted its recommendations for greater freedom and diversity in the Regional Programme. The critique of centralization was explicitly accepted by the Governors who affirmed their support for the nurturing of local talent and the representation of local points of view. Regional programmes were needed not only to contrast with London programmes but also to meet the legitimate demands of local tastes and humour. All in all the Governors believed that, in endorsing Siepmann's report, they were offering a 'Charter of Rights' for the regional services.[88]

It had taken much time and effort to establish a workable structure of consultation and discussion between London and the regions. It took time to work out how much and what kind of programmes the regions could best deliver, and the appropriate staffing ratios for such work. Capital expenditure on the renovation of regional studios and equipment took time to work its way through the system. But above all it took London some years to face up to the dangers inherent in the original policy of centralization, and to accept that regional broadcasting's contribution was different in kind from that of the National Programme – not the same but worse. The acceptance of this was the turning point. Though relations between the regions and London were never entirely smooth – as Reith remarked on several occasions, a uniformly easy relationship with Head Office must mean that one party or the other was not

" FUNNY; I COULD HAVE SWORN THAT WAS A REGIONAL COUGH! "

doing its job properly – there was more respect on both sides for the work of the other in the later thirties. And this, in turn, bore fruit in innovative and exciting programmes from the regions in the last few years before the outbreak of war.

CHAPTER FIFTEEN

Manchester and its Programmes

———————⟨✦⟩———————

EACH OF the regions, as it established itself, had a distinctive character and particular problems in relation to its own work and that of the National Programme. It was not just a question of the devaluation of provincial culture by a metropolitan culture. There was also, as we have seen, a continuous tension arising from the hegemony of *English* culture and resistance to its imposition in Scotland, Wales and Northern Ireland. Demands for programmes in the Welsh and Gaelic languages were one way in which this issue was focused from the beginning of 'regional' broadcasting in Wales and Scotland. In both countries the claims to a specific national identity and to particular cultural, religious and communal values as the marks of that identity had a direct bearing on the kinds of music, plays, entertainment and religious services broadcast by the programme-makers for Wales and Scotland. It was the same in Northern Ireland, though there the problems of an implacably divided community created a continuing internal dilemma along with the usual ones in the external relationship with London.

The term 'regional broadcasting' as applied to Scotland, Wales and Northern Ireland was a misnomer which helped to blur political issues that reached well beyond broadcasting. In England itself the three main regions – West, Midland and North – had different characteristics and interests which were in part the product of the features of the area each served, and in part of the fortuitous interests and abilities of the staff in each region. West Region, largely rural, took the lead in agricultural and farming programmes but otherwise appears to have been a tranquil backwater before the war. Siepmann's report on the work of each particular region, while generally favourable (with the exception of Northern Ireland, which he dealt with in an appendix) was rather scathing about the West, and he even recommended closing it down. Midland, based in Birmingham, was one of the most important production centres with a higher programme output than any other region. There were some novel and important programme developments in Midland which we shall touch on later, but it lacked a strong sense of its own regional identity and was probably closer to the 'London outlook' than any of the other regions. As Siepmann noted, the further away you got from London, the more fiercely independent – or bloodyminded, depending on your point of view – the regions tended to become.[1] It was North Region which, of all the English regions, had a most clearly developed character and style of broadcasting before the war.

There is litle doubt that, by the end of the thirties, some of the most interesting and original ideas in programme-making were coming from Manchester. North Region took the lead in the development of the radio feature or documentary and – along with Midland – in the presentation and discussion of public life and affairs. These developments, important in themselves, have a larger significance when set alongside what was simultaneously happening (or rather, *not* happening) in the National Programme. As the programme-makers in London fell silent on social and political issues under the combined pressure of continuing external political harassment and the dead hand of internal administrative policy, their colleagues in Manchester and Midland had greater freedom – within the limits of the mandate to the regions – to deal with such matters, from a regional perspective. Public life, stifled at the centre, continued to flourish in the margins. Moreover, the audience for North Region included a very large number of working-class listeners, and programmes about and for those listeners gave Manchester's programme service a distinctively different edge to the largely middle-class character of the National Programme. We can trace a set of social and cultural relations being worked out between broadcasters and audience in Manchester which differed sharply from that established between London and the national audience.

Manchester was by far the largest of all the regions – not in terms of geographical size, but in terms of the audience it addressed. By the mid-thirties the number of licences taken out annually in North Region was well over two million; twice as many as for Midland, four times greater than Scotland or West Region, eight times more than Wales and almost thirty times larger than Northern Ireland. In his report Siepmann noted that the opportunities, and the difficulties, faced by North Region were unique. Not even Scotland, in his view, faced comparable problems.[2] Manchester's kingdom covered not merely a very large area, but very wide differences of local culture, language and habits. The fiefdom extended from the Scottish borders to the southern edges of Lancashire and Yorkshire, taking in (for a time at least) the Peak District, the Potteries and Lincolnshire. It contained a remarkable number of sub-regional cultures and loyalties; not just in such obvious and ancient rivalries as that between the red rose of Lancashire and the white rose of Yorkshire, but between neighbouring towns and cities. In the North East, Northumberland and Durham had a quite separate character and the distinctive Geordie accent made Newcastle comedians incomprehensible to listeners in Lancashire and Yorkshire. The region contained a high concentration of important towns and cities, each with its own proper sense of civic dignity and pride. Those, like Sheffield, which had lost their own local station felt it as a blow to local importance and independence.

In 1927 Ted Liveing, then Head of Manchester 2ZY, and soon to be Director of North Region, offered a general account of the social and cultural character of Northern England and the range of resources it could tap for broadcasting.[3] It was a paper exercise designed to impress on London the scope and possibilities of the new region. Class differences, he suggested, were far less marked than in the South. There was far more contact between workers and entrepreneurs in the North, and less social distinctions in speech and custom between them. The middle-class merchant kept much the same hours as his employees and both enjoyed their 'high tea' on return home at about six o'clock. Masters and men both went to bed not long after ten in the evening. The merchant classes had few intellectual interests. The great influx of Jewish and continental blood in Liverpool and Manchester had helped to keep alive musical and artistic interests. The typical Northerner, according to Liveing, was virile, shrewd and impulsive; blunt and outspoken, sensitive and kindhearted, 'with all the crudities and egotism, but with all the drive and vigour, that are to be found in a race that is socially in a state of development.'

Liveing went on to review the resources available to broadcasting. For religious services there were a great many famous cathedral and churches. There was an abundance of musical talent, ranging from the Hallé and the Leeds Symphony Orchestra, through to many smaller orchestras, chamber music combinations and solo instrumental artistes. Many of the best-known concert and operatic artists of the day were natives of Lancashire. There was Sir Thomas Beecham's Manchester Operatic Society, and a wealth of choral combinations, most notably the Sheffield Choral Musical Union organized by Sir Henry Coward and the Hallé Chorus. The region's brass bands were famous – St Hilda's Colliery, the Lowell Springs and the Besses O' the Barn being outstanding. From an educational point of view there were large and modern universities at Manchester, Sheffield, Liverpool and Leeds. As for entertainment, though the theatre business was controlled by London entrepreneurs, drama still flourished in the North. The repertory movement was strong in Manchester and Yorkshire. The many seaside resorts and spas offered a wide range of light music and entertainment, while the facilities offered by Blackpool were so varied and valuable that Liveing described them in a separate appendix.

Anticipating some of the ominous implications of the new stress on centralization, Liveing was at pains to emphasize the importance of broadcasting in preserving local culture:

> The trend of modern times is to centralize more and more in London the intellectual, artistic and musical life of the nation. While this had been a very natural evolution in the last few centuries and has been in the interests of national efficiency, the movement has increased at an alarming rate since the war. There is now a very significant danger that the provinces will eventually be so heavily denuded of their talent, more particularly in music and drama, that they will become culturally barren and will not continue to supply the capital with the life-blood that it needs. The BBC is rapidly becoming the most powerful and dominating organization in the cultural life of the country. It will soon be in a position to make or break provincial culture.

Accordingly Liveing strongly urged that the fullest efforts should be made to foster, not only the national life of the country through the National Programme, but to develop the resources of the regions through contrasted programmes with a distinctive regional character every night of the week. In the years that followed, this task was energetically pursued by Liveing and the staff in the Manchester office.

In general the programme-makers tried to establish a coherent image of the region as a whole, and to hold together the variety of local idioms and customs in a unifying image of the North as a particular place and people with a distinctive way of life. The symbolic representation of Northernness had two separate but related versions of place and people: there was the industrial North and there was Northern pastoral. The region contained most of the major heavy industries that had been the mainstay of the first industrial revolution in the previous century: coal, iron, steel, cotton, wool, railways. This was the North that Priestley described as 'a cynically devastated countryside, sooty dismal little towns, and still sootier grim fortress-like cities'.[4] The effects of the recession were far more deeply felt here throughout the thirties than in that other England described by Priestley, of new towns and new industries in the South Midlands, London and the home counties. When Paul Bloomfield, fresh from the new BBC staff training school in London, was sent to do a spell in the regions in the late thirties he was struck by the difference between Birmingham and Manchester: 'In three and a half months in Birmingham I had seen only two beggars and no workless loungers whatever. On my first stroll in Manchester I saw hundreds of men, the good tough northern brand of Englishman, sitting or wandering about, workless. It was a profoundly depressing sight.'⁵

The other image of the North on radio was of its hills and fells, its dales and moorlands – the Lake District, the Yorkshire Dales, the Cheviot Hills, the Pennines, the Peak District. Thus it is invoked by the poet-narrator in Geoffrey Bridson's *Steel*:

> O my beloved North Country!
> Lonely and hard, barren and wintry wasteland.
> What is the grandeur of your superb fells?
> The towering barrier of your hills, the fine sweep of your silent moors?
> Such are the brave ways that I have known so long;
> The cry of birds, the circle of your dark rocks,
> The glitter of water in hidden valleys,
> The rough stone of your tumbling, rambling walls ...
> The tangly mass of bracken that shelters the deep road,
> Root and tuft of a straggling heath,
> Colourless grass that bends to the west wind –
> These have been dear to me. They shall be remembered.
> They are the fells, the features and character of a magnificent North.⁶

Here an immemorial folk – mostly shepherds or dry stone wall builders, it seems – pursued their traditional crafts and customs and spoke an immemorial dialect. Working folk in the towns and cities were seen as coming from this stock, and as having the same roots, cast of mind, character and loyalties. These two images of the North – part myth, part truth – were reproduced again and again in the outside broadcasts, plays and features put out from Manchester.

One major way in which the North was projected was through Outside Broadcasts. Just as in the National Programme OBs gathered up a diverse range of events and unobtrusively worked them together as visions of a common national life, they had a similar affirmative role in the programme output of Manchester. They helped to anchor a coherent image, in all its variety, of North Region's way of life. Outside Broadcasts escaped the statute of limitation imposed by Head Office on regional programme-making. It was one of the few areas that was virtually trouble-free from the start for it was, after all, one of the most obvious ways of producing programmes at little cost that were self-evidently of local and regional interest. In this area of production Manchester kept pace with London and, in certain respects, overtook it. In the initial publicity for the new regional service from the North great play was made of the 'flying-squad' of Outside Broadcast engineers who could, at a moment's notice, arrange a broadcast from any part of the region. By the mid-thirties it was conceded that the regions, and the North in particular, led the way in the development of OB techniques.

In the autumn of 1930 Liveing sent Reith a detailed report on the Outside Broadcast activities of Manchester in its first full year as the central station for North Region.[7] In twelve months it had produced over 300 programmes. Sport included rugby league, cricket, football, golf and racing. Religious services had been relayed from churches high and low all over the region. Entertainment had been tapped from the Tower Circus in Blackpool and from Belle Vue and the Variety Palace in Manchester. There had been panto from the Grand Theatre in Leeds and opera from the Manchester Opera House. Speeches and civic ceremonies included the opening of a new library in Burnley, a banquet in Hull for Miss Amy Johnson, the Lancashire Cotton Fair, the North of England Education Conference at Harrogate and the 100th anniversary of the Liverpool–Manchester railway. Concerts had been taken from Manchester, Liverpool and Leeds, the Bradford Triennial Music Festival and the Buxton Music Festival. Light music had been relayed from the splendid theatre organ in the Blackpool Tower Ballroom and from cafés and restaurants in Manchester, Blackpool and Newcastle. During the summer seaside music was heard from Whitby, Scarborough, Morecambe, Bridlington and, of course, Blackpool. All this was, by now, routine.

But Liveing noted not only a large increase in volume – some undertaken to placate local sensitivities as their own stations were closed down – but a general growth of new ideas and techniques in the use of OB resources. These included the incorporation of OB material into radio plays for realistic effect; the development of OBs to reflect the industrial life of the region; the use of OB points, instead of studios, for eye-witness accounts of sporting and other events. Extremely complex arrangements had been made to give texture and realism to the coverage of the TT races from the Isle of Man and the launch, from Liverpool, of a great passenger liner.

By 1929 Manchester had four studios and a principal control room with the latest dramatic control panel as used by Sieveking and others in London. The control panel was used to coordinate an ambitious programme called *The Port of Liverpool*, transmitted in October 1929, which offered a 'sound picture' of the city's history. The framework of the programme was a play specially written by Matthew Anderson, a local historian, into which were mixed 'descriptive sounds' from the port and the city. OB points were rigged up at the Pier Head, the organ of the cathedral and in the Town Hall. Actors in one of the studios performed a scene recreating the departure of settlers for Canada which was then faded to the Pier Head for the sounds of river traffic and the noise of ships' sirens booming out over the Mersey. A final account of the spiritual life of the city dissolved into an organ recital from the cathedral which concluded the play. The broadcast, Liveing claimed, created widespread interest among listeners and was warmly applauded by the press. On an even larger scale was *North Region Diversions* broadcast on 3 September 1930. It used over thirty microphones from various OB points in Liverpool, Manchester, Blackpool, a woollen mill near Leeds and a colliery near Newcastle to build up a sound picture of the whole region at work and play. In spite of elaborate rehearsals the programme was unfortunately marred by technical hitches and equipment failure. It was, Liveing admitted, 'below standard'. But in conception, at least, it pointed to new possibilities in OB techniques and greater depth in the portrayal of the life and character of the region.

The unsung hero behind most of this work was Victor Smythe, who had been with the station since 1924 and who was to provide invaluable service for the region over many years in the organization of all aspects of outside broadcasting. Siepmann, on one of his periodic regional tours to keep their Talks activities up to scratch, commended Smythe to Reith, in a confidential report, as very active, conscientious and immensely keen. It was Smythe who extended the 'built OB' from an occasional one-off thing into a programme series developed round a common theme. *Links in the Chain* was the first such series and it offered sound pictures of an essential link in transport or communication not normally accessible or visible to the public. The perennial concern of broadcasting to take its audience 'behind the scenes' found its first developed expression in programmes about a railway marshalling-yard, the workings of the sorting offices of a large city post office and the departure of a passenger steamer to Belfast.[8] Similar series soon followed. There was *Microphone Tour* and *North Regional Radio Routes*, in both of which a number of places were visited for their atmosphere and local colour. Midland Region ran a popular series in 1934 called *The Microphone at Large* which visited those kinds of town and village – Chipping Camden, Oakham and Ross on Wye – so dear, after the war, to *Down Your Way*.

Such programmes had the charm of novelty at first, but the charm soon faded for the interest of pictures of life in sound but not vision was limited. Moreover they lacked an essential ingredient: human interest. They were all about places, not people. The discovery that ordinary people talking about themselves, their everyday working lives and interests, could be the basis of programmes that were not only informative but entertaining and pleasurable for listeners was the most important contribution to broadcasting made by North Region before the war. The catalyst of this development was the arrival of Archie Harding as Director of Programmes in 1933.

Harding has been described as 'an Oxford intellectual Marxist'[9] and 'a middle-class champion of the proletariat, bitten by that awful bug which gives a man delusions about the North, making him believe that everything and everybody north of a line between the Severn and the Wash is better and more full of integrity than everything and everybody south of that line.'[10] As soon as he arrived there he set about recruiting a group of highly talented people – journalists, actors and writers – to programme-making, encouraging them to find new ways of expressing the character of Northern England and its people. Under Harding's influence North Region's programmes began to realize the task delegated to the regions – of reflecting the life and variety of the area they served – by establishing a relationship with the audience that was radically different from that between the National Programme in London and its nationwide audience.

The original model for Harding's ideas as to what feature programmes from the regions should aspire to was a programme made in 1930 called *The Western Land*. This was a scripted feature about life and work in Cornwall as told by a farmer, a fisherman, a tin-miner and a flower grower. It was broadcast from St Hilary's, Cornwall, and relayed to London by landline. The *Manchester Guardian* called it 'a promising experiment in "sound pictures" which might be extended, to the listener's profit, to other countrysides or to urban places where workers spend their leisure.'[11] To listeners at that time it sounded just like four people conversing at ease among themselves with sounds from the village and the countryside heard in the background. Harding thought it one of the most remarkable programmes ever broadcast, and he deeply regretted that there was such little chance of this kind of programme ever becoming a regular feature of the National Programme. He regarded the BBC as the one national organization in a position systematically to collect and present the great wealth of material all over Britain, of which *The Western Land* formed a part.[12] His first effort in this direction was the feature series *Harry Hopeful* which began on North Region in 1935.[13]

For this project Harding enlisted the services of an aspiring young Manchester poet and writer, D. G. Bridson. There were no mobile recording facilities in Manchester at this time. What Harding wanted to create in the studio were sound pictures of people and places as if they had been shot on location. Bridson conceived of an imaginary central character, Harry Hopeful, an out-of-work glass-blower's assistant on the tramp in search of work, meeting and talking to real people in the real places he visited. Bridson was fortunate in finding a 'natural' for the part, Frank Nicholls, a clock-mender from Irlam who was already a regular perfomer in Manchester's *Children's Hour*. The locations chosen included well-known beauty spots – the Dales, the North Yorkshire moors, the Peak District. Together Bridson and Nicholls went to these places and talked to the local people whom they had invited to take part in the programmes. As Nicholls talked to them (he had that rare ability to put people at their ease and draw them out in conversation) Bridson made detailed notes of what they said. Later, he worked this material into a script, a copy of which was sent to each participant. A few weeks later he and Nicholls returned with portable wireless equipment and a radio engineer. The microphone was then set up in the homes of the participants and they each rehearsed their part with Nicholls while Bridson listened on headphones in the car outside. Thus the speakers were accustomed to the microphone in familiar surroundings and adjustments could be made, if necessary, to make the script sound more natural. Later the full cast was assembled in Manchester's main studio. After one complete run-through came the live broadcast itself, performed before an invited audience which included the families and friends of the participants.

The first programme was broadcast on 23 May 1935 and featured 'Harry Hopeful's Day in the Yorkshire Dales'. It included what Bridson called 'shots' of the Swaledale Veterans' Choir singing local ballads, a short talk by a shepherd working at High Abbotside, a local bard, a postman talking about his round over the high moors, and so on. It was greeted with great enthusiasm in the BBC. 'Enjoyed every minute. Harry Hopeful was excellent. You were very lucky in finding such live personalities to put the stuff over. There was no doubt abut the genuineness of them all,' wrote E. L. Guilford, Director of the newly revived Newcastle station. Maschwitz congratulated Bridson on an 'extremely good programme'. This kind of thing was 'the regional goods all right' and he hoped there would be more of it. Siepmann praised the Dales programme as an admirable innovation and the nearest thing to real and typical regional performance he had yet heard. The whole thing had, he felt, a great air of spontaneity, though he was intrigued as to how it was done – was the audience literally there, was the laughter and applause real or recorded, and were they genuine characters or actors?

Harry Hopeful was one of the very first programmes from the regions to raise the quality of material above the level of anecdotal talks or dialect plays. It was proof of a newfound cultural vitality and resourcefulness in the provinces. For Bridson, as for Harding, the series fulfilled two deeply-held beliefs: that broadcasting should reflect the lives and opinions of ordinary people and, more particularly, that it should project the real character of North Region. The success of the programme established Bridson's reputation as a new and original radio talent and helped clinch for him the post of Features Programme Assistant (NR) in 1936.

Bridson was to have a long and very distinguished career in the BBC as a writer and producer for radio, and his work in Manchester before the war reflected his wide and varied interests. He wrote and produced verse dramas, literary and poetic features, anniversary programmes and historical features. Many of these are described in his own excellent biography. But central to his work was a concern to put over a new image of the North. In this respect

Harry Hopeful and the four programmes he made about the region's major industries in the next few years may be seen as the clearest expressions of this intention.

His first big industrial feature, *Steel*, was made shortly after Manchester had acquired its own Mobile Recording Unit.[14] Now that he could use actuality inserts Bridson had in mind a really ambitious programme for radio along the lines of the recent documentary film, *Coalface*.[15] He planned to surpass the film which had, in his view, mishandled some very interesting possibilities in choral speech and singing. *Steel* would combine poetic narrative, music and choral verse with recorded actuality 'sound shots' from a steel foundry. The whole thing, he wrote in a memorandum, 'should build up not so much a mere recorded actuality programme as an aesthetically significant and emotionally stirring programme on lines and on a scale previously untouched by the Corporation.' He commissioned an original orchestral score from the Sheffield composer, Desmond MacMahon – the first time this had been done for a radio feature. Sound recordings were made at the East Hecla factory of Hadfields Ltd (other big steel companies were piqued that they had not been chosen) and Sheffield was agog at the thought of a big radio programme about the industry which made their city famous.

MacMahon's symphonic suite was an integral part of the programme. It was played as an overture and then skilfully married into the poetic text that Bridson had written using chanted verse and sung choruses. The feature was presented as a symphony in four movements: *allegretto, andante, allegro scherzo* and *allegro finale*. The first movement begins by invoking the elemental qualities of the land and the men of the North country. A poetic *mise-en-scène* moves from the moors and granite outcrops circling Sheffield to daybreak in the town itself as the men make their way from various districts to the factory gates to clock on for the morning shift. A chanted chorus invoking the might and power of 'industry's resounding roar' is overtaken by the music which brings the movement to a climactic end. The second and third movements recreate the industrial processes which transform the scrap and pig iron into milled steel. We hear nothing from the men who work in the factory. Music and verse choruses, intermingled with recorded sound, conjure up instead a heroic vision of the abstract power and energy of modern industry as the mainstay of an emerging new age and a new social order. The final movement begins with a quiet invocation by the poet of what the region means to him which is overtaken by a finale that surges to a closing crescendo invoking a vision of a new destiny and a limitless future.

The programme was again very well received within the BBC, but local reaction was mixed. The Mayor of Sheffield offered his thanks of behalf of the people of the city and praised it as a magnificent idea excellently carried out. The Deputy Chairman of Hadfields offered his congratulations with only one reservation: 'it was perhaps a little too much of a fantasy, but that [response] is only to be expected from a hard-headed lot of people who spend most of their lives in the manufacture and manipulation of steel.' The *Daily Independent* was more blunt: 'Sheffield Laughed when BBC went Poetic over Steel' ran the headline, and the article went on to complain that all this poetry and word-spinning made the programme lack conviction.[16] Bridson took the point. While he continued to write and produce features that combined verse and music, these methods were now confined to literary and historical subjects. For his three subsequent industrial features – *Cotton, Wool* and *Coal* – he returned to the methods of *Harry Hopeful*, recruiting the young Joan Littlewood, fresh from RADA, as the presenter.

The last of the three, *Coal*, was particularly tricky.[17] To begin with there was a great deal of difficulty in finding a suitable pit on which to base the programme. Bridson wanted to get the North East accent as a change from those of Yorkshire and Landcashire heard in the previous two programmes. He also wanted to tap the very rich vein of Tyneside colliery songs. Beyond that he wanted a mine where the conditions were not too good (otherwise the miners would not believe it), and where the management would cooperate in a programme that boosted British coal at the same time as enlisting sympathy for the miners. The task of finding a suitable location was passed to Roger Wilson, the region's publicity officer. He eventually came up with Messrs Straker and Lowe, owners of Brancepath Colliery, Wilmington, Co. Durham. In a note to Bridson, Wilson assured him that Wilmington was a small town and that the pit was mechanized so there was plenty of unemployment which he could work into the picture. Moreover Brancepath had its own brass band, one of the best in the area.

Though a pit had now been settled on, the difficulties were by no means over. It soon transpired that the wage rates in the mine were slightly above average for the area, a fact that mystified the union people since the arrangement had been reached 'somewhat independently' of them. Wilson was very keen to make friends with the unions in order, as he put it, to 'secure our rear', and he felt it essential that the Durham Miners Association should be consulted. On the other hand, he did not want them brought in too early since they might cramp the whole programme. He recommended seeing their representatives officially when the script was well under way and 'we know the ground we propose to stick to'.

While all this was going on Bridson requisitioned London to authorize the purchase of two sets of overalls and two pairs of gumboots for himself and Joan Littlewood. Thus prepared they set off for Wilmington:

A month's work went into making the programme during which time Joan and I familiarized ourselves with every aspect of the miner's life. We went on shift

343

with the men by night and morning; we helped with the hewing, loading and putting; we got the dirt engrained in our scalps and every pore of our bodies. Joan lived with a miner's family – the son had been killed in the pit – while I put up in no greater comfort at the local miner's pub. By the time *Coal* came on the air, there wasn't a miner at the pit who didn't know us and treat us as one of themselves.[18]

As the programme took shape Bridson wanted to make sure that both the owners and the unions felt they had been fairly represented. He sent a draft script for comment to Captain Howe, the manager of Brancepath, with a cover note adding that 'we always find it best to prepare a script from the men's angle first and then have it vetted by the managers'. At the same time he contacted the President and Secretary of the Durham Miners Association. The script was returned by management with minimal changes and as the day of performance drew near, Wilson primed the local press and wrote to Wilmington's MP asking him to listen and inviting his comments on the programme.

Coal was performed on 17 November 1938 and evoked an immediate and sympathetic response from all over the country, particularly for one of the participants, a hewer who had been out of work for so long that his body had gone soft. He was unable to return to work at the coalface when a job did eventually come up. Money poured in to the Newcastle office, especially from listeners in the home counties, and Bridson arranged for it to be distributed among the miners in such a way that it did not come to the attention of the Means Test officials. The remainder was distributed among the families of men on short time to buy Christmas presents for their children.

In his own account of these industrial features, written many years after they were made, Bridson suggests that in intention and in effect they were simple and transparent. They were something new at that time and they proved that everyone had something to say and a point of view that deserved a hearing.[19] For Bridson the techniques he used served only, as in *Harry Hopeful*, to let people speak for themselves within the framework of a live studio broadcast. The production file of *Coal* however reveals the undisclosed strategies that organized the ground eventually occupied by the programme as broadcast. These hidden expediencies were not apparent in the seemingly artless presentation of the performance itself.

Meanwhile other techniques of social documentation were being developed in Manchester, which relied on the use of recorded actuality material for their effect. The pioneer of this kind of programme was Olive Shapley who joined the staff in Manchester in late 1934 to work, at first, on *Children's Hour*. In her first few years there she, like everyone else, gained a thorough grounding in all aspects of radio work. She helped in the studio production of some of

Bridson's programmes. She breathed new life into *Children's Hour*. She produced some of the radio plays written for the region. There was greater scope for individual initiative, more flexibility between different areas of production, more cooperation between programme-makers in Manchester at that time than in London.

In 1937 the Manchester studios were refitted with the latest equipment, including the new and improved Dramatic Control Panel already in use in London. Shapley was immediately fascinated by its possibilities when combined with the Mobile Recording Unit, and began to concentrate her work on making programmes in which recorded actuality was mixed, through the panel, with studio presentation and commentary. The recording van was twenty-seven feet long and weighed, when fully loaded, more than seven tons. Its maximum speed was twenty miles an hour. Inside were two turntables, each operated by a technician. The recording time of each disc was a maximum of four minutes. As one disc came to an end, recording was continued on the other turntable, thus securing uninterrupted continuity of a sort. The new studio equipment could accommodate up to six discs at a time, with remote control to lower the pick-up head onto the precise groove at which to begin the required recorded insert.[20]

Two recording vans has originally been commissioned by London to collect topical items for inclusion in the news bulletins. But they were unsuited for this and were passed over to the regions. Wales, Scotland and West Region however had many hilly and narrow roads which the vans could not negotiate. So by the time one of them arrived in Manchester there was some uncertainty as to whether they had any useful purpose at all. Bridson had used it for *Steel* but only for background effects. It was Olive Shapley who first took the van all over the region to record people talking in their homes, at work and on the streets. Single-handed, she brought to maturity the use of recorded actuality as the basis of the radio feature in those last few years before the war.

Her programmes broke new grounds for radio both in technique and in their subject matter. There were programmes about homeless people, about shopping, about the barge people who worked the canals, about long distance lorry drivers, about an all-night transport café. There was *Broadcasting with the Lid off*, a trip behind the scenes to show a day in the life of the Manchester office.[21] When London got wind of this there was much indignation at the indecency of baring the BBC bosom to the microphone. Head Office wanted to cancel it, but it was too late to withdraw it from the schedules. Opinion among the Manchester staff about the merits of the programme varied greatly but there was a general view that it had been worth doing. A report on it to Basil Nicolls (Controller of Programmes, London) assured him that by a different method it would have been possible to present the BBC as a more efficient and glamorous institution but it was felt such fantasies should be discouraged. Nicolls accepted the report with the comment that there was no objection to the BBC unbending – *occasionally*.

The structure of Shapley's early programmes was very straightforward, consisting of a narrative commentary to introduce and link the recorded material which formed the substance of the programme. This is how Wilfred Pickles introduced *Pounds, Shillings and Pence. A Study in Shopping*:

> Good evening everybody. Before we get going in this shopping programme there are one or two things I want to tell you about it. Now it's what I'd call a 'homely' programme. No flourish of trumpets about it, you know, but the sort of programme you'll recognize yourselves in maybe. The records you're going to hear were made at a little town called Sowerby Bridge. Sowerby Brigg I call it, coming from that part of the country myself.[22]

And here is how Olive Shapley herself introduced *Canal Journey*:

> On this occasion I went after the human story – as the newspapers say – and tried to get the canal people I met to tell in their own words something of what their life is like. In spite of all jokes to the contrary they are not a very voluble race and some of them found it hard to believe that anyone could find the details of their ordinary life interesting and, when they had been reassured on this point, it wasn't very easy for them to put their ideas into words. All the records you'll hear were made without script or rehearsal.[23]

The presenters she used regularly were Jimmie Miller (Ewan MacColl), Wilfred Pickles and Joan Littlewood. For *Homeless People*, broadcast on 6 September 1938, she used Miller and Pickles. The commentary she wrote was, as always, simple and direct:

> MILLER: Do you know what happens to you if you apply for a night's lodging in a casual ward? To begin with you're booked in: then you're searched to make sure you have no money (at least no more than a shilling); then you get your supper, you're given a bath and you go to bed. Next morning you get another meal and eight ounces of bread and two ounces of cheese to take away with you. You can't come back within a month; if you do, you have to stay four days and work in the institution. Normally you sleep in a dormitory. If you're noisy you may be put in a cubicle on your own, and if you're very noisy you may be 'put out' and then you pass into the hands of the police. That's not a common occurrence.[24]

The programme continued with recordings which showed something of the routines of a casual ward, and then went to visit a children's home in Cheadle, a hospital for the incurably sick in Scorton, North Yorkshire, a training centre for young tramps in County Durham, the South Shields Seamen's

Institute and lastly the Prudhoe Street Mission in Newcastle which was thus described by Miller in the closing commentary of the programme.

> After the hymn they go straight into the Refuge itself – a big, bare room, the floor scrubbed to whiteness, smelling faintly of disinfectant – and they lie there all morning. Men of all ages and types. War heroes who have never won back to work and security since 1918. Young lads tramping, perhaps from Glasgow to London, still young and silly enough to have hope and trust. Old men lying like sacks or heaps of rags on the hard floor – no mattresses, no covering.
>
> We came out into the bustle and light of Saturday evening shopping in Newcastle: gleaming fruit and succulent meat and melting pastries; soft beds and rich carpets; warm, bright clothes and strong, shapely shoes – all this a few feet away behind frail pieces of glass, yet as inaccessible to those lying on the Refuge floor as if they had been stars in the sky.

The mode of address of these programmes should be compared with that of *'Opping 'Oliday* and the London talks on housing and unemployment. It can readily be seen that the language here works in a quite different way. It is more informal, relaxed and intimate. It sets up a more equal relationship between the speaker, the subject of the programme and the audience. Such reportage, combined with her sympathetic skill as an interviewer (a quite new technique which she had to discover for herself), led one contemporary critic to describe Shapley's programmes as 'little masterpieces of understanding and authenticity'.

Even when dealing with a by now familiar 'documentary' topic for radio, such as mining, Shapley found a fresh and original way to present the subject. For *Miners' Wives*, broadcast 29 March 1939, the first part of the programme followed an established documentary pattern.[25] It was a factual presentation of daily life in Cragshead, a large mining village near Durham. Shapley spoke the commentary which was built round recordings of folk dancing, amateur dramatics, a WEA class, Saturday at the pictures – all fairly standard fare by now. But for the second half of the programme she had taken one of the participants, Mrs Emmerson, the wife of a checkweighman in Cragshead, to Marles-les-Mines a mining village in northern France. For a week the two of them lived with a miner's family while Mrs Emmerson got to know the people and the place. Back home she gave a talk, which made up the second half of the programme, on her impressions of the way of life in Marles-les-Mines compared with her own village community. The programme created quite a stir in the northern press (illness nearly prevented Mrs Emmerson from making the trip), who noted that this was the very first time that the BBC had allowed anyone, other than a small number of their own staff, to go abroad at their expense to contribute to one of their programmes.

There are no recordings of any of these programmes, but fortunately there are of two of the last programmes Shapley made before the outbreak of war. Both were technically more ambitious and on a larger scale than anything she had done before. *They Speak for Themselves* was billed in *Radio Times* as a radio enquiry into Mass Observation – 'that new idea with which we have had to reckon so surprisingly in the last year'.[26] This hour-long programme combined all the technical resources of radio available at that time; studio presentation and discussion, combined with recorded actuality overlaid with musical links and dramatized reconstructions of recent events.[27] It was presented by Tom Harrisson and Charles Madge, the founders of the movement, and it is worth noting that the only serious comment on radio, as far as we know, about the critical implications of the Munich crisis, between the event itself and the outbreak of war, comes in this North Region feature programme. The introduction to the programme and a later section, which uses actors to reconstruct the swings in public opinion at the time of the crisis, both point to the information gap between rulers and ruled, and the ignorance of the British public about what was happening in Europe and the aims of British policy. Though these points emerged unobtrusively – Munich was not the major focus of the programme – such references to the topic could not have been made in London. *They Speak for Themselves* and *The Classic Soil*, Shapley's next production, both dealt with major social topics that were beyond the scope of London at the time.

There is a strong likeness between the unemphatic reportage of Olive Shapley – her 'feel' for her subjects – and Elizabeth Gaskell's novels of Manchester life in the 1840s. *The Classic Soil* returned to the Manchester of those years for an hour-long programme comparing working-class life then with their circumstances a hundred years later.[28] The authority used as the basis for the comparison was not, however, Mrs Gaskell but that other famous observer and analyst of Manchester in the 1840s, Frederick Engels. Extracts from *The Condition of the Working Class in England* were read in the studio by a German resident in Manchester who was born in Engels' home town. The passages described the appalling housing conditions, the wretched clothes and the miserable diet of the newformed proletariat who inhabited that 'classic soil upon which the industrial revolution grew to full estate'. These accounts formed the basis for a comparison with the housing, diet and clothing of working people in Manchester and Salford in 1939. The programme was conceived and written by Joan Littlewood and produced by Olive Shapley who made all the many recordings used to build up a richly textured account of contemporary working-class life and experience.

The programme covered all levels of working-class experience from the relatively well-to-do, through those who just managed to make ends meet, to those below the poverty line for whom mere existence was an unrelenting struggle. It is full of subtle contrasts and shading that are funny and deso-

348

lating in turn. Men and women, young and old, all give their testimony. There are no cutaways to officialdom, to the voices of authority. There are the characteristic little vignettes that mark Shapley's style – of children queuing for a penn'orth of chips, or playing in the cobbled streets of Salford built when Engels wrote his book. There is a delightful little scene of street traders selling old clothes in Salford ('Tuppence a pair of bloomers! Come on, who'll buy my lovely bloomers? —— *pause* —— Don't you ladies wear bloomers in Salford?' *Shrieks of laughter* ...). There is a terrible sequence in which a mother, in a voice numb with grief, describes how she watched for eighteen months as her fourteen-year-old daughter wasted away from consumption – an illness brought on in the first place and made fatal by the damp and squalor of the tenement block in which the family lived.

It was, said Shapley, recalling it forty years after it was made, a 'shameful programme' because it was so onesided.[29] Manchester Corporation and Head Office both took exception to its lack of balance. For though the programme showed that conditions had improved for some – there is a housewife who describes the joys of her new council flat and the wonders of her new electric carpet cleaner – the overwhelming impression is one of resilience in the face of unremitting proverty. The last words of the programme belong to a young girl who works in one of the cotton mills. Her words sum up the experience, the circumstances and the expectations of a class and of a generation:

> I work in the cotton mill in the card room. I've had to work hard ever since I left school, and me mother and father before me. That's all there is for me – work, eat and sleep. What else is there? If you don't work you don't eat. I know when I was out of work for two years I walked the shoes off me feet, and if I hadn't found work when I did (*pause*) I'd've done away with meself. I'm thankful enough to be working now. Although it's hard, I never grumble. All I ask is steady work to keep meself in bread and butter. I don't want money and plenty of luxuries. All I want is a comfortable living. But what's the good of looking into the future? I've enough to do to worry about tomorrow.

The features written and produced by Bridson and Shapley in the second half of the thirties had no equivalents elsewhere in the BBC. They were acknowledged in London to be the leading programme-makers in their field. Their work however must be seen as part of a wider pattern of developments in the general programme output of North Region in those years. The distinctive brand of regionalism produced by Manchester was one which foregrounded ordinary working people both within the programmes and as a major part of the audience for whom those programmes were made. This double focus on the everyday lives and tastes of the majority was in sharp contrast with the National Programme throughout the thirties. In the National Programme working people appeared in programmes either as 'victims' (as occasionally uncomfortable reminders of how the other half lived), or as stereotyped representatives of 'the man in the street'. When the man in the street made his appearance – as he sometimes did in London's talks or features – he was handled with an uneasy facetiousness which served to underline the differences between 'them' and 'us'. Working people were only marginally present in London's output and only marginally recognized as members of the 'great audience' for the National Programme. In Manchester they were acknowledged as the majority audience for the regional service and were catered for accordingly.

This was not a simple task simply accomplished for the BBC, as Briggs observes, 'by the nature of its social context never found it easy fully to penetrate the working-class world which provided it with by far the largest part of its audience.' The background of BBC staff, the impersonality of its announcers, which clashed so sharply with 'the powerful working-class instinct to stress the personal in every aspect of human relationships', and above all the BBC's language – so alien and remote in accent, vocabulary and style – all combined to maintain a gulf between the institution and its working – class listeners.[30] In Manchester all these barriers had to be be acknowledged and overcome.

The social composition of the North Region staff did not escape comment in the Northern press. 'Tuner', the radio critic of a Bradford newspaper, after complaining generally of 'the class monopoly' of the BBC whose policy was completely controlled by 'the public school mind', went on to draw attention to the fact that key posts in Manchester were held by Southerners.[31] They should, he felt, be occupied by men with a true Northern pedigree. It is noticeable that from the mid-thirties the key posts in Manchester did go to men born in the region. When Harding left in 1936 to return to London as a co-director of 'St Beadles', the new staff training school, he was replaced as Director of Programmes by John Salt, grandson of the famous Sir Titus Salt of Saltaire. In the following year when Liveing retired as Director of North Region he was replaced, after some delay, by John Coatman who quit as Chief News Editor to return to his native Lancashire. Both made plain their intention to maintain the distinctive character of the region and to provide a service that pleased listeners. For Coatman the North Region microphone was the shared property of the Manchester staff and the people of the region. He wanted, by personal contacts as well as by programmes, to identify himself with Northern listeners.[32]

One way in which Machester tried to do this was in programmes that gave people access to the microphone to express their views. *Northern Cockpit* which began in 1935 was a half-way house between a radio talk and a discussion, and was introduced as 'a sort of radio parliament in which social problems are not so much debated as elucidated by means of relevant statements.' Each programme was a symposium of short talks on a subject of regional interest. Topics included 'Back to the Land', 'Cotton', 'Canvassing', 'Problems of Dialect in the North' and 'The Servant Problem'. What is striking about the scripts is the way in which experts and ordinary people contributed on an equal footing. The programme on Canvassing included a housewife, her husband, a canvasser, a sales manager and an economist. Each was given equal weight. The economist was not used to shape the argument or to comment on other contributions, but simply to provide a wider perspective. Within the limitations of the subjects, fairly radical opinions could be expressed. In the programme on 'The Servant Problem' a middle-class housewife advocated the communal organization of housing estates, with communal creches, common kitchens, no personal servants, but special 'sitters-in' to hold the baby when its parents went to the common cinema. Her aim was to free all those women who wished to do other things from the bondage of household work. This contributor was described, confidentially, as 'almost communist in political theory, but fundamentally conventional'.[33]

The idea of a radio parliament was taken up by Midland Region with *Midland Parliament*. This programme dealt more specifically with industrial issues and relations between workers and management. One of the regular working-class speakers, G. H. Jones, noted the suspicion among large sections of working people that the BBC had a natural bias towards the employing class. The programme helped to correct that view he felt for, although the employers generally had three out of five debaters round the table, he and his fellow spokesmen for the workers were always able to express their views as freely and as frankly as they wished. In a *Radio Times* article Jones declared:

> I like to think that for the short space of time I am before the microphone I am expressing the opinions of many people who would otherwise be inarticulate, and that it is my privilege to voice their protest against the folly of the present system of society which so complacently permits poverty to remain side by side with great wealth. I like to think too, of my words as mental bombs flying through space, destroying the accepted notions which deprive the working class not only of material welfare but of cultural development.[34]

Three important programmes, noted by Briggs, developed in Manchester in the late thirties were *Why Do You Believe That?*, *Public Enquiry* and *Burbleton*.[35] The first two were based on American programmes which Roger Wilson had observed on a visit to the United States to study serious broadcasting over there. *Why Do You Believe That?*, based on the Chicago Round Table programmes, was 'a Socratic dialogue' with three partners in discussion, one of whom was a steelworker from Scunthorpe. *Public Enquiry*, which began in June 1939, was offered to listeners as a companion programme to the already established *Burbleton*.

Both programmes aimed to deal with a wide range of contemporary local issues – the rates, council spending, education, corporation services, local elections and so on. *Burbleton* was a cross between a dramatized documentary and a soap opera. It was the name of an imaginary Northern borough, with a mayor called Alderman Wool, devised and written by T. Thompson, a Lancashire short story writer. Listeners heard farmers chatting at the field gate, wives conversing over the garden rails and customers at the Crown and Anchor ('the most democratic place in the country') all talking with refreshing candour about the topics of the moment in their small Northern town. The *Yorkshire Evening Post* had much praise for the programme and concluded its review by declaring that 'if anyone last night wanted all the arguments for and against municipal trading, there they were served up with a rich sauce of humour that was a sheer joy to the listener.'[36]

Public Enquiry began with a discussion of the rates. Before an invited audience of four hundred people, the pros and cons were discussed for twenty minutes each in Manchester's Central Library by Councillor S. P. Dawson and Alderman Wright Robinson. After that, the topic was thrown open and questions and comments taken from the floor. In the absence of omni-directional microphones at that time, microphone were strung across the gallery where the audience sat to pick up their contributions. The *Manchester Guardian*'s correspondent who was part of the audience noted that interruptions during the speeches were probably more numerous than they would have been if the microphones had not been there, and that the chance of getting heard 'over the air' by people at home seemed a dominating idea in the meeting.[37] The idea though was regarded as such a success that there were plans to transfer the programme to the National Programme. The war however scotched that plan, but in 1946 it was revived on the post-war Home Serivice.

The microphone was not however accessible to all shades of Northern opinion. In Manchester as in London the right to speak did not extend to working-class militants. Manchester had its own William Ferrie incident in 1934, a few weeks after that fiasco in London. George Staunton, a local Manchester man, was asked to give a brief account of the recent Hunger March in which he had taken part. The script that Staunton came up with was a stirring plea for unity in the ranks of the working class against the Unemployment Bill, Fascism and war. He ended with this rallying cry: 'Workers! Build a mighty united front and smash the government of hunger and war!' This was judged to be highly propagandist and provocative, and a departure from what had been asked for, namely a purely descriptive little talk. Someone in the Manchester office undertook to rewrite the script and came up with this ending: 'We came back from the march as fit as we left home – with a few exceptions as to feet – and our moral [sic] was good. We had the satisfaction of feeling that we had at last shown London a bit of what the unemployed in Lancashire were feeling, and had shown them too, how a great march of this kind could be well organized and disciplined.'[38] Mr Staunton refused to utter such twaddle, and the *Daily Worker* pointed the moral of the tale – 'Gentlemen only need apply. BBC bans workers' statements.'[39]

But the same newspaper had warm praise for *The Chartists' March*, a feature programme produced by John Pudney and written by Jimmie Miller (Ewan MacColl). It was transmitted on 13 May 1938 to commemorate the centenary of that great working-class political movement. Ewan MacColl and Joan Littlewood were both recruited, quite separately, by Kenneth Adam and Archie Harding, as occasional actors, presenters and writers for North Region. Their main energies at the time were absorbed in an effort to develop in Manchester a politically engaged theatre with a popular appeal to working people who would ordinarily never dream of going to watch a play. Though their contributions to radio were far more muted than their Red Megaphone and Living Newspaper productions they still had a distinctly populist radical edge to them.[40] It was Littlewood who chose Engels as the historical point of reference for *The Classic Soil*. In a memorandum explaining her choice she described *The Condition of the Working Class in England* as 'an accurate and careful study of [working-class] conditions which also contains some passages of very fine prose.' The word 'accurate' is pencilled out in the memorandum.[41]

The ways in which working-class life was presented in Manchester features and documentaries could sometimes give offence. We have seen how *Coal*, throughout its pre-production, was carefully orchestrated to avoid any possibility of antagonism between management, unions and workforce. In his efforts to find a suitable pit on which to base the programme, Roger Wilson, then North Region's publicity officer, had contacted Arthur Raistrick of Newcastle University's Geology Department for advice. In his reply Raistrick mentioned, among other things, his hope that this programme would avoid the local prejudice against the BBC which had been created against the previous programme in the occasional series, *Wool*.

Wool was based on Salt's Mill of Saltaire in the West Riding of Yorkshire and doubtless John Salt, the newly appointed Director of Programmes, helped set up that connection for Bridson. Raistrick's family came from Saltaire and many of his relatives worked in the mill. He had listened to the programme at home and at one point in it the girls in the burling and mending rooms were heard singing at their work. Raistrick commented:

All my family, cousins, aunts etc. work or have worked in the mill and some were there at the time. Singing has *never* been allowed, and next day when it started they were told firmly to keep that for the BBC. Most people in the district regard that programme as 'faked' and my own family tell me that they have never listened since to any works broadcast because they will be faked like Salts.[42]

If this anecdote is to believed – and there is a long history of such disciplinary rules enforced by fines in the textiles industry – it suggests that these industrial programmes by Bridson were somewhat romantic and sentimental, shading out the harsher aspects of working-class life and presenting a docile and respectful workforce with a fatalistic view of life. When *Wool* is read or listened to carefully, it reveals a range of incidental remarks that Bridson picked up from those who worked at the mill which hint at the tedium, risk of injury and danger to health of the wool business. There is a young lad of fifteen who, in his first week at work, could not sleep at night for the noise of the weaving shed ringing in his ears. There are passing references to fines for mistakes, to the risk of injury from flying shuttles that came loose, to the strain on the eyes in the burling and mending room where most of the girls wore glasses. One could go through the script picking out this 'hidden discourse' to produce a narrative with a very different emphasis to that which Bridson gave his programme, with its stress on the cheery resilience of working folk and their capacity to endure lean times.

There is no doubt that these programmes do manipulate working-class attitudes and sentiments, but to dismiss them as inauthentic or as ideologically suspect would be to miss much of their point. For, along with the *Harry Hopeful* series, they were the very first programmes in broadcasting to take the experience of ordinary people as a source of entertainment and pleasure. The most remarkable thing about the *Harry Hopeful* series was the sound of a live studio audience laughing, applauding and joining in. It was quite unlike anything that had been heard on radio at that time and it showed that radio could create its own public and participatory pleasures from the stuff of everyday life and experience. The most popular shows on radio and television, from *Have a Go!* to *That's Life!*, are the heirs to this discovery.

When Grace Wyndham Goldie laid down her pen as *The Listener*'s radio critic in 1939, she chose to celebrate regional broadcasting in her farewell article.

Let me before I die give one last shout about the importance of regional broadcasting. It is, I assure you, worth shouting about. Its effect on English life is only just beginning to be felt and is already enormous. It is a side of broadcasting which I never see publicly discussed and the value of which I never see publicly recognized ... In London the search is for the best possible play, feature, actor, talk or entertainment and to provide it for listeners. But in the regions there is something else. For it is the business of regional broadcasting to be expressive of the region. It is its business to be a channel for regional talent. But there is more than that. For it is also the business of the regions to express the everyday life of the region, its daily work, its past, its attitude of mind, and above all the quality of the people.[43]

At its best North Region regularly succeeded in making enjoyable, unpretentious programmes for its largely working-class audience. The voices of Wilfred Pickles, Frank Nicholls and others who performed in plays and features, spoke to and for the listeners in the North and did much to compensate for the official voices of the BBC's staff announcers. Whenever Manchester made programmes about local places and people it was a matter of pride for those who lived there and headline news in the local newspapers. When Olive Shapley took Mrs Emmerson to Marles-les-Mines as part of the preparation for *Miners' Wives*, it was a nine days wonder in the Newcastle press.[44] Her discreet, sympathetic and finely observed programmes avoided any prescriptive official definition of their subject matter. A note in *Radio Times* on *Homeless People* promised that 'no BBC voice will intrude at all'.[45] That democratic impulse at the heart of all this activity, to let people speak for themselves, to show the ordinary lives and pleasures of ordinary people, was well served by the pioneering efforts of programme-makers in Manchester in those brief golden years before the war.

CHAPTER SIXTEEN

The Listener

———⊲❋⊳———

THUS FAR we have considered the formation of broadcasting from the public, institutional side. It is time now to abandon such perspectives and come at broadcasting from the other side, from the point of reception, and to try to understand what having a radio meant, in real life contexts, to real people. Listeners' immediate point of contact with broadcasting was with a piece of equipment, the wireless receiving apparatus, whose construction and design was in constant flux until the mid-thirties. When broadcasting started up in 1923 'listening in' was very much a hit and miss affair. The BBC's low-powered transmitters and the primitive nature of the receiving equipment called for elaborate Heath Robinson contraptions in the back gardens of sub-urban Britain and on the rooftops of houses. To receive a programme in the early twenties an aerial up the 100 feet long was called for, suspended between two masts, either in the garden or on the roof. Failing that an elaborate cat's cradle device could be used indoors.[1] The receiving equipment looked more like something out of contemporary science fiction than a simple household object. No attempt was made to box in and conceal the technical components of the receiver which looked like what it was, a weird and wonderful scientific gadget.

Many people first heard the wild waves calling through the earphones of a crystal set. This crude listening device needed no electricty to power it, was simple to construct and cheap in comparison with valve sets. They were dependent on the power of the transmitting signal and were incapable of separating signals of equivalent strength unless these were widely separated on the waveband. It was impossible to amplify the sound of the signal, hence listening in on headphones was as solitary an activity then as the stereo Walkman is today. These were, by the end of the twenties, superseded by valve sets which needed a power supply to provide the thermionic valve with enough energy to amplify the incoming radio signal.[2] At first these were equally capricious in maintaining a clear and steady transmission of broadcast output. Just what a performance listening in on such contraptions was can be seen from the recollections gathered by Shaun Moores:

(1) I had to sit with my arms folded while he was fiddling with his crystal. If you even moved he'd be going 'shush, shush', you know. You couldn't even go in the kitchen and peel potatoes, because he used to say he could hear the sound of the droppings in the sink above what was coming through the headphones.

(2) I'd put the earphones on, and then anything my wife wanted to listen to, I'd turn one earphone outwards and she used to lean her head against mine – put her ear to it. Then we both used to listen together.

(3) There was a basin my brother would put on the living room table, and then he'd get the earphones. There'd be my other brothers and my sister crowding round this basin and listening to the sound coming out.
S.M.   Sorry, I'm still not clear – what exactly was this basin doing?
Well, my brother used to put the earphones in the basin and the sound was amplified by it. I can vividly remember the family crowding round and listening with their ears all close up to this basin on the table. The sound must only have been very faint, but it meant that more than one person could listen at a time.[3]

It is noticeable that control of the gadget rested with male members of the family; the father, husband, brother:

Only one of us could listen in and that was my husband. The rest of us were sat like mummies. We used to row over it when we were courting. I used to say, 'I'm not coming down to your house just to sit around like a stupid fool.' He always had these earphones on, messing with the wire, trying to get different stations. He'd be saying, 'I've got another one', but of course we could never hear it – you could never get those earphones off his head.[4]

Early radio meant something quite different for men and women. Sinclair Russell, writing in *The Broadcaster* in October 1922, took it for granted that women would not be interested in 'the mechanical side' of broadcasting 'for the natural indifference of the fair sex to any knowledge of what "makes the wheels go round" is inevitable'.[5] *Wireless Magazine* had a female columnist who wrote under the by-line, 'Wireless Femininities', which was illustrated with a picture of an earphoned lady of leisure sipping a cup of tea in an arm-chair. In February 1925 she discussed the different attitudes of the sexes to radio:

> To women wireless is a joy, a distraction, a companion, or an excitement; but it is never what it is to men – a toy.
> It seems to women that the last thing men want to do with their wireless set is listen in. They want to play with it and fiddle with it incessantly, just as they do with their cars ...
> One visitor always pulls out the set every time he comes and plays with the catswhisker, 'to see how it's working today'. But I've never known him listen in for five consecutive minutes – with the grand exception of last election night.
> My sympathies go out to a friend of mine who says she never hears any broadcasting because her husband is such an efficient wireless hobbyist. 'Which means that whenever there's grand opera, which I adore,' she sighs, 'he's taking down the old set, or putting up a new one, or sitting in front of it twiddling buttons and things to make it work better for listening in. Listening in!'[6]

For him wireless was a new craze, a scientific toy; for her it was a mysterious gadget and an imposed silence. Throughout the twenties radio was predominantly a hobby (or an obsession) indulged in by some male member of the household who was more concerned with tinkering with the equipment itself and with picking up a signal, any signal no matter what, rather than the pleasures of listening as such. Wireless was more a source of domestic strife than harmony.

A number of technical problems had to be overcome before listening to radio could become a simple, trouble-free social activity. Throughout the twenties radio receivers could, if not properly tuned in, create such severe interference in the immediate vicinity as to prevent other sets in the neighbourhood from producing anything other than a high-pitched whistling sound. The problem of 'oscillation' was a great social nuisance throughout the twenties.[7] Seventy-five per cent of all the correspondence received by the BBC from listeners before 1930 was on the subject, and Peter Eckersley wrote a pamphlet explaining its causes and admonishing listeners *not* to oscillate. But the problem was not overcome until the early thirties when it was eliminated by technical improvements in the design of radio sets. The growth of mains electricity increased the chances of interference from other domestic electrical appliances, and most electrical goods had to be fitted with suppressors. In 1932 60 per cent of complaints about reception problems received by the BBC concerned interference from urban tram services.

Not until the mid-thirties did the radio set become something that anyone could operate, offering good quality sound and interference-free reception. The first truly modern design was the celebrated Ekco set, produced by E. K.

Cole's company. It ran on mains electricity and its shell was made from moulded bakelite. It had two knobs for wavelengths and tuning, and one for volume. The frequencies of BBC and all major European stations were shown on the tuning dial. It created a sensation at Radiolympia, the annual trade fair, in 1934. A year later the Philips Company produced the Philco, billed as the People's Set. It cost just over five pounds and was designed to be within the purchase of any wage-earner. Its curved black bakelite case was reminiscent of the People's Car, the Volkswagen, which came into mass production in Germany at the same time.[8] The radio set had, for the first time, become a standardized, reasonably inexpensive, mass-produced commodity.

Marx thought of the commodity as a social hieroglyphic the true significance of which he decoded in terms of the hidden exploitative relations of its production. But the commodity, as a consumer good, also contains within itself its hidden relations of consumption. Consumer durables are, in Adrian Forty's phrase, objects of desire – the nature of the need or desire they are intended to satisfy is inscribed in their design.[9] The design of radio sets went quickly through three stages in the ten years that led up to the Ekco set. At first there was no attempt to encase the working parts of the equipment, whose delicate valves, diodes, capacitors and resistors were nakedly displayed to be twiddled and fiddled with by the amateur enthusiast. Competition in the industry in the early years focused on technical improvements in the reception and amplification of the signal. The buyer was assumed to be the male radio hobbyist.

By the late twenties the technical design of sets was becoming standardized. The moving coil loudspeaker first appeared in 1927 and soon replaced the moving magnet loudspeaker in all but the cheapest sets. By 1930 valve technology had developed to the point where two or three valves were all that were needed for the satisfactory amplification of the signal. The most significant improvement was the introduction of the exotically named 'supersonic heterodyne' which readjusted the incoming signal to a lower frequency for improved amplification and tuning.[10] These improvements made the working parts of the receiving apparatus smaller, more compact and portable. As manufacturers were less able to compete in terms of significant technical differences in their products, their attention turned to the hitherto neglected aspects of styling and design.

But how should the equipment be encased so as to make it attractive to purchasers? Such a question required thought about where the product would be placed and used, and its relationship with other objects in the environment. As early as May 1924, Reith, trying to encourage listeners actually to listen, had advised readers of *Radio Times* to avoid being over-preoccupied with the receiving equipment:

We say 'Come and listen to my wireless set', and we lead our friends into a room where there obtrude on the attention wires and valves and boxes and switches, and, to crown all, a horn. The attention is distracted by all this paraphernalia and by the tuning preliminaries which ensue. And then we all sit with our eyes glued to the loudspeaker and come to the conclusion that the sound is metallic and unsatisfying, and that we do not like our music tinned. Whereas, our minds are obsessed and distracted by the agency, and the music has not had a fair chance.

Tell your friends to 'Come and listen to the Unfinished Symphony', and let the music come on then mysteriously and spontaneously from behind some invisible source. Camouflage the loudspeaker, hide it behind a screen, in a cabinet, on the top of a bookcase – anywhere where people will not sit and stare at it.[11]

Most manufacturers, as they turned to housing the apparatus, followed Reith's thinking and tried to camouflage the radio set as a piece of domestic furniture. From the late twenties the radio industry began to encase its products in wooden cabinets which were, in most cases, designed by outside firms of cabinet-makers and made to look like other pieces of furniture. Taken to its limits this approach led some manufacturers to conceal their sets in other items of furniture – in an armchair, or art deco grandfather clock, for instance. This could lead to confusion, and stories circulated of the radio set being mistaken for the cocktail cabinet.[12]

The aim of such designs was unobtrusively to assimilate the radio set into the familiar environment of people's homes. But Adrian Forty argues that this approach 'did not fulfil the popular idea of radio as the symbol of future progress: it was supposed to represent everything that living rooms, and lives, lacked; sets that simply imitated what was already there could not fully satisfy people's expectation.'[13] One firm that broke from this design style was the Murphy company which manufactured good quality sets in the medium price range. The company approached Gordon Russell, one of the leading designers of modern furniture, who came up with a design for a wooden case that looked like, but was clearly distinct from, other pieces of contemporary furniture and was immediately recognizable for what it was. At the same time the Pye company produced a distinctively designed sunrise motif, reflecting the prevailing art deco style, for the loudspeaker grille of the wooden cabinets which housed their radio sets.

The third stage in the design of radio receivers was the production of a set that looked like nothing else in the room, that stood out as distinctively new. This was the intended effect of the revolutionary sets produced by the Ekco company from 1934 onwards. In that year Cole invited leading modern architects to submit designs in competition, and those of Serge Chermayeff and Wells Coates were chosen and put into production. The shell of both

designs was made of moulded bakelite, one of the earliest plastics manufactured by the petrochemical industries to replace traditional wood and metal
materials. The shape of both cases was impractical, if not impossible, to reproduce in wood. Thus shape and substance came together to connote the new.
Wells Coates' famous design, with its circular shape, its chromium-plated
grille, its prominent tuning dial and conspicuous knobs, proclaimed itself as an
unequivocally modern product, which bore no resemblance at all to furniture.
It set the standard that has been followed through to the present in the manufacture and design of radio and television sets as mediators of modernity.[14]

Radio sets were not cheap. The Pye 'Sunrise' model, one of the most
popular and attractive in the early thirties, cost between £15 and £30, and
Ekco sets were in the same price range. The Wells Coates set was significantly
cheaper at 10 guineas and the Philco People's set sold at 5 to 6 guineas – a
price that can be taken as standard for a reliable, inexpensive mains set at a
time when the average working wage was between £2 and £4 a week.[15]
Besides price, the other key factor in buying a set was whether the household
was wired for mains electricity. At the end of the First World War only 6 per
cent of houses were connected to an electricity supply.[16] In 1926 the Central
Electricty Board was set up to develop the national grid and, by 1939, two
households in three were connected to it. Such gross figures are misleading.
Illustrations of mains sets in the thirties tend as often to show them plugged
into the light socket as into the wall. Before 1930 the vast majority of
households were wired only for electric lighting. In the building boom of the
thirties it was standard to wire flats and houses for electricity but even then
the majority had no more than one 5 amp socket into which an electric iron
might be plugged. At most only a third of new houses had more than two electric sockets, and these houses were in the upper price bracket.[17]

Many working-class households purchased a battery-powered radio in the
thirties more from necessity than preference, for the heavy wet celled accumu-
lator which supplied the energy needed to be regularly recharged at the local
garage or radio shop. It was a hazard as well as a nuisance:

(1) I remember when I used to take those batteries to be recharged. I was only a
young girl. I used to take this glass-looking battery to the cycle shop. My
mother used to tell me to keep it away from my clothes, because there was acid
in them, and I used to walk up the street very gingerly with it.

(2) I remember once when a battery leaked. It was on the dresser and it leaked
all over the carpet and left a big white patch. My mother was furious.

(3) We used to have the radio on the sideboard in the living room – my mother
used to be going mad... In case it took the polish off the sideboard. My mother
didn't like it on there. She was always polishing and that. Well, your home was

your palace in them days. I don't think she was as interested in radio as my dad.[18]

In 1931 radio manufacturers began a campaign to get the public more 'mains-minded' and power units that plugged into the mains were produced to replace accumulators. By 1933 the sale of mains-powered sets was beginning to overtake the sale of battery-powered sets, but they did not finally disappear until after the Second World War when almost all houses were wired for mains electricity, voltages were standardized and the possibilities of domestic electrical appliances became practicable. Before the war the supply industry concentrated on overcoming problems of the high cost of electricity, difficulties in its distribution and customers' fear of it (a not uncommon attitude at the time) by promoting an image of electricity as uniquely modern and safe, as promising a bright, clean, efficient, cheerful, toil-free world.[19] The promise outpaced the reality. Electric domestic appliances were expensive and poorly designed. Electric cookers, fires and vacuum cleaners had tiny sales. The electric refrigerator and washing machine barely existed. The one electrical appliance to achieve huge mass sales before the war was the radio set, with nine million licences taken out in 1939. The only other items to come close to it were the electric iron, of which there were an estimated 6.5 million in use by the end of the thirties and, a long way behind that, the electric vacuum cleaner.

The social distribution of ownership of radios before the war is impossible to describe with precision.[20] What is certain is that three-quarters of British households had a radio by 1939, and the BBC's serivce reached into all sections of society. Three million households had a radio set in 1930. By 1939 this figure had tripled. Even in the severest years of the depression the continuing steep rise in the purchase of radio sets showed no sign of falling off. Only in the late thirties did the rate of increase flatten off to a plateau of nine million households with radio sets. By this time those without sets were either the very poor or those who lived out of range of satisfactory reception. 'Twenty million people are underfed', wrote George Orwell after his trek to Wigan Pier, 'but literally everyone in England has access to a radio. What we have lost in food we have gained in electricity.' Characteristically, he interpreted this development as a form of social control:

Whole sections of the working class who have been plundered of all they really need are being compensated, in part, by cheap luxuries which mitigate the surface of life... It is quite likely that fish-and-chips, art-silk stockings, tinned salmon, cut-price chocolate ... the movies, the radio, strong tea and the football pools have between them averted revolution.[21]

Other social investigators came to similar conclusions from different premises. At the end of the thirties the BBC's Board of Governors invited Hilda Jennings and Winifred Gill to conduct a small-scale investigation into the impact of radio on everyday life. They concentrated their efforts on a working-class district of Bristol, and their report argued strongly that radio had improved the attractiveness of home life for working-class families. Before the coming of radio:

> The street and public house offered the main scope for recreation outside the home. On Sunday afternoons and fine summer evenings the whole family would stand at the street door or sit on chairs on the pavement. When tension in a street ran high, quarrels easily arose and quickly spread. Witnesses told the survey worker that 'There was a row every night in some streets.' The rougher children 'ran the streets'. Rival street gangs raided each other or even pursued victims into their own homes.[22]

Seebohm Rowntree's social survey of working-class life in York, conducted at exactly the same time, made similar points. Rowntree listed radio as one of the 'undreamed of forms of recreation [which] science, industry and public enterprise have placed within the reach of the workers' and contrasted the wide range of leisure activities available at the end of the thirties with the limited resources of forty years earlier. In those days,

> A large proportion of young working people spent their evenings lounging about in the neighbourhood of their houses or promenading up and down certain streets in the city. The main street was so thronged with them that it was difficult to make one's way through it and a number of policemen were required to keep people moving and to prevent the horse-play between youths and girls from becoming too boisterous. Youths used to boast how many girls they had 'got off with' during the evening... Drunken men and women were constantly to be seen in the streets. On Saturday nights special policemen were drafted into the poorer districts of the city in order to deal with the fights and brawls which took place outside the public-houses at closing time.[23]

Both reports offered a cosy, contemporary domestic contrast, to which radio was a contributory factor, compared with a more brutalized street life before the advent of broadcasting.

As part of his survey Rowntree asked the members of a number of families to record what they usually did each day of the week in the summer and winter months. This is what some of them wrote:

1. MONDAY   6 am to 12 (noon) usual household duties. In the afternoon and evening read, knit, sew and listen to the wireless. (Machine-minder's wife, aged 40. No children).

2. SATURDAY   If not working, stay in bed until 10 am. Wash, shave, have dinner, attend a football match. After tea, listen in to 'In Town Tonight', Music Hall, News, Dance Music. (Factory worker, aged 45. Four grown-up children.)

3. WEDNESDAY   A friend and his wife come down to spend the evening with us, and we play cards and dominoes. If there is a variety or dance band on the wireless we turn it on. Spend 1s. for sweets and 1s. for cigarettes. (Labourer, aged 38. One young son.)

4. SUNDAY   No one in the house gets up before 10 am. The wife immediately starts getting the dinner ready and we both have a cup of tea. After dinner we both laze about, either reading or sleeping. Sunday is the worst day in the week, absolutely dead. After tea we roll up the carpet, find a foreign station on the wireless giving a dance band, and we dance most of the evening, sometimes playing cards for an hour before going to bed. Spend about 1s. on sweets and 1s. on cigarettes. (as 3.)[24]

Summing up the general impression of radio gained from his inquiries, Rowntree observed that again and again the wireless was seen as a companionable thing: ' "It is a good companion." It is used "to keep the family company." "Wireless is a companion to anyone alone in a room with some hand occupation, e.g. knitting or sewing." "It is used to take the boredom off work".'[25] Jennings and Gill noted that many of the people they interviewed remarked how often they heard friends or neighbours say: ' "Well, I want to be home by nine. There's a good programme on," or, speaking of their own habits: – "We don't bother to go out on a Saturday night when the winter programmes begin. We just settle down by the fire".'[26]

'A lot of people were right homebirds in them days,' an elderly woman told Shaun Moores. 'A lot of people were quite content to sit in. In fact, my father had beer in at the weekend rather than going to the pub.'[27] If people now tended to stay in more and go to the pub less radio provided new topical and social resources. Formerly, Jennings and Gill suggested, the interests and experiences of family members was limited to the doings and illnesses of neighbours, weddings, births and funerals in the district and commotions in the street. These, along with the ups and downs of family life, provided the main topics of conversation. But now,

Broadcasting has supplied not only a new way of spending leisure by family 'listening-in', but a vastly wider range of conversation. This was agreed on all sides. One listener gives a picture of his home. 'You get the family sat in the house of a night and there's a talk on the wireless. Someone doesn't agree and pulls it to pieces. Then they all has a go and gets outside of it [sic]. I've known them argue for hours.'[28]

Orwell's catalogue of 'cheap luxuries' which mitigated the surface of life were the precise cultural indicators of a class that had, on the whole and for the first time in its history, risen above the realm of necessity. The possession of a radio set pointed to a marginal surplus of disposable income and time for its purchase and enjoyment as an affordable pleasure. The spread of radio throughout the whole of Britain in the pre-war period to the point of ubiquity indicated that its ownership could not be thought of as a social luxury, but as a social necessity that catered for quite new kinds of needs.

Raymond Williams has coined the phrase 'mobile privatization' to describe two apparently paradoxical yet deeply connected tendencies in modern life: on the one hand, increasing mobility: on the other, a growing emphasis on the pleasure of privacy and self-sufficiency in the small family home.[29] The phenomenon of 'suburbia' embodied this process. The growth of the suburbs was one of the most distinctive features of the inter-war period. Between the wars over four million houses were built. The boom came in the thirties when three million houses, mainly for private sale, were constructed.[30] This enormous demand can be understood in relation to what has been called 'the basic demographic development of the twentieth century', namely the adoption of a pattern of small families by all social classes – a trend with profound implications for living standards, the status of women and children, and attitudes towards home and family.[31]

For the first time in two centuries the overall rate of population growth declined in the inter-war period. Within that there was a shift in population growth from the old industrial areas to the rapidly developing new industrial zones in the Midlands and South-East which absorbed 60 per cent of the total population growth between the wars. Greater London grew from 7.5 to 8.5 million in this period.[32] But in the same period an increase in the marriage rate coupled with a reduction in family size led to a rise in the number of households at a faster rate than the increase in population. The total number of families in England and Wales rose from 8 million in 1911 to 10 million in 1931, an increase of 25 per cent, while the total population rose only by 11 per cent.[33] It was this discrepancy that fuelled the pressure and demand in the housing market.

Smaller families meant that income had to be spent on fewer people, and that proportionately less of it went on basic necessities such as food. There was an opportunity to make savings and to spend the small surplus income on consumer goods and semi-luxuries.[34] As family size declined birth tended to be concentrated in the early years of married life so that, in principle, married women had greater freedom to take up work outside the home. As married couples could now look forward to a longer period of living together without young children to care for and fewer of them, one consequence was the domestication of men and their greater involvement in housework, home improvement and shopping.[35] Leisure activities were increasingly shared – cinema-going, the day trip, a night out at the pub. The cinemas of the period were designed as pleasure palaces for both sexes and public houses built in the 1930s with lounge bars and modern toilets were aimed not only at men, but their wives and girlfriends. Another consequence of fewer children was a more comfortable house, in which people were becoming home-centred and 'privatized'. Though these trends were in motion well before the inter-war period, they became achievable realities for millions in this period. The clearest sign of this process was in the newly growing culture of suburbia: in the sectors of the working class relocated in newly built council estates on the outskirts of towns; in the private housing that stretched out along, and branched off from, the arterial roads leading into the towns and cities of southern and central England.

Urbane, metropolitan culture has always been hostile to suburban culture and its style – 'by-pass variegated', as Osbert Lancaster called it. In *Vile Bodies* Waugh offered glimpses of it in contrast with the frenetic lifestyle of the Bright Young Things. Travelling by train, the hero, Adam, overhears some members of the Ladies' Conservative Association at Chesham Bois planning to complain to their MP about the scandalous midnight party at 10 Downing Street reported in the day's popular press – a party from which Adam is recovering. Adam's fiancée, Nina, joyriding in a light aeroplane is afforded a more distant prospect of suburbia:

> Nina looked down and saw inclined at an odd angle a horizon of straggling red suburb; arterial roads dotted with little cars; factories some of them working, others empty and decaying; a disused canal; some distant hills sown with bungalows; wireless masts and overhead power cables; men and women were indiscernible except as tiny spots; they were marrying and shopping and making money and having children. The scene lurched and tilted again as the aeroplane struck a current of air.
> 'I think I am going to be sick,' said Nina.[36]

Elsewhere, contemporary attitudes readjusted to this new phenomenon. *Punch* had always tended to portray the lifestyle of the upper sectors of the bourgeoisie. Before the First World War its cartoons had poked fun at the pretentiousness of middle-class manners; the social-climbing hostess was a frequent target. Their 'middling' position was enhanced by the juxtaposition of these cartoons with others illustrating the low life of the streets and the easy sophistication of 'society'. But by the late twenties *Punch* was depicting an almost exclusively middle-and lower-middle-class world of servant problems and car crashes, golf and bridge and cutely precocious children, whose inhabitants tended more and more to a semidetached existence.

Suburbia was becoming an emblem of the normal, workaday world, though with different connotations for different writers. For Graham Greene it was noisy and dishonest: witness the appalling road-house, dominated by a loud and bogus major, in *The Confidential Agent*. It was an object of interest to those two intrepid explorers of contemporary Britain, Priestley and Orwell. For Priestley, with his comfortable middle-brow view of the world, suburbia was the place in which the Everyman of the twentieth century exhibited his basic humanity. For Orwell, with his acutely sensitive nose for the nuances of class difference, it was the breeding ground of something that had never before existed in Britain: people of indeterminate social class:

> In 1910 every human being in these islands could be 'placed' in an instant by his clothes, manners and accent. This is no longer the case. Above all it is no longer the case in the new townships that have developed as a result of cheap motor cars and the southward shift of industry. The place to look for the germs of the future England is in the light-industry areas and along the arterial roads. In Slough, Dagenham, Barnet, Letchworth, Hayes – everywhere, indeed, on the outskirts of great towns – the old pattern is gradually changing into something new. In those vast wildernesses of glass and brick the sharp distinctions of the older kind of town, with its slums and mansions, or of the country, with its manor houses and squalid cottages, no longer exist. There are wide gradations of income, but it is the same kind of life that is being lived at different levels, in labour-saving flats or council houses, along the concrete roads and in the naked democracy of the swimming pools. It is a rather restless, cultureless life, centring round tinned food, *Picture Post*, the radio and the internal combustion engine.[37]

Radio was not merely a taken-for-granted element in this new way of life; it embodied it. This was the riddle of its commodity form. The cheap radio receiver was, as Williams puts it, 'a significant index of a general condition and response'[38] embodied in the mobile privatization of suburban living. We have had glimpses, in the preceding accounts, of other ways of life: of the culture of poverty, for instance, described for an audience that lived elsewhere, in talks series on the slums and unemployment. Urbane, metropolitan culture was routinely tapped through the late night music of the smart dance bands in Mayfair hotels, and caught occasionally in the sophisticated revues of the Maschwitz era of light entertainment. But neither of these were the heartland of the vast radio audience of the thirties. Radio, as part of the emerging mod-

Wife (*reading extract*) " 'THEN ON THROUGH ONE OF THOSE DREARY SUBURBS WITH EACH DOLEFUL LITTLE HOUSE AS DEPRESSING AS ITS OWNER.' "

Unshaken Householder. "PSHAW! IT'S EVIDENT SHE KNOWS NOTHING OF THE BALMORAL ESTATE."

ern way of life – mobile, family-centred, suburban, classless – was deeply implicated in its normalization, but it had first to discover how it was part of that new way of living. That, above all, meant understanding and accommodating to the conditions of listening.

From the beginning the broadcasters knew that they must try to make programmes that fitted into that context. *Broadcasting from Within*, by C. A. Lewis in 1924, was the first account by a programme-maker about programme-making and the problems they faced:

> Broadcasting is entertainment in the home. This in itself is a new field which has only hitherto been trodden by the player piano and gramophone. Home conditions are different from any other. Public entertainment takes place when people are gathered together for the express purpose of seeing or hearing a certain thing. They are in a mood to enjoy what they receive. They go there with that end in view. But the ghostliest of ghost stories told in the studio with the lights out does not thrill the listener whose baby is yelling under the table. It is nothing to create a studio atmosphere. The programme has to get into the home atmosphere.[39]

There were articles in *Radio Times* in those years which argued that radio might counter all the modern attractions offered by agencies outside the home and which threatened to undermine it. The listening habit could restore a more rational use of leisure time and 'reinstate the old love of home and family which has been such a bulwark against aggression of all kinds for the British people.'[40] The ideology of Home, Hearth and Happiness was annually invoked each Yuletide which was, from the very first broadcast Christmas, celebrated as a family festival. But although the broadcasters pragmatically recognized that they addressed a home-based audience, they had not yet begun to produce a home-centred culture of radio. Radio, in its first few years, was treated as part of a network of local, neighbourhood activities, with a wider social context and range than the home itself.

The way in which it was used as a noticeboard to announce forthcoming jubilees, fêtes and bazaars; amateur dramatic and musical performances; the meetings and reunions of all kinds of societies, associations and institutions, points up radio's involvement in the support of a wide and varied range of activities outside the home. Even during the General Strike such standing arrangements were routinely given out from London for the whole country. Thus the seven o'clock bulletin on 18 May 1926 ended with the announcement of the following functions as still on: The Sixteenth Annual May Lecture of the Institute of Metals, two performances of *The Human Touch* at King George's Hall, the Annual Conference of the National Association of Head Teachers, the Services and Meetings in celebration of the 67th Anniversary of the Universities' Mission to Central Africa, the examinations of the College of Violinists, the sixth Montgomery County Musical Festival, the Ramsey Hunt Hospital Carnival in aid of the Peterborough and District War Memorial Hospital and the May Meetings of the London District Council of the Spiritualist Union. The Dinner of the National Federation of Iron and Steel Manufacturers, the Dunmow Flitch and the 1250th Anniversary Celebrations of the See of Hereford were all, for the moment, postponed.[41]

The transition from Company to Corporation marks the point at which broadcasting became self-conscious, and a set of institutional relations replaced the initial interpersonal relations of the local stations. A new model listener was required to take full advantage of what radio now offered. The whole concept of a national system of public service broadcasting, with its central commitment to raising the general level of knowledge and taste, rested upon a set of expectations invested by the BBC in 'the great audience'. Listeners must help to make the ideal work by attentive listening, by a careful selection from the goods on offer: 'On the other side of the microphone the listener must recognize that a definite obligation rests on him to chose intelligently from the programmes offered to him.' The listener must *listen*: 'If you only listen with half an ear, you haven't a quarter of a right to criticize.' Leaving the radio on all the time, as background noise was frowned upon. 'Think of your favourite occupation. Don't you like a change sometimes? Give the wireless a rest sometimes.'[42]

The policy of mixed programming on a single channel presupposed that listeners would select from the varied bill of fare on offer. 'The broadcast programmes are, in this respect, very like the British Museum or the National Gallery or a great library,' Filson Young suggested. 'No one who uses a library would dream of beginning on the first shelf and going steadily through in the order of shelves in the cases.'[43] The important thing was 'constructive listening'. Some might think, it was conceded in *The Listener*, that the notion of constructive listening 'had a slightly forbidding ring, that it seemed to demand too much of the innocent licence-holder'.[44] But listeners were advised to be constructive because they were, in a sense, their own programme-builders. They were expected to look at the week's broadcasts as a whole and make a definite choice of the items most likely to please them, instead of just turning on the wireless in an idle hour and finding perhaps that neither National nor Regional could satisfy their tastes.

Listening was now a serious business: 'The remoteness of broadcasting and the fact that it appeals to one sense alone, imply a considerable effort on the part of its audience to establish a rapt connection with the programme.'[45] When a newspaper poll in 1931 revealed that radio drama was the least popular category of programme, *Radio Times* reported the following response from Val Gielgud:

He impenitently admits that until the habit of listening with concentration becomes more general than it is at present, the audience for plays is bound to continue a small one. Radio drama, by its demand upon the listener's imagination, implies a concentrated degree of listening which is as yet confined to an enthusiastic minority. As soon as the wireless play is generally regarded not as a substitute for the stage or screen play, but as a distinct form of art demanding a distinct form of approach on the part of the listener, the audience for drama will be as large as it is now faithful and enthusiastic.[46]

Advice was at hand on how to acquire the habit of concentrated listening. 'Make sure your set is working properly *before* you settle down to listen. Listen as carefully at home as you do in a theatre or concert hall. You can't get the best out of a programme if your mind is wandering, or if you are playing bridge or reading. Give it your full attention. Try turning out the lights so that your eye is not caught by familiar objects in the room. Your imagination will be twice as vivid.'[47] Listeners should prepare themselves for listening to a radio play by being in their favourite armchair five minutes before the start of the programme as they would at the theatre. And how should one listen to chamber music?

By imagining oneself present in the room with the few performers, as if overhearing friends playing music together. Try to be quiet and attentive all the time, and do not listen with just 'half an ear', as one may perhaps to a music-hall song or a dance band. Listen to the twining together of the strands of music – how one friend plays a tune, which is taken up by his fellow, and then by another, and so on until they have all had it in turn; how it is tossed from one to another like a ball, to be flung and caught again and again; how the lines now run apart, now converge, and scatter harmoniously like the ribands on a maypole. Imagine at the end, as the last chord fades away the players nodding to each other with a smile as if to say, 'Jolly good fun, that!' or 'That goes better every time!'[48]

Programme-building, in the early thirties, was designed to encourage attentive listening and to discourage the lazy listener. There was no standard length for programmes, no fixed times for them nor continuity between them in the schedules. Each announcer seemed concerned only with the one programme item that he announced, wrote Maurice Gorham, and innocent of any knowledge of what had gone before or what was to come.[49] There was no announcer's chat, previews of what was to come later, to maintain a smooth flow from one item to the next. Instead the spaces between programmes were deliberately left as little oases of silence broken only by the tick of a studio clock to reassure listeners that their sets had not broken down. The gaps between programmes were partly to allow for overruns (a recurring problem with all outside broadcast relays of music and variety), but more particularly they were intended to let people switch off rather than stay on, or to let them recompose themselves after a particularly stirring drama or concert. 'If a tragic or pathetic play ends at one minute to nine, the listener who has been gripped by it does not want to hear an unemotional voice reading the Weather Forecast at nine o'clock!'[50] Listeners were exhorted by Filson Young to make good use of the breaks between programmes: 'Silence would be wasted if it merely represented a blank, and something negative. It is a positive thing in itself; it is a definite opportunity to sit without the distraction of voice and sound, and think the thoughts that are within oneself – it may be the concert that is coming, or something quite different. For it would certainly be a poor way of spending an evening to think only the thoughts that are supplied by other people or suggested by what they were doing.'[51]

The concept of programme-building in the early thirties was remote from the present-day art of scheduling designed to capture and keep large television audiences during peak viewing hours. The idea then was to cater for all tastes, minority and majority, *over a period of time* – a month was the period sometimes quoted. The balance was not maintained in the daily or weekly bill of fare. One need not expect to find variety or light entertainment in supply every night of the week. Fixed scheduling was, with the exception of the nightly news bulletins, deliberately shunned. It was not easy to keep track of a talks series, for instance, when its time and place varied quite markedly; perhaps Tuesday at 8.35 this week and next week Thursday at 7.20. Through such means the BBC aimed to keep its audience on its toes, to stop it falling into idle habits and taking the output on offer for granted. If you wanted to keep track of what was on, you needed *Radio Times* to plan your listening in advance.

Underlying all this was a fear of standardization: standardized programming made standardized minds. 'It is something to bear in mind', a *Radio Times* editorial in 1931 declared,

> when we feel adversely critical towards programmes: were they not designed, we might pause and ask ourselves, as part of a scheme aimed to please each of us at some time or another, aimed, in fact, to allow us as listeners to retain our separate entities as thinking men and women? A people's strength lies ultimately in its individuality. Individuality is the expression of spirit, and spirit lives in each of us separately – not as a crowd. Nothing must be allowed to swamp that individuality.[52]

The greatest threat to that precious individuality posed by broadcasting was its power to standardize the minds of millions, and the editorial pointed its finger at the United States by way of illustration: 'A grotesque idea of the possibilities in this direction is provided by the mental picture of America leaping out of bed at a signal from the wireless and solemnly going through its morning exercises at the command of a voice from the air.'[53] The BBC's flexible programme arrangements, with its small number of fixed points, was explicitly contrasted with the rigidity of American programming, in which precisely the same artists appeared at precisely the same time in programmes advertising precisely the same products. Cultural critics of television in the early sixties took it to task for adjusting to rather than enriching everyday life: 'It takes the flow of time for granted and is received by audiences who are not attending particularly to particular moments of communication. Continuity thus serves to compound the trivialising tendencies of the universality of the media... Time, which could have been forcibly punctuated by broadcasting, has instead been patterned to a rhythm of acceptability.'[54] It was precisely those kinds of objections that programme-building in the early thirties was intended to forestall.

In the era of uplift BBC officials suppressed the social characteristics of their medium and its communicative context. Early radio had accepted the idea of entertainment in the home and the need to get into the home atmosphere. That was now overlooked, and radio was thought of as an *occasional* resource, like the theatre, cinema or concert hall. Listeners were expected to behave in the same way as they did in such contexts; to be silent, to pay attention, to invest the event with a sense of occasion. But it is unlikely that any large part of audience behaved itself as ideally it was supposed to. Radio and television have no sense of occasion, of a time and place set apart from ordinary life and affairs. Most people most of the time, irrespective of class, gender or education, treated the wireless as no more than a domestic utility for relaxation and entertainment – a convenience, a commodity, a cheerful noise in the background – which occasionally in moments of national crisis, mourning, celebration or sport became compulsive listening for the whole population. This account, from a survey of listening in South Wales in the late thirties, capture the realities of family listening:

Seven Toscanini concerts will during the month of May be thankfully received by many homes in this area. There will be homes where he will be treated respectfully by people of a minority which is growing. But in most of our homes he will have to 'rough it', and take his chance in the hurly-burly with Music Halls, Sing-Songs, Serials – and all the fun o' the fair. As he conducts women will knit or sew whilst waiting patiently for something they would much prefer, but can't get because the most musically minded son of the house insists on having what his father says is 'nothing more than a row'. The concert is interrupted by the coming and going in the room of other members of the family, each of whom asks: 'What's the row now?' Father growls 'ask me another' and the solitary listener groans inwardly. Neighbours call, enter the room and, not knowing Toscanini, state and discuss their business without lowering their voices.[55]

One can just imagine the response of such families to the BBC's advice on how to listen to chamber music.

From the mid-thirties onwards there was a renewed emphasis on the domestic context in which listening took place. But where previously listeners were thought of as caught up in a network of local activities and associations of which radio was a part, what was now stressed were the pleasures of privacy. A special Fireside Number of *Radio Times* in November 1935 affirmed the home as a retreat burrowed deeply away from the pressures of work and urban life:

> To come home from work on a November evening through the wet confusion of the city, the humid press of bus or tram, the rain-dimmed streets that lead to the lights of your own home; to close the door behind you, with the curtains drawn against the rain, and the fire glowing in the hearth – that is one of the real pleasures of life. And it is when you are settled by your own fireside that you most appreciate the entertainment that broadcasting can bring.[56]

The tired businessman or weary office worker were models frequently invoked to typify the ordinary listener for whom relaxation in the comfort of their own home after a hard day's work was a well-earned right. A Listeners' Own Number of *Radio Times* in April 1938 imagined the radio audience as Mr and Mrs Listener with their four children and Fido the dog, who also listens. 'All the family have different tastes, so too that vastly greater family of listeners whom they symbolize.'[57] Later in the same year a Home Number of *Radio Times* asked readers to try to imagine what it would have been like 'if radio had not been simple enough and cheap enough to use at home – if we had to do our listening in a crowd, as we go to the theatre and cinema. Broadcasting would have become a mass entertainment as the theatre and cinema are. It might have been grander, more imposing, more sophisticated, but would it have been so intimate, so friendly?'[58] The front cover of the issue had a cartoon of an ivy-clad Broadcasting House as a suburban cottage, complete with garden washing line and commuter husband with briefcase returning home to his wife who stands ready to greet him at the creeper-entwined porch. 'Broadcasting House', the editorial declared, doesn't really look so homely, but it might well do. When all is said and done, broadcasting, with all its elaborate mechanisms, is based on and aimed at, the home.' Radio, as Simon Frith has argued, was beginning to play a significant role in the organization of work and leisure.[59]

We have seen that, in the later thirties, greater care was taken to organize daily output on more routine, regular lines. Popular programmes were increasingly given fixed time slots. *Monday Night at Seven*, as its name implied, was an early and successful attempt to produce a fireside show that recurred at a known time and could be pleasurably anticipated as a predictable enjoyment in the week. The Programme Planning Department was beginning to adjust daily output to chime in with the time routines of day-to-day life through the weekend and the working week. In this they were immeasurably helped by the establishment of Listener Research and the information it began to supply, from 1936 onwards, about listening habits and tastes.

The fact that Listener Research was not established until 1936 is sometimes pointed to as proof of how little interest the BBC took in its audience before the war. But Mark Pegg is right to point out that the BBC was not alone in lacking detailed information about the habits and tastes of the population.[60] Apart from census returns there was a serious lack of detailed data from official sources or from academic or commercial institutions. The bulk of the information produced about social conditions between the wars came from unofficial sources and from privately-funded research. When the BBC began systematic research into the audience it was a pioneer in the emerging field of opinion sampling and market research. A crucial move in this direction was the appointment of Sir Stephen Tallents to the newly-created post of Controller (Public Relations) in the summer of 1935.

Tallents came from the Empire Marketing Board, where he had sponsored John Grierson and the use of documentary film to promote its activities, and the Post Office where he had been in charge of Public Relations. He was a leader in the field of corporate image management, and it was for this that he was recruited by Reith in 1935 at a time when the Corporation's public image was sagging badly. Press comments on his appointment linked it to the need for listener research, and the *Manchester Guardian* commented that 'he will aim at bringing the public and the broadcasting authorities into closer touch. He will ask the listener what he wants and reflect his views'.[61] Tallents immediately began to draw up plans for listener research which he described in a letter to his son:

> We want to know more than we do about the habits and tastes of listeners in different parts of the country and at different times of the year ... As to people's habits, there is a lot of information to be got indirectly from indirect sources such as gas and electric light companies – and even water companies, for the water engineer at Portsmouth has just sent us a graph showing how everyone ceased to use water for cooking, washing etc while the broadcast of the King's Funeral was on.'[62]

It needed more patient diplomacy within the BBC to persuade senior personnel of the necessity for audience research and some remained unconvinced.

But Reith, though apprehensive lest quantative research findings should unduly influence the quality of programmes and programming, was won over, and in 1936 Robert Silvey was appointed to prepare a programme of research into the habits and tastes of the audiences for radio. Information about habits was needed in order to have reliable data about who was (and who was not) available for listening, where and when. The first two inquiries that Silvey organized looked into 'Winter Listening Habits' and 'Summer Listening Habits'. In each case the intention was to discover the times that listeners, in summer and winter, turned on their radio sets and when they turned them off through each day of the week. Listening levels at half-hourly intervals through the day were examined and, in the summertime survey, there was a separate questionnaire to survey audience tastes across the range of programme output.[63]

These two inquiries were the first to employ random sampling techniques. Three thousand households were chosen at random from GPO licensing files covering all the BBC Regions. Opponents of listener research in the BBC had argued that each listener was an individual about whom one could not generalize, but such arguments were undermined by the data. A profile of listening habits for men and women, young and old, of different social classes, in different parts of the country and in urban and rural environments, on different days of the week at different times of the year began to emerge. There were hardly any regional differences in taste for programmes and very few differences between men and women. While there were social differences (e.g. a higher proportion of middle-class than of working-class listeners liked listening to Shakespeare, and a higher proportion of working-class than middle-class listeners wanted more Variety programmes) these differences were outweighed by the general trend of responses. The proportion of middle-class listeners who wanted more Variety (65 per cent) was greater than those who liked listening to Shakespeare (56 per cent). There were significant differences in Sunday listening habits: 47 per cent of working-class and 28 per cent of middle-class listeners tuned in to Radios Luxembourg and Normandie.

If much of the data seemed to confirm what common sense might have predicted, that does not undercut its importance. It enabled the structural framework of broadcasting – the arrangement of programme output through the days of the week, through the seasons of the year – to be arranged on a rational basis. Programme schedules could now be more confidently planned in relation to reliable information about who was available for listening, where and when. The value of data about listening habits is cumulative. As such surveys are made regularly through the years a pattern begins to emerge of the long-term continuities and changes in the daily routines of the populations of modern societies.

376

The other major kind of information that Listener Research began to provide was about audience tastes.[64] The most familiar form of such research is in terms of ratings – the proportion of listeners or viewers who hear or watch a particular programme or channel. The earliest research into audience preferences provided data of a different kind. It was designed to measure not the size of audiences for particular programmes, but the relative sizes of audiences for different kinds of output within the work of a particular department. The department that received most attention from Silvey's unit in the three years before the war was Variety. A special survey of the audience for variety in 1937 was launched with an appeal for volunteers to take part in the project given out by John Watt, Head of Variety, after a Saturday night broadcast of *Music Hall*: 47,000 replies were received in response to Watt's broadcast and appeals in *Radio Times* and *The Listener*. Over a three-month period, from October to December, 2000 selected volunteers were asked to complete weekly listening logs provided by Listener Research, supplemented with extra questionnaires to elicit opinions on the output of the Variety Department. A second survey, in mid 1938, took a random sample of listeners who were asked to state their preferences for various types of variety programmes. Finally, a third survey over a four-month period between December 1938 and March 1939 asked volunteers to comment on programmes of all kinds, including variety.

We have briefly noted the main findings of this research and its impact on the activities of the Variety Department and on programme planning. Here we wish to consider the more general implications of the data in relation to serialization of programmes. Seriality is perhaps the most important specific characteristic of broadcast output, and its implications to this day are widely misunderstood. Series and serial production is the most efficient, cost-effective way of meeting the enormous demands of continuous output. It allows for difference in content – daily or weekly – within a standardized, indefinitely reproducible programme format and is used across the whole range of output. Today's radio and television news, current affairs programmes, sports magazine programmes, soap operas, drama series, situation comedies, chat shows and discussion programmes all employ a standard template from which to produce a varying content within a fixed overall structure.

Seriality is closely linked to programme continuity and regularity in scheduling. A special study of *Monday Night at Seven* began to reveal their interlocking implications. First, it established that the appeal of such shows (confirmed in relation to *Band Waggon*) accumulated over time. In the first five weeks of the series the audience rose from 67 to 70 per cent, and by the eleventh week had reached a steady 77 per cent. *Monday Night at Seven* was immediately followed by *The Plums* and, while the average audience for this show was 66 per cent, Listener Research noted that 'the audience curves' for both programmes moved in sympathy to a remarkable extent. Thus producers discovered the importance of what was later known as 'the inheritance effect' and the general advantages of continuity and regularity in scheduling.[65] Indeed there was evidence that a popular show like *Monday Night at Seven* could alter the normal pattern of weekday listening. The average size of the Monday evening audience (55 per cent) was significantly higher than on any other day bar Saturday (70 per cent). It is difficult to be certain whether Saturday night was simply a more popular time for listening than other evenings, or whether it was made so by the transmission of the BBC's most successful entertainment programmes. But Listener Research attributed the higher audience figures for Monday evenings to *Monday Night At Seven* and concluded from this that the potential audience for listening on other weekday evenings was considerably greater than the current figures, and might be boosted by strategically placed popular shows. This received some confirmation when, on one occasion, *Palace of Varieties* was broadcast on a Tuesday rather than, as usual, on Saturday. In spite of the change, the size of its audience remained the same. By 1939 *Band Waggon* on Wednesdays was drawing a larger audience than *Music Hall* on Saturdays.[66]

In 1939 participants in the General Listening Barometer were asked to complete a questionnaire which solicited their views on the increasing use of serial formats not only in entertainment programmes but in drama and in talk. In the previous year Val Gielgud's Drama Department had ventured into serialized productions with a twelve-part version of *The Three Musketeers.* It was an immediate success, and the forerunner of an endless supply of dramatizations in weekly parts of the popular classics of English and European literature. In the same year the first drama thriller specially written for radio, *Send For Paul Temple* by Francis Durbridge, was produced by Midland Region and transmitted on the National Programme. It too was an instant hit, and Paul Temple along with Dick Barton were famous radio names in the forties and fifties. Though Talks had always gone in for serialized productions of a kind in its six- or twelve-part symposiums on particular topics, these had never been given fixed time slots in the schedules. But it had begun to experiment with the regular magazine format discovered by Variety's *In Town Tonight*, with *The World Goes By* compered by Freddy Grisewood. Listeners were now asked whether the policy of serial production was (a) a change for the better, (b) should be carried further, or (c) was being overdone. Ninety-one per cent favoured the change, 63 per cent wanted more of it, and 85 per cent assured Listener Research that the BBC was not over-egging the pudding.[67]

Programme planners tended to interpret the findings as a sign of listeners' preference for series of all kinds and producers in every department were encouraged to arrange their programmes in series, even if that meant simply broadcasting the same type of programme – a symphony concert, say – at a regular weekly time. Repetition alone however was no guarantee of success. There was more to it than the same thing at the same time on a regular basis. Some kinds of entertainment, concert party for instance, had been presented in weekly showcases since the early thirties but without ever acquiring huge audiences. The General Listening Barometer in 1939 showed that light music features such as *The Pig And Whistle* or miscellanies like *Lucky Dip* had relatively small audiences compared with the most popular series whose success was due to a number of related characteristics.[68] Slickness and continuity in presentation and the use of the same compères, presenters and entertainers were combined, in the best pre-war entertainment, with the creation of a basic format that allowed the development of a shared set of references and associations that grew from week to week.

The appeal of such shows cannot be attributed to the appeal of the predictable and the familiar to a lazy and undiscriminating audience. Rather they were predicated on active audience involvement and interaction with pleasures that accumulated and deepened the more you listened. Listener Research suggested that even with so-called background listening – light music and dance music – audiences listened with more discrimination than had been hitherto assumed. It was conventional wisdom in the BBC that when people were not listening attentively they would scarcely discriminate between one kind of undemanding music and another. But a survey in 1939 discovered a strong liking for melodic, properly orchestrated arrangements over run-of-the-mill dance music, and a general preference for compères and thematically arranged material over straight performances by individual bands or orchestras. *Dancing Through* with Geraldo and his orchestra (63 per cent) was preferred above *Music From the Movies* (54 per cent), which scored higher than *The Signature Tune Is* (46 per cent) which simply featured different well-known bands. Listener Research concluded that 'though the listening we are dealing with here may be "background" listening, it is certainly not "tap" listening. There is plenty of evidence of the exercise by listeners of active discrimination in the choice of "background" programmes, particularly in the evenings.'[69]

Before the war the attitude of the production departments to Listener Research varied greatly. It was strongly supported by Drama and Variety, and by 1938 John Watt was making extensive use of its findings to plan the winter programme of entertainment. Talks took a long spoon to sup with it, while the Music Department loathed the increasing reliance on its data by the Programme Planning Department. For the planners Listener Research very quickly became an essential aid in organizing output although, as we have seen, there were severe constraints on the extent to which they could readjust the balance of output from the production departments in the light of what they now knew about audience habits and tastes. But if, overall, its initial impact was restricted, it was the long-term commitment to audience research systematically and routinely that was important. It was the clearest acknowledgment of the necessity of basing the activities of broadcasting on real knowledge and understanding of their audiences, not on what the broadcasters thought they might want or need. When the Second World War made attention to those needs and wants an urgent imperative, the findings of Listener Research were an indispensable tool in the BBC's wartime task of maintaining the nation's morale.

Notes

———⊛———

PREFACE

1 A full history of the BBC may be found in the four volumes (to date) by Asa Briggs. This huge pioneering study covers all aspects of the institutional development of broadcasting and is the indispensable, authoritative source for any historical study of the subject. Our history could not have been written without the prior existence of Briggs' accounts which relieve us, in countless instances, from having to describe and contextualize the larger institutional framework within which our study of programme policy and production is situated. See Asa Briggs, *The History of Broadcasting in the United Kingdom*, volume 1, *The Birth of Broadcasting*; volume 2, *The Golden Age of Wireless*; volume 3, *The War of Words*; volume 4, *Sound and Vision* (Oxford University Press, Oxford, 1960, 1965, 1970, 1979).
2 On engineering, see E. Pawley, *BBC Engineering, 1922–1972* (BBC, London, 1972).
3 See Gerard Mansell, *Let Truth be Told. Fifty Years of BBC External Broadcasting* (Weidenfeld & Nicolson, London, 1982).
4 On religion, see Kenneth Wolfe, *The Churches and the British Broadcasting Corporation, 1922–1966* (SCM Press, London, 1984). Many of the themes in our book – on the politics of the production of information, entertainment and culture – are paralleled in Wolfe's study of 'the politics of broadcast religion', the subtitle of his book. On education, see John Robinson, *Learning Over the Air* (BBC, London, 1982).
5 On the development of television in the pre-war period, see Briggs, *The Golden Age of Wireless*, pp. 517–622.
6 For a sociological account of the management structure of the BBC and staff relations, see Tom Burns, *The BBC, Public Institution, Private World* (Macmillan, London, 1977). Although concerned with the BBC in the sixties and seventies, Burns is concerned to link the organization of the BBC at that time with its establishment under Reith in the pre-war period.

7   There is a considerable body of literature on radio drama (almost wholly treating it as a singular, authored product to the exclusion of serials and serialized plays). See Val Gielgud, *British Radio Drama, 1922–1956* (London, 1956). John Drakakis (ed.), *British Radio Drama* (Cambridge University Press, Cambridge, 1981). Ian Rodger, *Radio Drama* (Macmillan, London, 1982).

8   For an historical account of the treatment of health and medicine on radio and television, see Anne Karpf, *Doctoring the Media* (Routledge, London, 1988).

CHAPTER 1   *Public service broadcasting*

1   Cf. Kevin Wilson, *Technologies of Control: the New Interactive Media for the Home* (University of Wisconsin Press, Wisconsin, 1988), for a critical review of these developments.

2   John Reith, *Broadcast over Britain* (Hodder & Stoughton, London 1924), p. 23.

3   [The Peacock Report], *Report of the Committee on Financing the BBC* (HMSO, London, 1986), p. 130.

4   [The Pilkington Report], *Report of the Broadcasting Committee* (HMSO, London, 1960), p. 13.

5   Tom Burns, *The BBC, Public Institution, Private World* (Macmillan, London, 1977), pp. 36–7.

6   Cf. Jean Seaton, in James Curran and Jean Seaton, *Power without Responsibility. The Press and Broadcasting in Britain*, 3rd edition (Routledge, London, 1988), pp. 117–35. Krishan Kumar, 'Holding the middle ground: the BBC, the public and the professional broadcaster', in *Mass Communication and Society*, James Curran et al. (eds) (Edward Arnold and the Open Unversity Press, London, 1977), pp. 235–6.

7   Asa Briggs, *The History of Broadcasting in the United Kingdom*, Volume 1, *The Birth of Broadcasting* (Oxford University Press, Oxford, 1961), p. 235.

8   This is a gross summary of complex developments charted in Briggs, *The Birth of Broadcasting*.

9   The General Post Office was, in the 1920s, the largest British industry and the most successful revenue-producing department of state whose surplus revenue went straight to the Exchequer. This double role gave rise to increasing criticism of ministerial control over what was essentially a profit-oriented industry. Demands that the Post Office should be privatized led to the setting-up of the first Committee of Inquiry into its activities (The Bridgman Report, Cmnd. 4149, 1932). There is no doubt that the major concern of the Post Office with increasing its own profitability ran counter to the interests of broadcasting from the very beginning. There was intermittent pressure from Reith on the government to transfer reponsibility for broadcasting to another, preferably high-ranking, Ministry. For a useful discussion of the relations between the BBC and the Post Office, see 'Ministerial Control of British Broadcasting', Arthur Burrows, 26 June 1942, WAC R31/58.

10 [The Sykes Report], *The Broadcasting Committee Report* (HMSO, London, 1923), p. 6.

11 Ibid., p. 6.

12 Ibid., pp. 12–14.

13 John Reith, 'Memorandum of Information on the Scope and Conduct of the Broadcasting Service' (BBC Written Archives, Caversham), 1925, p. 3. This brief document

Notes

should be compared with Reith's book, *Broadcast over Britain* (Hodder & Stoughton, London, 1924) passages from which are reproduced verbatim in the Memorandum.

14 Reith, 'Memorandum of Information', p. 4.

15 Ibid., p. 4.

16 Ibid., p. 10.

17 John Reith, *Into the Wind*, (Hodder & Stoughton, London, 1949). pp. 99–100.

18 Reith, 'Memorandum of Information', p. 10.

19 Briggs, *Birth of Broadcasting*, p. 329

20 Raymond Williams, *Culture and Society* (Pelican Books, Harmondsworth, 1963), p. 315.

21 In *Broadcast over Britain* (p. 217) Reith wrote that 'Broadcasting is a servant of culture and culture has been called the study of perfection'. In *Culture and Anarchy* Arnold declared, 'Culture, which is the study of perfection, leads us ... to conceive of true human perfection as a *harmonious* perfection, developing all sides of our humanity; and as *general* perfection, developing all parts of our society,' Quoted in Williams, *Culture and Society*, p. 124.

22 [The Annan Report], *Report of the Committee on the Future of Broadcasting* (HMSO, London, 1977), p. 14.

23 Ibid., p. 80.

24 Ibid., p. 263.

25 Ibid., pp. 79, 114.

26 The classic account of this process in Britain is Edward Thompson's celebrated *The Making of the English Working Class* (Pelican Books, Harmondsworth, 1968).

27 The concept is taken from Jurgen Habermas, *The Structural Transformation of the Public Sphere* (Polity Press, Cambridge, 1989).

28 A. D. Lindsay, *The Essentials of Democracy* (Oxford University Press, London: Humphrey Milford, 1929), p. 7.

29 Walter Lippmann, *Liberty and the News*, (Harcourt, Brace and Howe New York, 1920), p. 38.

30 For a critical view, see George Boyce, 'The Fourth Estate: the reappraisal of a concept', in *Newspaper History: From the 17th Century to the Present Day*, George Boyce et al. (eds) (Sage/Constable, London, 1978), pp. 19–40.

31 Norman Angell, *After All* (Hamish Hamilton, London, 1951), quoted in D. L. LeMahieu, *A Culture For Democracy* (Oxford University Press, Oxford, 1988), p. 112.

32 Quoted in Margaret Mathieson, *The Preachers of Culture* (Allen & Unwin, London, 1975), p. 74. See Brian Doyle, *English and Englishness*, (Routledge, London, 1989), for a critical discussion of the Newbolt Report.

33 Mathieson, *The Preachers of Culture*, p. 78.

34 George Sampson, *English for the English* (Cambridge University Press, Cambridge, 1925), quoted in Mathieson, *The Preachers of Culture*, p. 75.

35 Lewis Mumford, *Technics and Civilization* (New York, 1934), quoted in Charles Loch Mowatt, *Britain between the Wars, 1918–1940* (Methuen, University Paperbacks, London, 1968), p. 231.

36 Forsyth Hardy (ed.), *Grierson on Documentary* (Faber & Faber, London, 1966), p. 207.

37 *BBC Year Book* (BBC, London, 1933), p. 37.

38 Ibid., p. 14.

39 See Briggs, *The Birth of Broadcasting*, for details.

40 Williams, *Culture and Society*, p. 18 and passim.
41 Theodor Adorno and Max Horheimer, *Dialectic of Enlightenment* (Verso, London, 1979).
42 F. R. Leavis, *Mass Civilisation and Minority Culture*, (The Minority Press, Cambridge, 1930).
43 Arthur Calder-Marshall, *The Changing Scene* (Chapman and Hall, London, 1937), p. 91.

CHAPTER 2 *The containment of controversy*

1 *Hansard*, vol. 199, 12 November 1926.
2 As M.E. Dimmock notes (*British Public Utilities and National Development*, Allen & Unwin, London, 1933) the responsibilities of the Postmaster General did not normally involve broad political questions or controversial issues. A former Labour Postmaster General, Vernon Hartshorn, expressed his regret, in a Supply Committee debate, that the Post Office was regarded in this country and by governments as a sort of second-rate Department, as no more than a stepping-stone to higher things. He noted that five different people, including himself, had held the post in the three years since broadcasting began (*Hansard*, vol. 186, 20 July 1925, col. 1876). Most of those appointed came to office with no previous knowledge of the Post Office, and their time was fully occupied with learning to master the administrative intricacies of the country's postal, telephone and telegraph services. All these factors militated against the Post Office's will or ability to exercise authority over the content of broadcasting with any clarity or consistency.
3 Briggs, *The Birth of Broadcasting* (Oxford Unversity Press, London, 1961). p. 167.
4 Ibid., p. 169.
5 Ibid., pp. 164–83, for an account of the deliberations of the Sykes Committee. The BBC Written Archives hold verbatim transcriptions of the Committee meetings.
6 Briggs, *The Birth of Broadcasting*, pp. 169–70.
7 BBC WAC R4/6/2/1, p. 50.
8 BBC WAC R4/6/2/2, p. 51.
9 Briggs, *The Birth of Broadcasting*, p. 130.
10 Ibid., pp. 132–3.
11 Ibid., p. 263.
12 *BBC Year Book* (BBC, London, 1928), p. 144.
13 Burrows to Reuters, 21 November 1923. BBC WAC R28/170.
14 Burrows to Reuters, 7 November 1924, ibid. On the Zinovieff letter cf. Mowatt, *Britain between the Wars*, (Methuen University Paperbacks, London, 1968), pp. 187–94.
15 Clements to Burrows, 10 November 1924. BBC WAC R28/170.
16 F. J. Brown to Reith, 12 June 1924 ibid.
17 Brown to Reith, 1 October 1924, ibid.
18 Reith to Brown, 3 October 1924, ibid.
19 Brown to Reith, 13 October 1924, ibid.
20 'What's in the Air', *Radio Times*, 16 November 1923.
21 Ibid., 30 November 1923

22 Briggs, *The Birth of Broadcasting*, p. 269.
23 H. E. Weston to Reith, 19 August 1924. BBC WAC R34/534/1.
24 Reith to Brown, 3 October 1924, ibid. This letter, Reith began, was 'in virtual continuation of my official letter of today's date'. Cf. n. 18 above.
25 All details can be found in BBC WAC R34/534/1. Cf. Briggs, *The Birth of Broadcasting*, pp. 268–9.
26 Reith to Hon. V. Phillipps, 27 October 1925. BBC WAC, ibid.
27 Reith to GPO, 15 October 1925, and previous correspondence. BBC WAC R34/317/1.
28 'What's in the Air', *Radio Times*, 23 November 1923.
29 Ibid., 16 November 1923.
30 Ibid., 7 December 1923.
31 John Reith, *Into the Wind* (Hodder & Stoughton, London, 1949), p. 98.
32 A long-forgotten issue. Briggs refers to it only when Baldwin finally killed it (*The Birth of Broadcasting*, pp. (342–3), and neither Reith (*Into the Wind*), nor Peter Eckersley (*The Power behind the Microphone*, Jonathan Cape, London, 1941) refer to it in their accounts of the early days. Roger Eckersley simply notes that the BBC 'failed wholly with the House of Commons in spite of many efforts' (*The BBC and All That*, Marston, Low, London, 1946, p. 62). When the topic was resurrected by politicians in the late fifties, there was no acknowledgement of the BBC's early claims to broadcast Parliament. Cf. Charles Wilson, *Parliaments, Peoples and Mass Media* (Cassell, London, 1970).
33 'Should Parliament be Broadcast?', *Radio Times*, 23 November 1923.
34 'When Parliament is Broadcast', *Radio Times*, 17 April 1925.
35 *The Times*, 26 March 1925.
36 *Morning Post*, 27 March 1925.
37 *Daily Mail*, 26 March 1925.
38 *Radio Times*, 26 February 1926.
39 Briggs, *The Birth of Broadcasting*, p. 343.
40 Charles Stuart (ed.), *The Reith Diaries* (Collins, London, 1975), p. 134.
41 [Crawford Report], *Report of the Broadcasting Committee* (HMSO, London, 1926), p. 13.
42 Christopher Farman, *May 1926, The General Strike. Britain's Aborted Revolution* (Panther Books, London, 1974). Margaret Morris (ed.), *The General Strike* (Penguin Books, Harmondsworth, 1976). Michael Tracey, *The Production of Political Television* (Routledge Direct Editions, London, 1977), ch. 8. The account that follows is largely drawn from Briggs, *The Birth of Broadcasting*, pp. 360–384, still the best account of the BBC and the strike.
43 Briggs, *The Birth of Broadcasting*, p. 365.
44 Morris, *The General Strike*, p. 251.
45 *Radio Times*, 28 May 1926.
46 Briggs, *The Birth of Broadcasting*, p. 374.
47 Ibid., pp. 380–3.
48 Stuart, *The Reith Diaries*, p. 139.
49 Both letters in BBC WAC R34/317/1.
50 Briggs, *The Birth of Broadcasting*, p. 383.
51 In BBC WAC R34/317/1.
52 Stuart, *The Reith Diaries*, p. 139.

53 Briggs, *The Birth of Broadcasting*, p. 116.
54 Ibid., p. 229.
55 Ibid., p. 355.
56 See Asa Briggs, *The History of Broadcasting in the United Kingdom*, volume 2, *The Golden Age of Wireless* (Oxford University Press, Oxford, 1965), p. 484, for a detailed breakdown of the allocation of licence fees revenue on an annual basis.
57 The BBC received its portion of the licence fee annually and in arrears. That is, it received payment in any one year based on the number of licences issued the previous year and its income therefore did not keep pace with the current licence position. An article in the *BBC Hand Book* (1929, pp. 46–52) calculated that in this way the BBC lost approximately £87,000 in the financial year ending 31 March 1928. The BBC was taxed on its income after the Post Office and the Treasury had taken their share. On top of this the Post Office received considerable further revenue from the BBC for the 4000 miles of landline it rented, at the same rate as private subscribers, for the SB link-ups and outside broadcasts from its stations and hook-up points.
58 Briggs, *The Birth of Broadcasting*, pp. 402–3.
59 Ibid., pp. 354–5.
60 Stuart, *The Reith Diaries*, p. 141.
61 Ibid.
62 The text of Clarendon's letter was read out in the House of Commons by Sir William Mitchell Thompson, the Postmaster General, during the Committee of Supply debate in the Commons, 12 November 1926.
63 *Hansard*, 1926, vol. 199, 12 November 1926, cols 1571–6.
64 Ibid., cols 1581–3.
65 Ibid., cols 1584–9.
66 Stuart, *The Reith Diaries*, pp. 141–2.

CHAPTER 3 *The management of news and political debate*

1 Keith Middlemas, *Politics in Industrial Society* (André Deutsch, London, 1980), p. 373.
2 Ibid., p. 337–70.
3 D. G. Anderson, *Fascists, Communists and the National Government. Civil Liberties in Great Britain, 1931–1937* (University of Missouri Press, Columbia and London, 1983).
4 Political and Economic Planning (PEP), *A Report on the Press* (London, 1938), p. 200.
5 Middlemas, *Politics in Industrial Society*, p. 356.
6 A. Briggs, *The Birth of Broadcasting* (Oxford University Press, London, 1961), p. 359
7 All these details from 'Home Bulletins' (undated). BBC WAC, R28/29.
8 Reith to GPO 16 January 1928. This letter, and the Post Office's reply, is to be found in BBC WAC, R31/4/2 and R34/317/1.
9 The text of Baldwin's reply to Fraser in the Commons is given in 'The broadcasting of controversial matter (excluding religious broadcasts): history and present practice' (Broadcasting Policy 5, November, 1942), p. 6, para. 21. This fifty-page internal document was compiled by Arthur Burrows to brief the BBC Directorate as it prepared to retrieve the political independence of the BBC from government control at the end of the war. It is a detailed and reliable account of relationships between the BBC,

governments and parties from the earliest days through to the outbreak of war. Hereafter referred to as BBC WAC, BP 5.

10 Senior staff sent Reith their responses to the Post Office's letter. Roger Eckersley felt that 'The need for circumspection and a quiet start is obvious. The strict need for impartiality as in the past is equally realised, in fact, under new conditions is more necessary than ever.' R. Eckersley to Reith, 8 March 1928. Peter Eckersley, characteristically, was horrified to hear it said that we would never have a Communist speaking – a most invidious doctrine, in his opinion. P. Eckersley, 6 March 1928. BBC WAC, R34/317/1. A small Controversy Committee was set up in March 1928, but was dissolved in November 1929. WAC, BP 5, paras 23, 31. For details of its deliberations, see WAC, R34/318.

11 Strutt to Matheson, 6 November 1926, BBC WAC, R28/16/2.

12 Strutt to Matheson, 3 March 1927, ibid.

13 Matheson to Eckersley, 4 May 1927, ibid.

14 Briggs, *The Birth of Broadcasting*, p. 358.

15 For Post Office announcements in the bulletins, see BBC WAC, R28/82/1–4.

16 See 'News Service. Review of the Year 1930', BBC WAC, R28/177/3. Hereafter, Review of News 1930. In 1928, in a Richmal Crompton story, we find William ingeniously getting rid of a boring elderly relative, who is overstaying his welcome in the Brown household, with a fake SOS message – intoned through Robert's new wireless – that his house has been burgled and he must return home at once. 'One Good Turn', in *William the Good* (Macmillan, London, 1984).

17 'News Service, Review of the Year 1931', p. 5. BBC WAC, R28/79. Hereafter, Review of News 1931.

18 Review of News 1930, pp. 3–4.

19 Reporting this incident to the Assistant Director of Programmes, Rose-Troup noted: 'While we welcome this close liaison with Government Departments, we shall naturally continue to watch all such communications very carefully so as not to be overloaded with official announcements of matters not of vital importance.' Rose-Troup, 1 December 1930. BBC WAC, R28/16/2. See also Review of News 1930.

20 C. L. Mowatt, *Britain between the Wars* (Methuen University Paperbacks London, 1968), pp. 363–4. Middlemas, *Politics in Industrial Society*, p. 210.

21 Review of News 1931, p. 3.

22 Ibid., p. 1.

23 The men of the fleet in harbour at Invergordon first heard of cuts in their pay from the wireless and the newspapers before the Admiralty had informed them of, or explained, its intentions. Mowatt, *Britain between the Wars*, pp. 404–5. This request to News Section was, presumably, to forestall that happening again.

24 All these details from Review of News 1931.

25 Review of News 1930, pp. 4–5.

26 Review of News 1931, pp. 2–3.

27 Both letters in R28/16/2.

28 Peter Kingsford, *The Hunger Marchers in Britain, 1920–1940* (Lawrence & Wishart, London, 1982) pp. 139–65.

29 Wal Hannington, *Unemployed Struggles* (Lawrence & Wishart, London, 1977).

30 Kingsford, *The Hunger Marchers in Britain*, pp. 156–8.

31 Anderson, *Fascists, Communists and the National Government*, p. 76. See also Sylvia

Scaffardi, *Fire under the Carpet. Working for Civil Liberties in the 1930s* (Lawrence & Wishart, London, 1986).

32 'Aide Memoire. Emergency Organisation', Graves, undated, but very likely, 11 November 1934. See Graves to Tallents, 19 November 1934. BBC WAC, R34/888/1.

33 *Time and Tide*, 10 October 1931.

34 Review of News 1931, pp. 1–2.

35 'Attitude of News Agencies', Rose-Troup to Reith, 1 December 1931. BBC WAC, R28/16/2.

36 Memo to Reith, 21 January 1932, BBC WAC, R28/39/1.

37 On Princess Marina, the Peterson-Gains fight and the Royal Press office, see BBC WAC, R28/39/1. On the row with the Lobby, R28/16/2. On racing results, R28/211/1–3.

38 'Record of interview at 10 Downing Street'. BBC WAC, R28/16/2.

39 BBC WAC, R28/39/1.

40 The account that follows has been compiled from BBC WAC, BP 5. See paras 24–46.

CHAPTER 4 *Broadcasting and unemployment*

1 J. Curran and J. Seaton, *Power Without Responsibility* (Routledge, London, 1988) Chapter 8.

2 T. Burns, *The BBC. Public Institution, Private World* (Macmillan, London, 1977), p. 17.

3 K. Kumar, 'Holding the middle ground', in *Mass Communication and Society*, J. Curran et al. (eds) (Edward Arnold/Open University, London, 1977), pp. 235–6.

4 Jonathan Dimbleby, *Richard Dimbleby* (Hodder & Stoughton, London, 1975), pp. 66–7.

5 A. Briggs, *The Golden Age of Wireless* (Oxford University Press, London, 1965), p. 42.

6 For the involvement of the writers in the politics of the time, see Samuel Hynes, *The Auden Generation. Literature and Politics in England in the 1930s* (Faber & Faber, London, 1976).

7 John Stevenson, *Social Conditions in Britain Between the Wars* (Penguin Books, Harmondsworth, 1977), pp. 57–8.

8 Briggs, *The Golden Age of Wireless*, p. 41.

9 The texts of these three talks series were all printed in *The Listener*.

10 William Beveridge, *Unemployment. A Problem of Industry* (Longman, London, 1909).

11 *The Listener*, 13 July 1932, p. 37.

12 For details of the various schemes, see C. L. Mowatt, *Britain between the Wars* (Methuen, London, 1965), pp. 488–90, and Wal Hannington, *The Problem of the Distressed Areas* (Gollancz, Left Books, London 1937), for a very different account.

13 Mais was a public schoolmaster, a writer of travel books and an occasional broadcaster. In 1931 he had given a series of talks, *The Unknown Island*, in which he described a walking tour of some of the lesser known beauty spots in Britain. On the basis of those broadcasts he was asked to report on the unemployed.

14 *The Listener*, 28 December 1932, pp. 917–8.

15 *The Listener*, 11 January 1933, p. 37.

16 *The Listener*, 25 January 1933, p. 118.

17 Chapter 3, above, pp. 46–7.

18 Hannington, *The Problem of the Distressed Areas*, p. 197.
19 *Manchester Guardian*, 12 January 1933.
20 *Daily Worker*, 20 January 1933.
21 *The Times*, 21 January 1933.
22 *Manchester Guardian*, 26 January 1933.
23 *Manchester Guardian*, 28 January 1933. The protest may have amounted to a strongly worded letter about the series to *Radio Times* (24 February 1933, p. 459) from the Stockport WEA complaining of 'the exclusion of the spokesmen of the unemployed from the microphone'.
24 Siepmann to Buchan, 2 February 1933. BBC WAC, R34/559.
25 *Blackleg*, Mary Stocks and John Orchard. Producer, Olive Shapley. North Region, 1 February 1939. BBC WAC, NR Scripts.
26 *The Listener*, 1 February 1933, pp. 163–4.
27 *The Listener*, 22 March 1933, p. 452.
28 *The Listener*, 1 March 1933, p. 326.
29 Cf. Reith to Buchan, 21 December 1932. BBC WAC, R34/559.
30 *The Everyman*, 2 February 1933.
31 *Daily Worker*, 11 February 1933.
32 Quoted by Marshall in the seventh talk in the series, 'Dark Spots in Manchester', *The Listener*, 1 March 1933, p. 327.
33 *Radio Times*, 17 March 1933, p. 655.
34 *The Listener*, 15 February 1933, p. 234.
35 *The Listener*, 1 March 1933, p. 327.
36 In between *S.O.S.* and *Time To Spare, The Listener* had commissioned and published a series of articles (not broadcast) in which representative types of unemployed were asked to describe the psychological effect of unemployment – what it did to their social life, their intellectual faculties, their interest in public affairs and their hopes for the future. It was then published as a book: H. L. Beales and R. S. Lambert, *Memoirs of the Unemployed* (Gollancz, London, 1934).
37 Felix Greene, 'The Tragedy of *Time to Spare*', *Radio Times*, 25 May 1934.
38 *The Listener*, 11 April 1934, p. 620. The BBC received nearly 4500 letters from listeners asking to be put in touch with a distressed family, offering help in the form of a small weekly sum of money, or to pay the family milk bill, or to provide clothes for the children. Other offers included help in the form of holidays or provisions, or voluntary work in the clubs and occupational centres. £1552 was received in small donations which Greene arranged to be distributed amongst the speakers, other families and the clubs and occupational centres. Greene to Siepmann, 26 June 1934. BBC WAC, R51/605/1.
39 *Daily Worker*, 5 May 1934.
40 *Hansard*, vol. 289, vol. VII, 1933–4, 14 May 1934, cols 1524–6 for the nub of the exchange between Dagger and Hudson.
41 The details of MacDonald's intervention and Reith's response are from an interview with Felix Greene, 3 July 1979.
42 The following account is constructed from WAC, R51/605/1.
43 *The Listener*, 4 July 1934.
44 Siepmann to Reith, 2 July 1934 and 3 July 1934. BBC WAC, R51/605/1.
45 Greene, *Radio Times*, 23 May 1934. Greene himself was under considerable pressure. He had annoyed Hudson in a letter, presumably replying to demands for information

following Hudson's allegations in the House, and back came a reply from J. A. N. Barlow, the Prime Minister's private secretary, calling it 'a piece of impertinence which has given very great offence'. Barlow had tried to persuade Hudson that it was merely 'a foolish outburst by an inexperienced and rather bumptious fledgling'. He went on to criticize Greene's *Radio Times* article as giving the impression that the speakers in the series were typical of the two million unemployed, which was not true. Reith replied that 'due action has been taken over Greene'. BBC WAC, R51/605/1. Greene's own recollection, forty-five years later, was of Reith's unwavering support throughout the affair (Interview, 1979).

46 *Daily Herald*, 4 June 1934.
47 Greene to Davies, 14 June 1934. BBC WAC, R51/605/1.
48 Howard Marshall, *Slum* (Heinemann, London, 1933), pp. 3–4.
49 Greene, *Radio Times*, 25 May 1934, and Interview, 1979.
50 These details from Noreen Branson and Margot Heinemann, *Britain in the Nineteen Thirties* (Panther Books, London, 1973), pp. 69–74.
51 This account of talks for the unemployed is constructed from BBC WAC, R51/605.
52 'To the Unemployed', *The Listener*, 5 October 1934, p. 561.
53 BBC WAC, R51/605.
54 For details of the Talks Department see chapter 8, below pp. 153–61.
55 The account that follows is constructed from BBC WAC, R51/607.
56 Rose-Troup to Liveing, 12 February 1936. BBC WAC, R51/560.
57 Tom Jeffery, 'Mass Observation: a short history' (Birmingham University, Centre for Contemporary Cultural Studies, Stencilled Paper, 1977), p. 3.
58 Quoted in Stevenson, *Social Conditions in Britain between the Wars*, p. 47.
59 Hynes, *The Auden Generation*, pp. 268–9.
60 B. Reid, 'The Left Book Club in the thirties', in J. Clark et al., *Culture and Crisis in Britain in the 30s* (Lawrence and Wishart, London, 1979), p. 194.
61 J. Stevenson, *Social Conditions in Britain Between the Wars* (Penguin Books, Harmondsworth, 1977), p. 55.

CHAPTER 5 *Broadcasting and foreign affairs*

1 See Asa Briggs, *Governing the BBC* (BBC, London, 1979), and B. Haworth, 'The British Broadcasting Corporation, Nazi Germany and the Foreign Office', *The Historical Journal of Film, Radio and Television*, vol. 1 (1981), no. 1. What follows is drawn largely from Haworth.
2 Stuart, *The Reith Diaries* (Collins, London, 1975), pp. 116–17.
3 On this affair see BBC WAC, R51/83 and BP 5, paras, 54–62. Also Briggs, *Governing the BBC*, pp. 198–201.
4 Eden's memorandum is in BBC WAC R51/83.
5 Briggs, *Governing the BBC*, p. 200.
6 BBC WAC, BP 5, para. 58.
7 Charles Curran, *A Seamless Robe* (Collins, London, 1979), pp. 63–4.
8 BBC WAC, BP 5, para. 61.
9 [The Ullswater Report], *Report of the Broadcasting Committee* (HMSO, London, 1936), para. 52, p. 18.
10 Ibid., para, 86, p. 28.

Notes

11 For an account of this programme, see chapter 7, pp. 139–40.
12 *Daily Mail*, 13 January 1937.
13 *The Listener*, 7 July 1938, pp. 5–6.
14 'The BBC and Left-Wing Bias' (undated), BBC WAC, R34/523.
15 Dimbleby, *Richard Dimbleby*, p. 76.
16 This correspondence is in BBC WAC, R41/201 PCS.
17 Broadcast in the main news bulletin, January 15 1937, See *'Civil War from Both Sides'*, *The Listener*, 20 January 1937, p. 126.
18 *Daily Worker*, 22 March 1937.
19 Dimbleby, *Richard Dimbleby* (Hodder & Stoughton, London, 1975), p. 77.
20 *The History of The Times*, vol. 4 (Times Publishing Co., London, 1952), p. 910.
21 *News Review*, 27 January 1938.
22 *Manchester Guardian*, 12 February 1938.
23 *History of The Times*, p. 910n.
24 *Report of the Press*, 1938, p. 202.
25 Details of this incident from BBC WAC, R34/512.
26 Coatman to Nicolls, 5 October 1938. BBC WAC, R34/325.
27 Briggs, *The Golden Age of Wireless* (Oxford University Press, London 1961), p. 233.
28 BBC WAC, BP 5, para. 75.
29 Ibid., para. 74.
30 These details from BBC WAC, R34/534/3.
31 Tallents to Reith, 15 March 1938. BBC WAC, ibid.
32 Control Board Minutes, minute 250, 5 April 1938. BBC WAC, R3/3/13.
33 The replies to this request for national heartening are in BBC WAC, R34/486. Cf. this account of them with Briggs, *The Golden Age of Wireless*, pp. 655–7.
34 Briggs, *The Golden Age of Wireless*, p. 656.
35 Details of this scheme from BBC WAC, R28/94.
36 See Nicolls memoranda, 30 May 1938 and 3 June 1938. BBC WAC, R34/534/3.
37 A view endorsed by R. H. Crossman, after a recent visit to Czechoslakia. Commenting on the fundamental differences between the British and American press, he observed that whereas here crises broke upon readers more or less unannounced, American readers were prepared for them in advance by a succession of news stories printed ahead of the actual crisis. Crossman thought the BBC could do more to educate people beforehand, and so have them understand what was happening and enable them to come to a better judgement on things when they did happen. Memorandum of a meeting with R. H. Crossman, 2 June 1938. BBC WAC, R28/58/1.
38 All these details from BBC WAC, R34/600/10.
39 'Crisis Broadcasts', D.O.S. to C.P., 24 October 1938. BBC WAC, R34/325.
40 Jardine Brown to Tallents, 28 September 1938. BBC WAC, R28/297.
41 Undated, in BBC WAC, R34/325.
42 'The BBC and National Defence', 5 October 1938. BBC WAC, R34/325.
43 On 11 June 1935, Reith and three senior officials discussed broadcasting and war, including air-raid precautions for the BBC. Stuart, *The Reith Diaries*, p. 167. By 1938 evidence of planning for war is liberally scattered through the minutes of the meetings of the Board of Governors (BG), Control Board (CB), Controllers' Meetings (CM) and Programme Board (PB). Staff arrangements, including wartime pay scales, were finalized in late September (cf. CM minute 468, 23 September 1938, and CB minute 561, 27 September 1938. BBC WAC, R3/10/2 and R3/13/3).

NOTES

44 We have found no further details, in the Written Archives, of the particular incidents mentioned by Coatman. But in another policy paper by Burrows government 'pressure' on the BBC in the aftermath of *The Citizen and His Government* is discussed. Noting that the practice of informal consultation with Government Departments increased thereafter, Burrows cites two discussion programmes that were cancelled as a result of government intervention. One between an Arab and Jewish speaker on the publication of the Palestine Commission Report was cancelled, in July 1937, on the instruction of the Cabinet. The other was a debate between Leo Amery, Harold Nicholson and G. Glasgow on 'The German Claim to Colonies', scheduled for March 1938. It was cancelled 'after consultation with the Foreign Office', in the light of the Austrian crisis, while *The Way of Peace* continued. See Broadcasting Policy 7. Editorial Control (BP 7), para. 12. In BBC WAC, R34/274.
45 PB, minute 154, 29 September 1938. BBC WAC, R34/600/10.
46 Ibid., minute 157, 6 October 1938 and minute 167, 13 October 1938.
47 CB, minute 87, 7 October 1938. BBC WAC, R3/13/3.
48 PB, minute 208, 3 November 1938. BBC WAC, R34/600/10.
49 Ibid., minute 226, 17 November 1936.
50 Details of PB discussion are from BBC WAC, R34/346.
51 For details of this talks series, see chapter 8, p. 172.
52 Ryan to Tallents, 12 November 1938. BBC WAC, R41/132/1.
53 *The Times*, 29 March 1939.
54 See *The Times*, leading article 25 February 1939. The correspondence is fully documented in BBC WAC, Press Cuttings from which the quotes that follow are taken.
55 *Daily Mail*, 15 February 1939.
56 Cf. *Nottingham Journal*, 15 April 1939.
57 27 February 1939. BBC WAC, R41/132/1.
58 Enlarged CB, minute 136, 3 March 1939. BBC WAC, R3/13/3.
59 The full text of Churchill's broadcast was printed in *The Times*, 17 October 1938.
60 The following account, including the correspondence with Churchill, Attlee and Tryon, is drawn from BBC WAC, R34/534/3.
61 Ibid., Churchill to Ogilvie, 21 February 1939. Ogilvie to Churchill 24 February 1939.
62 Ibid., Ogilvie to Attlee, 14 March 1939. Attlee to Ogilvie, 16 March 1939. Ogilvie to Attlee, 18 March 1939.
63 The account that follows is drawn from BBC WAC, R34/486.
64 Ibid., Dimbleby to Boyd, 17 April 1939.
65 Ibid., Siepmann to Nicolls, 20 April 1939.
66 Ibid., 'Whitehall Inefficiency', Nicolls to Graves, 10 May 1939.
67 Compare this account with Briggs, *The Golden Age of Wireless*, pp. 657–8.
68 Briggs, *The Golden Age of Wireless*, p. 365.
69 T. Harrison and C. Madge, *Britain By Mass Observation* (Penguin Special, Harmondsworth, 1939), p. 25.

CHAPTER 6   *News values and practices*

1 A. R. Burrows to Carey Clements, 6 December 1923. BBC WAC, R28/169.
2 Burrows to Clements, 5 December 1924, 27 May 1924, ibid.

3 Burrows to Clements, 1 September 1924, 3 September 1924, ibid.
4 Burrows to Clements, 7 November 1924, ibid.
5 Burrows to Clements, 1 September 1924, ibid.
6 Clements to Carpendale, 15 February 1924, ibid.
7 Clements to Burrows, 2 September 1924, ibid.
8 For a useful account of the changes of style and content brought about by the new journalism in the twenties, see D. L. LeMahieu, *A Culture for Democracy* (Oxford University Press, Oxford, 1988), pp. 17–43.
9 John Reith, *Into the Wind* (Hodder and Stoughton, London, 1949), p. 136.
10 A. Briggs, *The Birth of Broadcasting* (Oxford University Press, London, 1961), p. 368. Cf. pp. 366–75 for his account of the bulletins, their content and wider implications. For an excellent inside account, see C. F. Atkinson, 'Report on the organization and day work of the emergency news staff. May 4th to May 18th, 1926', by C. F. Atkinson, May 18 1926. BBC WAC, CO/37.
11 The two evening transmissions were general news bulletins (GNBs) and included other home and overseas new. The three daytime bulletins dealt only with the strike.
12 Briggs, *The Birth of broadcasting*, p. 368.
13 2nd GNB 9.30 pm, 7 May 1926. BBC WAC, CO/32/1 (all the bulletins are in this file).
14 4 pm bulletin, 5 May 1926, ibid.
15 4 pm bulletin, 6 May 1926, ibid.
16 1 pm bulletin, 10 May 1926, ibid.
17 1st GNB, 7 pm, 7 May 1926, ibid.
18 Bill Schwarz, 'The language of constitutionalism: Baldwinite conservatism', in *Formations of Nation and People*, ed. James Donald (Routledge & Kegan Paul, London: 1984), p. 18.
19 C. Stuart, *The Reith Diaries* (Collins, London, 1975), pp. 94–5.
20 Atkinson, 'Report on the Emergency', BBC WAC, CO/37.
21 R. H. Eckersley to Managing Director, 17 May 1926. BBC WAC, R28/177/1.
22 Emergency News Service (C. F. Atkinson) to Director of Publicity, 17 May 1926, ibid. See also Stobart to Eckersley, 17 May 1927.
23 Matheson to Reith, 18 May 1927, ibid.
24 Strutt to Matheson, 14 October 1927, ibid.
25 Eckersley to Matheson, 9 May 1928, ibid.
26 The *Westminster Gazette* was a Liberal weekly newspaper of the old school, famous for the lengthy editorials written by its editor J. A. Spender. It was converted to a daily in 1921 but ran at a heavy loss and was merged in 1928 into the *Daily News*, Commenting on its failure, Spender remarked: 'The appeal, therefore, was deliberately to the few. The trouble was that they were so very few, as newspapers reckon numbers' (quoted in LeMahieu, *A Culture for Democracy*, p. 18, n. 34). Not the best model for a broadcast news service, but the newspaper was the antithesis of the kind of journalism that Matheson wished to avoid.
27 Philip Macer-Wright, 'Suggestions for the improvement of the BBC News Service', 24 September 1928. BBC WAC, R28/177/1.
28 On News Reel, cf. Briggs, *The Golden Age of Wireless*, p. 155. *Programme Record*, vol. 5, p. 127 (a series of bound volumes of programmes as broadcast in the Written Archives). There is a one-page, undated compilation on Newsreels in BBC WAC, R28/79/1.

29 *Radio Times*, 6 October 1933, p. 66.
30 'Do You Like Talks?', by the BBC Director of Talks, *News Chronicle*, 17 May 1934.
31 Undated News Reel compilation, BBC WAC, R28/79/1.
32 *The Times*, Broadcasting Number, 14 August 1934. Quoted in Briggs, *The Golden Age of Wireless*, p. 155.
33 News Service. Review of the Year 1930. BBC WAC, R28/177/3
34 Ibid. It is worth remembering that the News Section had only begun to compile its own bulletins two months earlier (the first was broadcast on 10 February 1930) and was still very inexperienced.
35 *Sunday Chronicle*, 20 April 1930.
36 *Sunday Graphic*, 20 April 1930.
37 *Newspaper World*, 3 May 1930.
38 Originally John Coatman was appointed Chief News Editor within the Talks Department, but this created strains with Siepmann, and it was not long before Coatman secured the independence of News from Talks (R. S. Lambert, *Ariel and All His Quality* (Gollancz, London, 1940), pp. 84–5. J. Dimbleby, *Richard Dimbleby* (Hodder & Stoughton, London, 1975), pp. 63–4.
39 *News Chronicle*, 5 April 1935.
40 Lambert, *Ariel And All His Quality*, p. 84.
41 Briggs, *The Golden Age of Wireless*, p. 147.
42 It is clear that Coatman found the new adminstrative structure irksome, and a memorandum from Reith ťo Graves (Controller of Programmes) spelt out in fascinating detail how the structure of command was supposed to work and what Graves's authority was in relation to Coatman (DG to CP, 'C.N.E.'s Memorandum 30.12.35', 2 January 1936, BBC WAC, R28/177/3). Broadcast news editing, Lambert observed, being essentially topical, did not lend itself to the cumbrous censorial process which controlled Talks (*Ariel and All His Quality*, p. 85.)
43 *Newspaper World*, 25 May 1935.
44 *News Chronicle*, 1 March 1935.
45 Script, undated, in BBC WAC, R41/132/1.
46 *Manchester Guardian*, 8 February 1935.
47 Script, undated, in BBC WAC, R41/132/1.
48 *The Observer*, 23 June 1935.
49 Quoted in Briggs, *The Golden Age of Wireless*, p. 159.
50 See Dimbleby (*Richard Dimbleby*, pp. 64ff), for a good account of the pre-war News Department, from which the following details are taken.
51 The following details are from HSNE (Home Service News Editor) to CP (Controller of Programmes), 19 August 1938. BBC WAC, R28/177/4.
52 Dimbleby, *Richard Dimbleby*, for the full letter and a fuller account of Richard Dimbleby's early days in the News Department.
53 John Coatman, 'Broadcasting News', *Quarterly Review*, January 1937, pp. 118–128. *Radio Times*, 7 September 1934, has an article on *Echo des Tages*: 'Broadcasting the News of the Day', by Edward Roderich Dietze, 'Germany's pioneer of news recordings', p. 614.
54 E. Pawley, *BBC Engineering 1922–1976* (BBC, London, 1976), p. 188.
55 The original request for this, he claimed, went back to November 1934. It was delivered at the end of 1938. Dimbleby would later claim that 'the whole vast network

of BBC news recording has developed from the introduction of that solitary vehicle' (*Richard Dimbleby*, p. 69).

56 HSNE to CP, 14 October 1938. BBC WAC, R28/177/4, p. 12.
57 Ibid., pp. 13–14.
58 The news bulletins for 30 September 1938 are on microfiche in the Written Archives.
59 David H. Culbert, *News for Everyman. Radio and Foreign Affairs in Thirties America* (Greenwood Press, Westport, Conn., 1976), p. 5.
60 Erik Barnouw *The Golden Web*, A History of Broadcasting in the United States, vol. II *1933 to 1955* (Oxford University Press, New York, 1968), p. 76.
61 Ibid., p. 78.
62 Culbert, *News for Everyman*, p. 74.
63 Ibid., pp. 72, 74.
64 'Crisis Broadcasts', 24 October 1938. BBC WAC, R34/325.
65 'News Agencies During the Crisis', 4 November 1938. BBC WAC, R28/297.
66 HSNE to CP, 14 October 1938. BBC WAC, R28/177/4. pp. 4ff.
67 This account is from Dimbleby, *Richard Dimbleby*, pp. 77–80.
68 Ibid., pp. 78–9.
69 Ibid., p. 79.

CHAPTER 7 *Features and social documentaries*

1 Felix Felton, *The Radio-Play. Its Techniques and Possibilities* (Sylvan Press, London, 1949), p. 99. Full details, as far as possible, are given of programmes mentioned in this chapter. Scripts and production files are in the Written Archives. Recordings extant on tape or disc are kept in the BBC Sound Archives, London (SAL). References for recorded programmes are taken from the BBC Sound Archives Catalogue, March 1985.
2 *Radio Times*, 31 August 1928, p. 367.
3 Lance Sieveking, *The Stuff of Radio* (Cassell & Co, London, 1934), p. 15.
4 See 'Feature Programmes', undated, p. 3, BBC WAC, R19/352/1.
5 Sieveking, *The Stuff of Radio*, p. 31.
6 Ibid., pp. 16–24.
7 Ibid., pp. 383–2.
8 Ibid., pp. 401–2.
9 Cf *Multiple Studio Blues*, Regional Programme, 24 November 1938. BBC SAL, LP23219. Essentially an in-joke, the programme was an affectionate parody of the Sieveking style feature produced at the drama control panel. In particular it was a send-up of *Steel*, by D. G. Bridson (chapter 15, pp. 342–3).
10 R. D. Charques, 'Is there a future for radio drama?', *Radio Times*, 17 January 1930.
11 Cf. Val Gielgud, *Years in a Mirror* (The Bodley Head, London, 1965), p. 52.
12 George Orwell, 'Inside The Whale' (1940), in *The Collected Essays, Journalism and Letters of George Orwell*, vol. 1, *An Age Like This* (Secker and Warburg, London, 1968), pp. 508–9.
13 22 November 1929, London.
14 First broadcast 6 March 1929, London.
15 22 September 1930, National Programme.

16 2 April 1928, London.
17 *Radio Times*, 3 March 1928.
18 *Cambridge Left*, Summer 1933, Quoted in S. Hynes, *The Auden Generation* (Faber and Faber, London, 1966), p. 100.
19 Sieveking, *The Stuff of Radio*, p. 32.
20 *The Testament of François Villon*, 23 October 1931, National Programme. Further details in *Radio Times*, 16 October 1931, p. 175 and 23 October 1931, p. 262.
21 Broadcast respectively on 21 November 1929, 11 June 1931, 31 December 1932.
22 *Radio Times*, 15 November 1929, p. 493. Ewan MacColl in 'Some notes on the Radio Ballads' (unpublished, undated), calls this 'the most savage document ever to be broadcast ... what emerged from Harding's feature was a picture of Vienna torn and bleeding after the collapse of the Austro-Hungarian Empire,'
23 *The Listener*, 10 June 1931, pp. 966–7.
24 *Crisis in Spain*, composed by E. A. Harding, produced by Lance Sieveking, p. 11. BBC WAC, Scripts. A Staff Training School recording of the complete programme, produced by Harding as a teaching exercise and faithful to the original except for its slow pace, was made in 1938. BBC SAL, T28022.
25 Script in BBC WAC, R19/825/1.
26 D. G. Bridson, *Prospero and Ariel* (Gollancz, London, 1972), p. 22.
27 Hilda Matheson, *Broadcasting* (Thornton Butterworth, London, 1933), p. 97.
28 *Radio Times*, 10 February 1933, p. 325.
29 Ibid., 3 February 1933.
30 *The Listener*, 18 January 1933, p. 74.
31 Gustav Klaus, *The Literature of Labour* (Harvester Press, Brighton, 1985), pp. 128–76.
32 *The Listener*, 18 January 1933, pp. 73–4.
33 See below chapter 8, pp. 161–3.
34 *The Listener*, 5 April 1934, pp. 700–1.
35 W. T. Rault, 'Wanted! A microphone at large', *Radio Times*, 26 February 1932.
36 Ibid., 6 December 1929, pp. 695–6.
37 Ibid., 8 January 1932.
38 Ibid., 9 February 1934.
39 Ibid., 2 March 1934.
40 Ibid., 1 June 1934.
41 Ibid., pp. 666–7.
42 Felton, *The Radio-Play*, pp. 99–100.
43 Script on microfiche, BBC WAC. All the recorded actuality inserts, but not the programme as whole, are on BBC SAL, MT451.
44 Stuart Hall, 'Television and culture', *Sight and Sound*, summer 1976.
45 'Here's Hopping!', *Radio Times*, 7 September 1934, p. 616.
46 A very different contemporary description of hop picking in Kent can be got from Orwell's diary of his experience as a hop-picker. See 'Hop-picking' (1931), in *The Collected Essays, Journalism and Letters of George Orwell*, vol. 1. An Age Like This, 1920–1940', (London, Secker Warburg, 1968), pp. 52–71. Orwell's more abrasive account, while making it clear that the hop pickers had a good time, brings out the stringent rules imposed by the farmers, their sharp practices at weighing, and the tactics of the pickers to get fair measure. In the radio programme, one of the two brief talks is by an unemployed clerk who worked as a check-weighman for 30 shillings a week. He describes the arrival at the field of the pickers: 'Gnarled ancients tottered along hand

in hand with chubby little infants, lisping coarse phrases which I do not propose to repeat ...' Obviously seeing himself as a cut above the pickers, the clerk's tale ends with him fleeing the district, on the advice of the village constable, because his predecessor the year before was thrown in the duck pond. The reasons for this rough treatment, unexplained in the programme, become clear from Orwell's diary – the checker was regarded by the pickers as in league with the farmer to cheat them of their earnings at the weigh-in.

47   The documentary film-makers by this time had all attached themselves to nationalized industries or quasi-public utilities and were making programmes on similar themes: cf. *Housing Problems* for the gas industry, *Night Mail* for the GPO, etc. For histories of the documentary film movement, see Rachael Low, *The History of the British Film, 1929–1939: Documentary and Educational Films of the 1930s* (George Allen & Unwin, London, 1985). Elizabeth Sussex, *The Rise and Fall of British Documentary* (University of California Press, Berkeley, 1975).

48   John Salt to P. D., 6 February 1935. BBC WAC, R19/352/1.

49   Ibid. The gas industry found compensation in the documentary film, *Housing Problems*, which presented it as an agent of change, progress and modernity.

50   *Radio Times*, 14 December 1934, p. 900.

51   Ibid., 9 March 1935.

52   Ibid., 16 March 1935. An article by Gilliam in *Radio Times*, 8 March 1935, notes that the programme contained a large percentage of actual sound, done by means of a mobile recording van. He describes it as 'a planned sound picture ... with actual "sound shots" of the men and machines that carry on essential services in the teeth of the gale.'

53   Ibid., 10 July 1935.

54   John Grierson, Preface to Paul Rotha, *Documentary Film* (Faber and Faber, London, 1936), pp. 8–9.

55   Auden wrote *Hadrian's Wall*, produced by John Pudney, 25 November 1937. See BBC WAC, NR Scripts and N2/47. It contains the much anthologized lyric, *Roman Wall Blues*: 'Over the heather the wet wind blows, I've lice in my tunic and a cold in my nose ... etc.

56   Barbara Coulton, *Louis MacNeice in the BBC* (Faber & Faber, London, 1980), p. 44.

57   Ibid. Bridson, *Prospero and Ariel*; Rayner Heppenstall, *Portrait of the Artist as a Professional Man* (Peter Owen, London, 1967).

58   17 July 1937. BBC SAL, T1846.

59   29 November 1936, BBC SAL, T28006.

60   Lambert, *Ariel and all his Quality*, p. 76.

61   Grace Wyndham Goldie, 'J'Accuse ...', *The Listener*, 19 January 1938, p. 134.

62   See chapter 15, below.

63   Gilliam to all Regional Directors, 1 March 1939. BBC WAC, R19/352/1.

CHAPTER 8   *Forms of talk*

1   S. A. Moseley, *Broadcasting in my time* (Richard Cowan, London, 1935), p. 35

2   R. S. Lambert, *Ariel and All His Quality* (Gollancz, London, 1940), p. 64. We have relied a great deal on Lambert's account of 'The Talking Machine'. It is the best con-

temporary description and commentary on the complex history of the Talks Department. A. Briggs (*Golden Age of Wireless*, Oxford University Press, London, 1961, p. 14) notes that most insider accounts of the period were written by 'rebels' and therefore need putting in context. Later, however, he felt that he should have paid more attention to what they had to say ('Problems and possibilities in the writing of broadcasting history', *Media Culture & Society*, vol. 2, no. 1 (1980), p. 11). Lambert, of course, had some grounds for resentment of his treatment by the BBC high command. He had featured in the notorious 'Talking Mongoose Case' (for an outline see A. Briggs, *Governing The BBC*, BBC, London, 1979, pp. 201–6 and Lambert's own account in *Ariel and All His Quality*) but this did not mar, in our opinion, the overall quality or accuracy of his accounts of pre-war broadcasting.

3 Lambert, *Ariel and All His Quality*, p. 63.
4 S. A. Moseley, *Broadcasting in My Time* (Richard Cowan, London, 1935), p. 35.
5 See *Radio Times*, 6 April 1934, p. 5; 13 April 1934, pp. 85, 89; 27 April 1934, p. 261.
6 Ibid, 5 January 1934, p. 48.
7 Hilda Matheson, *Broadcasting* (Thornton Butterworth, London, 1939) p. 97.
8 Ibid., pp. 95–6.
9 Memorandum III attached to letter from Murray to Pulvermacher, 30 April 1935. BBC WAC R34/523.
10 Lionel Fielden, *The Natural Bent* (André Deutsch, London, 1960), p. 115. See A. Briggs, *The Golden Age of Wireless* (Oxford University Press, London, 1965), pp. 141–2; Lambert, *Ariel and All His Quality*, pp. 68–75; Moseley, *Broadcasting in My Time*, p. 36. The particular issue on which Matheson resigned, in January 1932, was Reith's refusal to allow Harold Nicholson to praise *Ulysses* on radio. Matheson had been the lover of Nicholson's wife, Vita Sackville-West, and had given them both regular opportunities to broadcast on life and literature. Through Vita she recruited Virginia Woolf to the microphone. On leaving the BBC she became Vita Sackville-West's secretary for several years. All details from Victoria Glendinning, *Vita. The Life of Vita Sackville-West* (Weidenfeld & Nicolson, London, 1983).
11 Lambert, *Ariel and All His Quality*, pp. 76–7. A classic instance of a newspaper vendetta against the BBC while a Labour Government was in power began in the *Morning Post* on 26 February 1931 with the headlines 'BBC's Socialist Bias', 'Widespread Disquiet'. The subsequent article attacked the BBC (a) for allowing the *Daily Herald* 'free publicity' (the *Herald* had been allowed to run a ballot over the airwaves to discover its readers' favourite programmes), and (b) for printing in *The Listener* opposite a reprinted radio talk by Stanley Baldwin on unemployment a misleading advertisement for a left-wing book on the subject. The advertisement was undoubtedly misleading (see *The Listener*, 25 February 1931, pp. 304–5) and the magazine immediately apologized for an error of judgement. The *Post* sniffily concluded that that might carry more weight 'if the whole tendency of the use by the BBC of the tremendous power of publicity which they enjoy had not been markedly biased in favour of the Socialist Government and Party'.

Next day the headlines ran: 'The BBC Does it Again'. '"Mistake" After "Mistake"'. 'Growing Public Uneasiness'. Now the issue was a talk the previous night, on Russia by Maurice Dobb, 'A well-known supporter of the Communist point of view' (For Dobb's talk in the *Whither Mankind* series, see *The Listener*, 4 March 1931, pp. 356–7). A leader denouncing The Socialistic BBC was matched by one in

Notes

the *Daily Herald* – Behind The Times – jeering at the *Morning Post*'s stupidity and declaring that the exact opposite was the truth: 'So timid, so orthodox is the BBC that it declines to allow any original thinker to broadcast his views'.

The following day, 28 February 1931, the headlines read 'The BBC's Socialist "Dope"'. 'Outcry Aroused by Communist's Russian Broadcast. A Record That Speaks For Itself'. Dobb had now become 'a well-known Communist' and the *Herald* was accused of inserting its yesterday's leader into its later editions (i.e. after the *Morning Post*'s attack on Dobb) in order to save the BBC from the consequences of having let loose a Communist on the air. To the rest of the article, which did no more than puff up the previous day's story, was added a column and a half of readers' letters protesting at the 'BBC's Socialist Activities'.

The next two days had well-filled columns of letters all in the same vein and on 3 March there was the splendid cartoon of a Bolshevik commissar reading from a script at the microphone. On 10 March the ritual column or so of letters was headlined 'Wireless Given Up In Disgust'. 'More Complaints of BBC Socialism'. '"Notorious Bias"'. 'Demand for Thorough Revision of Methods'. Thereafter, the *Morning Post* spluttered into (temporary) silence. Similar examples can be found in the press cuttings collection and Lambert's account should be seen as a precise and accurate description of how the press made mischief at the BBC's expense.

12 Programme Board Minutes, 3 January 1935, 7 February, 1935. BBC WAC, R34/600/7.
13 This account is taken from BBC WAC, R51/187.
14 Greene to Reith, 23 January 1935, ibid. For the William Ferrie incident see below chapter 13, pp. 290–91.
15 But a few months later the Board of Governors was prepared to defend (almost) to the last the right of Mosley and Pollitt to broadcast (Chapter 5, *The Citizen and His Government* affair). This paradox is best understood by seeing the Board's decision on *What Price Freedom?* as a tightening of control on what was seen as an unruly department. It was moreover a purely internal matter. The idea for *The Citizen and His Government*, however, had come from one of the BBC's advisory bodies, the Adult Education Advisory Committee, whose chairman, Principal J. H. Nicholson of University College Hull, strongly supported the proposal. Moreover this was an educational, not a general talks series.
16 Fielden to Siepmann, 13 February 1935. BBC WAC, R51/187.
17 Reith to Gladstone Murray, 20 February 1935, ibid.
18 Siepmann to Reith, Reith to Siepmann, 10 and 11 March 1935, ibid.
19 Board of Governors, 12 June 1935. BBC WAC, R1/1/4.
20 Hilda Matheson, 'The record of the BBC', *Political Quarterly*, vol. 6, no. 4 (1935), pp. 512, 514.
21 Fielden, *The Natural Bent*, p. 142.
22 In July 1935, Dawnay was explaining to the Ullswater Committee 'our theory in relation to Talks Branch'. 'We want representatives of different interests and different points of view, from the pretty extreme left to the pretty extreme right.... At this moment I am deliberately looking for a man whom I might describe as a member of the Golders Green intelligentsia. We lack such a man. At the moment we do not lack the rather reactionary Tory type of mind.' Verbal evidence, 19 July 1935. BBC WAC, R4/7/18/12.

23 Lambert, *Ariel and All His Quality*, p. 82.
24 Briggs, *Golden Age of Wireless*, p. 148.
25 Ibid.
26 Paul Bloomfield, *BBC* (Eyre and Spottiswoode, London, 1941), p. 172.
27 Lambert, *Ariel and All His Quality*, p. 87.
28 *BBC Hand Book*, 1928, p. 124.
29 Matheson, *Broadcasting*, pp. 75–6.
30 Ibid., pp. 70–1.
31 Ibid., pp. 99–100.
32 Briggs, *The Golden Age of Wireless*, p. 126.
33 John Hilton, *This and That*, 1 August 1937. BBC SAL, LP20767.
34 Bloomfield, *BBC*, p. 84.
35 Reith to de la Mare, 16 February 1933. BBC WAC, R51/339.
36 *BBC Year Book*, 1930, pp. 229–30.
37 McLaren to Healy, 6 April 1936. BBC WAC, Radio Contributors: Maurice Healy.
38 *The Listener*, 1936, vol. 15, p. 701.
39 Ibid., p. 911.
40 Rendall to Laski, 30 January 1933. BBC WAC, Radio Contributors: Harold Laski.
41 Cox to Barnes, 27 August 1937. 1 September 1937. BBC WAC, Radio Contributors: Sir William Beveridge.
42 Matheson to Eckersley, 21 February 1928. BBC WAC, R51/118.
43 *BBC Hand Book*, 1929, p. 41.
44 Beveridge to Adams, 4 March 1932. BBC WAC, Radio Contributors: Sir William Beveridge.
45 Adams to Healy, 4 October 1935. BBC WAC, Radio Contributors: Maurice Healy.
46 Gladstone Murray to C. P., 19 November 1935. BBC WAC, R51/118.
47 Siepmann to Laski, 30 July 1935. BBC WAC, Radio Contributors: Harold Laski.
48 Adams to Maconachie, 13 March 1936. BBC WAC, R51/118.
49 Wilson to Maconachie, 14 December 1936. BBC WAC, ibid.
50 Wilson, '"Men Talking": notes on the experience gained in running this series, January–April, 1937', undated, 1937. BBC WAC, R51/319.
51 Maconachie to Nicolls, 23 April 1937. BBC WAC, ibid.
52 Wilson to Maconachie, 22 July 1937. BBC WAC, ibid. The young lawyer referred to was Edgar Lustgarten who became famous in the fifties as the presenter of a popular crime series on television.
53 Maconachie to Wilson, 13 February 1937. BBC WAC, R51/118.
54 Matheson, 10 October 1928. BBC WAC, ibid.
55 Eckersley, 24 July 1929. BBC WAC, ibid.
56 Translation of article from *Berliner Tageblatt* attached to memorandum from Matheson to D. P., 20 August 1929. BBC WAC, ibid.
57 Rendall to Empire Programme Director, undated, 1933. BBC WAC, ibid.
58 BBC WAC, BP 5, p. 43.
59 Maconachie to Nicolls, 4 March 1938. BBC WAC, R51/397.
60 Nicolls, to North Region Director, 4 March 1938. BBC WAC, R51/354.
61 *The Listener*, 1929, vol. 1, p. 68.
62 Luker to Gibson, 11 October 1937. BBC WAC, R51/319.
63 Luker to Maconachie, 13 November 1937. BBC WAC, ibid.
64 Education Officer, Leeds, 18 October 1937. BBC WAC, ibid.

65 Luker to Quigley, 26, October 1937. BBC WAC, ibid.
66 Gloag, notes on series (undated), 1937. BBC WAC, ibid.
67 Note on a conversation between Salmon and Last, 11 October 1938. BBC WAC, R34/325.
68 Luker to Maconachie, 25 November 1938. BBC WAC, R51/397.
69 Felton, 9 June 1938. BBC WAC, R51/99.
70 Bloomfield, *BBC*, pp. 183–210.
71 Hodge to Salmon, 28 September 1937. BBC WAC, Radio Contributors: Herbert Hodge.
72 Eric Maschwitz, *No Chip on my Shoulder* (Jenkins, London, 1957), p. 67.
73 J. C. Cannell, *In Town Tonight* (George Harrap and Co., London, 1935), p. 8.
74 Ibid., p. 162.
75 *Owt Abaht Owt*, 7 December 1934. BBC WAC, Scripts.
76 Frederick Grisewood, *The World Goes By* (Secker and Warburg, London, 1953), p. 199.
77 Briggs, *Golden Age of Wireless*, p. 123.
78 Arthur Lloyd-James, *The Broadcast Word* (Kegan Paul and Trench Trubner, London, 1935). Briggs, *The Golden Age of Wireless*, pp. 467–9.

CHAPTER 9 *Music policy*

1 See Cyril Ehrlich, *The Music Profession in Britain Since the Eighteenth Century* (Oxford University Press, Oxford, 1985).
2 E. D. Mackerness, *'Somewhere Further North' – A History of Music in Sheffield* (University of Sheffield, Sheffield, 1974).
3 The obvious exception being opera, which did not easily adapt to wireless broadcasting. There were continuing experiments in the search for the best method of presenting opera on wireless from 1928 onwards when *Pelléas et Mélisande* was broadcast from the studio with Filson Young as narrator to explain to listeners the story of the opera and the changing of the scenes (BBC WAC, Radio Contributors: Filson Young. Cf. R27/375/1–7 on Opera Policy from 1930 to 1954). There was a feeling that small-scale music, especially chamber concerts, came over better than large-scale works, and some felt that big choral music did not altogether succeed on radio. The rival merits of studio broadcasts and public performances of music were much debated.
4 *Radio Times*, 5 October 1923.
5 Ibid., 1 February 1924, p. 232.
6 Ibid., 20 February 1925, p. 387.
7 A. Briggs, *The Birth of Broadcasting* (Oxford University Press, London, 1961), p. 279. For listeners' responses, see *Radio Times*, letters, 7 August 1926.
8 Henry Hall, *Here's to the Next Time* (Odhams, London, 1956), p. 64.
9 E. D. Mackerness, *A Social History of English Music* (Routledge & Kegan Paul, London, 1966), p. 251.
10 14 October 1937. BBC WAC, R72/475/3.
11 Minutes of the Ullswater Committee, Folio J, 5 June 1935, p. 382. BBC WAC, R4/7/18/5
12 *Radio Times*, 28 September 1923.

13 Ibid., 12 October, 1923, p. 114.
14 P. McFarlane, *Copyright. The Development and Exercise of the Performing Right* (J. Olford Publications, London, 1980), pp. 113–14.
15 A. Briggs, *The Golden Age of Wireless*, p. 86.
16 Maschwitz, 5 November 1935. BBC WAC, R27/475/1.
17 'The Power Behind Your Dance Music', *Radio Pictorial*, 27 April 1935, p. 15.
18 Variety Department. Minutes of Meeting, 4 May 1936. BBC WAC, R27/475/1.
19 Hall, *Here's to the Next Time*, p. 150.
20 Variety Department. Minutes of Meeting, 4 May 1936. BBC WAC, R27/475/1. On the situation in the USA, see John Ryan, *The Production of Culture in the Music Industry* (University Press of America, Lanham, MD, 1985).
21 Jardine Brown to Nicolls, 11 December 1936. BBC WAC, R27/475/2.
22 Crutwell to Jardine Brown, Limitation of Vocal Numbers, BBC WAC, R27/179.
23 'Song plugging and the Society of Popular Music Publishers', 7 November 1938. BBC WAC, R27/471.
24 Watt to Wellington, 7 December 1939. BBC WAC, R27/475/4.
25 'What is this Crooning?', *Radio Pictorial*, 26 January 1934, p. 16.
26 'Singing on the Air', *Radio Pictorial*, 22 June 1934, p. 17.
27 All details from BBC WAC, R34/281.
28 Dance Music and Vocal Numbers, 2 July 1937. BBC WAC, R27/71/2.
29 This story is constructed from BBC WAC, R27/496.
30 Graves to Nicolls, 20 April 1937. BBC WAC, ibid.
31 Broadcast Dance Music, 4 June 1937. BBC WAC, R27/71/2.
32 All details from Dance Music and Vocal Numbers, 2 July 1937. BBC WAC, R27/71/2.
33 The pop song as we know it did not exist before the war. The voice, in dance music numbers, functioned as one solo instrument among others and like them, had its own solo turn in numbers that featured vocalists. The singer as named star, or as the key figure in a band, was a later development. The first British singer with a named radio showcase of her own was Vera Lynn – *Sincerely Yours, Vera Lynn* was a favourite wartime programme. See also chapter 13, n. 74, p. 410.
34 Details of the Music Department are from Nicholas Kenyon, *The BBC Symphony Orchestra* (BBC, London, 1981), pp. 64ff. See also Boult's own account in Adrian Boult, *My Own Trumpet* (Hamish Hamilton, London, 1972).
35 Kenyon, *The BBC Symphony Orchestra* (BBC, London, 1981), p. 130.
36 This account of the music appreciation movement is from E. D. Mackerness, *A Social History of English Music* (Routledge & Kegan Paul, London, 1966).
37 *BBC Hand Book* 1928, p. 85.
38 *Radio Times*, 12 October 1923.
39 Briggs, *Birth of Broadcasting*, pp. 262, 284, 254.
40 Percy Scholes, *Everybody's Guide to Broadcast Music* (Oxford University Press and Hodder & Stoughton, Oxford and London, 1925).
41 Details of this programme from BBC WAC, R27/106.
42 Filson Young, 30 November 1934, ibid.
43 Boult to Dawnay, 11 November 1934, ibid.
44 Boult to Graves, 5 November 1935, ibid.
45 For histories of the Henry Wood Promenade Concerts, see Ates Orga, *The Proms* (David & Charles, London, 1974) and David Cox, *The Henry Wood Proms* (BBC, London, 1980) from whom this assessment is derived.

46 Cox, *The Henry Wood Proms*, p. 88.

47 For a full account of the formation of the Symphony Orchestra, see Kenyon, *The BBC Symphony Orchestra*.

48 Boult to Nicolls, 17 March 1931. BBC WAC, R27/431.

49 Meeting of 18 October 1934. BBC WAC, R27/100.

50 Sir Walford Davies, 26 June 1935. BBC WAC, R4/7/18/7, Folio N, pp. 639–54.

51 Even more importantly the broadcasting of music, from studios or public places, demanded the rapid development of new technical, engineering and production skills – improvements in microphones and microphone placements, careful attention to the acoustic properties of voices, instruments and the studio or site from which the broadcast was given. Balancing the sound of an orchestra was a skilled art and, by the early thirties, the Music Department had insisted that it should be done only by those who combined technical and musical proficiency for such work. On these developments, see E. Pawley, *BBC Engineering, 1922–1972* (BBC, London, 1972), pp. 41–5, 108–26. Cf. also Philip Elliott and Geoff Matthews, 'Broadcasting culture: innovation, accommodation and routinization in the early BBC, in *Impacts and Influences*, ed. James Curran et al. (Methuen, London, 1987), pp. 234–58.

52 *BBC Hand Book*, 1928, p. 92.

53 Cf. Reginald Nettel, *The Orchestra In England* (Jonathan Cape, London, 1946), pp. 247–9, on Henry Wood's efforts to overcome 'the long established deputy system'.

54 Boult, Written Memorandum to Ullswater Committee, pp. 5–6, BBC WAC, R4/7/6/1.

55 Supplementary evidence to Crawford Committee, p. 12. BBC WAC, R4/2/2.

56 Eckersley to Reith, Music Five Year Plan, 31 December 1934. BBC WAC, R27/11. A nice example of the impact of Soviet centralized planning on the British intelligentsia. Somewhere in the Talks Department a Five Year Plan for Poetry, from the ancient Greeks to the present day, was germinating. Mercifully, perhaps, it never came to fruition.

57 Bliss to Boult, 16 August 1934. BBC WAC, R27/249/1.

58 Dawnay to Bliss, 10 September 1934. BBC WAC, ibid.

59 This decision was released as a public announcement. Full text in Cox, *The Henry Wood Proms*, pp. 106–7.

60 Briggs, *Golden Age of Wireless*, pp. 52–3.

61 Listener Research Report, 26 June 1939. BBC WAC, R9/5/3.

62 All details from Boult to Ogilvie, Decentralization, 25 October 1939. BBC WAC, R27/219.

CHAPTER 10 *Musical tastes*

1 On *Musica Practica*, see Roland Barthes, *Image-Music-Text* (Fontana, London, 1977, pp. 149–54. For a discussion of Barthes' distinction between music that is played and music that is listened to, see Michael Chanan, 'The trajectory of Western Music or, as Mahler said, the music is not in the notes', *Media Culture & Society*, vol. 3, no. 3 (1981), pp. 219–42.

2 Quoted in Percy Scholes, *The Mirror of Music*, vol. 2. (Novello and Oxford University Press, Sevenoaks and London, 1947), p. 798. A good sketch of contemporary musical responses to the coming of radio is given on pp. 795–800.

3 Ibid., p. 797.

4 Constant Lambert, *Music Ho!* (Faber & Faber, London, 1966), p. 109.
5 Quoted in Susan Briggs, *Those Radio Times* (Weidenfeld & Nicolson, London, 1981), p. 108.
6 Lambert, *Music Ho!*, p. 201.
7 Susan Briggs, *Those Radio Times*, p. 109.
8 *Radio Times*, Letters, 14 February 1934.
9 Bliss to Nicolls, Music Policy, 30 December 1941, BBC WAC, R27/245/1.
10 Letter to Scholes, in Percy Scholes, *Everybody's Guide to Broadcast Music* (Oxford University Press and Hodder and Stoughton, Oxford and London, 1925), p. 39.
11 Albert McCarthy, *The Dance Band Era* (Studio Vista, London, 1971), p. 48.
12 *Melody Maker*, November 1928.
13 *Melody Maker*, October 1928, p. 1051.
14 Ibid., September 1928, p. 937.
15 Ibid., March 1929.
16 *Radio Magazine*, March 1934, p. 24.
17 *Melody Maker*, February 1932, pp. 105–6.
18 Ibid., April 1932, pp. 275–7.
19 *Radio Magazine*, February 1934, p. 3.
20 'The North puts gaiety into our dance music', *Radio Pictorial*, February 1935. p. 9.
21 For an authoritative discussion of the bands, see McCarthy, *The Dance Band Era*.
22 *Radio Times*, 14 February 1936, p. 11; 21 February 1936, p. 36; 28 February 1936, p. 11.
23 'Seeing the invisible audience', *Radio Magazine*, October 1934, p. 17.
24 Scholes, *Everybody's Guide to Broadcast Music*, pp. 42, 43, 26.
25 Basil Maine, *Reflected Music* (Methuen, London, 1930), pp. 131–3.
26 Scholes, *Everybody's Guide to Broadcast Music*, p. 43.
27 *Radio Times*, Letter, 10 November 1935.
28 Percy Scholes, *The Radio Times Music Handbook* (Oxford University Press, Oxford, 1935), p. vii.
29 Maine, *Reflected Music*, p. 131.
30 Ibid., p. 132. Letter from Leeds listener, 15 May 1935. BBC WAC, R41/114/1.
31 Percy Scholes, *The Oxford Companion to Music*, 9th edition (Oxford University Press, London, 1955), p. 169, col. a.
32 'Plans for 1931–2', 17 September 1931. BBC WAC, R27/67.
33 *BBC Hand Book*, 1928, p. 98.
34 'Plans for 1931–2', 17 September 1931. BBC WAC, R27/67.
35 'Music Five Year Plan', 31 December 1934. BBC WAC, R27/100.
36 *Musical Times*, 1 January 1929, p. 69.
37 Ibid., 1 March 1930, p. 259.
38 Scholes, *Mirror of Music*, vol. 2, p. 797n.
39 Details from BBC WAC, R27/46/1.
40 *Musical Times*, 1 May 1931, pp. 444–5.
41 Scholes, *Mirror of Music*, vol. 2, p. 797 col. a.
42 'Music Five Year Plan', 31 December 1934. BBC WAC, R27/100.
43 Adam, 9 July 1937. Siepmann, 15 July 1937. BBC WAC, R27/46/2.
44 M. O. to D. P. P., 19 August 1940. BBC WAC, ibid.
45 Otto Karolyi, *Introducing Music* (Pelican Books, Harmondsworth, 1965), p. 111.

46 On this distinction, see Scholes, *The Oxford Companion to Music*, pp. 839–42.
47 Ibid., p. 218, col. b.
48 *Britannica* (1962), vol. 16, p. 16.
49 Pierre Bourdieu, *Distinction. A Social Critique of the Judgement of Taste* (Routledge & Kegan Paul, London, 1984), pp. 56–7.

CHAPTER 11 *Time and money, entertainment and culture*

1 *Radio Times*, 12 October 1923, p. 23.
2 *BBC Hand Book*, 1928, p. 34.
3 *Radio Times*, 20 July 1928, p. 4.
4 Harry Tate, *Popular Wireless*, 28 December 1929.
5 C. B. Cochran, *The Graphic*, 1 March 1929.
6 Ivor Brown, *The Saturday Review*, 23 July 1927.
7 George Graves, *Radio Times*, 4 November 1925.
8 Harry Lauder, *Radio Times*, 15 January 1926, p. 145.
9 Will Hay, *BBC Hand Book*, 1929, pp. 185–6.
10 *Radio Times*, 16 January 1931, p. 111.
11 R. H. Eckersley to Midland Reginal Director, 21 January 1937. BBC WAC, R34/283.
12 Quoted in a letter of complaint from Rev. E. E. Sibley, 20 January 1935. The public apology is quoted in the BBC's reply to the letter. BBC WAC, R34/292/2.
13 Programme Board, 24 January 1935. BBC WAC, R34/600.
14 Controller of Programmes to C. Brewer, 21 July 1937. BBC WAC, R34/292/2.
15 John Watt (ed.), *Radio Variety* (Dent, London, 1939), see Introduction.
16 A. Briggs, *Golden Age of Wireless* (Oxford University Press, London, 1965). pp. 82–3.
17 'Report on Payment of Artists at Coliseum and Alhambra', undated BBC WAC, R30 Stoll Negotiations.
18 Cock to Eckersley, 4 January 1933. BBC WAC, R30 General Theatre Corporation: Studio Ban on Artists.
19 Cock to Eckersley, 12 January 1933. BBC WAC, ibid.
20 Details about Radio Luxembourg are from Martin Head, 'The beginning of Radio Luxembourg: 1930–1939' (Dissertation, Polytechnic of Central London, 1980). See also Briggs, *The Golden Age of Wireless*, pp. 352–69.
21 Head, 'The beginning of Radio Luxembourg', p. 19.
22 Ibid., p. 20.
23 Ibid., p. 24.
24 Ibid., p. 25.
25 J. B. Priestley, *The Star*, 16 January 1935.
26 A. H. Brown, 1937. BBC WAC, Radio Contributors: Elsie and Doris Waters. Other information on fees are from contributor files.
27 Head, 'The beginning of Radio Luxembourg', p. 36.
28 Seebohm Rowntree, *Poverty and Progress* (Longmans, Green and Co., London, 1941), p. 409.
29 Details of the BBC's Sunday policy are from Kenneth Wolfe, *The Churches and the British Broadcasting Corporation, 1922–1956* (SCM Press, London, 1984), pp. 66–75.
30 Ibid., p. 67.

31 Ibid., p. 69.
32 Report of the Programme Revision Committee, 1934. BBC WAC, R34/874. Cf. Briggs, *The Golden Age of Wireless*, pp. 48–52.
33 Reith, 7 March, 1935. BBC WAC, R34/609.
34 Briggs, *The Golden Age of Wireless*, p. 53.
35 For Silvey's account of the history of audience research, see R. Silvey, *Who's Listening: The Story of BBC Audience Research* (Allen & Unwin, London, 1974).
36 Programme Board, 21 March 1935. BBC WAC, R34/600.
37 Reports of Variety Listening Barometer, 1937. BBC WAC R9/5/117, and of General Listening Barometer, 1939. Report no. 14, R9/5/5.
38 'Notes on October–December Programme Schedules', Programme Board, 23 June 1938. BBC WAC, R34/600.
39 Report to Music Advisory Committee, 1939. BBC WAC, R29/199.
40 Briggs, *The Golden Age of Wireless*, pp. 179–80.
41 Opera Position, undated, 1935. BBC WAC, R27/375/1.
42 'Music Policy', Appendix B: p. 12, 1941. BBC WAC, R27/245/1.
43 BBC WAC, R34/874.
44 General Listening Barometer, January 1939. BBC WAC, R9/5/5.
45 Figures derived from BBC *Year Books, Hand Books, Annuals*, 1928–39.
46 Figures derived from annual reports to BBC from Deloitte, Griffiths & Co. 1927–34 and BBC *Annuals* and *Year Books*, 1935–9.
47 A. Peacock and R. Weir. *The Composer in the Market Place* (Faber & Faber, London, 1975), p. 82.
48 Ibid., p. 141.
49 We would like to thank Mr D. J. Perry for his most helpful advice in interpreting these figures. The summaries of programme expenditure for 1934 and 1937 are in BBC WAC, R20/83.
50 This account is from 'Music Productions Unit', 31 August 1938. BBC WAC, R27/375/1.
51 Ibid.
52 'Notes on October–December Programme Schedules', Programme Board, 23 June 1938. BBC WAC, R34/600.
53 Programme Board, 1939, Minute 492, R34/600.
54 'Notes on the October–December Programme Schedules', Programme Board, 23 June 1938. BBC WAC, R34/600.
55 For a fuller analysis and discussion of programme expenditure see David Cardiff, 'Time, money and culture: BBC programme finances 1927–1939', *Media Culture & Society*, vol. 5, nos 3/4 (1983), pp. 373–93.

CHAPTER 12 *Styles of variety*

1 Barry Took, *Laughter in the Air* (Robson Books, London 1976), p. 9.
2 Critic of the *London Star*, cited in *The Performer*, 10 February, 1932.
3 Both letters in *Radio Times*, 22 October 1926, p. 223.
4 Programme Board, 26 July 1929, Minute 3. BBC WAC, R34/600. *BBC Year Book*, 1930, p. 237.

Notes

5 Charles Brewer, *The Spice of Variety* (Frederick Muller, London, 1948).

6 *Radio Times*, 26 February 1932, p. 494, and *Daily Mirror*, 28 March 1932.

7 *Radio Times*, 21 July 1925, p. 361.

8 Sidney Moseley, *Who's Who in Broadcasting*. See entry for Mabel Constanduros.

9 Ted Ray, *Raising the Laughs* (Werner Laurie, London, 1952), p. 67.

10 *Radio Times*, 3 August 1928, p. 191.

11 Ibid., 30 January 1931, pp. 231–2.

12 Eric Midwinter, *Make 'em Laugh* (George Allen & Unwin, London, 1979), p. 60.

13 P. G. Wodehouse, 'Jeeves and the song of songs', in *The World of Jeeves*, (Barrie & Jenkins, London, 1976).

14 Hughie Green, *Opportunity Knocked* (Frederick Muller, London, 1965).

15 Cyril Fletcher, *Nice One Cyril* (Corgi Books, London, 1980), chapter 2.

16 Max Beerbohm, *Last Theatres: 1904–1910* (Rupert Hart-Davis, London, 1970).

17 W. McQueen-Pope, *Gaiety: Theatre of Enchantment*, (W. H. Allen, London, 1949).

18 *Radio Times*, 26 June 1931, p. 728. See also Took, *Laughter in the Air*, p. 6.

19 Susan Briggs, *Those Radio Times*, p. 8.

20 *Radio Times*, 19 December 1924, p. 589.

21 Ibid., 3 August 1928, p. 191.

22 *Vaudeville*. 1931. BBC WAC, Scripts.

23 Ibid.

24 *From the Files*. 1932. BBC WAC, Scripts.

25 *BBC Year Book*, 1932, p. 199.

26 Erving Goffman, *Asylums* (Pelican Books, Harmondsworth, 1968).

27 Eric Midwinter, *Make 'em Laugh*.

28 *Cads' College*, 1938. BBC WAC, Scripts.

29 *Manchester Guardian*, 11 March 1934.

30 Maschwitz, 15 December 1933. BBC WAC R20/150.

31 *Evening News*, 30 August 1935.

32 Maschwitz, 15 December 1933. BBC WAC, R20/150.

33 Eric Maschwitz, *No Chip on My Shoulder* (Jenkins, London, 1957), p. 71.

34 Lance Sieveking, *The Eye of the Beholder* (Hulton Press, London, 1957), p. 188.

35 John Snagge and Michael Barsley, *Those Vintage Days of Radio* (Pitman Publishing, London, 1972), p. 106.

36 *By Royal Appointment*. BBC WAC Scripts.

37 *Café Colette*, 1940. BBC WAC Scripts.

38 *Red Sarafan*, 1935. BBC WAC Scripts.

39 *Daily Worker*, 6 December 1935.

40 Sheridan Morley, *A Talent To Amuse* (Heinemann, London, 1969).

41 Eric Barker, *Steady, Barker!* (Secker & Warburg, London, 1956). Sheila Van Damm, *We Never Closed* (Robert Hale, London, 1967).

42 *Radio Times*, 23 December 1932.

43 *The Writer*, August 1929.

44 *BBC Year Book*, 1932, p. 200.

45 *A Seat In The Park*. BBC WAC Scripts.

46 *BBC Year Book*, 1932, p. 200.

47 *World For Sale*. BBC WAC Scripts.

48 *The World We Listen In*. BBC WAC Scripts.

49   *Manchester Guardian*, 11 January 1932. *Daily Herald*, 9 January 1932.
50   *BBC Annual*, 1936, p. 43.
51   *BBC Year Book*, 1934, p. 117.
52   *BBC Annual*, 1935, p. 57.
53   *BBC Annual*, 1936, pp. 58, 59.
54   Maschwitz, *No Chip on my Shoulder*, p. 67.
55   *Monday Night At Seven*. BBC WAC Scripts.
56   Assistant Director of Programmes, 9 July 1930. BBC WAC R19/989.
57   *BBC Year Book*, 1940, pp. 80–3.
58   Programme Board, 14 March 1935. BBC WAC R34/600.
59   Recalled by the show's producer in *Radio Times*, 7 January 1949, p. 5.
60   *The Times*, 7 November 1936.
61   *Radio Times*, 29 October 1937, p. 9.
62   Programme Board, 1937, Minute 425. BBC WAC, R34/600.
63   *Mr Muddlecombe, J. P.*, 1937. BBC WAC Scripts.
64   *Cad's College*, 1938 (2nd episode), BBC WAC Scripts.
65   Arthur Askey, *Before Your Very Eyes* (Woburn Press, London, 1975), pp. 93–4.
66   Ibid., p. 95.
67   *Band Waggon* scripts, BBC WAC.
68   Askey, *Before Your Very Eyes*, p. 96.
69   *Band Waggon* scripts. BBC WAC.
70   Askey, *Before Your Very Eyes*, pp. 98–9.
71   Variety Listening Barometer, Report No. 6, 9 March 1938. BBC WAC, LR/9/5/117.

CHAPTER 13   *The national culture*

1   Valerie Chancellor, *History For Their Masters: Opinion in the English History Text-Book, 1800–1914* (Adams & Dart, London, 1970). Margaret Mathieson, *The Preachers of Culture* (Unwin Educational, London, 1975).
2   David Cannadine, 'The context, performance and meaning of ritual: the British monarchy and the "Invention of Tradition"', in *The Invention of Tradition*, ed. E. Hobsbawm and T. Ranger (Cambridge University Press, Cambridge, 1983).
3   M. Bommes and P. Wright, 'Charms of residence; the public and the past', in *Making Histories*, ed. R. Johnson et al. (Hutchinson, London, 1982).
4   R. Vaughan Williams, *National Music* (Oxford University Press, Oxford, 1963).
5   David Chaney, 'A symbolic mirror of ourselves: civic ritual in mass society', in *Media Culture & Society. A Critical Reader*, ed. R. Collins et al. (Sage Publications, London, 1986), p. 249.
6   An article on Outside Broadcasts in *Radio Times*, 8 January 1932 (p. 56), claimed that the 10,000th OB had been notched up on 24 November 1931.
7   *Radio Times*, 20 January 1928.
8   Anthony Giddens, *Central Problems in Social Theory* (Macmillan, London, 1979), p. 201.
9   *Radio Times*, 11 May 1934.
10 Ibid., 20 December 1924.
11 Quoted in *Voices out of the Air. The Royal Christmas Broadcasts, 1932–1981*, ed. Tom Fleming (Heinemann, London, 1981), pp. 5–6.

Notes

12 A. Briggs, *Birth of Broadcasting* (Oxford University Press, London, 1961), pp. 290–1.
13 Quoted in Mark Pegg, *Broadcasting and Society, 1918–1939* (Croom Helm, London, 1983), p. 192.
14 C. Stuart, *The Reith Diaries* (Collins, London, 1975), p. 133.
15 Reith, *Memorandum of Information* (1925), p. 4. WAC.
16 Robert Wood, *A World in Your Ear* (Macmillan, London, 1979), pp. 66–72.
17 Ibid., pp. 82–3.
18 Fleming (ed.), *Voices Out of the Air*, pp. 14–15.
19 Ibid., p.17.
20 Wood, *A World in Your Ear*, pp. 83–6.
21 Ibid., pp. 101–12.
22 Humphrey Jennings and Charles Madge (eds), *May the Twelfth: Mass Observation Day-Survey, 1937* (Faber & Faber, London, 1987), pp. 270, 275, 280. From 'Reactions to Radio', pp. 267–94.
23 *BBC Year Book*, 1930, p. 82.
24 Empire Day 1935. BBC WAC, Scripts. Quoted in 'An examination of the BBC Empire Service, its establishment and function, 1932–1939', Monica Delaney (BA Media Studies Dissertation, Polytechnic of Central London, 1979), p. 21.
25 *Radio Times*, 21 December 1934, p. 974.
26 *All The World Over*, 1932. BBC WAC, Scripts.
27 Scripts for both programmes in BBC WAC.
28 Review in *Manchester Guardian*, 27 December 1933.
29 Rex Cathcart, *The Most Contrary Region. The BBC in Northern Ireland, 1924–1984* (The Blackstaff Press, Belfast, 1984), pp. 65–6.
30 Ibid., pp. 5–6.
31 Ibid., pp. 63–4.
32 Programme Director (Northern Ireland) to AC(P), 18 March 1937. BBC WAC, R34/239.
33 Rose-Troup to DT, 20 April 1932, King-Bull to Gielgud, 22 February 1930. BBC WAC, R51/134. L. Fielden to C. Cliffe, undated, 1937. R47, Empire Day 1937.
34 BBC WAC, R19/874.
35 Quoted in *Fifty Years of Vaudeville*, Ernest Short (Eyre & Spottiswoode, London, 1946), p. 169.
36 Martin J. Wiener, *English Culture and the Decline of the Industrial Spirit, 1850–1980* (Penguin Books, Harmondsworth, 1985).
37 Ibid., pp. 72–5.
38 Ibid., cf. pp. 98–126.
39 *The Listener*, 4 October 1933, p. 482. All talks in this series except, obviously, William Ferrie's, were printed in *The Listener*.
40 *The Listener*, 1934, vol. 11, p. 410.
41 *Daily Herald*, 6 March 1934.
42 BBC WAC, BP. 7, p. 2.
43 *The Listener*, 1934, vol. 11, p. 491.
44 Details of this programme in BBC WAC, R51/341.
45 Cock, 7 November 1929. BBC WAC, R34/918/1.
46 *Radio Times*, 3 July 1931, p. 3.
47 Ibid., 27 February 1931.
48 Ibid., 23 February 1934.

49 Graves to D. V., 2 February 1936. BBC WAC, R34/918.
50 Programme Board, 7 February 1936. BBC WAC R34/600.
51 Constanduros to Gielgud, 20 May 1938. BBC WAC, Radio Contributors: Mabel Constanduros.
52 *Radio Times*, 50th Anniversary Souvenir, 1973, p. 38.
53 D. O. S. to Mr Pringle, 19 September 1938. BBC WAC, R19/1191.
54 Ronald Frankau, in a script of *Music Hall* (21 December 1940), confessed, 'We never get any sleep, because in the earliest hours of every morning we have to listen to American jokes, and then spend the remaining pre-dawn translating them into English – for you', BBC WAC Scripts.
55 *BBC Year Book*, 1931, p. 193.
56 *Radio Times*, 5 February 1934, p. 298.
57 From recording of transmission on 2 May 1938. BBC SAL, LP23261–2.
58 *Baghdad On the Subway*, BBC WAC Scripts.
59 *Radio Pictorial*, 19 June 1934,
60 *Radio Pictorial*, 17 June 1938, p. 9.
61 All details from early numbers of *Radio Pictorial*.
62 The Mais programme is quoted in a demonstration record made in the late thirties by the J. Walter Thompson Advertising Company, to persuade their clients of the importance of radio as an advertising medium. We are grateful to Martin Head who drew our attention to this and other fascinating promotions of 1930s commercial radio.
63 Script of 5 January 1936. BBC WAC, E18 V.I.R. Radio Luxembourg.
64 The Official Rule Book of The League of Ovaltineys. Quoted in Head, 'The Beginning of Radio Luxembourg', pp. 64–5.
65 Ibid., p. 49.
66 Ibid., Appendix H, p. 2.
67 Claude Cockburn, *The Devil's Decade* (Sidgwick and Jackson, London, 1973), p. 103.
68 Compton Mackenzie, quoted in John Montgomery, *The Twenties* (George Allen & Unwin, London, 1975), p. 59.
69 Cyril Ehrlich, (Oxford University Press, Oxford, 1985), *The Music Profession in Britain since the Eighteenth Century*, p. 16.
70 Scholes, *Oxford Companion to Music*, p. 487b.
71 Sir Edward Bairstow in evidence to the Ullswater Committee, 26 June 1935. BBC WAC, R4/7/18/7.
72 Ehrlich, *The Music Profession in Britain*, pp. 216–7.
73 Details from BBC WAC, R27/179.
74 Note on Informal Meeting, 9 June 1937, between representatives of the British Authors and Composers Association and the BBC. BBC WAC, R27/179. Graves had defined a British song by the nationality of its composers, but the words and music of most of the contemporary products of Charing Cross Road were mid-Atlantic in style. A British song, before the war, meant something rather more traditional as is evident from the popular series, *Songs of the British Isles*, which began in 1938 and ran through into the war. Freddie Grisewood occasionally compered the programme as Our Bill, a Cotswold rustic, and sang in them. There was an earthy sprinkling of dialect songs of the Muckbottom Fair variety in the weekly selections. A medley of Scottish songs included some sung in Gaelic as well as 'ordinary Scottish airs of the "Annie Laurie" type'. A programme for 16 July 1939 included Men of Harlech, The Vicar of Bray,

Notes

Country Gardens, Widecombe Fair, Londonderry Air, a Sea Shanty pot-pourri and Auld Lang Syne to wash it all down (all details from BBC WAC, R27/480). The contemporary popular song, as the vehicle for a star British singer, did not develop on radio until the Second World War.

75 Thus, Boult writes to D. P., 23 February 1933, after a meeting with the Music Programme Advisory Panel in which the Department had come under fire for its 'senseless predilection for Vienna and Berlin': 'I repeatedly made the point that English professionals were, generally speaking, not good enough for our most important performances, and that for less important things we were encouraging them as far as we possibly could,' BBC WAC, R27/249/1.
76 Boult to Reith, 13 May 1933. Boult to D. P., 12 May 1933. BBC WAC, R27/432.
77 Memorandum by Dr Adrian Boult, submitted to The Broadcasting Committee, 1935 by the British Broadcasting Corporation, pp. 1–6. BBC WAC, R4/7/6/1.
78 *BBC Year Book*, 1930, p. 241.
79 *Monthly Musical Record*, 1 September 1931, pp. 262–3.
80 Cf. Kenyon, *The BBC Symphony Orchestra*, p. 80ff.
81 Howgill to Boult, 31 October 1933. BBC WAC, R55/1.
82 See chapter 15, pp. 342–3.
83 Donald Mitchell, *Britten and Auden in the Thirties* (Faber & Faber, London, 1981), pp. 105–7, 126–7, 165–8.
84 Cox, *The Henry Wood Proms*, p. 94.
85 Boult, 13 May 1935. BBC WAC, R41/114/1.
86 The following account is from BBC WAC, R27/33/1. On the formation of the British Council see Philip Taylor, *The Projection of Britain* (Cambridge University Press, Cambridge, 1981), pp. 125–78.

CHAPTER 14 Local and regional broadcasting

1 P. Eckersley, *The Power Behind the Microphone* (Jonathan Cape, London, 1941), pp. 62–80.
2 J. Reith, *Broadcast over Britain* (Hodder & Stonghton, London, 1924), p. 62. Cf. Eckersley, *Power behind the Microphone*, pp. 68–70.
3 Reith, *Broadcast over Britain*, p. 63.
4 Report by D. P. on Visit to Newcastle, 10/11 January 1924. BBC WAC, R13/361.
5 Robert Wood, *A World in Your Ear* (Macmillan, London, 1979), p. 38.
6 Station Director's Talks, 24 August 1924. BBC WAC, NRS 24A Microfiche.
7 C. A. Lewis, *Broadcasting from Within* (George Newnes, London, 1924), p. 59.
8 Ibid., p. 60.
9 *Radio Times*, 11 April 1924, p. 146.
10 *Radio Times*, 22 January 1926, p. 125.
11 *Radio Times*, 23 November 1923.
12 D. P.'s Report on Visit to Manchester, 8/9 January 1924. BBC WAC, R13/360.
13 29 August 1924. BBC WAC, NRS/24A, Microfiche.
14 21 November 1924, ibid.
15 *Radio Times*, 11 December 1925, p. 548.
16 Quarterly Report on Newcastle Station, Sept.–Dec. 1925. BBC WAC, R13/361.

NOTES

17 Asa Briggs, 'Local and Regional in Northern Sound Broadcasting', *Northern History*, vol. X (1975), pp. 172–3.
18 21 November 1924, 5 December 1924. BBC WAC, NRS/24A, Microfiche.
19 *Radio Times*, 14 August 1925, p. 320.
20 Ibid., 29 January 1926.
21 Ibid., 8 January 1926.
22 Ibid., 30 April 1926, p. 239.
23 Ibid., 29 January 1926, p. 243. 5 February 1926, p. 291. 19 February 1926, p. 392.
24 Ibid., 21 May 1926, p. 330. 28 May 1926, p. 350.
25 Ibid., 6 November 1925, p. 292.
26 *Sunday Chronicle*, 17 January 1926.
27 All details from BBC WAC, R13/361.
28 16 July 1924. BBC WAC, NRS/24A, Microfiche.
29 Ibid., 3 October 1924.
30 Ibid., 24 August 1924.
31 Ibid., 29 April 1925.
32 Cf. Ian Hartley, *2ZY to NBH. An Informal History of the BBC in Manchester and the North West* (Willow Publishing, Altrincham, 1987), p. 27.
33 Programme Meetings, 7 June 1926, 14 June 1926. BBC WAC, R13/360.
34 Reith, *Broadcast Over Britain*, p. 64.
35 *Radio Times*, 10 July 1925, p. 103.
36 Briggs, *Birth of Broadcasting*, p. 182.
37 Reith to Carpendale, 7 December 1923. BBC WAC, R34/731/1.
38 Briggs, *Birth of Broadcasting*, p. 206.
39 Ibid., p. 393.
40 Ibid., pp. 206–7.
41 Ibid., p. 208.
42 Programme Meetings, 15 October 1926. BBC WAC, R13/360.
43 Stobart to Reith, 26 November 1926, ibid.
44 Briggs, *Birth of Broadcasting*, p. 256.
45 Ibid., pp. 291–5 for these details.
46 Clarke to Reith, 22 October 1926. BBC WAC, R34/738/1. We have tried to find the book of instructions referred to in Clarke's memorandum, but without success.
47 Reith to Station Directors, 1 November 1926, ibid.
48 Programme Meetings, 13 September 1926. BBC WAC, R13/360.
49 P. Eckersley, *The Power Behind the Microphone* (Jonathan Cape, London. 1941), p. 172.
50 Ibid., p. 172. Briggs merely notes that Eckersley left the BBC in 1929 'for personal reasons' (*Golden Age of Wireless*, p. 19) which suggests a voluntary departure. This ignores Eckersley's own account which makes it clear that he was forced to resign when Reith ordered his dismissal (*Power Behind the Microphone*, p. 152). Eckersley was 'hurt and angry', and felt one reason for his dismissal was that he was 'not sufficiently subservient' (pp. 152, 153).
51 Ibid., p. 58.
52 Roger Eckersley, *The BBC and All That* (London, Low, Marston, 1946).
53 Briggs, *Golden Age of Wireless*, p. 19.
54 BBC WAC, R13/365/1.

Notes

55 Eckersley, *Power Behind the Microphone*, pp. 81–103. Briggs, *Birth of Broadcasting*, pp. 318–22.
56 Stobart to A. C (P). 21 May 1928. BBC WAC, R34/738/2.
57 *Sheffield Mail*, 20 October 1926.
58 Sharp to Reith, 13 January 1926. BBC WAC, R13/365/1.
59 Reith to All Station Directors, 9 October 1925. BBC WAC, R34/731/1.
60 This account is put together from BBC WAC, R13/365/1–2.
61 The Distribution of the Service, November 1926. BBC WAC, R34/738/1.
62 Ibid.
63 *BBC Hand Book*, 1929, p. 57.
64 A separate Welsh region was established in 1937. Cf. Briggs, *Golden Age of Wireless*, pp. 321–3. Also, 'The Broadcast Service in Wales', *BBC Year Book*, 1933, pp. 65–8.
65 Eckersley to Reith, 13 November 1928. BBC WAC, R34 738/2.
66 Briggs, *Golden Age of Wireless*, p. 307.
67 Eckersley to Regional Directors, 28 November 1928. BBC WAC, R34/738/2.
68 Eckersley to Reith, 15 November 1928. BBC WAC, ibid.
69 Programme Activities, Liveing to Eckersley, undated [December 1928]. BBC WAC, ibid.
70 Regional Programmes, Cleghorn Thomson to Eckersley, 6 December 1928, ibid.
71 Cleghorn Thomson to Eckersley, 5 February 1929. BBC WAC, R34/738/3.
72 Reith to Regional Directors, 25 April 1929. BBC WAC, ibid.
73 Siepmann to Reith, 12 May 1932. BBC WAC, R34/731/2.
74 Liveing to Reith, 13 June 1932. BBC WAC, R34/738/4.
75 Briggs, *Golden Age of Wireless*, p. 37.
76 Ibid., p. 328.
77 Ibid., p. 326.
78 Liveing to Nicolls, 13 August 1934. BBC WAC, R13/357/1.
79 Note on the Staffing of the Regions, 24 June 1935. BBC WAC, R4/7/6/3.
80 Nicolls to All Regional Directors, 25 February 1935. BBC WAC, R34/731/2.
81 Note on the Staffing of the Regions. BBC WAC, R4/7/6/3.
82 BBC WAC, R4/7/18/7 Fol. N.
83 BBC WAC, R4/7/18/5 Fol. J.
84 Memorandum by Dr Adrian Boult, submitted to the Broadcasting Committee, 1935 by the British Broadcasting Corporation. BBC WAC, R4/7/6/1.
85 Regional Policy, undated (1936). BBC WAC R4/7/7.
86 Briggs, *Golden Age of Wireless*, p. 490.
87 C. A. Siepmann, Report on the Regions, January 1936. BBC WAC, R34/734/1.
88 Briggs, *Golden Age of Wireless*, pp. 334–6.

CHAPTER 15 *Manchester and its programmes*

1 C. A. Siepmann, Report on the Regions, January 1936. BBC WAC, R34/734/1.
2 Ibid.
3 Broadcasting in the North of England under the Regional Scheme, September 1927. BBC WAC, R34/738/1.
4 J. B. Priestley, *An English Journey* (Penguin Books, Harmondsworth, 1978).
5 P. Bloomfield, *BBC* (Eyre and Spottiswoods, London, 1941), p. 149.

6 *Steel*, 23 February 1937. BBC SAL, T28010.
7 Outside Broadcast Activities in North Region, 24 September 1930. BBC WAC, R13/357/1.
8 *Radio Times*, 10 March 1933.
9 D. Bridson, *Prospero and Ariel* (Gollancz, London, 1972), p. 28.
10 Bloomfield, *BBC*, pp. 50–51.
11 *Manchester Guardian, 28 October 1930*.
12 Harding to Gielgud, 3 November 1930. BBC WAC, R19/352/1.
13 There were two series of this programme. The account that follows is compiled from Bridson, *Prospero and Ariel*, pp. 53–6, and BBC WAC, N2/50. There are several scripts in WAC and two complete recordings: 'Saltersgate to Staithes, or Harry Hopeful's Day in Cleveland', 22 October 1935, SAL, LP771f1–3, and 'Cressbrook to Ashbourne, or Harry Hopeful's Day in the Derbyshire Dales', 13 April 1936, SAL, T1048.
14 23 February 1937. This account is compiled from BBC WAC, N2/124. Complete recording, BBC SAL, T28010.
15 *Coalface* was the first documentary film with a sound track. It had a musical score by Benjamin Britten and verse and choruses by W.H. Auden. In 1938 Bridson produced *Coronation Scot*, which aimed to be 'even more exciting than the *Night Mail* documentary film' (BBC WAC, N28 for production details). The activities of the film documentarists were a point of reference and stimulus for radio features and documentary producers.
16 *Daily Independent*, 24 February 1937. The *Sheffield Telegraph* took a more judicious view of the programme and there was an interesting discussion of the programme, for and against, in its letters columns.
17 17 November 1938. This account is compiled from BBC WAC, N2/16. The disc recordings contain extracts, not the complete programme. BBC SAL, LP31338f1.
18 Bridson, *Prospero and Ariel*, p. 69.
19 Ibid., p. 70.
20 Technical details from Pawley, *BBC Engineering*, pp. 189–90.
21 12 January 1939. Details from BBC WAC, N2/11.
22 30 April 1938. BBC WAC, NR Scripts.
23 25 August 1939. BBC WAC, NR Scripts.
24 6 September 1938. BBC WAC, NR Scripts.
25 29 March 1939. BBC WAC, NR Scripts.
26 *Radio Times*, 19 May 1939, p. 4.
27 1 June 1939. BBC WAC, NR Scripts. Complete recording, SAL, T28038.
28 6 July 1939. BBC WAC, NR Scripts. Complete recording, SAL, LP25677.
29 Interview with Olive Shapley, July 1980.
30 Briggs, *Golden Age of Wireless*, p. 40.
31 *Yorkshire Observer*, 10 July 1935.
32 Regionalism in Broadcasting, *Yorkshire Post*, 9 May 1938.
33 Wilson to Maconachie, June 1937. BBC WAC, R51/319.
34 *Radio Times*, 12 June 1937.
35 Briggs, *Golden Age of Wireless*, pp. 151–2.
36 *Yorkshire Evening Post*, 16 May 1939.
37 *Manchester Guardian*, 15 June 1939.

38 Text from *Manchester Guardian*, 14 March 1934.
39 *Daily Worker*, 15 March 1934.
40 Ewan MacColl, 'Grass roots of Theatre Workshop', *Theatre Quarterly*, vol. VII, no. 9 (1973), pp. 58–68. Howard Gurney and Ewan MacColl, *Agit-Prop to Theatre Workshop* (Manchester University Press, Manchester, 1986).
41 The memorandum is with the script. BBC WAC, NR Scripts.
42 Letter in BBC WAC, N2/16.
43 *The Listener*, 6 March 1939.
44 *Daily Dispatch*, 8 February 1938.
45 *Radio Times*, 26 August 1938.

CHAPTER 16 *The Listener*

1   Jonathan Hill, *The Cat's Whisker. 50 Years of Wireless Design* (Oresko Books, London. 1978), p. 36.
2   On crystal and valve sets, see Mark Pegg, *Broadcasting and Society*, 1918 – 1939 (Croom Helm, London, 1983), pp. 36–40.
3   Shaun Moores, '"The box on the dresser": memories of early radio and everyday life', *Media Culture & Society*, vol. 10, no. 1 (1988), p. 30.
4   Ibid., pp. 29–30.
5   Susan Briggs, *Those Radio Times* (Weidenfeld & Nicolson, London, 1981), p. 29.
6   Ibid.
7   Pegg, *Broadcasting and Society*, p. 40.
8   See Hill, *The Cat's Whisker*, pp. 73–8.
9   Adrian Forty, *Objects of Desire. Design and Society, 1750–1980.* (Thames & Hudson, London, 1986), pp. 11–13, 200–6, on the design of radio sets.
10 Pegg, *Broadcasting and Society*, p. 39.
11 Quoted in Susan Briggs, *Those Radio Times*, pp. 28–9.
12 Forty, *Objects of Desire*, p. 202. See illustration p. 12.
13 Ibid.
14 Ibid., pp. 203–5.
15 Prices of sets from Hill, *The Cat's Whisker*.
16 Forty, *Objects of Desire*, p. 188.
17 Ibid., p. 189.
18 Moores, '" The box on the dresser"', p. 29.
19 Forty, *Objects of Desire*, pp. 188–9.
20 On the growth of licence fees and the regional distribution of sets before the war, see Pegg, *Broadcasting and Society*, pp. 6–17.
21 George Orwell, *The Road to Wigan Pier* (Heinemann Educational, London, 1965), ch. V, pp. 90–1.
22 Hilda Jennings and Winifred Gill, *Broadcasting in Everyday Life*, (BBC, London, 1939), p. 10.
23 B. Seebohm Rowntree, *Poverty And Progress* (Longmans, Green and Co., London, 1941), p. 469.
24 Ibid., pp. 430, 432, 433, 444.
25 Ibid., p. 411. Jennings and Gill noted very similar responses.

26 Jennings and Gill, *Broadcasting in Everyday Life*, p. 13.
27 Moores, ' "The box on the dresser" ', p. 25.
28 Jennings and Gill, *Broadcasting in Everyday Life*, p. 23.
29 Raymond Williams, *Television. Technology and Cultural Form*, (Fontana, London, 1974), p. 26.
30 John Stevenson, *British Society 1914–45* (Pegnuin Books, Harmondsworth, 1984), p. 221.
31 Ibid., p. 142
32 Ibid., p. 144.
33 Ibid., p. 163.
34 Ibid., pp. 163–4.
35 Ibid., pp. 165–6.
36 Evelyn Waugh, *Vile Bodies* (Chapman and Hall, London, 1930), p. 223.
37 Orwell, 'The Lion and the Unicorn' (1941), *The Collected Essays, Journalism and Letters of George Orwell*, pp. 77–8.
38 Williams, *Television. Technology and Cultural Form*, pp. 27–8.
39 C. A. Lewis, *Broadcasting from Within* (George Newnes, London, 1924), pp. 47–8.
40 *Radio Times*, 2 May 1924.
41 1st General News Bulletin, 7.00 pm, 18 May 1926. BBC WAC, CO/32/4.
42 *BBC Year Book*, 1930, pp. 60–1. Also Filson Young, 'Intelligent Listening', pp. 231–2.
43 Filson Young, *Shall I Listen?* (Constable, London, 1933), p. 264. Filson Young had a position in the BBC as 'programme consultant' until his death in 1938 and was encouraged to express his opinions both within the BBC and in *Radio Times* on all aspects of programmes. His views were, to some extent, those of the BBC, though Briggs notes that in his later years he was increasingly unpopular in Broadcasting House (Briggs, *The Golden Age of Wireless*, p. 71).
44 *The Listener*, Editorial, 30 September 1936.
45 Ibid.
46 *Radio Times*, 20 February 1931, p. 414.
47 *BBC Year Book*, 1930, p. 60.
48 *BBC Hand Book*, 1929, p. 175.
49 Maurice Gorham, *Sound and Fury* (Marshall, London, 1948), p. 52.
50 *BBC Year Book*, 1932, p. 115.
51 Young, *Shall I Listen?*, p. 264.
52 *Radio Times*, 19 January 1931, p. 108.
53 Ibid.
54 P. Abrams, 'Television and radio', in *Discrimination and Popular Culture*, ed. D. Thompson (Penguin Books, Harmondsworth, 1973), p. 113.
55 Jack Jones, 'Survey of the Social Effects of the Coming of Broadcasting (South Wales)', (BBC, 1938), p. 8.
56 *Radio Times*, Fireside Number, 15 November 1935.
57 Ibid., Listener's Own Number, 15 April 1938.
58 Ibid., Home Number, 18 November 1938.
59 Simon Frith, 'The pleasures of the hearth: the making of BBC light entertainment', in *Formations of Pleasure*, ed. James Donald (Routledge Kegan Paul, London, 1983).
60 Pegg, *Broadcasting and Society*, p. 99.

61 *Manchester Guardian*, 9 July 1935. Quoted in David Chaney, 'Audience research and the BBC in the 1930s: a mass medium comes into being', in *Impacts and Influences*, ed. James Curran et al. (Methuen, London, 1987) pp. 259–77. The article has a useful sketch of Tallents' career before joining the BBC.
62 Quoted in Briggs, *The Golden Age of Wireless*, p. 266.
63 See Pegg, *Broadcasting and Society*, pp. 129–40
64 Ibid., pp. 113–29.
65 Report on the Variety Listening Barometer, Interim Reports 5 and 6. BBC WAC, LR9/5/117.
66 Ibid., Main Report, Part 1, p. 3.
67 General Listening Barometer, returns for February 1939. BBC WAC, R9/5/5.
68 Interim Report, no. 5, BBC WAC, R9/5/5. It is worth noting that on the question 'Should the policy [of serialization] be carried further?' 72 per cent of working-class respondents were for and 26 per cent against, compared with 48 per cent of middle-class respondents for and 44 per cent against.
69 Report on the Variety Listening Barometer, Main Report Part 2, pp. 55–62. BBC WAC, LR9/5/117.

Sources and Bibliography

———⟶❋⟵———

BBC SOURCES

The primary source for this history has been the holdings on all aspects of broadcasting in the BBC Written Archives at Caversham, referred to in the footnotes as BBC WAC. The great bulk of pre-war material has now been shelf-listed and catalogued. An indexed précis of shelf-holdings currently covers the music and policy catalogues and is being extended to other areas. Apart from drama scripts which are still held in London, extant scripts for all other areas of production are held at Caversham either in manuscript or on microfiche. There are complete runs from the beginning of *Radio Times* (including regional variations), *The Listener* and the *BBC Hand Books, Year Books* and *Annuals* (as they were variously called) all of which are invaluable sources of information on all aspects of broadcasting. We used the Northern Edition of *Radio Times* because of our particular interest in the activities of the northern stations in the twenties and of Manchester in the thirties. The full minutes of the pre-war parliamentary Committees of Inquiry into broadcasting are also part of Caversham's collection.

Recordings of pre-war programmes are held in the BBC Sound Archives, Broadcasting House, London (referenced in the notes as BBC SAL). The sound archives are regarded still as an internal BBC resource for use in programme-making and are not open to the public for research purposes. Those wishing to hear pre-war radio may do so at the National Sound Archives, 29 Exhibition Road, London SW6. There is little recorded material before 1935, but from then on – although the material represents only a tiny fraction of the total volume of output – some idea may be gleaned of what radio sounded like in the last few years before the war.

The BBC's Photograph library, again not open to the public, has a precious collection of publicity photographs, mainly from the thirties, which illustrate – rather like the recorded programmes – significant aspects of pre-war programme-making. It also has a collection of publicity pictures of leading members of staff.

Sources and Bibliography

OFFICIAL SOURCES

[Annan Report] *Report of the Committee on the Future of Broadcasting*, Cmnd. 6753 HMSO, London, 1977).
[Crawford Report] *Report of the Broadcasting Committee*, Cmnd. 2599 (HMSO, London, 1925).
[Peacock Report] *Report of the Committee on Financing the BBC*, Cmnd. 9284 (HMSO, London, 1986).
[Pilkington Report] *Report of the Broadcasting Committee*, Cmnd. 1753 (HMSO, London, 1960).
[Sykes Report] *Broadcasting Committee Report*, Cmnd. 1951 (HMSO, London, 1923).
[Ullswater Report] *Report of the Broadcasting Committee*, Cmnd. 5091 (HMSO, London, 1936).
Hansard is essential for all aspects of political broadcasting.

CONTEMPORARY PERIODICALS

Radio Pictorial and *Radio Magazine* both started in January 1934 and are illuminating on all aspects of the culture of popular radio. *Melody Maker, Musical Times* and the *Monthly Music Record* were all consulted for contemporary musical responses to the impact of radio. *Punch* for the period was checked for illustrative material.

BIBLIOGRAPHY

Abrams, P., 'Television and radio', in *Discrimination and Popular Culture*, D. Thompson (ed.) (Penguin Books, Harmondsworth, 1973).
Adorno, T. and Horkheimer, M., *Dialectic of Enlightenment (Verso, London, 1979)*.
Anderson, D. G., *Fascists, Communists and the National Government. Civil Liberties in Great Britain, 1931–1937* (University of Minnesota Press, Columbia and London, 1983).
Angell, N., *After All* (Hamish Hamilton, London, 1951).
Askey, A., *Before Your Very Eyes* (Woburn Press, London, 1975).
Barker, E., *Steady Barker!* (Secker & Warburg, London, 1956).
Barnouw, E., *The Golden Web. A History of Broadcasting in the United States*, volume 2 *1935–1955* (Oxford University Press, New York, 1968).
Barthes, R., *Image-Music-Text* (Fontana, London, 1977).
Beales, H. L. and Lambert, R. S., *Memoirs of the Unemployed* (Gollancz, London, 1934).
Beerbohm, M., *Last Theatres: 1904–1910* (Rupert Hart-Davis, London, 1970).
Beveridge, W., *Unemployment. A Problem of Industry* (Longman, London, 1909).
Bloomfield, P., *BBC* (Eyre & Spottiswoode, London, 1941).
Bommes, M. and Wright, P., 'Charms of residence: the public and the past', in *Making Histories*, ed. R. Johnson et al. (Hutchinson, London, 1982).
Boult, A., *My Own Trumpet* (Hamish Hamilton, London, 1972).
Bourdieu, P., *Distinction. A Social Critique of the Judgement of Taste*, (Routledge and Kegan Paul, London, 1984).
Boyce, G., 'The Fourth Estate: the reappraisal of a concept', in *Newspaper History: From*

419

the 17th Century to the Present Day, ed. G. Boyce et al. (Sage/Constable, London, 1978).

Branson, N. and Heinmann, M., *Britain in the Nineteen Thirties* (Panther Books, London, 1973).

Brewer, C., *The Spice of Variety* (Frederick Muller, London, 1948).

Bridson, D., *Prospero and Ariel* (Gollancz, London, 1972).

Briggs, A., *The Birth of Broadcasting, The History of Broadcasting in the United Kingdom*, volume 1 (Oxford University Press, London, 1961).

Briggs, A., *The Golden Age of Wireless, The History of Broadcasting in the United Kingdom*, volume 2 (Oxford University Press, London, 1965).

Briggs, A., *Governing the BBC* (BBC, London, 1979).

Briggs, A., 'Local and Regional in Northern sound broadcasting', *Northern History*, vol. X (1975).

Briggs, A., 'Problems and possibilities in the writing of broadcasting history', *Media Culture & Society*, vol. 2, no. 1 (1980).

Briggs, S., *Those Radio Times* (Weidenfeld and Nicolson, London, 1981).

Burns, T. *BBC. Public Institution, Private World* (Macmillan, London, 1977).

Calder-Marshall, A., *The Changing Scene* (Chapman and Hall, London, 1937).

Cannadine, D., 'The context, performance and meaning of ritual: the British monarchy and the "Invention of Tradition"', in *The Invention of Tradition*, E. Hobsbawm and T. Ranger (eds) (Cambridge University Press, Cambridge, 1983).

Cannell, J. C., *In Town Tonight* (George Harrap and Co., London. 1935).

Cardiff, D., 'Time, money and culture: BBC programme finances, 1927–1939', *Media Culture & Society*, vol. 5, no. 3/4 (1983).

Cardiff, D. and Scannell, P., 'Broadcasting and national unity', in *Impacts and Influences*, J. Curran et al. (eds) (Methuen, London, 1987).

Cathcart, R., *The Most Contrary Region. The BBC in Northern Ireland, 1924–1984* (The Blackstaff Press, Belfast, 1984).

Chancellor, V., *History For Their Masters: Opinion in the English History Text-Book, 1800–1914* (Adams & Dart, London, 1970).

Chaney, D., 'A symbolic mirror of ourselves: civic ritual in mass society', in *Media Culture & Society, A Critical Reader*, R. Collins et al. (eds) (Sage, London, 1986).

Chaney, D., 'Audience research and the BBC in the 1930s: a mass medium comes into being', in *Impacts and Influences*, J. Curran et al. (eds) (Methuen, London, 1987).

Chanan, M., 'The trajectory of western music or, as Mahler said, the music is not in the notes', *Media Culture & Society*, vol. 3 no. 3 (1981).

Clark, J. et al. *Culture and Crisis in Britain in the 30s* (Lawrence and Wishart, London, 1979).

Cockburn, C., *The Devil's Decade* (Sidgwick & Jackson, London, 1973).

Collins, R. et al. (eds), *Media Culture & Society. A Critical Reader* (Sage, London, 1986).

Coulton, B., *Louis MacNeice in the BBC* (Faber and Faber, London, 1980).

Cox, D., *The Henry Wood Proms* (BBC, London, 1980).

Crompton, R., *William The Good* (Macmillan, London, 1984).

Culbert, D. H. *News for Everyman. Radio and Foreign Affairs in Thirties America* (Greenwood Press, Westport, Conn., 1976).

Curran, C., *A Seamless Robe* (Collins, London 1979).

Curran, J. et al. (eds), *Mass Communication and Society* (Edward Arnold/Open University Press, London, 1977).

Curran, J. et al. (eds), *Impacts and Influences* (Methuen, London, 1987).

Sources and Bibliography

Curran, J. and Seaton, J., *Power without Responsibility. The Press and Broadcasting in Great Britain*, 3rd edition (Routledge, London, 1988).

Delaney, M., 'An examination of the BBC Empire Service: its establishment and function, 1932–1939' (Media Studies Dissertation, Polytechnic of Central London, 1979).

Dimbleby, J., *Richard Dimbleby* (Hodder and Stoughton, London, 1975).

Dimmock, M. E., *British Public Utilities and National Development* (Allen and Unwin, London, 1933).

Donald, J. (ed.) *Formations of Pleasure* (Routledge and Kegan Paul, London, 1983).

Donald, J. (ed.) *Formations of Nation and People* (Routledge and Kegan Paul, London, 1984).

Doyle, B., *English and Englishness* (Routledge, London 1989).

Drakakis, J. (ed.), *British Radio Drama* (Cambridge University Press, Cambridge, 1981).

Eckersley, P., *The Power Behind The Microphone* (Jonathan Cape, London, 1941).

Eckersley, R., *The BBC and All That* (Marston Low, London, 1946).

Ehrlich, C., *The Music Profession in Britain since the Eighteenth Century* (Oxford University Press, Oxford, 1985).

Elliott, P. and Matthews, G., 'Broadcasting culture: innovation, accommodation and routinization in the early BBC', in *Impacts and Influences*, J. Curran et al. (eds) (Methuen, London, 1987).

Farman, C., *May 1926. The General Strike. Britain's Aborted Revolution* (Panther Books, London, 1974).

Felton, F., *The Radio-Play. Its Techniques and Possibilities* (Sylvan Press, London, 1949).

Fielden, L., *The Natural Bent* (André Deutsch, London, 1960).

Fleming, Tom (ed.) *Voices out of the Air. The Royal Christmas Broadcasts 1932–1981* (Heinemann, London, 1981)

Fletcher, C. *Nice One Cyril* (Corgi, Books, London, 1980).

Forty, A., *Objects of Desire. Design and Society, 1750–1980* (Thames and Hudson, London, 1986).

Giddens, A., *Central Problems in Social Theory* (Macmillan, London 1979).

Gielgud, V., *British Radio Drama, 1922–1956* (Harrap, London, 1956).

Gielgud, V., *Years in a Mirror* (The Bodley Head, London, 1965).

Glendinning, V., *Vita. The Life of Vita Sackville-West* (Weidenfeld & Nicolson, London, 1983).

Goffman, E., *Asylums* (Pelican Books, Harmondsworth, 1968).

Gorham, M., *Sound and Fury* (Marshall, London, 1948).

Green, H., *Opportunity Knocked* (Frederick Muller, London, 1965).

Grisewood, F., *The World Goes By* (Secker and Warburg, London, 1952).

Gurney, H. and MacColl, E., *Agit-Prop to Theatre Workshop* (Manchester University Press, Manchester, 1986).

Habermas, J., *The Structural Transformation of the Public Sphere* (Polity Press, Cambridge, 1989).

Hall, H., *Here's to the Next Time* (Odhams, London, 1956).

Hall, S., 'Television and culture', *Sight and Sound*, Summer 1976.

Hannington, W., *The Problem of the Distressed Areas* (Gollancz, Left Books, London, 1937).

Hannington, W., *Unemployed Struggles* (Lawrence and Wishart, London, 1977).

Hardy, F., *Grierson on Documentary* (Faber and Faber, London, 1966).

Harrison, T. and Madge, C., *Britain by Mass Observation* (Penguin Special, Harmondsworth, 1939).

Hartley, I., *2ZY to NBH, An Informal History of the BBC in Manchester and the North* (Willow Press, Altrincham, 1987).

Haworth, B., 'The British Broadcasting Corporation, Nazi Germany and the Foreign Office', *The Historical Journal of Film, Radio and Television*, vol, 1, no. 1 (1981).

Head, M., 'The beginning of Radio Luxembourg' (Media Studies Dissertation, Polytechnic of Central London, 1980).

Heppenstall, R., *Portrait of the Artist as a Professional Man* (Peter Owen, London, 1967).

Hill, J., *The Cat's Whisker. Fifty Years of Wireless Design* (Oresko Books, London, 1978).

History of The Times, The, vol. IV (Times Publishing Co. London, 1952).

Hobsbawm, E. and Ranger, T., *The Invention of Tradition* (Cambridge University Press, Cambridge, 1983).

Hynes, S., *The Auden Generation. Literature and Politics in England in the 1930s* (Faber and Faber, London, 1966).

Jeffery, T., 'Mass Observation: a short history' (Centre for Contemporary Cultural Studies, stencilled paper, Birmingham University, 1977).

Jennings, Hilda and Gill, Winifred, *Broadcasting in Everyday Life* (BBC, London, 1939).

Jennings, Humphrey and Madge, Charles (eds), *May the Twelfth. Mass Observation Day Survey, 1937* (Faber and Faber, London, 1987).

Johnson, R. et al., *Making Histories* (Hutchinson, London, 1982).

Karolyi, O., *Introducing Music* (Pelican Books, Harmondsworth, 1965).

Karpf, A., *Doctoring the Media* (Routledge, London, 1988).

Kenyon, N., *The BBC Symphony Orchestra* (BBC, London, 1981).

Kingsford, P., *The Hunger Marchers in Britain, 1920–1940* (Lawrence and Wishart, London, 1977).

Klaus, G, *The Literature of Labour* (Harvester Press, Brighton, 1985).

Kumar, K. 'Holding the middle ground: the BBC, the public and the professional broadcaster', in *Mass Communication and Society*, J. Curran et al. (eds) (Edward Arnold/Open University Press, London, 1977).

Lambert, C., *Music Ho!* (Faber and Faber, London, 1966).

Lambert, R. S., *Ariel and All His Quality* (Gollancz, London, 1940).

Leavis, F. R., *Mass Civilisation and Minority Culture* (Minority Press, Cambridge, 1930).

LeMahieu, D. L., *A Culture for Democracy* (Oxford University Press, Oxford, 1988).

Lewis, C. A., *Broadcasting from Within* (George Newnes, London, 1924).

Lindsay, A. D., *Essentials of Democracy* (Oxford University Press, London, 1929).

Lippmann, W., *Liberty and the News* (Harcourt, Brace & Howe, New York, 1920).

Lloyd-James, A., *The Broadcast Word* (Kegan Paul & Trench Trubner, London, 1935).

Low, R., *The History of the British Film 1929–1939: Documentary and Educational Films of the 1930s* (George Allen & Unwin, London, 1985).

MacColl, E., 'Grass roots of Theatre Workshop', *Theatre Quarterly*, vol. 8, no. 9 (1973).

Mackerness, E. D., *A Social History of English Music* (Routledge & Kegan Paul, London, 1966).

Mackerness, E. D., *'Somewhere Further North'. A History of Music in Sheffield* (University of Sheffield, Sheffield, 1974).

Maine, B., *Reflected Music* (Methuen, London, 1930).

Mansell, G., *Let Truth be Told. Fifty Years of BBC External Broadcasting* (Weidenfeld and Nicolson, London, 1982).

Marshall, H., *Slum* (Heinemann, London, 1933).

Maschwitz, E., *No Chip on my Shoulder* (Jenkins, London, 1957).

Matheson, H., *Broadcasting* (Thornton Butterworth, London, 1933).

Matheson, H., 'The record of the BBC', *Political Quarterly*, vol. 6, no. 4 (1935).

Mathieson, M., *The Preachers of Culture* (Allen & Unwin, London, 1975).

McCarthy, A., *The Dance Band Era* (Studio Vista, London, 1971).

McFarlane, P., *Copyright. The Development and Exercise of the Performing* Right (J. Olford Publications., London, 1980).

McQueen-Pope, W., *Gaiety, Theatre of Enchantment* (W. H. Allen, London, 1949).

Middlemas, K., *Politics in Industrial Society* (André Deutsch, London, 1980).

Midwinter, E., *Make 'em Laugh* (George Allen & Unwin, London, 1979).

Mitchell, D., *Britten and Auden in the Thirties* (Faber and Faber, London, 1981).

Montgomery, J., *The Twenties* (George Allen and Unwin, London, 1957).

Moores, S., ' "The box on the dresser": memories of early radio and everyday life', *Media Culture & Society*, vol. 10, no. 1 (1988).

Morley, S., *A Talent to Amuse* (Heinemann, London, 1969).

Morris, M. (ed.), *The General Strike* (Penguin Books, Harmondsworth, 1976).

Moseley, S. A. (ed.), *Who's Who in Broadcasting* (Pitman, London, 1933).

Moseley, S. A., *Broadcasting in my Time* (Richard Cowan, London, 1935).

Mowatt, C. L., *Britain between the Wars, 1918–1940* (Methuen University Paperbacks, London, 1968).

Mumford, L., *Technics and Civilization* (New York, 1934).

Nettel, R., *The Orchestra in England* (Jonathan Cape, London, 1946).

Orga, A., *The Proms* (David and Charles, London, 1974).

Orwell, G., *The Road to Wigan Pier* (Heinemann Education, London, 1965).

Orwell, G., *Collected Essays. Journalism and Letters of George Orwell*. vol. 1, *An Age Like This* (Secker and Warburg, London, 1968).

Pawley, E., *BBC Engineering, 1922–1972* (BBC, London, 1972).

Peacock, A. and Weir, R., *The Composer in the Market Place* (Faber and Faber, London, 1978).

Pegg, M., *Broadcasting and Society, 1918–1939* (Croom Helm, London, 1983).

Political and Economic Planning (PEP), *Report on the British Press* (London, 1938).

Priestley, J. B., *An English Journey* (Penguin Books, Harmondsworth, 1978).

Ray, T., *Raising the Laughs* (Werner Laurie, London, 1952).

Reid, B., 'The Left Book Club in the thirties', *Culture and Crisis in the Thirties'*, J. Clark et al. (eds) (Lawrence and Wishart, London, 1979).

Reith, J., *Broadcast over Britain* (Hodder and Stoughton, London, 1924).

Reith, J., *Into the Wind* (Hodder and Stoughton, London, 1949).

Robinson, J., *Learning Over the Air* (BBC, London, 1982).

Rodger, I., *Radio Drama* (Macmillan, London, 1982).

Rotha, P., *Documentary Film* (Faber and Faber, London, 1936).

Rowntree, S., *Poverty and Progress* (Longmans, Green and Co. London, 1941).

Ryan, J., *The Production of Culture in the Music Industry* (University Press of America, Lanham MD, 1985).

Sampson, G., *English for the English* (Cambridge University Press, Cambridge, 1925).

Scaffardi, S., *Fire under the Carpet. Working for Civil Liberties in the 1930s* (Lawrence and Wishart, London, 1986).

Scholes, P., *Everybody's Guide to Broadcast Music* (Oxford University Press and Hodder & Stoughton, Oxford and London, 1925).

Scholes, P., *The Radio Times Music Handbook* (Oxford University Press, Oxford, 1935).

Scholes, P., *The Mirror of Music*, 2 vols (Novello and Oxford University Press, Sevenoaks and London, 1947).

Scholes, P., *The Oxford Companion to Music*, 9th edition (Oxford University Press, London, 1955).

Schwarz, B., 'The language of constitutionalism: Baldwinite conservatism', in *Formations of Nation and People*, J. Donald (ed.) (Routledge and Kegan Paul, London, 1984).

Short, E., *Fifty Years of Vaudeville* (Eyre and Spottiswoode, London, 1946).

Sieveking, L., *The Stuff of Radio* (Cassell and Co., London, 1934).

Sieveking, L., *The Eye of the Beholder* (Hulton Press, London, 1957).

Silvey, R., *Who's Listening? The Story of BBC Audience Research* (Allen & Unwin, London, 1977).

Snagge, J. and Barsley, M., *Those Vintage Days of Radio* (Pitman Publishing, London, 1972).

Stevenson, J., *Social Conditions in Britain Between the Wars* (Penguin Books, Harmondsworth, 1977).

Stevenson, J., *British Society, 1914–1945* (Penguin Books, Harmondsworth, 1984).

Stuart, C., *The Reith Diaries* (Collins, London, 1975).

Sussex, E., *The Rise and Fall of British Documentary* (University of California Press, Berkeley, 1975).

Taylor, P., *The Projection of Britain* (Cambridge University Press, Cambridge, 1981).

Thompson, D., *Discrimination and Popular Culture* (Penguin Books, Harmondsworth, 1973).

Thompson, E. P., *The Making of the English Working Class* (Pelican Books, Harmondsworth, 1968).

Took, B., *Laughter in the Air* (Robson Books, London, 1976).

Tracey, M., *The Production of Political Television* (Routledge Direct Editions, London 1979).

Van Damm, S., *We Never Closed* (Robert Hale, London, 1967).

Vaughan Williams, R., *National Music* (Oxford University Press, Oxford, 1963).

Watt, J., *Radio Variety* (Dent, London, 1939).

Waugh, E., *Vile Bodies* (Chapman and Hall, London, 1930).

Wiener, M., *English Culture and the Decline of the Industrial Spirit, 1850–1950* (Penguin Books, Harmondsworth, 1985).

Williams, R., *Culture and Society* (Pelican Books, Harmondsworth, 1963).

Williams, R., *Television: Technology and Cultural Form* (Fontana, London, 1974).

Wilson, C., *Parliaments, People and Mass Media* (Cassell & Co, London, 1970).

Wilson, K., *Technologies of Control: the New Interactive Media for the Home* (University of Wisconsin Press, Wisconsin, 1988).

Wodehouse, P. G., *The World of Jeeves* (Barnes and Jenkins, London, 1976).

Wolfe, K., *The Churches and the British Broadcasting Corporation, 1922–1956* (SCM Press, London, 1984).

Wood, R., *A World in Your Ear* (Macmillan, London, 1979).

Young, F., *Shall I Listen?* (Constable, London, 1933).

Index

N.B.C. (National Broadcasting
Corporation), 130, 295
Nansen, Fridtjof, 84
Nash, George, 203
National, The, 129
National Character, The, 290
National Council for Civil Liberties, 47
National Council for Social Services, 59,
69
national culture, 277–303
National Federation of Employers'
Organizations, 44
National Federation of Music Societies,
328
National Government, 45, 47–8, 61, 95,
156
National Grid, 148–9, 361
National Joint Council, 55
National Lectures, 163–4, 166
National Programme, xi, 14, 16–17,
63–4, 72, 93, 121, 189, 192, 194, 203,
216, 223, 244, 280, 292, 294, 303–4,
323, 326, 328–9, 333–4, 336–7, 340,
349–50, 352, 378; finance, 238–40
National Service, 96–8
National Trust, The, 277
National Unemployed Workers
Movement, 40, 60–1
Neagle, Anna, 258
Nelson, Mrs, 175
New Year Over Europe, 139–40
New Year Programmes, 135, 285, 289
New York, 129; Stock Exchange, 49
New York Times, The, 127
Newbolt Report, The, 12
Newcastle, 67, 142, 305–7, 310–11, 319,
338–9, 341, 344, 355
Newman, Greatrex, 252
Newport Players Society, 308
news, 6, 24–31, 34, 39–56, 78, 80, 85, 87,
91, 103–33, 155, 175, 307; bulletins,
36, 41, 45, 78, 82–3, 85, 88, 91, 97,
105–6, 108–14, 116–18, 120–2,
125–6, 203, 311, 313, 345, 369;
flashes, 125; news talks, 89, 121;
'no news', 118
news agencies, 25–6, 41, 43, 45, 49, 80,
82, 87, 105–7, 112–13, 118, 121–2,
125, 130–1

News Chronicle, The, 119
News Department (formerly News
Section), 44–5, 47–8, 78, 80, 88–90,
93, 96, 105, 112–3, 116–7, 120, 122–3,
130–1, 155
News from Yesterday, 119
Newspaper Proprietors' Association, 25,
41, 82, 230
Newspaper World, The, 118
newsreels, 119, 122
Nicholls, Frank, 340–1, 355
Nicolls, Basil, 85–7, 89, 97–8, 100,
124–5, 170–1, 307, 309, 311–13, 327,
345–6
Nicolson, Harold, 82, 154
Nightingale, Florence, 84
Night Mail, xiii, 301
Nine Sharp, 289
Noah's Ark, 100
Noble, Roy, 211
Noble, Sir William, 24
Norman, R. C., 83, 95–6
North American Representative, 86, 130,
160
North Region, 62, 140, 146, 151–2, 173,
175, 211, 288–9, 304–8, 321, 326–8,
333–55
North Region Director, 82, 88, 121, 171,
339
North Region Diversions, 339
North Regional Radio Routes, 339
Northcliffe, Lord, 12
Northern Cockpit, 350
Northern Ireland, 16, 116, 203, 279,
287–8, 304–8, 323, 326–7, 333–4
Northern Studio Orchestra, 175
'Not for broadcasting' caption, 48–9
Nottingham, 80, 305–6, 317, 319
Novello, Ivor, 258

Observer, The, 120
Off Duty, 69
Ogilvie, Frederick, 93–5
Old Age Pensions, 94, 96
Oliver, Paul, 296
Opera, 235–6, 241–3, 308–9, 338
Operetta, 242
'Opping 'Oliday, 147–9, 151, 347
Opportunity Knocks, 252

Index

Promenade Concerts, 121, 193, 198–9, 202, 206, 235–6, 301–2
pronunciation, 176
propaganda, 27, 31, 85, 96–7
proportional representation, 168
Public Assistance, 67–8
Public Enquiry, 351–2
Public Order Act, 1936, 40
Pudney, John, 100, 150, 353
Pudovkin, Vsevolod, 135
Punch, 138, 171, 251, 366–7
'Pure Radio', 135–40
Putney, London, 109
'Puzzle Corner', 266, 272
Pye sets, 361

Quarrell Island, 146
Question Time, 30
Queen Mary, The, 119, 282
Queen's Hall, The, 205–6
quiz programmes, 100, 268, 310, 315

R.U.R., 138
radio cars, 123–4, 132
Radio Circle, 315
Radio Luxembourg, 228–32, 295–8, 376
Radio Magazine, 211–12
Radio Newsreel, 116–17
Radio Normandie, 230, 295, 376
Radio Pictorial, 189, 210–11, 231, 295
Radio Relay Services, 230
Radio Times, xiii, 24, 27, 29–30, 33, 52, 63, 68, 98, 100, 113, 117, 135, 137–9, 141, 145–6, 148–9, 164, 172, 175, 182–5, 195, 206–7, 211, 216, 224, 246, 248, 278, 292–5, 308–9, 311, 313, 348, 351, 355, 359–60, 369–71, 374, 377
Radio Times Music Handbook, 214, 216
Radio Toulouse, 318
Radiolympia, 279, 359
Raistrick, Arthur, 353
Rankin, John, 64
Ray, Ted, 250, 297–8
reception, 14, 321
recording, 105, 117–18, 123–4, 134, 146, 340, 342, 345
Red Sarafan, 257
regional broadcasting, 172, 304–55; orchestras, 203, 212, 322–3, 328–9; Regional Scheme, 318–19, 322

Regional Directors' Meeting, 323
Regional Education Officers, 69
Regional Programme, 14, 16, 69, 121, 194, 223, 244, 304, 323, 327, 330
Reith, Sir, John, British Broadcasting Company, 7–9, 14–16; Charter, 8–9, 14–16, 35–8, 41; commercial broadcasting, 230; controversy, 31–2, 34–5, 41–2, 50, 52; entertainment, 224, 272, 359–60; features, 135–40; finance, 35; foreign affairs, 72–4, 81, 84; General Strike, 7, 29, 32–3, 35, 47–8, 100, 108, 111; music, 185, 193–5, 198, 202, 206, 300, 302; news, 107–8, 113–14, 118, 124; politics, 31–2, 34, 52, 55, 57, 61, 65–7; public relations, 50, 375–6; public service, 7; regions, 305, 307, 313–27, 330, 338–9; resignation, 17, 24–5, 27–30, 85; Royal Family, 280–1; Sundays, 232; talks, 153, 158–9, 168, 291
relay stations, 15, 305, 319, 321
religious broadcasting, 162, 232, 338
Rendall, R. A., 160, 170
Report on the Press, 40
reporting, 25, 80, 121–4, 139, 151, 154, 347
Republic of Austria, The, 138–9
request programmes, 268, 310, 313
Research Unit, 135, 138
Retail Distributors' Association, 126
Revue Musicale, 301
Revue Section, 116, 229, 260
revues, 235, 241, 255, 258, 260–2, 309, 367
Reuters, 25–6, 41, 43, 49, 87, 106, 108–9, 112–13, 116, 130–1
Reynold's News, 73
Rhondda Valley, 62, 64
Richmond, Admiral, 82
Richmond and Twickenham Times, The, 122
Road to Wigan Pier, The, xiii, 58, 141, 358
Robinson, Wright, 352
Ronald, Sir Landon, 183, 236
Roosters, The, 252
Robey, George, 231, 295
Robinson, Stanford, 241–3
Robinson Family, The, 249

437